June 28th 1943.

ne General Secretary,
.A.Trades and Labour Council,
nion Centre,
OHANNESBURG.

ear Sir,

I am attaching, as requested, three additional pies of our Constitution. I regret the delay in this tter, but I have no full-time staff available and have en extremely busy preparing our memorandum for the Wittersrand Gold Mines Native Wages' Commission.

In this connection I am also attaching a py of our memorandum, which I recommend to your Council's st careful consideration. My Union will appreciate it very ch if your Council would see their way clear to support our presentations. Your particular attention is drawn to the ction on "Trade Unionism" (Pages 40 to 42), which we feel e your Council will be able to support without any reser-ions whatsoever.

Yours faithfully,

JAMES MAJORO,
HON. SECRETARY:

miners, this ... in support ... at the Confer...

POLIC... ...ER JA...

10/-

Miners Strike ...

In spite of police violence and terror, over fifty thous... the Witwatersrand carried out the decision of a special Uni... August 4, to come out on strike as from Monday, August I... They are demanding a minimum wage of ten shillings ... and conditions. More workers are coming out on strike on th...

... mine, last Tuesday morning, police opened ... six were shot dead and other ... African Mine ... opean

GEORGE LIVI. ROOM 69, City Dee...
"I was running away from the p...
hitting everybody with batons. ...
the back and elbows. They were ...
knees and on their heads. Ther...
me who were injured and admitt...
anyone assaulting the police. ...
assaulting the miners. The Afr...
tabs on their shoulders. I thi...
tabs on their shoulders. The p...
could catch. Many people were ...
hitting the people as though t...
killed them. They did not choo...
were assaulted. They did not c...
be working underground or not....
Yes, I supported the strike. ...
The wages we get are very smal...
have to do very hard work und...
strike if there were another ...
since that time. The food is ...
strike. Many people were dism...
were from my room. Yes, I thi...
did not hear of any complaint...
ask any of the miners who wer...
to tell you the truth. They w...

...ny old residents of the Location
...y rendered houseless and
...less or subjected to persecution
persecution.
...detailed report of complaints
...supplied You Sir, You would be
...nded to learn of such treatment
...meted out or rather that such acts
...ld be perpetrated by Officials
...rusted with the welfare, care and
...tody of a subject race
...the reconstruction of your Committees
...Worship. May I suggest that a
...ecial Committee be appointed
...deal with Location Matters as
...medium between the Council
...nd the Location inhabitants.
The present system is wholly
unsatisfactory and compels the
Council to abide by the ruling
of a Location Subt... Committee
This would be welcomed by the inhabitants
of the Location and would no doubt
ensure better management, order,
peace, progress + contentment.
Your Obedient Servant

...y Mail, Wednesday, August 14, 1946.

...tle's FILM GUIDE
"THE CALL OF THE WILD"
20th Century
Castle LAGER

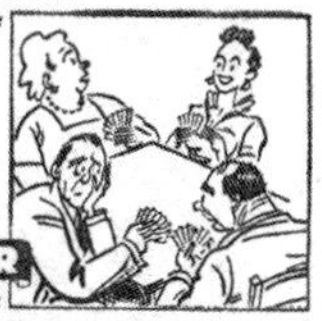

D...

Established 1902.
Price 2d.

4,000 STRIKERS TO MARC... JOHANNES...

Four Ministers Will Deal With Dispute

THE Prime Minister, General Smuts, has ...pointed a Cabinet sub-...mmittee to deal with the ...tive mineworkers' strike. The committee consists of ... Minister of Mines, Mr. F. Waterson; the Minister ... Labour, Dr. Colin Steyn; ... Minister of Justice, Mr. ... G. Lawrence, and the ...ister of Native Affairs, ...or Piet van der Byl. ...e Government is giving ...nt attention to the ...e. The Cabinet sub-...ittee was in communi-...n throughout yesterday ... the mine owners, and ...with the native mine-...rs through the Native ...issioners of the De-...ent of Native Affairs.

Natives Armed with Knives, Iron Bars, Choppers

Polic... to ... Back...

...D with choppers, iron bars, knives and an ... ...ons, 4,000 native strikers, forming a six-m... to ... ...n Johannesburg from West Springs yest...

They were intercepte... When they refused to turn ... police. Three of them w... received minor injuries.

Four natives were k... number were injured, and ... result of clashes between t... day.

Detectives from M... documents from the A... yesterday arrested its ... the Riotous Assemblie... strike. Subsequently ... union were arrested.

Other arrests inclu... alleged Communist, a... dorp. They will appe...

Thirteen Rand mines ... On some mines where wor... additional compounds bec...

The clash between 30... intended to march from t... nesburg took place on the ... Witpoort shaft of the Bra... march is not known.

With few exceptions the strik... armed themselves with sti... iron bars, choppers, knives ... other dangerous weapons.

NATIVE UNIONS THREATEN ...NERAL STRIKE

...TECTIVES ARREST ...RX AT MEETING

...native trade unions affiliated to the Transvaal ... of Non-European Trade Unions decided at a ...erday afternoon that they would all go on strike ...urs in sympathy with the native mineworkers.

...M. Basner, Native ...n the Senate, was ...

...matic incidents at ...ncluded the arrest ... of J. B. Marx, ...e African Mine-...

...as debating two ...er all the native

Police Avert Trouble at Benoni

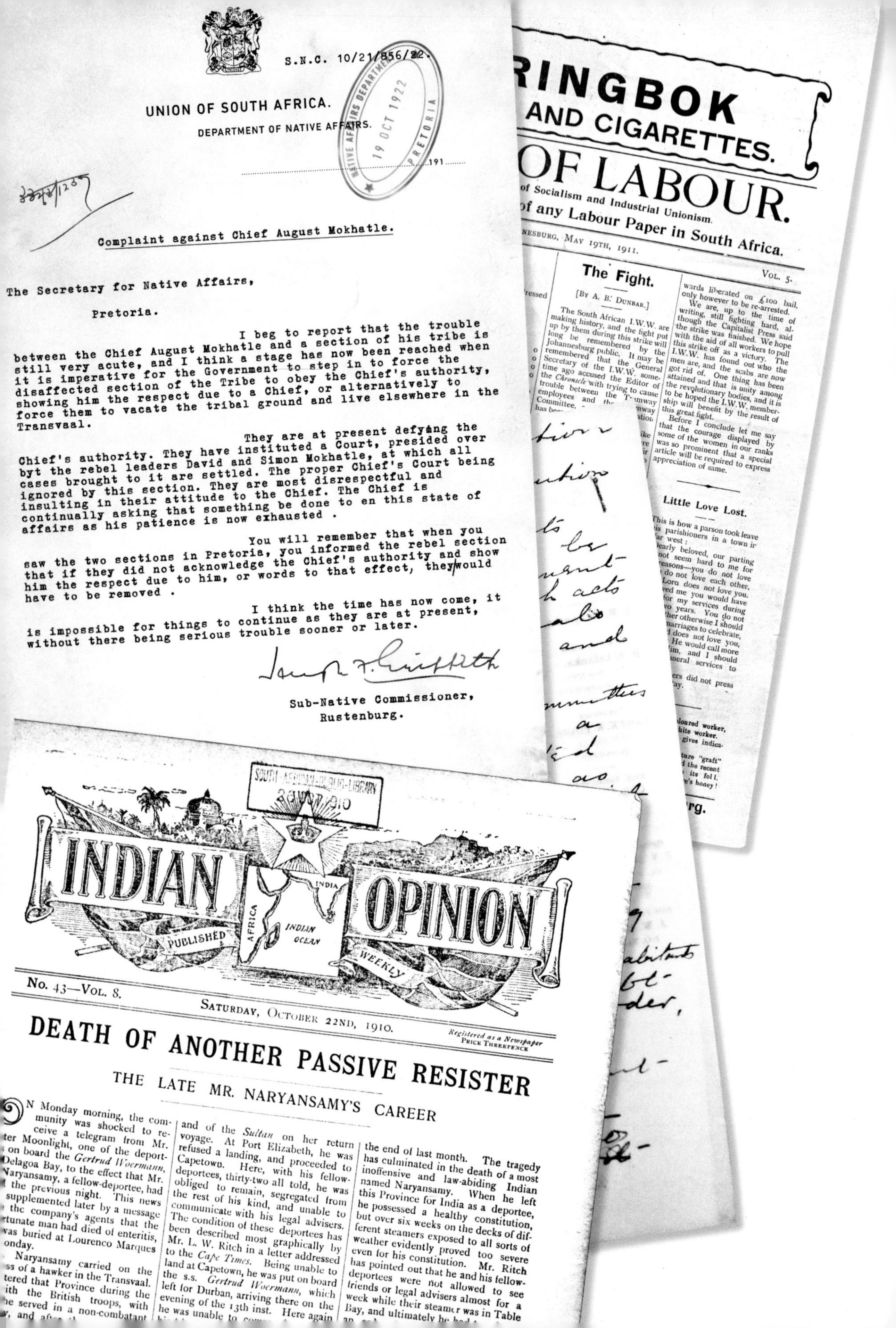

S.N.C. 10/21/856/22.

UNION OF SOUTH AFRICA.

DEPARTMENT OF NATIVE AFFAIRS.

NATIVE AFFAIRS DEPARTMENT 19 OCT 1922 PRETORIA

.......191.......

Complaint against Chief August Mokhatle.

The Secretary for Native Affairs,

Pretoria.

I beg to report that the trouble between the Chief August Mokhatle and a section of his tribe is still very acute, and I think a stage has now been reached when it is imperative for the Government to step in to force the disaffected section of the Tribe to obey the Chief's authority, showing him the respect due to a Chief, or alternatively to force them to vacate the tribal ground and live elsewhere in the Transvaal.

They are at present defying the Chief's authority. They have instituted a Court, presided over byt the rebel leaders David and Simon Mokhatle, at which all cases brought to it are settled. The proper Chief's Court being ignored by this section. They are most disrespectful and insulting in their attitude to the Chief. The Chief is continually asking that something be done to en this state of affairs as his patience is now exhausted .

You will remember that when you saw the two sections in Pretoria, you informed the rebel section that if they did not acknowledge the Chief's authority and show him the respect due to him, or words to that effect, they would have to be removed .

I think the time has now come, it is impossible for things to continue as they are at present, without there being serious trouble sooner or later.

Joseph F. Griffith

Sub-Native Commissioner,
Rustenburg.

...RINGBOK ... AND CIGARETTES.

...OF LABOUR.

...of Socialism and Industrial Unionism.

...of any Labour Paper in South Africa.

...NESBURG, MAY 19TH, 1911. VOL. 5.

The Fight.

[BY A. B. DUNBAR.]

The South African I.W.W. are making history, and the fight put up by them during this strike will long be remembered by the Johannesburg public. It may be remembered that the General Secretary of the I.W.W. some time ago accused the Editor of the *Chronicle* with trying to cause trouble between the Tramway employees and the ... Committee, ... has been ...

... wards liberated on £100 bail, only however to be re-arrested. We are, up to the time of writing, still fighting hard, although the Capitalist Press said the strike was finished. We hope with the aid of all workers to pull this strike off as a victory. The I.W.W. has found out who the men are, and the scabs are now got rid of. One thing has been attained and that is unity among the revolutionary bodies, and it is to be hoped the I.W.W. membership will benefit by the result of this great fight.

Before I conclude let me say that the courage displayed by some of the women in our ranks was so prominent that a special article will be required to express appreciation of same.

Little Love Lost.

This is how a parson took leave ...is parishioners in a town ir ...ar west: ...early beloved, our parting ...not seem hard to me for ...reasons—you do not love ... do not love each other, ... Lord does not love you. ...ved me you would have ... for my services during ...wo years. You do not ...ther otherwise I should ... marriages to celebrate, ... does not love you, ... He would call more ...him, and I should ...uneral services to ...

...ers did not press ...ay.

...loured worker, ...hite worker. ... gives indica-...

...ture "graft" ...d the recent ... its fol l. ...'s honey!

...rg.

SOUTH AFRICAN PUBLIC LIBRARY 3 NOV 1910

INDIAN OPINION
PUBLISHED WEEKLY
AFRICA
INDIA
INDIAN OCEAN

No. 43—VOL. 8. SATURDAY, OCTOBER 22ND, 1910.

Registered as a Newspaper PRICE THREEPENCE

DEATH OF ANOTHER PASSIVE RESISTER

THE LATE MR. NARYANSAMY'S CAREER

ON Monday morning, the community was shocked to receive a telegram from Mr. ...ter Moonlight, one of the deport... on board the *Gertrud Woermann*, ...Delagoa Bay, to the effect that Mr. Naryansamy, a fellow-deportee, had ... the previous night. This news ... supplemented later by a message ... the company's agents that the ...rtunate man had died of enteritis, ...was buried at Lourenco Marques ...onday.

Naryansamy carried on the ...ss of a hawker in the Transvaal. ...tered that Province during the ...ith the British troops, with ...he served in a non-combatant ..., and after ...

and of the *Sultan* on her return voyage. At Port Elizabeth, he was refused a landing, and proceeded to Capetown. Here, with his fellow-deportees, thirty-two all told, he was obliged to remain, segregated from the rest of his kind, and unable to communicate with his legal advisers. The condition of these deportees has been described most graphically by Mr. L. W. Ritch in a letter addressed to the *Cape Times*. Being unable to land at Capetown, he was put on board the s.s. *Gertrud Woermann*, which left for Durban, arriving there on the evening of the 13th inst. Here again he was unable to ...

the end of last month. The tragedy has culminated in the death of a most inoffensive and law-abiding Indian named Naryansamy. When he left this Province for India as a deportee, he possessed a healthy constitution, but over six weeks on the decks of different steamers exposed to all sorts of weather evidently proved too severe even for his constitution. Mr. Ritch has pointed out that he and his fellow-deportees were not allowed to see friends or legal advisers almost for a week while their steamer was in Table Bay, and ultimately he had ...

ALL RISE

RESISTANCE AND REBELLION
IN SOUTH AFRICA
1910 – 1948

A GRAPHIC HISTORY

————————

Richard Conyngham

With artwork by:

Saaid Rahbeeni
The Trantraal Brothers
Liz Clarke
Dada Khanyisa
Tumi Mamabolo
Mark Modimola

First published in Africa by Jacana Media (Pty) Ltd in 2021

10 Orange Street
Sunnyside
Auckland Park 2092
South Africa
+2711 628 3200
www.jacana.co.za

Cover, preliminary-pages artwork, and contributors portraits by Liz Clarke
Editing by André Trantraal
Copy-editing by Lara Jacob and Jill Bell
Proofreading by Megan Mance
Design by Gaelen Pinnock | polygram.co.za

Printed by Shumani RSA

See a complete list of Jacana titles at www.jacana.co.za

For my mum, Heather, who gave me pictures,
and for my dad, John, who gave me words

Contents

Acknowledgments

This book would never have been created had it not been for the vision of one of South Africa's great resisters, Zackie Achmat. In 2014, Zackie and I visited the archive of the Supreme Court of Appeal for the first time, but decades before this he had already recognized resistance case records as a vital yet neglected source of social, political, and legal history. I would like to begin by thanking him for his wisdom and mentorship.

Much of the initial development of *All Rise* took place on a pomegranate farm in the Klein Karoo. Thank you to Jack Lewis, Omar Burjaq, Rosie, and Socs for their hospitality and companionship.

I owe an enormous debt to Edwin Cameron and Hlonipha Mokoena for their discerning guidance and generous, insightful forewords, to André Trantraal and Verushka Louw for their editorial expertise, tireless availability and devoted friendship, and to Gaelen Pinnock, designer extraordinaire, for pulling together the book's many parts with patience and agility.

Additionally, I would like to acknowledge the many friends, colleagues and mentors who, over the years, selflessly read, reviewed, and supported the development of this project. They are Gill Benjamin, Yana van Leeve, Nick Friedman, Julian Simcock, Brad Brockman, SarahBelle Selig, Bridget Impey, Megan Mance, Jessica Powers, Tau Tavengwa, Hugh Corder, Trevor Getz, Dunbar Moodie, Uma Dhupelia-Mesthrie, Goolam Vahed, Julia Wells, Andrew Manson, Alexia Chamberlain, Claire Bruns Hugo, Nomaliqhwa Hadebe, Nigel Richard, Lara Jacob, Jonny Wilkinson, Catherine Meyburgh, Gabriele Mohale, Helen Joannides, Andre Hoffman, Melanie Geustyn, Jeremy Krikler, Robert Inglis, Shabnaaz Gani, Nura Suleiman, David Simonsz, Frankie Murrey, Shay Heydenrych, Annie Nisenson, Bhavya Dore, Gita Dore, Vasantha Surya, Nathan Geffen, Doron Isaacs, Jared Rossouw, Steve Narain, Cian Martin, Matt Eb, Motlatji Ditodi, Kira Schlesinger, Oli Fegan, Adelina Marroquin Candelaria, Adrian Kombe, Moeketsi Thatho, and Chenaimoyo Chiwaya.

Thank you, too, to the organizations that helped to finance the project. The Bertha Foundation was the primary funder and the first to recognize the book's potential. I would also like to acknowledge the generous contributions by Adrian Enthoven, the National Arts Council, the Arts and Culture Trust, and the Academic and Non-Fiction Authors' Association of South Africa.

Lastly, and most of all, thank you to my parents, Heather and John, my sister Sarah, and my partner Alejandra. From day one, their love, tolerance, and sober counsel kept this project afloat.

Foreword

I am excited and honored to be able to contribute one of the forewords to this splendid book of history. It is quite unlike any other I have come across in South Africa. It uses artwork to bridge gaps where photographs, perhaps even words, would have fallen short. It eschews the predictable and the obvious—lighting instead upon remarkable lives that have receded into the backstage of history. And through the diversity of its characters, creators, and artistic styles, it achieves something broader—it celebrates the rich history of South Africa itself.

I know this, having followed the contributors' progress over the past seven years. They chose a difficult path but they stuck to it. "Big-name" historical figures, whether resistance heroes or oppressive villains, would have been easier to research and more attractive to publishers.

Here, instead, we are presented with six vividly recounted, significant, as-yet-untold stories about working-class South Africans who lived during the pre-apartheid era. Reading about these resisters, one wonders how their truly extraordinary contributions could have slipped so far from our popular consciousness. They are women and men who, in different contexts, with tremendous personal courage, exercised their right to resist authority. In doing so, some of them broke unjust laws—and owing to this fact alone, their identities have survived in our country's official record.

Richard Conyngham and his gifted collaborators have cracked open these obscure legal documents in an ambitious effort to unearth the deeper, textured events that gave rise to them. This was not a straightforward task. The language of the law, sometimes aloof and pompous, often dry and opaque, does not easily lend itself to storytelling.

But from a simple legal perspective, this book's achievement is significant. When we look back at twentieth-century South Africa, both before and during apartheid, it is tempting to assume that the legal system as a whole—its judges, lawyers, the courts, even the law itself—were unmitigatedly complicit in systemically oppressing people of color. For the most part, this is of course true—but not entirely. The author and artists' great achievement is to have found the resistances, the rebellions, the innovative battles that South Africans fought against oppression.

The pages that follow offer you, the reader, a nuanced picture, reflecting a principle that is no less true today than it was then: that the law, when used properly, even in times of great injustice, can produce outcomes that are just.

So open the book with anticipation of delight and joy. Your journey through these pages will be vivid, informative, and revealing. This is an exciting and wonderful contribution to our history.

EDWIN CAMERON

Retired Justice of the Constitutional
Court of South Africa; former Justice
of the Supreme Court of Appeal
May 2021

Foreword

Black Act… Miners' Strike… Native Commissioners… Militant Trade Unions… It was a long century and this one promises to be longer still. The story of resistance in South Africa offers few comfortable and palatable summations; not least of which is the story of the legal system and its culpability, or not, in the endorsement of segregation and later apartheid laws.

No amount of platitudes can soften the blows that many felt when the justice system affirmed unjust laws and regulations. Yet, what these graphic stories show is that even when it was darkest, the law offered a refuge against unmitigated injustice. This is the singular pleasure of reading these stories and then writing a foreword—it is that through even its most convoluted and warped turns, the rightness and justice of the law triumphed. That these stories affirm that narrative is a given; their other joy is that they offer you, the reader, a new reason for revisiting our post-apartheid Constitution so that you may appreciate anew the grand human achievement that it is.

So many of the protagonists in these stories are people—men, women, lawyers, judges—whom we would never have heard of. Some of them are now only familiar through their collective identities—the Bafokeng, for example. What these graphic, beautifully illustrated stories tell is of the particularities that created their identities.

The struggle of African women to be exempted from pass laws is one such story. As a country we annually commemorate the brave acts of the women who marched to Pretoria in 1956 but we no longer think about their predecessors, the women who in 1925 defied the newly promulgated pass laws and the limits placed on their freedom of movement. "The Widow of Marabastad" stands in for so many women who risked their lives working as washerwomen, only to be told that they could no longer be out late at night without a pass. The dignity and determination of the widow, Helena Detody, reveals the character and grit that it took to challenge these unjust laws and be willing, as Helena says, to take on the "King of England."

"Courage under fire" is a well-worn cliché, but in the case of the story of the working-class white men who challenged the mining magnates as well as the government of Jan Christiaan Smuts, the cliché is apposite. These men were living in revolutionary times when worker resistance to exploitation was traversing the world causing economic, social as well as political upheaval.

The stories of the tram and mine workers illustrate the nature of the exclusionary job reservation that benefited white workers while at the same time highlighting the iron fists with which successive Union governments crushed resistance. The sharp class divides and the untenable separation between the wealthy northern suburbs and the working-class southern suburbs of Johannesburg function as the backdrop for these stories about the injustices of incommunicado detentions and capital punishment.

Even within this world of immigrant white working-class men, honor, solidarity, and fortitude were valorized virtues and with each story, the reader is invited to sympathize with the characters' struggles to maintain composure in the face of repression. One of the highlights for me was the manner in which the stories are dramatized and mapped onto the streets of the emerging city of Johannesburg. Fox and Loveday is a corner that I have also stood on and now it has a new meaning for me.

The debt that we owe as a country to migrants is incalculable. The countless waves of refugees, indentured laborers, rural hopefuls, and adventurous wealth seekers have all shaped the manner in which we think about the country's past. Yet, on their arrival many of these migrants were met with cold and undisguised fear and rejection. Each legislature in South Africa attempted to give meaning to such terms as "Asiatics" and "undesirable persons." The stories included in this book are testament to the personal costs borne by immigrants as successive governments attempted to expel them or limit their rights.

The summary arrests and the arbitrary deportations were tools used to make the immigrant feel as unwelcome as possible. Even in this century this is a common story, but back then such deportations were often without recourse. Without the intervention of the courts, many such expulsions would have gone unnoticed. The merchant whose shop is boarded up and is never seen again may well have been more common. We read these stories now and shudder at the inhumanity and callousness with which these South Africans were treated simply because they were migrants or the children of migrants.

It would be too easy to imagine that the stories contained in this book are about congratulating ourselves for having left this past behind. That is not the easy route that you, the reader, are being invited to take. Instead, I would suggest that perhaps you should think of these stories as re-enactments of the past as well as auguries of the present. We are still grappling with the meaning of the word "justice" and our fallibility as human beings. The real value of these stories, I would say, is the manner in which they bring to the present what may be our buried guilt and shame about the manner in which our country destroyed and trampled on so many lives.

Although this may seem like a heavy burden to carry, I think this is where the present also becomes a relief. These stories are an affirmation of the reasons why our Constitution is not just a legal nicety but a moral imperative. It should therefore be a joyous experience to know that, at least in this moment, no one is sitting in a prison cell awaiting their march to the gallows. This is therefore a book that is not only educational; it is also inspirational and I can only hope that many readers will enjoy not just reading it but passing it on to others.

HLONIPHA MOKOENA

Associate Professor, WiSER
(Wits Institute for Social &
Economic Research)
May 2021

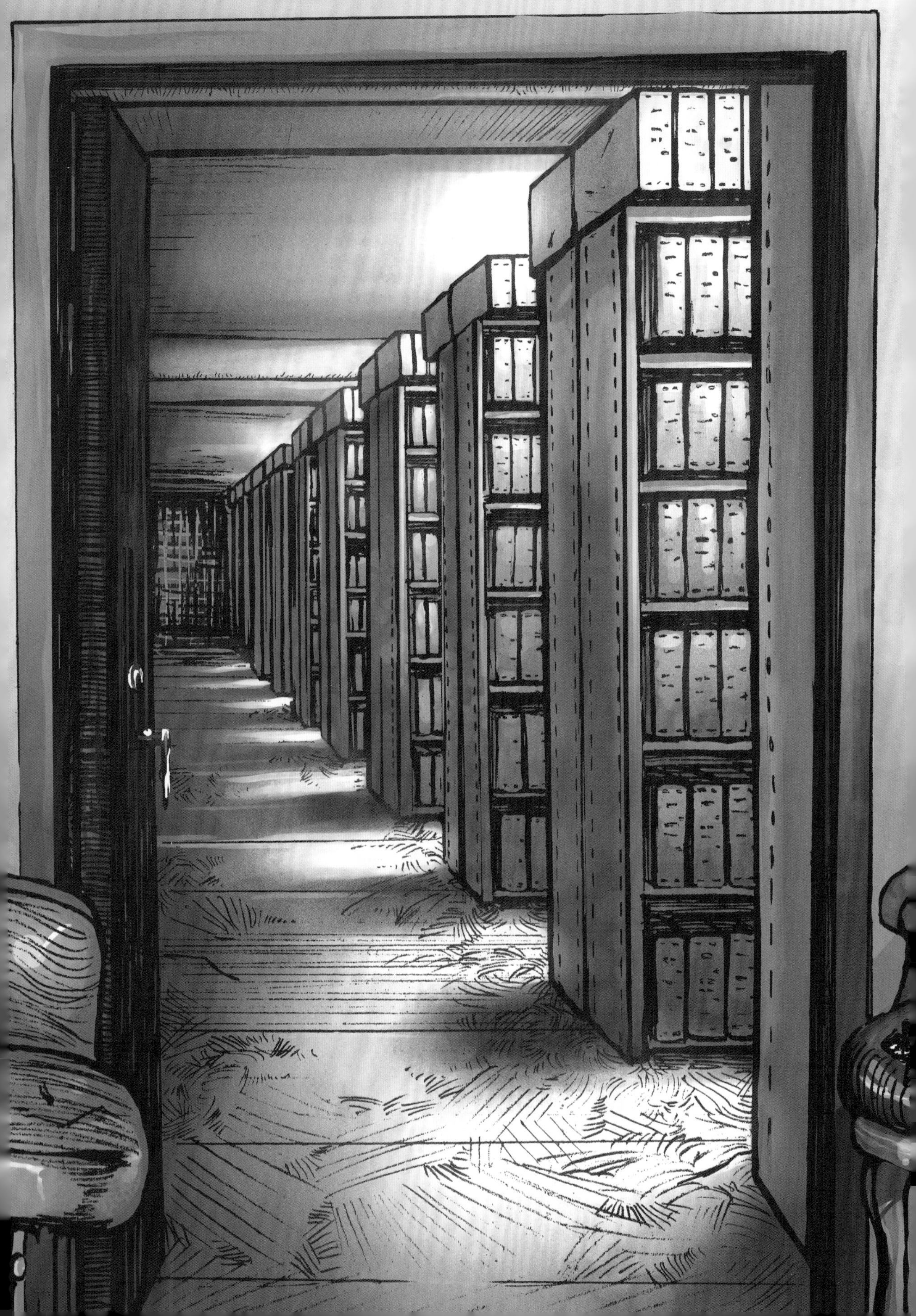

Introduction: A Dusty Basement

Imagine a room full of forgotten stories which few readers know about. The room is not a library. The stories are not in books. To find this place, you need to travel to the basement of an old court building in the city of Bloemfontein. It is there, beyond a heavy iron door, at the end of a passage lined with broken antique furniture, that the stories in this book were found.

Before South Africa's Constitutional Court opened its doors to a newly democratic nation in 1995, the Appellate Division, which today is known as the Supreme Court of Appeal, was the highest court in the land. It was established in June 1910, days after the country's two dominant colonizing forces—the British and the Dutch-speaking Boers—had come together for the first time to govern one unified nation. They had chosen Bloemfontein, the court's home, as a political halfway house between the seat of the executive in Pretoria, a city of Boer heritage, and the Houses of Parliament in Cape Town, where the British had long held sway.

Today, in the Supreme Court of Appeal's basement archive, there are thousands of cardboard boxes containing more than a century of case records. When you flick the light switch and the room's fluorescent tubes putter to life, row upon row of shelved rectangular sleeves are revealed. They sit like an audience waiting for a procession of readers to enter the room. But very few do. Occasionally a judge or law clerk, sometimes a researcher, but more often than not the archive goes for weeks without a visitor, patiently gathering dust.

The oldest cardboard boxes crack like bones when you loosen them. Inside, yellowed pages are bound with string and rusty staples. Words flow in typewriter fonts or the elaborate, heavy-inked handwriting of an earlier time. In letters, petitions, affidavits, transcripts, exhibits of evidence, and judgments, these words tell the stories of disputes won and lost. In one sleeve, it is a wife against a husband. In the next, a worker against a boss. One shelf up, a victim against a perpetrator. Further along, a citizen against the government.

When you carefully consider these case records—what gave rise to them, who was involved, and ultimately how they were decided—not only are you looking back in time but also accessing a history beyond the court itself. The disputes that reach the highest court of any country are a reflection of its society. They expose its fault lines and points of friction. Cases of resistance against authority are arguably the most illuminating, as they point to the struggles that motivated ordinary citizens to break the law, or to turn to it in the pursuit of justice.

All Rise is the product of years of research that began in the dusty basement of the Supreme Court of Appeal. It is a collection of illustrated stories of resistance and rebellion from the period loosely known as the "Union years"—between South Africa's unification in 1910 and the beginning of apartheid in 1948. This was a time of momentous upheaval in our country. Corporations and government bodies joined forces to attack the freedoms of working people. Passive resisters, strikers, rebels, and revolutionaries fought back in the streets and in the courts.

In the Supreme Court of South Africa
APPELLATE DIVISION.
On Appeal from the Transvaal Provincial Division of the said Court
BETWEEN
MAHOMED CHOTABHAI ... Appellant
AND
1. MINISTER OF JUSTICE and
2. REGISTRAR OF ASIATICS ... Respondents
RECORD OF PROCEEDINGS.

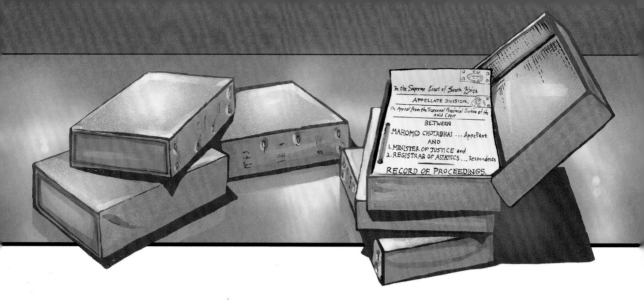

Books have been written about these events, but many are now out of print and most, if not all, have limited readership. Few foreground the anonymous men and women who took to the streets in protest. This is partly because working-class people left little written history of their own, but also because historians and their readers have generally overlooked their lives and contributions.

The basement archive of the former Appellate Division offers a unique opportunity to reconnect with these lost resisters and the faded worlds they inhabited. We—the author and illustrators—have chosen to revive these stories in the graphic form, rather than as a conventional written history. Our aim in doing so was to invite unlikely readers to open this book and once inside feel included by it. We hope to have done its characters justice, and that through our illustrations and words they will "rise" again, this time to receive the recognition they deserve—from a wide, diverse readership.

RICHARD CONYNGHAM

May 2021

A Note on Terminology

Many of the characters in this book would not have spoken English as a first language. South Africa currently has 11 official languages, among which English ranks as the sixth most-spoken at home. Weighing up readability against accuracy of representation, we have chosen to include a scattering of words in the characters' vernacular, with translations provided in the glossary on page 236.

Also included in the glossary are certain idiomatic words and phrases which may not be recognizable to all readers of the English language. Some can be categorized as particular to, or originating from, South Africa; others are universal but more technical or arcane in nature.

In the few instances where legislative acts, statutes or ordinances are mentioned for the first time, their full names are provided as footnotes.

During the period covered by this book, racist terms were so pervasive in South African society that they were even commonly used in newspapers and official documentation. Rather than deliberately avoid this historical fact, we have chosen to include certain terms—namely, "Asiatic," "Coolie," "Sammy," "Native," "Non-European," "tribe," and "tribal"—either in dialogue, where it was considered contextually accurate, or in keeping with the statutory language of the period. This in no way seeks to diminish the offensiveness of these words.

The names used for racial and ethnic groups have complex, contested meanings, to the extent that no nomenclature is perfect. For the purposes of this book, we have chosen to use the term "person of color" to refer to any person of African, Coloured, Indian or Chinese descent. For those readers who are unfamiliar with the South African context, the word "Coloured" denotes a person, native to Southern Africa, of mixed heritage, including Khoi, San, African, Asian, white and other descent.

In Chapter 5, the terms "chief" and "kgosi" are used interchangeably to denote the highest political authority within a specific traditional community. Historically, in Batswana society, both words were widely used. However, since the late 1990s, the Royal Bafokeng Administration has adopted the term "king" instead.

The Union of South Africa was a dominion of the British Empire. As a result, criminal prosecutions before its courts were instituted in the name of the Crown (cited in the format *Rex v. Accused*), and its currency was the pound sterling (£).

All place names in this book reflect their contemporary usage at the time the stories took place. These include South Africa's original four provinces (formerly colonies and republics)—Transvaal, Orange Free State, Natal, and Cape—which existed between 1910 and 1994, before they were reconfigured into the nine provinces of today.

Further, the stories also contain the following historical place names which are no longer in use: Port Natal (Durban), Bombay (Mumbai), Lourenço Marques (Maputo), Delagoa Bay (Maputo Bay), Portuguese East Africa (Mozambique), Basutoland (Lesotho), Tanganyika (mainland Tanzania), South West Africa (Namibia), Bechuanaland Protectorate (Botswana), and Southern Rhodesia (Zimbabwe).

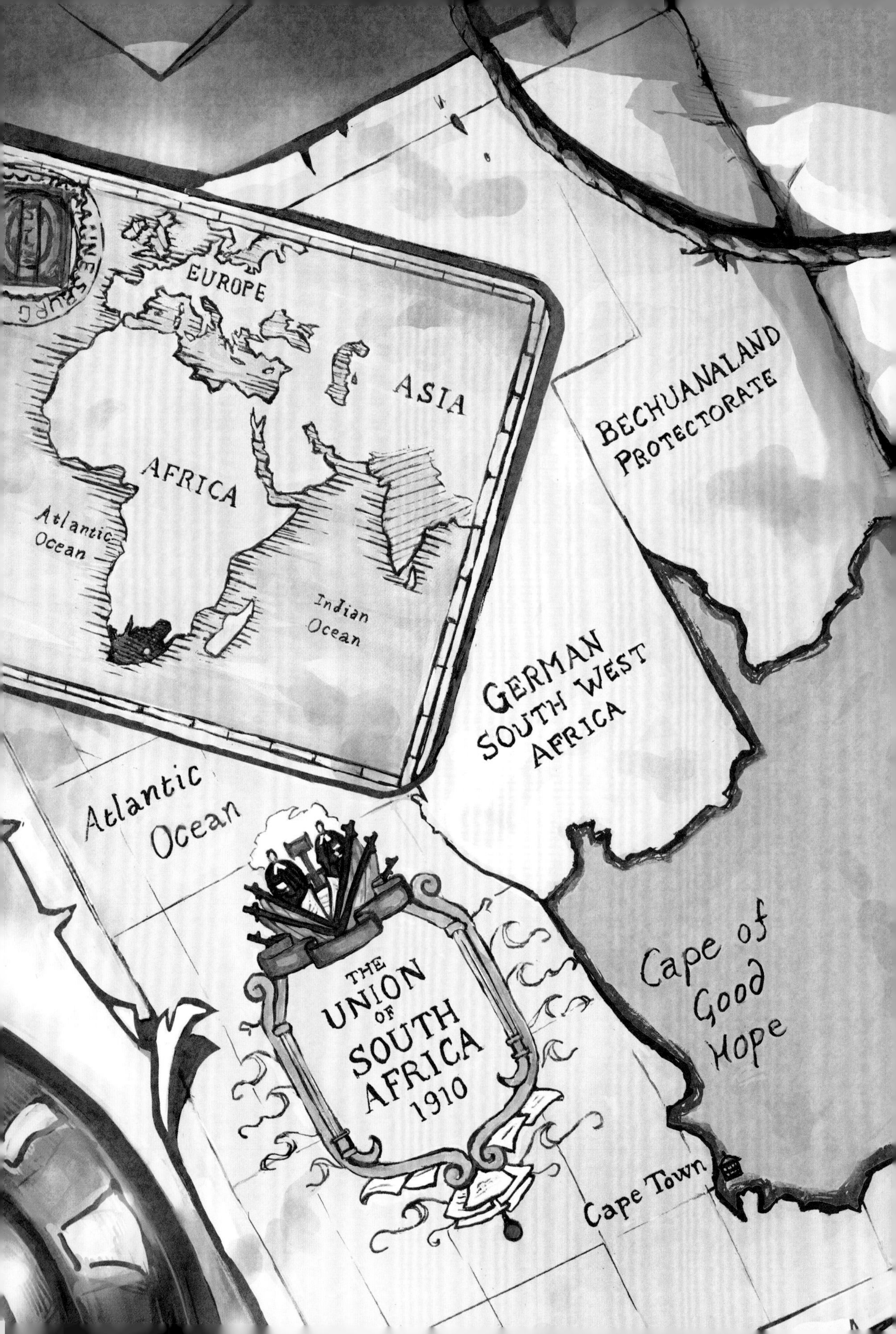
EUROPE
ASIA
AFRICA
Atlantic Ocean
Indian Ocean
BECHUANALAND PROTECTORATE
GERMAN SOUTH WEST AFRICA
Atlantic Ocean
THE UNION OF SOUTH AFRICA 1910
Cape of Good Hope
Cape Town

SOUTHERN RHODESIA
Transvaal
PORTUGUESE EAST AFRICA
Lourenço Marques
N
E
W
S
Indian Ocean
Phokeng
Pretoria
Johannesburg
SWAZI-LAND
Orange Free State
Natal
Bloemfontein
Maseru
BASUTO-LAND
Durban
East London
Port Elizabeth
12 August 1910

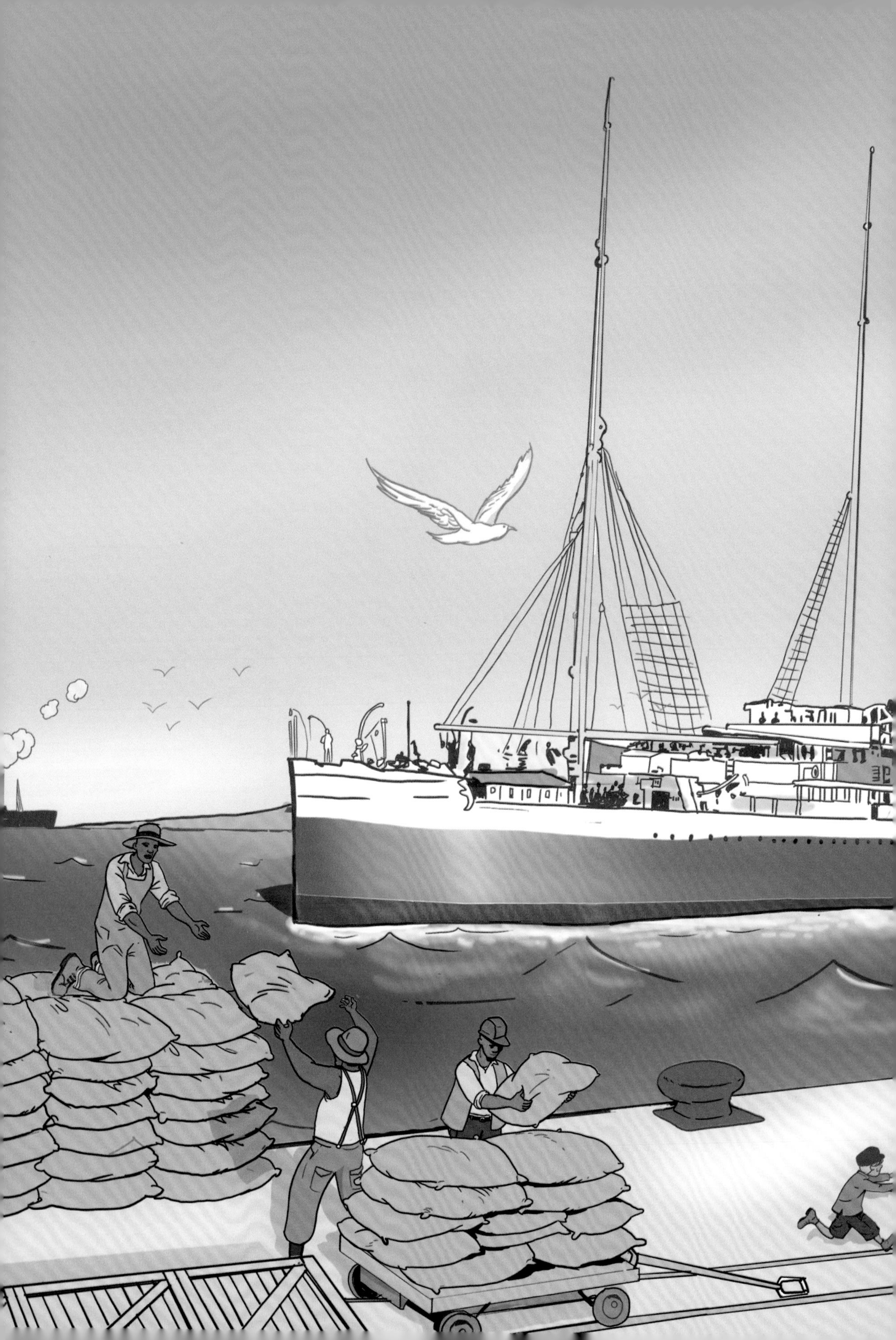

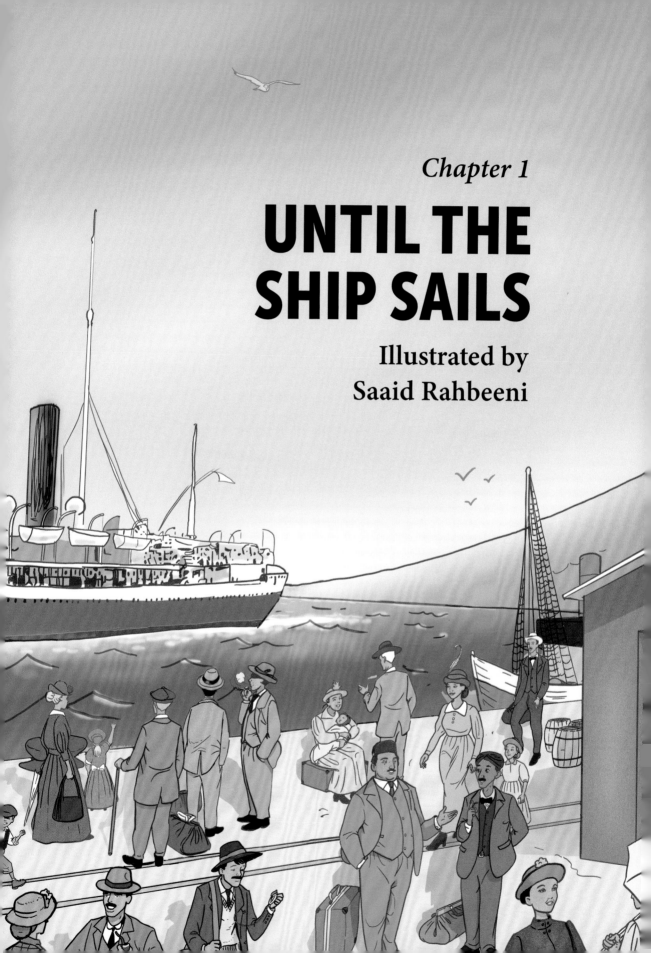

Chapter 1

UNTIL THE SHIP SAILS

Illustrated by
Saaid Rahbeeni

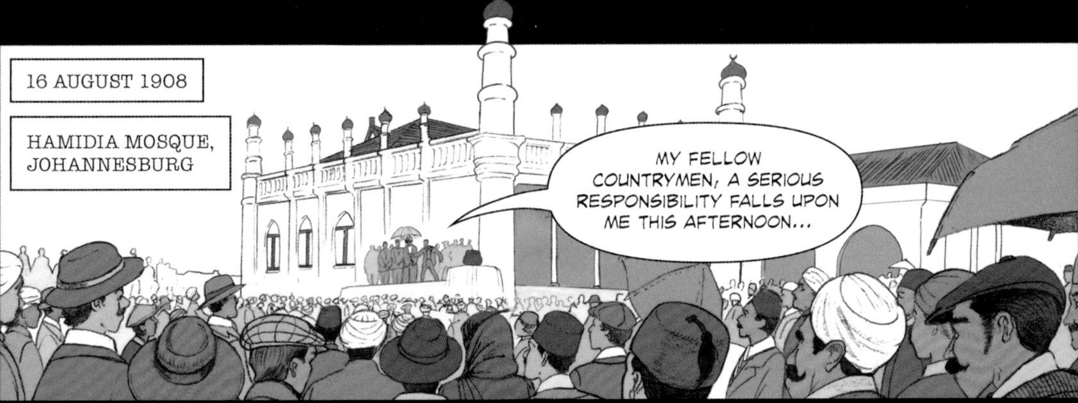
16 AUGUST 1908
HAMIDIA MOSQUE, JOHANNESBURG
MY FELLOW COUNTRYMEN, A SERIOUS RESPONSIBILITY FALLS UPON ME THIS AFTERNOON...

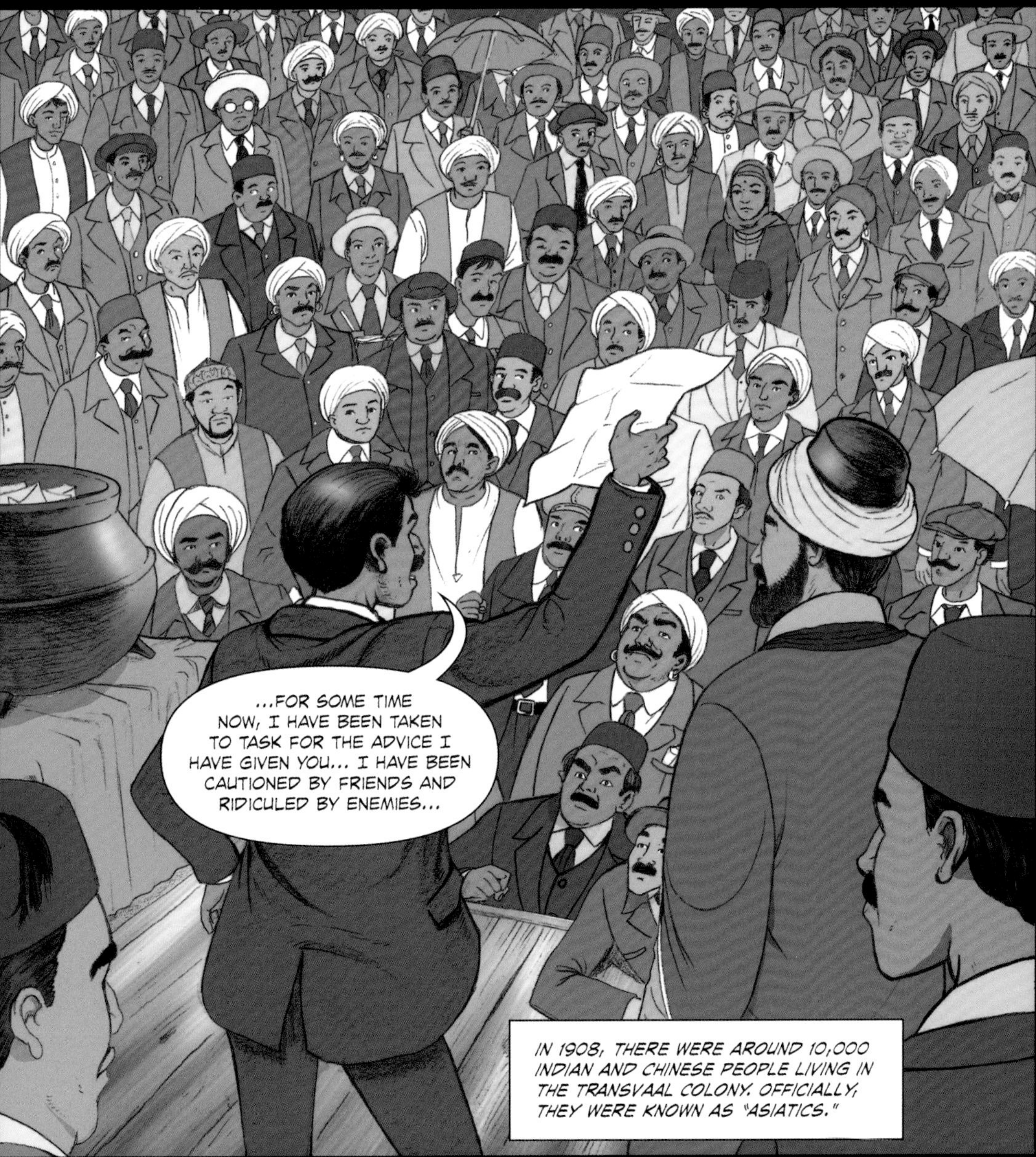
...FOR SOME TIME NOW, I HAVE BEEN TAKEN TO TASK FOR THE ADVICE I HAVE GIVEN YOU... I HAVE BEEN CAUTIONED BY FRIENDS AND RIDICULED BY ENEMIES...
IN 1908, THERE WERE AROUND 10,000 INDIAN AND CHINESE PEOPLE LIVING IN THE TRANSVAAL COLONY. OFFICIALLY, THEY WERE KNOWN AS "ASIATICS."

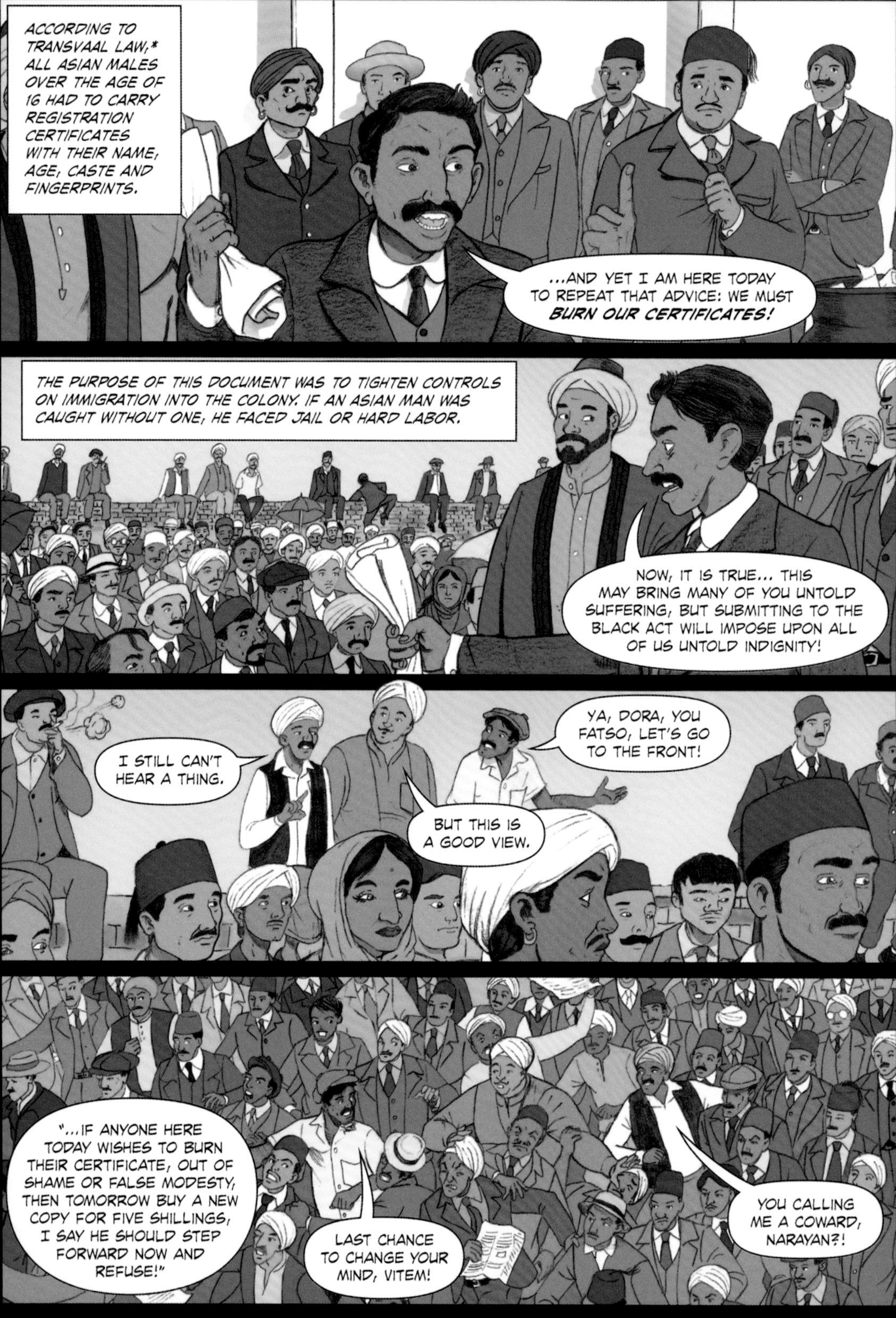
ACCORDING TO TRANSVAAL LAW,* ALL ASIAN MALES OVER THE AGE OF 16 HAD TO CARRY REGISTRATION CERTIFICATES WITH THEIR NAME, AGE, CASTE AND FINGERPRINTS.
...AND YET I AM HERE TODAY TO REPEAT THAT ADVICE: WE MUST BURN OUR CERTIFICATES!
THE PURPOSE OF THIS DOCUMENT WAS TO TIGHTEN CONTROLS ON IMMIGRATION INTO THE COLONY. IF AN ASIAN MAN WAS CAUGHT WITHOUT ONE, HE FACED JAIL OR HARD LABOR.
NOW, IT IS TRUE... THIS MAY BRING MANY OF YOU UNTOLD SUFFERING, BUT SUBMITTING TO THE BLACK ACT WILL IMPOSE UPON ALL OF US UNTOLD INDIGNITY!
I STILL CAN'T HEAR A THING.
BUT THIS IS A GOOD VIEW.
YA, DORA, YOU FATSO, LET'S GO TO THE FRONT!
"...IF ANYONE HERE TODAY WISHES TO BURN THEIR CERTIFICATE, OUT OF SHAME OR FALSE MODESTY, THEN TOMORROW BUY A NEW COPY FOR FIVE SHILLINGS, I SAY HE SHOULD STEP FORWARD NOW AND REFUSE!"
LAST CHANCE TO CHANGE YOUR MIND, VITEM!
YOU CALLING ME A COWARD, NARAYAN?!

* The Asiatic Law Amendment Act of 1907 (also known as "the Black Act").

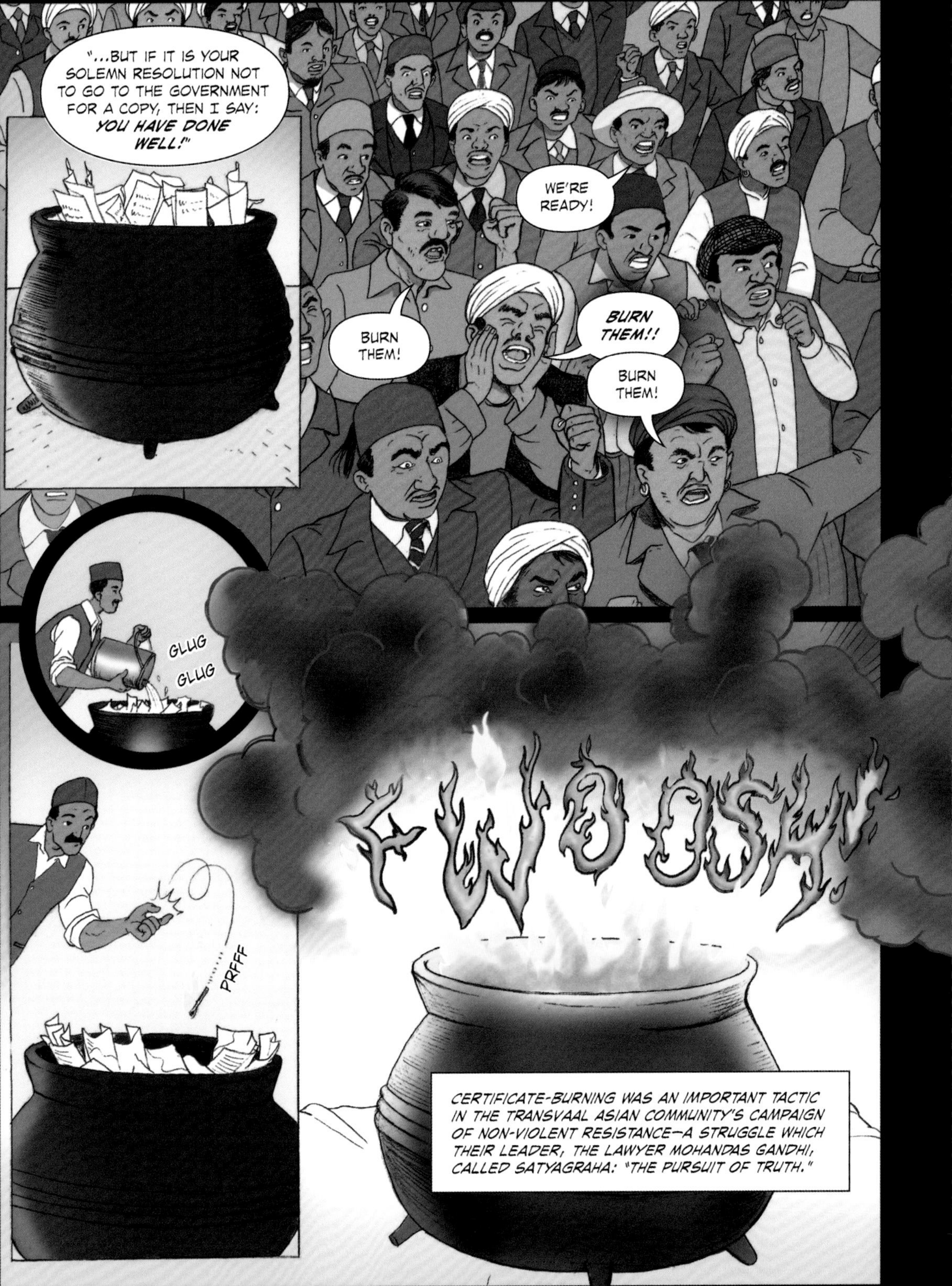
"...BUT IF IT IS YOUR SOLEMN RESOLUTION NOT TO GO TO THE GOVERNMENT FOR A COPY, THEN I SAY: ***YOU HAVE DONE WELL!***"
WE'RE READY!
BURN THEM!
BURN THEM!!
BURN THEM!
GLUG
GLUG
PRFFF
FWOOSH
CERTIFICATE-BURNING WAS AN IMPORTANT TACTIC IN THE TRANSVAAL ASIAN COMMUNITY'S CAMPAIGN OF NON-VIOLENT RESISTANCE—A STRUGGLE WHICH THEIR LEADER, THE LAWYER MOHANDAS GANDHI, CALLED SATYAGRAHA: "THE PURSUIT OF TRUTH."

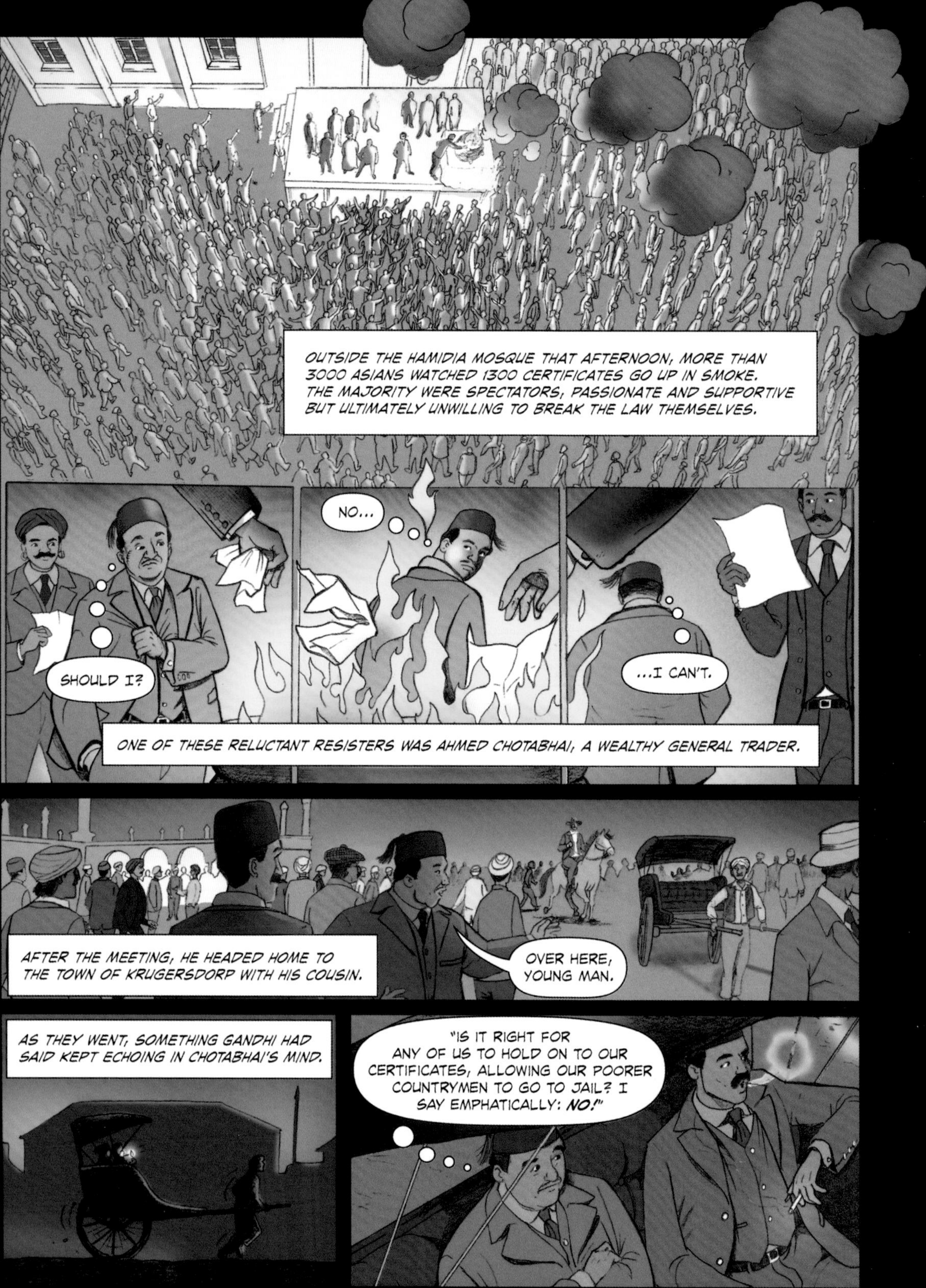

OUTSIDE THE HAMIDIA MOSQUE THAT AFTERNOON, MORE THAN 3000 ASIANS WATCHED 1300 CERTIFICATES GO UP IN SMOKE. THE MAJORITY WERE SPECTATORS, PASSIONATE AND SUPPORTIVE BUT ULTIMATELY UNWILLING TO BREAK THE LAW THEMSELVES.
SHOULD I?
NO...
...I CAN'T.
ONE OF THESE RELUCTANT RESISTERS WAS AHMED CHOTABHAI, A WEALTHY GENERAL TRADER.
AFTER THE MEETING, HE HEADED HOME TO THE TOWN OF KRUGERSDORP WITH HIS COUSIN.
OVER HERE, YOUNG MAN.
AS THEY WENT, SOMETHING GANDHI HAD SAID KEPT ECHOING IN CHOTABHAI'S MIND.
"IS IT RIGHT FOR ANY OF US TO HOLD ON TO OUR CERTIFICATES, ALLOWING OUR POORER COUNTRYMEN TO GO TO JAIL? I SAY EMPHATICALLY: NO!"

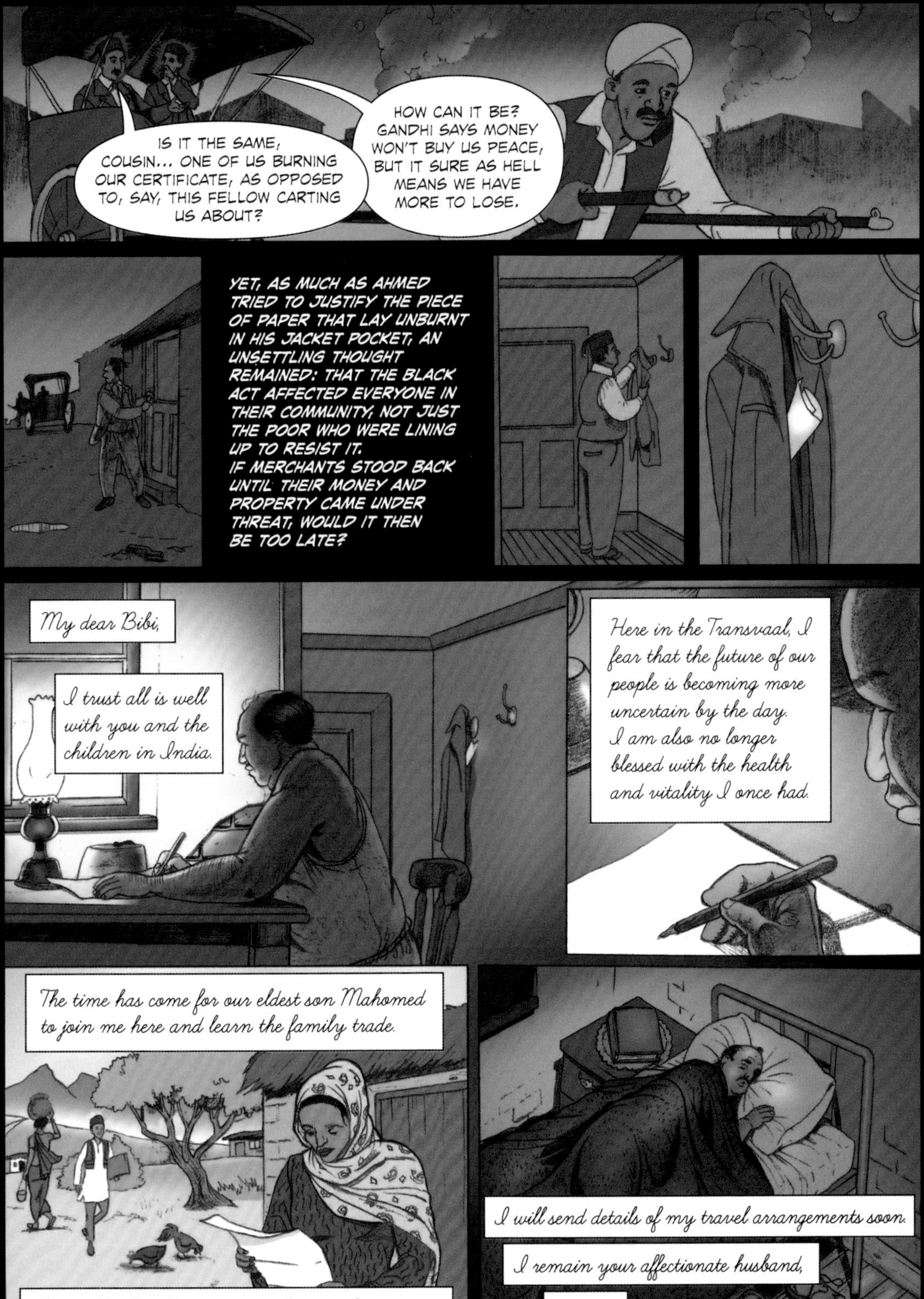
IS IT THE SAME, COUSIN... ONE OF US BURNING OUR CERTIFICATE, AS OPPOSED TO, SAY, THIS FELLOW CARTING US ABOUT?
HOW CAN IT BE? GANDHI SAYS MONEY WON'T BUY US PEACE, BUT IT SURE AS HELL MEANS WE HAVE MORE TO LOSE.
YET, AS MUCH AS AHMED TRIED TO JUSTIFY THE PIECE OF PAPER THAT LAY UNBURNT IN HIS JACKET POCKET, AN UNSETTLING THOUGHT REMAINED: THAT THE BLACK ACT AFFECTED EVERYONE IN THEIR COMMUNITY, NOT JUST THE POOR WHO WERE LINING UP TO RESIST IT. IF MERCHANTS STOOD BACK UNTIL THEIR MONEY AND PROPERTY CAME UNDER THREAT, WOULD IT THEN BE TOO LATE?
My dear Bibi,
I trust all is well with you and the children in India.
Here in the Transvaal, I fear that the future of our people is becoming more uncertain by the day. I am also no longer blessed with the health and vitality I once had.
The time has come for our eldest son Mahomed to join me here and learn the family trade.
Naturally I will accompany him on his voyage.
I will send details of my travel arrangements soon.
I remain your affectionate husband,
Ahmed

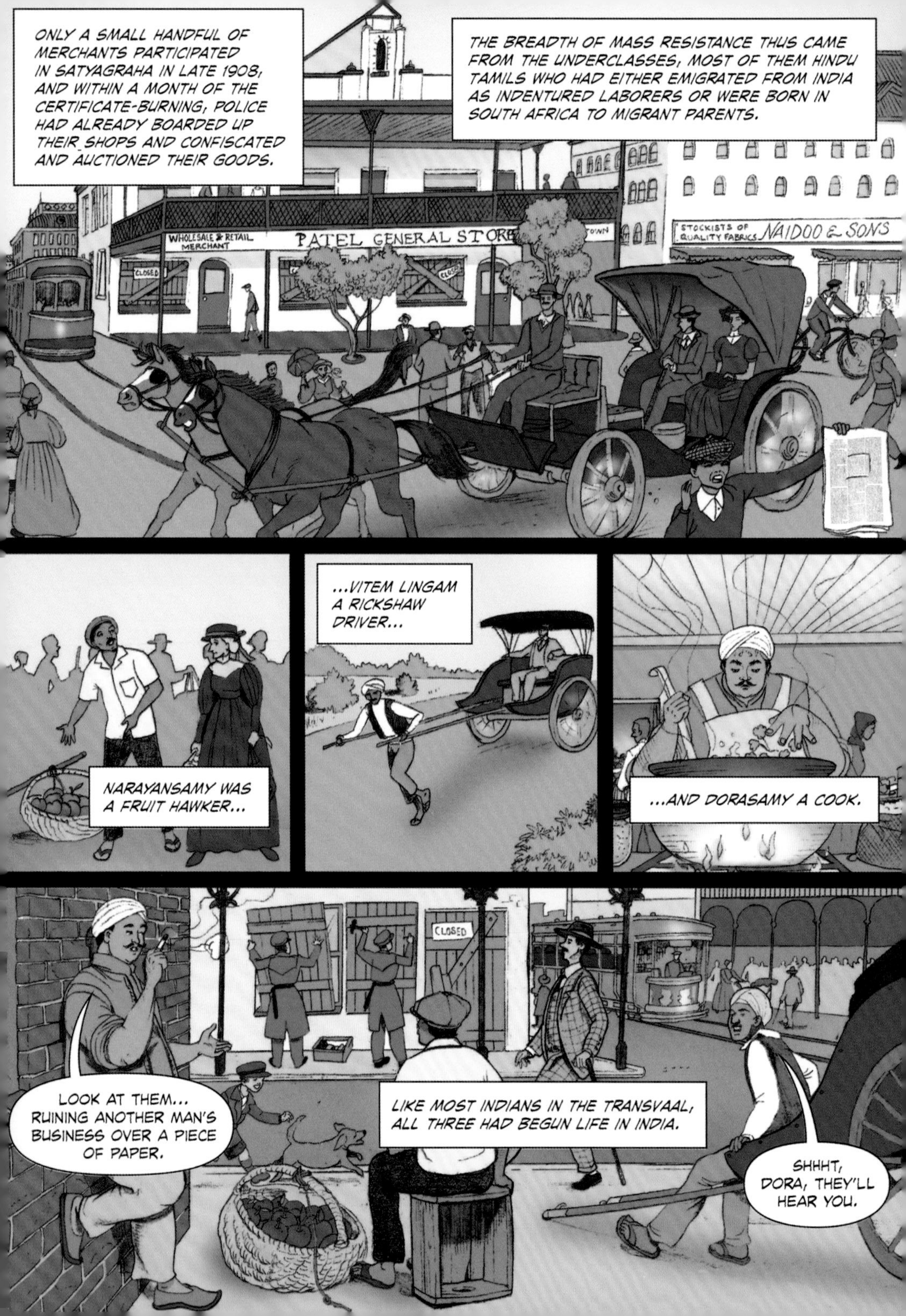
ONLY A SMALL HANDFUL OF MERCHANTS PARTICIPATED IN SATYAGRAHA IN LATE 1908, AND WITHIN A MONTH OF THE CERTIFICATE-BURNING, POLICE HAD ALREADY BOARDED UP THEIR SHOPS AND CONFISCATED AND AUCTIONED THEIR GOODS.
THE BREADTH OF MASS RESISTANCE THUS CAME FROM THE UNDERCLASSES, MOST OF THEM HINDU TAMILS WHO HAD EITHER EMIGRATED FROM INDIA AS INDENTURED LABORERS OR WERE BORN IN SOUTH AFRICA TO MIGRANT PARENTS.
WHOLESALE & RETAIL MERCHANT
PATEL GENERAL STORE
CLOSED
CLOSED
STOCKISTS OF QUALITY FABRICS
NAIDOO & SONS
NARAYANSAMY WAS A FRUIT HAWKER...
...VITEM LINGAM A RICKSHAW DRIVER...
...AND DORASAMY A COOK.
CLOSED
LOOK AT THEM... RUINING ANOTHER MAN'S BUSINESS OVER A PIECE OF PAPER.
LIKE MOST INDIANS IN THE TRANSVAAL, ALL THREE HAD BEGUN LIFE IN INDIA.
SHHHT, DORA, THEY'LL HEAR YOU.

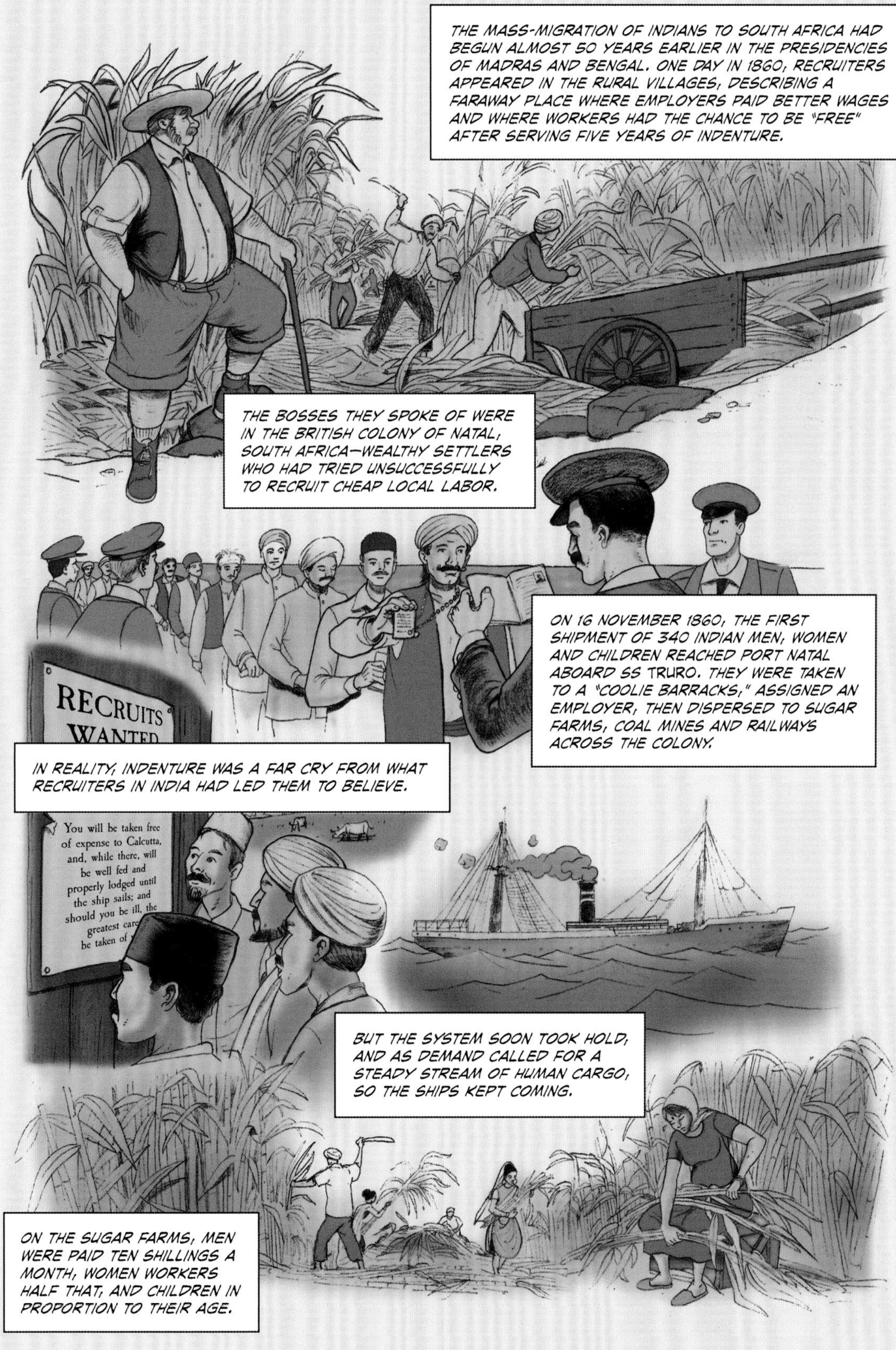
THE MASS-MIGRATION OF INDIANS TO SOUTH AFRICA HAD BEGUN ALMOST 50 YEARS EARLIER IN THE PRESIDENCIES OF MADRAS AND BENGAL. ONE DAY IN 1860, RECRUITERS APPEARED IN THE RURAL VILLAGES, DESCRIBING A FARAWAY PLACE WHERE EMPLOYERS PAID BETTER WAGES AND WHERE WORKERS HAD THE CHANCE TO BE "FREE" AFTER SERVING FIVE YEARS OF INDENTURE.
THE BOSSES THEY SPOKE OF WERE IN THE BRITISH COLONY OF NATAL, SOUTH AFRICA—WEALTHY SETTLERS WHO HAD TRIED UNSUCCESSFULLY TO RECRUIT CHEAP LOCAL LABOR.
ON 16 NOVEMBER 1860, THE FIRST SHIPMENT OF 340 INDIAN MEN, WOMEN AND CHILDREN REACHED PORT NATAL ABOARD SS TRURO. THEY WERE TAKEN TO A "COOLIE BARRACKS," ASSIGNED AN EMPLOYER, THEN DISPERSED TO SUGAR FARMS, COAL MINES AND RAILWAYS ACROSS THE COLONY.
RECRUITS WANTED
IN REALITY, INDENTURE WAS A FAR CRY FROM WHAT RECRUITERS IN INDIA HAD LED THEM TO BELIEVE.
You will be taken free of expense to Calcutta, and, while there, will be well fed and properly lodged until the ship sails; and should you be ill, the greatest
be taken of
BUT THE SYSTEM SOON TOOK HOLD, AND AS DEMAND CALLED FOR A STEADY STREAM OF HUMAN CARGO, SO THE SHIPS KEPT COMING.
ON THE SUGAR FARMS, MEN WERE PAID TEN SHILLINGS A MONTH, WOMEN WORKERS HALF THAT, AND CHILDREN IN PROPORTION TO THEIR AGE.

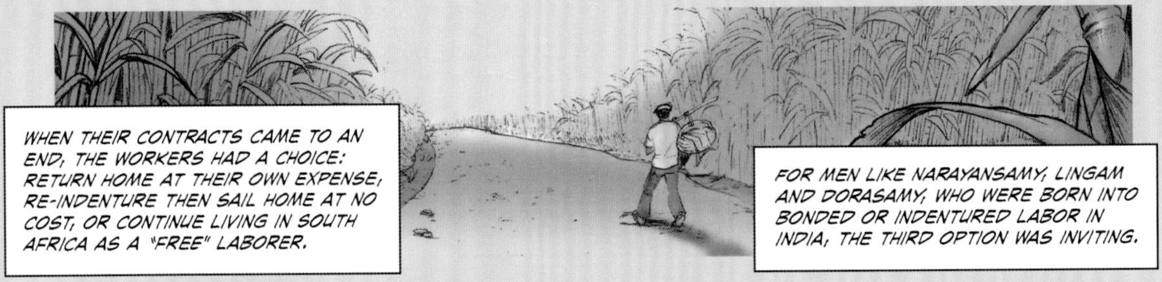
WHEN THEIR CONTRACTS CAME TO AN END, THE WORKERS HAD A CHOICE: RETURN HOME AT THEIR OWN EXPENSE, RE-INDENTURE THEN SAIL HOME AT NO COST, OR CONTINUE LIVING IN SOUTH AFRICA AS A "FREE" LABORER.
FOR MEN LIKE NARAYANSAMY, LINGAM AND DORASAMY, WHO WERE BORN INTO BONDED OR INDENTURED LABOR IN INDIA, THE THIRD OPTION WAS INVITING.

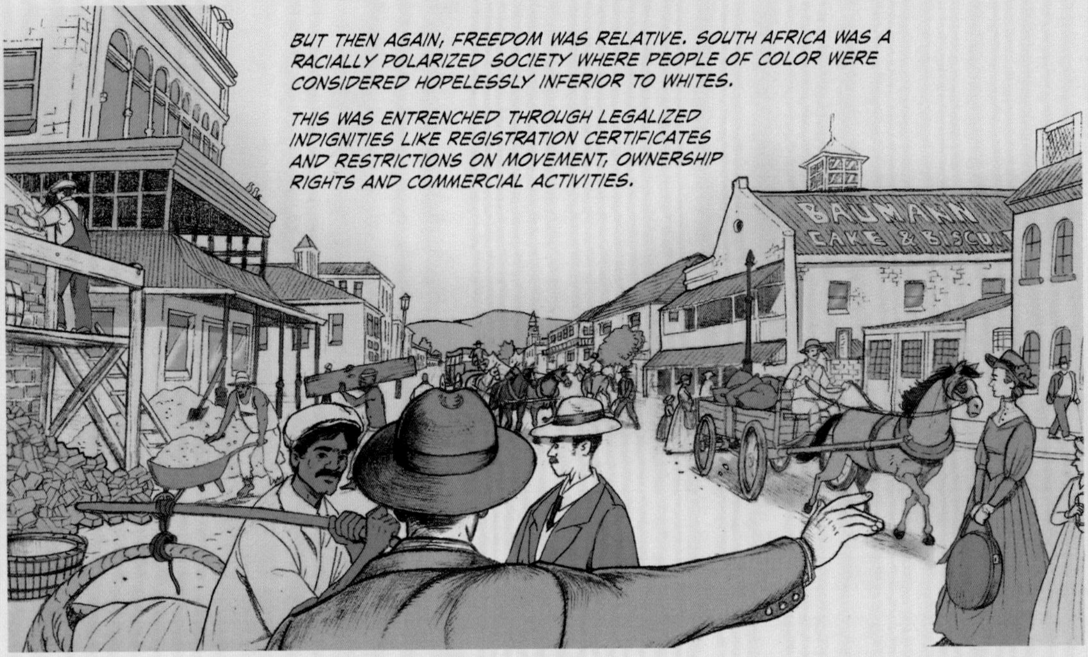
BUT THEN AGAIN, FREEDOM WAS RELATIVE. SOUTH AFRICA WAS A RACIALLY POLARIZED SOCIETY WHERE PEOPLE OF COLOR WERE CONSIDERED HOPELESSLY INFERIOR TO WHITES.
THIS WAS ENTRENCHED THROUGH LEGALIZED INDIGNITIES LIKE REGISTRATION CERTIFICATES AND RESTRICTIONS ON MOVEMENT, OWNERSHIP RIGHTS AND COMMERCIAL ACTIVITIES.
BAUMANN
CAKE & BISCUIT

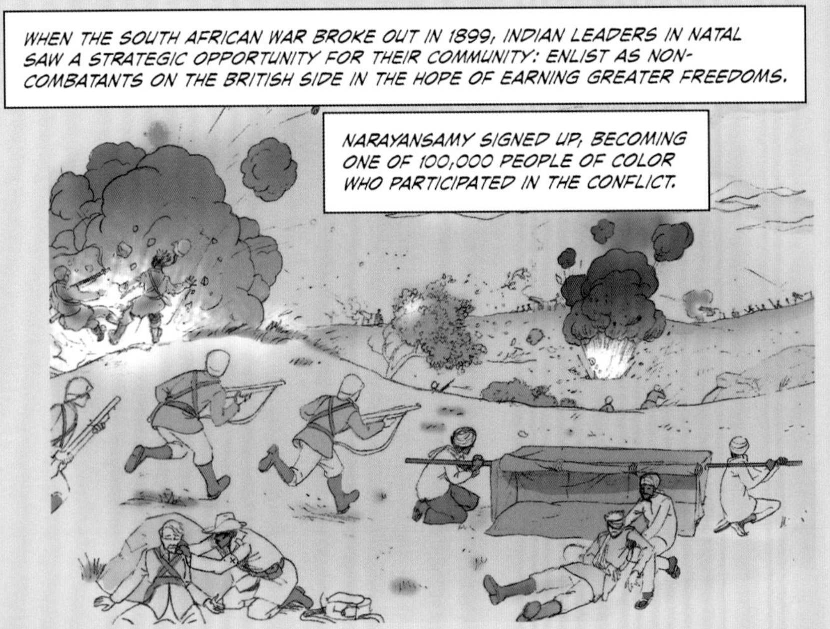
WHEN THE SOUTH AFRICAN WAR BROKE OUT IN 1899, INDIAN LEADERS IN NATAL SAW A STRATEGIC OPPORTUNITY FOR THEIR COMMUNITY: ENLIST AS NON-COMBATANTS ON THE BRITISH SIDE IN THE HOPE OF EARNING GREATER FREEDOMS.
NARAYANSAMY SIGNED UP, BECOMING ONE OF 100,000 PEOPLE OF COLOR WHO PARTICIPATED IN THE CONFLICT.

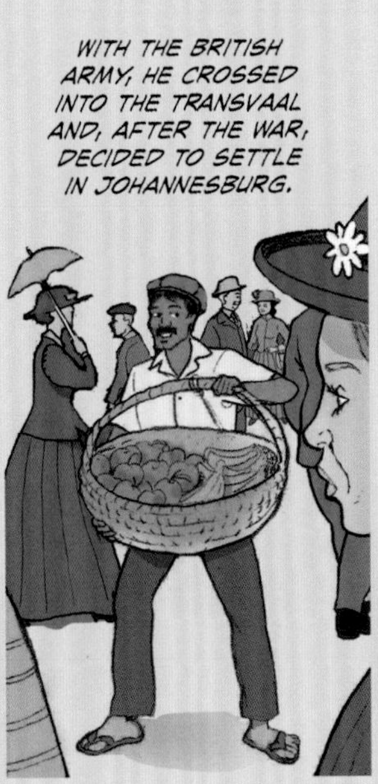
WITH THE BRITISH ARMY, HE CROSSED INTO THE TRANSVAAL AND, AFTER THE WAR, DECIDED TO SETTLE IN JOHANNESBURG.

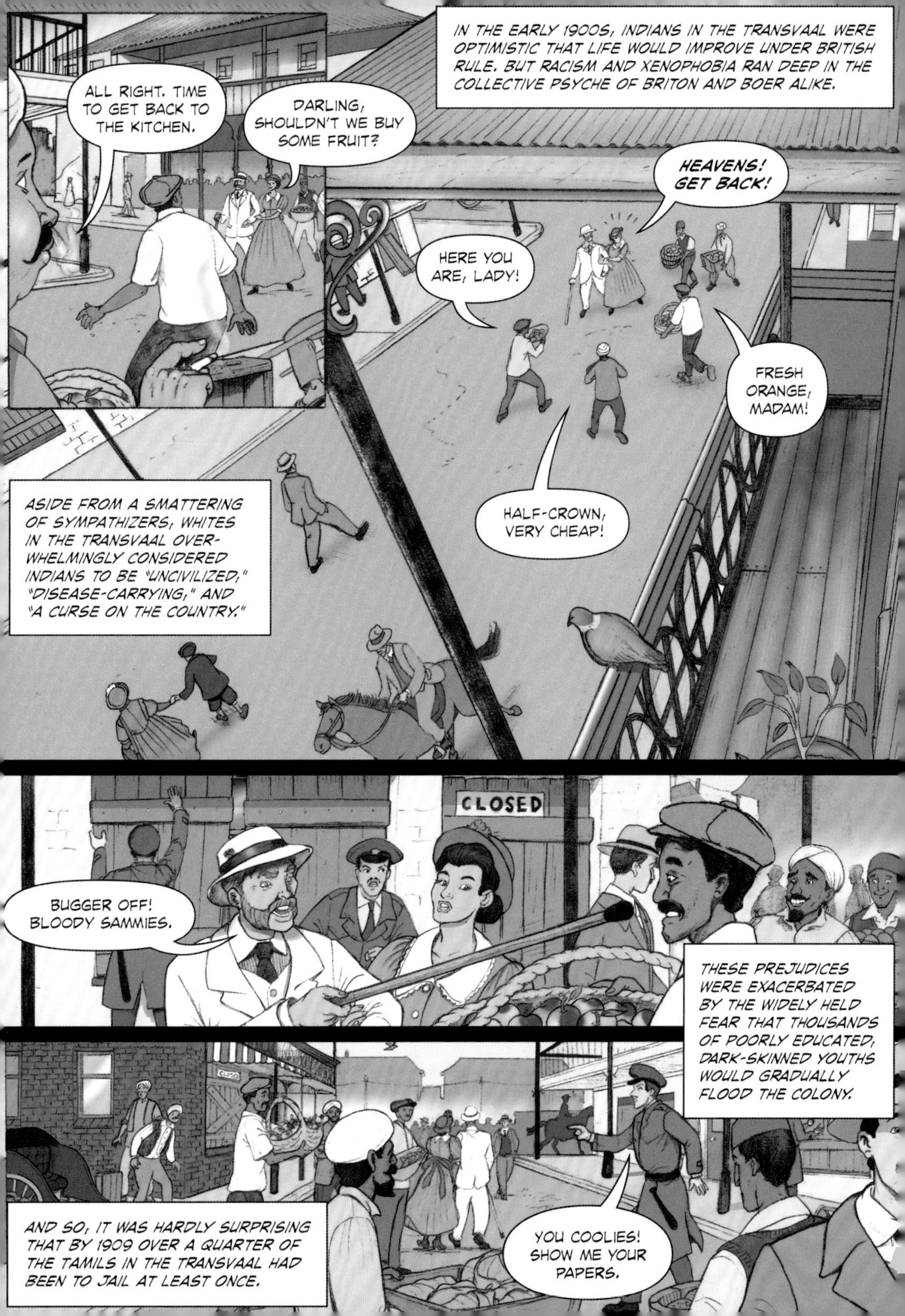

IN THE EARLY 1900S, INDIANS IN THE TRANSVAAL WERE OPTIMISTIC THAT LIFE WOULD IMPROVE UNDER BRITISH RULE. BUT RACISM AND XENOPHOBIA RAN DEEP IN THE COLLECTIVE PSYCHE OF BRITON AND BOER ALIKE.
ALL RIGHT. TIME TO GET BACK TO THE KITCHEN.
DARLING, SHOULDN'T WE BUY SOME FRUIT?
HEAVENS! GET BACK!
HERE YOU ARE, LADY!
FRESH ORANGE, MADAM!
HALF-CROWN, VERY CHEAP!
ASIDE FROM A SMATTERING OF SYMPATHIZERS, WHITES IN THE TRANSVAAL OVERWHELMINGLY CONSIDERED INDIANS TO BE "UNCIVILIZED," "DISEASE-CARRYING," AND "A CURSE ON THE COUNTRY."
CLOSED
BUGGER OFF! BLOODY SAMMIES.
THESE PREJUDICES WERE EXACERBATED BY THE WIDELY HELD FEAR THAT THOUSANDS OF POORLY EDUCATED, DARK-SKINNED YOUTHS WOULD GRADUALLY FLOOD THE COLONY.
AND SO, IT WAS HARDLY SURPRISING THAT BY 1909 OVER A QUARTER OF THE TAMILS IN THE TRANSVAAL HAD BEEN TO JAIL AT LEAST ONCE.
YOU COOLIES! SHOW ME YOUR PAPERS.

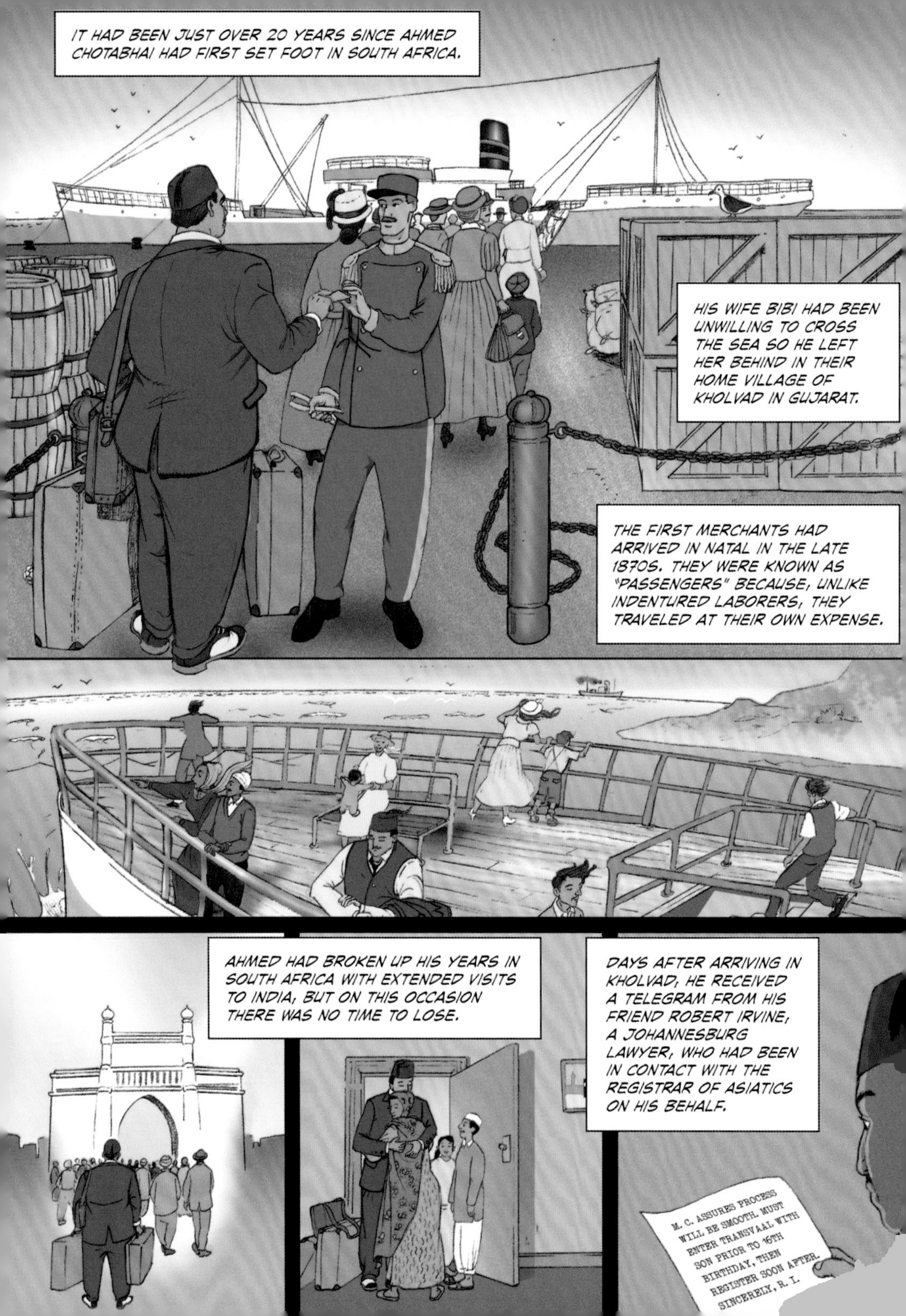
IT HAD BEEN JUST OVER 20 YEARS SINCE AHMED CHOTABHAI HAD FIRST SET FOOT IN SOUTH AFRICA.
HIS WIFE BIBI HAD BEEN UNWILLING TO CROSS THE SEA SO HE LEFT HER BEHIND IN THEIR HOME VILLAGE OF KHOLVAD IN GUJARAT.
THE FIRST MERCHANTS HAD ARRIVED IN NATAL IN THE LATE 1870S. THEY WERE KNOWN AS "PASSENGERS" BECAUSE, UNLIKE INDENTURED LABORERS, THEY TRAVELED AT THEIR OWN EXPENSE.
AHMED HAD BROKEN UP HIS YEARS IN SOUTH AFRICA WITH EXTENDED VISITS TO INDIA, BUT ON THIS OCCASION THERE WAS NO TIME TO LOSE.
DAYS AFTER ARRIVING IN KHOLVAD, HE RECEIVED A TELEGRAM FROM HIS FRIEND ROBERT IRVINE, A JOHANNESBURG LAWYER, WHO HAD BEEN IN CONTACT WITH THE REGISTRAR OF ASIATICS ON HIS BEHALF.
M. C. ASSURES PROCESS WILL BE SMOOTH. MUST ENTER TRANSVAAL WITH SON PRIOR TO 16TH BIRTHDAY, THEN REGISTER SOON AFTER. SINCERELY, R. I.

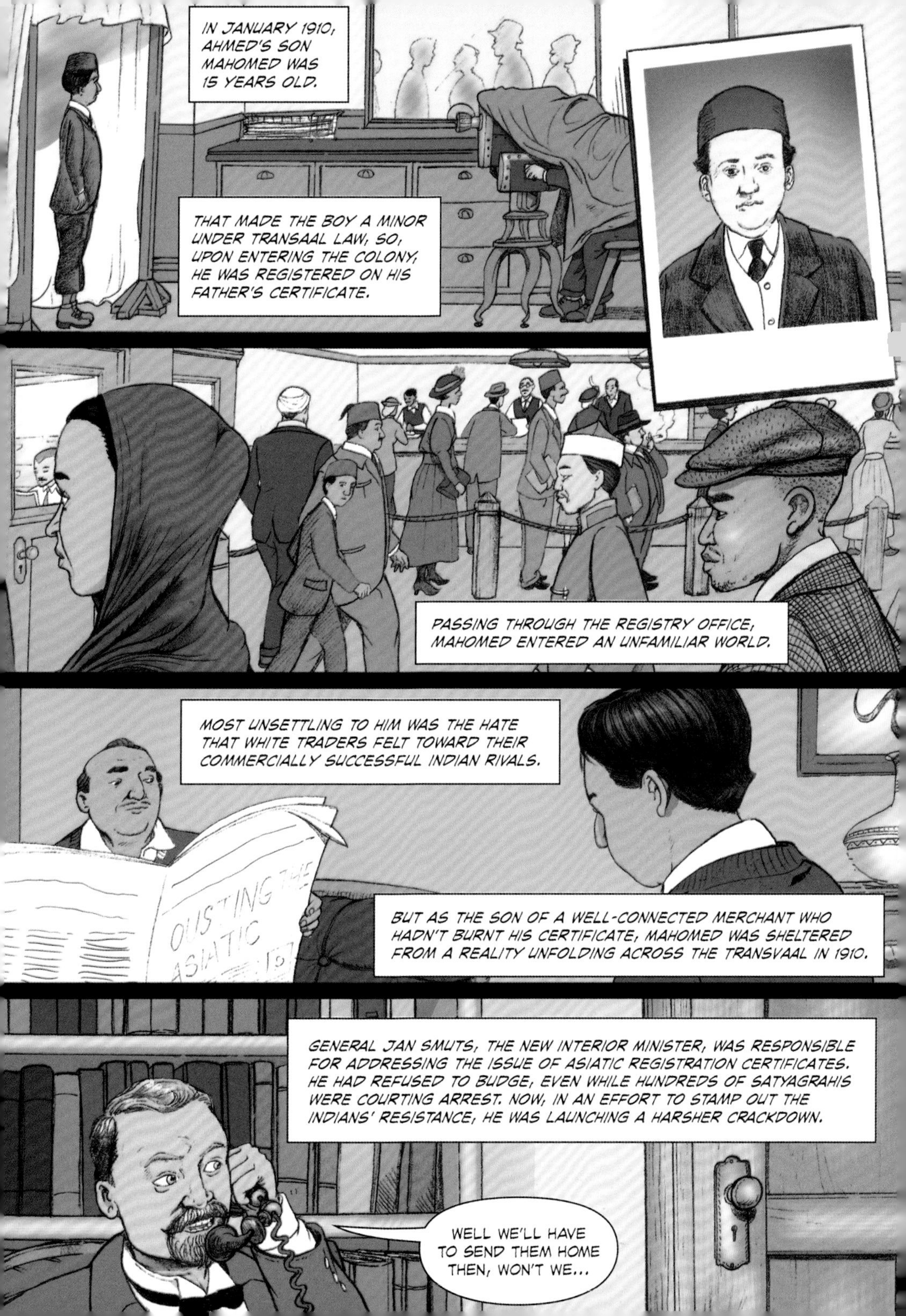

IN JANUARY 1910, AHMED'S SON MAHOMED WAS 15 YEARS OLD.
THAT MADE THE BOY A MINOR UNDER TRANSAAL LAW, SO, UPON ENTERING THE COLONY, HE WAS REGISTERED ON HIS FATHER'S CERTIFICATE.
PASSING THROUGH THE REGISTRY OFFICE, MAHOMED ENTERED AN UNFAMILIAR WORLD.
MOST UNSETTLING TO HIM WAS THE HATE THAT WHITE TRADERS FELT TOWARD THEIR COMMERCIALLY SUCCESSFUL INDIAN RIVALS.
OUSTING THE ASIATIC
BUT AS THE SON OF A WELL-CONNECTED MERCHANT WHO HADN'T BURNT HIS CERTIFICATE, MAHOMED WAS SHELTERED FROM A REALITY UNFOLDING ACROSS THE TRANSVAAL IN 1910.
GENERAL JAN SMUTS, THE NEW INTERIOR MINISTER, WAS RESPONSIBLE FOR ADDRESSING THE ISSUE OF ASIATIC REGISTRATION CERTIFICATES. HE HAD REFUSED TO BUDGE, EVEN WHILE HUNDREDS OF SATYAGRAHIS WERE COURTING ARREST. NOW, IN AN EFFORT TO STAMP OUT THE INDIANS' RESISTANCE, HE WAS LAUNCHING A HARSHER CRACKDOWN.
WELL WE'LL HAVE TO SEND THEM HOME THEN, WON'T WE...

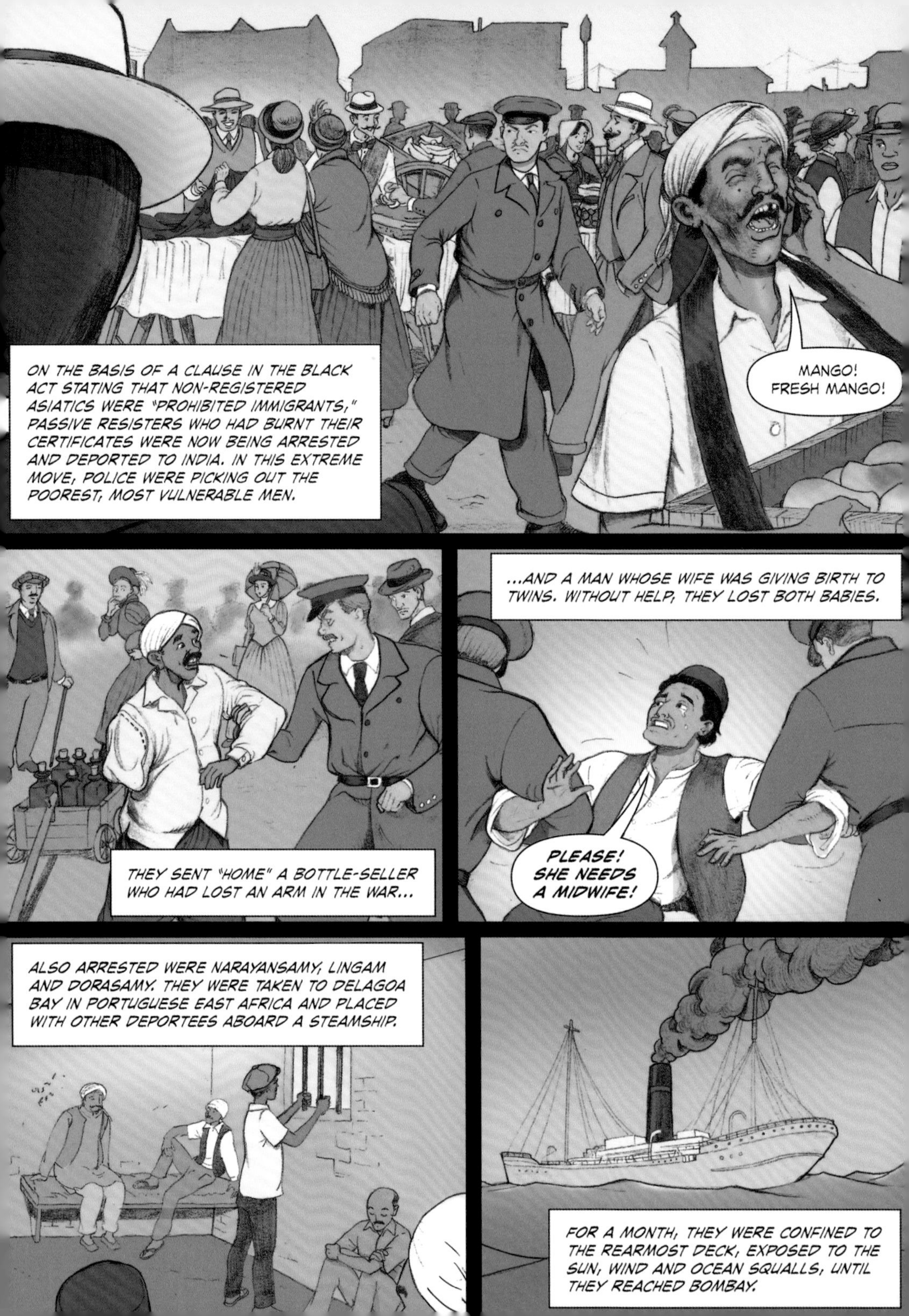
ON THE BASIS OF A CLAUSE IN THE BLACK ACT STATING THAT NON-REGISTERED ASIATICS WERE "PROHIBITED IMMIGRANTS," PASSIVE RESISTERS WHO HAD BURNT THEIR CERTIFICATES WERE NOW BEING ARRESTED AND DEPORTED TO INDIA. IN THIS EXTREME MOVE, POLICE WERE PICKING OUT THE POOREST, MOST VULNERABLE MEN.
MANGO! FRESH MANGO!
THEY SENT "HOME" A BOTTLE-SELLER WHO HAD LOST AN ARM IN THE WAR...
...AND A MAN WHOSE WIFE WAS GIVING BIRTH TO TWINS. WITHOUT HELP, THEY LOST BOTH BABIES.
PLEASE! SHE NEEDS A MIDWIFE!
ALSO ARRESTED WERE NARAYANSAMY, LINGAM AND DORASAMY. THEY WERE TAKEN TO DELAGOA BAY IN PORTUGUESE EAST AFRICA AND PLACED WITH OTHER DEPORTEES ABOARD A STEAMSHIP.
FOR A MONTH, THEY WERE CONFINED TO THE REARMOST DECK, EXPOSED TO THE SUN, WIND AND OCEAN SQUALLS, UNTIL THEY REACHED BOMBAY.

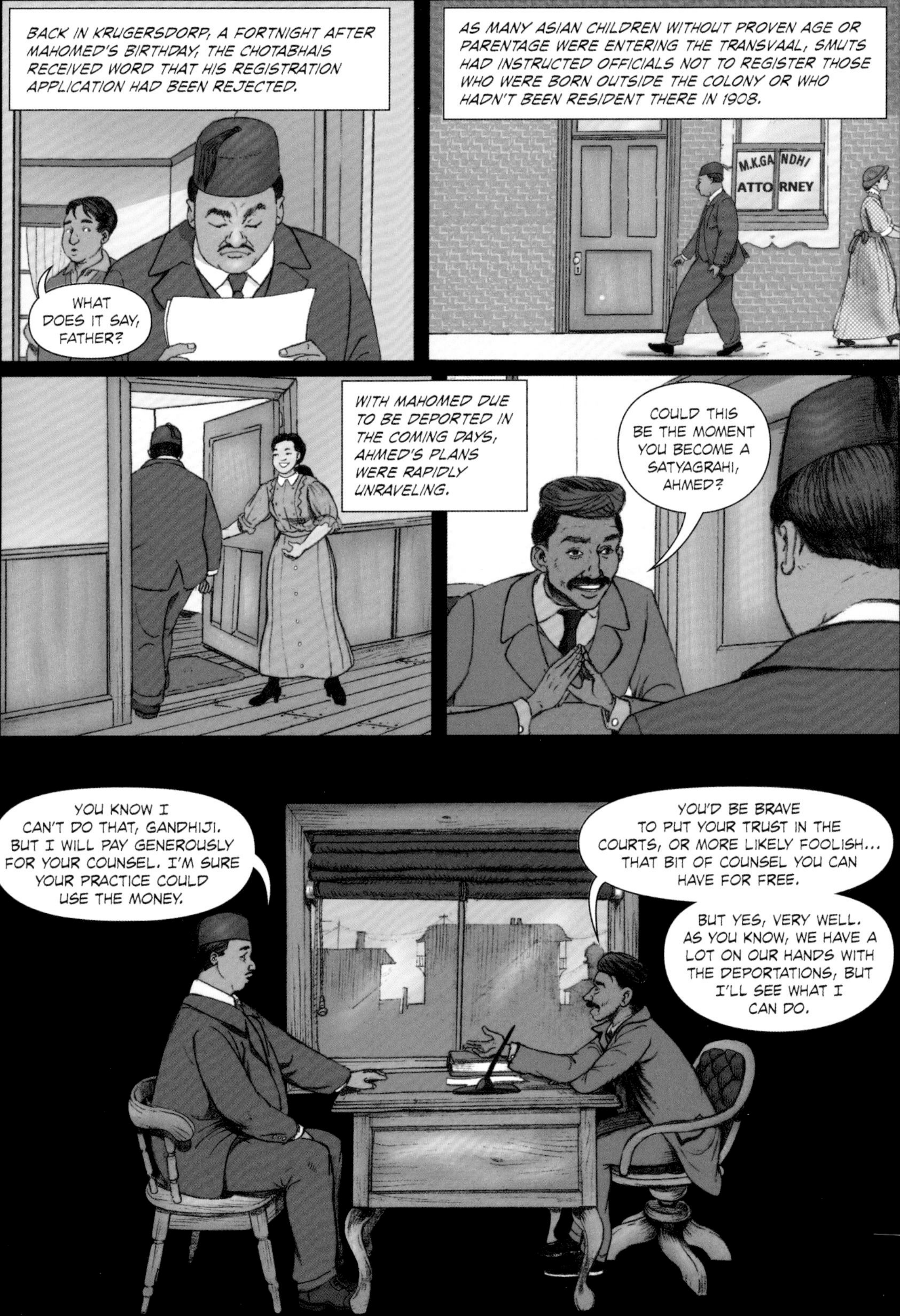
BACK IN KRUGERSDORP, A FORTNIGHT AFTER MAHOMED'S BIRTHDAY, THE CHOTABHAIS RECEIVED WORD THAT HIS REGISTRATION APPLICATION HAD BEEN REJECTED.
WHAT DOES IT SAY, FATHER?
AS MANY ASIAN CHILDREN WITHOUT PROVEN AGE OR PARENTAGE WERE ENTERING THE TRANSVAAL, SMUTS HAD INSTRUCTED OFFICIALS NOT TO REGISTER THOSE WHO WERE BORN OUTSIDE THE COLONY OR WHO HADN'T BEEN RESIDENT THERE IN 1908.
M.K.GANDHI
ATTORNEY
WITH MAHOMED DUE TO BE DEPORTED IN THE COMING DAYS, AHMED'S PLANS WERE RAPIDLY UNRAVELING.
COULD THIS BE THE MOMENT YOU BECOME A SATYAGRAHI, AHMED?
YOU KNOW I CAN'T DO THAT, GANDHIJI. BUT I WILL PAY GENEROUSLY FOR YOUR COUNSEL. I'M SURE YOUR PRACTICE COULD USE THE MONEY.
YOU'D BE BRAVE TO PUT YOUR TRUST IN THE COURTS, OR MORE LIKELY FOOLISH... THAT BIT OF COUNSEL YOU CAN HAVE FOR FREE.
BUT YES, VERY WELL. AS YOU KNOW, WE HAVE A LOT ON OUR HANDS WITH THE DEPORTATIONS, BUT I'LL SEE WHAT I CAN DO.

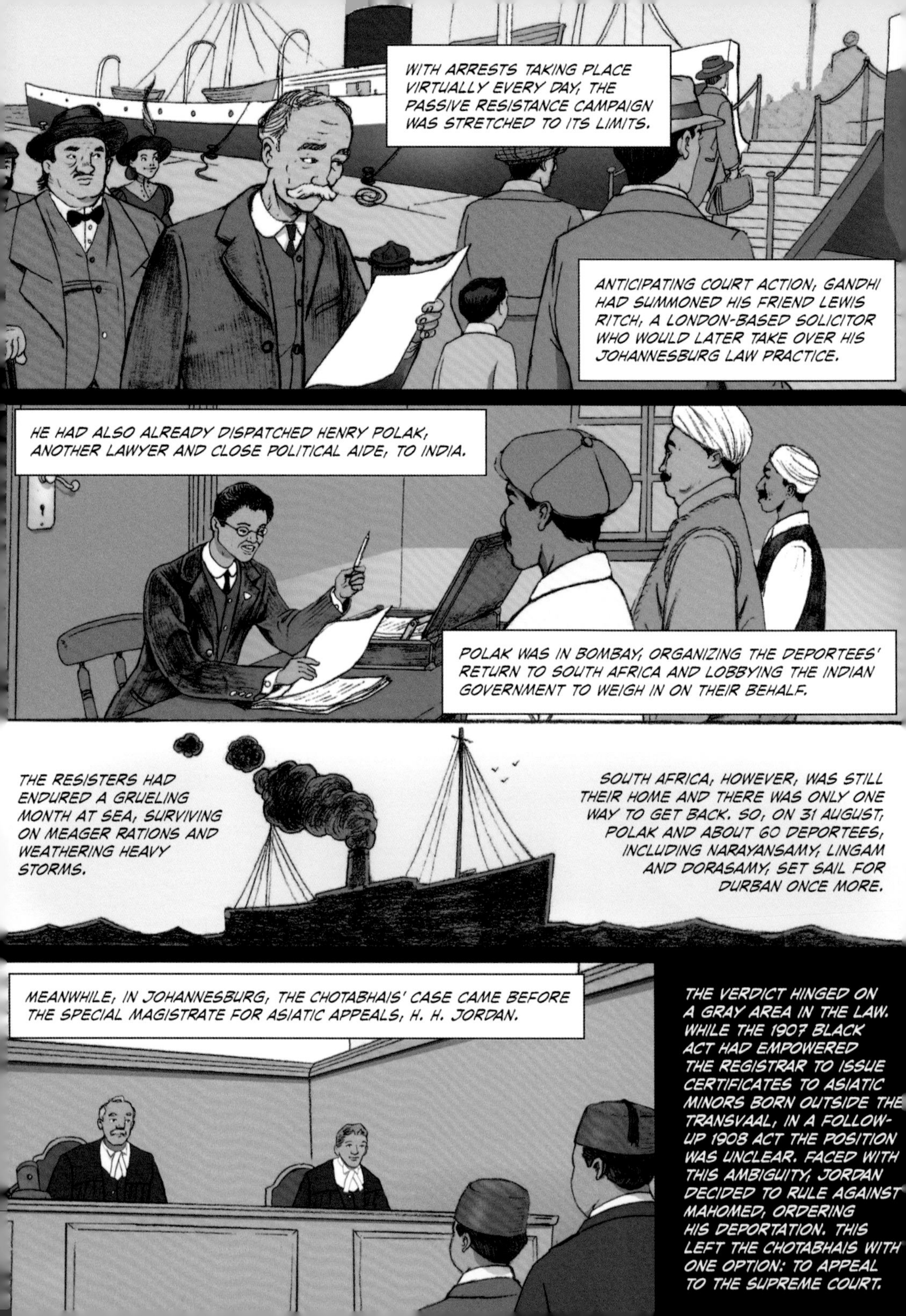
WITH ARRESTS TAKING PLACE VIRTUALLY EVERY DAY, THE PASSIVE RESISTANCE CAMPAIGN WAS STRETCHED TO ITS LIMITS.
ANTICIPATING COURT ACTION, GANDHI HAD SUMMONED HIS FRIEND LEWIS RITCH, A LONDON-BASED SOLICITOR WHO WOULD LATER TAKE OVER HIS JOHANNESBURG LAW PRACTICE.
HE HAD ALSO ALREADY DISPATCHED HENRY POLAK, ANOTHER LAWYER AND CLOSE POLITICAL AIDE, TO INDIA.
POLAK WAS IN BOMBAY, ORGANIZING THE DEPORTEES' RETURN TO SOUTH AFRICA AND LOBBYING THE INDIAN GOVERNMENT TO WEIGH IN ON THEIR BEHALF.
THE RESISTERS HAD ENDURED A GRUELING MONTH AT SEA, SURVIVING ON MEAGER RATIONS AND WEATHERING HEAVY STORMS.
SOUTH AFRICA, HOWEVER, WAS STILL THEIR HOME AND THERE WAS ONLY ONE WAY TO GET BACK. SO, ON 31 AUGUST, POLAK AND ABOUT 60 DEPORTEES, INCLUDING NARAYANSAMY, LINGAM AND DORASAMY, SET SAIL FOR DURBAN ONCE MORE.
MEANWHILE, IN JOHANNESBURG, THE CHOTABHAIS' CASE CAME BEFORE THE SPECIAL MAGISTRATE FOR ASIATIC APPEALS, H. H. JORDAN.
THE VERDICT HINGED ON A GRAY AREA IN THE LAW. WHILE THE 1907 BLACK ACT HAD EMPOWERED THE REGISTRAR TO ISSUE CERTIFICATES TO ASIATIC MINORS BORN OUTSIDE THE TRANSVAAL, IN A FOLLOW-UP 1908 ACT THE POSITION WAS UNCLEAR. FACED WITH THIS AMBIGUITY, JORDAN DECIDED TO RULE AGAINST MAHOMED, ORDERING HIS DEPORTATION. THIS LEFT THE CHOTABHAIS WITH ONE OPTION: TO APPEAL TO THE SUPREME COURT.

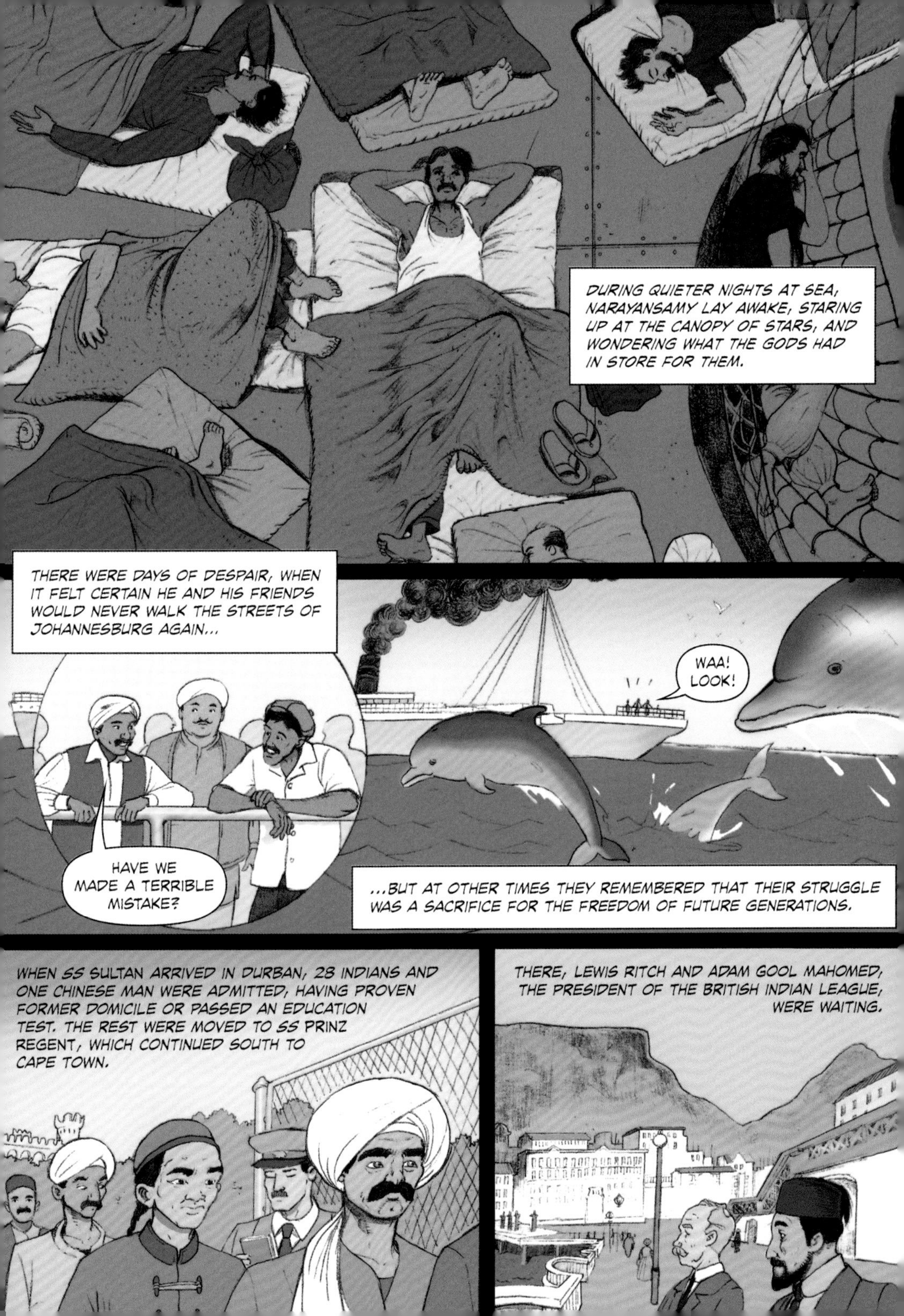
DURING QUIETER NIGHTS AT SEA, NARAYANSAMY LAY AWAKE, STARING UP AT THE CANOPY OF STARS, AND WONDERING WHAT THE GODS HAD IN STORE FOR THEM.
THERE WERE DAYS OF DESPAIR, WHEN IT FELT CERTAIN HE AND HIS FRIENDS WOULD NEVER WALK THE STREETS OF JOHANNESBURG AGAIN...
HAVE WE MADE A TERRIBLE MISTAKE?
WAA! LOOK!
...BUT AT OTHER TIMES THEY REMEMBERED THAT THEIR STRUGGLE WAS A SACRIFICE FOR THE FREEDOM OF FUTURE GENERATIONS.
WHEN SS SULTAN ARRIVED IN DURBAN, 28 INDIANS AND ONE CHINESE MAN WERE ADMITTED, HAVING PROVEN FORMER DOMICILE OR PASSED AN EDUCATION TEST. THE REST WERE MOVED TO SS PRINZ REGENT, WHICH CONTINUED SOUTH TO CAPE TOWN.
THERE, LEWIS RITCH AND ADAM GOOL MAHOMED, THE PRESIDENT OF THE BRITISH INDIAN LEAGUE, WERE WAITING.

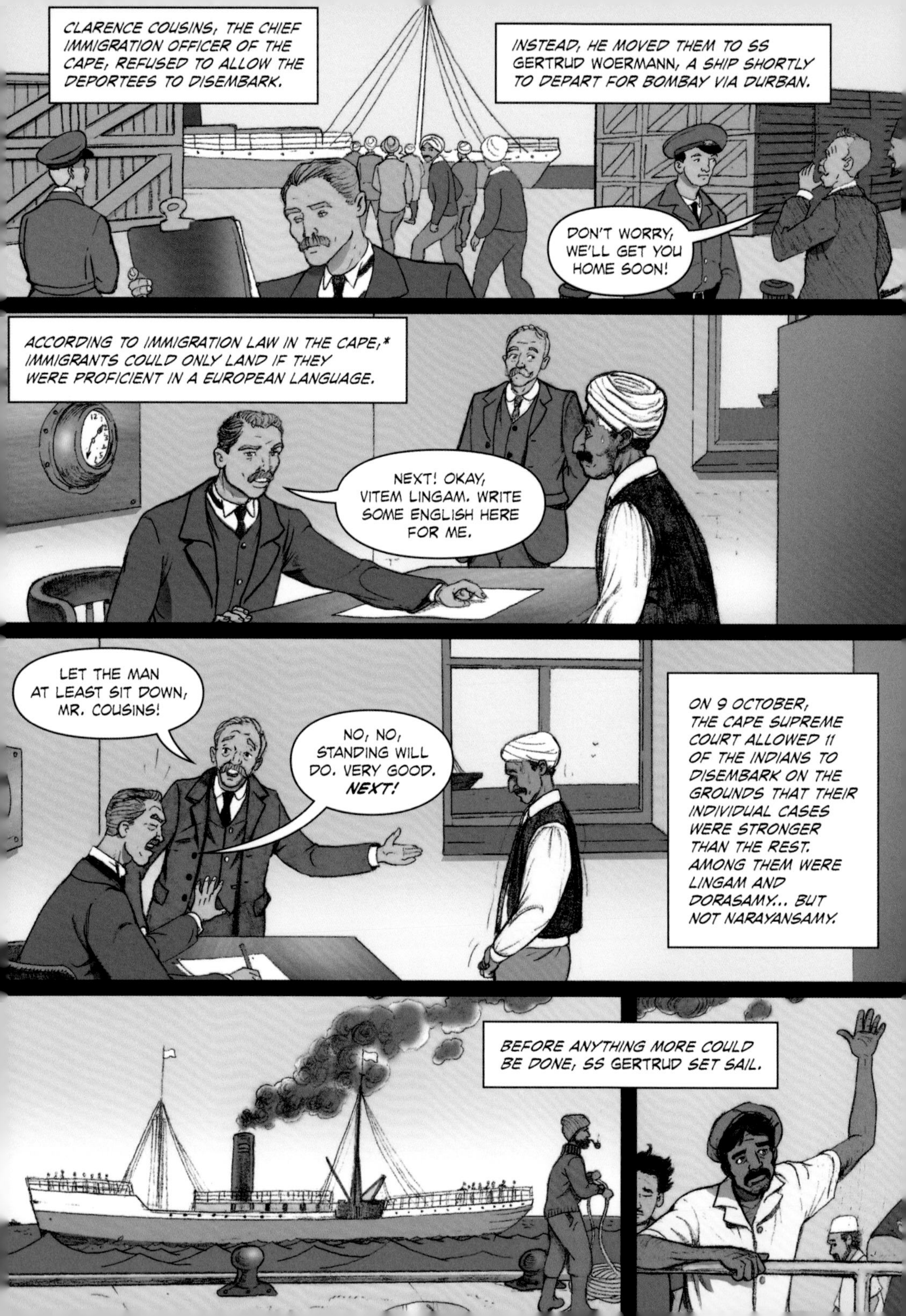
CLARENCE COUSINS, THE CHIEF IMMIGRATION OFFICER OF THE CAPE, REFUSED TO ALLOW THE DEPORTEES TO DISEMBARK.
INSTEAD, HE MOVED THEM TO SS GERTRUD WOERMANN, A SHIP SHORTLY TO DEPART FOR BOMBAY VIA DURBAN.
DON'T WORRY; WE'LL GET YOU HOME SOON!
ACCORDING TO IMMIGRATION LAW IN THE CAPE,* IMMIGRANTS COULD ONLY LAND IF THEY WERE PROFICIENT IN A EUROPEAN LANGUAGE.
NEXT! OKAY, VITEM LINGAM. WRITE SOME ENGLISH HERE FOR ME.
LET THE MAN AT LEAST SIT DOWN, MR. COUSINS!
NO, NO, STANDING WILL DO. VERY GOOD. NEXT!
ON 9 OCTOBER, THE CAPE SUPREME COURT ALLOWED 11 OF THE INDIANS TO DISEMBARK ON THE GROUNDS THAT THEIR INDIVIDUAL CASES WERE STRONGER THAN THE REST. AMONG THEM WERE LINGAM AND DORASAMY... BUT NOT NARAYANSAMY.
BEFORE ANYTHING MORE COULD BE DONE, SS GERTRUD SET SAIL.

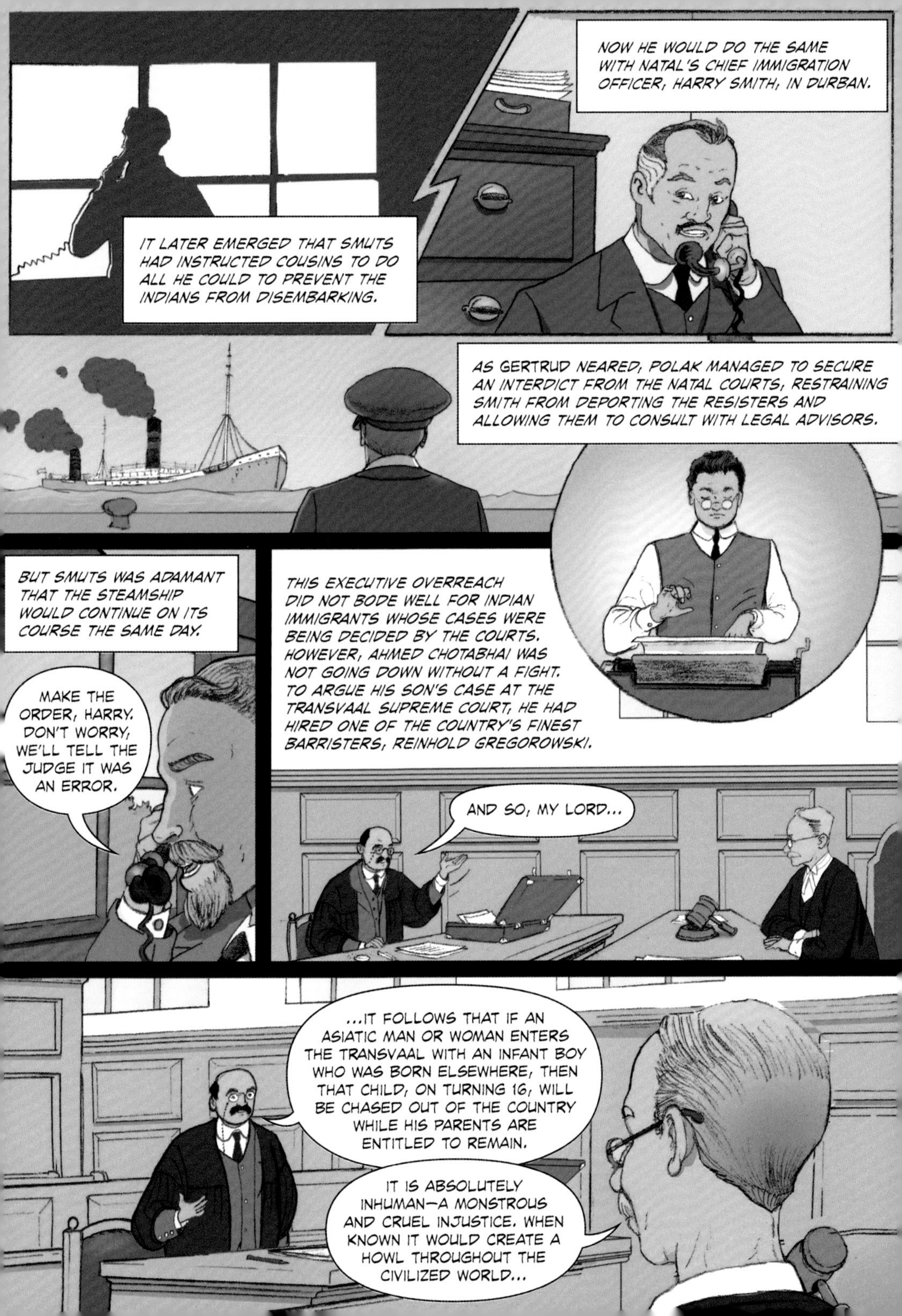
NOW HE WOULD DO THE SAME WITH NATAL'S CHIEF IMMIGRATION OFFICER, HARRY SMITH, IN DURBAN.
IT LATER EMERGED THAT SMUTS HAD INSTRUCTED COUSINS TO DO ALL HE COULD TO PREVENT THE INDIANS FROM DISEMBARKING.
AS GERTRUD NEARED, POLAK MANAGED TO SECURE AN INTERDICT FROM THE NATAL COURTS, RESTRAINING SMITH FROM DEPORTING THE RESISTERS AND ALLOWING THEM TO CONSULT WITH LEGAL ADVISORS.
BUT SMUTS WAS ADAMANT THAT THE STEAMSHIP WOULD CONTINUE ON ITS COURSE THE SAME DAY.
MAKE THE ORDER, HARRY. DON'T WORRY, WE'LL TELL THE JUDGE IT WAS AN ERROR.
THIS EXECUTIVE OVERREACH DID NOT BODE WELL FOR INDIAN IMMIGRANTS WHOSE CASES WERE BEING DECIDED BY THE COURTS. HOWEVER, AHMED CHOTABHAI WAS NOT GOING DOWN WITHOUT A FIGHT. TO ARGUE HIS SON'S CASE AT THE TRANSVAAL SUPREME COURT, HE HAD HIRED ONE OF THE COUNTRY'S FINEST BARRISTERS, REINHOLD GREGOROWSKI.
AND SO, MY LORD...
...IT FOLLOWS THAT IF AN ASIATIC MAN OR WOMAN ENTERS THE TRANSVAAL WITH AN INFANT BOY WHO WAS BORN ELSEWHERE, THEN THAT CHILD, ON TURNING 16, WILL BE CHASED OUT OF THE COUNTRY WHILE HIS PARENTS ARE ENTITLED TO REMAIN.
IT IS ABSOLUTELY INHUMAN—A MONSTROUS AND CRUEL INJUSTICE. WHEN KNOWN IT WOULD CREATE A HOWL THROUGHOUT THE CIVILIZED WORLD...

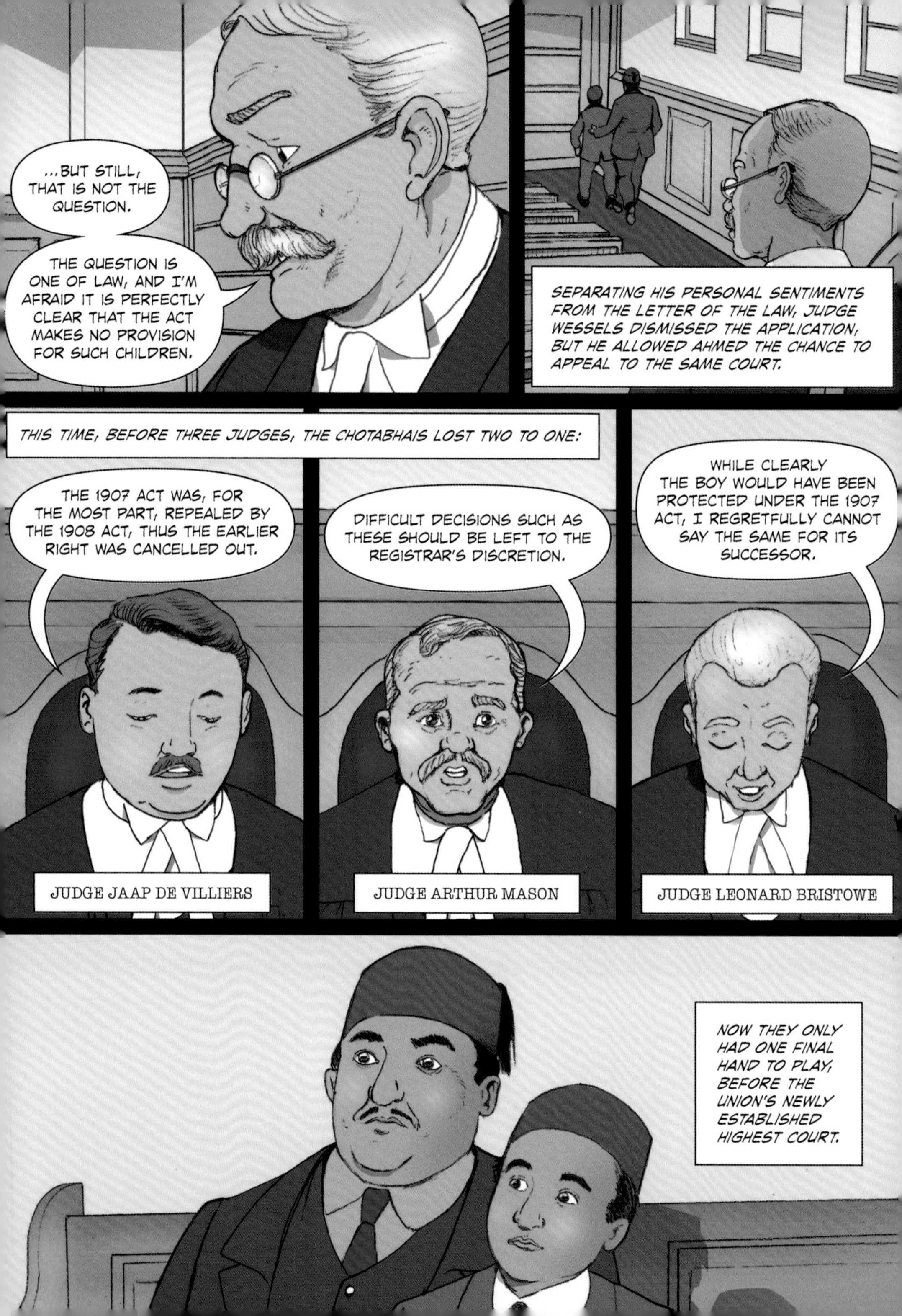

...BUT STILL, THAT IS NOT THE QUESTION.
THE QUESTION IS ONE OF LAW, AND I'M AFRAID IT IS PERFECTLY CLEAR THAT THE ACT MAKES NO PROVISION FOR SUCH CHILDREN.
SEPARATING HIS PERSONAL SENTIMENTS FROM THE LETTER OF THE LAW, JUDGE WESSELS DISMISSED THE APPLICATION, BUT HE ALLOWED AHMED THE CHANCE TO APPEAL TO THE SAME COURT.
THIS TIME, BEFORE THREE JUDGES, THE CHOTABHAIS LOST TWO TO ONE:
THE 1907 ACT WAS, FOR THE MOST PART, REPEALED BY THE 1908 ACT, THUS THE EARLIER RIGHT WAS CANCELLED OUT.
JUDGE JAAP DE VILLIERS
DIFFICULT DECISIONS SUCH AS THESE SHOULD BE LEFT TO THE REGISTRAR'S DISCRETION.
JUDGE ARTHUR MASON
WHILE CLEARLY THE BOY WOULD HAVE BEEN PROTECTED UNDER THE 1907 ACT, I REGRETFULLY CANNOT SAY THE SAME FOR ITS SUCCESSOR.
JUDGE LEONARD BRISTOWE
NOW THEY ONLY HAD ONE FINAL HAND TO PLAY, BEFORE THE UNION'S NEWLY ESTABLISHED HIGHEST COURT.

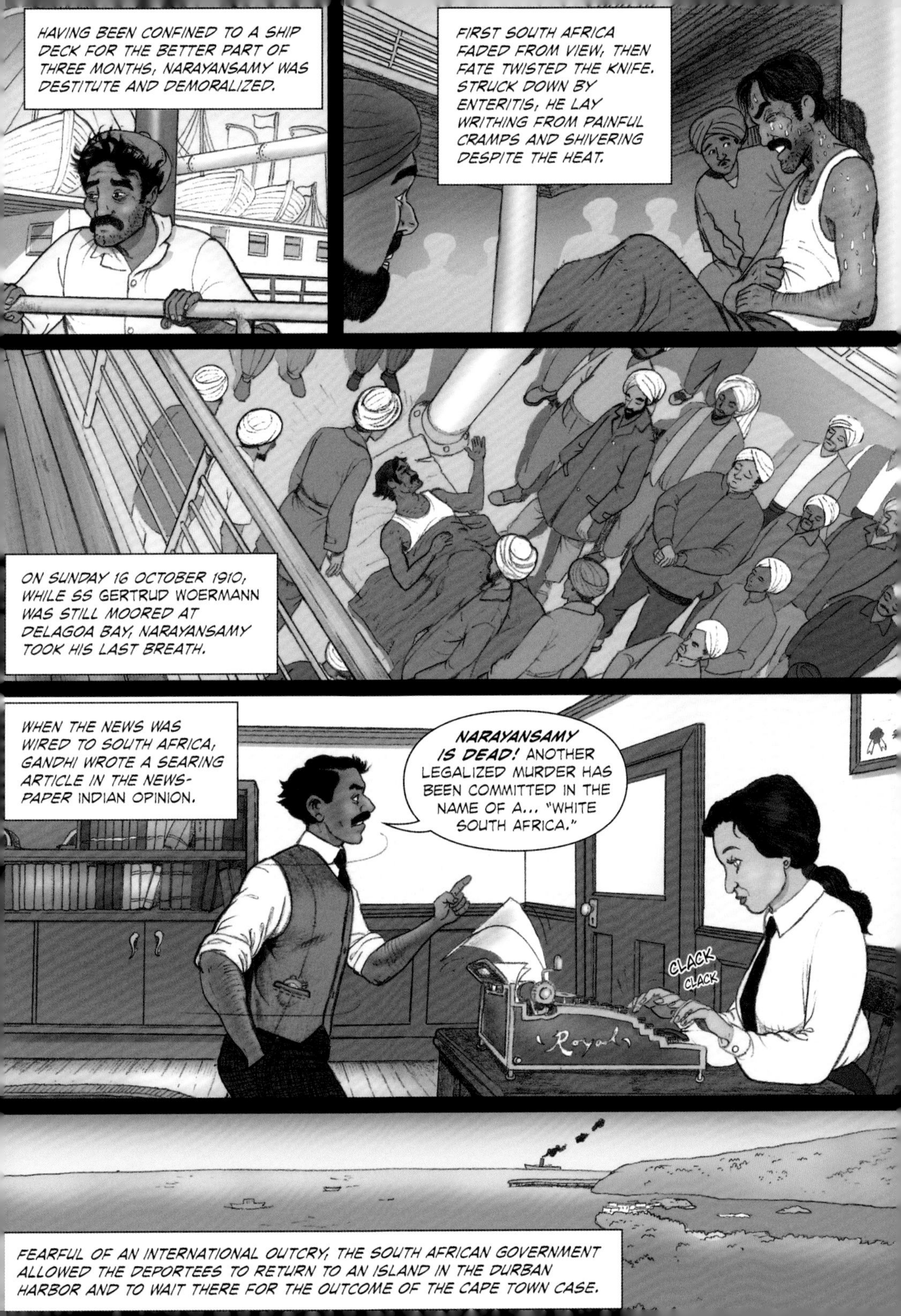
HAVING BEEN CONFINED TO A SHIP DECK FOR THE BETTER PART OF THREE MONTHS, NARAYANSAMY WAS DESTITUTE AND DEMORALIZED.
FIRST SOUTH AFRICA FADED FROM VIEW, THEN FATE TWISTED THE KNIFE. STRUCK DOWN BY ENTERITIS, HE LAY WRITHING FROM PAINFUL CRAMPS AND SHIVERING DESPITE THE HEAT.
ON SUNDAY 16 OCTOBER 1910, WHILE SS GERTRUD WOERMANN WAS STILL MOORED AT DELAGOA BAY, NARAYANSAMY TOOK HIS LAST BREATH.
WHEN THE NEWS WAS WIRED TO SOUTH AFRICA, GANDHI WROTE A SEARING ARTICLE IN THE NEWSPAPER INDIAN OPINION.
NARAYANSAMY IS DEAD! ANOTHER LEGALIZED MURDER HAS BEEN COMMITTED IN THE NAME OF A... "WHITE SOUTH AFRICA."
CLACK
CLACK
Royal
FEARFUL OF AN INTERNATIONAL OUTCRY, THE SOUTH AFRICAN GOVERNMENT ALLOWED THE DEPORTEES TO RETURN TO AN ISLAND IN THE DURBAN HARBOR AND TO WAIT THERE FOR THE OUTCOME OF THE CAPE TOWN CASE.

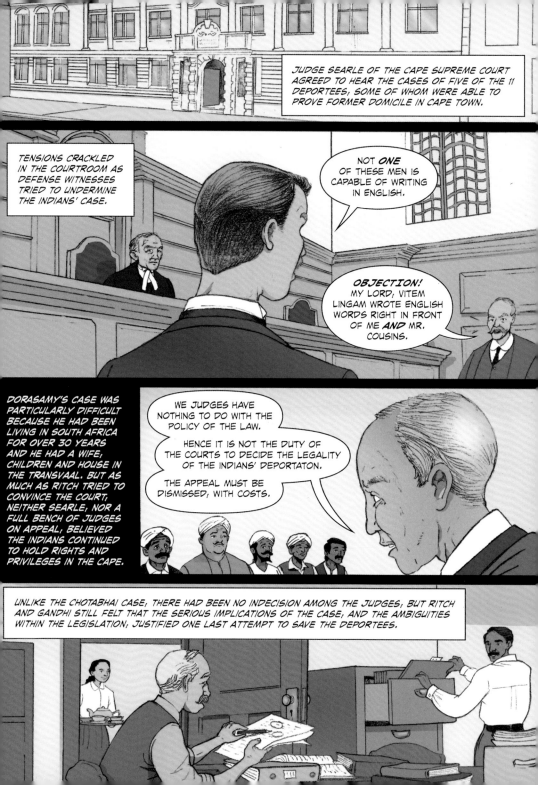

JUDGE SEARLE OF THE CAPE SUPREME COURT AGREED TO HEAR THE CASES OF FIVE OF THE 11 DEPORTEES, SOME OF WHOM WERE ABLE TO PROVE FORMER DOMICILE IN CAPE TOWN.

TENSIONS CRACKLED IN THE COURTROOM AS DEFENSE WITNESSES TRIED TO UNDERMINE THE INDIANS' CASE.

NOT *ONE* OF THESE MEN IS CAPABLE OF WRITING IN ENGLISH.

OBJECTION! MY LORD, VITEM LINGAM WROTE ENGLISH WORDS RIGHT IN FRONT OF ME *AND* MR. COUSINS.

DORASAMY'S CASE WAS PARTICULARLY DIFFICULT BECAUSE HE HAD BEEN LIVING IN SOUTH AFRICA FOR OVER 30 YEARS AND HE HAD A WIFE, CHILDREN AND HOUSE IN THE TRANSVAAL. BUT AS MUCH AS RITCH TRIED TO CONVINCE THE COURT, NEITHER SEARLE, NOR A FULL BENCH OF JUDGES ON APPEAL, BELIEVED THE INDIANS CONTINUED TO HOLD RIGHTS AND PRIVILEGES IN THE CAPE.

WE JUDGES HAVE NOTHING TO DO WITH THE POLICY OF THE LAW.

HENCE IT IS NOT THE DUTY OF THE COURTS TO DECIDE THE LEGALITY OF THE INDIANS' DEPORTATON.

THE APPEAL MUST BE DISMISSED, WITH COSTS.

UNLIKE THE CHOTABHAI CASE, THERE HAD BEEN NO INDECISION AMONG THE JUDGES, BUT RITCH AND GANDHI STILL FELT THAT THE SERIOUS IMPLICATIONS OF THE CASE, AND THE AMBIGUITIES WITHIN THE LEGISLATION, JUSTIFIED ONE LAST ATTEMPT TO SAVE THE DEPORTEES.

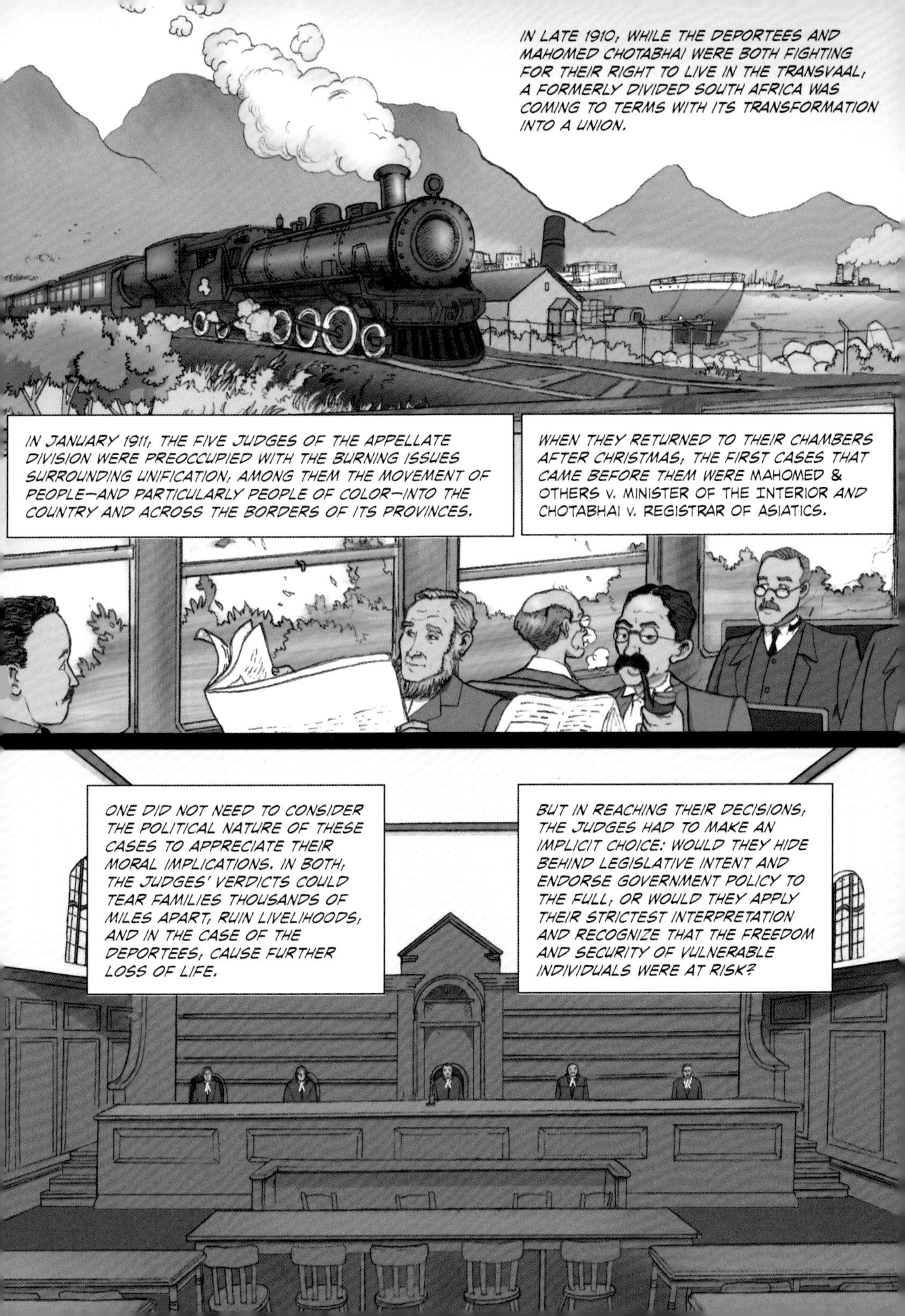
IN LATE 1910, WHILE THE DEPORTEES AND MAHOMED CHOTABHAI WERE BOTH FIGHTING FOR THEIR RIGHT TO LIVE IN THE TRANSVAAL, A FORMERLY DIVIDED SOUTH AFRICA WAS COMING TO TERMS WITH ITS TRANSFORMATION INTO A UNION.
IN JANUARY 1911, THE FIVE JUDGES OF THE APPELLATE DIVISION WERE PREOCCUPIED WITH THE BURNING ISSUES SURROUNDING UNIFICATION, AMONG THEM THE MOVEMENT OF PEOPLE—AND PARTICULARLY PEOPLE OF COLOR—INTO THE COUNTRY AND ACROSS THE BORDERS OF ITS PROVINCES.
WHEN THEY RETURNED TO THEIR CHAMBERS AFTER CHRISTMAS, THE FIRST CASES THAT CAME BEFORE THEM WERE MAHOMED & OTHERS v. MINISTER OF THE INTERIOR AND CHOTABHAI v. REGISTRAR OF ASIATICS.
ONE DID NOT NEED TO CONSIDER THE POLITICAL NATURE OF THESE CASES TO APPRECIATE THEIR MORAL IMPLICATIONS. IN BOTH, THE JUDGES' VERDICTS COULD TEAR FAMILIES THOUSANDS OF MILES APART, RUIN LIVELIHOODS, AND IN THE CASE OF THE DEPORTEES, CAUSE FURTHER LOSS OF LIFE.
BUT IN REACHING THEIR DECISIONS, THE JUDGES HAD TO MAKE AN IMPLICIT CHOICE: WOULD THEY HIDE BEHIND LEGISLATIVE INTENT AND ENDORSE GOVERNMENT POLICY TO THE FULL, OR WOULD THEY APPLY THEIR STRICTEST INTERPRETATION AND RECOGNIZE THAT THE FREEDOM AND SECURITY OF VULNERABLE INDIVIDUALS WERE AT RISK?

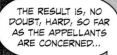

THE RESULT IS, NO DOUBT, HARD, SO FAR AS THE APPELLANTS ARE CONCERNED...

...BUT WHERE THE MEANING OF THE LEGISLATURE EXPRESSED IN A STATUTE IS CLEAR, THE COURT IS BOUND TO GIVE EFFECT TO IT.

HOWEVER DESIRABLE IT MAY BE TO RESTRICT INDIAN IMMIGRATION, THIS COURT MUST APPLY THE SAME RULES OF CONSTRUCTION WHICH IT WOULD TO ACTS WITH LESS DESIRABLE OBJECTS.

IN MAHOMED, THE APPELLATE DIVISION FOUND THAT THE APPLICANTS—DORASAMY, LINGAM, MOODALEY, VALOO PERUMAL AND ANTONIE TEAM—HAD FAILED TO JUSTIFY THEIR RIGHT TO ENTRY. THIS MEANT THAT THE FIVE MEN, AND HUNDREDS OF OTHER DEPORTED PASSIVE RESISTERS LIKE THEM, WERE BANISHED INDEFINITELY FROM THEIR HOME PROVINCE OF THE TRANSVAAL.

IN CHOTABHAI, ALL FIVE APPELLATE DIVISION JUDGES DECIDED THAT THE REGISTRAR SHOULD HAVE ALLOWED MAHOMED CHOTABHAI TO REGISTER. AFTER FOUR LEGAL DEFEATS, THE BOY'S CASE PREVAILED AT THE FINAL HURDLE. FROM THAT MOMENT, HE—AND OTHER ASIATIC CHILDREN IN HIS POSITION—HAD THE RIGHT TO LIVE IN THE TRANSVAAL WITH THEIR PARENTS.

AHMED CHOTABHAI DIED OF UNKNOWN CAUSES IN 1913. IN HIS WILL, HIS ESTATE OF 10,000 POUNDS WAS SPLIT BETWEEN HIS SONS MAHOMED AND ISMAIL, LEAVING 100 POUNDS TO HIS DAUGHTER FATMA AND NOTHING TO HIS WIFE BIBI.

NARAYANSAMY WAS BURIED IN LOURENÇO MARQUES ON 17 OCTOBER 1910, THE DAY AFTER HIS DEATH. NOTHING IS KNOWN OF THE FATE OF DORASAMY, LINGAM AND THEIR FELLOW SATYAGRAHIS BEYOND THE APPELLATE DIVISION'S DISMISSAL OF THEIR CASE ON 30 JANUARY 1911.

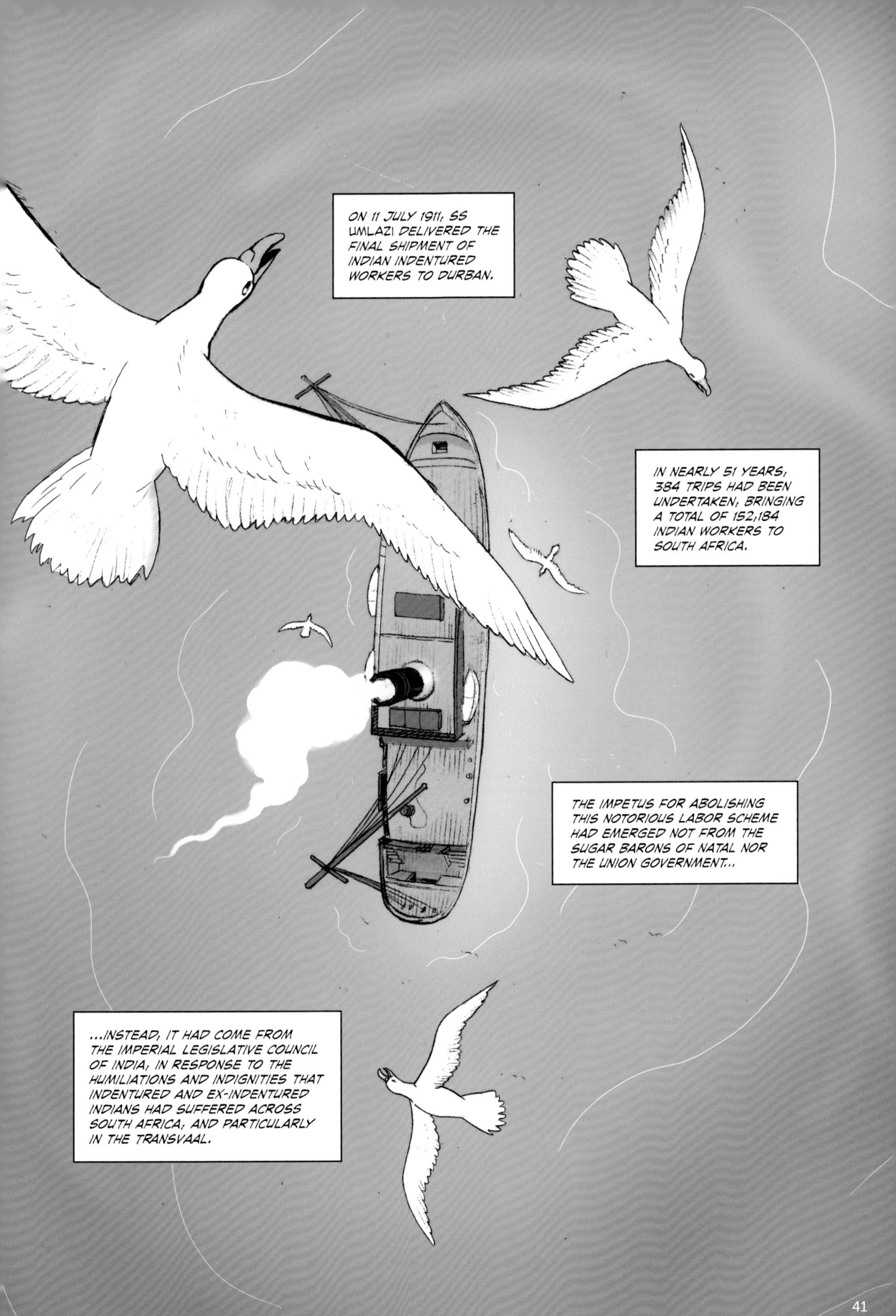
ON 11 JULY 1911, SS UMLAZI DELIVERED THE FINAL SHIPMENT OF INDIAN INDENTURED WORKERS TO DURBAN.
IN NEARLY 51 YEARS, 384 TRIPS HAD BEEN UNDERTAKEN, BRINGING A TOTAL OF 152,184 INDIAN WORKERS TO SOUTH AFRICA.
THE IMPETUS FOR ABOLISHING THIS NOTORIOUS LABOR SCHEME HAD EMERGED NOT FROM THE SUGAR BARONS OF NATAL NOR THE UNION GOVERNMENT...
...INSTEAD, IT HAD COME FROM THE IMPERIAL LEGISLATIVE COUNCIL OF INDIA, IN RESPONSE TO THE HUMILIATIONS AND INDIGNITIES THAT INDENTURED AND EX-INDENTURED INDIANS HAD SUFFERED ACROSS SOUTH AFRICA, AND PARTICULARLY IN THE TRANSVAAL.

BEHIND THE STORY: SOURCES AND SKETCHES

Chapter 1: Until the Ship Sails

Side by side in one of the boxes in the Supreme Court of Appeal's basement archive are two sleeves containing the court records of *Chotabhai v. Registrar of Astiatics* and *Mahomed & Others v. Minister of the Interior.* These documents were the basis of our research for the opening chapter. They included important biographical details for many of the characters; they outlined the events leading up to their parallel appeals in early 1911; and they laid bare, through exhibits and affidavits, the humiliation and inhumanity of the Asiatic registration process.

Beyond court records, the task of piecing together the peripheral history and social environment was made easier by crucial discoveries in the Registrar of Asiatics files; a small gathering of photographs—depicting key characters and events from the satyagraha campaign—which have survived in various South African and Indian archival collections; but above all, journalism and correspondence by members of the Transvaal and Natal Indian communities during the early twentieth century.

Mohandas Gandhi wrote prolifically during the 21 years he lived in South Africa (between 1893 and 1914). His speeches, letters, and dispatches from this period, which form part of his 100-volume collected works, read like a journal for the satyagraha campaign. Many of these writings originally appeared in the newspaper *Indian Opinion,* which Gandhi founded in 1903. Unflinching and detailed in its chronicling of the South African Indian community's activism and litigation, this source, more than any other, helped us to weave together the events in this story.

BRITISH INDIANS BURNING THEIR CERTIFICATES IN FRONT OF THE MOSQUE, JOHANNESBURG.

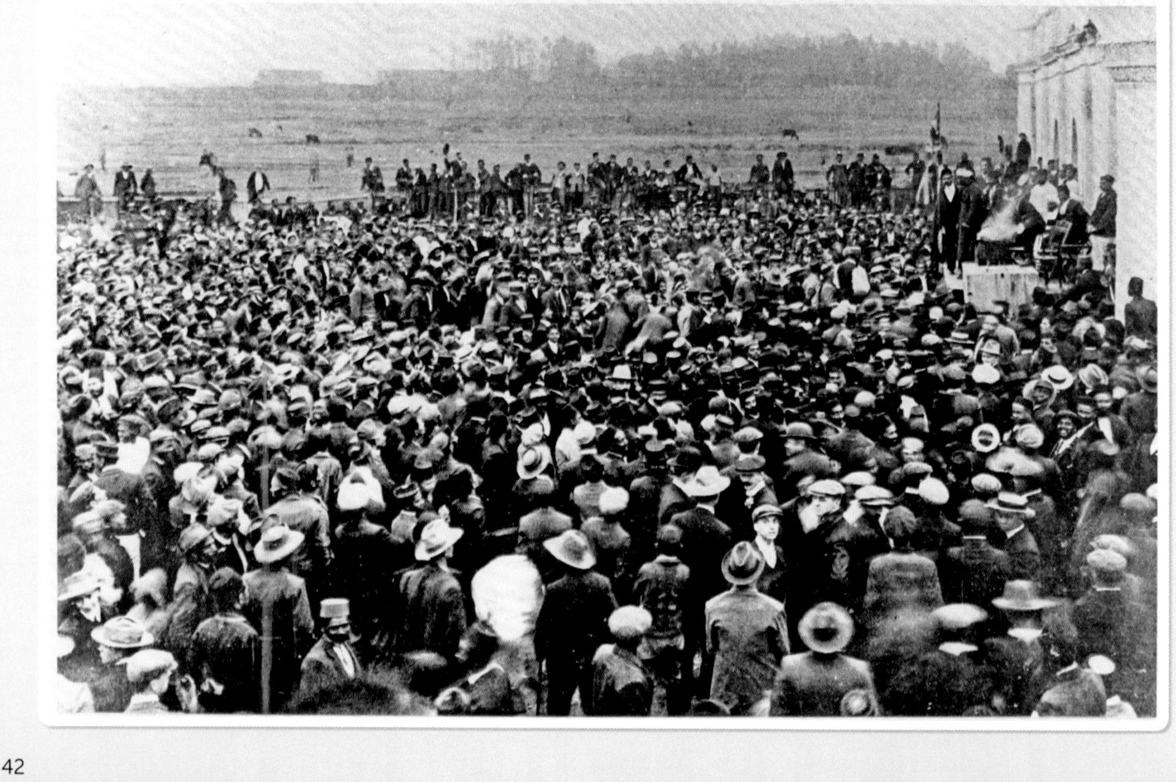

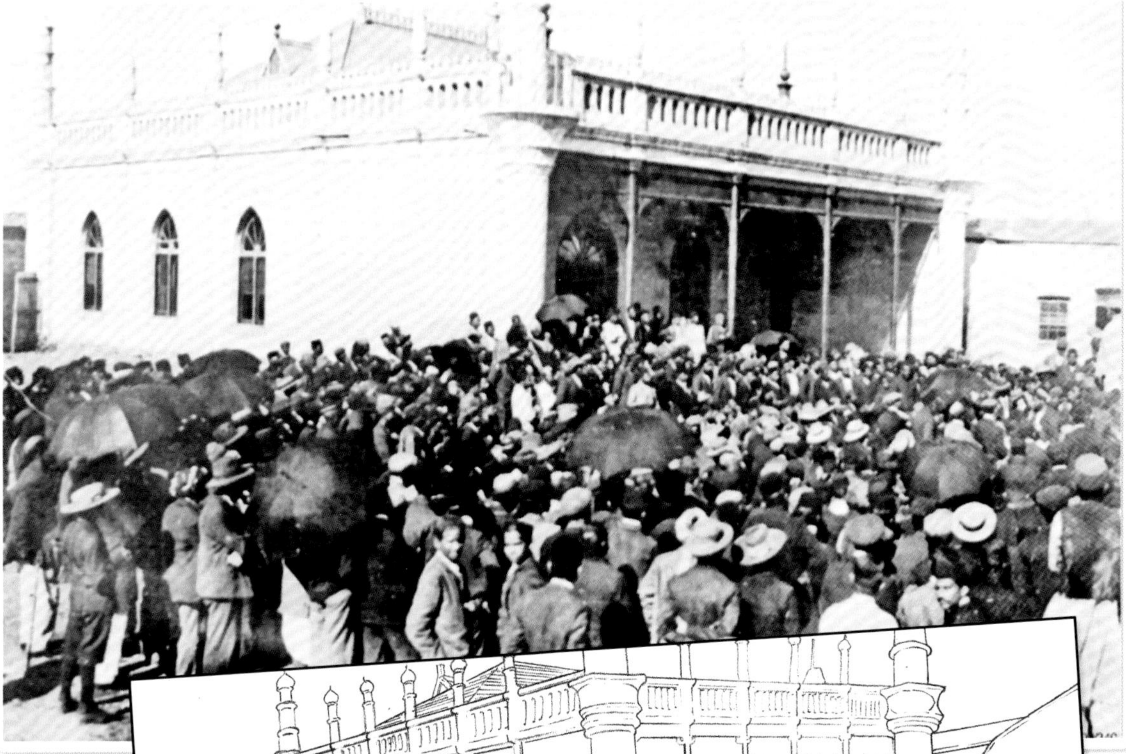

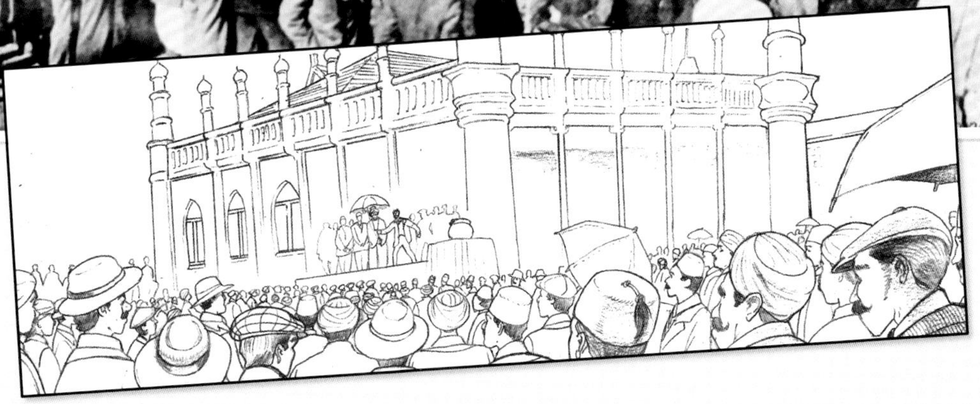

Left and above: "That afternoon, more than 3000 Asians watched 1300 certificates go up in smoke…" the iconic gathering which took place outside Johannesburg's Hamidia Mosque on 16 August 1908.

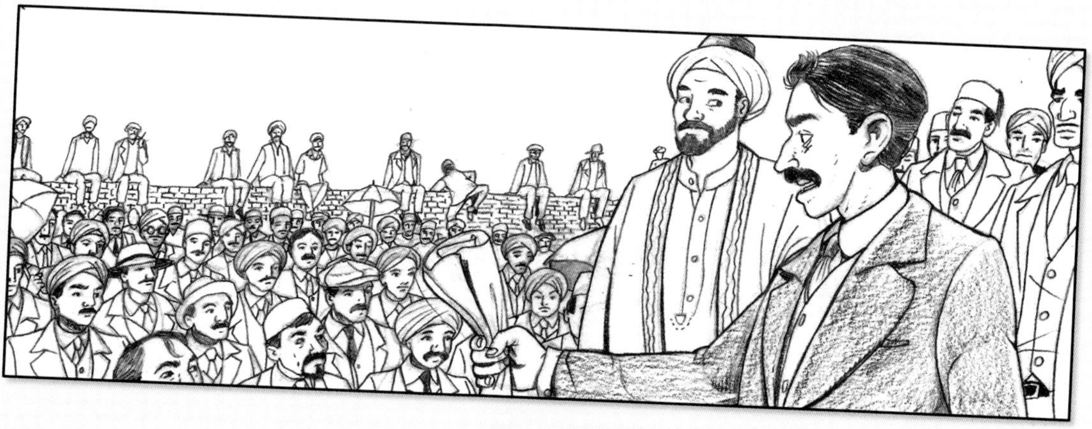

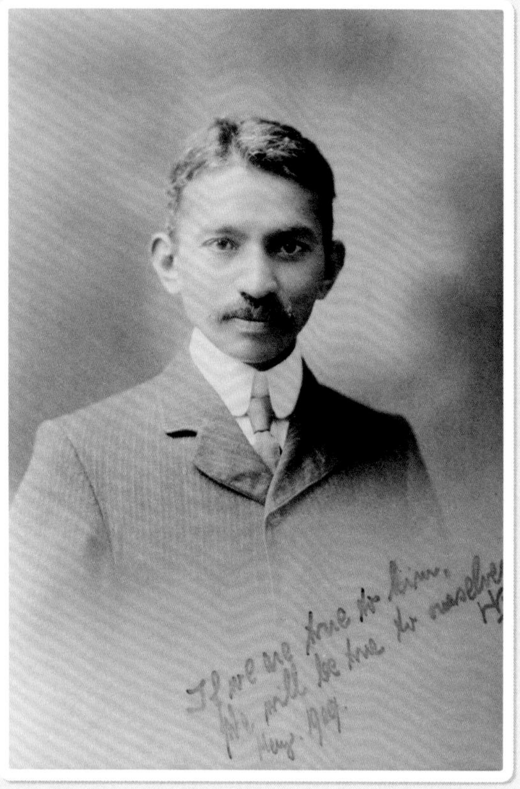

Mohandas Gandhi, lawyer, activist, and champion of satyagraha, in 1909.

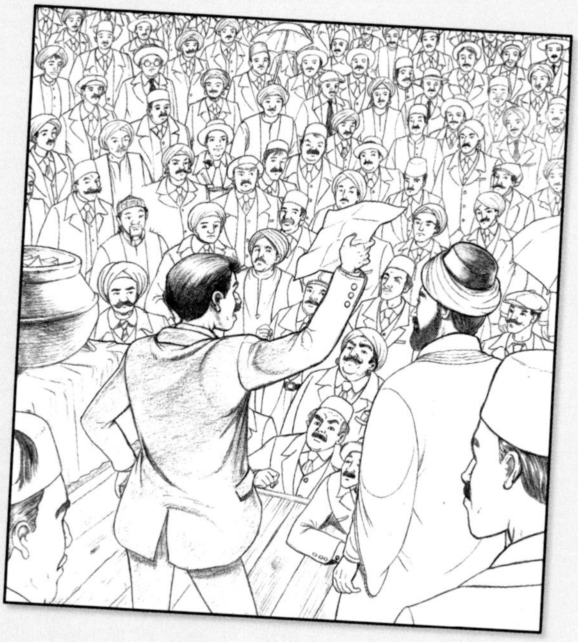

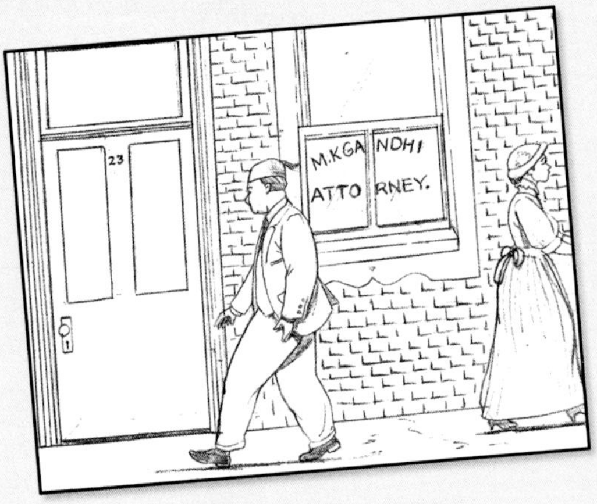
23
M.K.GA NDHI
ATTO RNEY.

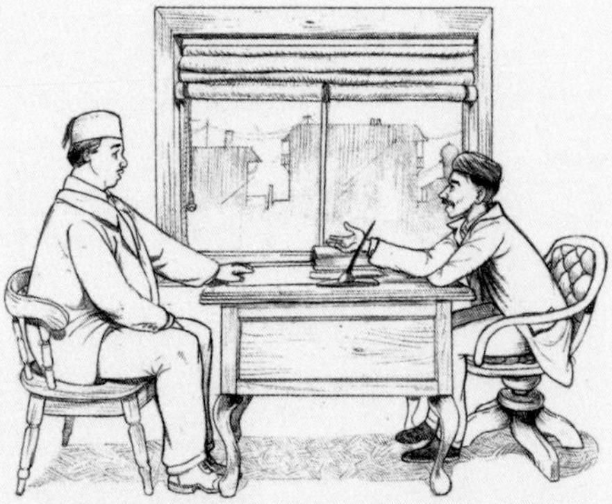

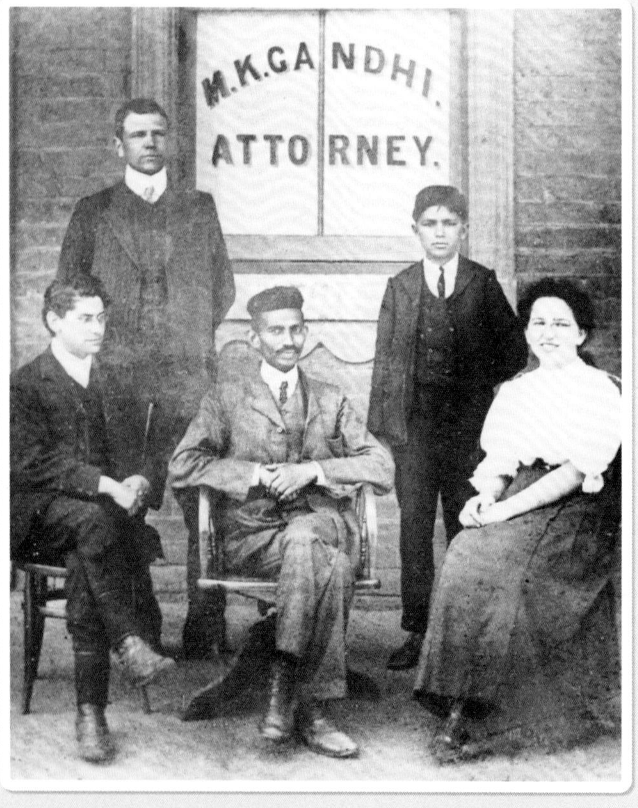
M.K.GA NDHI.
ATTO RNEY.

Left: Gandhi seated outside his law practice at 15 Rissik Street, Johannesburg, between his long-time colleagues, Henry Polak (*front left*) and Sonja Schlesin (*front right*).

Right: "As the son of a well-connected merchant who hadn't burnt his certificate, the boy was sheltered from a reality unfolding across the Transvaal in 1910..." a photo of Mahomed Chotabhai, attached to a 1922 immigration form, survives in South Africa's National Archives.

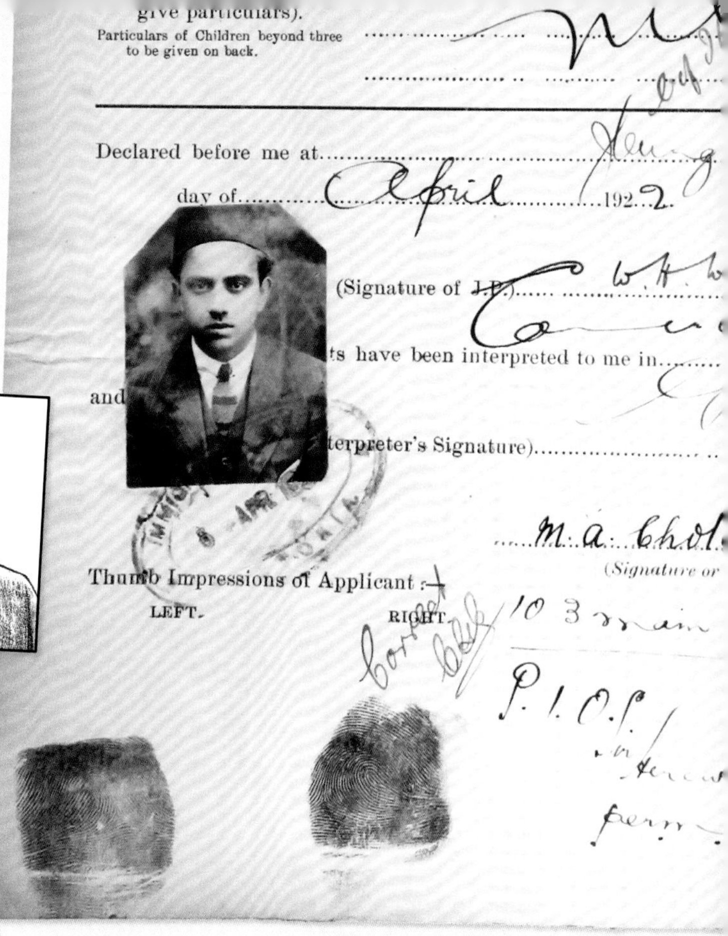

Particulars of Children beyond three to be given on back.
Declared before me at
day of April 1922
(Signature of J.P.)
ts have been interpreted to me in
and
terpreter's Signature)
M. A. Chot
(Signature or
Thumb Impressions of Applicant :
LEFT.
RIGHT.

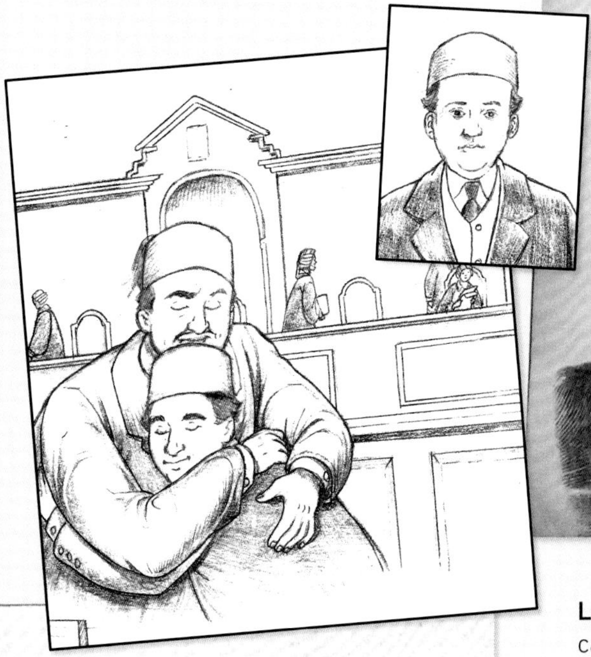

Left: Notes covering Mahomed Chotabhai's case, published in *Indian Opinion.*

Below: A few months after Mahomed's victory at the Appellate Division, Gandhi wrote this letter to the boy's father.

AUGUST 27TH, 1910

bhai with a view to getting the lad separately registered. Mr. Chamney said that could not be until he had attained majority. Application was therefore renewed on the boy attaining majority, but now Mr. Chamney said that the boy could not be registered as he was advised by the Law Department that Asiatic minors who were not resident in the Transvaal at the commencement of Act 36 of 1908 or who were not born in the Transvaal could not be registered although they entered the country with their parents whilst they were yet minors.

Poor Mr. Chhotabhai was paralysed. Was his own son to be expelled although he had meekly submitted to the Asiatic Act and was prepared to make his son do likewise? He began to look about himself and found that other parents were in the same predicament. Mr. Chhotabhai began to envy passive resisters their freedom. Was he to become a passive resister and tear his own certificate to pieces? His wealth, his age, his position, however, proved too strong for him and he began to seek the advice of lawyers.

The result was this appeal. Mr. Benson, after having proved the facts narrated by me, contended that Mr.

Messrs. ... indsamy P... 26 deporte... have now ... East Lond... Vereenigi... Their case... 24th insta... that two I... don their ... sideration.

The J... intends to ... minimum ... licence to ... months.

The cas... Govindsan... on to-day ... the 27th i...

Hin...

An orga... formation ... the doubl... loyalty and... ation and...

Dear MR. CHOTABHAI,

I am much obliged to you for your note of the 3rd instant enclosing a cheque for £300 in connection with you son's case. As I have already informed you, I do not desire to make personal use of your generous gift. It is my intention shortly to make over the Phoenix Farm, together with the machinery and the Press Buildings, which have been valued at £5,000, to trustees in trust for public purposes; and I propose, if I can induce our wealthy men to follow up your gift, to devote the money towards building a substantial school at Phoenix. Should, however, such support not be forthcoming, I propose to retain the sum to use, if required, for the objects of passive resistance, should its revival next year unfortunately become necessary.

Thanking you for your promise of co-operation in public work,

Yours sincerely,
M. K. GANDHI

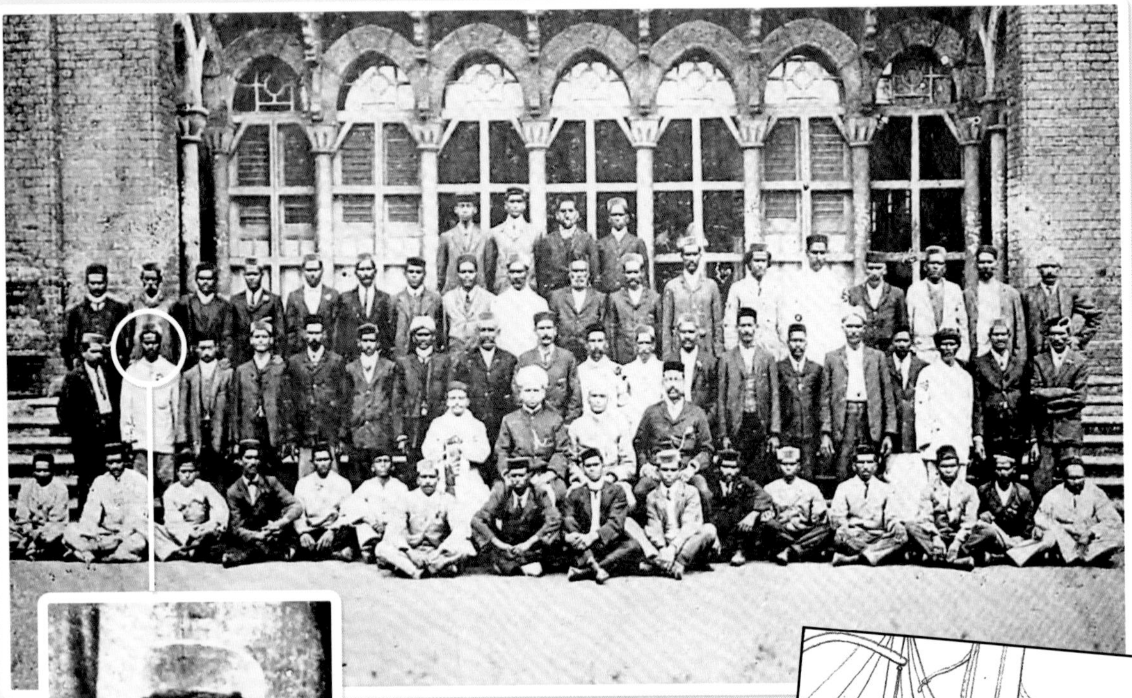

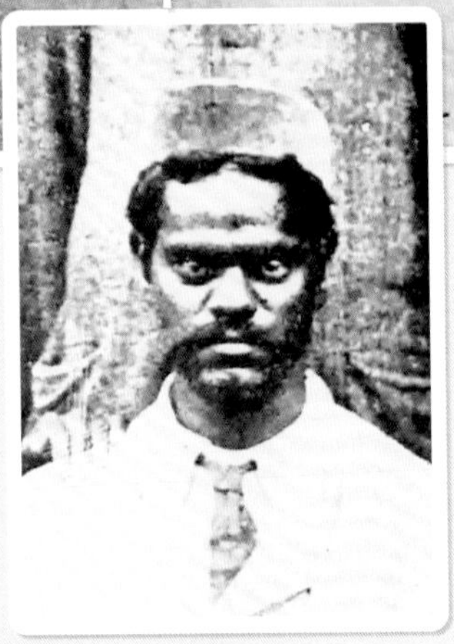

Above: While waiting to return to South Africa in mid-1910, the deported passive resisters were photographed by Chennai (formerly Madras)-based journal *Indian Review*.

Left: Narayansamy, the fruit hawker who died of enteritis aboard SS *Gertrud Woermann* on 16 October 1910.

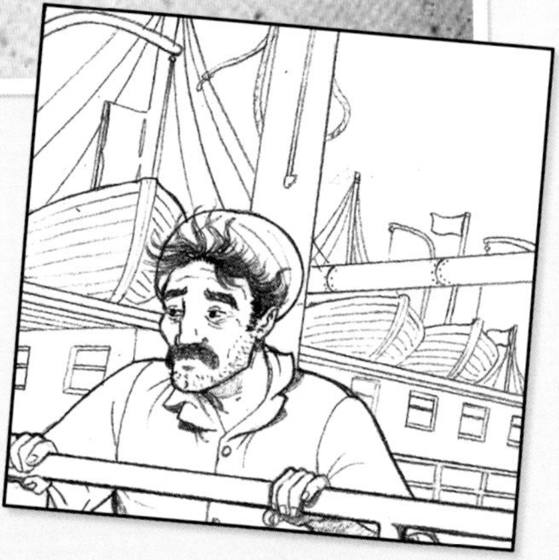

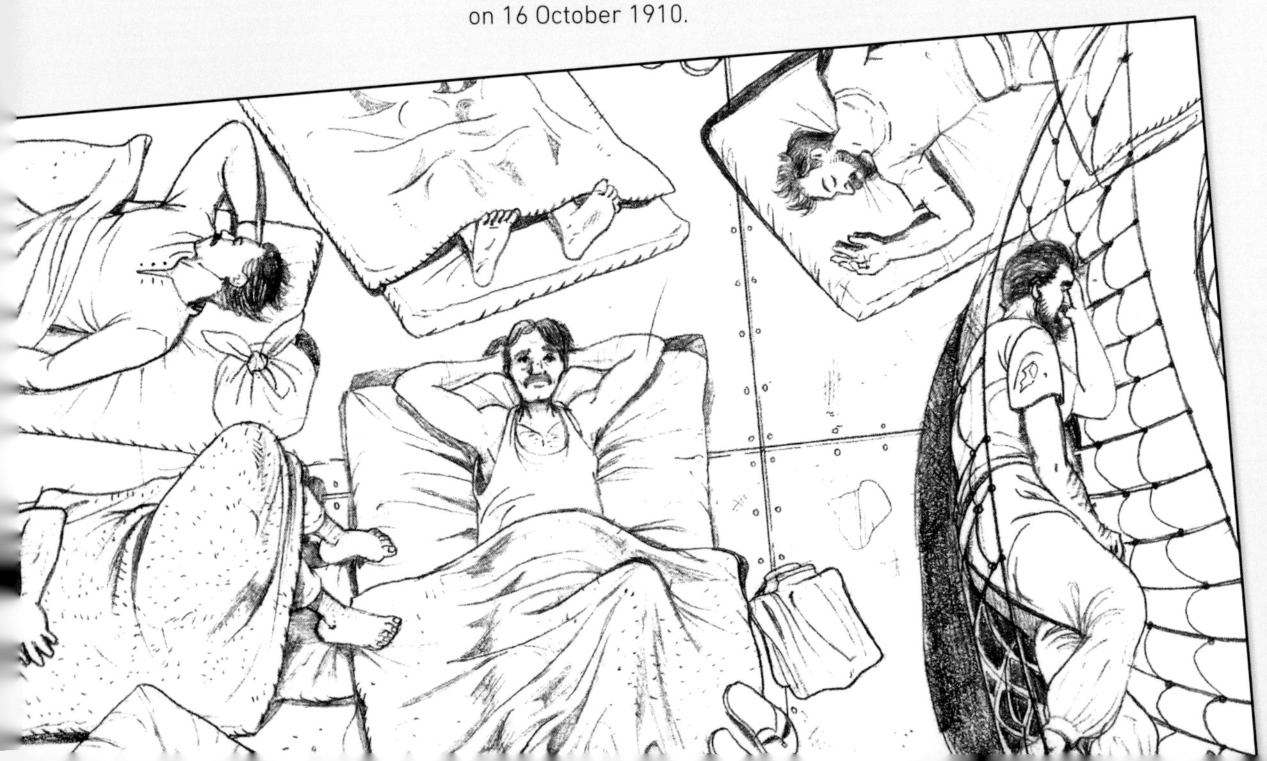

Left and below: Two articles published in *Indian Opinion* to mark Narayansamy's death. The column entitled "From the editor's chair" was likely written by Gandhi.

INDIAN OPINION
25 OCT 1910

From the Editor's Chair

LEGALISED MURDER

NARAYANSAMY is dead. Another legalised murder has been committed in the name of a "white South Africa." "Legalised murder" is, no doubt, a strong expression, but it fits the deed. If A deliberately brings about a state of things under which B dies, A is, we imagine, guilty of murder. We know that it was due to instructions from the Minister of the Interior that the deportees who arrived by the s.s. *Sultan* were refused a landing at various South African ports. We know that they were prevented even from seeing their legal advisers, and were reduced to a state of helplessness. And we know, too, that those rigid instructions which prevented the men from temporarily landing at any of the ports were not supplemented by others as to their care and good treatment during the period of enforced detention. Matters being thus, at whose door shall we place the death of Narayansamy? Such death caused by the act of a private individual would be termed murder; caused by the deed of a Government, acting under ostensible legal authority, we can but term legalised murder.

And thus to-day we mourn the death of Narayansamy, cruelly done to death, and offer our humble condolences to his unknown relatives. But there is a feeling of joy, too, for we feel that Narayansamy has died well. He has died as befits a true soldier—he has died fighting for the principles he held so dear. And it may be said of him, as it cannot of even the bravest and greatest of living passive resisters in the Transvaal, that he has completed his work. The honour of the Motherland has been safe in his keeping. And though the community to-day mourns an irreparable loss, it has gained in another direction. The supreme sacrifices offered by Narayansamy and Nagappan cannot but add to the sanctity of the struggle. The community must feel with added force that it dare not abandon its pursuit, but must press onward to the goal, regardless of the difficulties that beset its path. And thus Narayansamy and Nagappan have died, as they lived, doing their duty. And so, dead, they live in the memory of their mourning countrymen.

We give Mr. Narayansamy's portrait as a supplement with the present issue.

No. 43—VOL. 8.   SATURDAY, OCTOBER 22ND, 1910.   *Registered as a Newspaper* PRICE THREEPENCE

DEATH OF ANOTHER PASSIVE RESISTER

THE LATE MR. NARYANSAMY'S CAREER

ON Monday morning, the community was shocked to receive a telegram from Mr. Peter Moonlight, one of the deportees on board the *Gertrud Woermann*, at Delagoa Bay, to the effect that Mr. A. Naryansamy, a fellow-deportee, had died the previous night. This news was supplemented later by a message from the company's agents that the unfortunate man had died of enteritis, and was buried at Lourenco Marques on Monday.

Mr. Naryansamy carried on the business of a hawker in the Transvaal. He entered that Province during the war with the British troops, with whom he served in a non-combatant capacity, and after the war, he was admitted to residence and was duly registered. He was one of those who voluntarily registered, during the compromise of 1908, and he subsequently destroyed his certificate upon the discovery of General Smuts's repudiation of his obligations. He went to gaol as a passive resister. About the beginning of July last, Naryansamy was arrested again and illegally deported to India by a Portuguese agency and at the instance of the Union Government, and he landed in a destitute condition at Bombay, whence he was despatched, at the expense of the Bombay Government, to Madras, where he was the guest of the Indian South Africa League (Madras). He accompanied [the deportees] from Bombay for Durban, on 31st August, by the s.s. *Sultan*, with 82 fellow-sufferers. During the voyage he suffered from slight [illness,] but easily recovered, and [at the time] of his arrival at Durban, [after a] day's voyage, he apparently [was in] good health. He was not [allowed,] at the time, to land in [Natal] and as his claims had not [been suf]ficiently investigated, he [had to] proceed to Port Elizabeth, [on the] speedy departure of the [*Cro*]*wn Regent* to that port

and of the *Sultan* on her return voyage. At Port Elizabeth, he was refused a landing, and proceeded to Capetown. Here, with his fellow-deportees, thirty-two all told, he was obliged to remain, segregated from the rest of his kind, and unable to communicate with his legal advisers. The condition of these deportees has been described most graphically by Mr. L. W. Ritch in a letter addressed to the *Cape Times*. Being unable to land at Capetown, he was put on board the s.s. *Gertrud Woermann*, which left for Durban, arriving there on the 13th inst. Here again he was unable to communicate with his friends, and owing to the lawless action of the immigration authorities, the vessel bearing him was allowed to proceed to Delagoa Bay. The illness must have culminated during the voyage there.

Mr. Gandhi writes to the Press as follows under date the 17th instant :—

Sir,—Most of the newspapers published a telegram from Pretoria some days ago to the effect that at last the Asiatic question that has agitated the Colony for the last four years was about to be satisfactorily settled. This news was supposed to be officially inspired, but was immediately followed by the arrest of one of the staunchest and best-respected of Indians in this Province, namely, Mr. Sorabji, and his arrest was followed by that of three of his co-passive resisters equally brave, that is, Messrs. Thambi Naidoo, Sodha and Medh.

I should, however, not have trespassed upon your courtesy and the attention of the public in order merely to give the above information. But, in my humble opinion, it is due to the public to know something of the trials of those Indians and Chinese who, although lawful residents of the Transvaal and some of them born in South Africa, were deported to India, and returned per S. S. *Sultan* about

the end of last month. The tragedy has culminated in the death of a most inoffensive and law-abiding Indian named Naryansamy. When he left this Province for India as a deportee, he possessed a healthy constitution, but over six weeks on the decks of different steamers exposed to all sorts of weather evidently proved too severe even for his constitution. Mr. Ritch has pointed out that he and his fellow-deportees were not allowed to see friends or legal advisers almost for a week while their steamer was in Table Bay, and ultimately he had to obtain an order from the Supreme Court before he could see them. He has stated in a letter to the Cape papers that he found these men bootless and hatless and in some cases even without sufficient protection for the body, shivering on the open deck of that steamer. They were refused landing first at Durban, then at Port Elizabeth, then at the Cape, and again at Durban, the last time in defiance of an order of the Supreme Court restraining the Immigration Officer from removing them from the jurisdiction of the Provincial Division of Natal. The Officer, acting under instructions from the Minister of the Interior, and in his over-zeal to please his Chief, gave a meaning to the order of the Court which no common sense man would give, and in indecent haste sent these men to Delagoa Bay with the result that, as above stated, Naryansamy is no more. I have not hesitated to call the death of the late Nagappan legalised murder, and I fear that the death of Naryansamy must be classed in the same category. I have the warrant of our own Court for stating that deportation such as Naryansamy's under an administrative order, described by Mr. Laughton, K. C., as "Star-Chamber procedure," is illegal. Naryansamy and his fellows, very properly, as I think every lover of justice and fair-play would say, disregard such deportation, attempt to return to the country

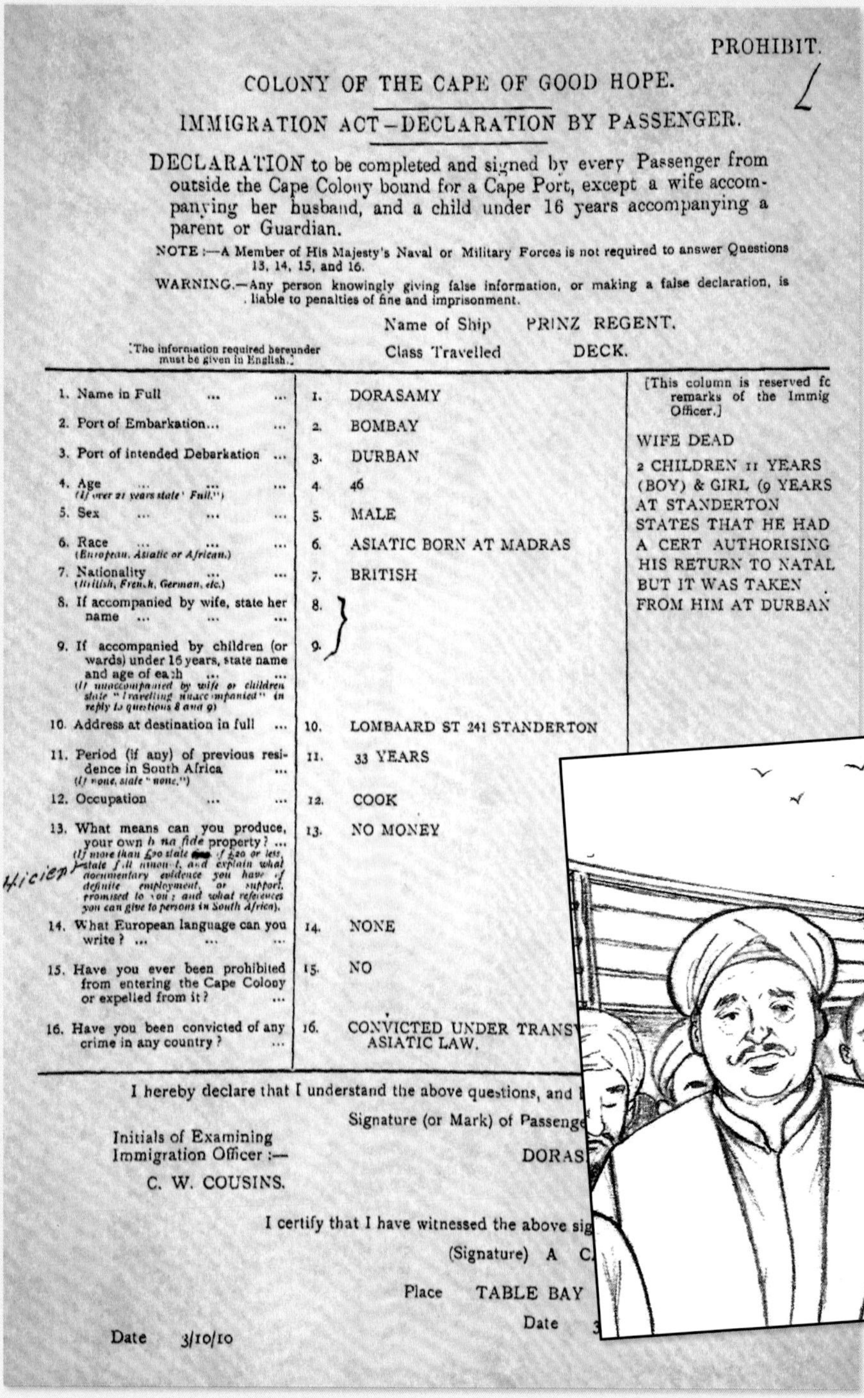

PROHIBIT.

COLONY OF THE CAPE OF GOOD HOPE.

IMMIGRATION ACT—DECLARATION BY PASSENGER.

DECLARATION to be completed and signed by every Passenger from outside the Cape Colony bound for a Cape Port, except a wife accompanying her husband, and a child under 16 years accompanying a parent or Guardian.

NOTE :—A Member of His Majesty's Naval or Military Forces is not required to answer Questions 13, 14, 15, and 16.

WARNING.—Any person knowingly giving false information, or making a false declaration, is liable to penalties of fine and imprisonment.

Name of Ship PRINZ REGENT.

[The information required hereunder must be given in English.] Class Travelled DECK.

		[This column is reserved fc remarks of the Immig Officer.]
1. Name in Full	1. DORASAMY	
2. Port of Embarkation... ...	2. BOMBAY	WIFE DEAD
3. Port of intended Debarkation ...	3. DURBAN	2 CHILDREN 11 YEARS
4. Age ... ... (If over 21 years state "Full.")	4. 46	(BOY) & GIRL (9 YEARS AT STANDERTON
5. Sex	5. MALE	STATES THAT HE HAD
6. Race ... ... (European, Asiatic or African.)	6. ASIATIC BORN AT MADRAS	A CERT AUTHORISING
7. Nationality ... ... (British, French, German, etc.)	7. BRITISH	HIS RETURN TO NATAL BUT IT WAS TAKEN
8. If accompanied by wife, state her name	8. }	FROM HIM AT DURBAN
9. If accompanied by children (or wards) under 16 years, state name and age of each ... ... (If unaccompanied by wife or children state "Travelling unaccompanied" in reply to questions 8 and 9)	9.	
10. Address at destination in full ...	10. LOMBAARD ST 241 STANDERTON	
11. Period (if any) of previous residence in South Africa ... (If none, state "none.")	11. 33 YEARS	
12. Occupation	12. COOK	
13. What means can you produce, your own bona fide property? ... (If more than £20 state ... if £20 or less, state full amount, and explain what documentary evidence you have of definite employment, or support, promised to you; and what references you can give to persons in South Africa).	13. NO MONEY	
14. What European language can you write?	14. NONE	
15. Have you ever been prohibited from entering the Cape Colony or expelled from it? ...	15. NO	
16. Have you been convicted of any crime in any country? ...	16. CONVICTED UNDER TRANS ASIATIC LAW.	

I hereby declare that I understand the above questions, and

Signature (or Mark) of Passenge

Initials of Examining Immigration Officer :—

C. W. COUSINS.

DORAS

I certify that I have witnessed the above sig

(Signature) A C.

Place TABLE BAY

Date 3

Date 3/10/10

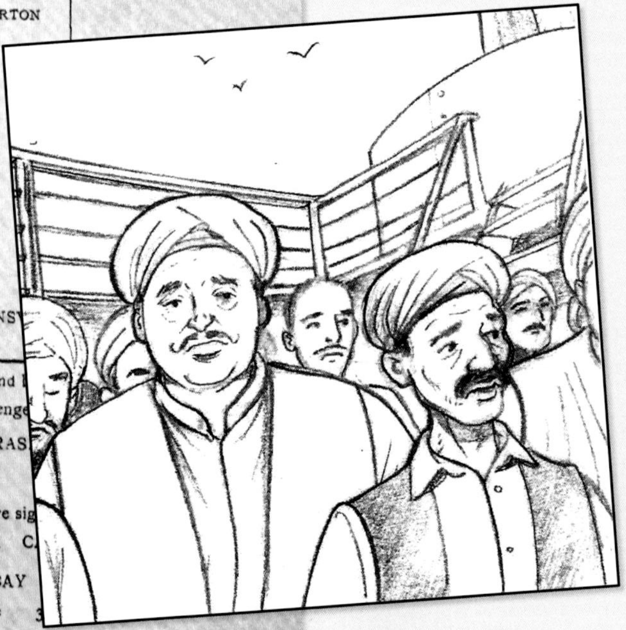

Left: Dorasamy's passenger declaration form filled out upon his arrival at Table Bay, Cape Town.

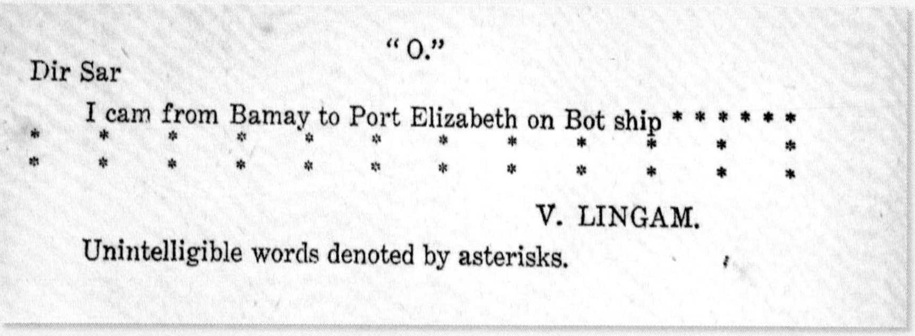

"O."

Dir Sar

I cam from Bamay to Port Elizabeth on Bot ship * * * * * *
* * * * * * * * * * * * *
* * * * * * * * * * * * *

V. LINGAM.

Unintelligible words denoted by asterisks.

Left: A transcription of Vitem Lingam's English literacy test at Cape Town harbor.

Henry Polak, the British-born lawyer and journalist who accompanied the deportees back to South Africa in 1910.

Sonja Schlesin, for years Gandhi's private secretary and a key satyagraha organizer, particularly in solidarity with Indian women.

Lewis Ritch, the London-trained solicitor who argued the deportees' case in Cape Town.

Clarence Wilfred Cousins, Cape Town's Chief Immigration Officer from 1905–1915.

General Jan Smuts (c. 1911), the Union government's first Minister of the Interior.

Johannes Wessels, the first judge to dismiss Mahomed Chotabhai's application at the Transvaal Supreme Court.

Lord Henry de Villiers, the first chief justice of the Appellate Division (1910-1914), who wrote the leading judgment in favor of Mahomed Chotabhai.

Sir James Rose Innes, the Appellate Division's second chief justice (1914–1927), who wrote the leading judgment dismissing the Indian deportees' appeal.

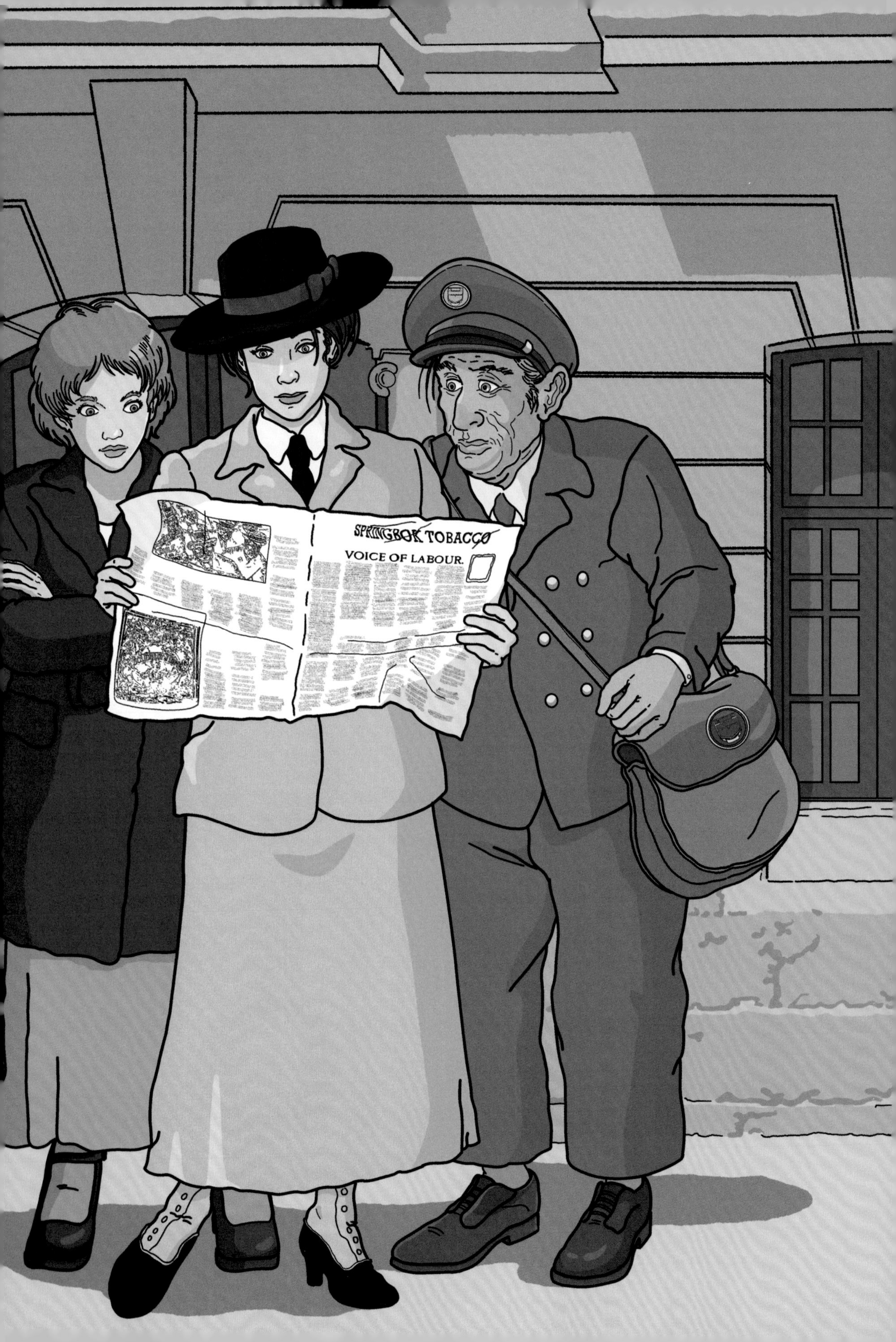
SPRINGBOK TOBACCO
VOICE OF LABOUR.

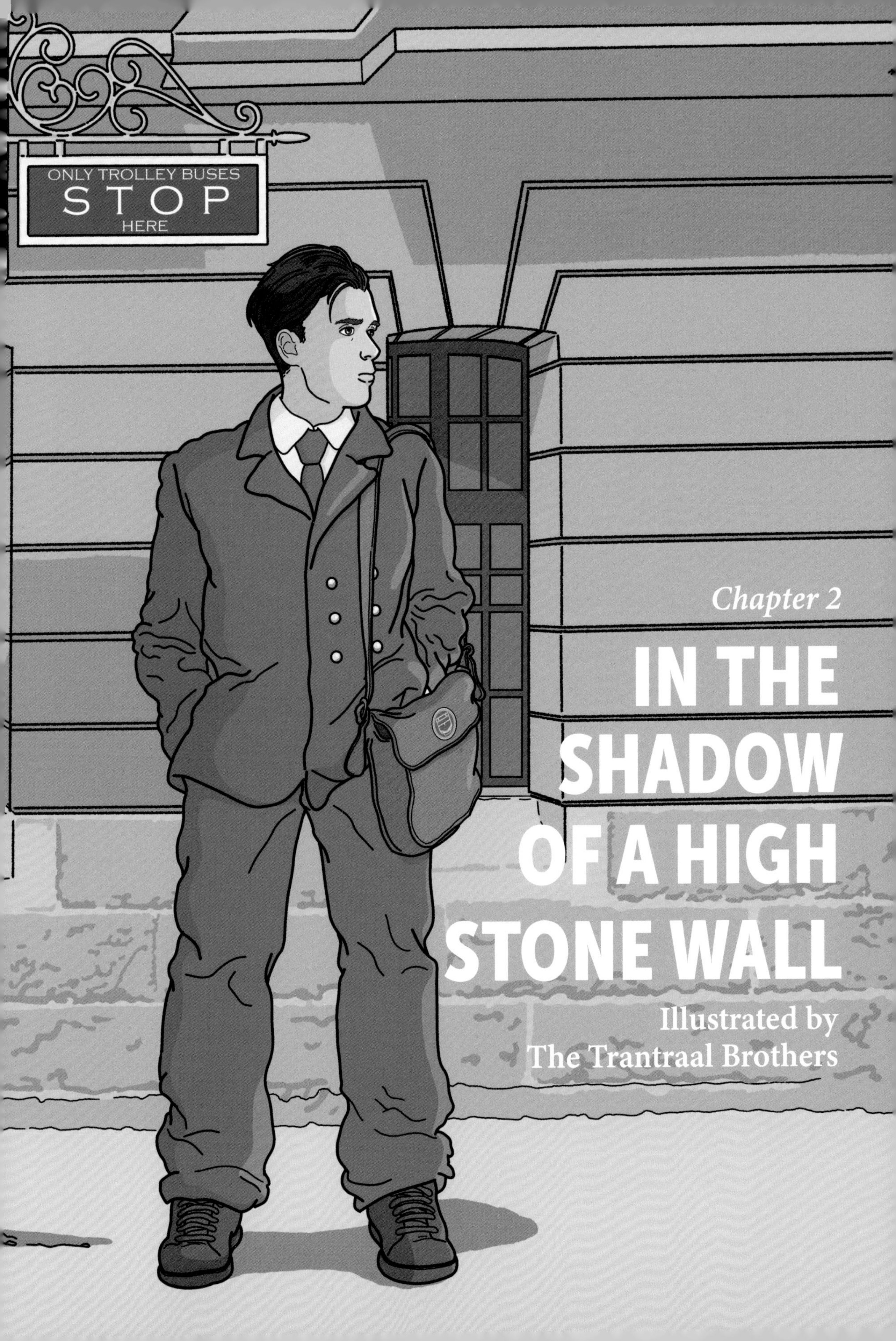
ONLY TROLLEY BUSES
STOP
HERE

Chapter 2

IN THE SHADOW OF A HIGH STONE WALL

Illustrated by
The Trantraal Brothers

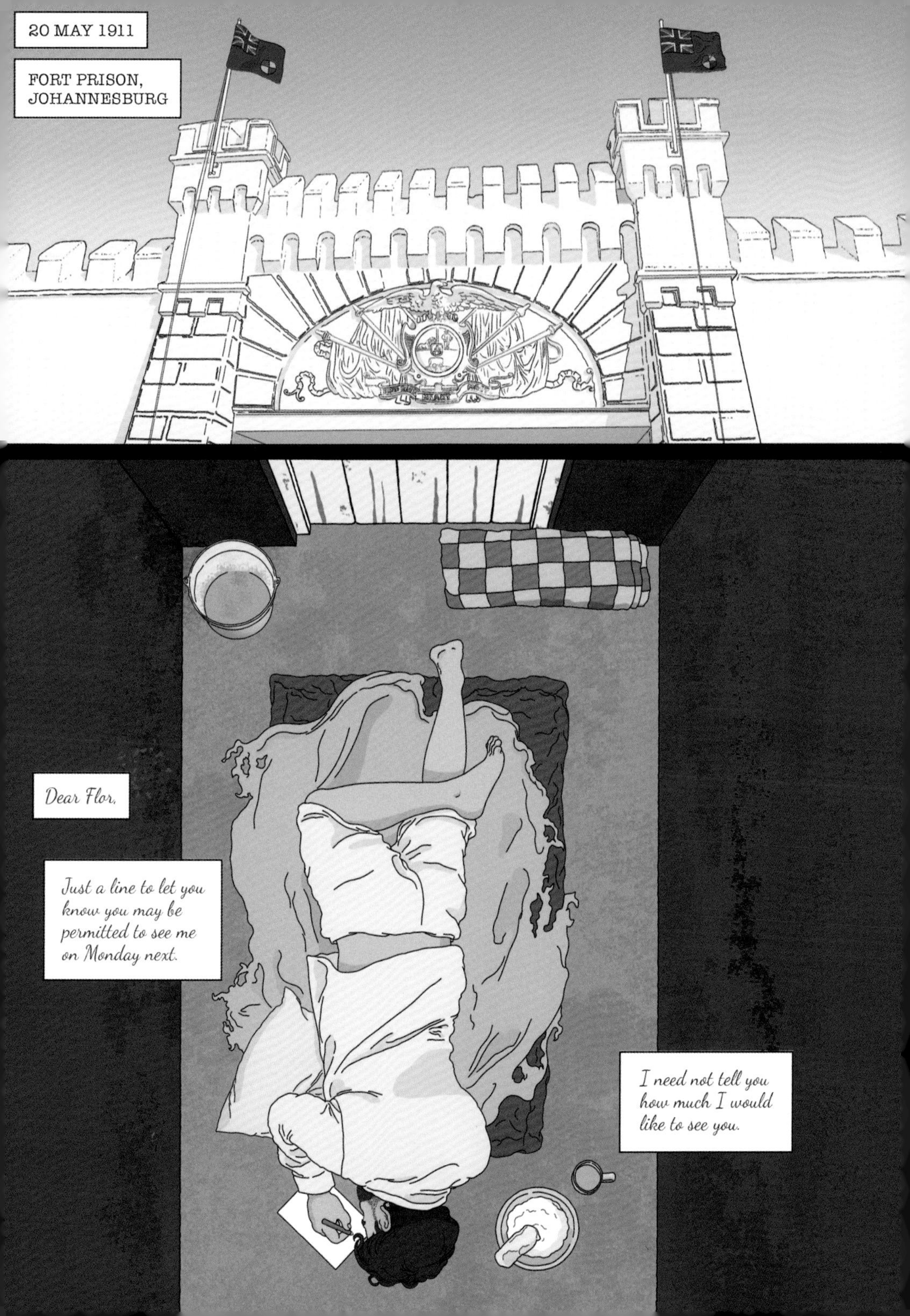
20 MAY 1911
FORT PRISON, JOHANNESBURG
Dear Flor,
Just a line to let you know you may be permitted to see me on Monday next.
I need not tell you how much I would like to see you.

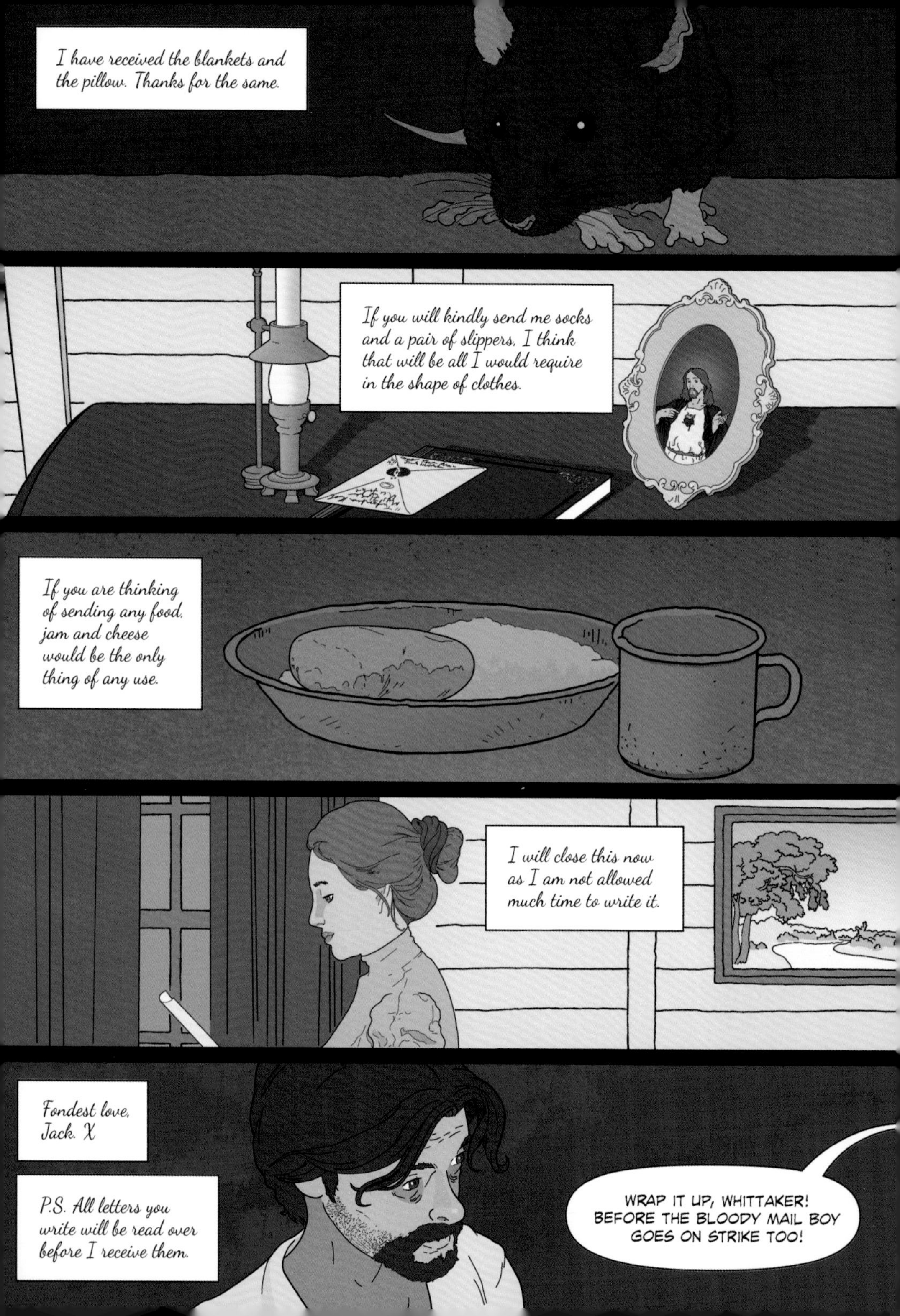
I have received the blankets and the pillow. Thanks for the same.
If you will kindly send me socks and a pair of slippers. I think that will be all I would require in the shape of clothes.
If you are thinking of sending any food, jam and cheese would be the only thing of any use.
I will close this now as I am not allowed much time to write it.
Fondest love, Jack. X
P.S. All letters you write will be read over before I receive them.
WRAP IT UP, WHITTAKER! BEFORE THE BLOODY MAIL BOY GOES ON STRIKE TOO!

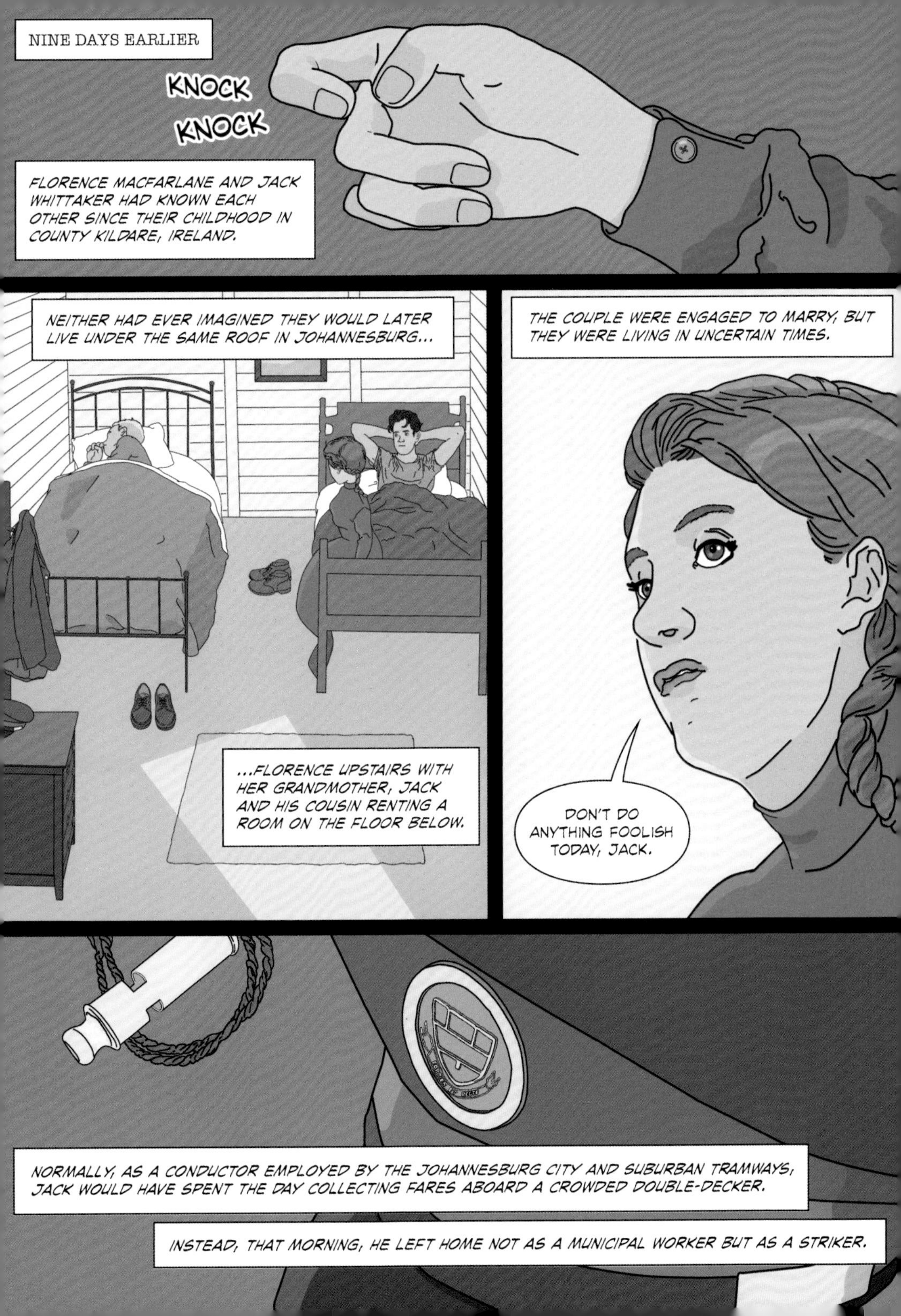
NINE DAYS EARLIER
KNOCK
KNOCK
FLORENCE MACFARLANE AND JACK WHITTAKER HAD KNOWN EACH OTHER SINCE THEIR CHILDHOOD IN COUNTY KILDARE, IRELAND.
NEITHER HAD EVER IMAGINED THEY WOULD LATER LIVE UNDER THE SAME ROOF IN JOHANNESBURG...
...FLORENCE UPSTAIRS WITH HER GRANDMOTHER, JACK AND HIS COUSIN RENTING A ROOM ON THE FLOOR BELOW.
THE COUPLE WERE ENGAGED TO MARRY, BUT THEY WERE LIVING IN UNCERTAIN TIMES.
DON'T DO ANYTHING FOOLISH TODAY, JACK.
NORMALLY, AS A CONDUCTOR EMPLOYED BY THE JOHANNESBURG CITY AND SUBURBAN TRAMWAYS, JACK WOULD HAVE SPENT THE DAY COLLECTING FARES ABOARD A CROWDED DOUBLE-DECKER.
INSTEAD, THAT MORNING, HE LEFT HOME NOT AS A MUNICIPAL WORKER BUT AS A STRIKER.

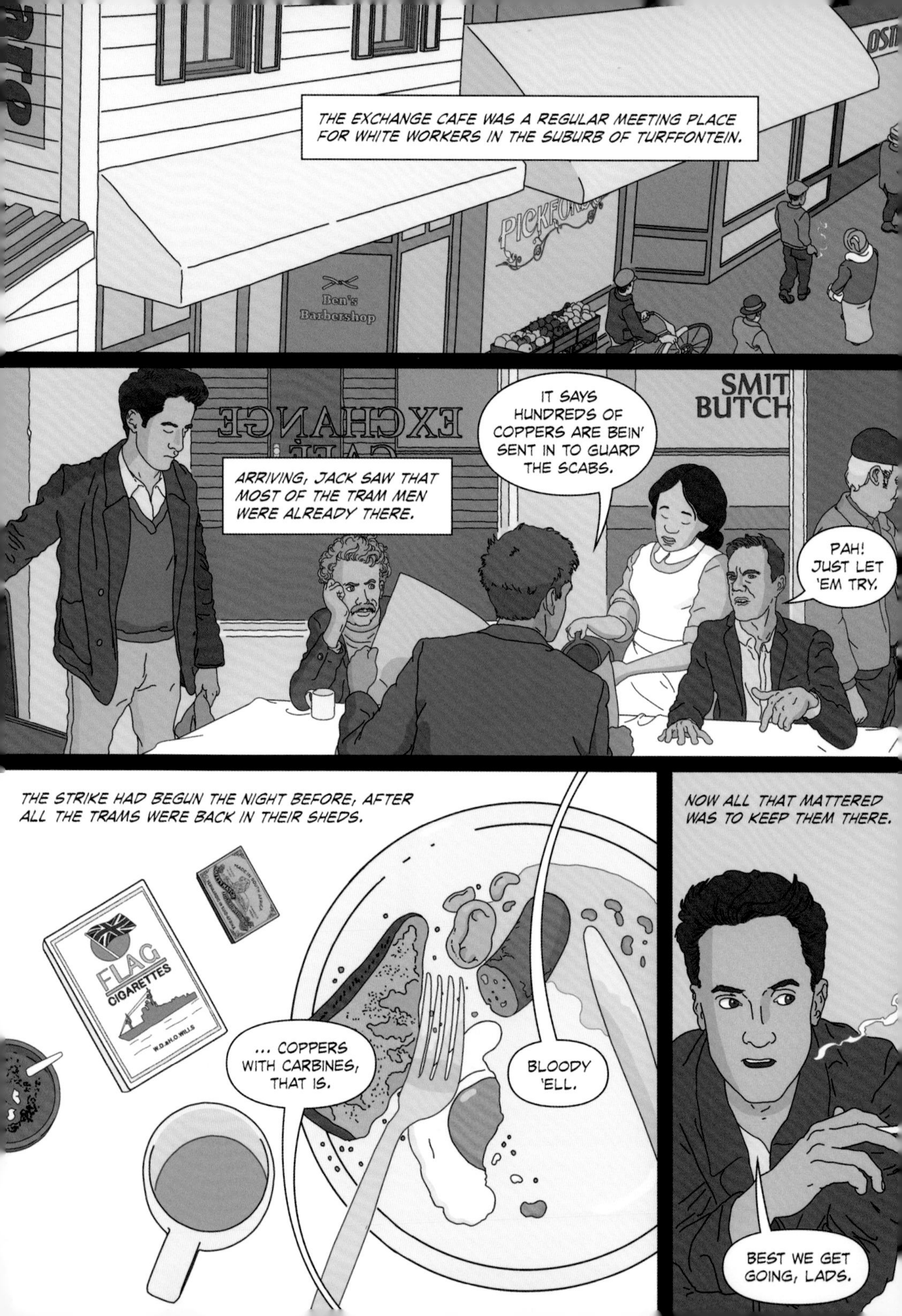
THE EXCHANGE CAFE WAS A REGULAR MEETING PLACE FOR WHITE WORKERS IN THE SUBURB OF TURFFONTEIN.
Ben's Barbershop
ARRIVING, JACK SAW THAT MOST OF THE TRAM MEN WERE ALREADY THERE.
IT SAYS HUNDREDS OF COPPERS ARE BEIN' SENT IN TO GUARD THE SCABS.
PAH! JUST LET 'EM TRY.
THE STRIKE HAD BEGUN THE NIGHT BEFORE, AFTER ALL THE TRAMS WERE BACK IN THEIR SHEDS.
FLAG CIGARETTES
W.D.&H.O. WILLS
... COPPERS WITH CARBINES, THAT IS.
BLOODY 'ELL.
NOW ALL THAT MATTERED WAS TO KEEP THEM THERE.
BEST WE GET GOING, LADS.

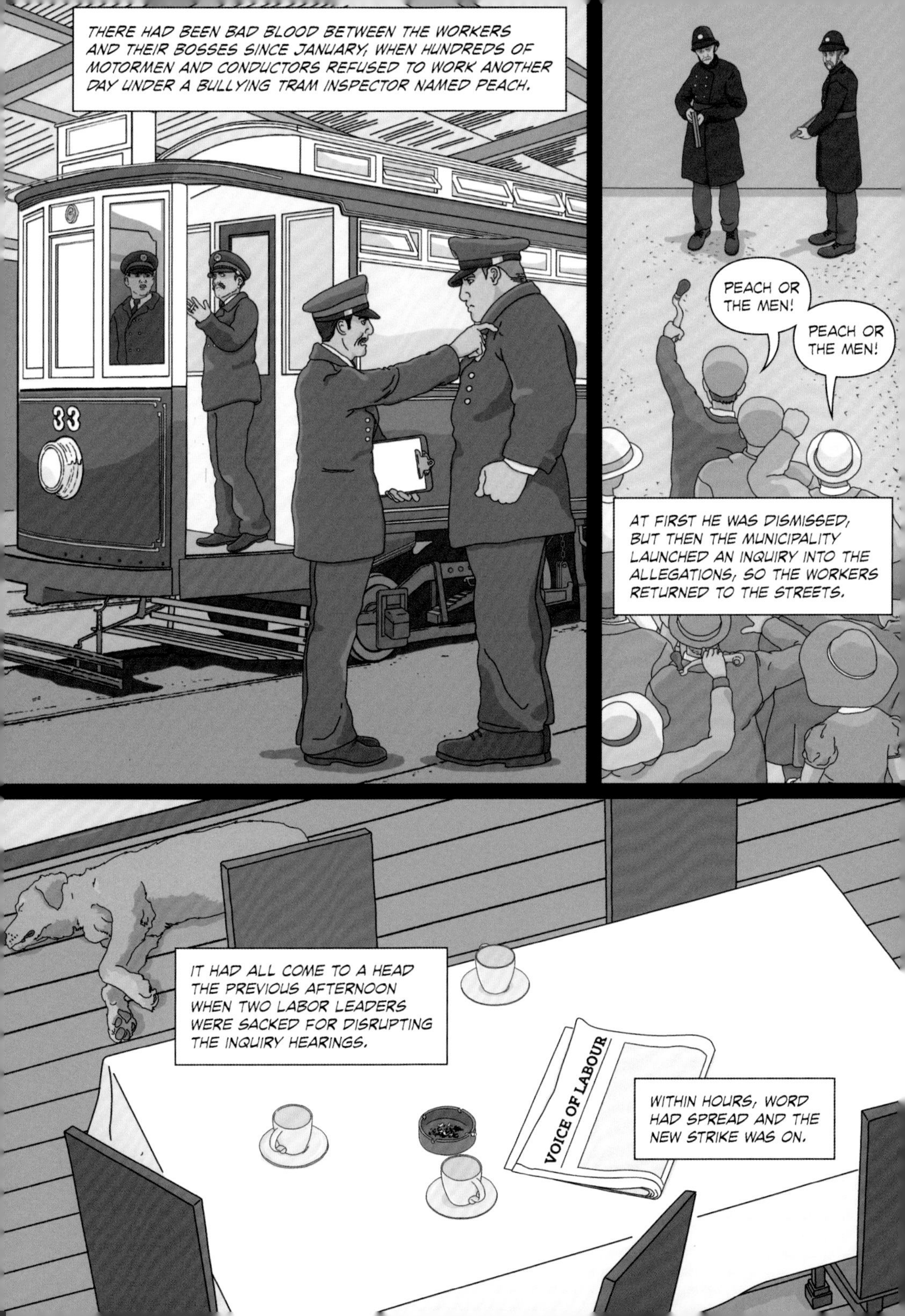

THERE HAD BEEN BAD BLOOD BETWEEN THE WORKERS AND THEIR BOSSES SINCE JANUARY, WHEN HUNDREDS OF MOTORMEN AND CONDUCTORS REFUSED TO WORK ANOTHER DAY UNDER A BULLYING TRAM INSPECTOR NAMED PEACH.
33
PEACH OR THE MEN!
PEACH OR THE MEN!
AT FIRST HE WAS DISMISSED, BUT THEN THE MUNICIPALITY LAUNCHED AN INQUIRY INTO THE ALLEGATIONS, SO THE WORKERS RETURNED TO THE STREETS.
IT HAD ALL COME TO A HEAD THE PREVIOUS AFTERNOON WHEN TWO LABOR LEADERS WERE SACKED FOR DISRUPTING THE INQUIRY HEARINGS.
VOICE OF LABOUR
WITHIN HOURS, WORD HAD SPREAD AND THE NEW STRIKE WAS ON.

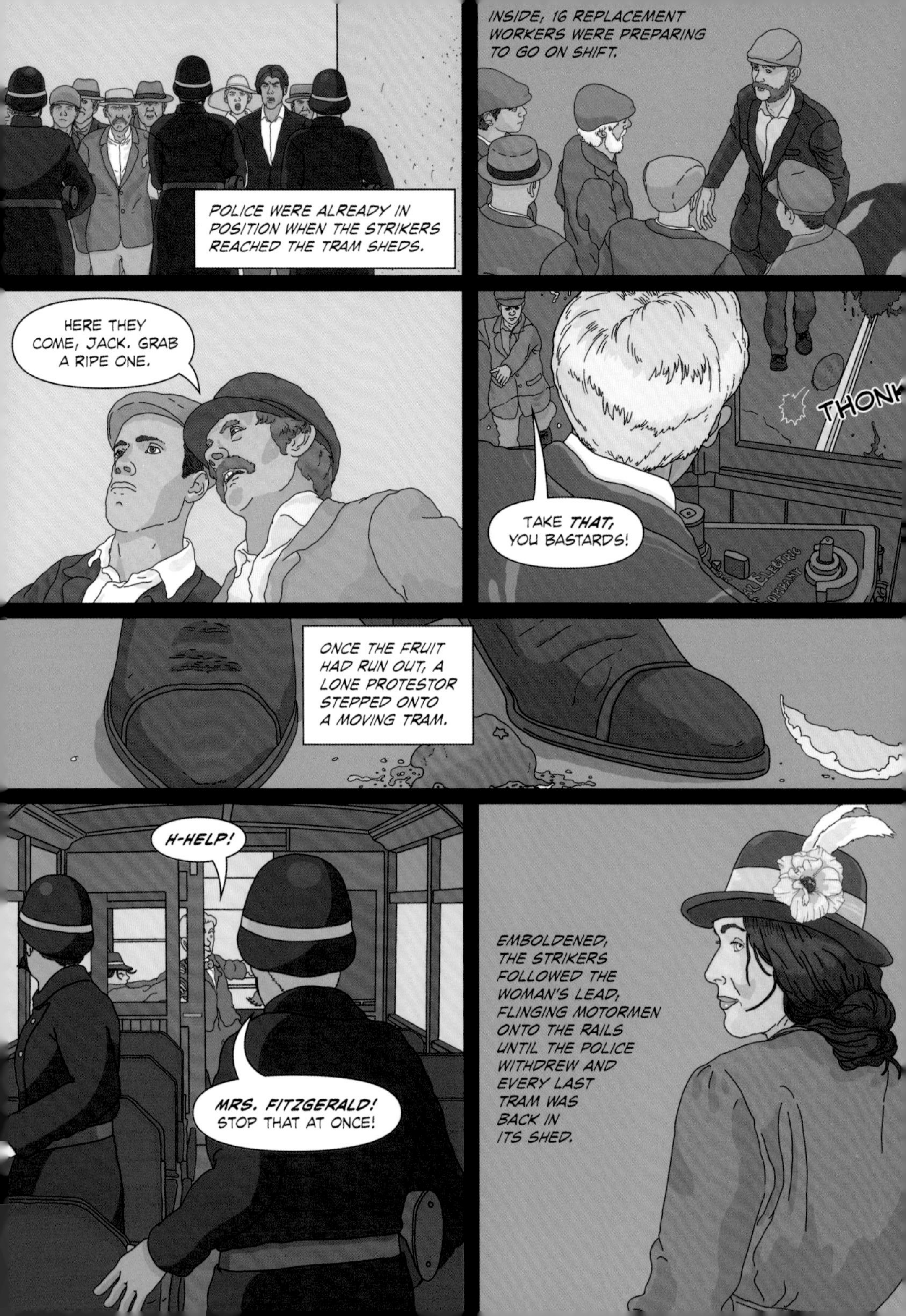
POLICE WERE ALREADY IN POSITION WHEN THE STRIKERS REACHED THE TRAM SHEDS.
INSIDE, 16 REPLACEMENT WORKERS WERE PREPARING TO GO ON SHIFT.
HERE THEY COME, JACK. GRAB A RIPE ONE.
THONK
TAKE THAT, YOU BASTARDS!
ONCE THE FRUIT HAD RUN OUT, A LONE PROTESTOR STEPPED ONTO A MOVING TRAM.
H-HELP!
MRS. FITZGERALD! STOP THAT AT ONCE!
EMBOLDENED, THE STRIKERS FOLLOWED THE WOMAN'S LEAD, FLINGING MOTORMEN ONTO THE RAILS UNTIL THE POLICE WITHDREW AND EVERY LAST TRAM WAS BACK IN ITS SHED.

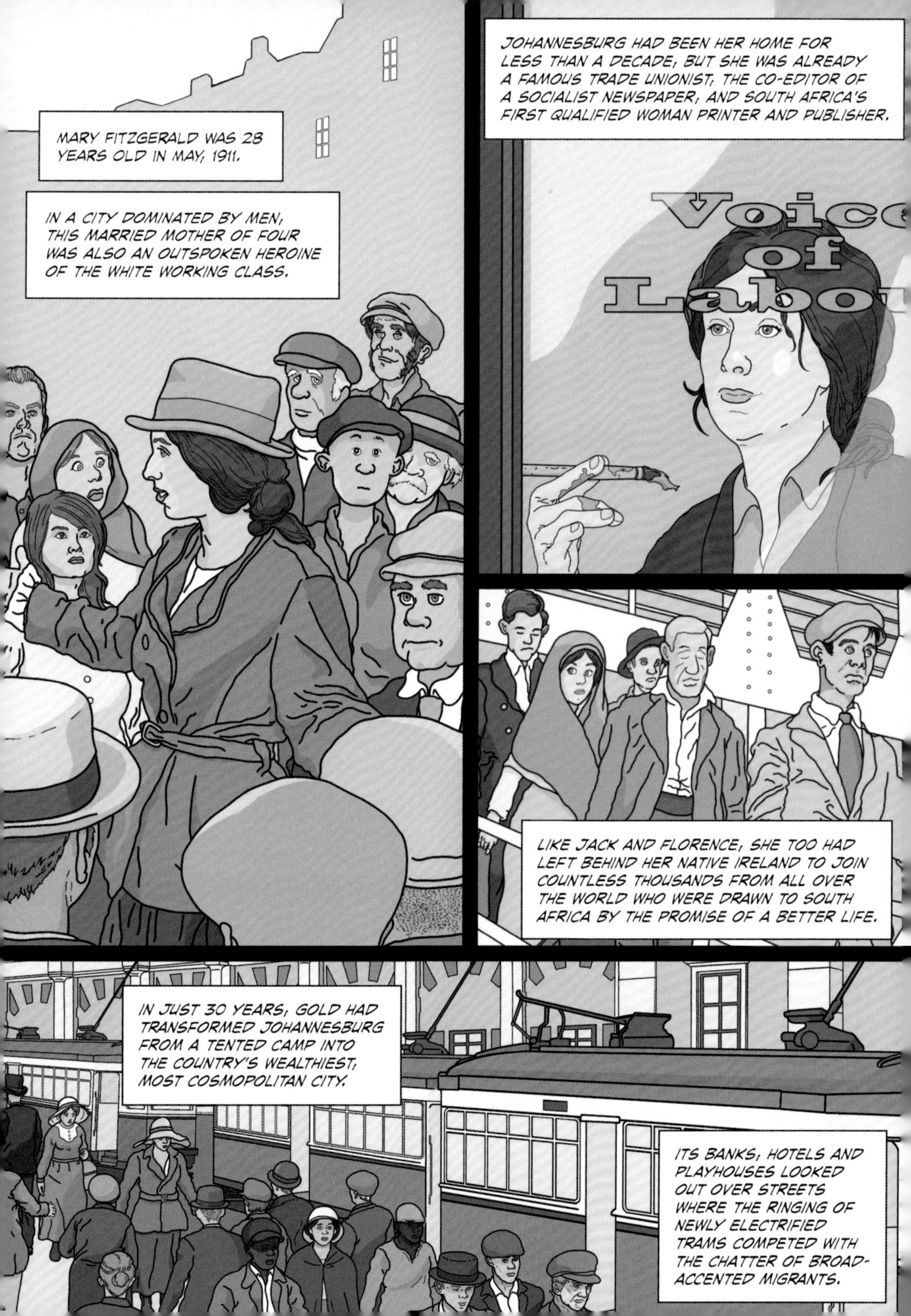
MARY FITZGERALD WAS 28 YEARS OLD IN MAY, 1911.
IN A CITY DOMINATED BY MEN, THIS MARRIED MOTHER OF FOUR WAS ALSO AN OUTSPOKEN HEROINE OF THE WHITE WORKING CLASS.
JOHANNESBURG HAD BEEN HER HOME FOR LESS THAN A DECADE, BUT SHE WAS ALREADY A FAMOUS TRADE UNIONIST, THE CO-EDITOR OF A SOCIALIST NEWSPAPER, AND SOUTH AFRICA'S FIRST QUALIFIED WOMAN PRINTER AND PUBLISHER.
Voice of Labo
LIKE JACK AND FLORENCE, SHE TOO HAD LEFT BEHIND HER NATIVE IRELAND TO JOIN COUNTLESS THOUSANDS FROM ALL OVER THE WORLD WHO WERE DRAWN TO SOUTH AFRICA BY THE PROMISE OF A BETTER LIFE.
IN JUST 30 YEARS, GOLD HAD TRANSFORMED JOHANNESBURG FROM A TENTED CAMP INTO THE COUNTRY'S WEALTHIEST, MOST COSMOPOLITAN CITY.
ITS BANKS, HOTELS AND PLAYHOUSES LOOKED OUT OVER STREETS WHERE THE RINGING OF NEWLY ELECTRIFIED TRAMS COMPETED WITH THE CHATTER OF BROAD-ACCENTED MIGRANTS.

BUT PRECIOUS MINERALS, CHEAP LABOR AND CAPITALIST GROWTH HAD ONLY BROUGHT POWER AND PROSPERITY TO A SELECT FEW.

WHILE THE CAPTAINS OF INDUSTRY, OR "RANDLORDS," SIPPED EXPENSIVE WINE IN THEIR DOWNTOWN CLUBS...

...THE UNEMPLOYED AND WAGE-EARNING POOR LIVED IN A HOSTILE UNDERWORLD OF BEER, GAMBLING AND PROSTITUTION.

WHITE WORKERS LIKE JACK DIDN'T HAVE IT EASY. FEW EARNED ENOUGH TO RAISE A FAMILY OR RENT A HOME.

BUT AFRICAN, COLOURED, INDIAN AND CHINESE WORKERS SUFFERED THE MOST.

EARNING A FRACTION OF THE LOWEST WHITE WORKERS' SALARIES, THEY LIVED EITHER IN SEGREGATED SLUMS OR SINGLE-SEX COMPOUNDS.

AFRICAN WORKERS FAR OUTNUMBERED WHITE WORKERS IN JOHANNESBURG. YET HAVING BEEN DRIVEN FROM RURAL AREAS BY COLONIAL TAXES AND LAND-OWNERSHIP RESTRICTIONS, THEY TOO WERE MIGRANTS SEEKING LOW-PAID EMPLOYMENT IN TOWNS AND CITIES.

THE TWO GROUPS HAD A COMMON ENEMY: THEIR BOSSES AND THE GOVERN-MENT. BUT EVEN THOUGH WHITE WORKING-CLASS IMMIGRANTS HAD BROUGHT OVER FROM EUROPE AND THE UNITED STATES A NON-RACIAL, NON-SEXIST MOVEMENT OF ORGANIZED LABOR, THEY REFUSED TO UNITE WITH AFRICAN WORKERS. MOST OF THEM WANTED SOUTH AFRICA TO BE A "WHITE MAN'S COUNTRY" RATHER THAN A "WORKERS' COUNTRY."

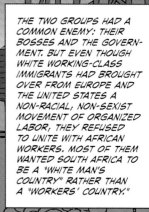

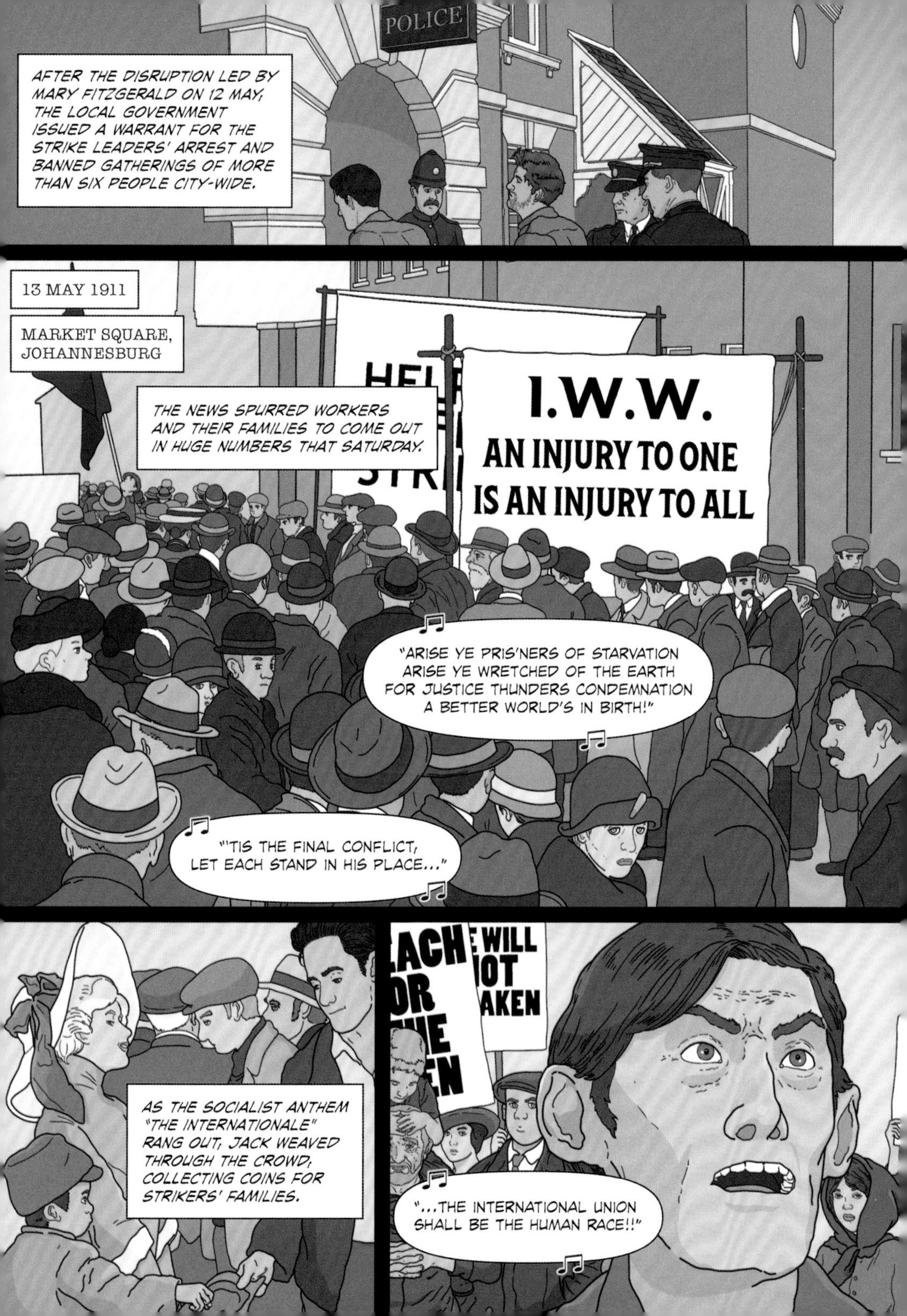
POLICE
AFTER THE DISRUPTION LED BY MARY FITZGERALD ON 12 MAY, THE LOCAL GOVERNMENT ISSUED A WARRANT FOR THE STRIKE LEADERS' ARREST AND BANNED GATHERINGS OF MORE THAN SIX PEOPLE CITY-WIDE.
13 MAY 1911
MARKET SQUARE, JOHANNESBURG
THE NEWS SPURRED WORKERS AND THEIR FAMILIES TO COME OUT IN HUGE NUMBERS THAT SATURDAY.
I.W.W. AN INJURY TO ONE IS AN INJURY TO ALL
"ARISE YE PRIS'NERS OF STARVATION ARISE YE WRETCHED OF THE EARTH FOR JUSTICE THUNDERS CONDEMNATION A BETTER WORLD'S IN BIRTH!"
"'TIS THE FINAL CONFLICT, LET EACH STAND IN HIS PLACE..."
AS THE SOCIALIST ANTHEM "THE INTERNATIONALE" RANG OUT, JACK WEAVED THROUGH THE CROWD, COLLECTING COINS FOR STRIKERS' FAMILIES.
"...THE INTERNATIONAL UNION SHALL BE THE HUMAN RACE!!"

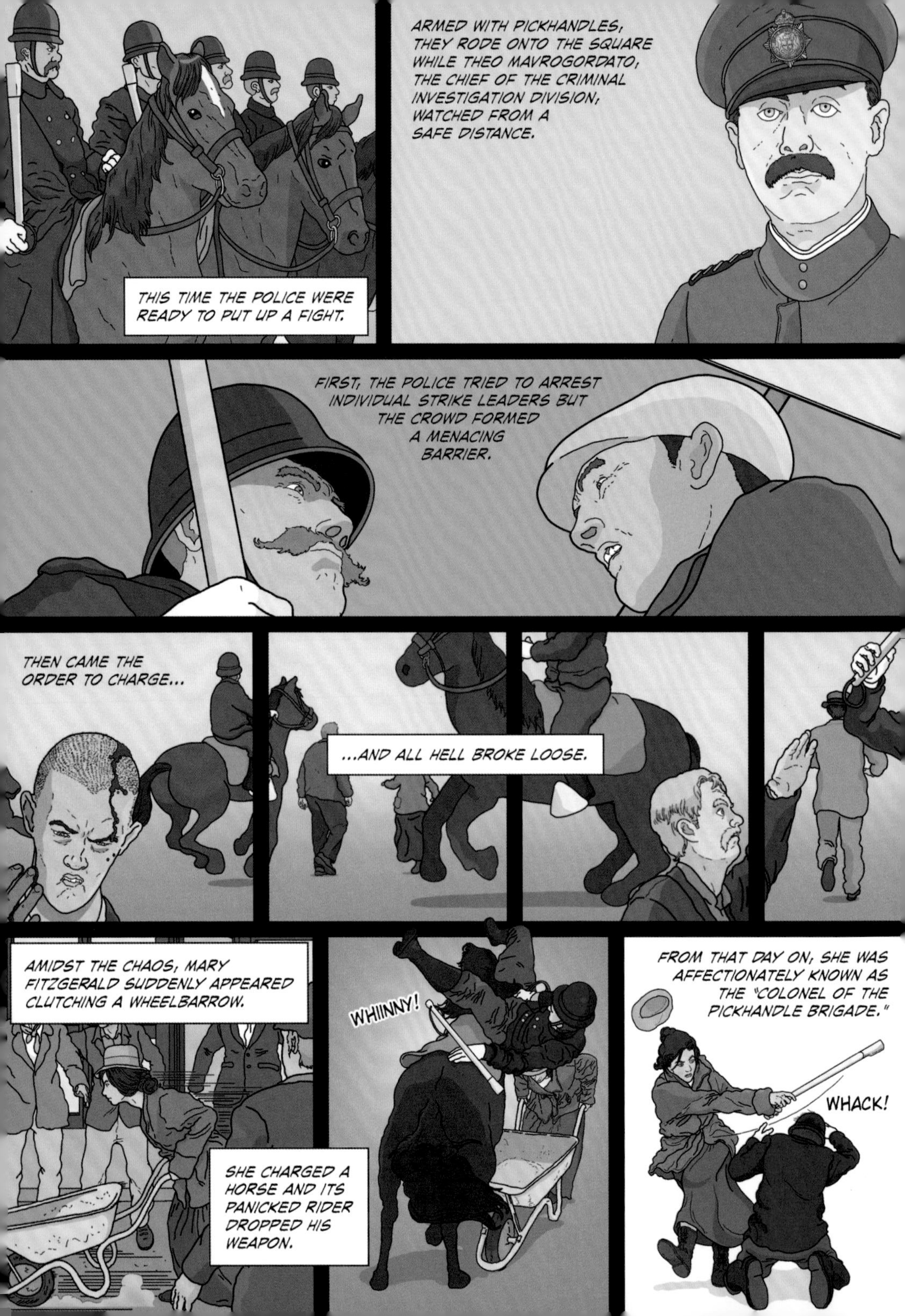
THIS TIME THE POLICE WERE READY TO PUT UP A FIGHT.
ARMED WITH PICKHANDLES, THEY RODE ONTO THE SQUARE WHILE THEO MAVROGORDATO, THE CHIEF OF THE CRIMINAL INVESTIGATION DIVISION, WATCHED FROM A SAFE DISTANCE.
FIRST, THE POLICE TRIED TO ARREST INDIVIDUAL STRIKE LEADERS BUT THE CROWD FORMED A MENACING BARRIER.
THEN CAME THE ORDER TO CHARGE...
...AND ALL HELL BROKE LOOSE.
AMIDST THE CHAOS, MARY FITZGERALD SUDDENLY APPEARED CLUTCHING A WHEELBARROW.
SHE CHARGED A HORSE AND ITS PANICKED RIDER DROPPED HIS WEAPON.
WHIINNY!
FROM THAT DAY ON, SHE WAS AFFECTIONATELY KNOWN AS THE "COLONEL OF THE PICKHANDLE BRIGADE."
WHACK!

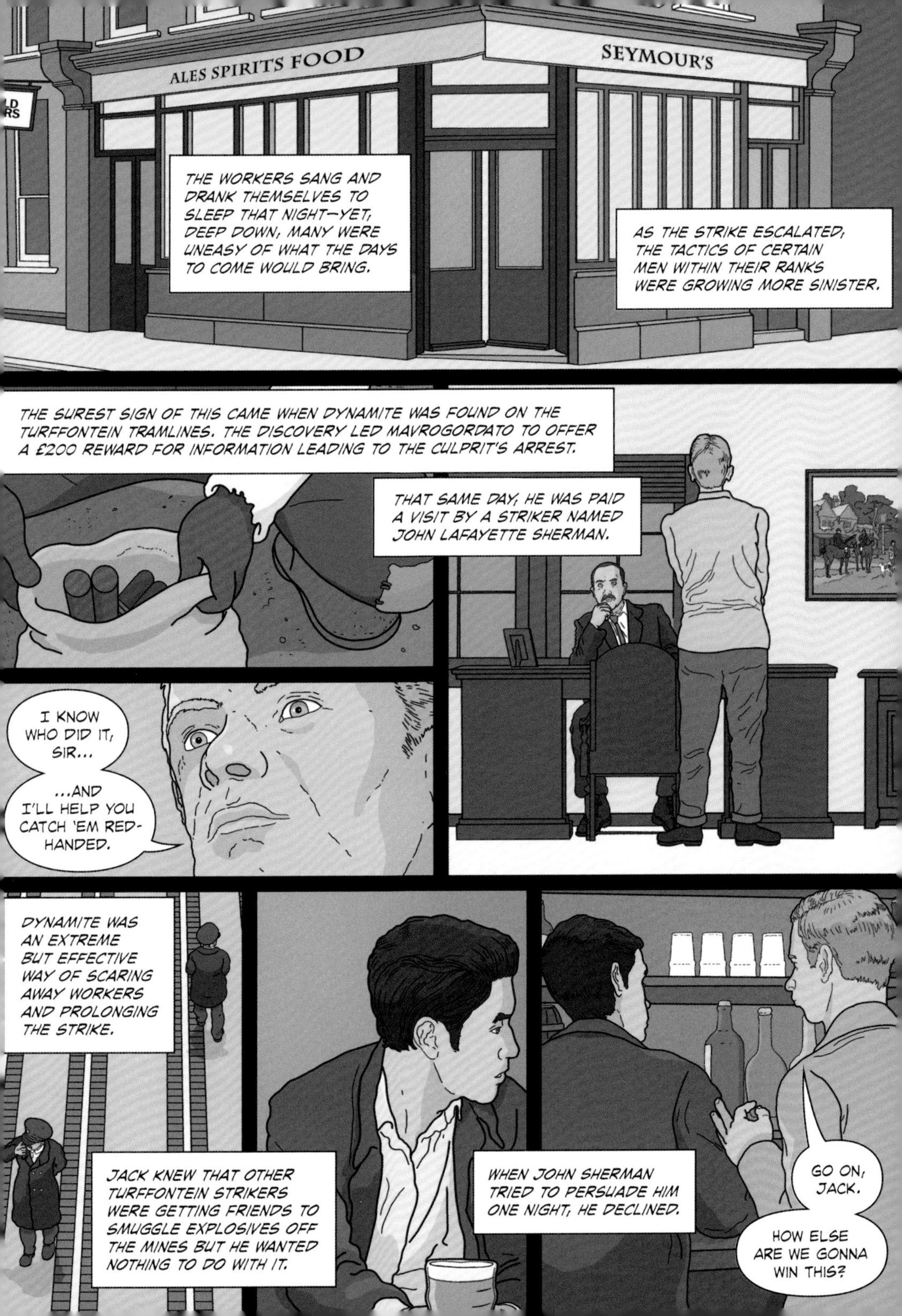

ALES SPIRITS FOOD
SEYMOUR'S
THE WORKERS SANG AND DRANK THEMSELVES TO SLEEP THAT NIGHT—YET, DEEP DOWN, MANY WERE UNEASY OF WHAT THE DAYS TO COME WOULD BRING.
AS THE STRIKE ESCALATED, THE TACTICS OF CERTAIN MEN WITHIN THEIR RANKS WERE GROWING MORE SINISTER.
THE SUREST SIGN OF THIS CAME WHEN DYNAMITE WAS FOUND ON THE TURFFONTEIN TRAMLINES. THE DISCOVERY LED MAVROGORDATO TO OFFER A £200 REWARD FOR INFORMATION LEADING TO THE CULPRIT'S ARREST.
THAT SAME DAY, HE WAS PAID A VISIT BY A STRIKER NAMED JOHN LAFAYETTE SHERMAN.
I KNOW WHO DID IT, SIR...
...AND I'LL HELP YOU CATCH 'EM RED-HANDED.
DYNAMITE WAS AN EXTREME BUT EFFECTIVE WAY OF SCARING AWAY WORKERS AND PROLONGING THE STRIKE.
JACK KNEW THAT OTHER TURFFONTEIN STRIKERS WERE GETTING FRIENDS TO SMUGGLE EXPLOSIVES OFF THE MINES BUT HE WANTED NOTHING TO DO WITH IT.
WHEN JOHN SHERMAN TRIED TO PERSUADE HIM ONE NIGHT, HE DECLINED.
GO ON, JACK.
HOW ELSE ARE WE GONNA WIN THIS?

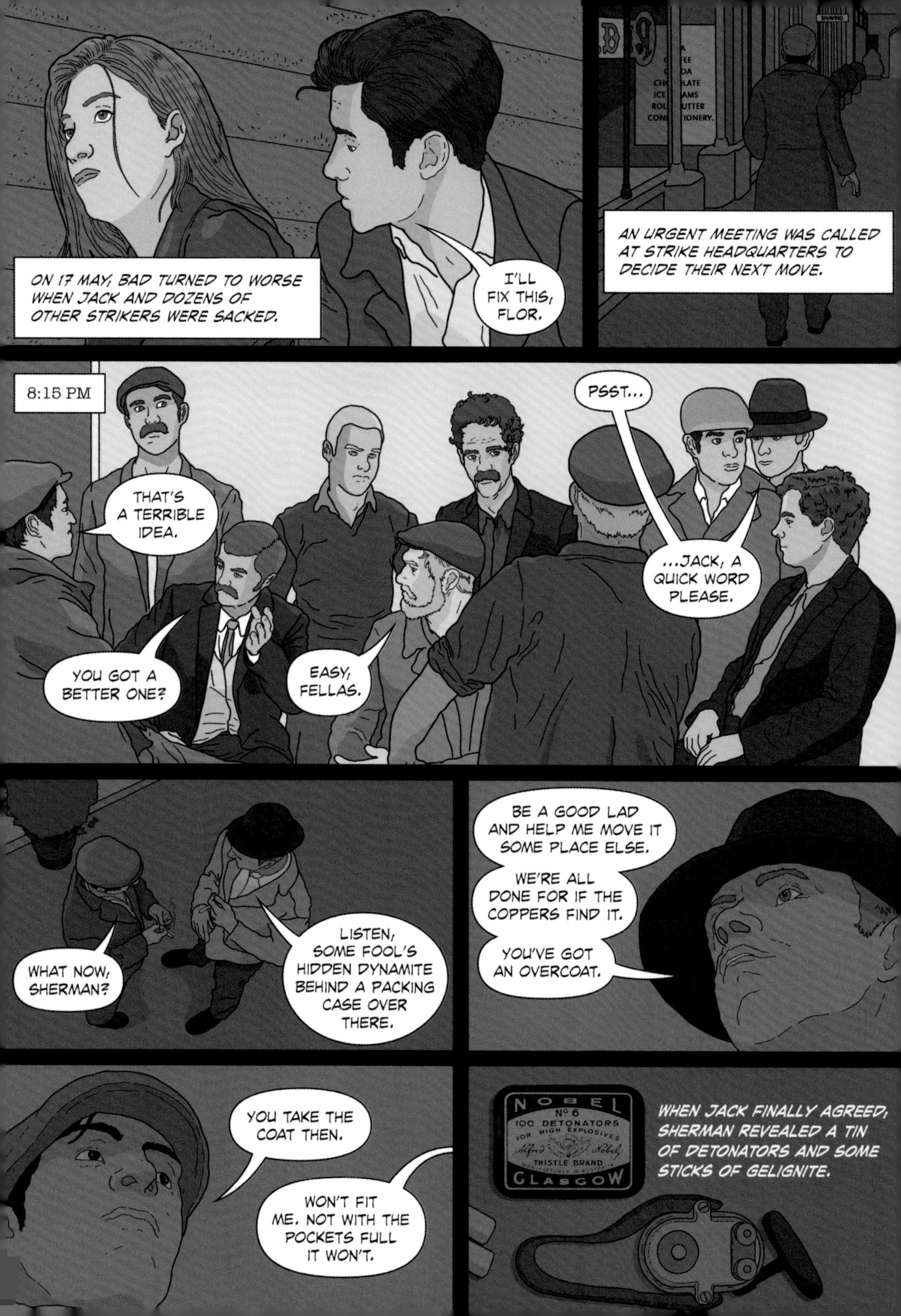
ON 17 MAY, BAD TURNED TO WORSE WHEN JACK AND DOZENS OF OTHER STRIKERS WERE SACKED.
I'LL FIX THIS, FLOR.
AN URGENT MEETING WAS CALLED AT STRIKE HEADQUARTERS TO DECIDE THEIR NEXT MOVE.
8:15 PM
THAT'S A TERRIBLE IDEA.
YOU GOT A BETTER ONE?
EASY, FELLAS.
PSST...
...JACK, A QUICK WORD PLEASE.
WHAT NOW, SHERMAN?
LISTEN, SOME FOOL'S HIDDEN DYNAMITE BEHIND A PACKING CASE OVER THERE.
BE A GOOD LAD AND HELP ME MOVE IT SOME PLACE ELSE.
WE'RE ALL DONE FOR IF THE COPPERS FIND IT.
YOU'VE GOT AN OVERCOAT.
YOU TAKE THE COAT THEN.
WON'T FIT ME. NOT WITH THE POCKETS FULL IT WON'T.
NOBEL
No 6
100 DETONATORS
FOR HIGH EXPLOSIVES
THISTLE BRAND
GLASGOW
WHEN JACK FINALLY AGREED, SHERMAN REVEALED A TIN OF DETONATORS AND SOME STICKS OF GELIGNITE.

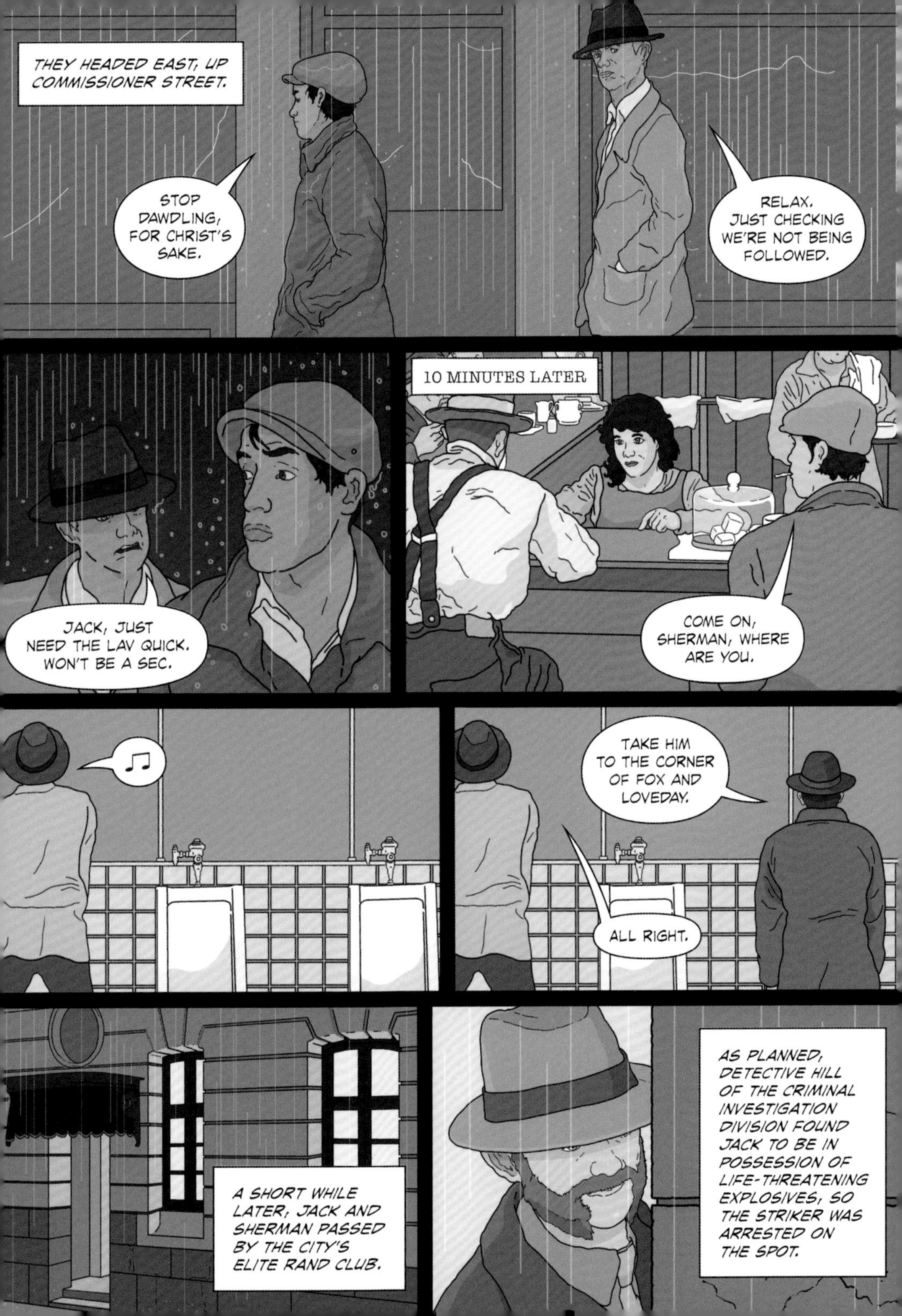
THEY HEADED EAST, UP COMMISSIONER STREET.
STOP DAWDLING, FOR CHRIST'S SAKE.
RELAX. JUST CHECKING WE'RE NOT BEING FOLLOWED.
JACK, JUST NEED THE LAV QUICK. WON'T BE A SEC.
10 MINUTES LATER
COME ON, SHERMAN, WHERE ARE YOU.
♫
TAKE HIM TO THE CORNER OF FOX AND LOVEDAY.
ALL RIGHT.
A SHORT WHILE LATER, JACK AND SHERMAN PASSED BY THE CITY'S ELITE RAND CLUB.
AS PLANNED, DETECTIVE HILL OF THE CRIMINAL INVESTIGATION DIVISION FOUND JACK TO BE IN POSSESSION OF LIFE-THREATENING EXPLOSIVES, SO THE STRIKER WAS ARRESTED ON THE SPOT.

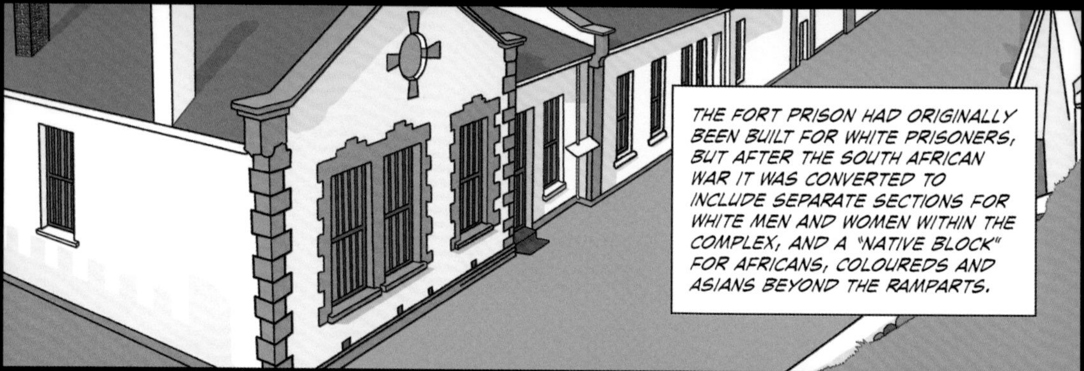
THE FORT PRISON HAD ORIGINALLY BEEN BUILT FOR WHITE PRISONERS, BUT AFTER THE SOUTH AFRICAN WAR IT WAS CONVERTED TO INCLUDE SEPARATE SECTIONS FOR WHITE MEN AND WOMEN WITHIN THE COMPLEX, AND A "NATIVE BLOCK" FOR AFRICANS, COLOUREDS AND ASIANS BEYOND THE RAMPARTS.

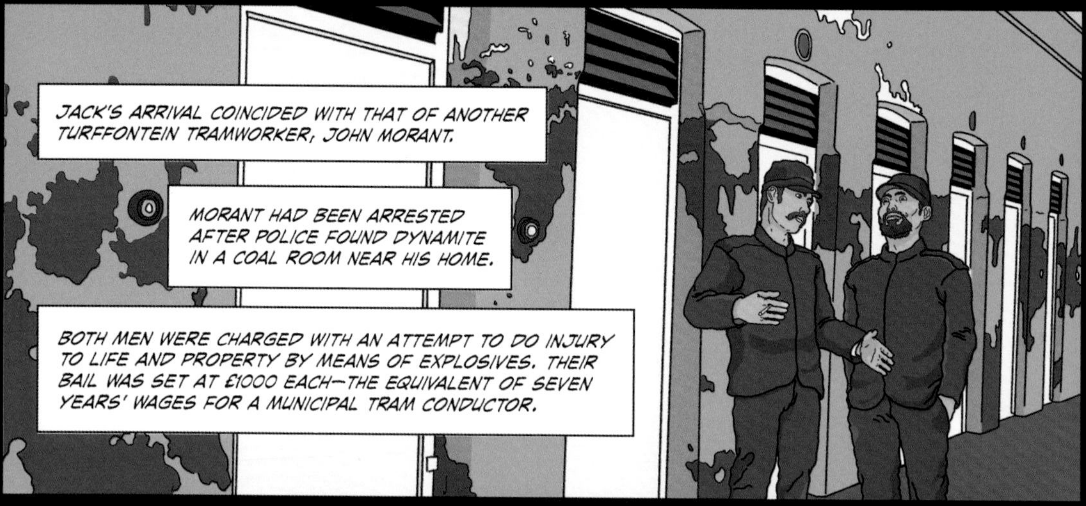
JACK'S ARRIVAL COINCIDED WITH THAT OF ANOTHER TURFFONTEIN TRAMWORKER, JOHN MORANT.
MORANT HAD BEEN ARRESTED AFTER POLICE FOUND DYNAMITE IN A COAL ROOM NEAR HIS HOME.
BOTH MEN WERE CHARGED WITH AN ATTEMPT TO DO INJURY TO LIFE AND PROPERTY BY MEANS OF EXPLOSIVES. THEIR BAIL WAS SET AT £1000 EACH—THE EQUIVALENT OF SEVEN YEARS' WAGES FOR A MUNICIPAL TRAM CONDUCTOR.

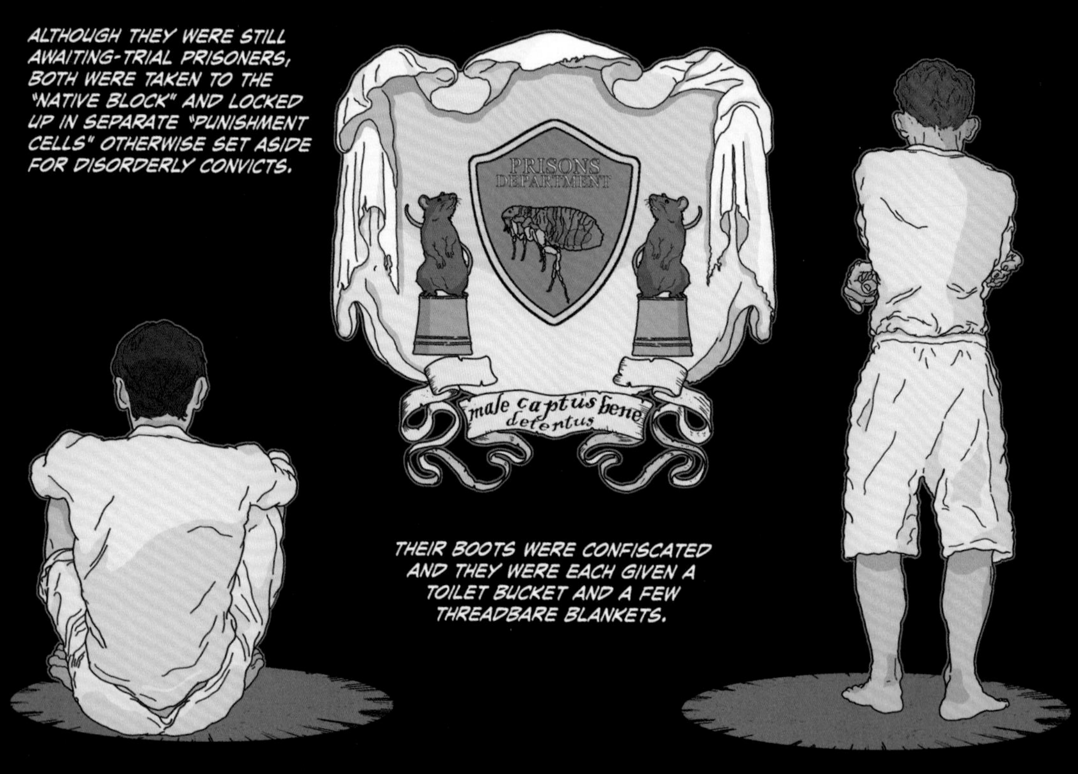
ALTHOUGH THEY WERE STILL AWAITING-TRIAL PRISONERS, BOTH WERE TAKEN TO THE "NATIVE BLOCK" AND LOCKED UP IN SEPARATE "PUNISHMENT CELLS" OTHERWISE SET ASIDE FOR DISORDERLY CONVICTS.
PRISONS DEPARTMENT
male captus bene detentus
THEIR BOOTS WERE CONFISCATED AND THEY WERE EACH GIVEN A TOILET BUCKET AND A FEW THREADBARE BLANKETS.

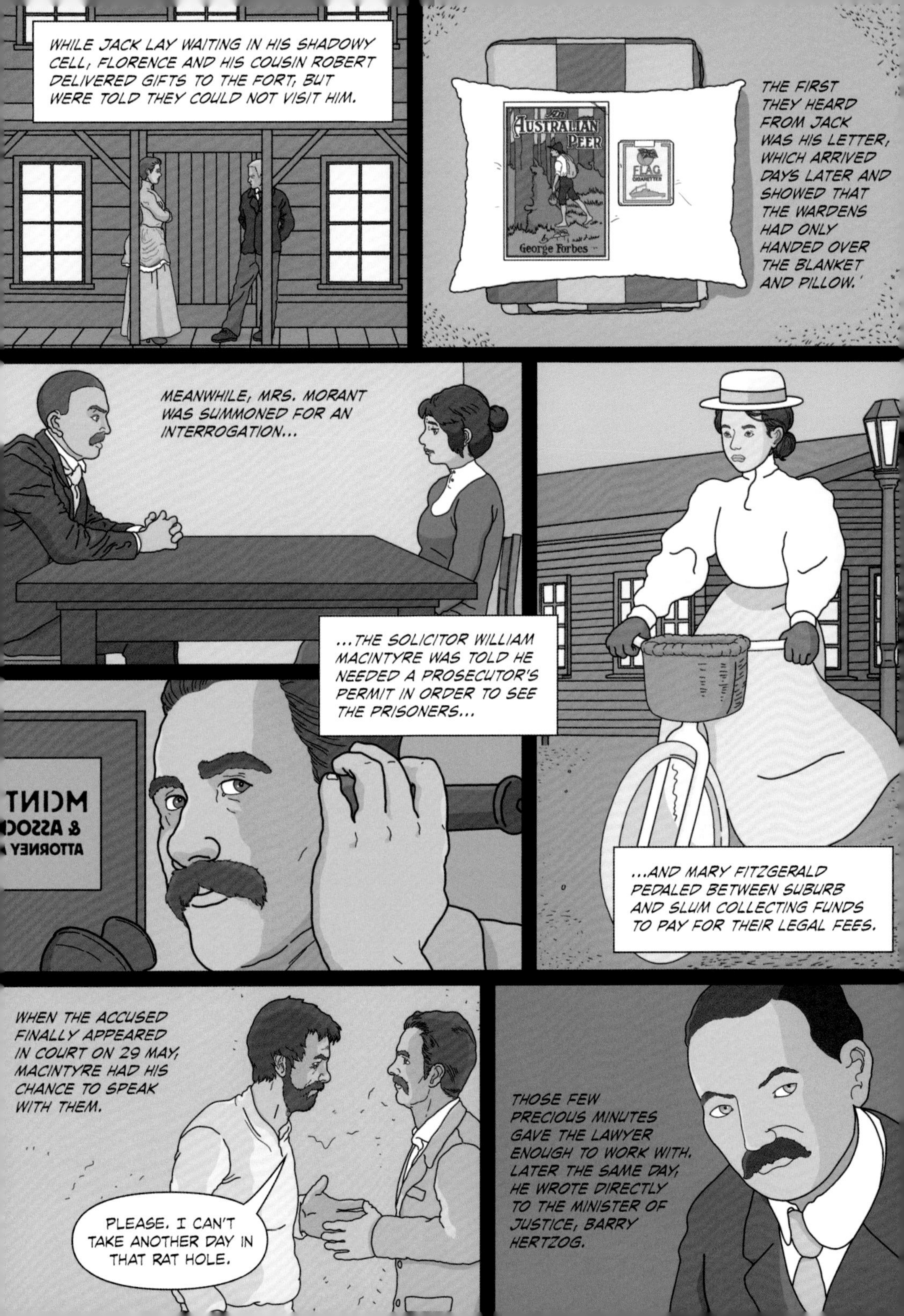
WHILE JACK LAY WAITING IN HIS SHADOWY CELL, FLORENCE AND HIS COUSIN ROBERT DELIVERED GIFTS TO THE FORT, BUT WERE TOLD THEY COULD NOT VISIT HIM.
AN AUSTRALIAN PEER
George Forbes
FLAG
THE FIRST THEY HEARD FROM JACK WAS HIS LETTER, WHICH ARRIVED DAYS LATER AND SHOWED THAT THE WARDENS HAD ONLY HANDED OVER THE BLANKET AND PILLOW.
MEANWHILE, MRS. MORANT WAS SUMMONED FOR AN INTERROGATION...
...THE SOLICITOR WILLIAM MACINTYRE WAS TOLD HE NEEDED A PROSECUTOR'S PERMIT IN ORDER TO SEE THE PRISONERS...
...AND MARY FITZGERALD PEDALED BETWEEN SUBURB AND SLUM COLLECTING FUNDS TO PAY FOR THEIR LEGAL FEES.
WHEN THE ACCUSED FINALLY APPEARED IN COURT ON 29 MAY, MACINTYRE HAD HIS CHANCE TO SPEAK WITH THEM.
PLEASE. I CAN'T TAKE ANOTHER DAY IN THAT RAT HOLE.
THOSE FEW PRECIOUS MINUTES GAVE THE LAWYER ENOUGH TO WORK WITH. LATER THE SAME DAY, HE WROTE DIRECTLY TO THE MINISTER OF JUSTICE, BARRY HERTZOG.

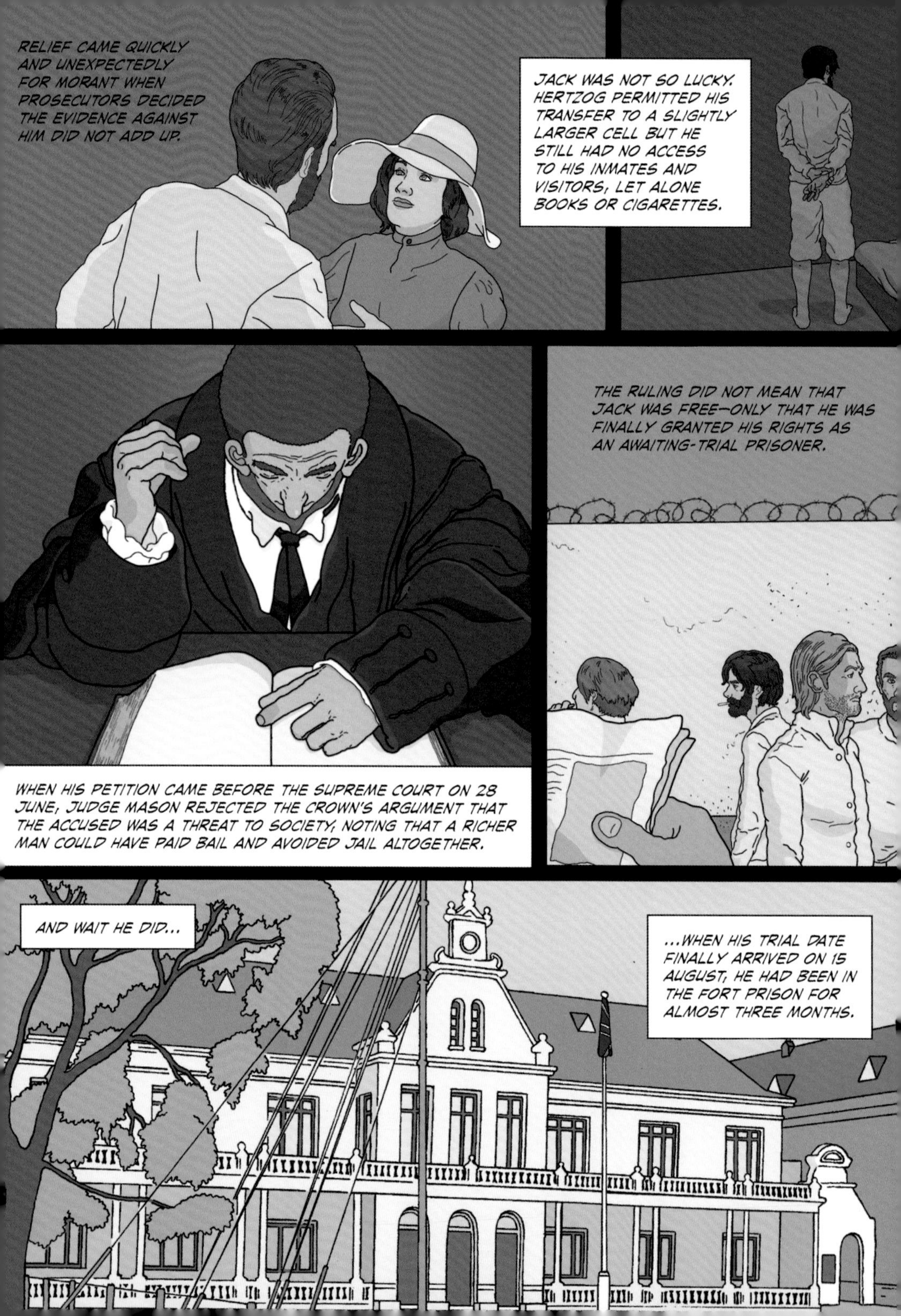
RELIEF CAME QUICKLY AND UNEXPECTEDLY FOR MORANT WHEN PROSECUTORS DECIDED THE EVIDENCE AGAINST HIM DID NOT ADD UP.
JACK WAS NOT SO LUCKY. HERTZOG PERMITTED HIS TRANSFER TO A SLIGHTLY LARGER CELL BUT HE STILL HAD NO ACCESS TO HIS INMATES AND VISITORS, LET ALONE BOOKS OR CIGARETTES.
WHEN HIS PETITION CAME BEFORE THE SUPREME COURT ON 28 JUNE, JUDGE MASON REJECTED THE CROWN'S ARGUMENT THAT THE ACCUSED WAS A THREAT TO SOCIETY, NOTING THAT A RICHER MAN COULD HAVE PAID BAIL AND AVOIDED JAIL ALTOGETHER.
THE RULING DID NOT MEAN THAT JACK WAS FREE—ONLY THAT HE WAS FINALLY GRANTED HIS RIGHTS AS AN AWAITING-TRIAL PRISONER.
AND WAIT HE DID...
...WHEN HIS TRIAL DATE FINALLY ARRIVED ON 15 AUGUST, HE HAD BEEN IN THE FORT PRISON FOR ALMOST THREE MONTHS.

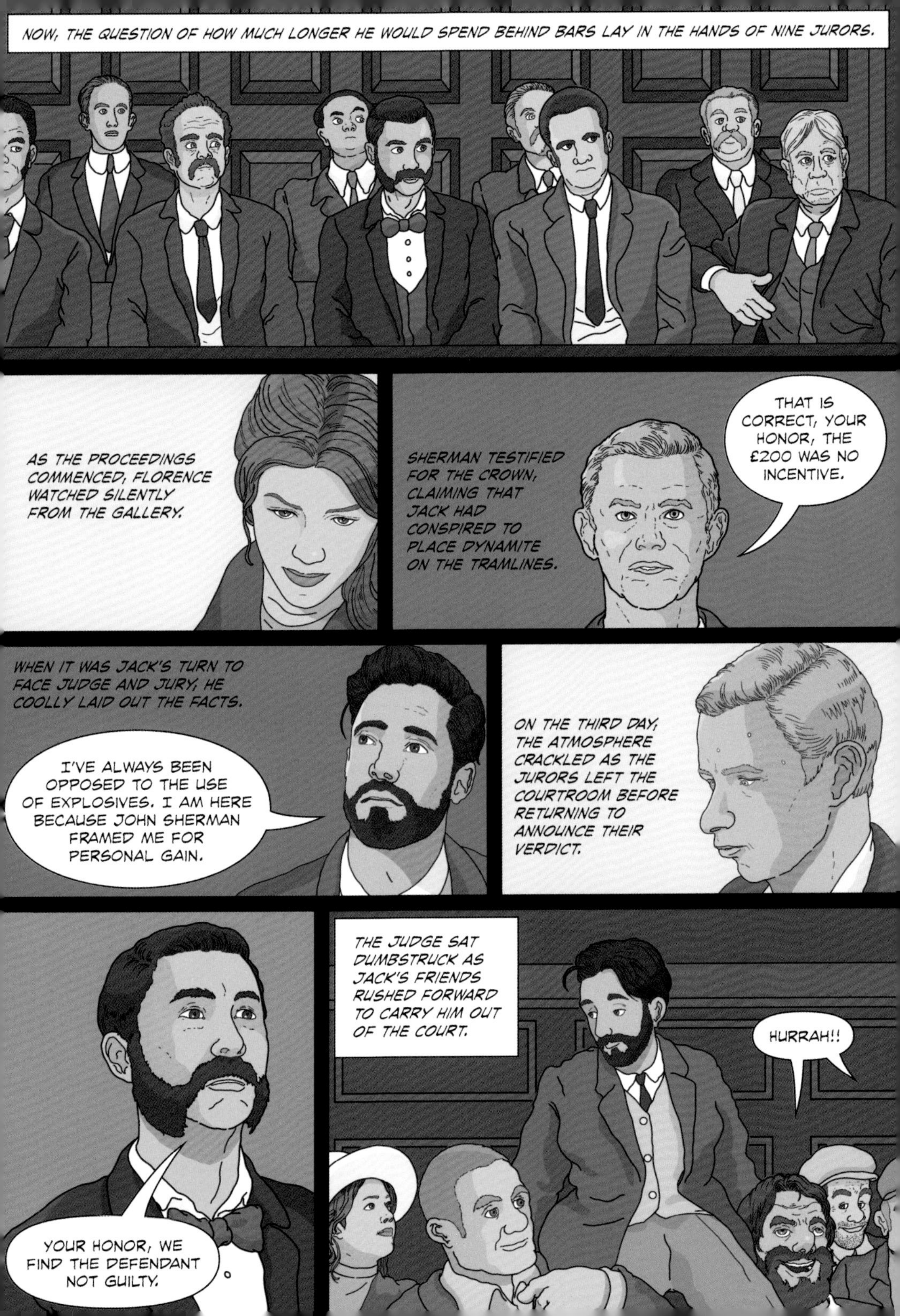
NOW, THE QUESTION OF HOW MUCH LONGER HE WOULD SPEND BEHIND BARS LAY IN THE HANDS OF NINE JURORS.
AS THE PROCEEDINGS COMMENCED, FLORENCE WATCHED SILENTLY FROM THE GALLERY.
SHERMAN TESTIFIED FOR THE CROWN, CLAIMING THAT JACK HAD CONSPIRED TO PLACE DYNAMITE ON THE TRAMLINES.
THAT IS CORRECT, YOUR HONOR, THE £200 WAS NO INCENTIVE.
WHEN IT WAS JACK'S TURN TO FACE JUDGE AND JURY, HE COOLLY LAID OUT THE FACTS.
I'VE ALWAYS BEEN OPPOSED TO THE USE OF EXPLOSIVES. I AM HERE BECAUSE JOHN SHERMAN FRAMED ME FOR PERSONAL GAIN.
ON THE THIRD DAY, THE ATMOSPHERE CRACKLED AS THE JURORS LEFT THE COURTROOM BEFORE RETURNING TO ANNOUNCE THEIR VERDICT.
YOUR HONOR, WE FIND THE DEFENDANT NOT GUILTY.
THE JUDGE SAT DUMBSTRUCK AS JACK'S FRIENDS RUSHED FORWARD TO CARRY HIM OUT OF THE COURT.
HURRAH!!

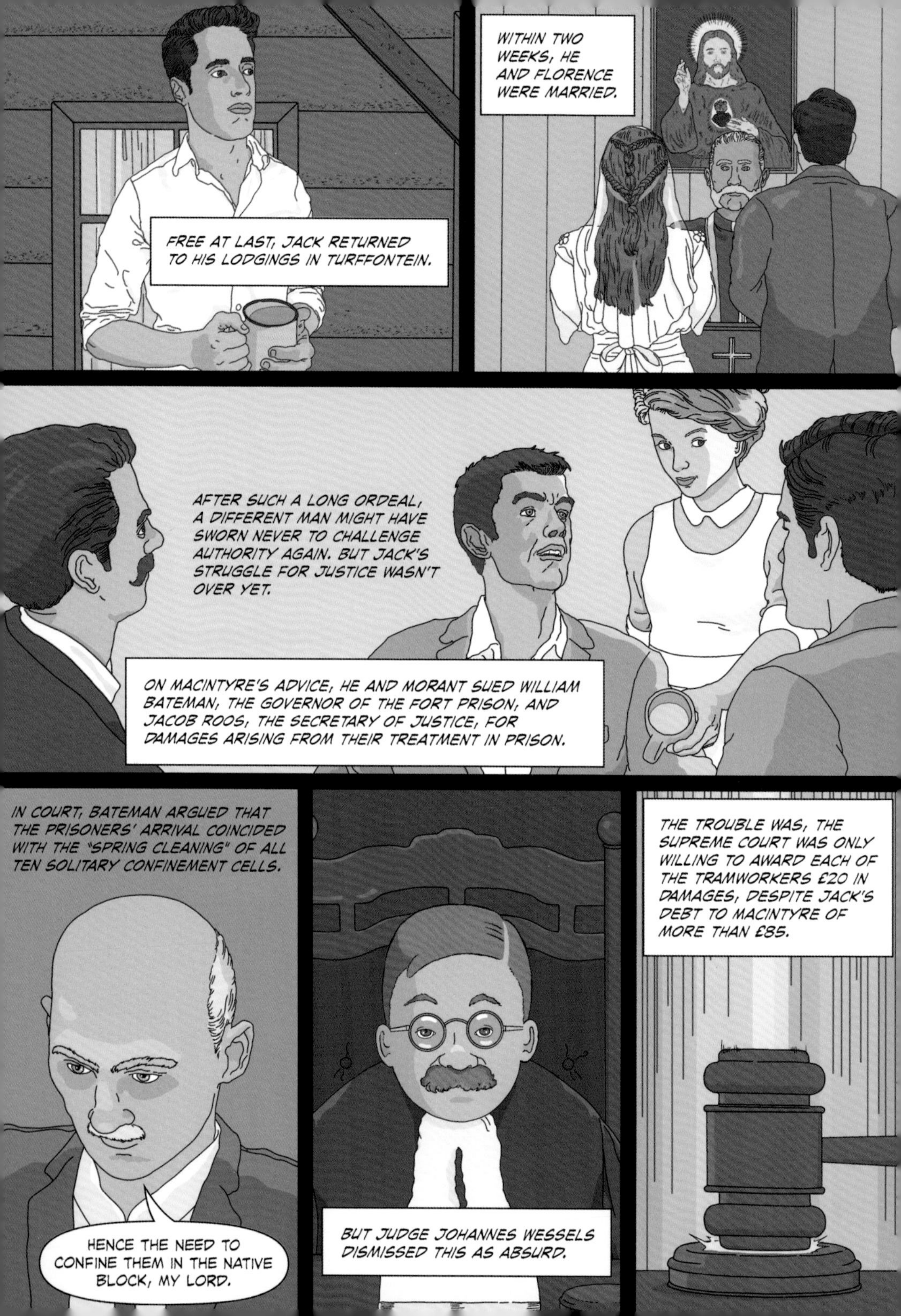
FREE AT LAST, JACK RETURNED TO HIS LODGINGS IN TURFFONTEIN.
WITHIN TWO WEEKS, HE AND FLORENCE WERE MARRIED.
AFTER SUCH A LONG ORDEAL, A DIFFERENT MAN MIGHT HAVE SWORN NEVER TO CHALLENGE AUTHORITY AGAIN. BUT JACK'S STRUGGLE FOR JUSTICE WASN'T OVER YET.
ON MACINTYRE'S ADVICE, HE AND MORANT SUED WILLIAM BATEMAN, THE GOVERNOR OF THE FORT PRISON, AND JACOB ROOS, THE SECRETARY OF JUSTICE, FOR DAMAGES ARISING FROM THEIR TREATMENT IN PRISON.
IN COURT, BATEMAN ARGUED THAT THE PRISONERS' ARRIVAL COINCIDED WITH THE "SPRING CLEANING" OF ALL TEN SOLITARY CONFINEMENT CELLS.
HENCE THE NEED TO CONFINE THEM IN THE NATIVE BLOCK, MY LORD.
BUT JUDGE JOHANNES WESSELS DISMISSED THIS AS ABSURD.
THE TROUBLE WAS, THE SUPREME COURT WAS ONLY WILLING TO AWARD EACH OF THE TRAMWORKERS £20 IN DAMAGES, DESPITE JACK'S DEBT TO MACINTYRE OF MORE THAN £85.

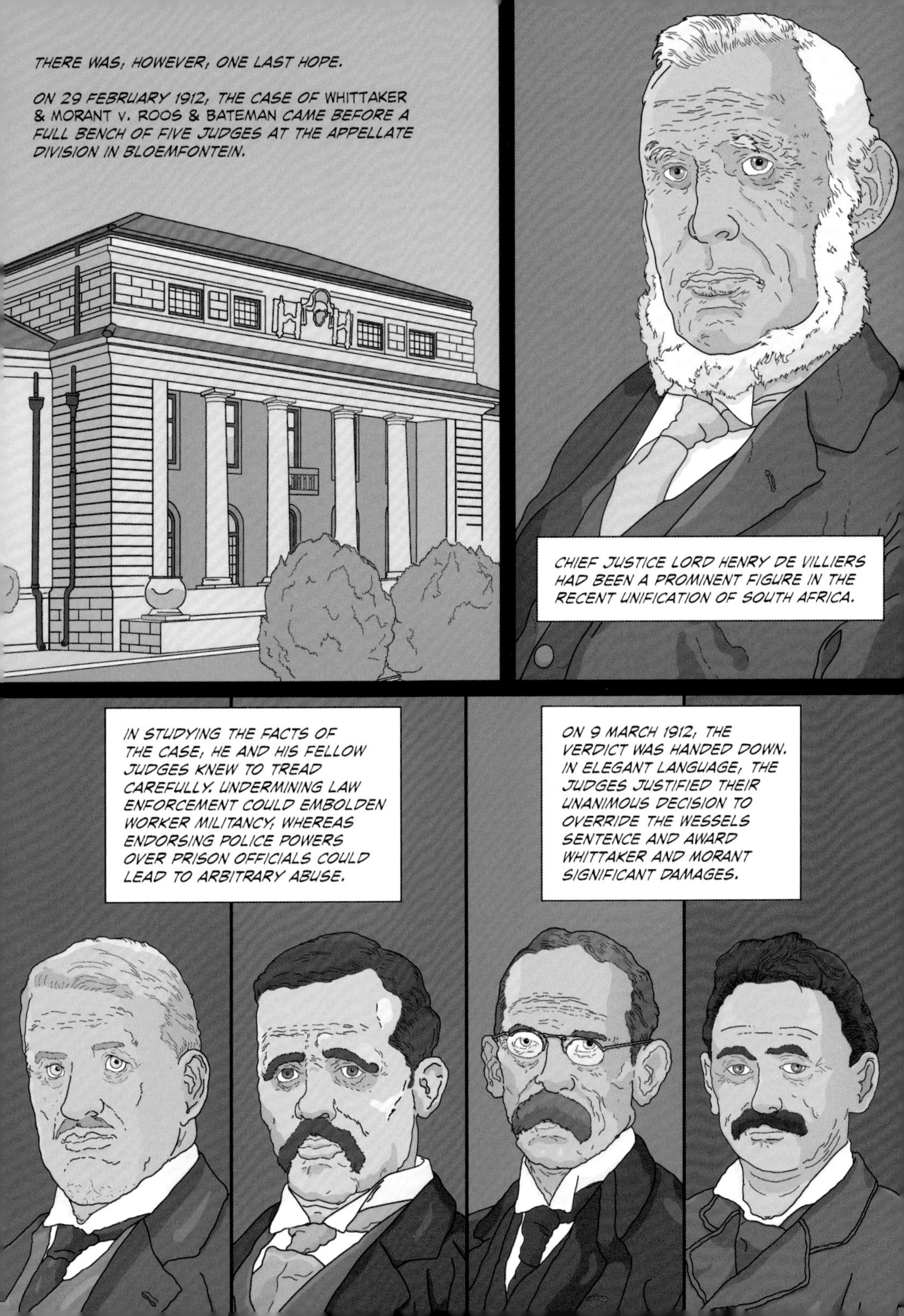
THERE WAS, HOWEVER, ONE LAST HOPE.
ON 29 FEBRUARY 1912, THE CASE OF WHITTAKER & MORANT v. ROOS & BATEMAN CAME BEFORE A FULL BENCH OF FIVE JUDGES AT THE APPELLATE DIVISION IN BLOEMFONTEIN.
CHIEF JUSTICE LORD HENRY DE VILLIERS HAD BEEN A PROMINENT FIGURE IN THE RECENT UNIFICATION OF SOUTH AFRICA.
IN STUDYING THE FACTS OF THE CASE, HE AND HIS FELLOW JUDGES KNEW TO TREAD CAREFULLY. UNDERMINING LAW ENFORCEMENT COULD EMBOLDEN WORKER MILITANCY, WHEREAS ENDORSING POLICE POWERS OVER PRISON OFFICIALS COULD LEAD TO ARBITRARY ABUSE.
ON 9 MARCH 1912, THE VERDICT WAS HANDED DOWN. IN ELEGANT LANGUAGE, THE JUDGES JUSTIFIED THEIR UNANIMOUS DECISION TO OVERRIDE THE WESSELS SENTENCE AND AWARD WHITTAKER AND MORANT SIGNIFICANT DAMAGES.

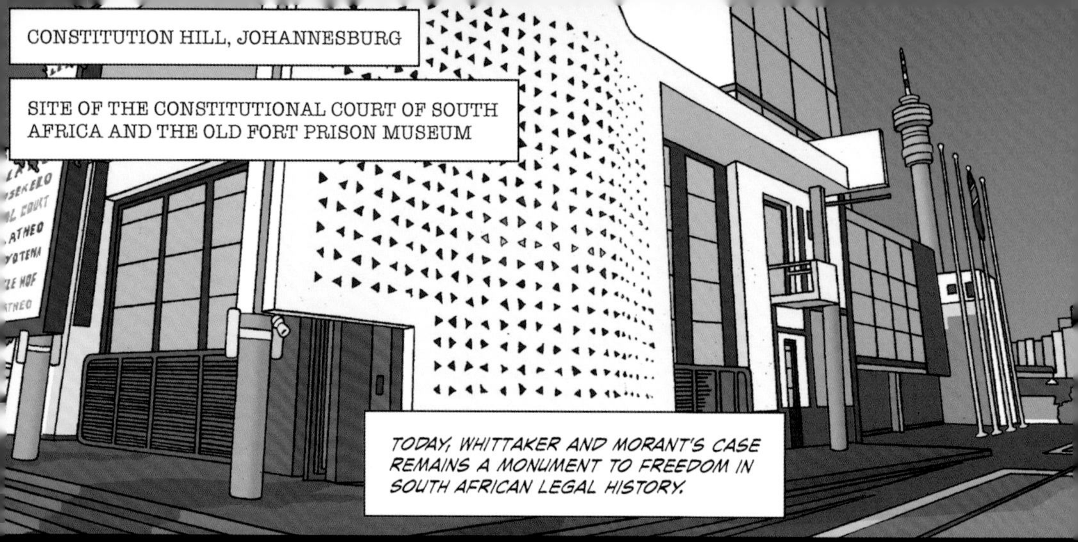
CONSTITUTION HILL, JOHANNESBURG
SITE OF THE CONSTITUTIONAL COURT OF SOUTH AFRICA AND THE OLD FORT PRISON MUSEUM
TODAY, WHITTAKER AND MORANT'S CASE REMAINS A MONUMENT TO FREEDOM IN SOUTH AFRICAN LEGAL HISTORY.

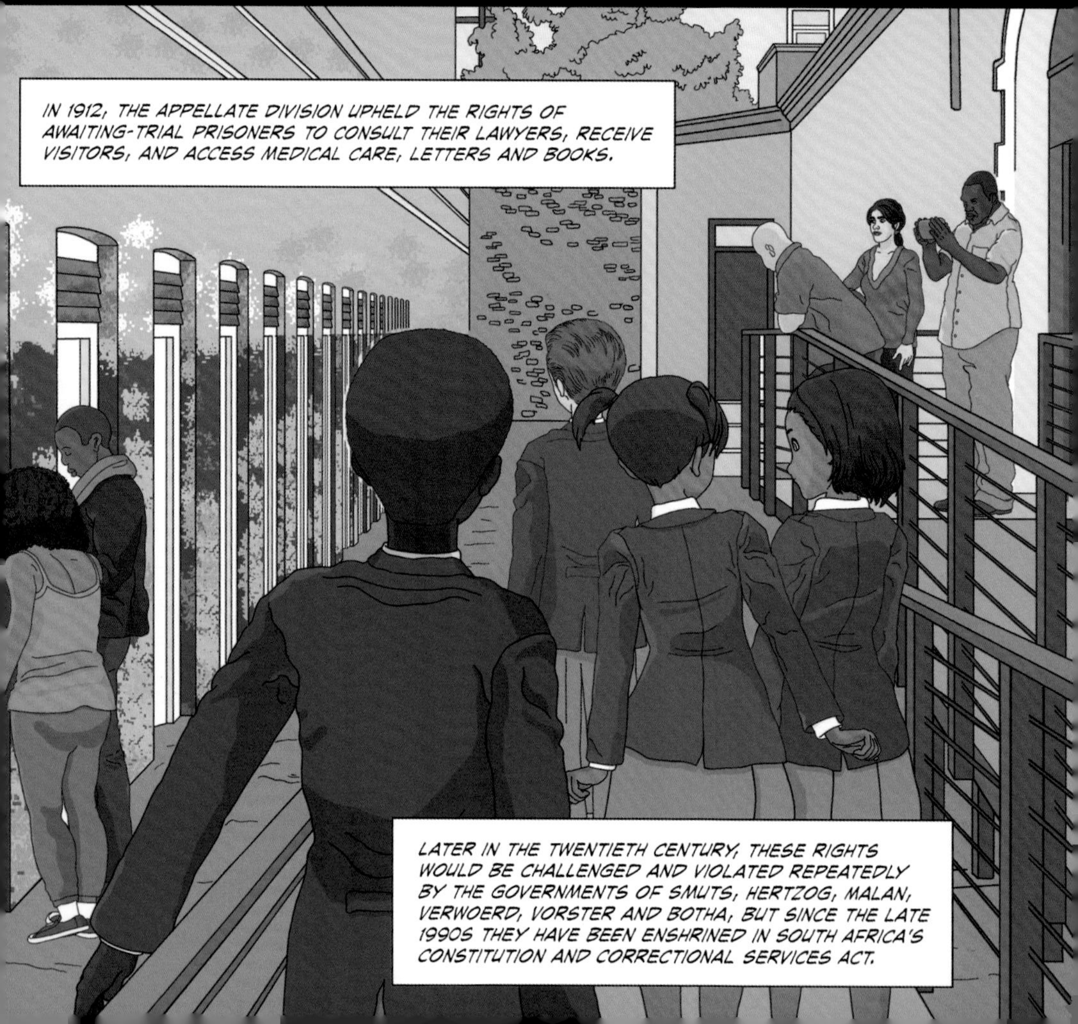
IN 1912, THE APPELLATE DIVISION UPHELD THE RIGHTS OF AWAITING-TRIAL PRISONERS TO CONSULT THEIR LAWYERS, RECEIVE VISITORS, AND ACCESS MEDICAL CARE, LETTERS AND BOOKS.
LATER IN THE TWENTIETH CENTURY, THESE RIGHTS WOULD BE CHALLENGED AND VIOLATED REPEATEDLY BY THE GOVERNMENTS OF SMUTS, HERTZOG, MALAN, VERWOERD, VORSTER AND BOTHA, BUT SINCE THE LATE 1990S THEY HAVE BEEN ENSHRINED IN SOUTH AFRICA'S CONSTITUTION AND CORRECTIONAL SERVICES ACT.

WHILE THE APPELLATE DIVISION JUDGES WERE DECIDING HIS FATE, JACK WHITTAKER FOUND WORK "LEARNING CYANIDE" ON THE MINES, EARNING 12 POUNDS AND 10 SHILLINGS A MONTH. BEYOND THIS AND THE COURT'S VERDICT, WE KNOW NOTHING OF HIS LATER LIFE.

ON THE WITWATERSRAND, THE DECADE TO FOLLOW AFTER 1912 WAS TO BE ONE OF THE MOST TURBULENT IN SOUTH AFRICAN LABOR HISTORY, CULMINATING IN THE 1922 RAND REVOLT. AS TO WHETHER JACK WAS ONE OF THE TENS OF THOUSANDS OF WORKERS WHO TOOK PART IN THIS ERA OF UNREST WE CAN ONLY SPECULATE.

THOUGH HIS PERSONAL STORY IS ALMOST ENTIRELY LOST TO US—LIKE THOSE OF MILLIONS OF WORKERS ALL OVER THE WORLD—HIS CONTRIBUTION AS A RESISTER LIVES ON IN THE BASEMENT OF THE SUPREME COURT OF APPEAL. THERE, TOO, ONE CAN FIND A SHEET OF PAPER CONTAINING JACK'S ONLY SURVIVING WORDS: THE LETTER HE WROTE TO FLORENCE FROM HIS PUNISHMENT CELL ON 20 MAY 1911.

BEHIND THE STORY: SOURCES AND SKETCHES

CHAPTER 2: IN THE SHADOW OF A HIGH STONE WALL

In contrast to the explosive decade of white working-class resistance that shook the Witwatersand from 1912 to 1922, the 1911 Johannesburg municipal tram workers' strike was relatively under-reported. In addition, throughout this period, most of the city's major newspapers tended to be one-sided in their coverage of the unrest, effectively publishing propaganda on behalf of the government and employers.

These considerations underscored the importance of two counter-balancing sources—*Voice of Labour*, the first socialist weekly in twentieth-century South Africa, and the two sets of court records that stemmed from Jack Whittaker's arrest in 1911: those for his initial criminal trial, and those for the later case which he and John Morant won in early 1912.

Like *Indian Opinion*, original copies of *Voice of Labour* are housed in the National Library of South Africa. Founded in 1908, the newspaper acted as a mouthpiece for the international syndicalist organization known as the Industrial Workers of the World. It kept a close eye on labor movements both locally and abroad; and often through first-hand reporting by Mary Fitzgerald herself, its coverage extended to the tram strike and Jack Whittaker's protracted legal battles. Reading *Voice of Labour* alongside the *Whittaker* court records, we were able to corroborate information and establish a richer, more "visual" understanding—in the absence of photographs—of the dramatic events which punctuated this story.

Right: Jack's letter to his fiancée Florence Macfarlane, written from his "punishment cell," was included as an exhibit of evidence in the case of *Whittaker & Morant v. Roos & Bateman.*

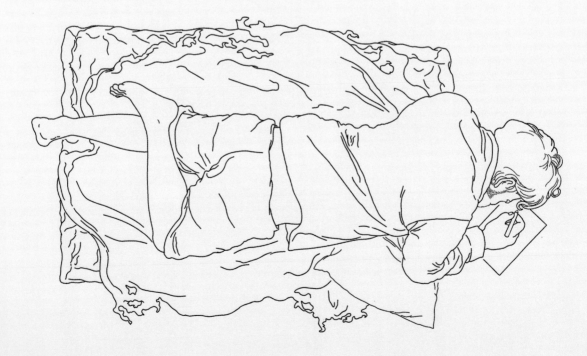

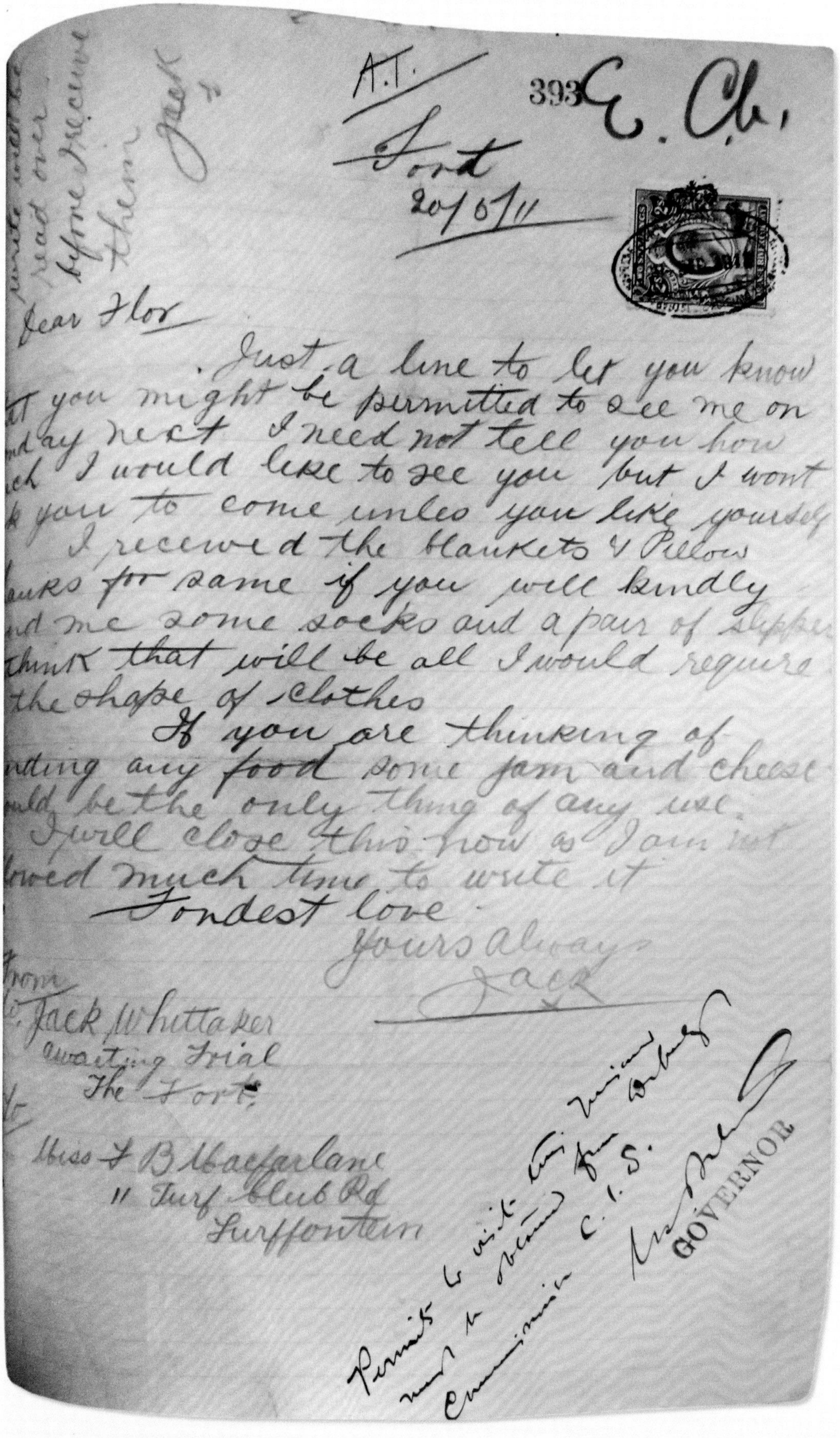
read over
before I receive
them
Jack
A.T.
Fort
20/6/11
393 E. Cb.
Dear Flor
Just a line to let you know
at you might be permitted to see me on
nday next I need not tell you how
ch I would like to see you but I wont
you to come unles you like yoursel
I received the blankets & Pillow
anks for same if you will kindly
d me some socks and a pair of slippe
think that will be all I would require
the shape of clothes
If you are thinking of
nding any food some jam and cheese
uld be the only thing of any use.
I will close this now as I am not
owed much time to write it
Fondest love
Yours Always
Jack
From
Jack Whittaker
awaiting Trial
The Fort.
Miss F B Macfarlane
11 Turf Club Rd
Turffontein
C.I.D.
GOVERNOR

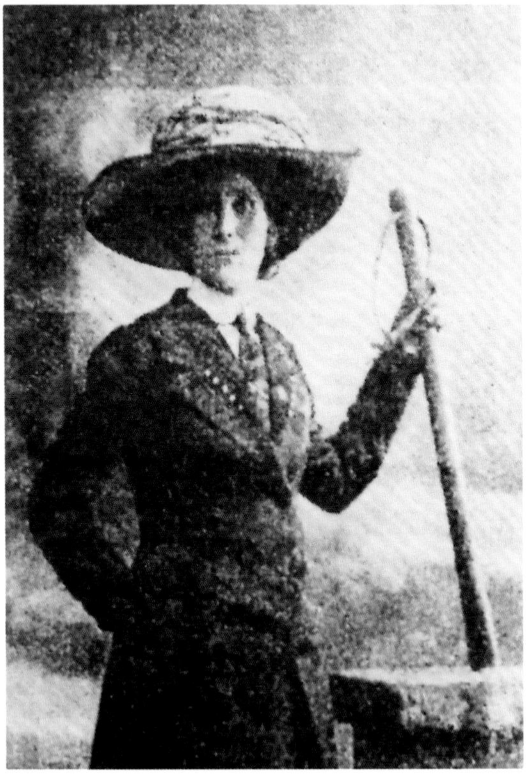

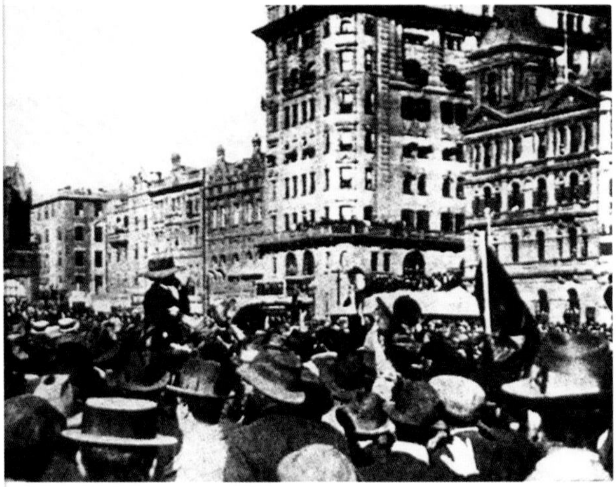

Mary Fitzgerald (popularly known as "Pickhandle" Mary) was a radical trade unionist, fiercely outspoken protestor, and the co-editor of *Voice of Labour*, who emerged as a driving force behind the struggles of Johannesburg's working-class during the early twentieth century.

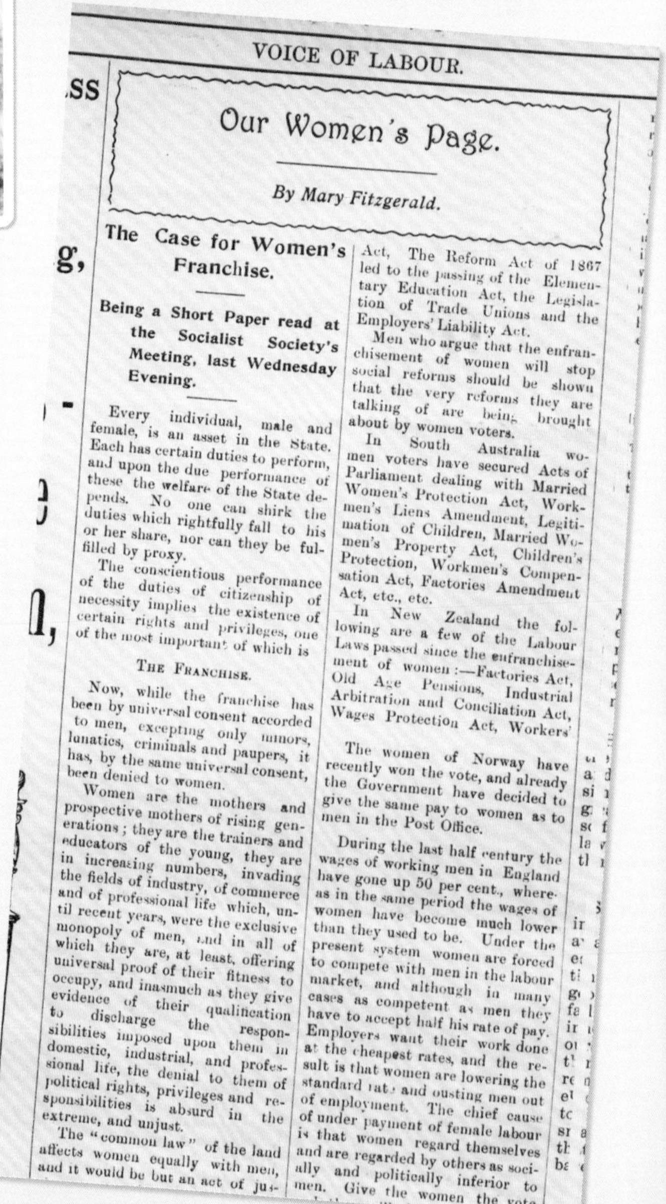

VOICE OF LABOUR.

Our Women's Page.

By Mary Fitzgerald.

The Case for Women's Franchise.

Being a Short Paper read at the Socialist Society's Meeting, last Wednesday Evening.

Every individual, male and female, is an asset in the State. Each has certain duties to perform, and upon the due performance of these the welfare of the State depends. No one can shirk the duties which rightfully fall to his or her share, nor can they be fulfilled by proxy.

The conscientious performance of the duties of citizenship of necessity implies the existence of certain rights and privileges, one of the most important of which is

THE FRANCHISE.

Now, while the franchise has been by universal consent accorded to men, excepting only minors, lunatics, criminals and paupers, it has, by the same universal consent, been denied to women.

Women are the mothers and prospective mothers of rising generations; they are the trainers and educators of the young, they are in increasing numbers, invading the fields of industry, of commerce and of professional life which, until recent years, were the exclusive monopoly of men, and in all of which they are, at least, offering universal proof of their fitness to occupy, and inasmuch as they give evidence of their qualification to discharge the responsibilities imposed upon them in domestic, industrial, and professional life, the denial to them of political rights, privileges and responsibilities is absurd in the extreme, and unjust.

The "common law" of the land affects women equally with men, and it would be but an act of jus-

Act, The Reform Act of 1867 led to the passing of the Elementary Education Act, the Legislation of Trade Unions and the Employers' Liability Act.

Men who argue that the enfranchisement of women will stop social reforms should be shown that the very reforms they are talking of are being brought about by women voters.

In South Australia women voters have secured Acts of Parliament dealing with Married Women's Protection Act, Workmen's Liens Amendment, Legitimation of Children, Married Women's Property Act, Children's Protection, Workmen's Compensation Act, Factories Amendment Act, etc., etc.

In New Zealand the following are a few of the Labour Laws passed since the enfranchisement of women:—Factories Act, Old Age Pensions, Industrial Arbitration and Conciliation Act, Wages Protection Act, Workers'

The women of Norway have recently won the vote, and already the Government have decided to give the same pay to women as to men in the Post Office.

During the last half century the wages of working men in England have gone up 50 per cent., whereas in the same period the wages of women have become much lower than they used to be. Under the present system women are forced to compete with men in the labour market, and although in many cases as competent as men they have to accept half his rate of pay. Employers want their work done at the cheapest rates, and the result is that women are lowering the standard rate and ousting men out of employment. The chief cause of under payment of female labour is that women regard themselves and are regarded by others as socially and politically inferior to men. Give the women the vote

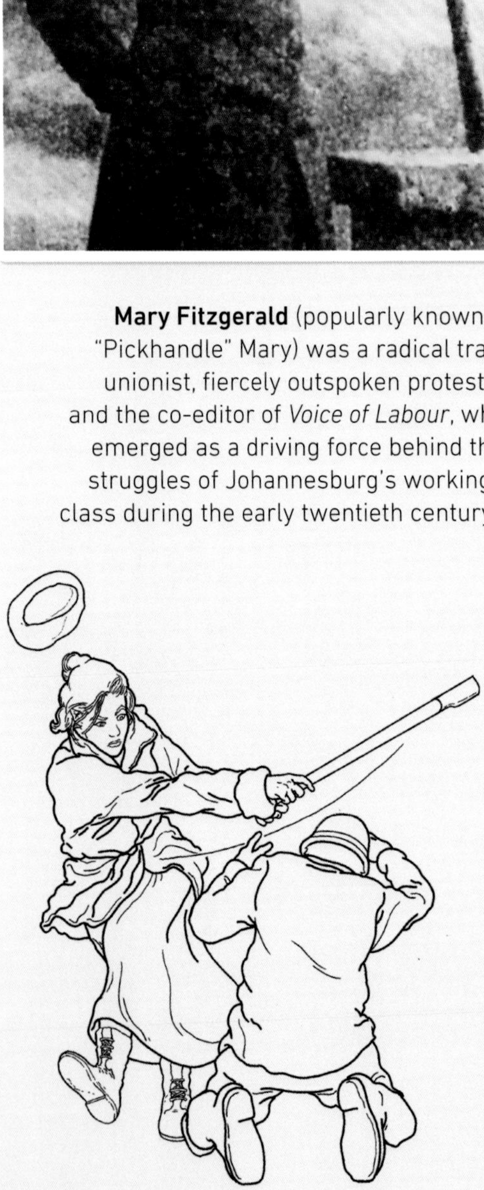

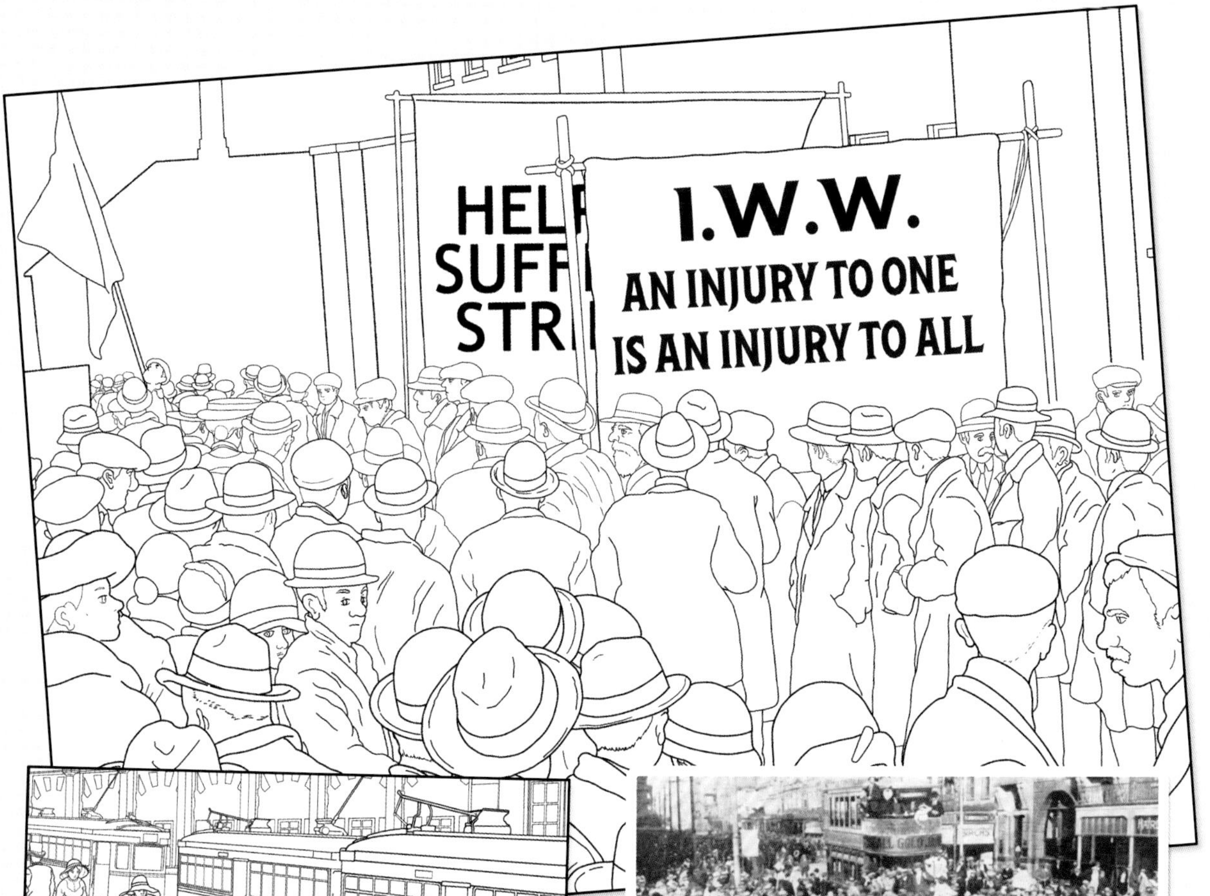
HEL
SUFF
STR
I.W.W.
AN INJURY TO ONE
IS AN INJURY TO ALL

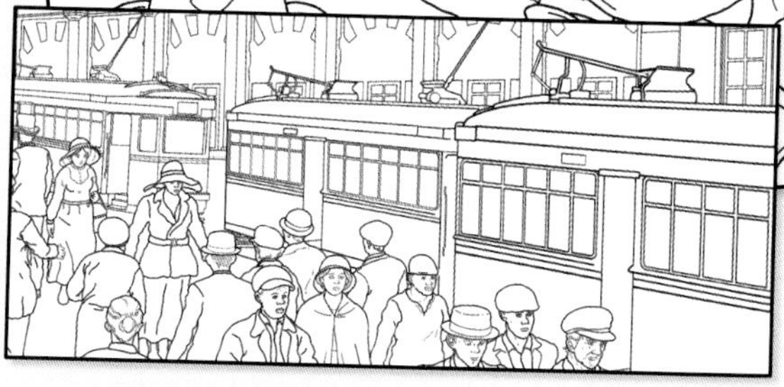

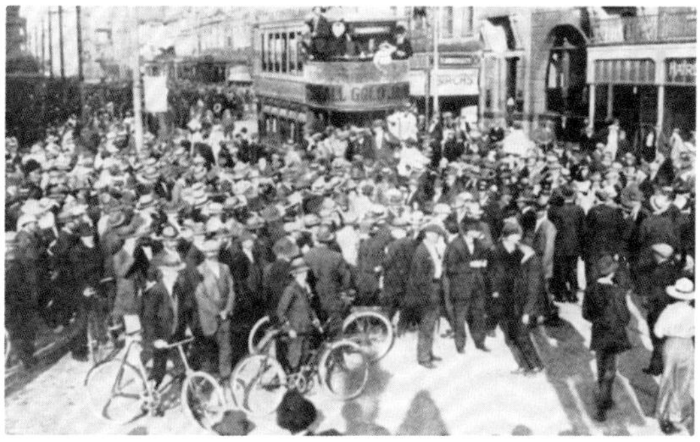

Right: "The ringing of newly electrified trams competed with the chatter of broad-accented migrants..." municipal strike action on Market Street (*above*) and the Market Square (*below*), in central Johannesburg during the early twentieth century.

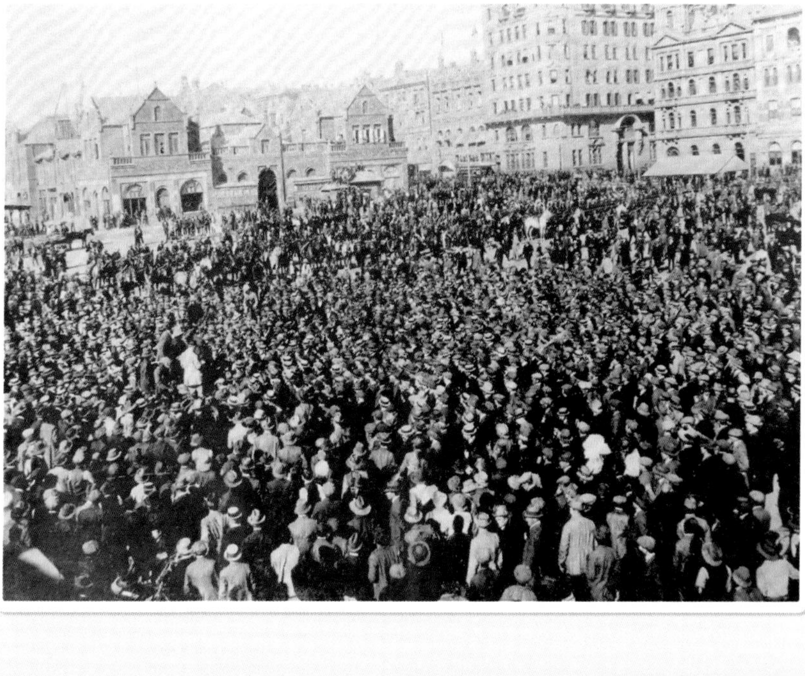

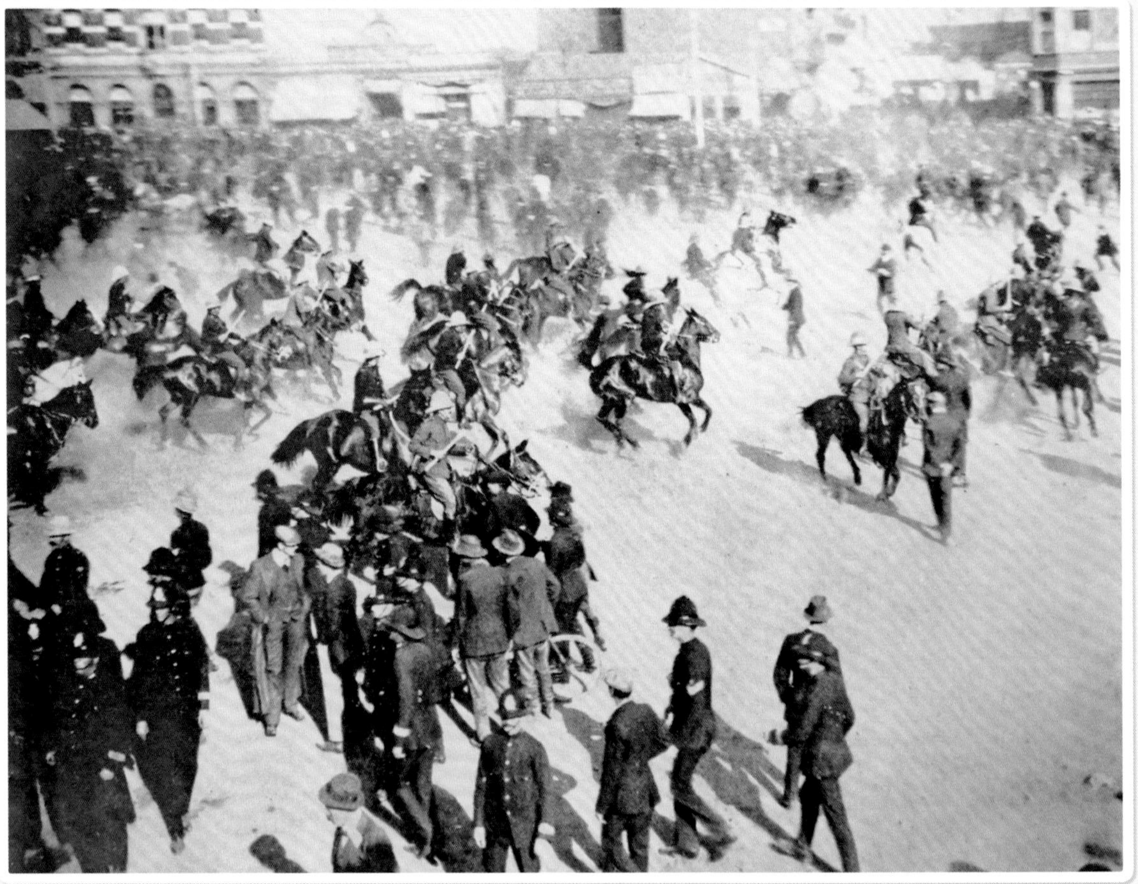

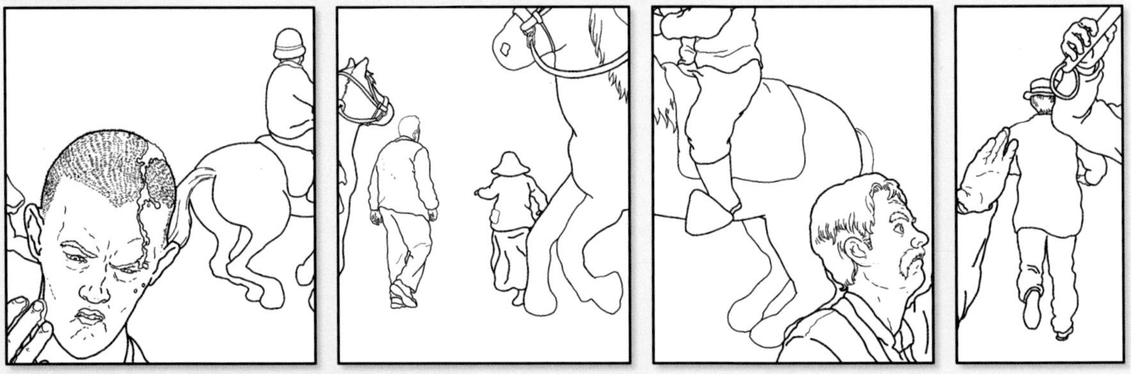

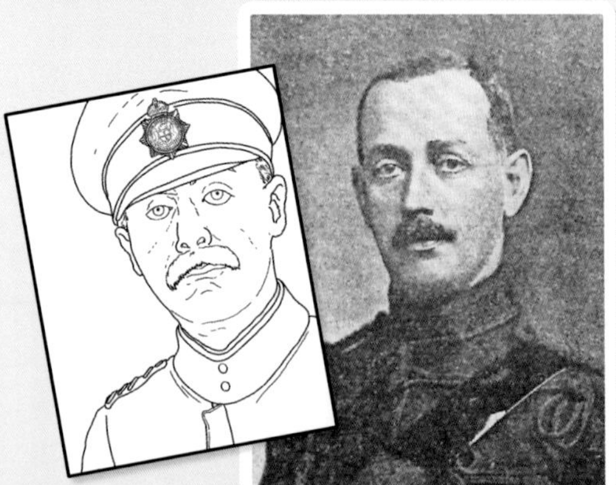

Above: "On the Witwatersrand, the decade to follow after 1912 was to be one of the most turbulent in South African labor history, culminating in the 1922 Rand Revolt..." police charging strikers on the Market Square in 1913.

Left: Theo Mavrogordato, the Johannesburg police chief who orchestrated the crackdown on striking tram workers in 1911.

The Story of John Layfayette Sherman.

Working Class Traitor and Spy.

Told from his own lips according to extracts from a record of the proceedings in the case of Rex versus William John Whittaker, certified to be correct by H. E. Alcock, Official Shorthand Writer of the Supreme Court, Witwatersrand Local Division.

Sherman's Career.

I am 29 years of age on the 9th of next May. I was in the Navy of the United States of America. I was in the police of Cape Colony and then the trams in Port Elizabeth. I was in the Cape Mounted Rifles 4½ years. Up to the time of the Tramway Strike I had been about 5 months in the employ of the tramways of the Johannesburg Municipality. I was working on the trams on the night of the 11th May (Thursday) the night the Tram Strike commenced. On the 12th there was an election of the Strike Committee. I was a member of the committee.

An "Affair."

In the C.M.R. I received an injustice and purchased my discharge. It was a private matter between the corporal and myself and a certain lady. It was a married lady. A charge was brought against me and I left.

Convicted for Theft.

I got a month for theft of furniture. Sentence was suspended to give me time to pay for the furniture.

A Police Spy.

I said that I acted as a spy on the men. I was giving the police information from the Saturday (the strike started on Thursday night). I was acting under Mr Mavrogordato's (the chief detective's) instructions. I was under the impression that I was acting in conjunction with the police all along. I was asked to go to a room at Goodman's Buildings one night. I suspected they were going to use dynamite. I had not heard all the conversation. I should have liked to have heard more of the conversation because I wanted to give the information to the police.

Suggesting Use of Dynamite.

I may have mentioned the use of dynamite for the purpose of gaining information.

Sherman Makes Money.

I knew that a reward of £200 would be paid to the man who gave information as to who placed the dynamite on the line. The reward was not offered until the Monday morning (15th). I cannot exactly say what time it would be when I first heard of the reward of £200, I think it was on the Monday or Tuesday (15th or 16th) It

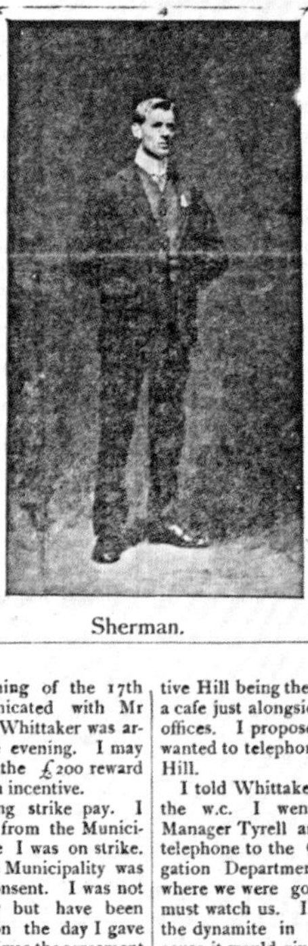

Sherman.

was on the morning of the 17th when I communicated with Mr Mavrogordato. Whittaker was arrested that same evening. I may have thought of the £200 reward but it was not an incentive.

I was receiving strike pay. I was getting pay from the Municipality at the time I was on strike. My pay from the Municipality was continued by consent. I was not paid continually but have been paid up since; on the day I gave information, that was the agreement with Councillor Moss. I was to be paid until this case was finished, I have made no offer to repay the money I received from the strike funds.

How Sherman Sold Whittaker

It was lunch time on the 16th that Whittaker told me about the dynamite. Next morning I communicated with Mr Mavrogordato I was acting under his instructions. At 9 p.m. (on the 17th) I went to Rosenberg's Arcade and met Whittaker who handed me a tin box. I took them to be detonators. I took the box in my hand and said "You have an overcoat on, you can keep them dry, put them in your pocket." I had my instructions not to wear an overcoat. We came out into Commissioner Street along to Harrison Street. We went to have a cup of coffee each. I had not an appointment until 9.30 p.m. and I wanted to keep him from laying the dynamite until that time. We stopped at each corner because I thought that was the best means of drawing suspicion away from us. I wanted to delay him until 9.30 when I would be certain of Detective Hill being there. We went to a cafe just alongside the Tramway offices. I proposed that because I wanted to telephone to Detective Hill.

I told Whittaker I was going to the w.c. I went into General Manager Tyrell and asked him to telephone to the Criminal Investigation Department. I told him where we were going and that he must watch us. I proposed laying the dynamite in Main Street because it would give me a chance to pass Detective Hill on the way.

At the corner of Harrison and Market Streets there were two detectives watching us. I recognised the two detectives. Whittaker also saw the detectives and from what I could understand he suspected they were detectives. He said "Are not those two detectives?" and I said I did not know but he had best not be in a hurry. We wa for some time. It was nearly past nine and I said "Come, had best go." It was arranged t I should signal to Detective H if Whittaker had the dynamite his possession. It was arrang previously to signal to Detecti Hill by lighting a cigarette. I signalled to Hill. It was arranged that I should attempt to rescue Whittaker- I did so. I was ordered to go to Pretoria by Detective Hill because it was not saf for me to stay.

Detective Hill's Story.

Sherman was introduced to me Mr. Mavrogordato who gave certain instructions. I made appointment with Sherman to m me between 9.30 and 9,45 p.m corner of Loveday and Fox st Sherman and Whittaker retu to the corner of Rissik and streets. I asked P.C. Shark assist me in affecting the arre this man Whittaker. We took him each having hold of an arm. Sherman followed and he made some kind of attempts on his own suggestion to rescue Whittaker, I gave Sherman a kick and told him to go away. He was trying to overdo the thing a bit. I think S man was very pleased that he caught this man. He said t was a reward of £200 offered he was the only person who given information. He expecte get the reward, I think I recol him once saying that, if he did the reward he should clear ou the country.

Sherman's Method.

Rory Beattie, a conductor the trams, said: During the strike I had a conversation with Sherman. He proposed that he and I should place dynamite from Market Square to the sheds on several parts of the rails in order to damage the cars that w going home. He explained h easy it was to lay dynamite. said he and another man on Booysen's road put dynamite the rails. He tried to entice further.

Blow them to Hell.

William Alfred Hughes, motorman, said: On the Fri Sherman came rushing up to door of Rosenberg's Arcade. got hold of my arm. There were a little over a dozen men there. He said—the very words he used were "The bastards want blowing to Hell."

Didn't Care a Damn.

Joseph Jackson, the bookkeep of Bradlow & Co. said: Sherm bought furniture on the hire p ment system. He paid £3 1 in five instalments, sold the fu ture and was prosecuted. On Monday after Whittaker's a I spoke to him about his acc He told me that when he go £200 he would have every

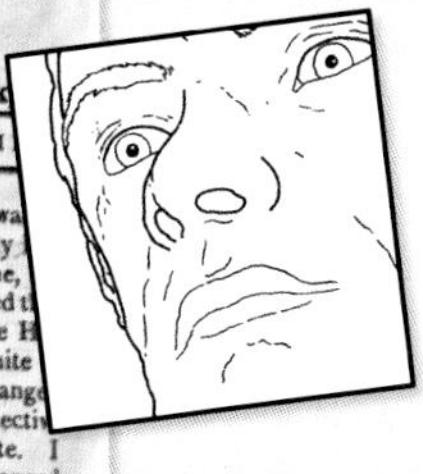

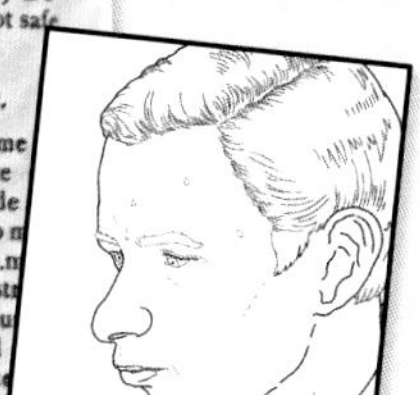

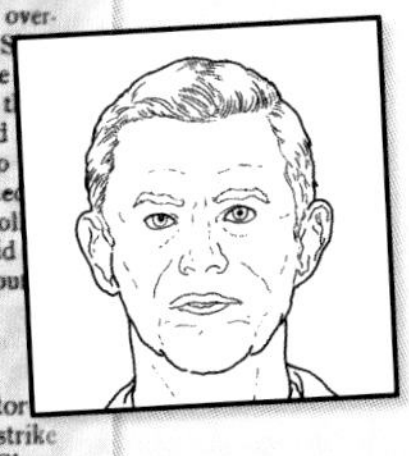

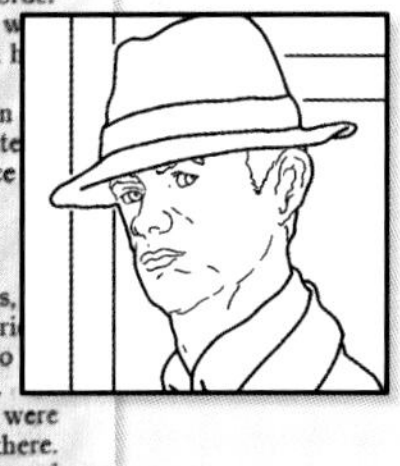

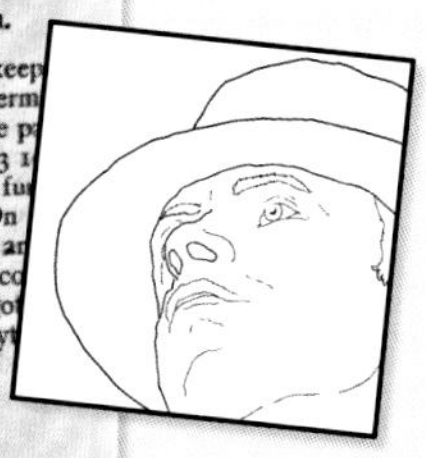

Above: A *Voice of Labour* article condemning John Lafayette Sherman, the "traitor and spy" who framed Jack Whittaker during the 1911 tram strike.

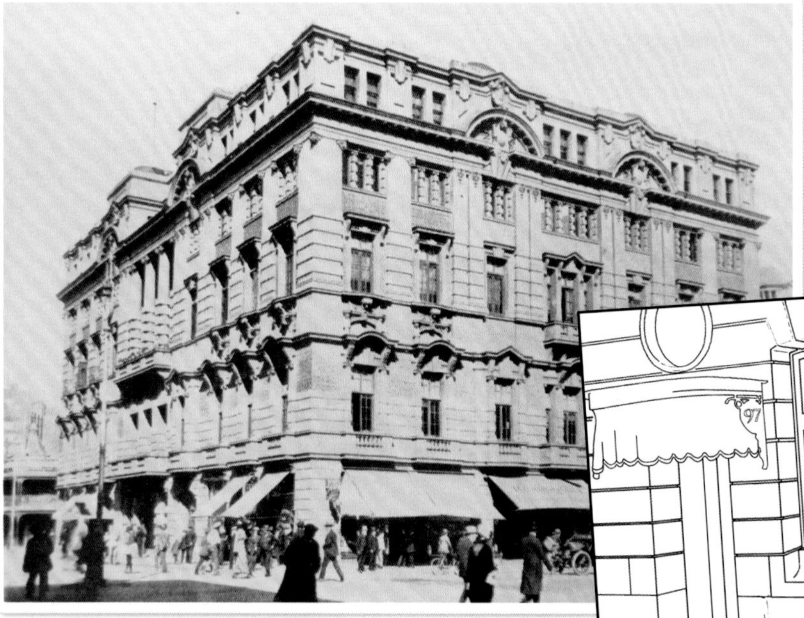

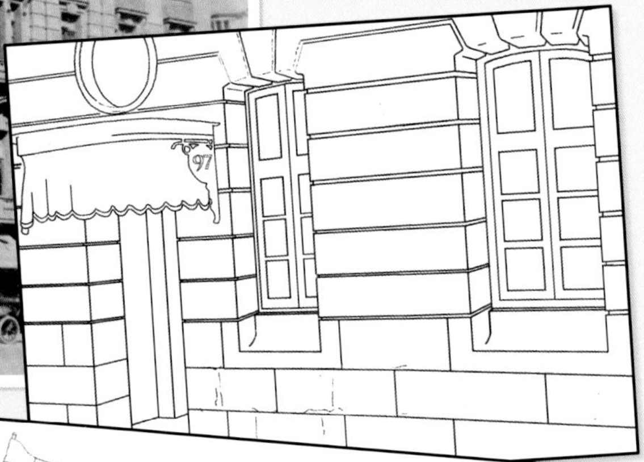

97

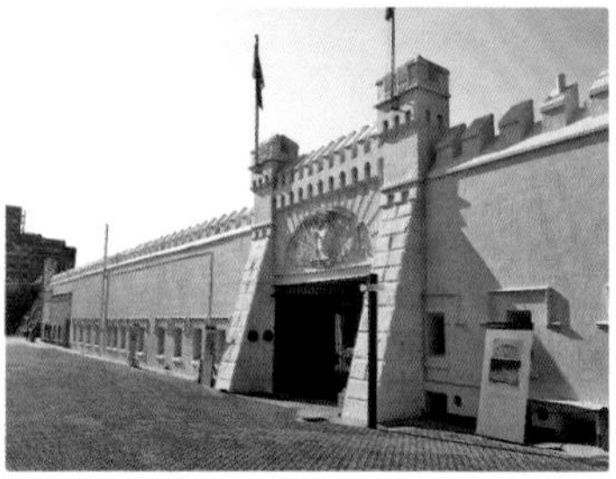

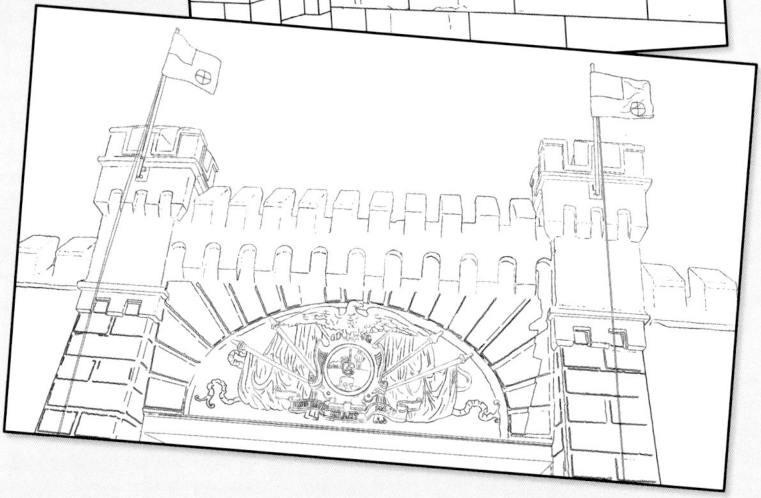

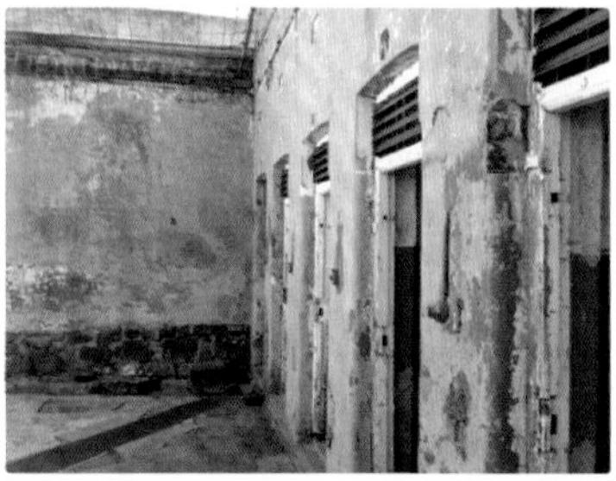

Top: On a rainy evening in May 1911, Jack Whittaker was arrested on the corner of Fox and Loveday, outside Johannesburg's elite Rand Club. **Above, left:** The Old Fort prison buildings, situated in what today is known as the Constitution Hill precinct, house permanent museum exhibitions. **Left:** The "punishment cells," where Jack Whittaker and John Morant were isolated, are now part of a museum tour.

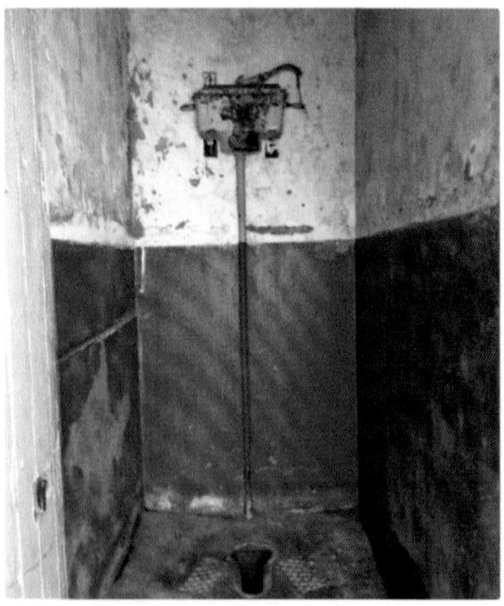

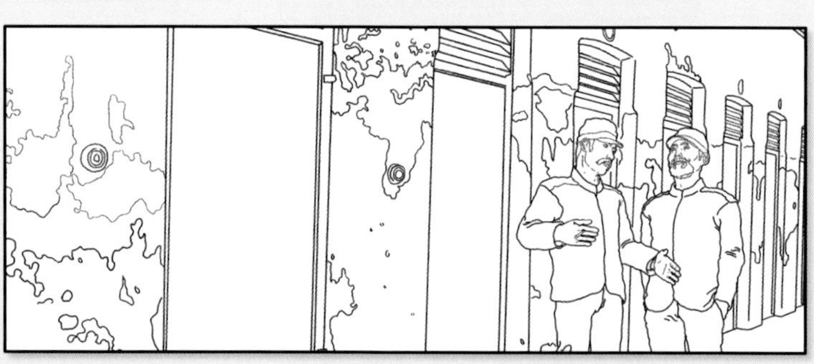

2 VOICE OF LABOUR. December 15th, 1911.

The Case of Whittaker.

Whittaker, in May last, was a Johannesburg Tramwayman on strike, J. F. Sherman was a friend and fellow striker of Whittaker's.

Sherman and others were using dynamite and some cars had been blown up. The Municipality offered £200 to anyone who would give information leading to the arrest of the dynamiters. Sherman set out to win this reward with the intention of using the money to skip the country.

Acting with the police the beguiling Sherman enticed Whittaker to a street corner where it was arranged that two detectives should secret themselves. Sherman got Whittaker to carry some dynamite for him and gave the detectives a prearranged signal to come and arrest Whittaker. Sherman danced with glee to think he should so easily earn a £200 reward.

Whittaker was taken to the "Fort" on May 18th and instead of being put in the section of the prison intended for prisoners awaiting trial, he was taken to the solitary confinement section and locked in a small dark cell about nine feet by four feet which was marked "Punishment Cell."

He had to use a bucket in this cell which was only taken away once in 24 hours at 6 a-m. Although he was a heavy smoker he wasn't allowed the comfort of one of the hundreds of cigarettes handed to the prison officials by his wife and friends. The cell was so small and the stretcher occupied so much of the space that he could only stand up or lie down. There was no window and the ventilation was bad. The only light came through a peephole in the door which was usually closed. The papers and books handed in by his wife and friends were not given him. He was allowed a prison book but could only read it when the peephole was open, and then he had to stand up and hold his book to the peephole

As a tram conductor Whittaker was used to an open air life and this treatment broke him up.

At first he was allowed two hours exercise in the 24 hours. Later on this was reduced to one hour only, but his health became so bad that the doctor ordered his return to the two hours exercise per diem.

On the second day the deputy governor visited him and he asked why he was so cruelly treated. The deputy governor said he didn't know but said he would send the governor.

On the third day the Governor came and was asked the same question. The Governor said it was not his fault. He was acting under instructions from the police.

Mr Van den Berg, the Magistrate, visited the prison and in answer to Whittaker's complaint said that his treatment was wrong but he (the Magistrate) had no power to do anything.

For about three weeks he was prevented from shaving and had to appear in Court unshaven.

Mrs. Whittaker and Mr McIntyre (Whittaker's legal adviser) visited the Governor at the Fort, Mr Mavrogordato at his office and wired and wrote letters to the Secretary of the Law Department at Pretoria. They were not allowed to see Whittaker. These minions of the law shifted the responsibility from the one to the other. At times they would promise a permit and then go back on their word.

At last the exasperated friends of Whittaker took action to compel the law officials to obey the law in respect of Whittaker. The case came before Judge Mason and the Crown argued that it was "in the interests of justice" that Whittaker should be kept away from Morant and his wife and friends. The Judge rightly pointed out the absurdity of this because had Whittaker not been a poor man he could have put up the £1,000 bail and secured freedom.

Continuing, Judge Mason said: "I know of some systems of jurisprudence (in Russia?) where prisoners awaiting trial are treated in that way. They are put in gaol, placed under restraints and put under solitary confinement of every kind in order to break down their resistance in maintaining their innocence. *That is entirely foreign to the administration of justice in a British country.*"

The Judge also pointed out how Whittaker was being punished before he was ever put on trial and attached blame to Mr Roos, Director of Prisons.

Not satisfied with this, Whittaker's persecutors (the Union Government of South Africa!!) appealed the case to the Supreme Court and the appeal was dismissed.

When Whittaker was tried for the alleged crime of dynamiting cars, he was proved innocent and discharged. He immediately took steps to obtain reasonable compensation for his illtreatment in prison with the result already known.

The Judges recognised that the treatment of Whittaker was illegal and that he had suffered, but pointed out that Whittaker was not the sort of man to whom heavy damages should be awarded. HE WAS ONLY A WORKING MAN! and £20 was quite enough for him. The order put the costs upon Whittaker, these amounting to several hundred pounds.

The verdict is an insult to the working class—an insult which must be avenged. Let everyone roll up on Sunday at 3 p.m. to 27 Goodman's Buildings and take steps to have the case appealed to the final court at Bloemfontein. This is the next legal step and also the last.

The working man who takes Court decisions like these lying down is unworthy. The blood of every honest self respecting worker ought to course more warmly through his veins, his pulse should beat quicker and the fire should light in his eyes on reading the class verdict of our Capitalist Judges, and his mind should be fixed on using with his fellow workers, their omnipotent power to secure justice for even the meanest of their class. An injury to one is the concern of all!

scientific and revolutionary education will be imparted under the direction of Mr Hird.

This College is the most worthy

Chicago, and Theodore Debs (brother of Eugene V. Debs) and J. O'Neal, both

The two

fitted for the respective posts they already hold

I.W.W. orators

Above: One of the articles covering Whittaker's story that were published in *Voice of Labour.*

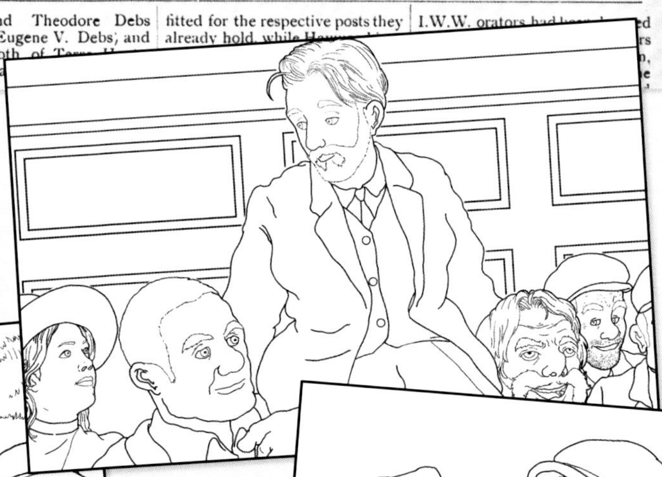

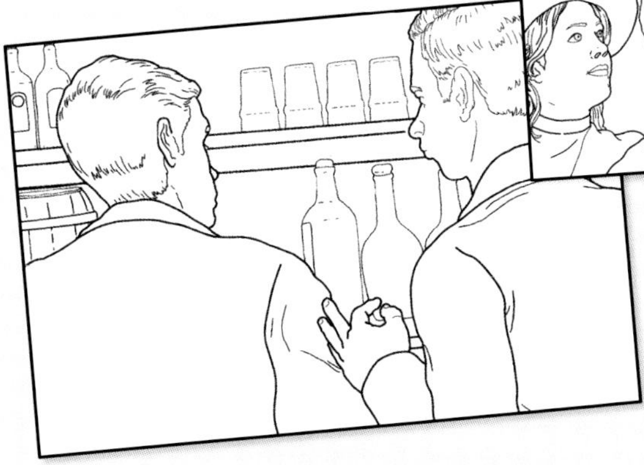

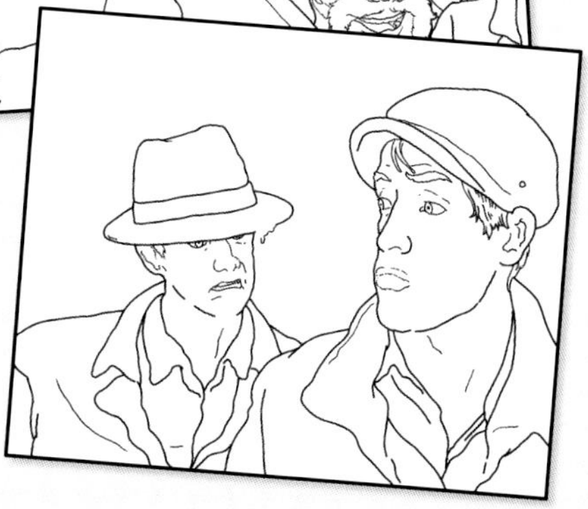

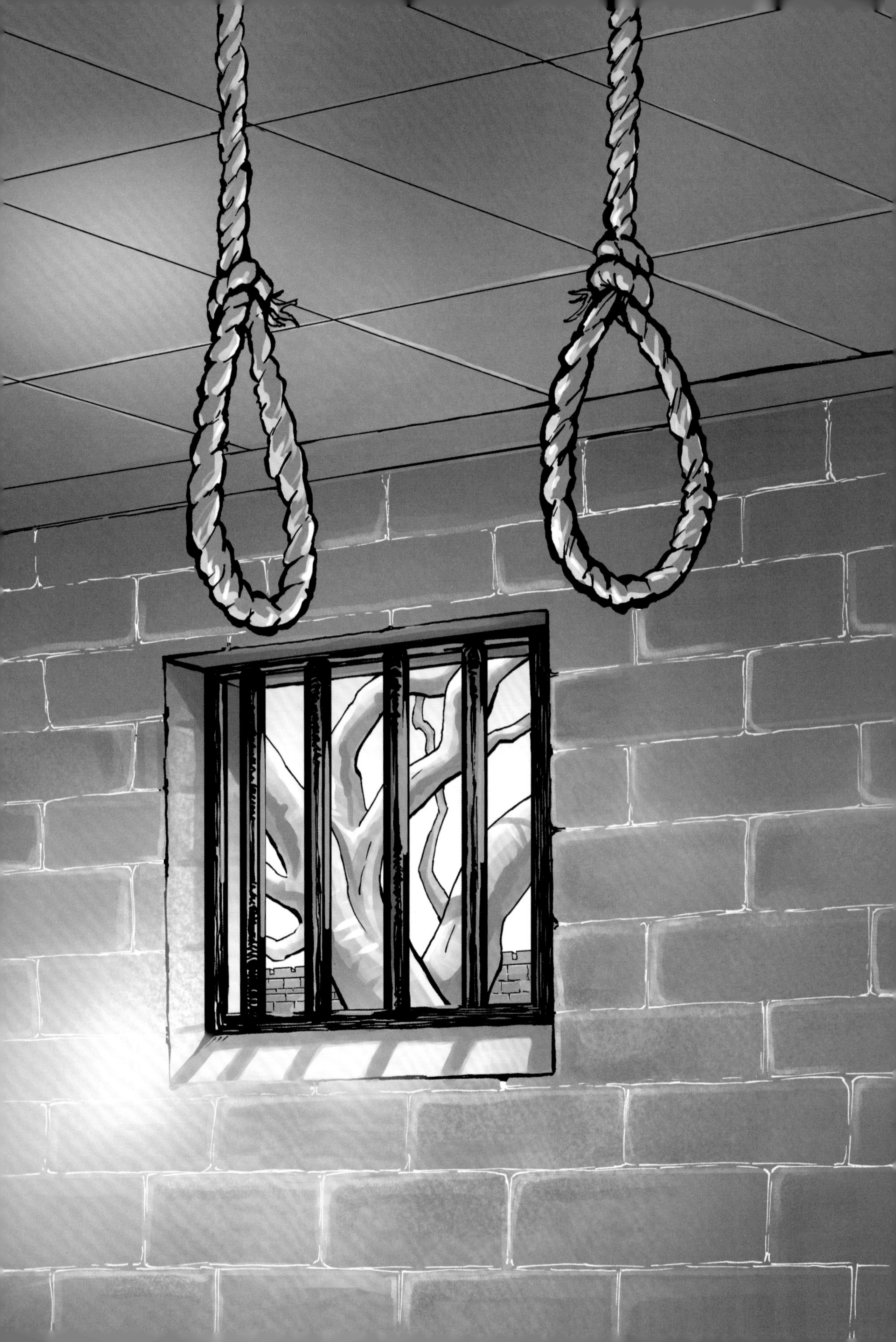

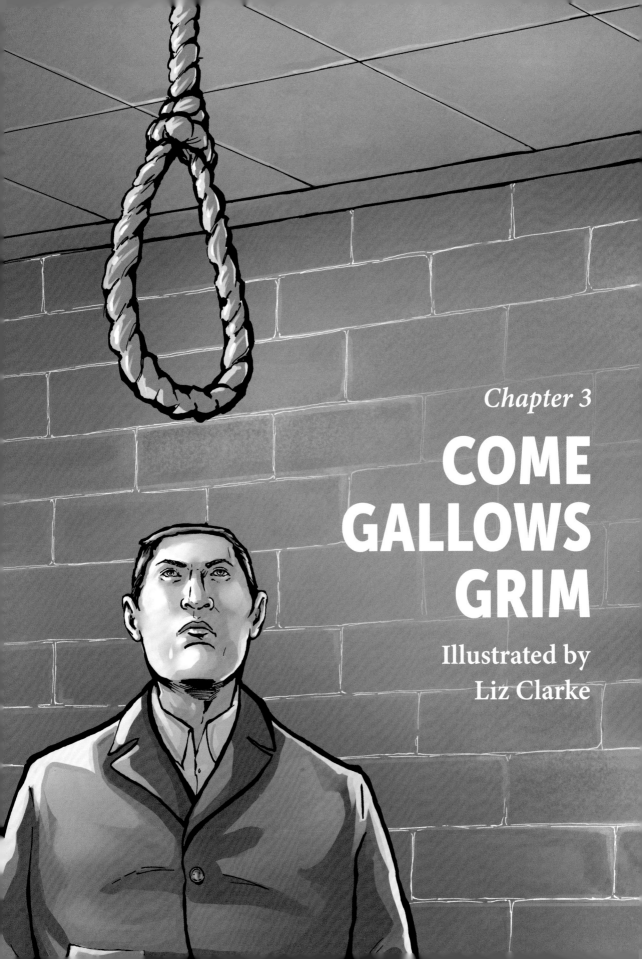

Chapter 3

COME GALLOWS GRIM

Illustrated by
Liz Clarke

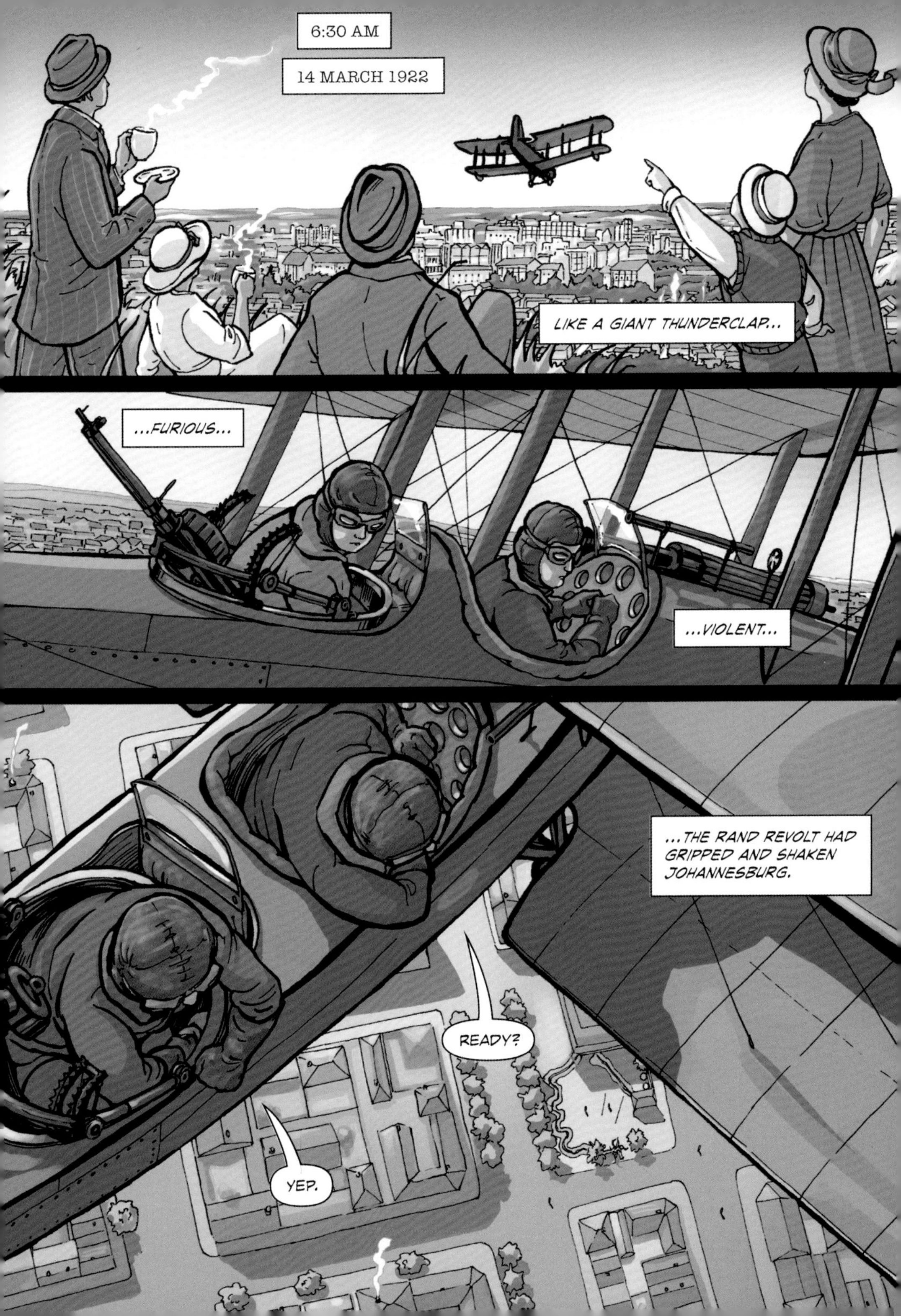

6:30 AM
14 MARCH 1922
LIKE A GIANT THUNDERCLAP...
...FURIOUS...
...VIOLENT...
...THE RAND REVOLT HAD GRIPPED AND SHAKEN JOHANNESBURG.
READY?
YEP.

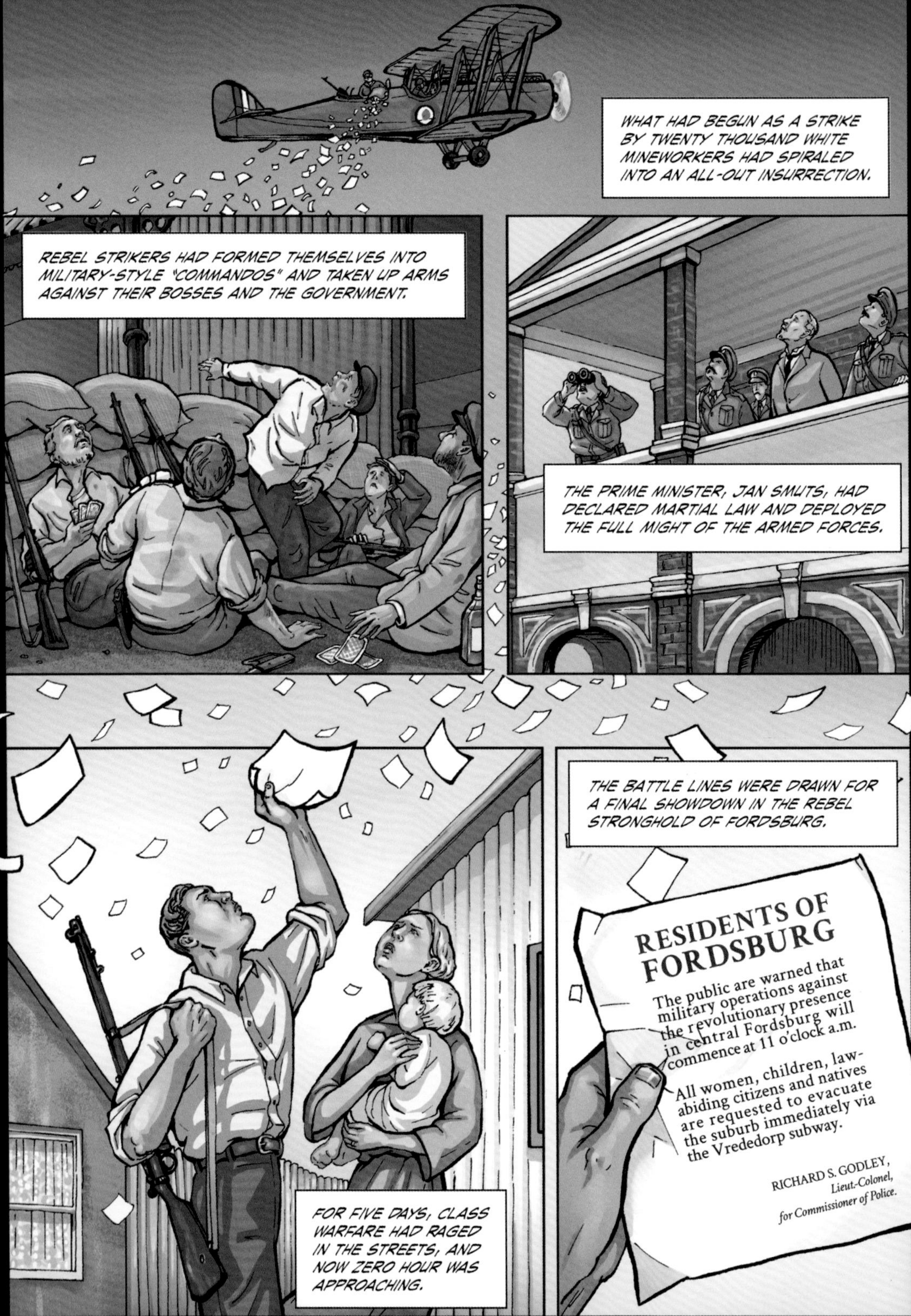
WHAT HAD BEGUN AS A STRIKE BY TWENTY THOUSAND WHITE MINEWORKERS HAD SPIRALED INTO AN ALL-OUT INSURRECTION.
REBEL STRIKERS HAD FORMED THEMSELVES INTO MILITARY-STYLE "COMMANDOS" AND TAKEN UP ARMS AGAINST THEIR BOSSES AND THE GOVERNMENT.
THE PRIME MINISTER, JAN SMUTS, HAD DECLARED MARTIAL LAW AND DEPLOYED THE FULL MIGHT OF THE ARMED FORCES.
FOR FIVE DAYS, CLASS WARFARE HAD RAGED IN THE STREETS, AND NOW ZERO HOUR WAS APPROACHING.
THE BATTLE LINES WERE DRAWN FOR A FINAL SHOWDOWN IN THE REBEL STRONGHOLD OF FORDSBURG.
RESIDENTS OF FORDSBURG
The public are warned that military operations against the revolutionary presence in central Fordsburg will commence at 11 o'clock a.m.
All women, children, law-abiding citizens and natives are requested to evacuate the suburb immediately via the Vrededorp subway.
RICHARD S. GODLEY,
Lieut.-Colonel,
for Commissioner of Police.

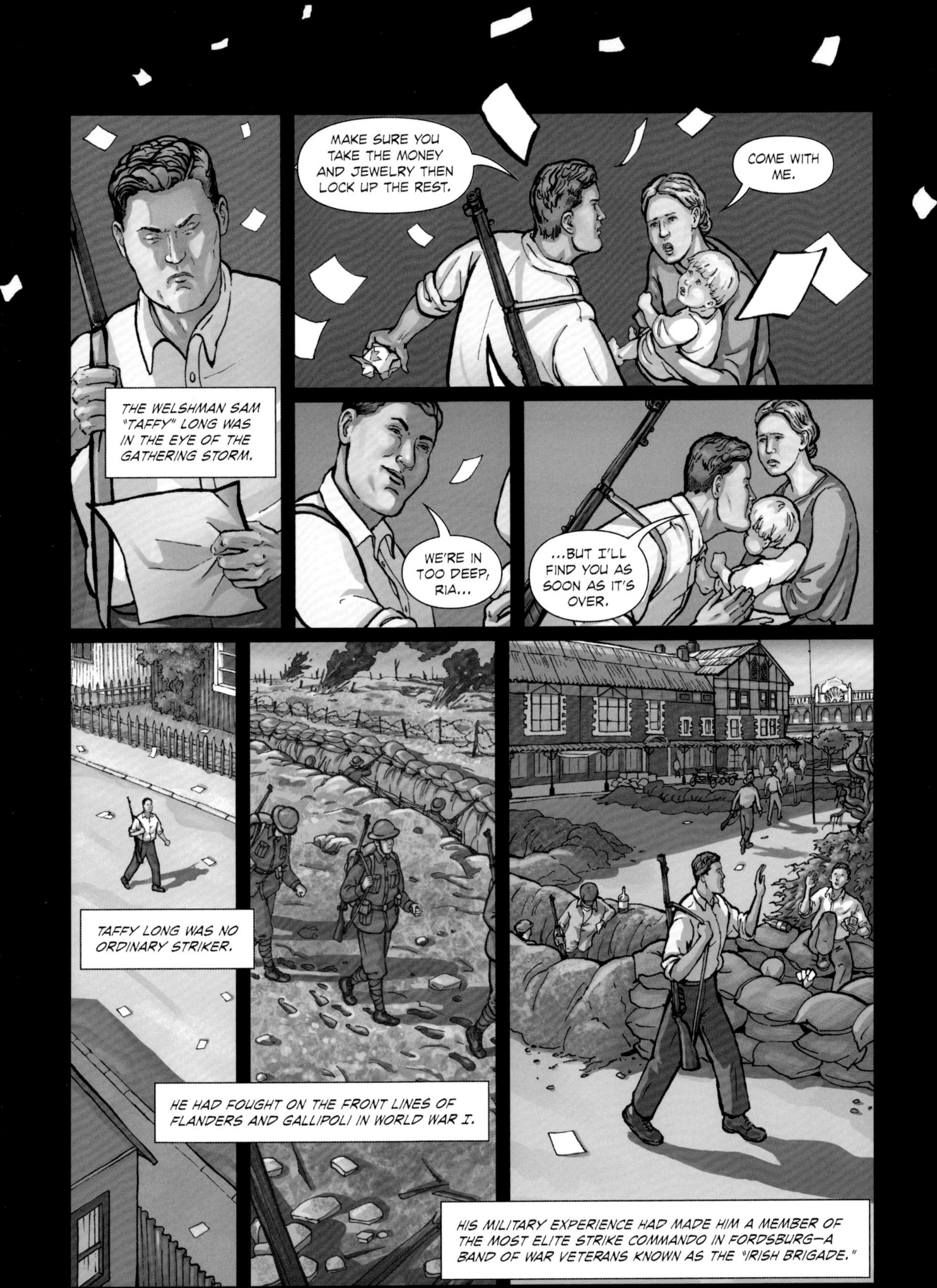
THE WELSHMAN SAM "TAFFY" LONG WAS IN THE EYE OF THE GATHERING STORM.
MAKE SURE YOU TAKE THE MONEY AND JEWELRY THEN LOCK UP THE REST.
COME WITH ME.
WE'RE IN TOO DEEP, RIA...
...BUT I'LL FIND YOU AS SOON AS IT'S OVER.
TAFFY LONG WAS NO ORDINARY STRIKER.
HE HAD FOUGHT ON THE FRONT LINES OF FLANDERS AND GALLIPOLI IN WORLD WAR I.
HIS MILITARY EXPERIENCE HAD MADE HIM A MEMBER OF THE MOST ELITE STRIKE COMMANDO IN FORDSBURG—A BAND OF WAR VETERANS KNOWN AS THE "IRISH BRIGADE."

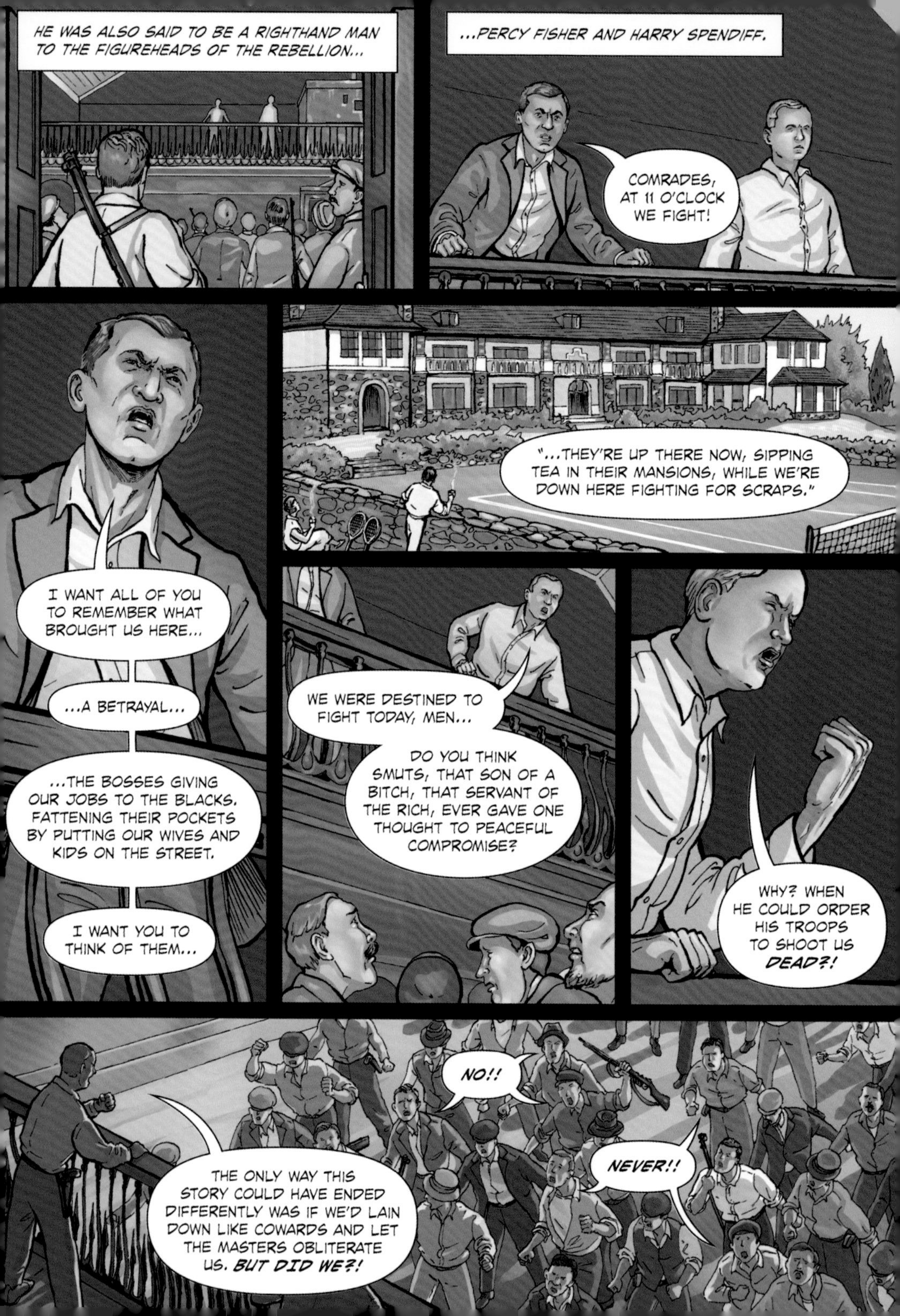
HE WAS ALSO SAID TO BE A RIGHTHAND MAN TO THE FIGUREHEADS OF THE REBELLION...
...PERCY FISHER AND HARRY SPENDIFF.
COMRADES, AT 11 O'CLOCK WE FIGHT!
I WANT ALL OF YOU TO REMEMBER WHAT BROUGHT US HERE...
...A BETRAYAL...
...THE BOSSES GIVING OUR JOBS TO THE BLACKS. FATTENING THEIR POCKETS BY PUTTING OUR WIVES AND KIDS ON THE STREET.
I WANT YOU TO THINK OF THEM...
"...THEY'RE UP THERE NOW, SIPPING TEA IN THEIR MANSIONS, WHILE WE'RE DOWN HERE FIGHTING FOR SCRAPS."
WE WERE DESTINED TO FIGHT TODAY, MEN...
DO YOU THINK SMUTS, THAT SON OF A BITCH, THAT SERVANT OF THE RICH, EVER GAVE ONE THOUGHT TO PEACEFUL COMPROMISE?
WHY? WHEN HE COULD ORDER HIS TROOPS TO SHOOT US *DEAD?!*
THE ONLY WAY THIS STORY COULD HAVE ENDED DIFFERENTLY WAS IF WE'D LAIN DOWN LIKE COWARDS AND LET THE MASTERS OBLITERATE US. *BUT DID WE?!*
NO!!
NEVER!!

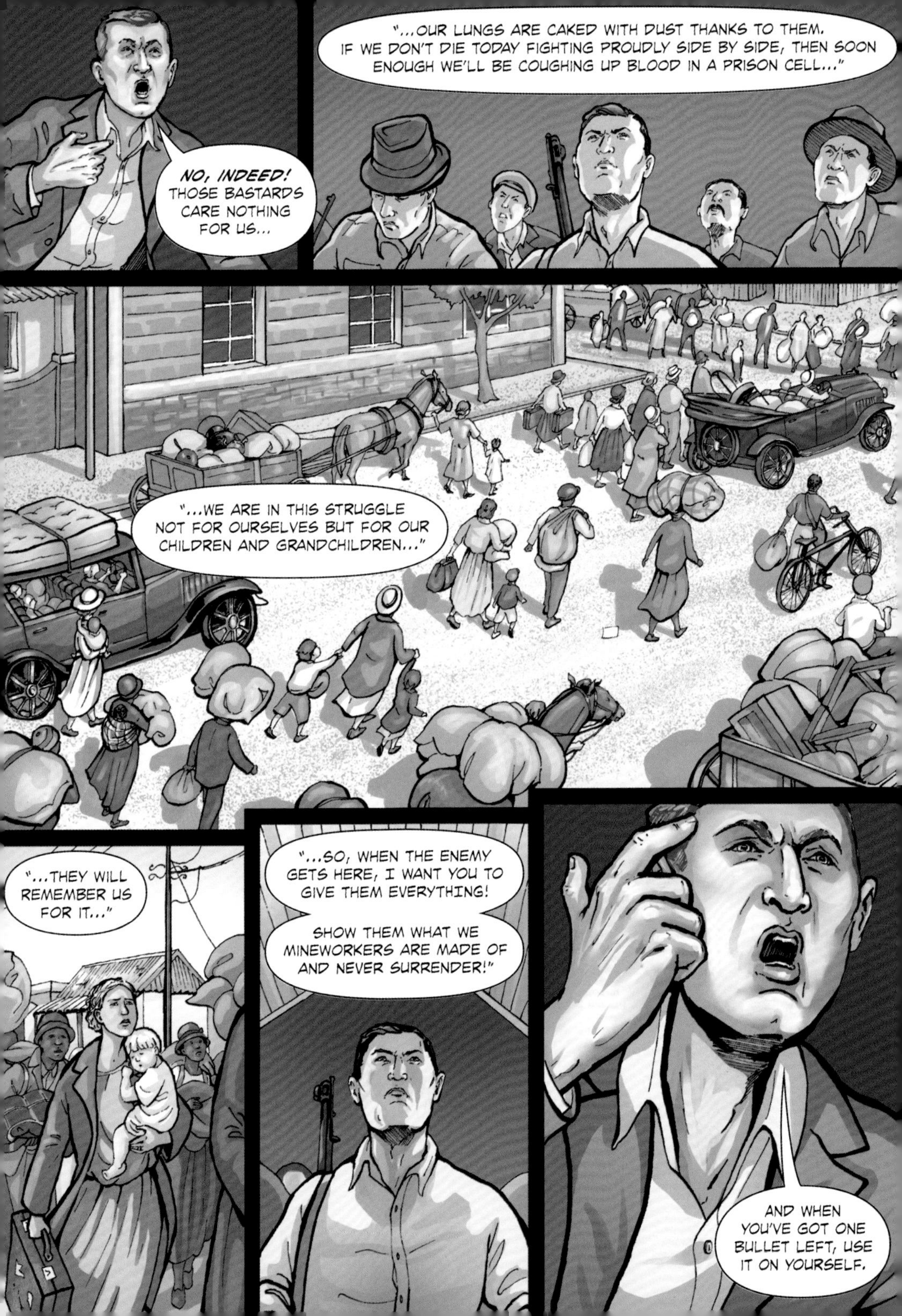
NO, INDEED! THOSE BASTARDS CARE NOTHING FOR US...
"...OUR LUNGS ARE CAKED WITH DUST THANKS TO THEM. IF WE DON'T DIE TODAY FIGHTING PROUDLY SIDE BY SIDE, THEN SOON ENOUGH WE'LL BE COUGHING UP BLOOD IN A PRISON CELL..."
"...WE ARE IN THIS STRUGGLE NOT FOR OURSELVES BUT FOR OUR CHILDREN AND GRANDCHILDREN..."
"...THEY WILL REMEMBER US FOR IT..."
"...SO, WHEN THE ENEMY GETS HERE, I WANT YOU TO GIVE THEM EVERYTHING!
SHOW THEM WHAT WE MINEWORKERS ARE MADE OF AND NEVER SURRENDER!"
AND WHEN YOU'VE GOT ONE BULLET LEFT, USE IT ON YOURSELF.

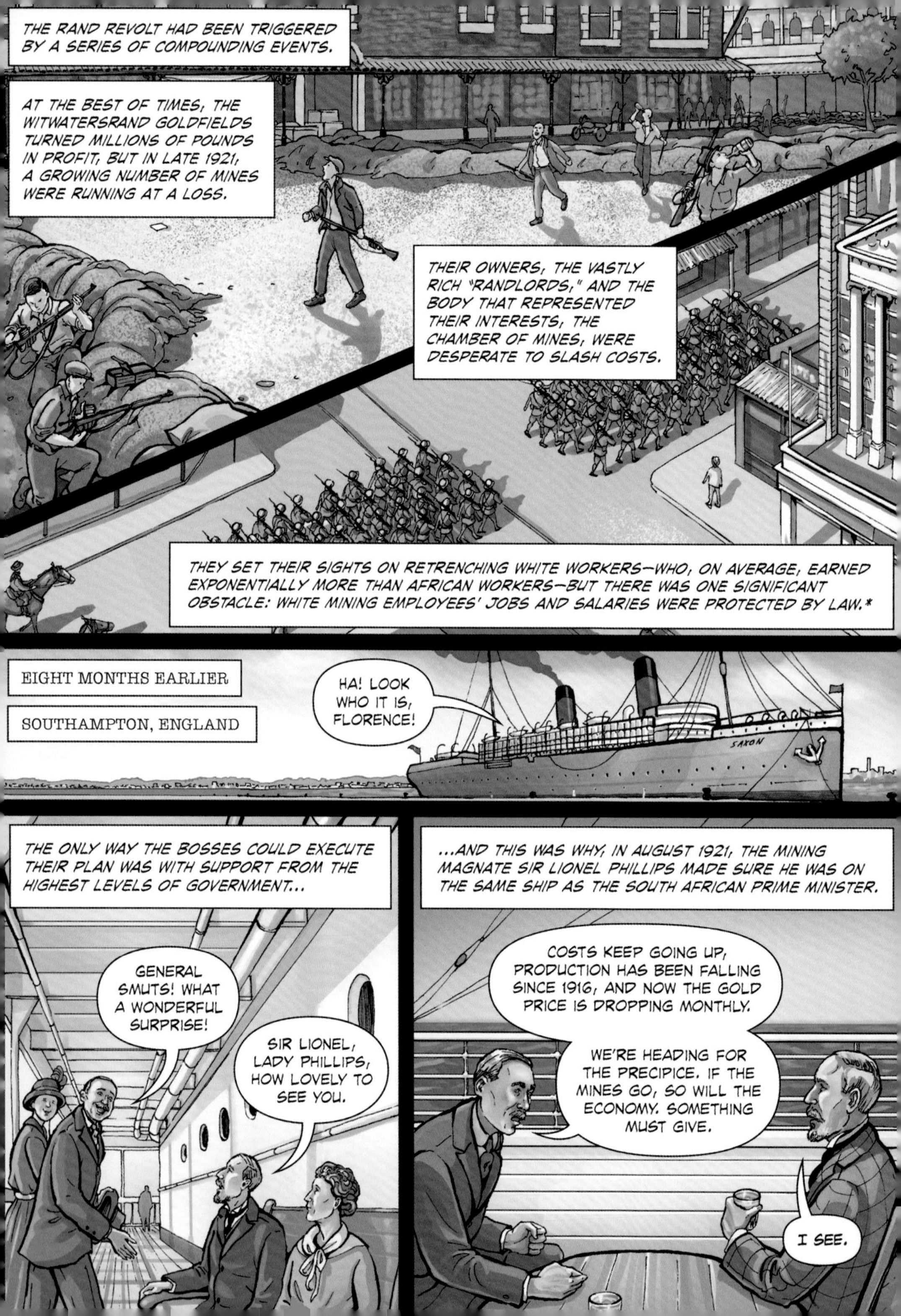

THE RAND REVOLT HAD BEEN TRIGGERED BY A SERIES OF COMPOUNDING EVENTS.
AT THE BEST OF TIMES, THE WITWATERSRAND GOLDFIELDS TURNED MILLIONS OF POUNDS IN PROFIT, BUT IN LATE 1921, A GROWING NUMBER OF MINES WERE RUNNING AT A LOSS.
THEIR OWNERS, THE VASTLY RICH "RANDLORDS," AND THE BODY THAT REPRESENTED THEIR INTERESTS, THE CHAMBER OF MINES, WERE DESPERATE TO SLASH COSTS.
THEY SET THEIR SIGHTS ON RETRENCHING WHITE WORKERS—WHO, ON AVERAGE, EARNED EXPONENTIALLY MORE THAN AFRICAN WORKERS—BUT THERE WAS ONE SIGNIFICANT OBSTACLE: WHITE MINING EMPLOYEES' JOBS AND SALARIES WERE PROTECTED BY LAW.*
EIGHT MONTHS EARLIER
SOUTHAMPTON, ENGLAND
HA! LOOK WHO IT IS, FLORENCE!
SAXON
THE ONLY WAY THE BOSSES COULD EXECUTE THEIR PLAN WAS WITH SUPPORT FROM THE HIGHEST LEVELS OF GOVERNMENT...
GENERAL SMUTS! WHAT A WONDERFUL SURPRISE!
SIR LIONEL, LADY PHILLIPS, HOW LOVELY TO SEE YOU.
...AND THIS WAS WHY, IN AUGUST 1921, THE MINING MAGNATE SIR LIONEL PHILLIPS MADE SURE HE WAS ON THE SAME SHIP AS THE SOUTH AFRICAN PRIME MINISTER.
COSTS KEEP GOING UP, PRODUCTION HAS BEEN FALLING SINCE 1916, AND NOW THE GOLD PRICE IS DROPPING MONTHLY.
WE'RE HEADING FOR THE PRECIPICE. IF THE MINES GO, SO WILL THE ECONOMY. SOMETHING MUST GIVE.
I SEE.

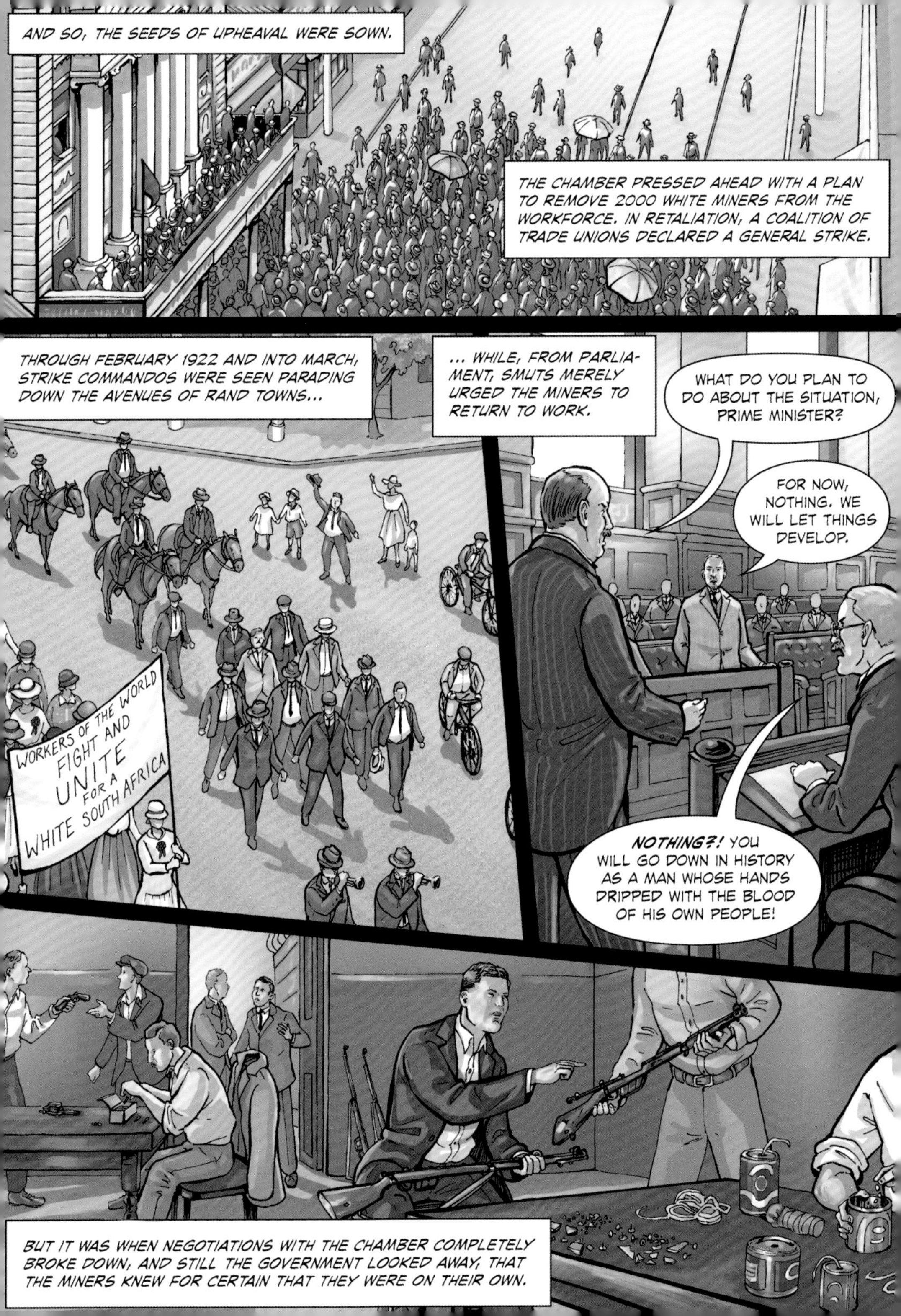
AND SO, THE SEEDS OF UPHEAVAL WERE SOWN.
THE CHAMBER PRESSED AHEAD WITH A PLAN TO REMOVE 2000 WHITE MINERS FROM THE WORKFORCE. IN RETALIATION, A COALITION OF TRADE UNIONS DECLARED A GENERAL STRIKE.
THROUGH FEBRUARY 1922 AND INTO MARCH, STRIKE COMMANDOS WERE SEEN PARADING DOWN THE AVENUES OF RAND TOWNS...
WORKERS OF THE WORLD FIGHT AND UNITE FOR A WHITE SOUTH AFRICA
... WHILE, FROM PARLIAMENT, SMUTS MERELY URGED THE MINERS TO RETURN TO WORK.
WHAT DO YOU PLAN TO DO ABOUT THE SITUATION, PRIME MINISTER?
FOR NOW, NOTHING. WE WILL LET THINGS DEVELOP.
NOTHING?! YOU WILL GO DOWN IN HISTORY AS A MAN WHOSE HANDS DRIPPED WITH THE BLOOD OF HIS OWN PEOPLE!
BUT IT WAS WHEN NEGOTIATIONS WITH THE CHAMBER COMPLETELY BROKE DOWN, AND STILL THE GOVERNMENT LOOKED AWAY, THAT THE MINERS KNEW FOR CERTAIN THAT THEY WERE ON THEIR OWN.

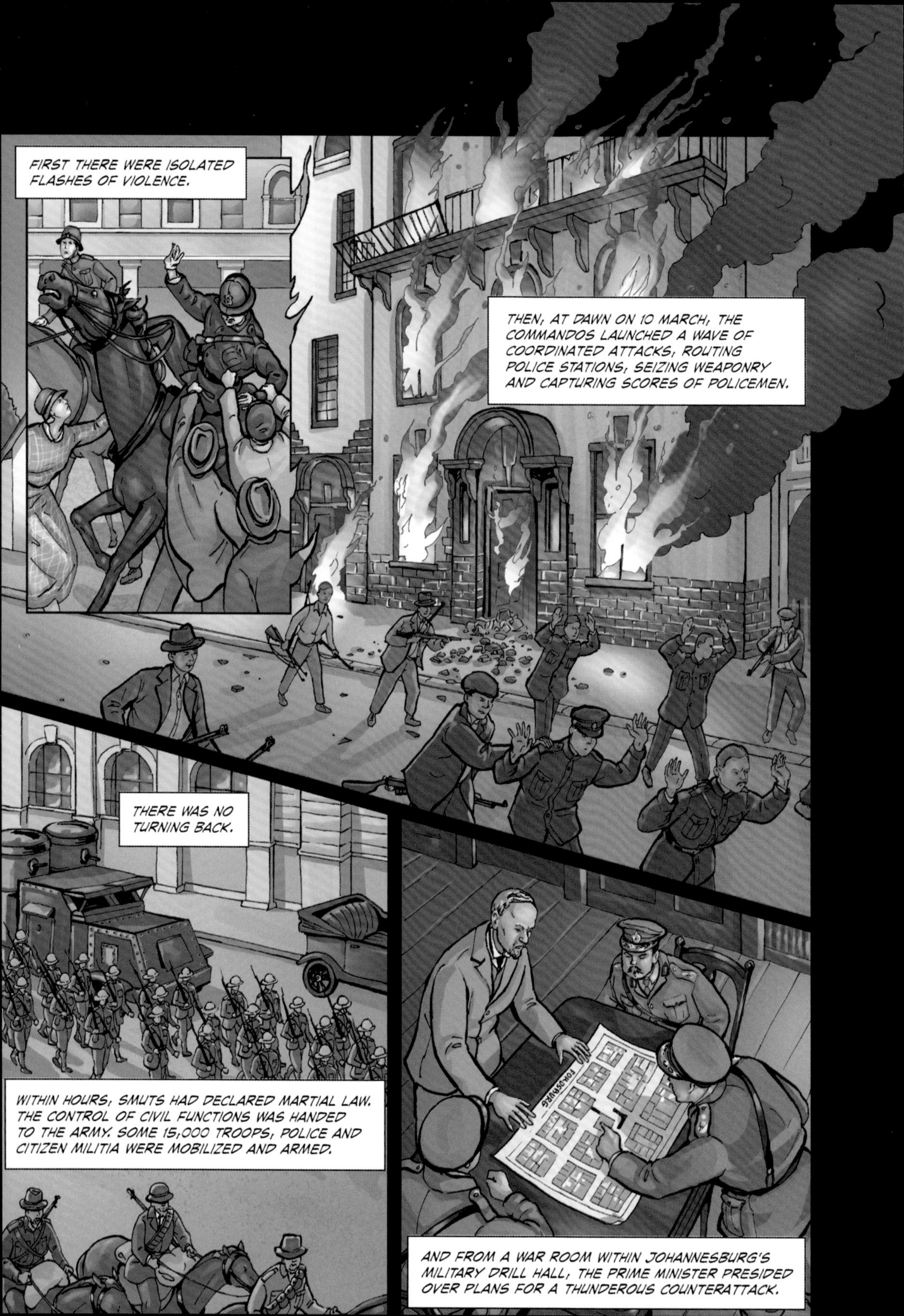
FIRST THERE WERE ISOLATED FLASHES OF VIOLENCE.
THEN, AT DAWN ON 10 MARCH, THE COMMANDOS LAUNCHED A WAVE OF COORDINATED ATTACKS, ROUTING POLICE STATIONS, SEIZING WEAPONRY AND CAPTURING SCORES OF POLICEMEN.
THERE WAS NO TURNING BACK.
WITHIN HOURS, SMUTS HAD DECLARED MARTIAL LAW. THE CONTROL OF CIVIL FUNCTIONS WAS HANDED TO THE ARMY. SOME 15,000 TROOPS, POLICE AND CITIZEN MILITIA WERE MOBILIZED AND ARMED.
AND FROM A WAR ROOM WITHIN JOHANNESBURG'S MILITARY DRILL HALL, THE PRIME MINISTER PRESIDED OVER PLANS FOR A THUNDEROUS COUNTERATTACK.

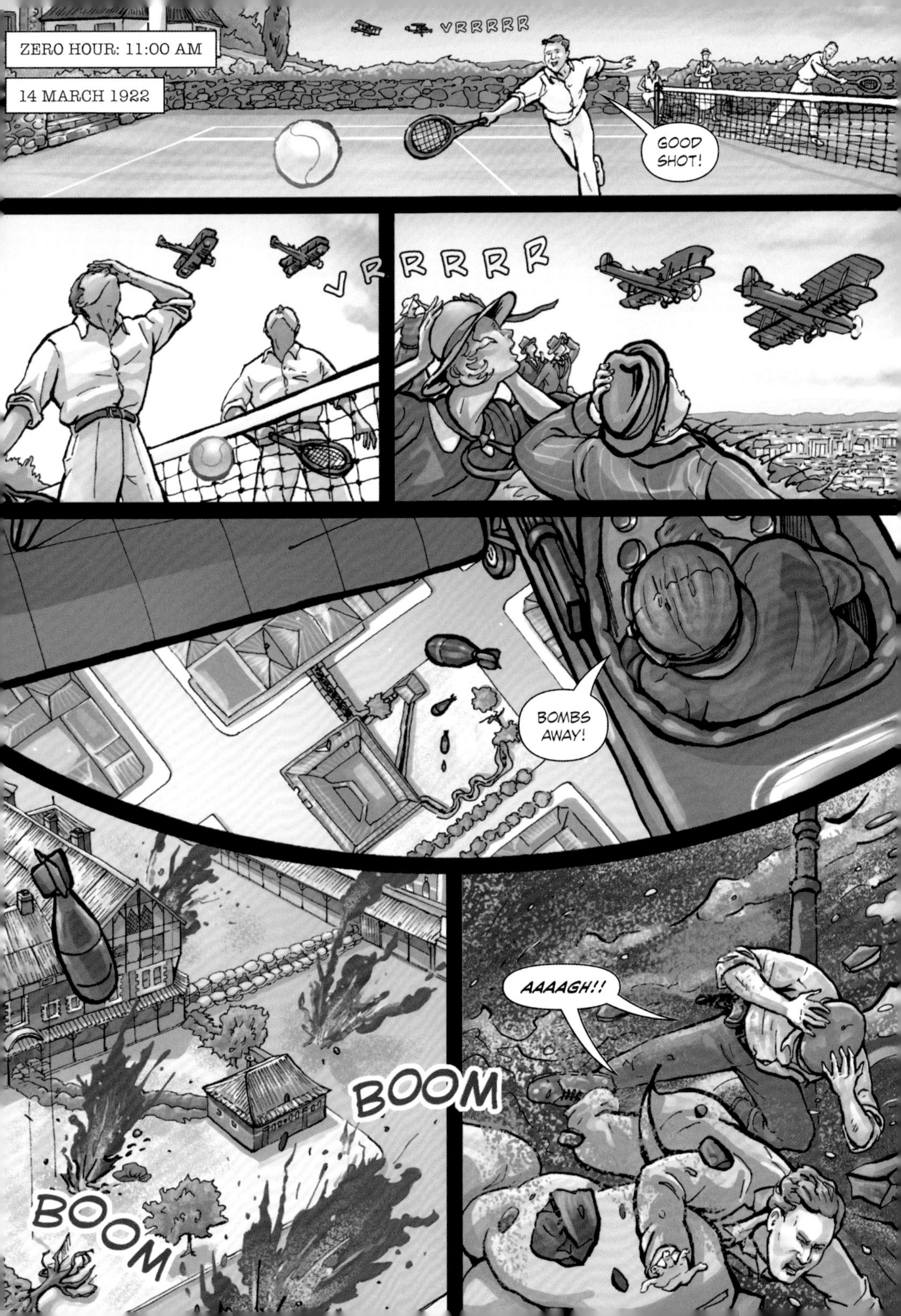
ZERO HOUR: 11:00 AM
14 MARCH 1922
VRRRRR
GOOD SHOT!
VRRRRRR
BOMBS AWAY!
BOOM
BOOM
AAAAGH!!

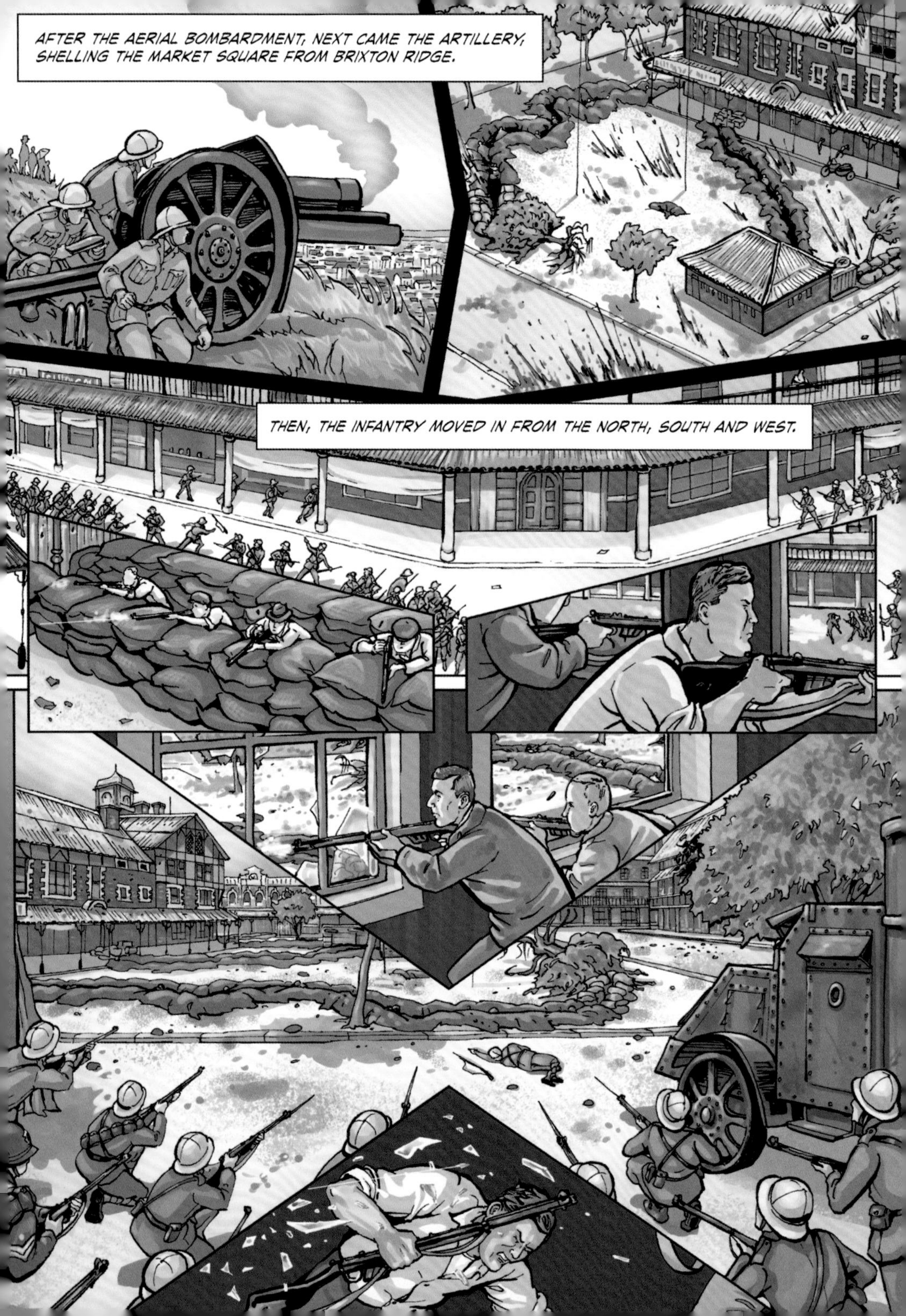
AFTER THE AERIAL BOMBARDMENT, NEXT CAME THE ARTILLERY, SHELLING THE MARKET SQUARE FROM BRIXTON RIDGE.
THEN, THE INFANTRY MOVED IN FROM THE NORTH, SOUTH AND WEST.

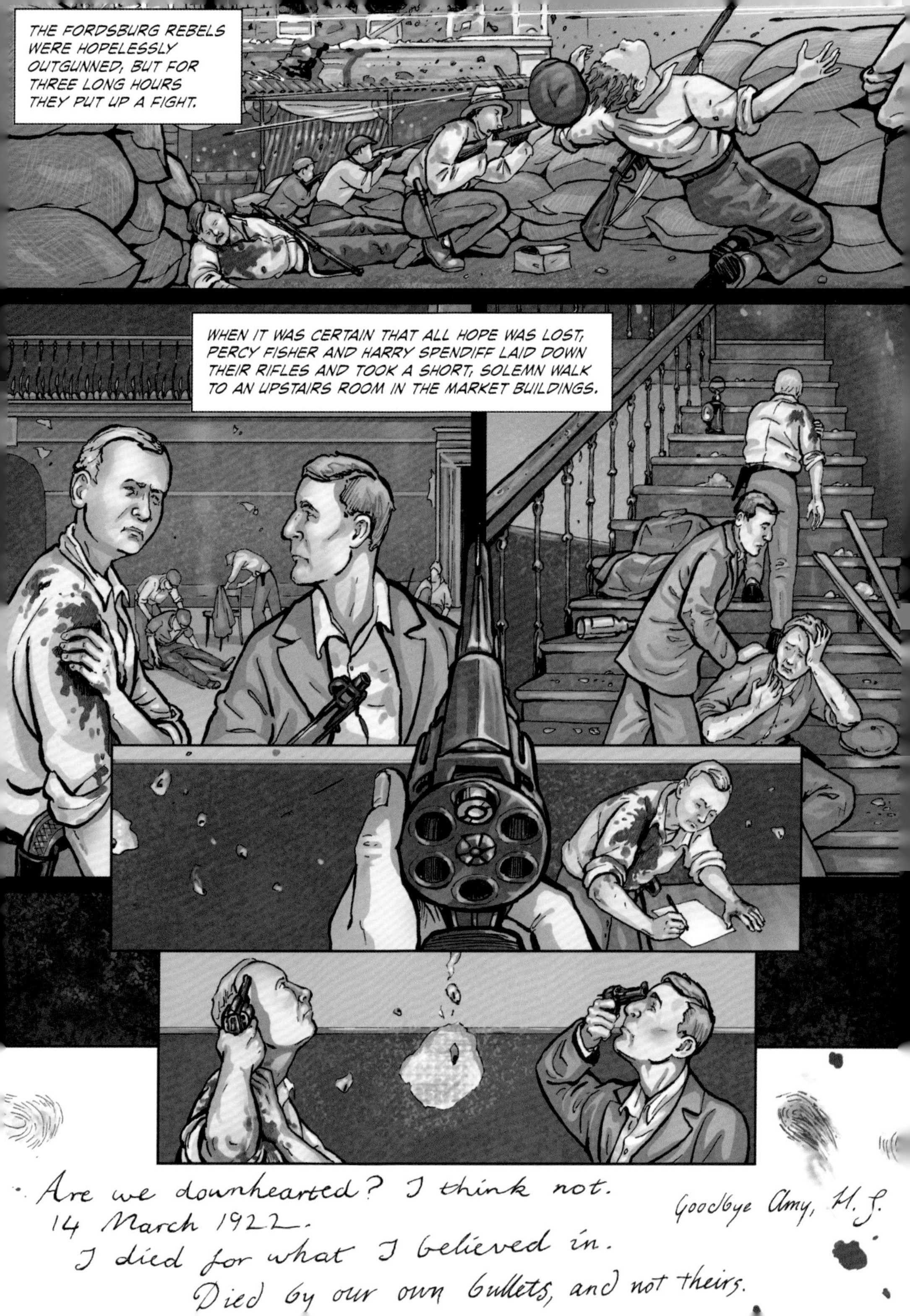
THE FORDSBURG REBELS WERE HOPELESSLY OUTGUNNED, BUT FOR THREE LONG HOURS THEY PUT UP A FIGHT.
WHEN IT WAS CERTAIN THAT ALL HOPE WAS LOST, PERCY FISHER AND HARRY SPENDIFF LAID DOWN THEIR RIFLES AND TOOK A SHORT, SOLEMN WALK TO AN UPSTAIRS ROOM IN THE MARKET BUILDINGS.
Are we downhearted? I think not.
14 March 1922.
I died for what I believed in.
Died by our own bullets, and not theirs.
Goodbye Amy, H. S.

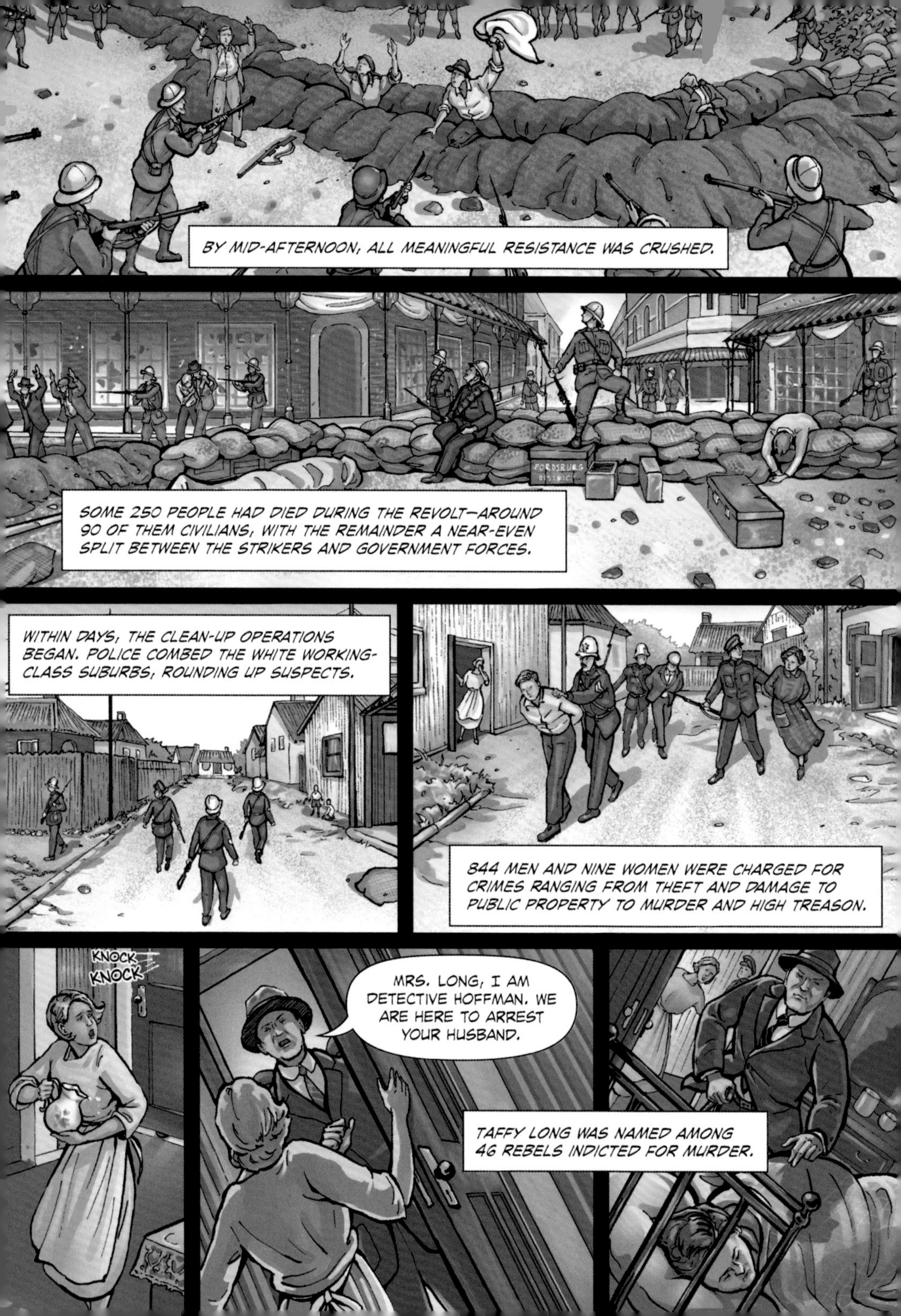
BY MID-AFTERNOON, ALL MEANINGFUL RESISTANCE WAS CRUSHED.
FORDSBURG DISTRICT
SOME 250 PEOPLE HAD DIED DURING THE REVOLT—AROUND 90 OF THEM CIVILIANS, WITH THE REMAINDER A NEAR-EVEN SPLIT BETWEEN THE STRIKERS AND GOVERNMENT FORCES.
WITHIN DAYS, THE CLEAN-UP OPERATIONS BEGAN. POLICE COMBED THE WHITE WORKING-CLASS SUBURBS, ROUNDING UP SUSPECTS.
844 MEN AND NINE WOMEN WERE CHARGED FOR CRIMES RANGING FROM THEFT AND DAMAGE TO PUBLIC PROPERTY TO MURDER AND HIGH TREASON.
KNOCK KNOCK
MRS. LONG, I AM DETECTIVE HOFFMAN. WE ARE HERE TO ARREST YOUR HUSBAND.
TAFFY LONG WAS NAMED AMONG 46 REBELS INDICTED FOR MURDER.

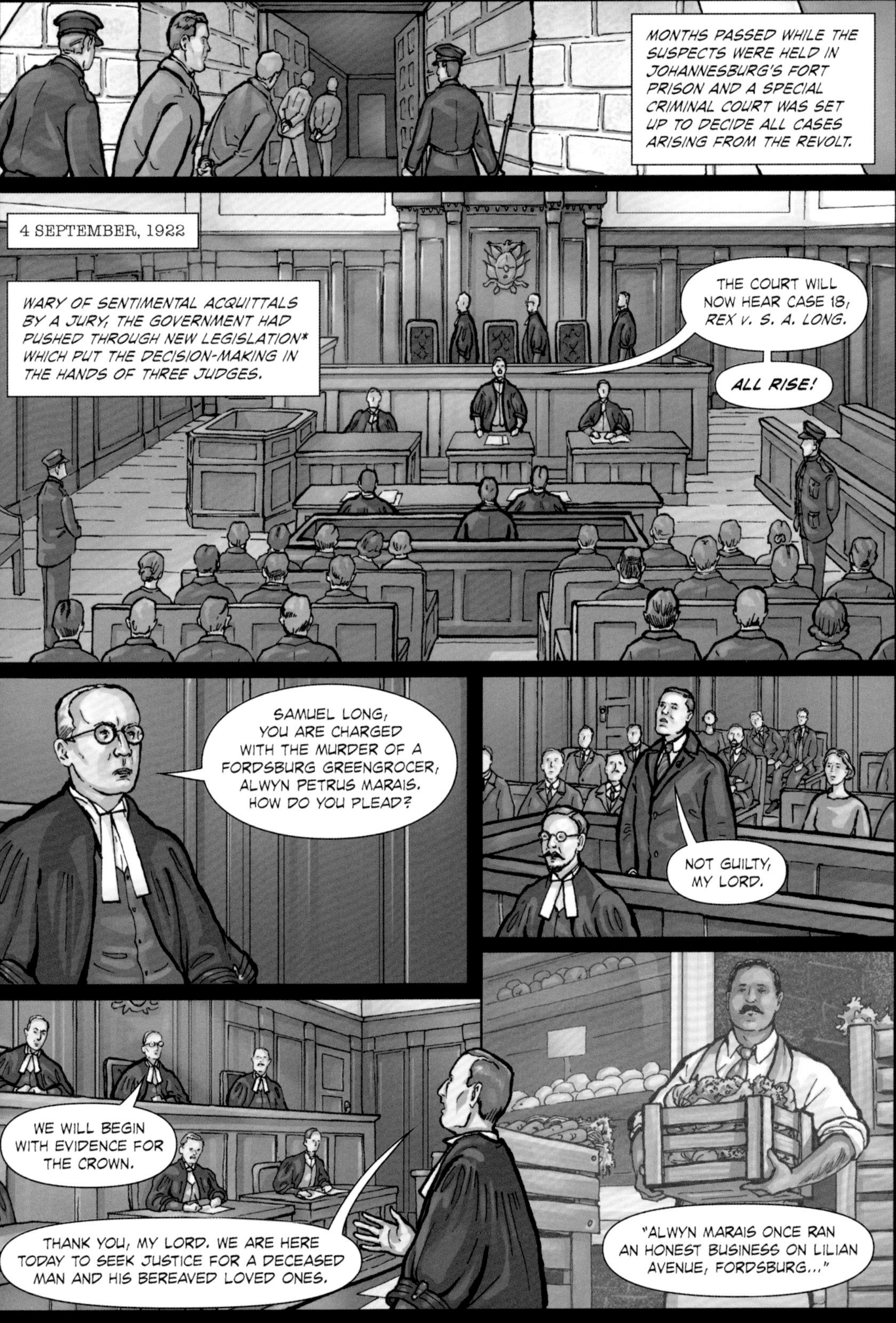
MONTHS PASSED WHILE THE SUSPECTS WERE HELD IN JOHANNESBURG'S FORT PRISON AND A SPECIAL CRIMINAL COURT WAS SET UP TO DECIDE ALL CASES ARISING FROM THE REVOLT.
4 SEPTEMBER, 1922
WARY OF SENTIMENTAL ACQUITTALS BY A JURY, THE GOVERNMENT HAD PUSHED THROUGH NEW LEGISLATION* WHICH PUT THE DECISION-MAKING IN THE HANDS OF THREE JUDGES.
THE COURT WILL NOW HEAR CASE 18, REX v. S. A. LONG.
ALL RISE!
SAMUEL LONG, YOU ARE CHARGED WITH THE MURDER OF A FORDSBURG GREENGROCER, ALWYN PETRUS MARAIS. HOW DO YOU PLEAD?
NOT GUILTY, MY LORD.
WE WILL BEGIN WITH EVIDENCE FOR THE CROWN.
THANK YOU, MY LORD. WE ARE HERE TODAY TO SEEK JUSTICE FOR A DECEASED MAN AND HIS BEREAVED LOVED ONES.
"ALWYN MARAIS ONCE RAN AN HONEST BUSINESS ON LILIAN AVENUE, FORDSBURG..."

* Indemnity and Trial of Offenders Act, No. 6 of 1922.

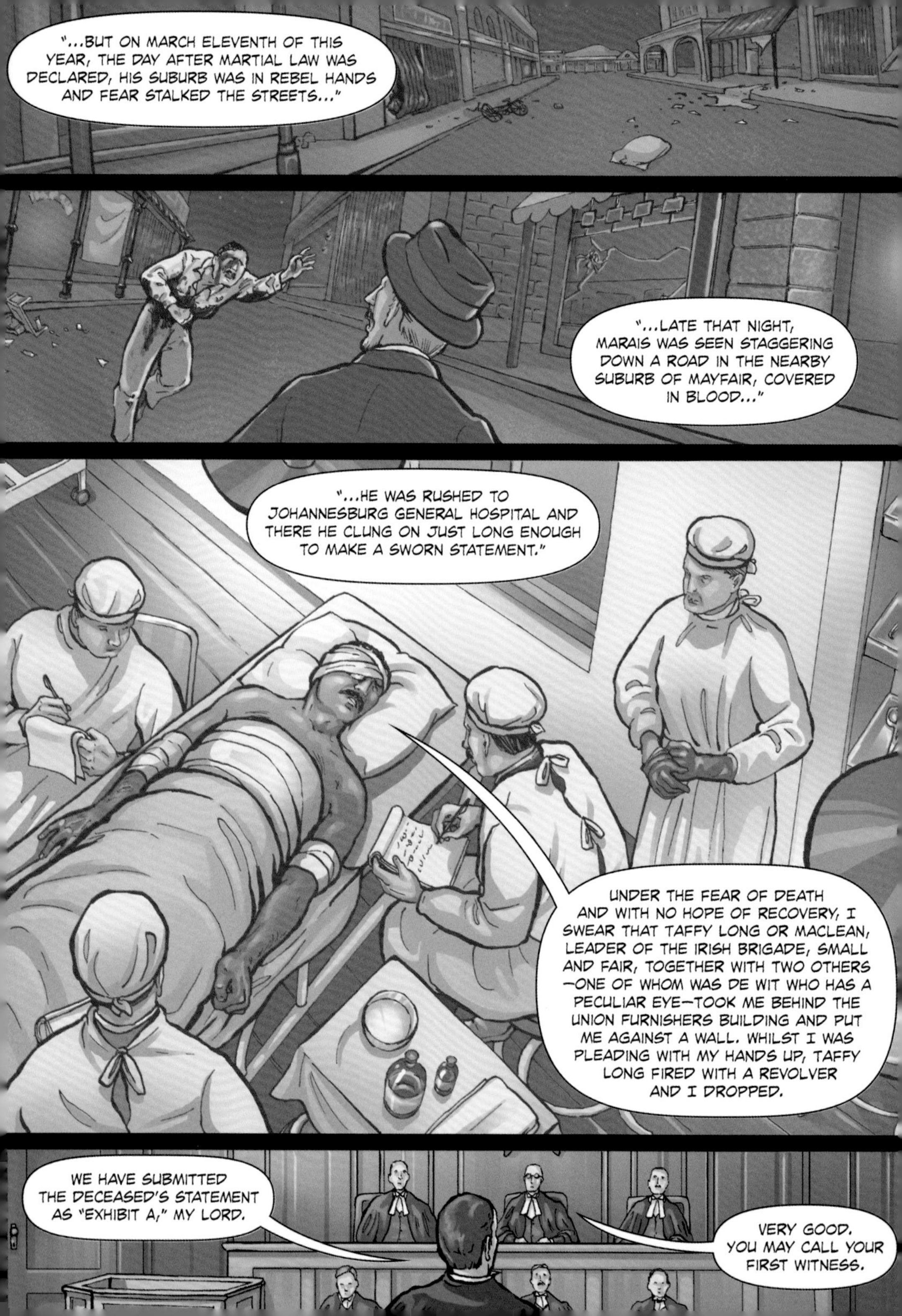
"...BUT ON MARCH ELEVENTH OF THIS YEAR, THE DAY AFTER MARTIAL LAW WAS DECLARED, HIS SUBURB WAS IN REBEL HANDS AND FEAR STALKED THE STREETS..."
"...LATE THAT NIGHT, MARAIS WAS SEEN STAGGERING DOWN A ROAD IN THE NEARBY SUBURB OF MAYFAIR, COVERED IN BLOOD..."
"...HE WAS RUSHED TO JOHANNESBURG GENERAL HOSPITAL AND THERE HE CLUNG ON JUST LONG ENOUGH TO MAKE A SWORN STATEMENT."
UNDER THE FEAR OF DEATH AND WITH NO HOPE OF RECOVERY, I SWEAR THAT TAFFY LONG OR MACLEAN, LEADER OF THE IRISH BRIGADE, SMALL AND FAIR, TOGETHER WITH TWO OTHERS —ONE OF WHOM WAS DE WIT WHO HAS A PECULIAR EYE—TOOK ME BEHIND THE UNION FURNISHERS BUILDING AND PUT ME AGAINST A WALL. WHILST I WAS PLEADING WITH MY HANDS UP, TAFFY LONG FIRED WITH A REVOLVER AND I DROPPED.
WE HAVE SUBMITTED THE DECEASED'S STATEMENT AS "EXHIBIT A," MY LORD.
VERY GOOD. YOU MAY CALL YOUR FIRST WITNESS.

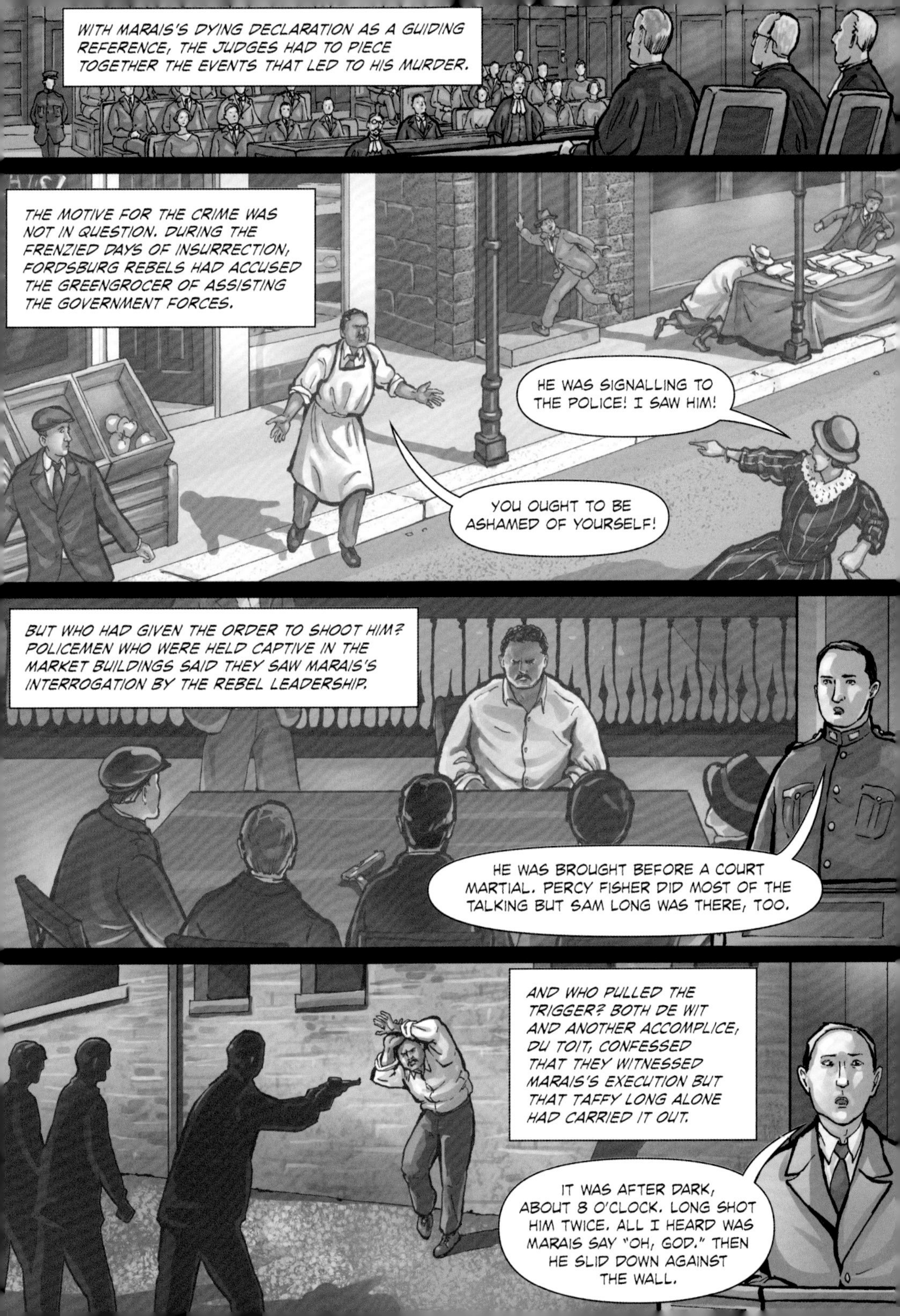
WITH MARAIS'S DYING DECLARATION AS A GUIDING REFERENCE, THE JUDGES HAD TO PIECE TOGETHER THE EVENTS THAT LED TO HIS MURDER.
THE MOTIVE FOR THE CRIME WAS NOT IN QUESTION. DURING THE FRENZIED DAYS OF INSURRECTION, FORDSBURG REBELS HAD ACCUSED THE GREENGROCER OF ASSISTING THE GOVERNMENT FORCES.
HE WAS SIGNALLING TO THE POLICE! I SAW HIM!
YOU OUGHT TO BE ASHAMED OF YOURSELF!
BUT WHO HAD GIVEN THE ORDER TO SHOOT HIM? POLICEMEN WHO WERE HELD CAPTIVE IN THE MARKET BUILDINGS SAID THEY SAW MARAIS'S INTERROGATION BY THE REBEL LEADERSHIP.
HE WAS BROUGHT BEFORE A COURT MARTIAL. PERCY FISHER DID MOST OF THE TALKING BUT SAM LONG WAS THERE, TOO.
AND WHO PULLED THE TRIGGER? BOTH DE WIT AND ANOTHER ACCOMPLICE, DU TOIT, CONFESSED THAT THEY WITNESSED MARAIS'S EXECUTION BUT THAT TAFFY LONG ALONE HAD CARRIED IT OUT.
IT WAS AFTER DARK, ABOUT 8 O'CLOCK. LONG SHOT HIM TWICE. ALL I HEARD WAS MARAIS SAY "OH, GOD." THEN HE SLID DOWN AGAINST THE WALL.

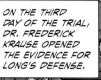

ON THE THIRD DAY OF THE TRIAL, DR. FREDERICK KRAUSE OPENED THE EVIDENCE FOR LONG'S DEFENSE.

MARAIS WAS IN THE THROES OF DEATH WHEN HIS WORDS WERE RECORDED.

IT IS NO WONDER HE CONFUSED HIS KILLER FOR AN INNOCENT MAN.

WITH THE GREATEST RESPECT TO THE DECEASED, MY LORD, SAMUEL LONG IS NEITHER "FAIR" NOR "SHORT."

DE WIT AND DU TOIT, WHO WERE PRESENT AT THE SCENE OF THE CRIME AND HAVE SINCE TURNED CROWN WITNESS, ARE FAIRER AND SHORTER!

AND, WHAT IS MORE... DU TOIT, NOT LONG, IS KNOWN BY THE NICKNAME "MACLEAN!"

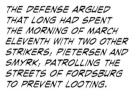

THE DEFENSE ARGUED THAT LONG HAD SPENT THE MORNING OF MARCH ELEVENTH WITH TWO OTHER STRIKERS, PIETERSEN AND SMYRK, PATROLLING THE STREETS OF FORDSBURG TO PREVENT LOOTING.

WHEN GUNFIRE RANG OUT FROM THE NEARBY MINE DUMPS, THEY TOOK COVER INDOORS.

THAT IS CORRECT... MY WIFE AND I INVITED THESE MEN INTO OUR HOME THAT DAY.

WE DRANK TEA AND SHARED STORIES OF THE GREAT WAR.

WE WAITED FOR NIGHTFALL TO BE SAFE.

THEN SMYRK AND I ACCOMPANIED LONG TO HIS HOUSE WHERE MRS. LONG OFFERED US DINNER.

THEY DIDN'T EAT.

SMYRK AND PIETERSEN LEFT AT 9:45, THEN MY HUSBAND AND I WENT TO BED.

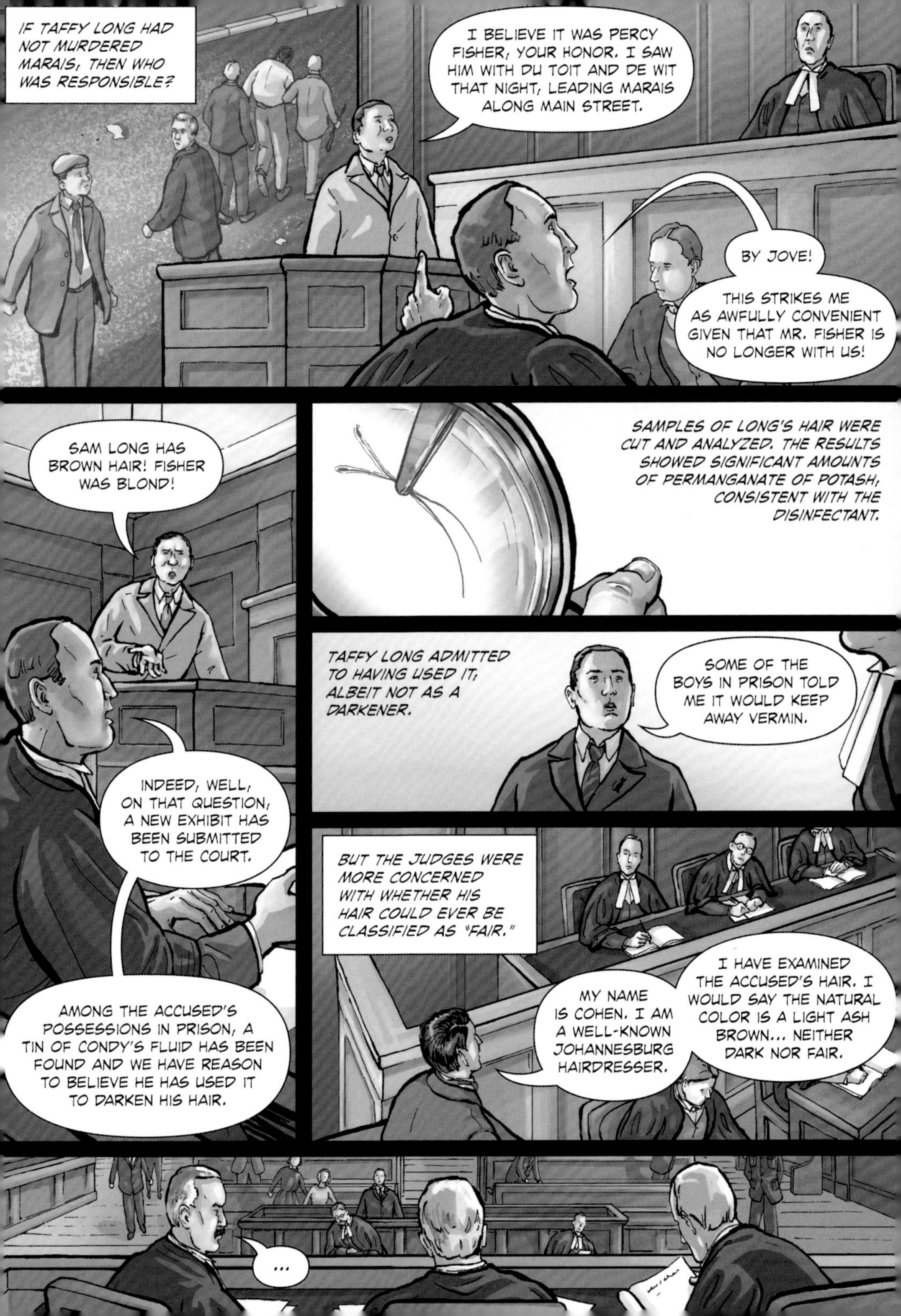
IF TAFFY LONG HAD NOT MURDERED MARAIS, THEN WHO WAS RESPONSIBLE?
I BELIEVE IT WAS PERCY FISHER, YOUR HONOR. I SAW HIM WITH DU TOIT AND DE WIT THAT NIGHT, LEADING MARAIS ALONG MAIN STREET.
BY JOVE!
THIS STRIKES ME AS AWFULLY CONVENIENT GIVEN THAT MR. FISHER IS NO LONGER WITH US!
SAM LONG HAS BROWN HAIR! FISHER WAS BLOND!
INDEED, WELL, ON THAT QUESTION, A NEW EXHIBIT HAS BEEN SUBMITTED TO THE COURT.
AMONG THE ACCUSED'S POSSESSIONS IN PRISON, A TIN OF CONDY'S FLUID HAS BEEN FOUND AND WE HAVE REASON TO BELIEVE HE HAS USED IT TO DARKEN HIS HAIR.
SAMPLES OF LONG'S HAIR WERE CUT AND ANALYZED. THE RESULTS SHOWED SIGNIFICANT AMOUNTS OF PERMANGANATE OF POTASH, CONSISTENT WITH THE DISINFECTANT.
TAFFY LONG ADMITTED TO HAVING USED IT, ALBEIT NOT AS A DARKENER.
SOME OF THE BOYS IN PRISON TOLD ME IT WOULD KEEP AWAY VERMIN.
BUT THE JUDGES WERE MORE CONCERNED WITH WHETHER HIS HAIR COULD EVER BE CLASSIFIED AS "FAIR."
MY NAME IS COHEN. I AM A WELL-KNOWN JOHANNESBURG HAIRDRESSER.
I HAVE EXAMINED THE ACCUSED'S HAIR. I WOULD SAY THE NATURAL COLOR IS A LIGHT ASH BROWN... NEITHER DARK NOR FAIR.
...

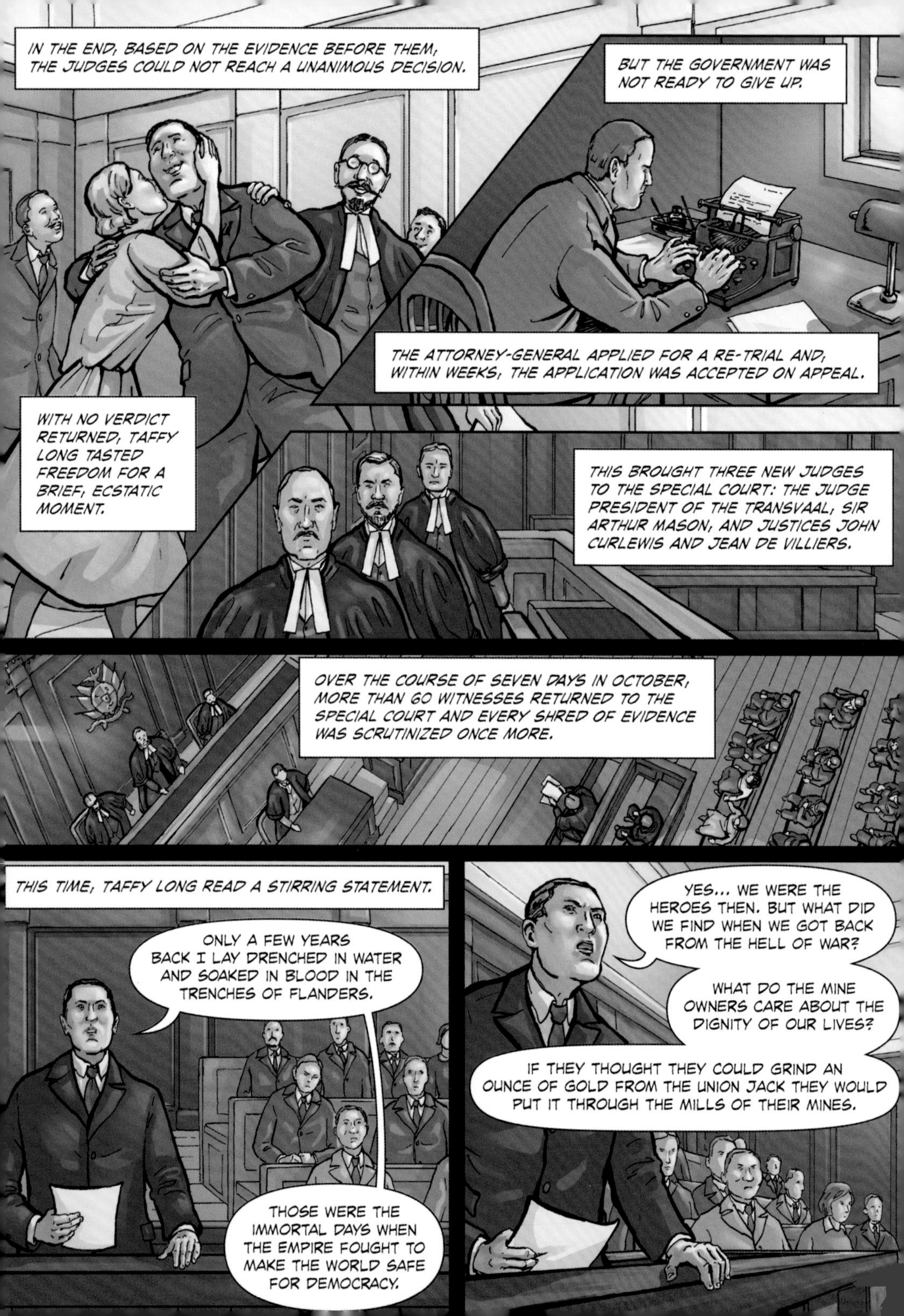
IN THE END, BASED ON THE EVIDENCE BEFORE THEM, THE JUDGES COULD NOT REACH A UNANIMOUS DECISION.
WITH NO VERDICT RETURNED, TAFFY LONG TASTED FREEDOM FOR A BRIEF, ECSTATIC MOMENT.
BUT THE GOVERNMENT WAS NOT READY TO GIVE UP.
THE ATTORNEY-GENERAL APPLIED FOR A RE-TRIAL AND, WITHIN WEEKS, THE APPLICATION WAS ACCEPTED ON APPEAL.
THIS BROUGHT THREE NEW JUDGES TO THE SPECIAL COURT: THE JUDGE PRESIDENT OF THE TRANSVAAL, SIR ARTHUR MASON, AND JUSTICES JOHN CURLEWIS AND JEAN DE VILLIERS.
OVER THE COURSE OF SEVEN DAYS IN OCTOBER, MORE THAN 60 WITNESSES RETURNED TO THE SPECIAL COURT AND EVERY SHRED OF EVIDENCE WAS SCRUTINIZED ONCE MORE.
THIS TIME, TAFFY LONG READ A STIRRING STATEMENT.
ONLY A FEW YEARS BACK I LAY DRENCHED IN WATER AND SOAKED IN BLOOD IN THE TRENCHES OF FLANDERS.
THOSE WERE THE IMMORTAL DAYS WHEN THE EMPIRE FOUGHT TO MAKE THE WORLD SAFE FOR DEMOCRACY.
YES... WE WERE THE HEROES THEN. BUT WHAT DID WE FIND WHEN WE GOT BACK FROM THE HELL OF WAR?
WHAT DO THE MINE OWNERS CARE ABOUT THE DIGNITY OF OUR LIVES?
IF THEY THOUGHT THEY COULD GRIND AN OUNCE OF GOLD FROM THE UNION JACK THEY WOULD PUT IT THROUGH THE MILLS OF THEIR MINES.

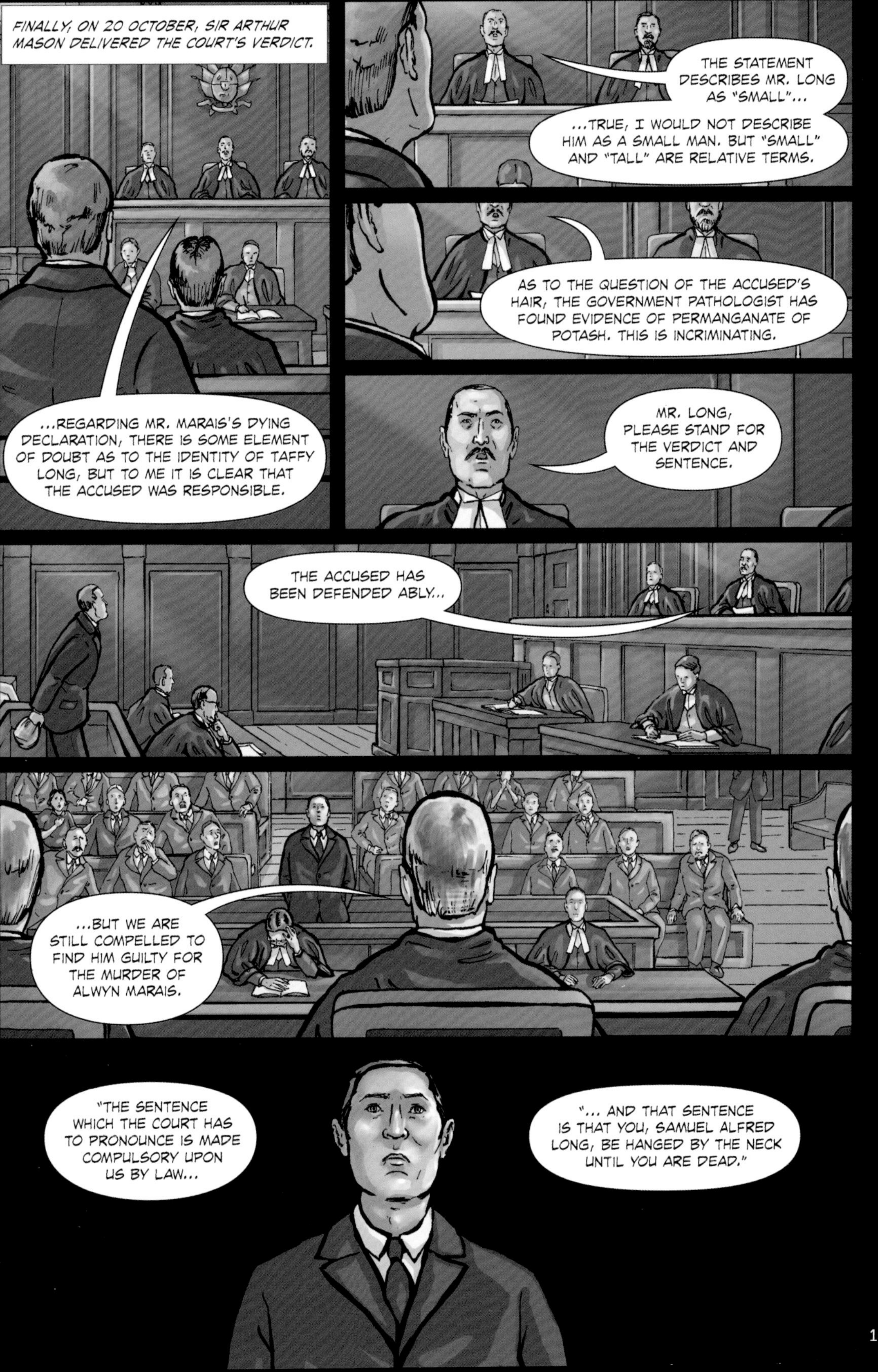
FINALLY, ON 20 OCTOBER, SIR ARTHUR MASON DELIVERED THE COURT'S VERDICT.
...REGARDING MR. MARAIS'S DYING DECLARATION, THERE IS SOME ELEMENT OF DOUBT AS TO THE IDENTITY OF TAFFY LONG, BUT TO ME IT IS CLEAR THAT THE ACCUSED WAS RESPONSIBLE.
THE STATEMENT DESCRIBES MR. LONG AS "SMALL"...
...TRUE, I WOULD NOT DESCRIBE HIM AS A SMALL MAN. BUT "SMALL" AND "TALL" ARE RELATIVE TERMS.
AS TO THE QUESTION OF THE ACCUSED'S HAIR, THE GOVERNMENT PATHOLOGIST HAS FOUND EVIDENCE OF PERMANGANATE OF POTASH. THIS IS INCRIMINATING.
MR. LONG, PLEASE STAND FOR THE VERDICT AND SENTENCE.
THE ACCUSED HAS BEEN DEFENDED ABLY...
...BUT WE ARE STILL COMPELLED TO FIND HIM GUILTY FOR THE MURDER OF ALWYN MARAIS.
"THE SENTENCE WHICH THE COURT HAS TO PRONOUNCE IS MADE COMPULSORY UPON US BY LAW...
"... AND THAT SENTENCE IS THAT YOU, SAMUEL ALFRED LONG, BE HANGED BY THE NECK UNTIL YOU ARE DEAD."

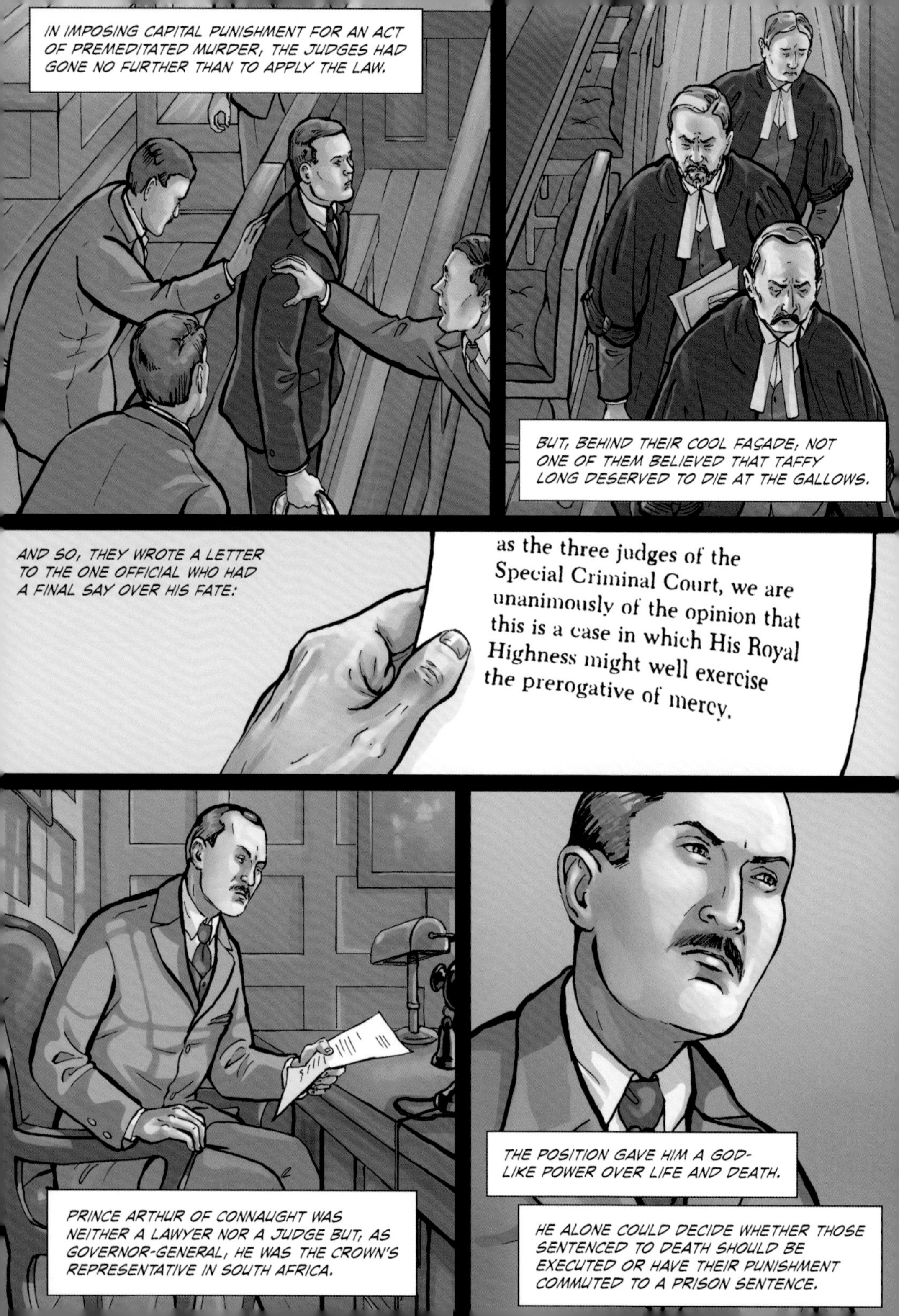
IN IMPOSING CAPITAL PUNISHMENT FOR AN ACT OF PREMEDITATED MURDER, THE JUDGES HAD GONE NO FURTHER THAN TO APPLY THE LAW.
BUT, BEHIND THEIR COOL FAÇADE, NOT ONE OF THEM BELIEVED THAT TAFFY LONG DESERVED TO DIE AT THE GALLOWS.
AND SO, THEY WROTE A LETTER TO THE ONE OFFICIAL WHO HAD A FINAL SAY OVER HIS FATE:
as the three judges of the Special Criminal Court, we are unanimously of the opinion that this is a case in which His Royal Highness might well exercise the prerogative of mercy.
PRINCE ARTHUR OF CONNAUGHT WAS NEITHER A LAWYER NOR A JUDGE BUT, AS GOVERNOR-GENERAL, HE WAS THE CROWN'S REPRESENTATIVE IN SOUTH AFRICA.
THE POSITION GAVE HIM A GOD-LIKE POWER OVER LIFE AND DEATH.
HE ALONE COULD DECIDE WHETHER THOSE SENTENCED TO DEATH SHOULD BE EXECUTED OR HAVE THEIR PUNISHMENT COMMUTED TO A PRISON SENTENCE.

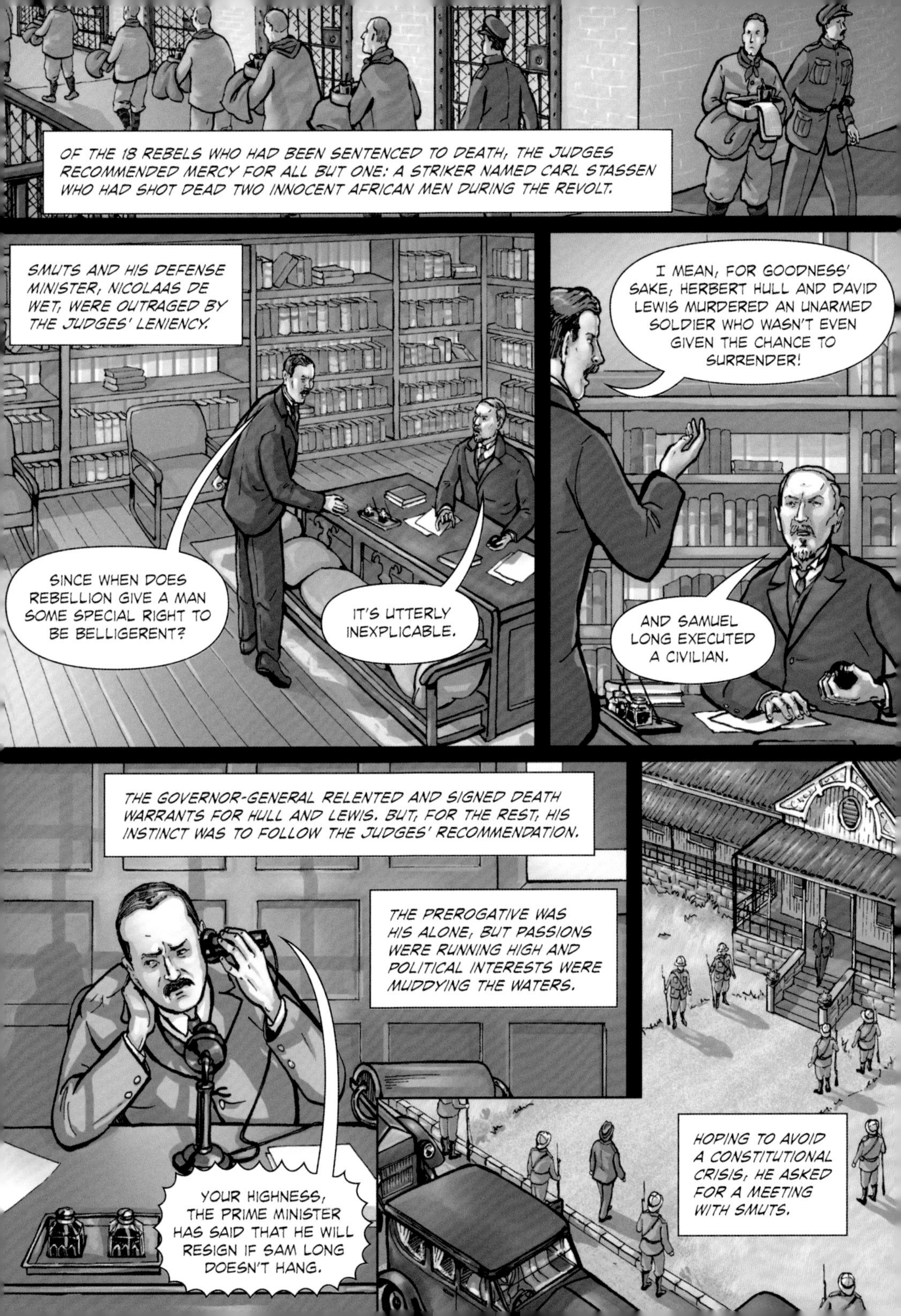
OF THE 18 REBELS WHO HAD BEEN SENTENCED TO DEATH, THE JUDGES RECOMMENDED MERCY FOR ALL BUT ONE: A STRIKER NAMED CARL STASSEN WHO HAD SHOT DEAD TWO INNOCENT AFRICAN MEN DURING THE REVOLT.
SMUTS AND HIS DEFENSE MINISTER, NICOLAAS DE WET, WERE OUTRAGED BY THE JUDGES' LENIENCY.
SINCE WHEN DOES REBELLION GIVE A MAN SOME SPECIAL RIGHT TO BE BELLIGERENT?
IT'S UTTERLY INEXPLICABLE.
I MEAN, FOR GOODNESS' SAKE, HERBERT HULL AND DAVID LEWIS MURDERED AN UNARMED SOLDIER WHO WASN'T EVEN GIVEN THE CHANCE TO SURRENDER!
AND SAMUEL LONG EXECUTED A CIVILIAN.
THE GOVERNOR-GENERAL RELENTED AND SIGNED DEATH WARRANTS FOR HULL AND LEWIS. BUT, FOR THE REST, HIS INSTINCT WAS TO FOLLOW THE JUDGES' RECOMMENDATION.
THE PREROGATIVE WAS HIS ALONE, BUT PASSIONS WERE RUNNING HIGH AND POLITICAL INTERESTS WERE MUDDYING THE WATERS.
YOUR HIGHNESS, THE PRIME MINISTER HAS SAID THAT HE WILL RESIGN IF SAM LONG DOESN'T HANG.
HOPING TO AVOID A CONSTITUTIONAL CRISIS, HE ASKED FOR A MEETING WITH SMUTS.

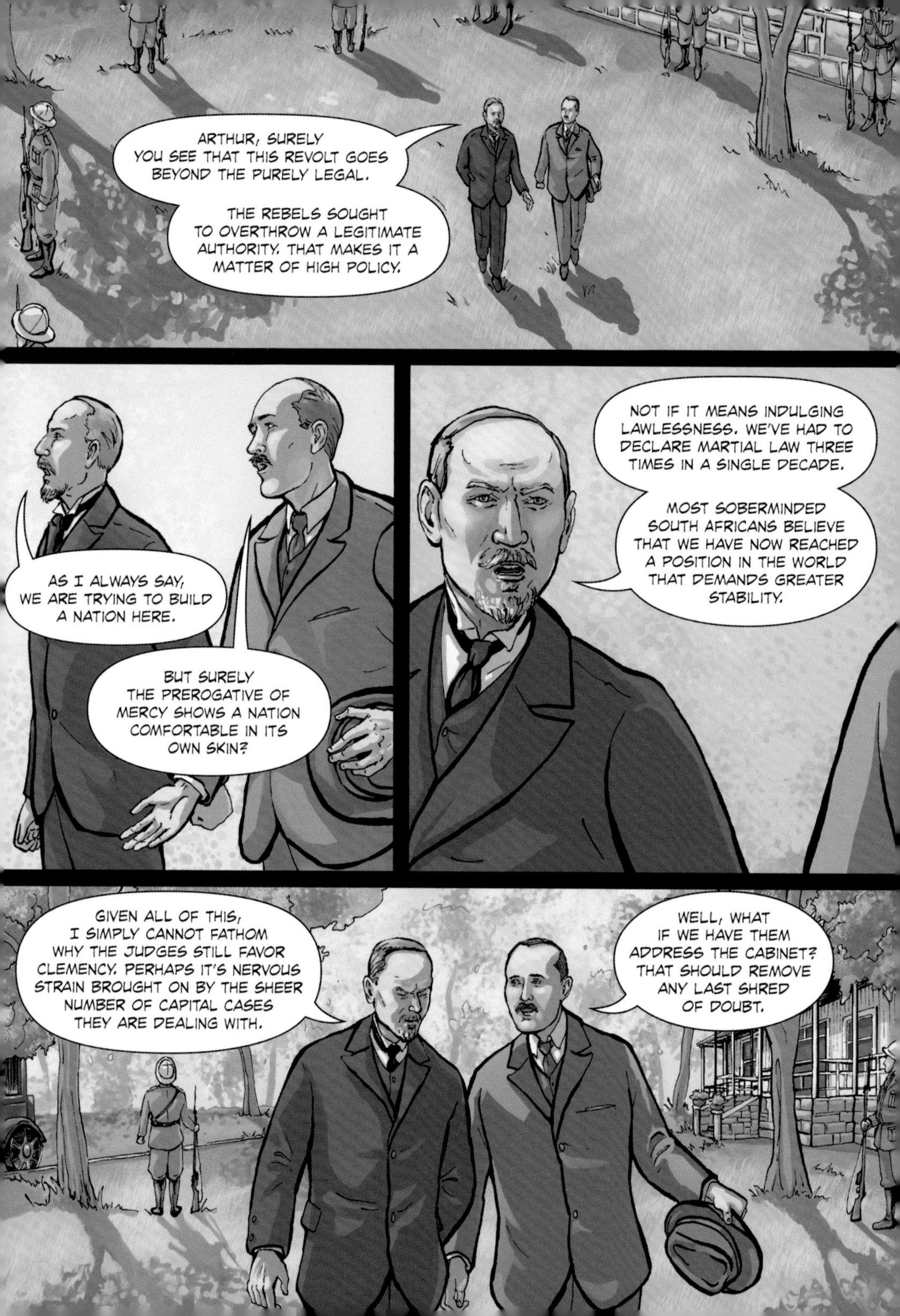
ARTHUR, SURELY YOU SEE THAT THIS REVOLT GOES BEYOND THE PURELY LEGAL.
THE REBELS SOUGHT TO OVERTHROW A LEGITIMATE AUTHORITY. THAT MAKES IT A MATTER OF HIGH POLICY.
AS I ALWAYS SAY, WE ARE TRYING TO BUILD A NATION HERE.
BUT SURELY THE PREROGATIVE OF MERCY SHOWS A NATION COMFORTABLE IN ITS OWN SKIN?
NOT IF IT MEANS INDULGING LAWLESSNESS. WE'VE HAD TO DECLARE MARTIAL LAW THREE TIMES IN A SINGLE DECADE.
MOST SOBERMINDED SOUTH AFRICANS BELIEVE THAT WE HAVE NOW REACHED A POSITION IN THE WORLD THAT DEMANDS GREATER STABILITY.
GIVEN ALL OF THIS, I SIMPLY CANNOT FATHOM WHY THE JUDGES STILL FAVOR CLEMENCY. PERHAPS IT'S NERVOUS STRAIN BROUGHT ON BY THE SHEER NUMBER OF CAPITAL CASES THEY ARE DEALING WITH.
WELL, WHAT IF WE HAVE THEM ADDRESS THE CABINET? THAT SHOULD REMOVE ANY LAST SHRED OF DOUBT.

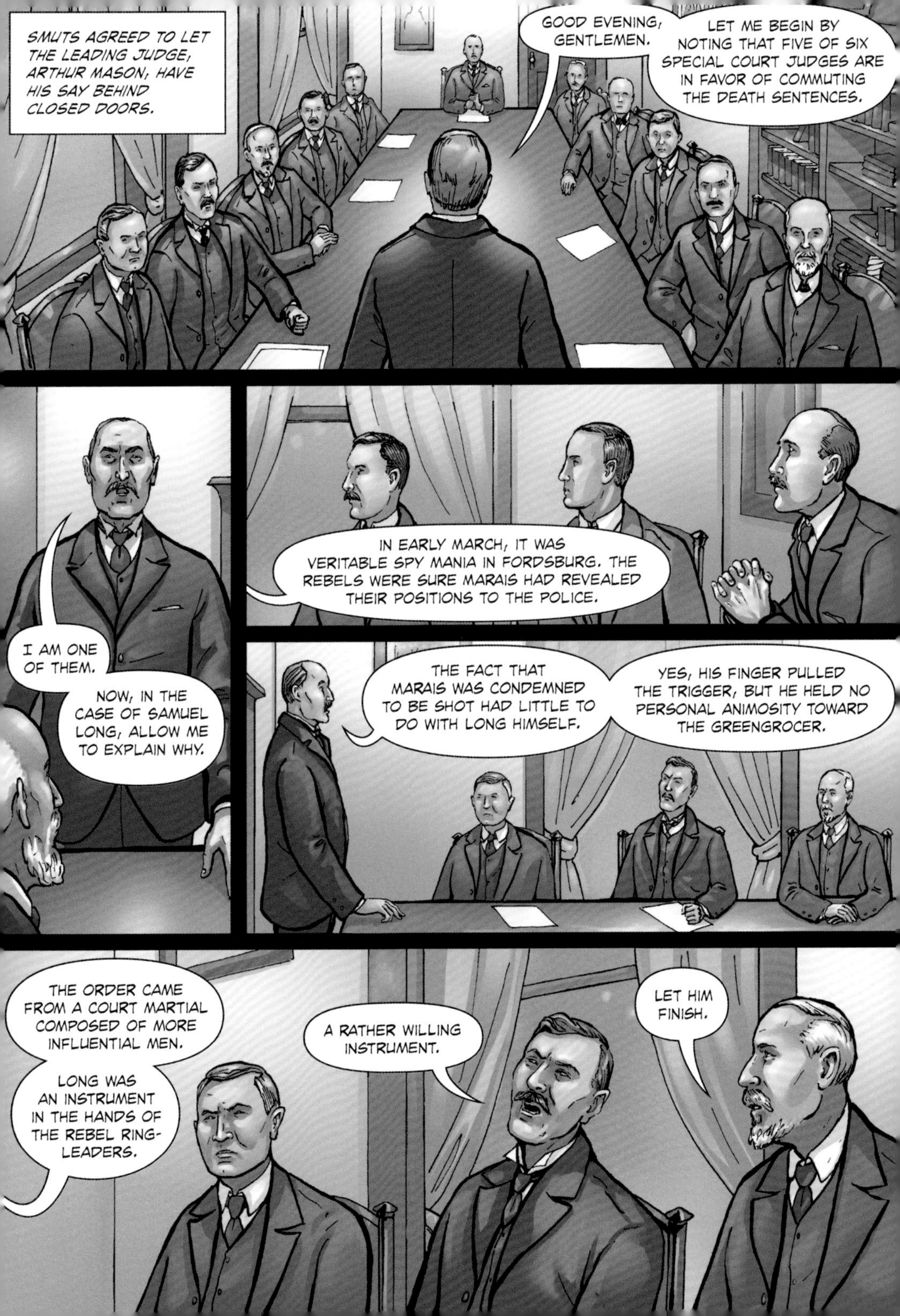
SMUTS AGREED TO LET THE LEADING JUDGE, ARTHUR MASON, HAVE HIS SAY BEHIND CLOSED DOORS.
GOOD EVENING, GENTLEMEN.
LET ME BEGIN BY NOTING THAT FIVE OF SIX SPECIAL COURT JUDGES ARE IN FAVOR OF COMMUTING THE DEATH SENTENCES.
I AM ONE OF THEM.
NOW, IN THE CASE OF SAMUEL LONG, ALLOW ME TO EXPLAIN WHY.
IN EARLY MARCH, IT WAS VERITABLE SPY MANIA IN FORDSBURG. THE REBELS WERE SURE MARAIS HAD REVEALED THEIR POSITIONS TO THE POLICE.
THE FACT THAT MARAIS WAS CONDEMNED TO BE SHOT HAD LITTLE TO DO WITH LONG HIMSELF.
YES, HIS FINGER PULLED THE TRIGGER, BUT HE HELD NO PERSONAL ANIMOSITY TOWARD THE GREENGROCER.
THE ORDER CAME FROM A COURT MARTIAL COMPOSED OF MORE INFLUENTIAL MEN.
LONG WAS AN INSTRUMENT IN THE HANDS OF THE REBEL RING-LEADERS.
A RATHER WILLING INSTRUMENT.
LET HIM FINISH.

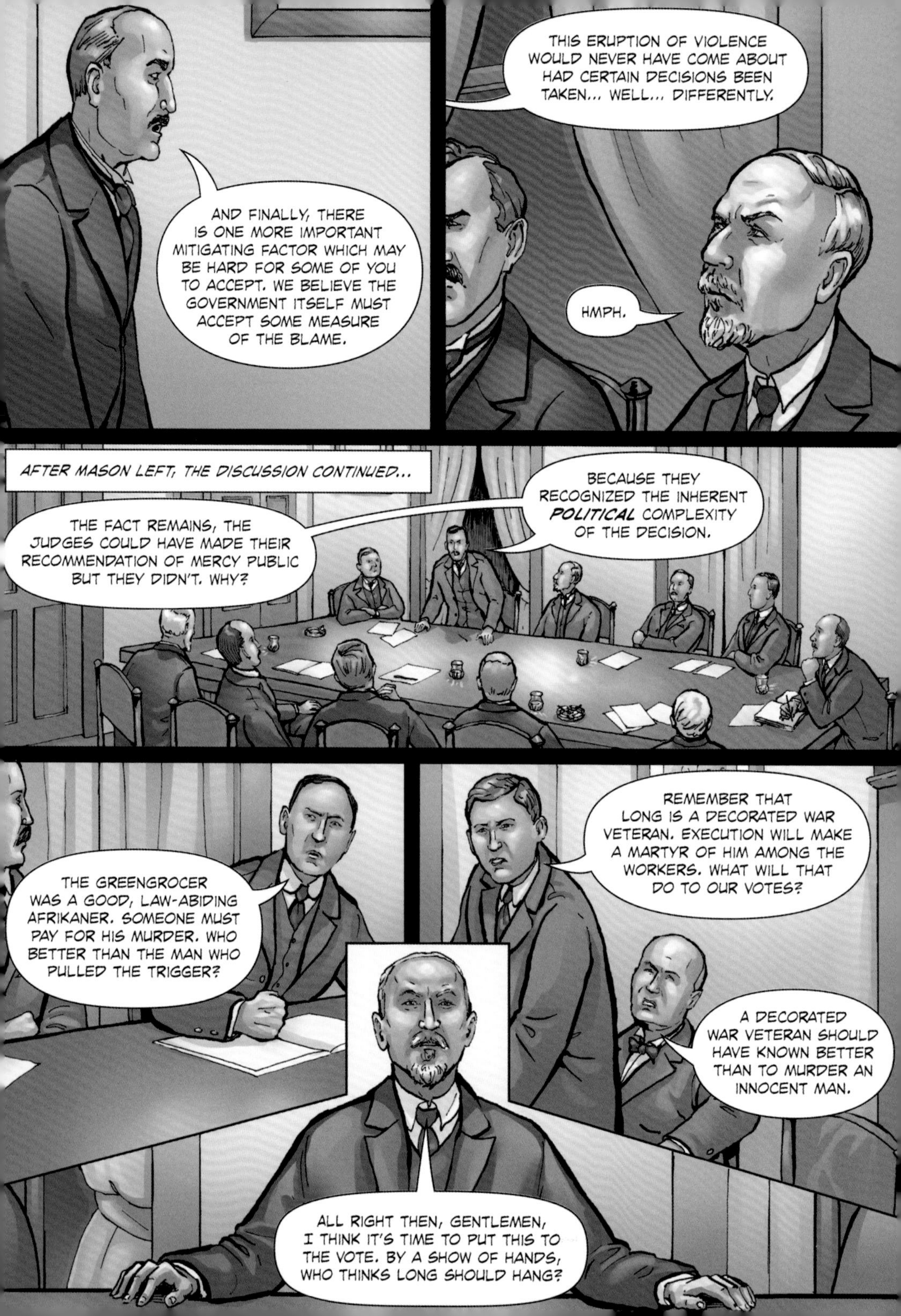
AND FINALLY, THERE IS ONE MORE IMPORTANT MITIGATING FACTOR WHICH MAY BE HARD FOR SOME OF YOU TO ACCEPT. WE BELIEVE THE GOVERNMENT ITSELF MUST ACCEPT SOME MEASURE OF THE BLAME.
THIS ERUPTION OF VIOLENCE WOULD NEVER HAVE COME ABOUT HAD CERTAIN DECISIONS BEEN TAKEN... WELL... DIFFERENTLY.
HMPH.
AFTER MASON LEFT, THE DISCUSSION CONTINUED...
THE FACT REMAINS, THE JUDGES COULD HAVE MADE THEIR RECOMMENDATION OF MERCY PUBLIC BUT THEY DIDN'T. WHY?
BECAUSE THEY RECOGNIZED THE INHERENT POLITICAL COMPLEXITY OF THE DECISION.
THE GREENGROCER WAS A GOOD, LAW-ABIDING AFRIKANER. SOMEONE MUST PAY FOR HIS MURDER. WHO BETTER THAN THE MAN WHO PULLED THE TRIGGER?
REMEMBER THAT LONG IS A DECORATED WAR VETERAN. EXECUTION WILL MAKE A MARTYR OF HIM AMONG THE WORKERS. WHAT WILL THAT DO TO OUR VOTES?
A DECORATED WAR VETERAN SHOULD HAVE KNOWN BETTER THAN TO MURDER AN INNOCENT MAN.
ALL RIGHT THEN, GENTLEMEN, I THINK IT'S TIME TO PUT THIS TO THE VOTE. BY A SHOW OF HANDS, WHO THINKS LONG SHOULD HANG?

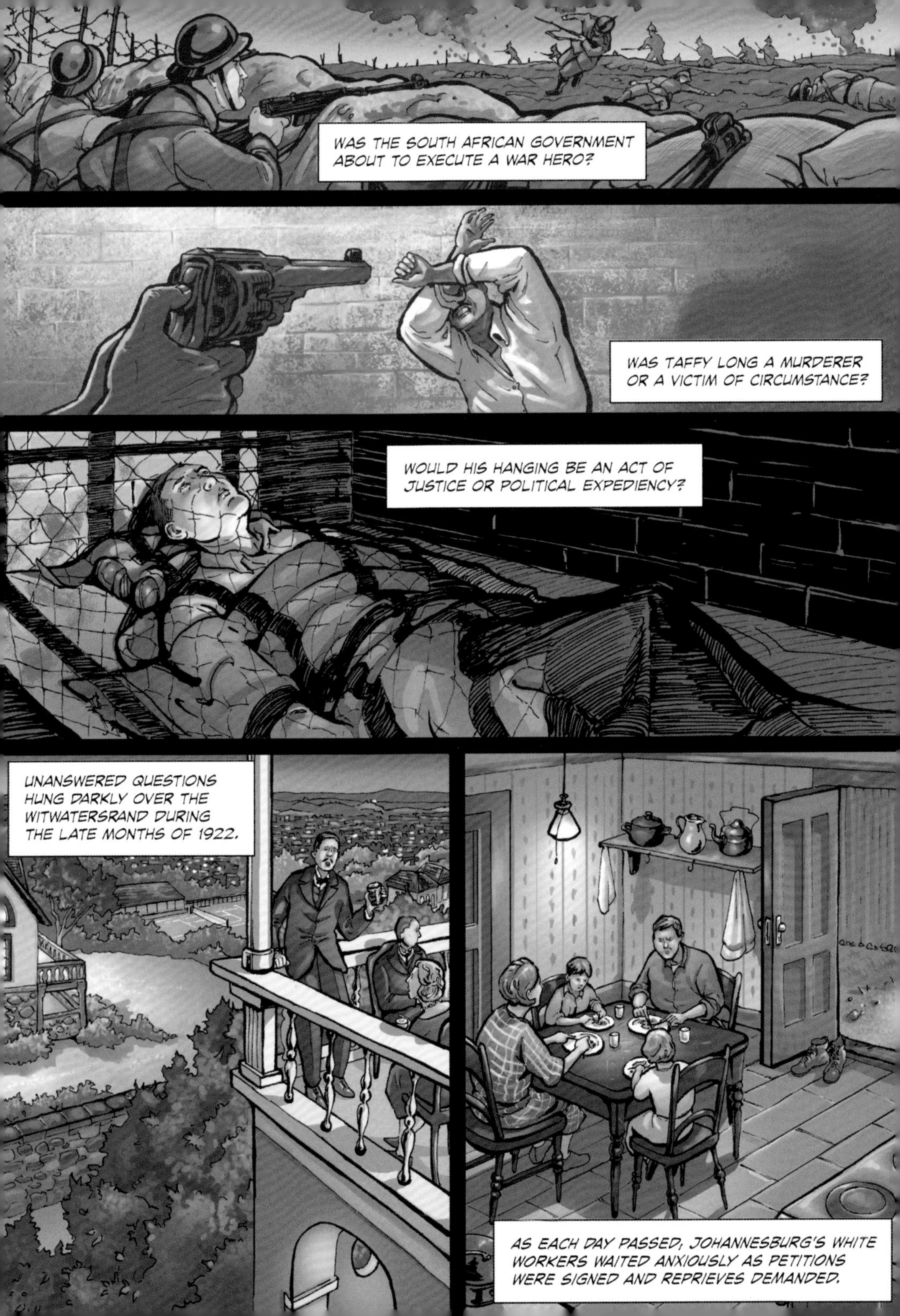
WAS THE SOUTH AFRICAN GOVERNMENT ABOUT TO EXECUTE A WAR HERO?
WAS TAFFY LONG A MURDERER OR A VICTIM OF CIRCUMSTANCE?
WOULD HIS HANGING BE AN ACT OF JUSTICE OR POLITICAL EXPEDIENCY?
UNANSWERED QUESTIONS HUNG DARKLY OVER THE WITWATERSRAND DURING THE LATE MONTHS OF 1922.
AS EACH DAY PASSED, JOHANNESBURG'S WHITE WORKERS WAITED ANXIOUSLY AS PETITIONS WERE SIGNED AND REPRIEVES DEMANDED.

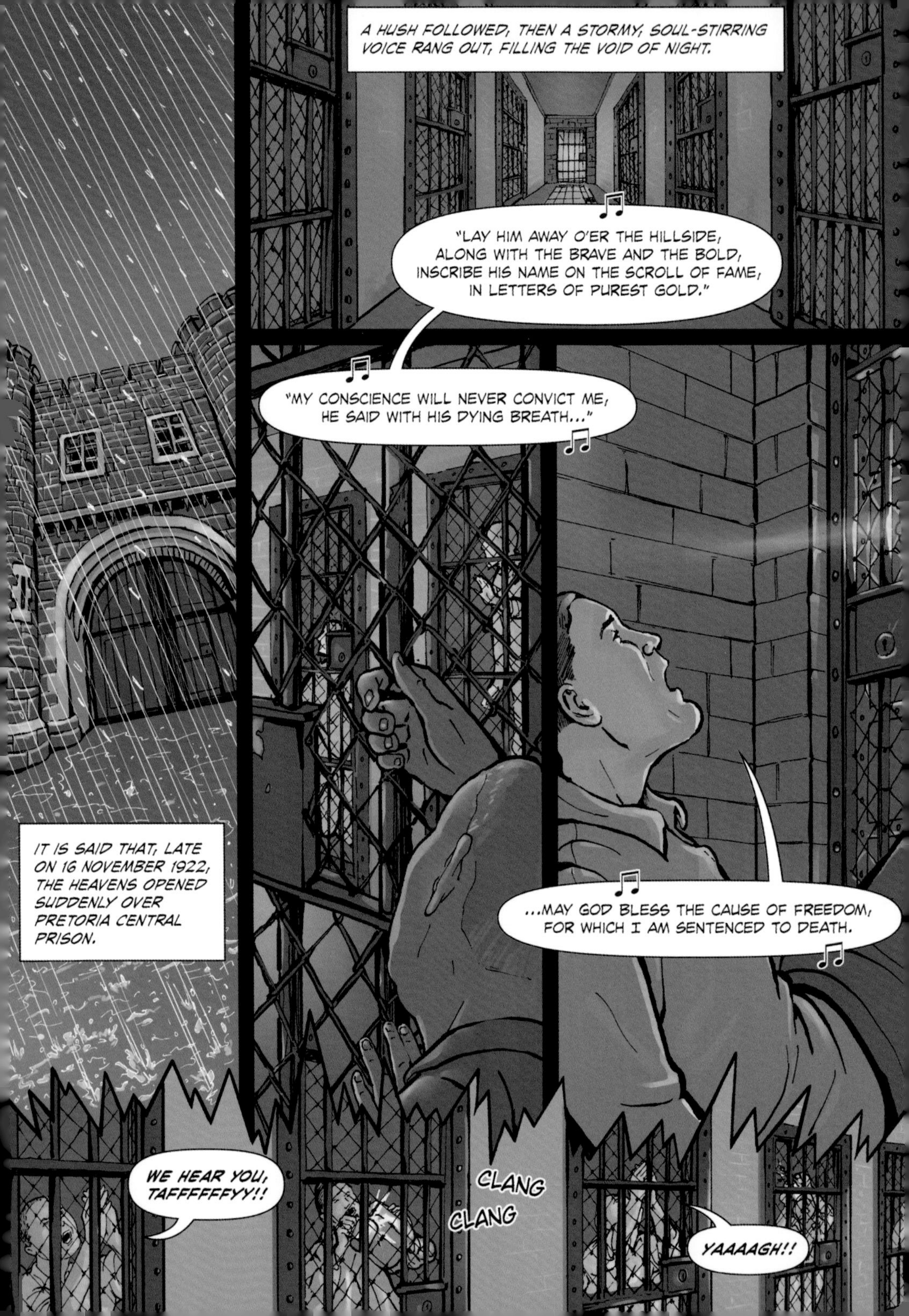
A HUSH FOLLOWED, THEN A STORMY, SOUL-STIRRING VOICE RANG OUT, FILLING THE VOID OF NIGHT.
"LAY HIM AWAY O'ER THE HILLSIDE, ALONG WITH THE BRAVE AND THE BOLD, INSCRIBE HIS NAME ON THE SCROLL OF FAME, IN LETTERS OF PUREST GOLD."
IT IS SAID THAT, LATE ON 16 NOVEMBER 1922, THE HEAVENS OPENED SUDDENLY OVER PRETORIA CENTRAL PRISON.
"MY CONSCIENCE WILL NEVER CONVICT ME, HE SAID WITH HIS DYING BREATH..."
...MAY GOD BLESS THE CAUSE OF FREEDOM, FOR WHICH I AM SENTENCED TO DEATH.
WE HEAR YOU, TAFFFFFFYY!!
CLANG
CLANG
YAAAAGH!!

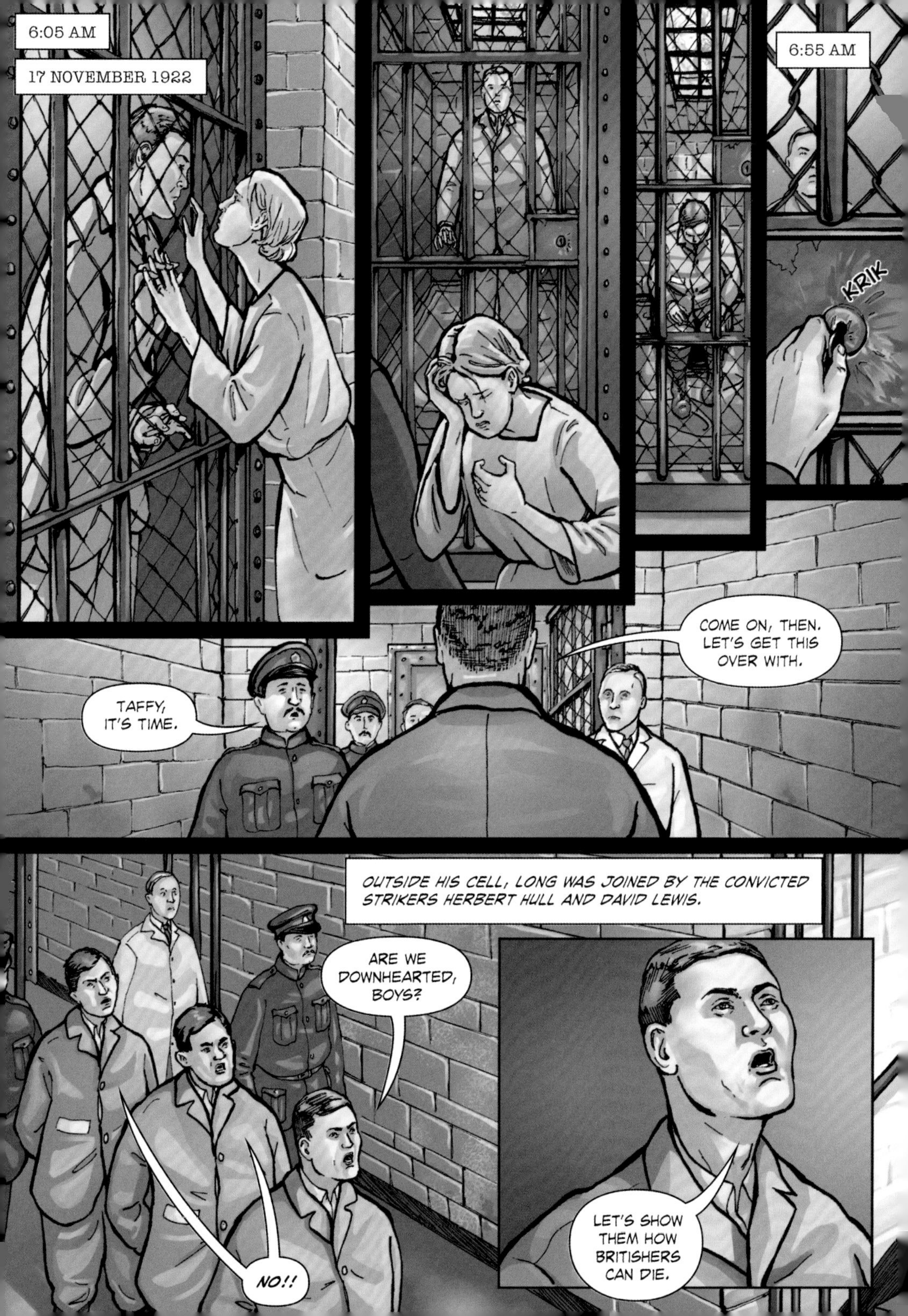
6:05 AM
17 NOVEMBER 1922
6:55 AM
KRIK
COME ON, THEN. LET'S GET THIS OVER WITH.
TAFFY, IT'S TIME.
OUTSIDE HIS CELL, LONG WAS JOINED BY THE CONVICTED STRIKERS HERBERT HULL AND DAVID LEWIS.
ARE WE DOWNHEARTED, BOYS?
NO!!
LET'S SHOW THEM HOW BRITISHERS CAN DIE.

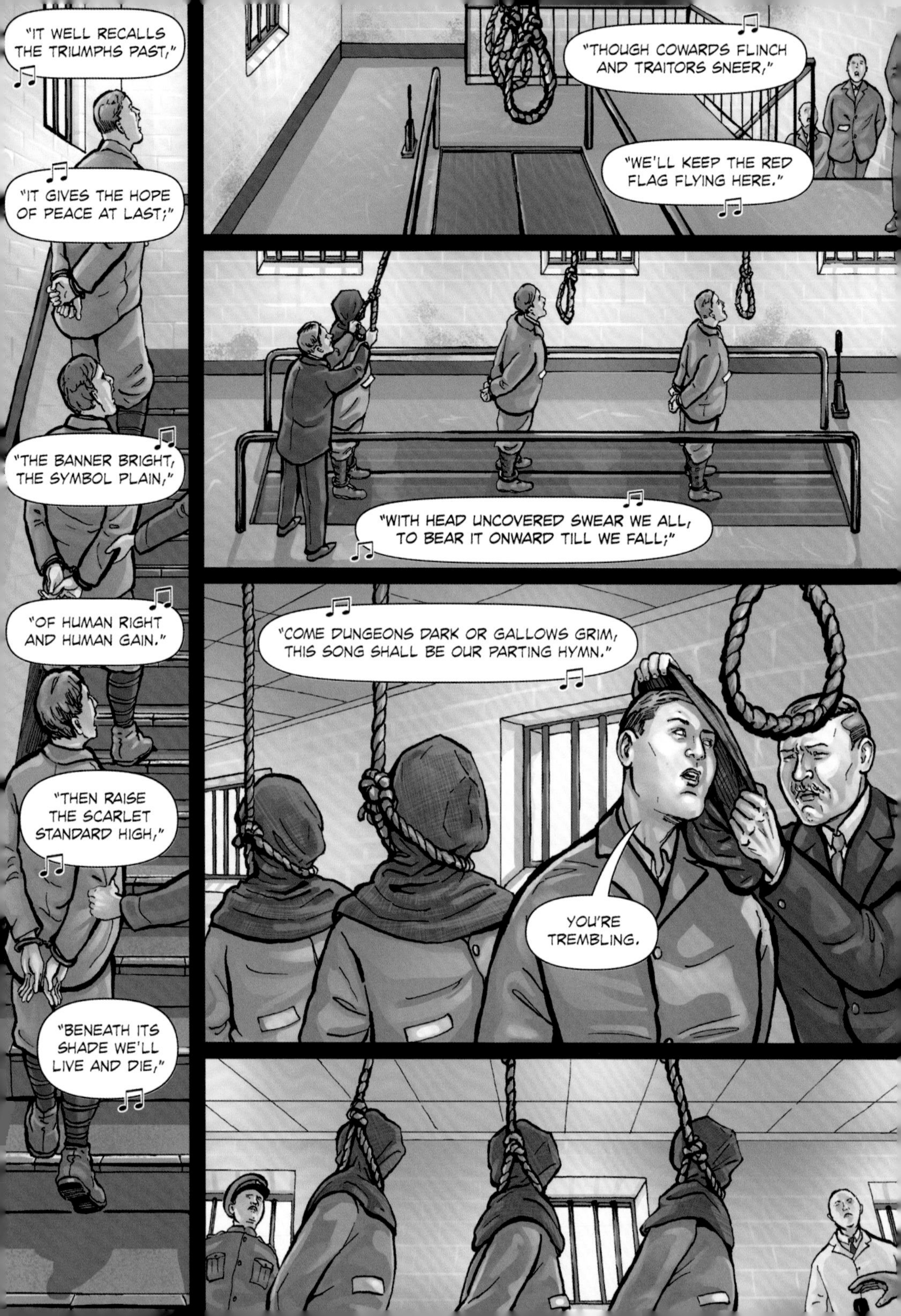

"IT WELL RECALLS THE TRIUMPHS PAST,"
"IT GIVES THE HOPE OF PEACE AT LAST;"
"THE BANNER BRIGHT, THE SYMBOL PLAIN,"
"OF HUMAN RIGHT AND HUMAN GAIN."
"THEN RAISE THE SCARLET STANDARD HIGH,"
"BENEATH ITS SHADE WE'LL LIVE AND DIE,"
"THOUGH COWARDS FLINCH AND TRAITORS SNEER,"
"WE'LL KEEP THE RED FLAG FLYING HERE."
"WITH HEAD UNCOVERED SWEAR WE ALL, TO BEAR IT ONWARD TILL WE FALL;"
"COME DUNGEONS DARK OR GALLOWS GRIM, THIS SONG SHALL BE OUR PARTING HYMN."
YOU'RE TREMBLING.

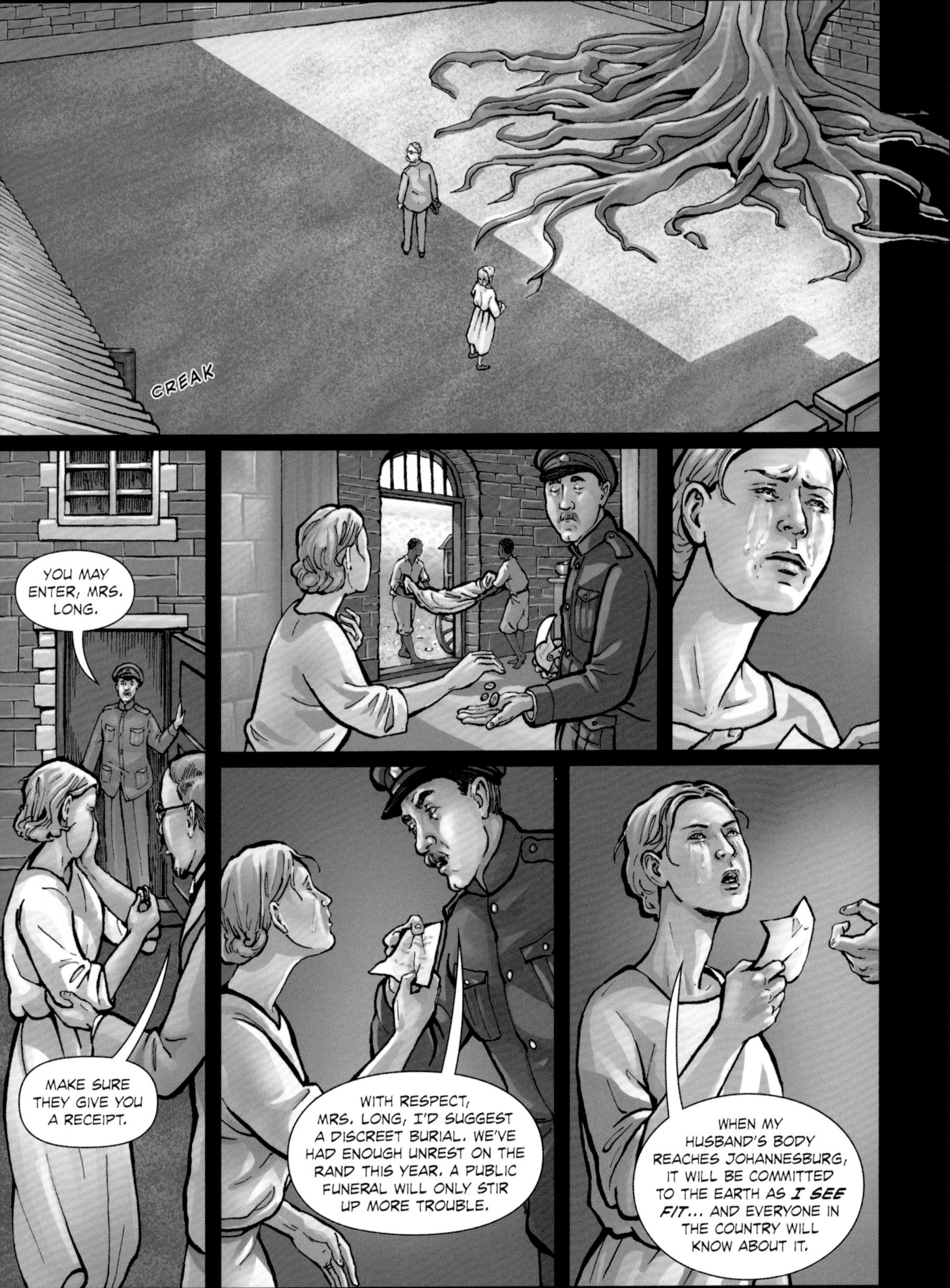
CREAK
YOU MAY ENTER, MRS. LONG.
MAKE SURE THEY GIVE YOU A RECEIPT.
WITH RESPECT, MRS. LONG, I'D SUGGEST A DISCREET BURIAL. WE'VE HAD ENOUGH UNREST ON THE RAND THIS YEAR. A PUBLIC FUNERAL WILL ONLY STIR UP MORE TROUBLE.
WHEN MY HUSBAND'S BODY REACHES JOHANNESBURG, IT WILL BE COMMITTED TO THE EARTH AS *I SEE FIT*... AND EVERYONE IN THE COUNTRY WILL KNOW ABOUT IT.

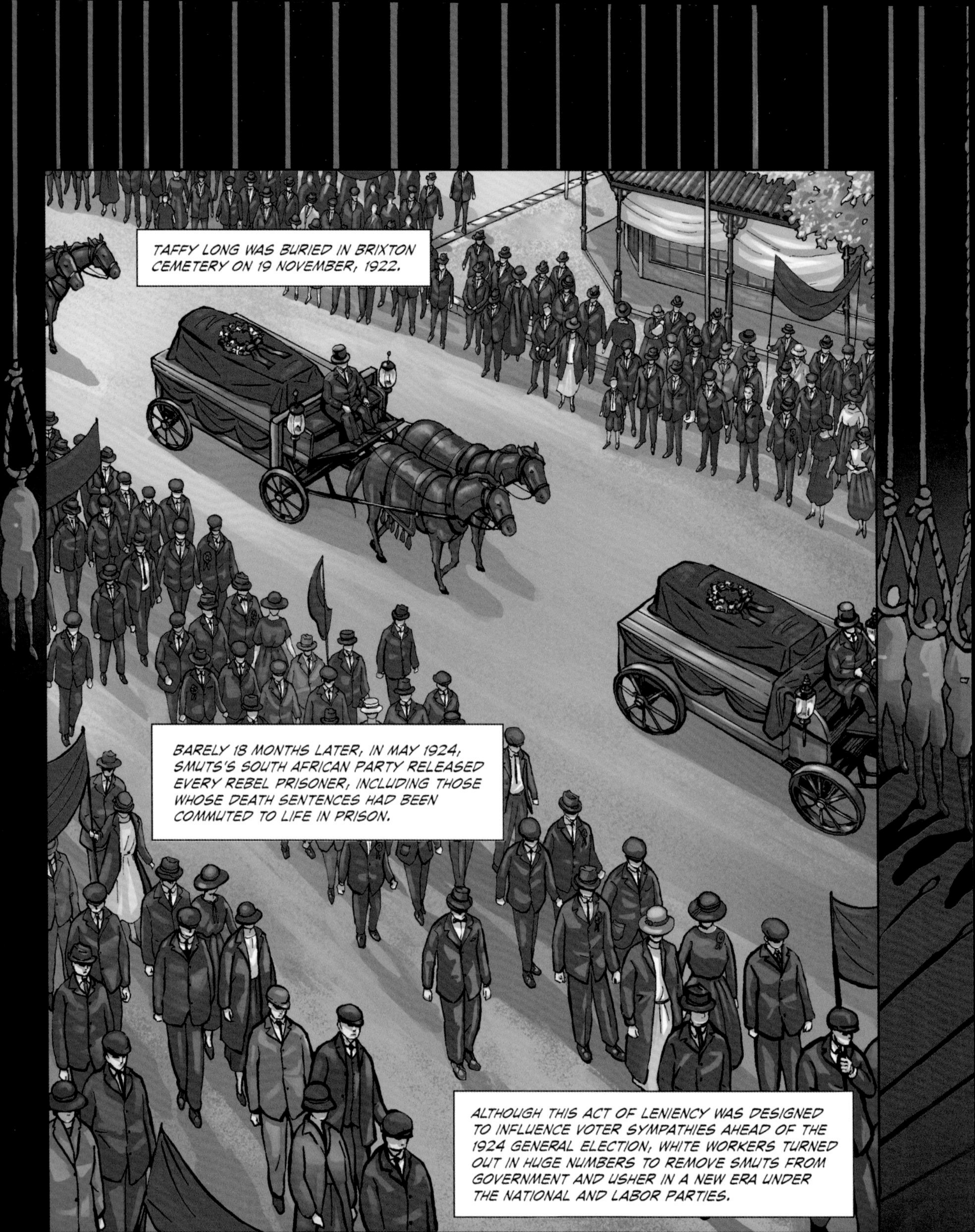
TAFFY LONG WAS BURIED IN BRIXTON CEMETERY ON 19 NOVEMBER, 1922.
BARELY 18 MONTHS LATER, IN MAY 1924, SMUTS'S SOUTH AFRICAN PARTY RELEASED EVERY REBEL PRISONER, INCLUDING THOSE WHOSE DEATH SENTENCES HAD BEEN COMMUTED TO LIFE IN PRISON.
ALTHOUGH THIS ACT OF LENIENCY WAS DESIGNED TO INFLUENCE VOTER SYMPATHIES AHEAD OF THE 1924 GENERAL ELECTION, WHITE WORKERS TURNED OUT IN HUGE NUMBERS TO REMOVE SMUTS FROM GOVERNMENT AND USHER IN A NEW ERA UNDER THE NATIONAL AND LABOR PARTIES.

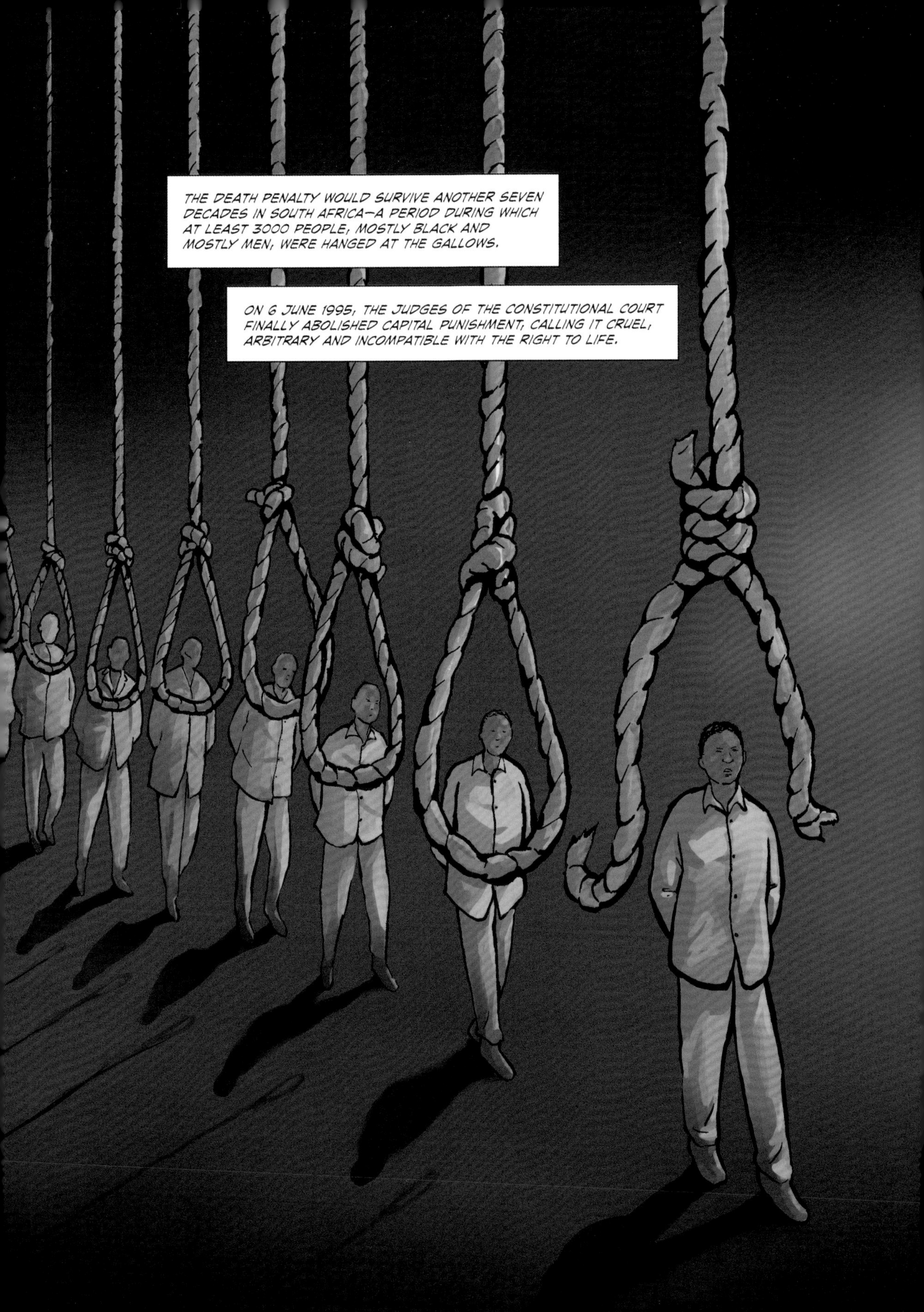
THE DEATH PENALTY WOULD SURVIVE ANOTHER SEVEN DECADES IN SOUTH AFRICA—A PERIOD DURING WHICH AT LEAST 3000 PEOPLE, MOSTLY BLACK AND MOSTLY MEN, WERE HANGED AT THE GALLOWS.
ON 6 JUNE 1995, THE JUDGES OF THE CONSTITUTIONAL COURT FINALLY ABOLISHED CAPITAL PUNISHMENT, CALLING IT CRUEL, ARBITRARY AND INCOMPATIBLE WITH THE RIGHT TO LIFE.

BEHIND THE STORY: SOURCES AND SKETCHES

CHAPTER 3: COME GALLOWS GRIM

Entering the world of the Rand Revolt for the first time can be a bewildering experience. It was a chaotic, life-or-death drama, which a century later has a cinematic, almost fictional quality. White workers rose up to overthrow the ruling order. Evacuation leaflets fell from the sky. The government bombed its citizens. Rebel leaders shot themselves in the midst of defeat. Events such as these are hard to believe, even if we know they really happened.

Chapter 3 is not the story of the Rand Revolt itself. It is the story of *Rex v. Samuel Alfred Long*—one among hundreds of devastating sagas that played out on the Witwatersrand in 1922. In order to revive it, we needed to wade through a wealth of source material. The records for Long's two trials before the Special Criminal Court contain over a thousand pages of witness testimony, and among them we discovered an extraordinary exhibit of evidence: samples of the defendant's hair.

For every aspect of the story, there was also no shortage of visual inspiration, largely on account of *The Star* newspaper, which published a collection of photographs taken during the revolt. The most crucial source of all, however, was a top-secret letter written in November 1922 by Prince Arthur of Connaught to the Duke of Devonshire in England. In it, the Governor-General details the "difficulties" he faced, caught between "impartial" judges and "biased" politicians, in deciding whether Long's case warranted the prerogative of mercy.

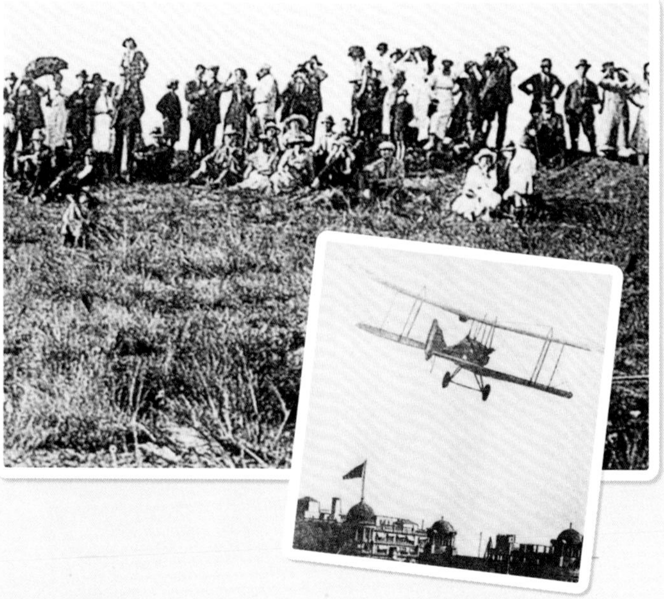

Below: Spectators watching the Battle of Fordsburg from Brixton Ridge, Johannesburg.

Overlay: One of the De Havilland aircraft that was used to drop leaflets and attack the rebel forces during the revolt.

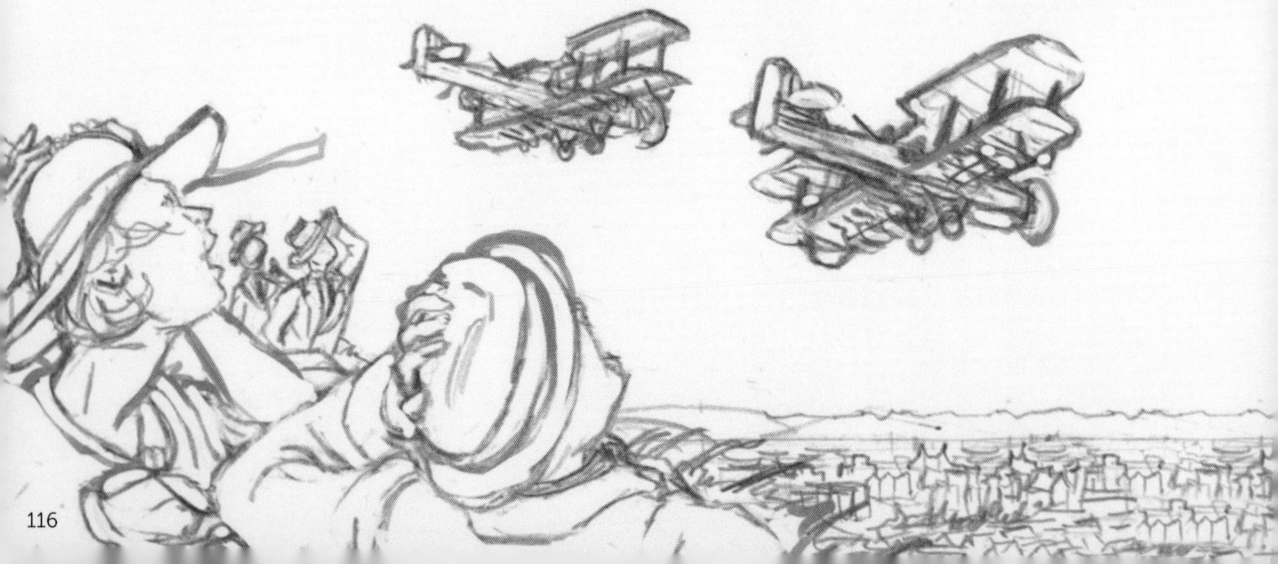

Sam "Taffy" Long, who fought on the front lines of the First World War prior to emigrating to South Africa, where he was executed in 1922.

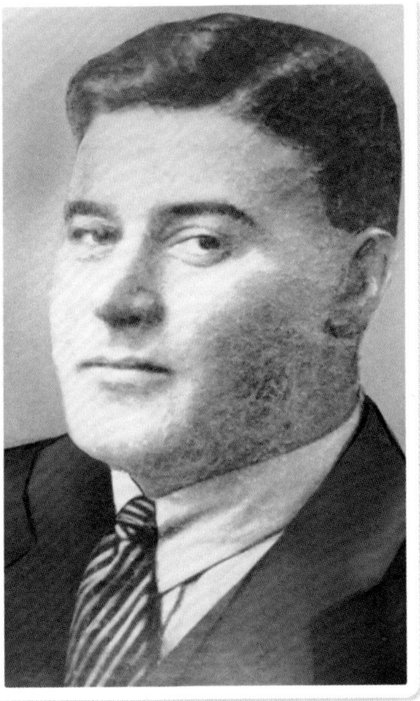

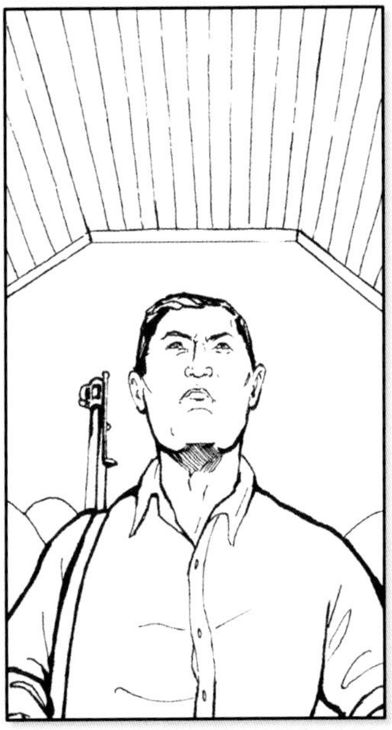

Maria Elizabeth "Ria" Long, whom Taffy married in July 1921, together with their infant son, Samuel Thomas.

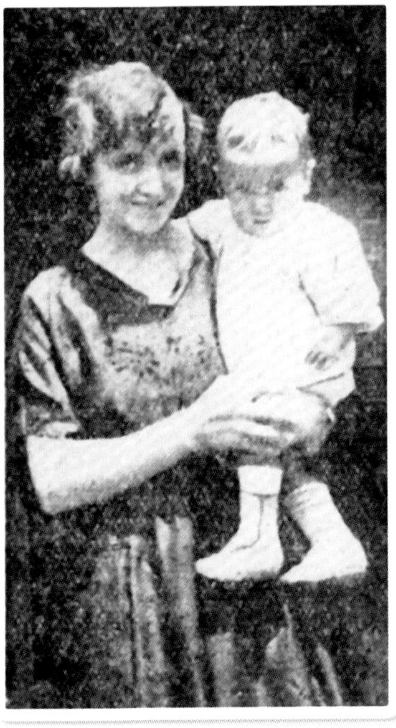

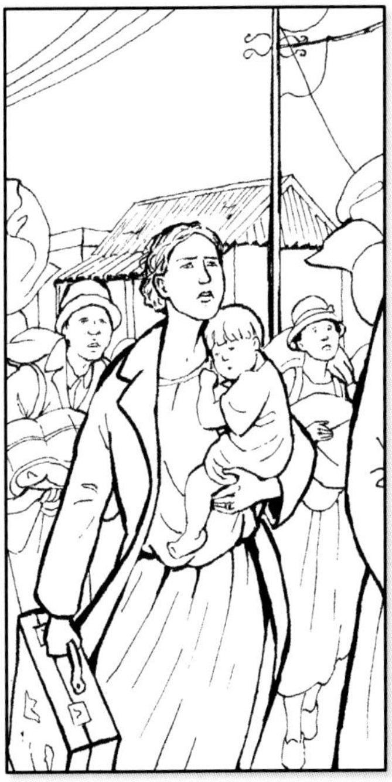

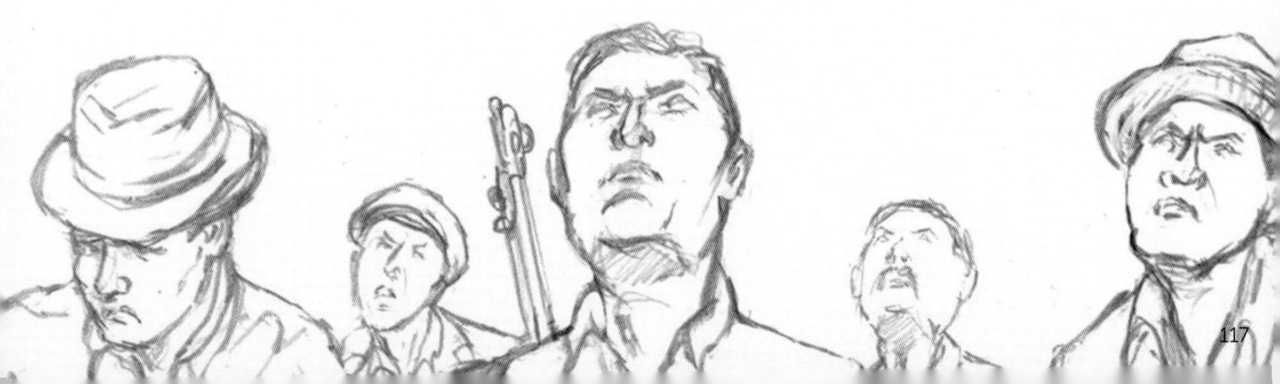

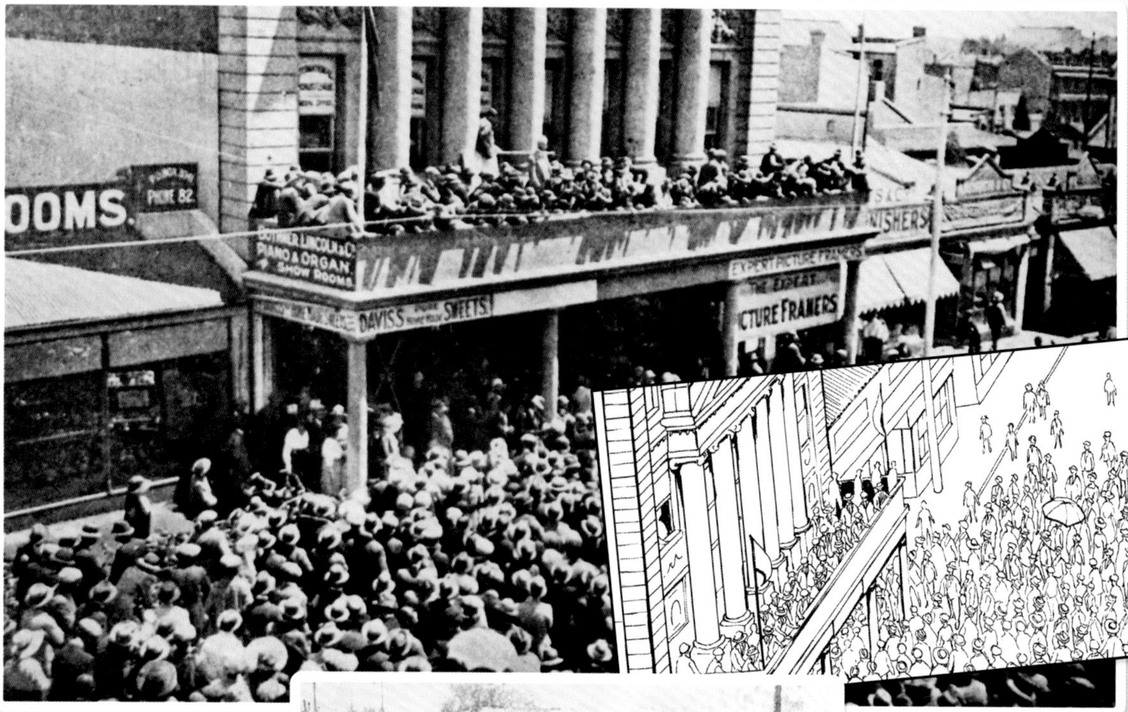
OOMS.
PHONE 82
PIANO & ORGAN
SHOW ROOMS
DAVISS
SWEETS
EXPERT PICTURE FRAMERS
CTURE FRAMERS

Above: Workers crowd outside the Johannesburg Trade Hall on 6 March, the day the general strike was announced.

Above, right: "Through February 1922 and into March, strike commandos were seen parading down the avenues of Rand towns..." horsemen of the Newlands Commando ride past a group of women supporters.

Right: The Fordsburg Police Station, destroyed by the rebels on 11 March 1922.

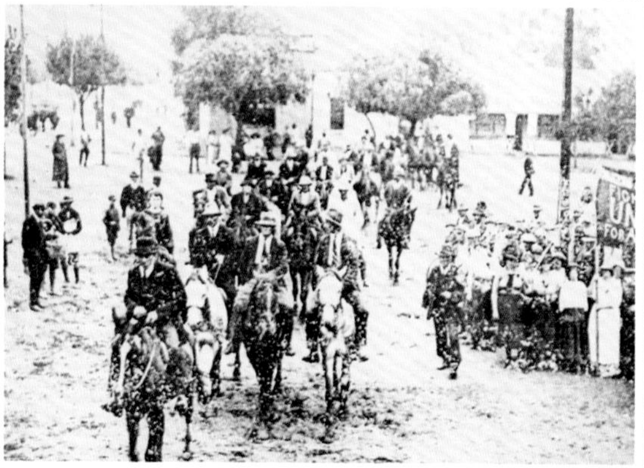

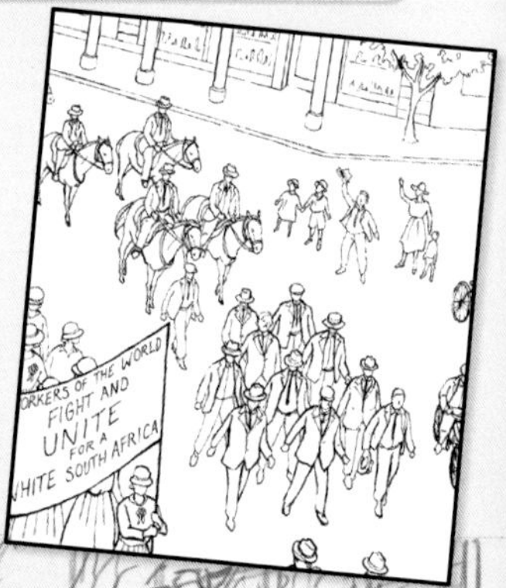
ORKERS OF THE WORLD
FIGHT AND
UNITE
FOR A
HITE SOUTH AFRICA

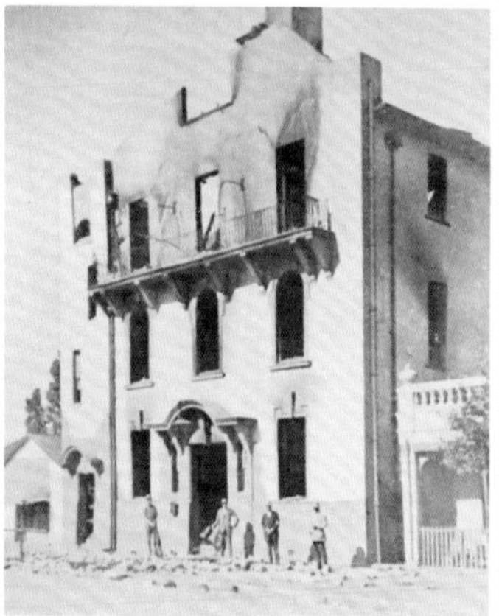

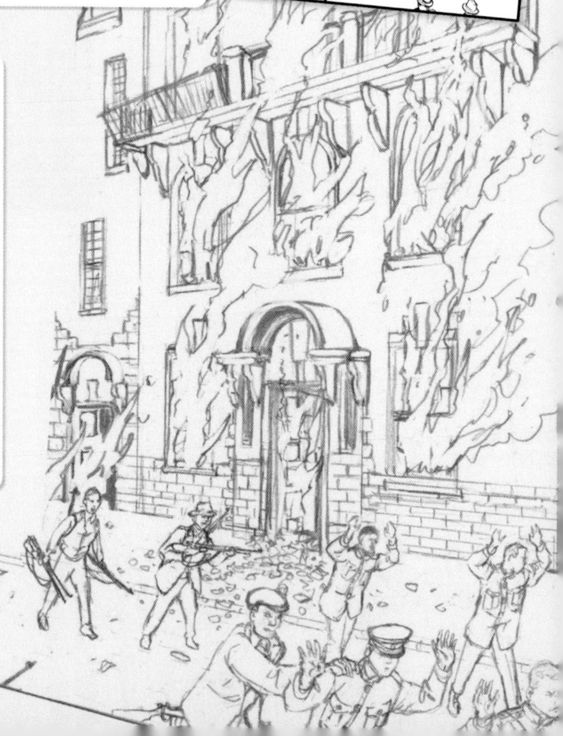

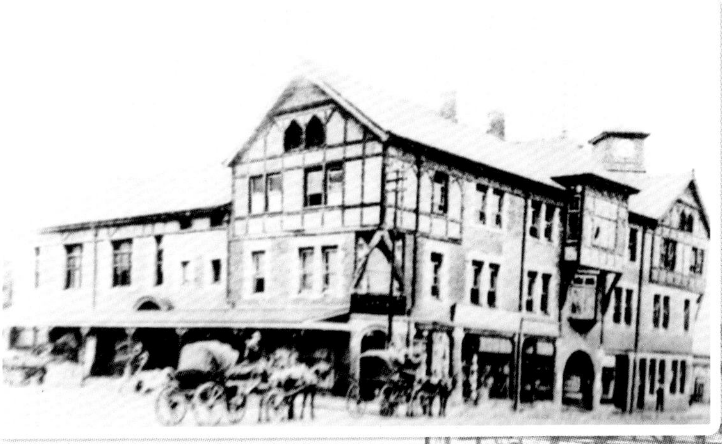

The Market Buildings, headquarters of the Fordsburg rebels under the leadership of Percy Fisher and Harry Spendiff.

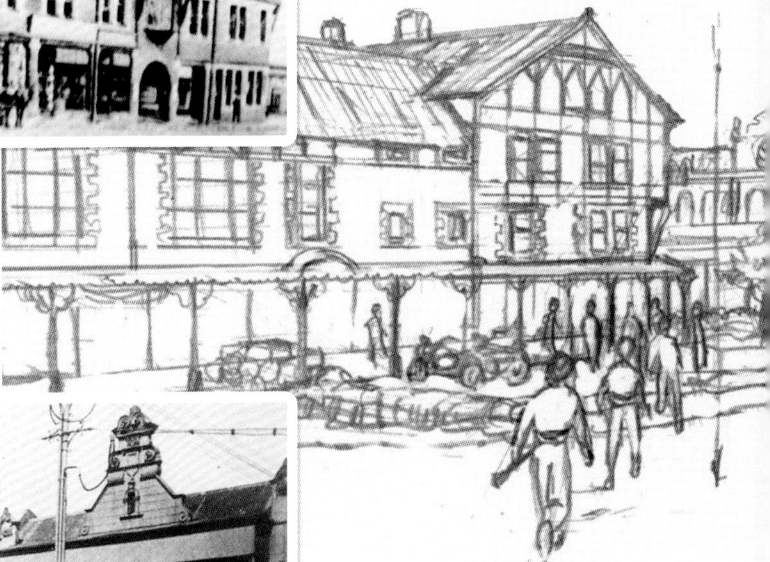

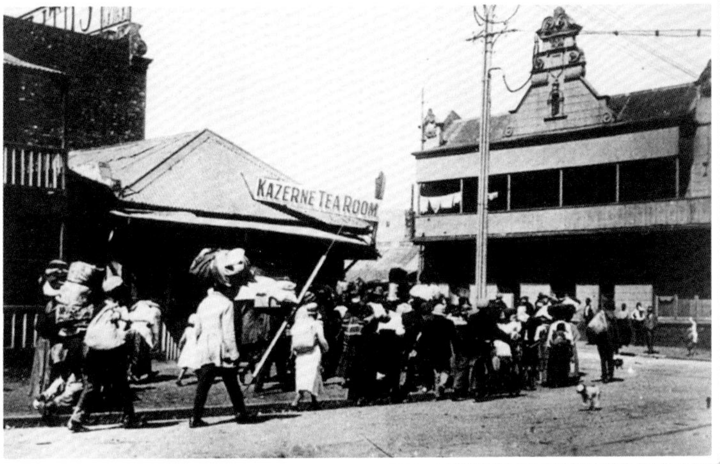
KAZERNE TEA ROOM

"All women, children, law-abiding citizens, and natives are requested to evacuate the suburb immediately..." residents flee Fordsburg in anticipation of the military offensive on the morning of 14 March 1922.

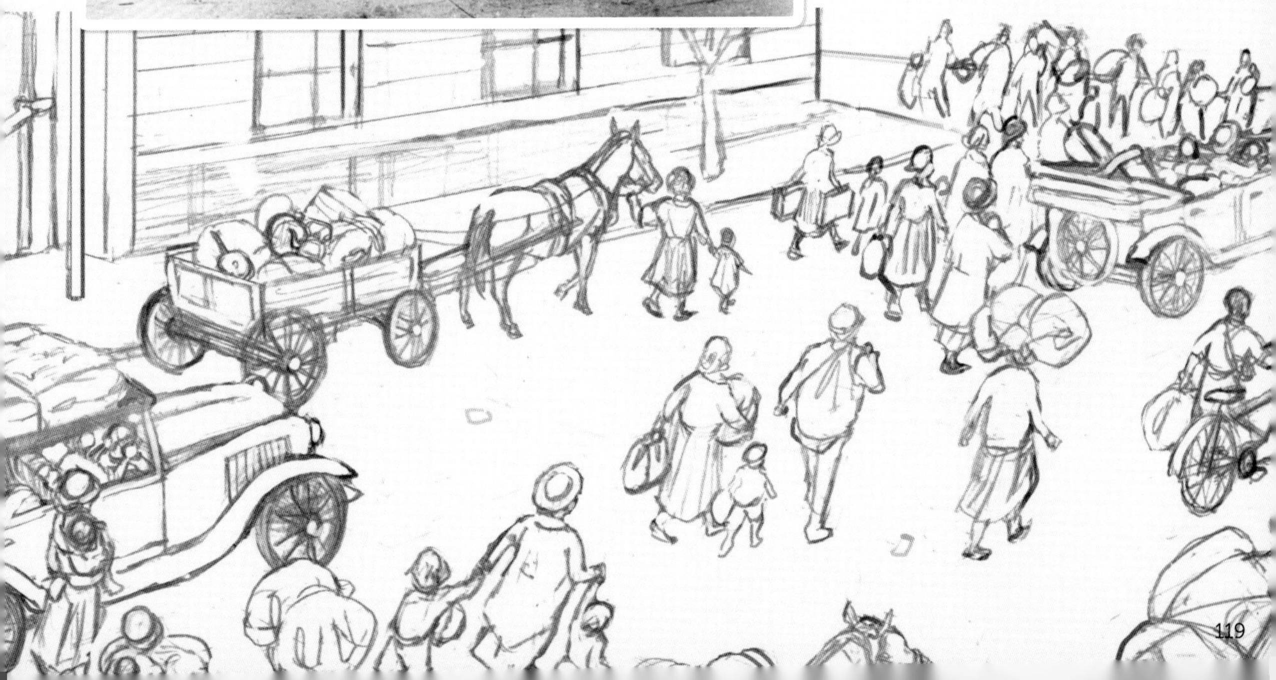

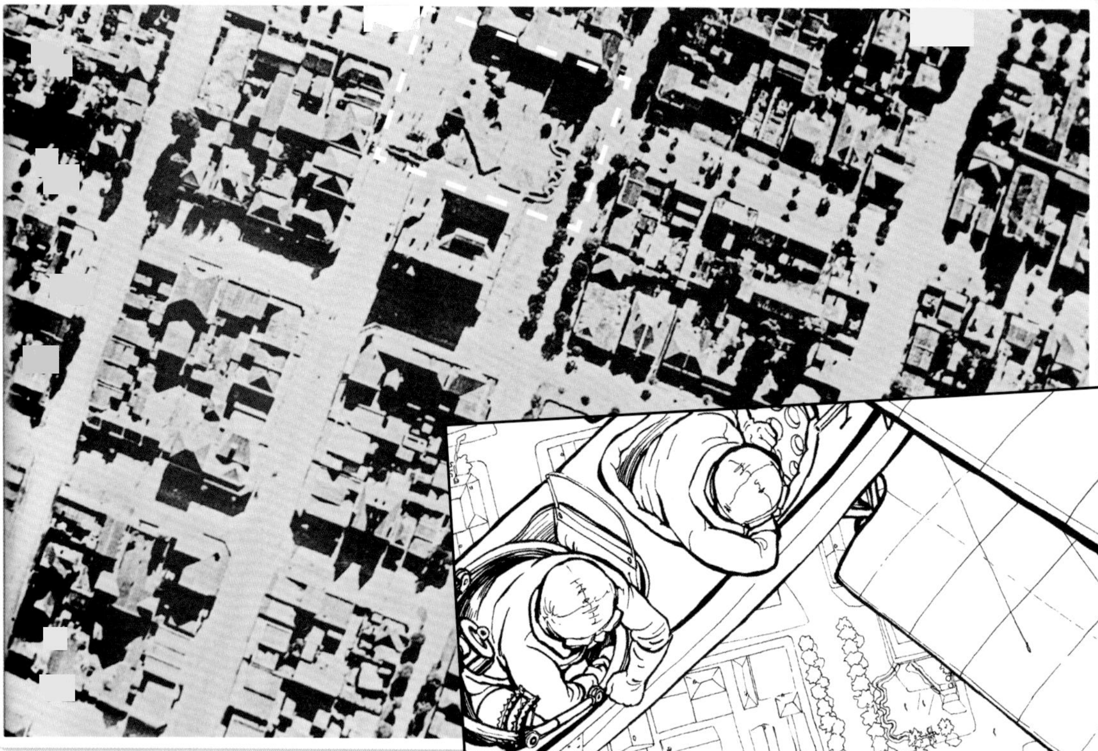

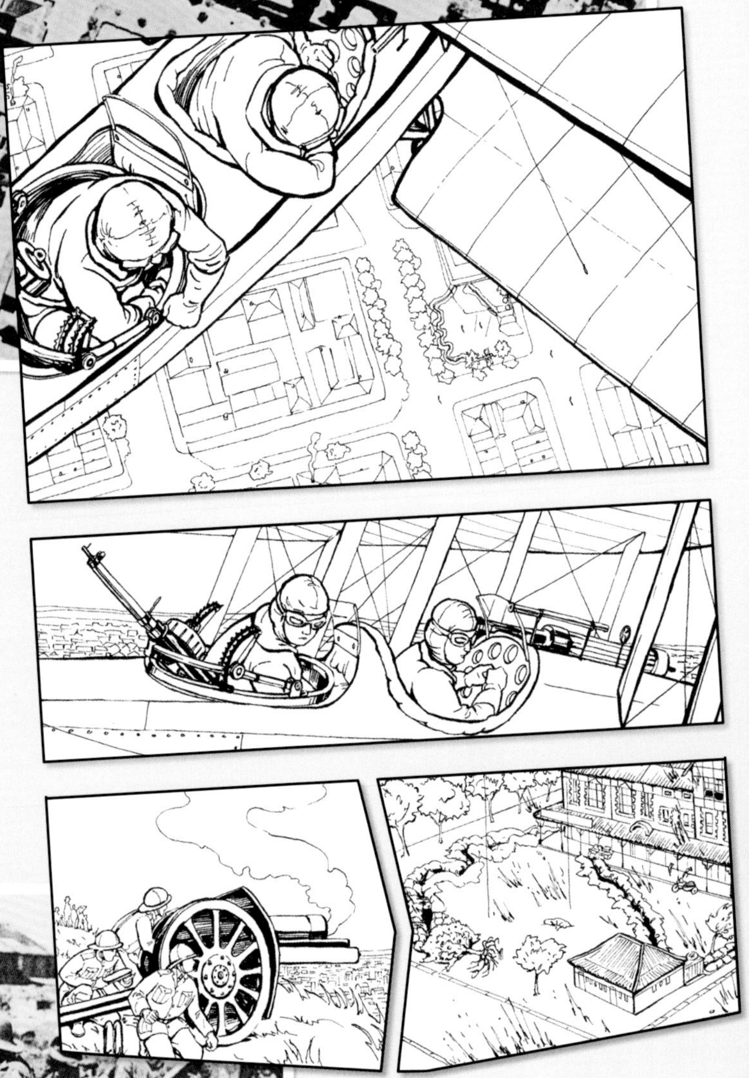

Above: A view over central Fordsburg during the revolt, taken from one of the fighter planes, with trenches and rebel forces visible outside the Market Buildings.

Below: After the aerial bombardment, the artillery shelled Market Square from Brixton Ridge.

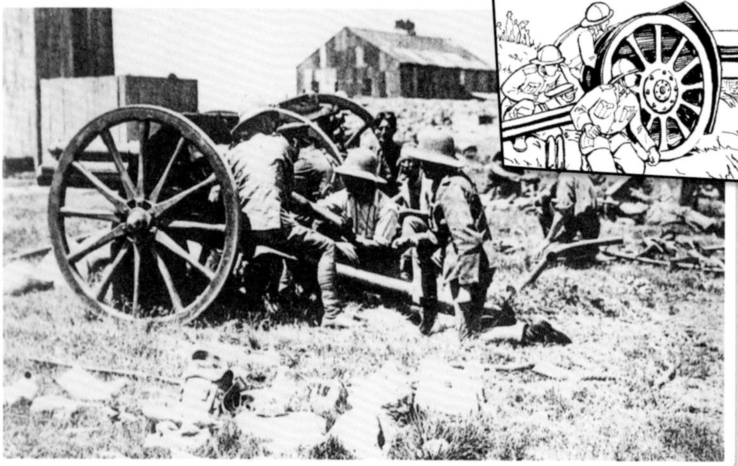

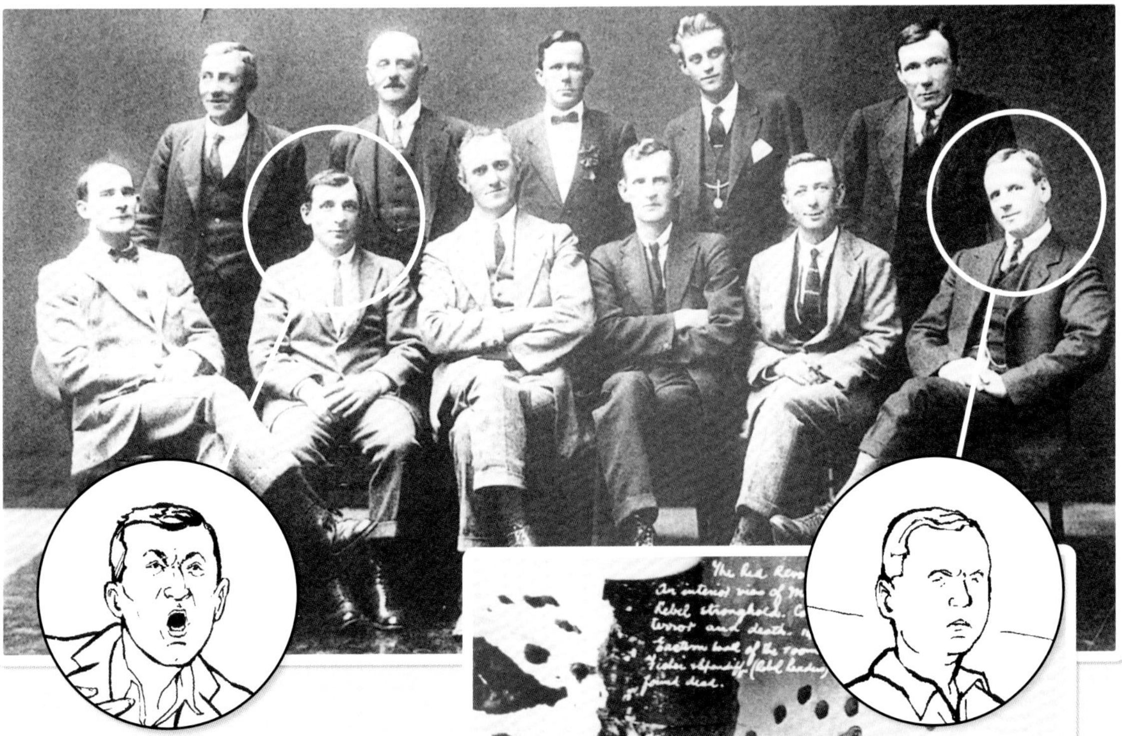

Percy Fisher

Harry Spendiff

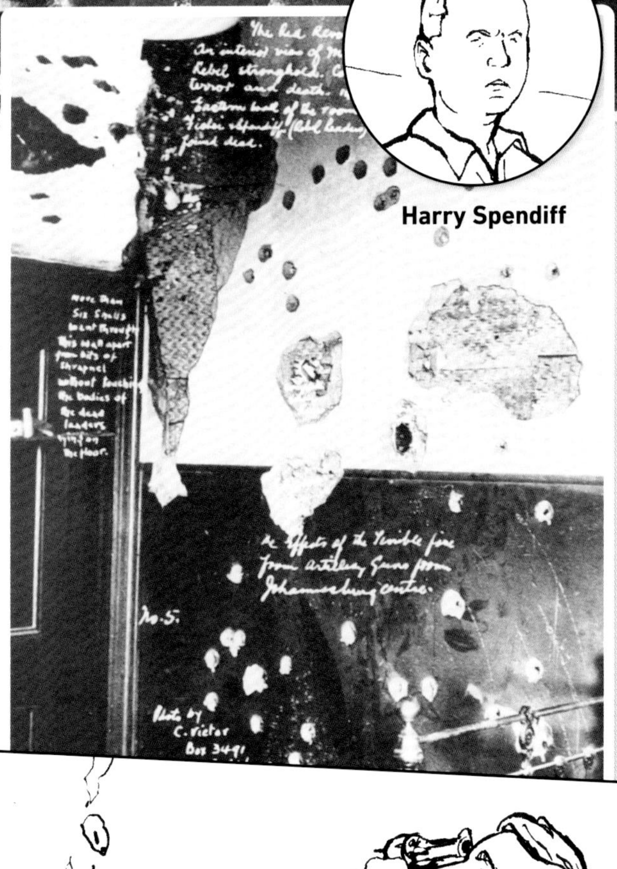
Rebel stronghold.
terror and death.
found dead.
more than Six Shells went through this wall apart from bits of shrapnel without touching the bodies of the dead leaders lying on the floor.
from Artillery Guns from Johannesburg centre.
No. 5.
Photo by C. Victor Box 3491.

Right: The upstairs room where Fisher and Spendiff, the figureheads of the rebellion, committed suicide.

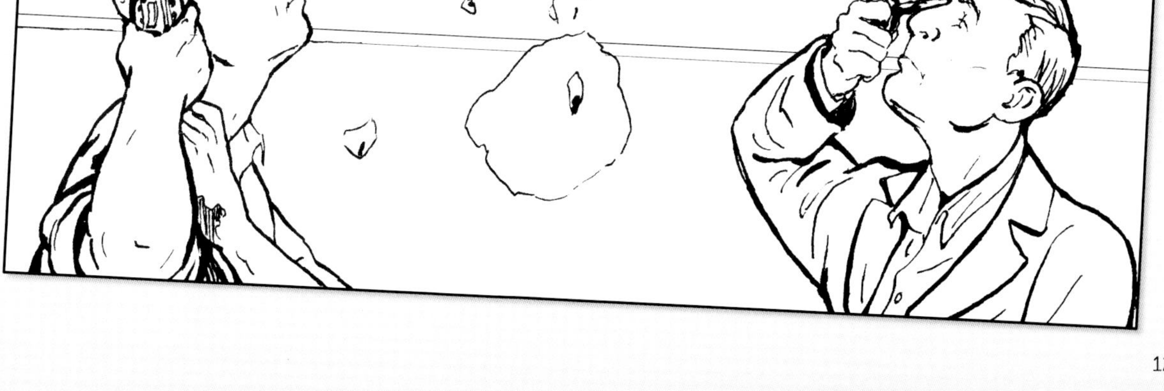

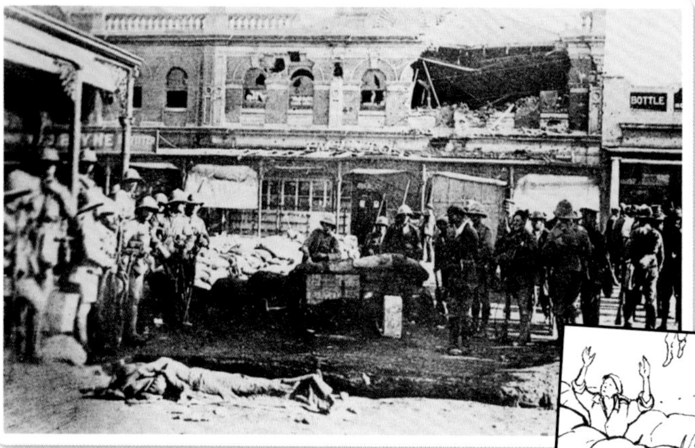
BOTTLE

Left and below, left: Fordsburg's Market Square after the revolt was suppressed.

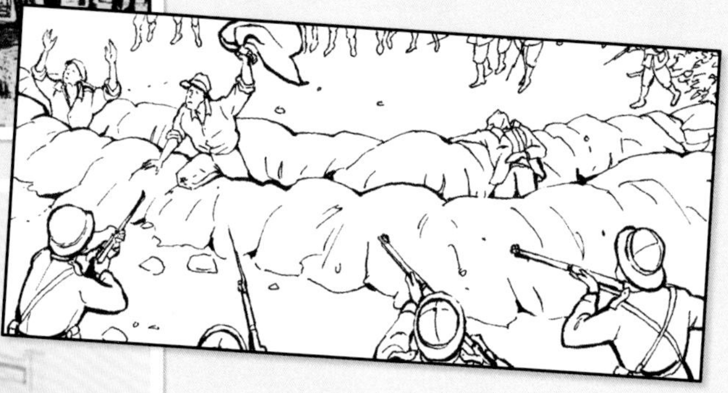

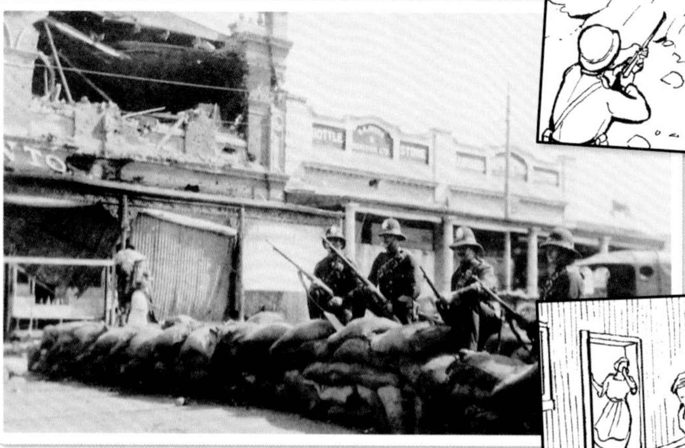

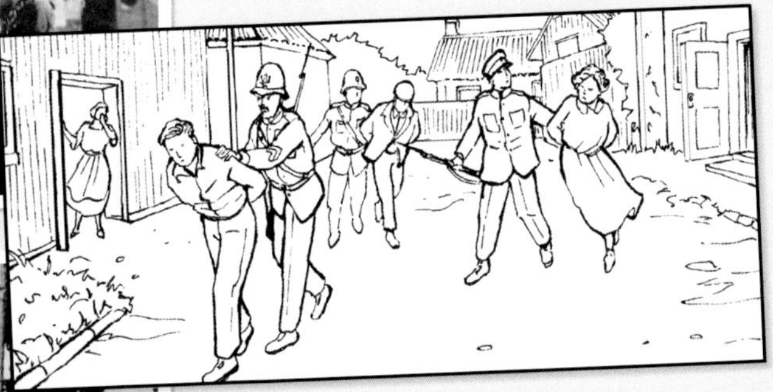

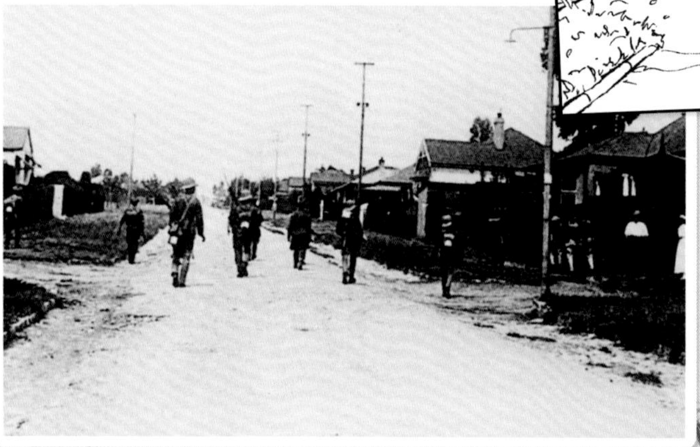

Left: Days after the revolt was crushed, police began to round up suspects from the white working-class suburbs.

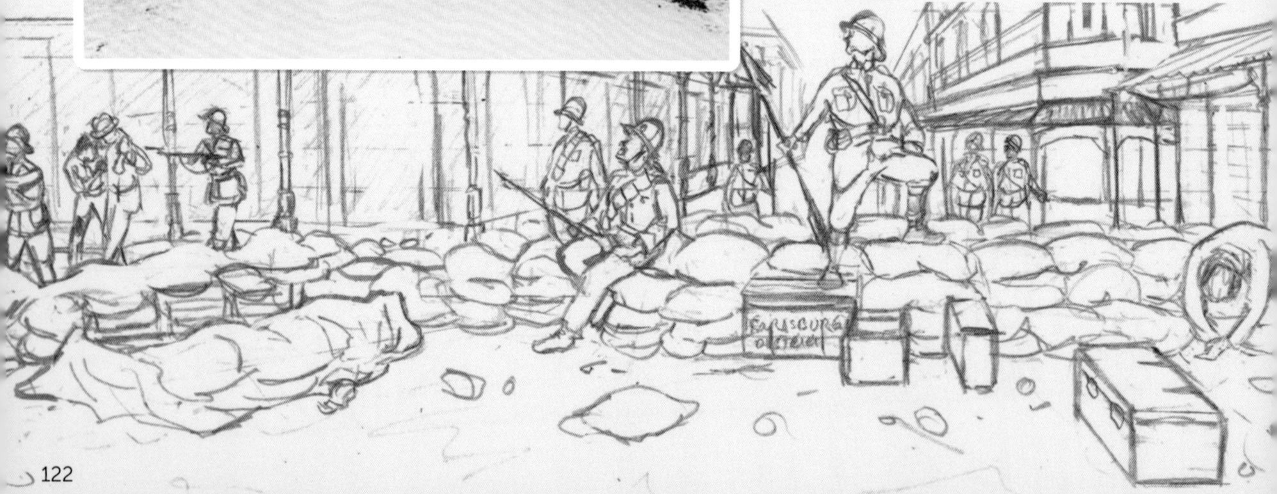

RAND DAILY MAIL, JOHANNESBURG, FRIDAY, MAY 19, 1922.

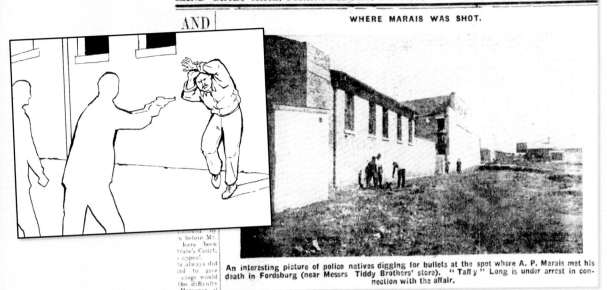

WHERE MARAIS WAS SHOT.

An interesting picture of police natives digging for bullets at the spot where A. P. Marais met his death in Fordsburg (near Messrs Tiddy Brothers' store). "Taffy" Long is under arrest in connection with the affair.

Above: Policemen search for evidence in a Fordsburg yard, "behind the Union Furnishers building," where the greengrocer Alwyn Marais was executed.

Below: "There is no difference in the color of his hair now from what it was when I first knew him. This is the photograph when we got married. He always kept his hair fairly long and bushy…" Exhibit "T," submitted as part of Long's defense during his wife Ria's cross-examination.

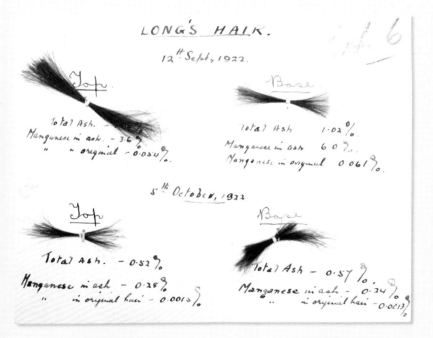

LONG'S HAIR.
12th Sept, 1922.
Top
Total Ash.
Manganese in ash. - 3.6%
" " original - 0.034%.
Base
Total Ash 1.02%
Manganese in ash 6.0%.
Manganese in original 0.061%.
5th October, 1922
Top
Total Ash. - 0.52%
Manganese in ash - 0.28%
" in original hair - 0.0013%
Base
Total Ash - 0.57%.
Manganese in ash - 0.24%
" in original hair - 0.0013%

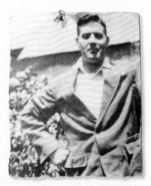

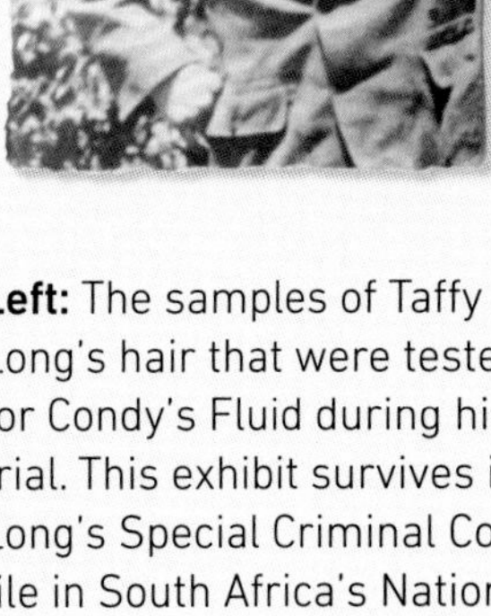

Left: The samples of Taffy Long's hair that were tested for Condy's Fluid during his trial. This exhibit survives in Long's Special Criminal Court file in South Africa's National Archives.

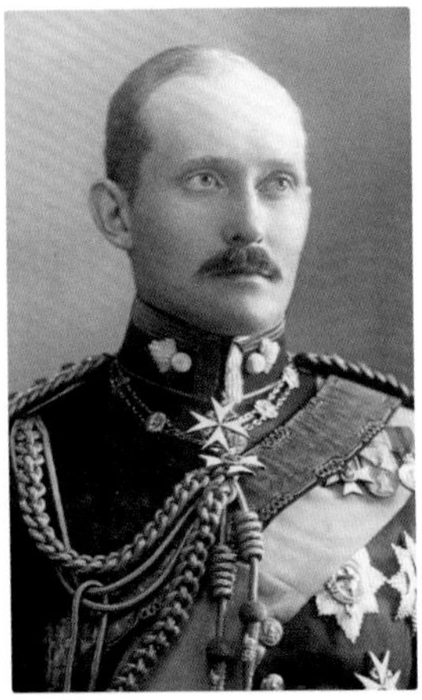

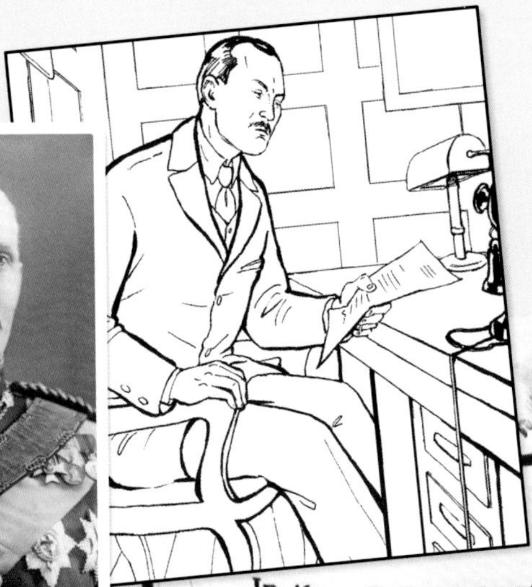

Prince Arthur of Connaught (*left*), South Africa's Governor-General from 1920-1924, who ultimately chose not to exercise the prerogative of mercy in the case of Taffy Long (*below*).

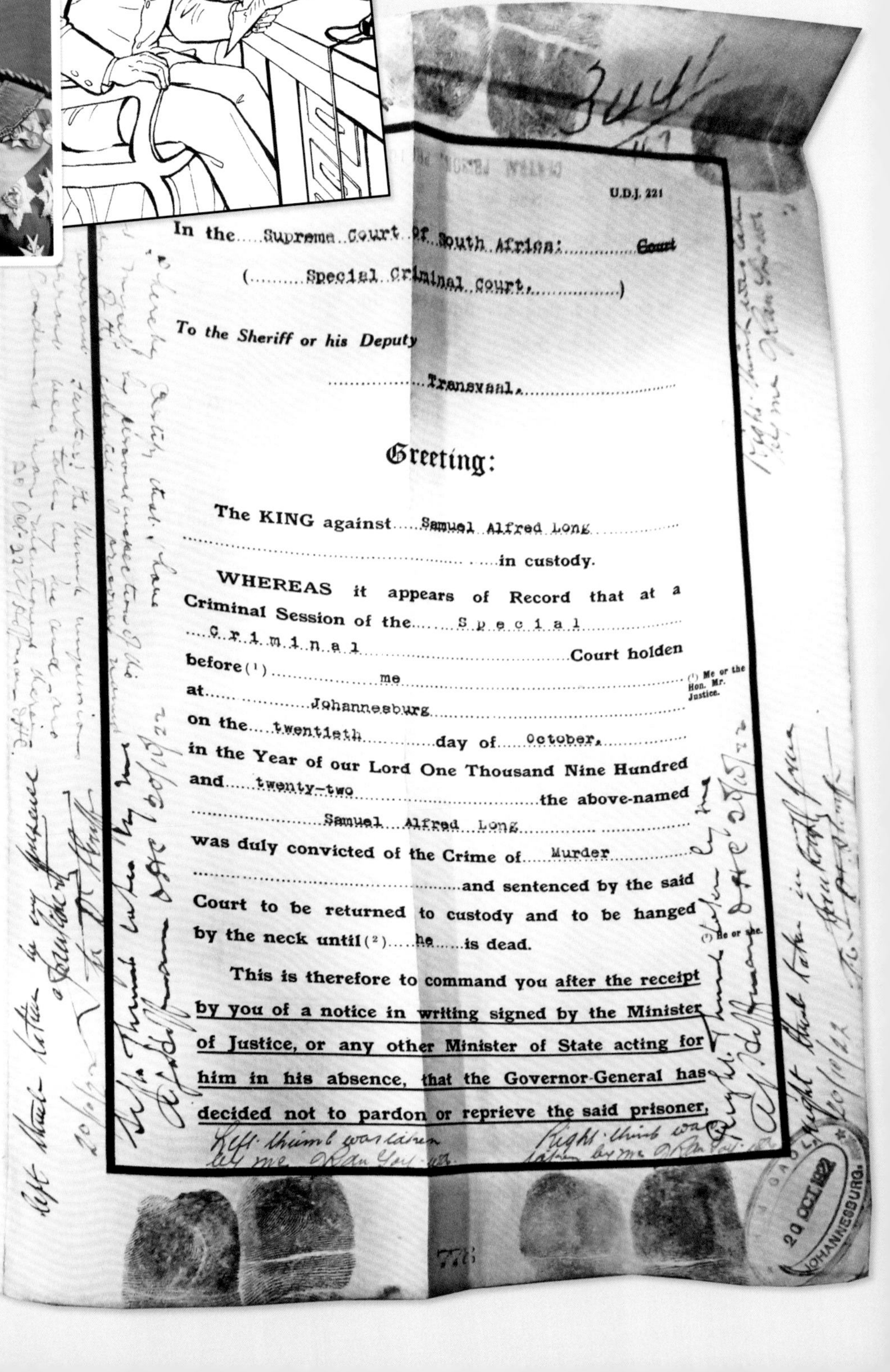

U.D.J. 221

In the Supreme Court of South Africa: ~~Court~~

(Special Criminal Court.)

To the Sheriff or his Deputy

Transvaal.

Greeting:

The KING against Samuel Alfred Long in custody.

WHEREAS it appears of Record that at a Criminal Session of the Special Criminal Court holden before(1) me at Johannesburg on the twentieth day of October, in the Year of our Lord One Thousand Nine Hundred and twenty-two the above-named Samuel Alfred Long was duly convicted of the Crime of Murder and sentenced by the said Court to be returned to custody and to be hanged by the neck until(2) he is dead.

This is therefore to command you after the receipt by you of a notice in writing signed by the Minister of Justice, or any other Minister of State acting for him in his absence, that the Governor-General has decided not to pardon or reprieve the said prisoner,

(1) Me or the Hon. Mr. Justice.

(2) He or she.

Left thumb was taken by me

Right thumb was taken by me

20 OCT 1922 JOHANNESBURG.

776

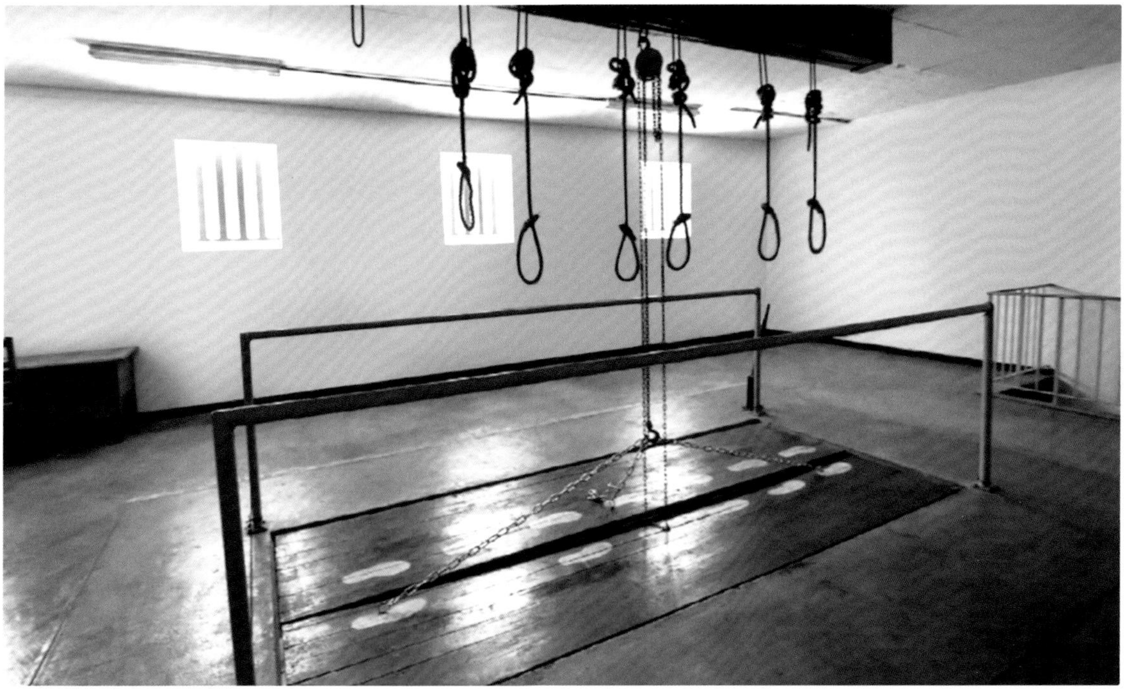

Above: The gallows at Kgosi Mampuru II Correctional Facility (formerly Pretoria Central Prison), now a public museum, where Taffy Long was hanged on 17 November 1922.

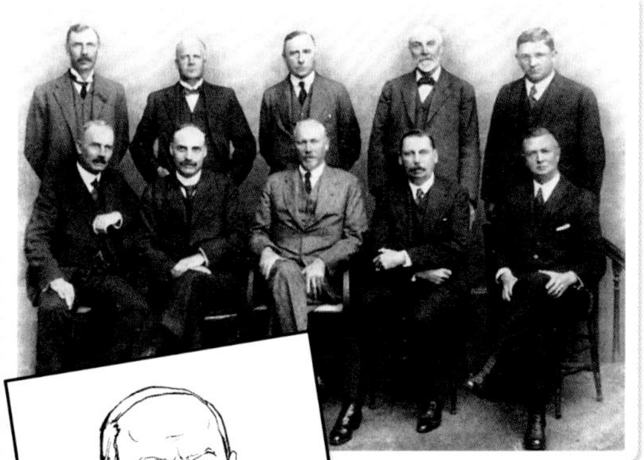

Left: The third cabinet of the Union of South Africa, and the first under Prime Minister Jan Smuts (*front, center*). During a meeting in late 1922, the majority voted in favor of Taffy Long's execution. Over the weeks building up to it, the Minister of Justice Nicolaas de Wet (*back, far left*) had argued vehemently against the prerogative of mercy.

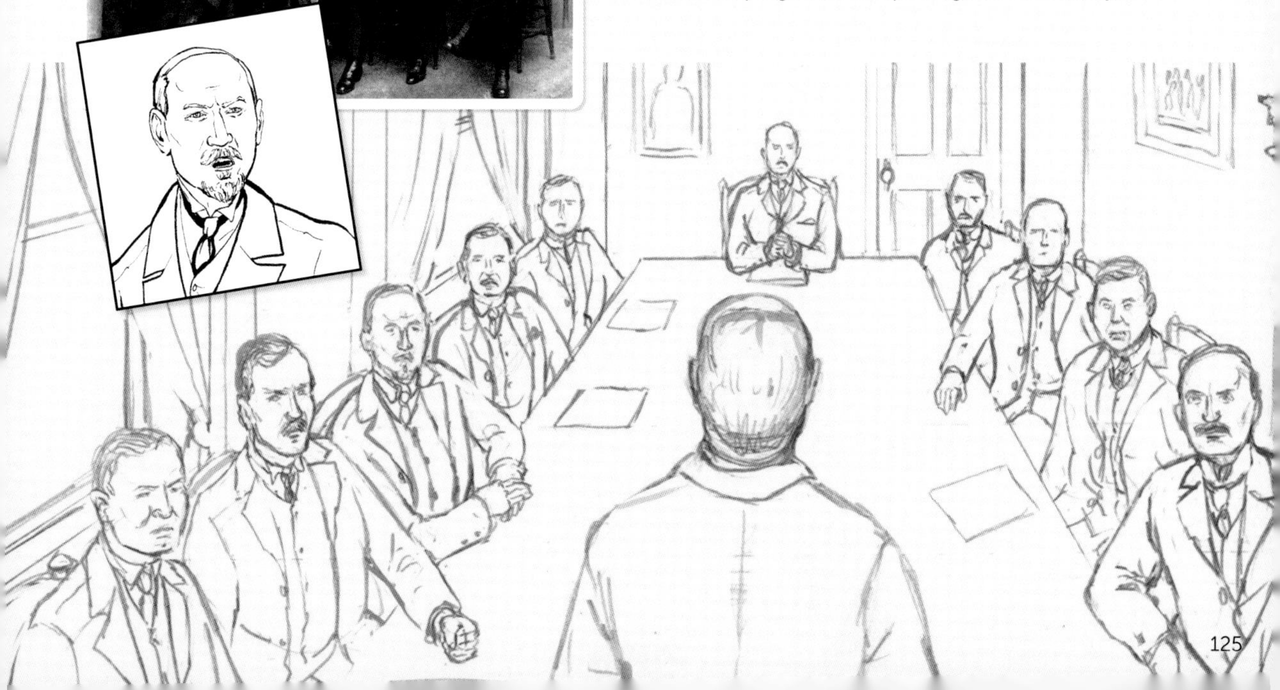

Chapter 4

THE WIDOW OF MARABASTAD

Illustrated by Dada Khanyisa

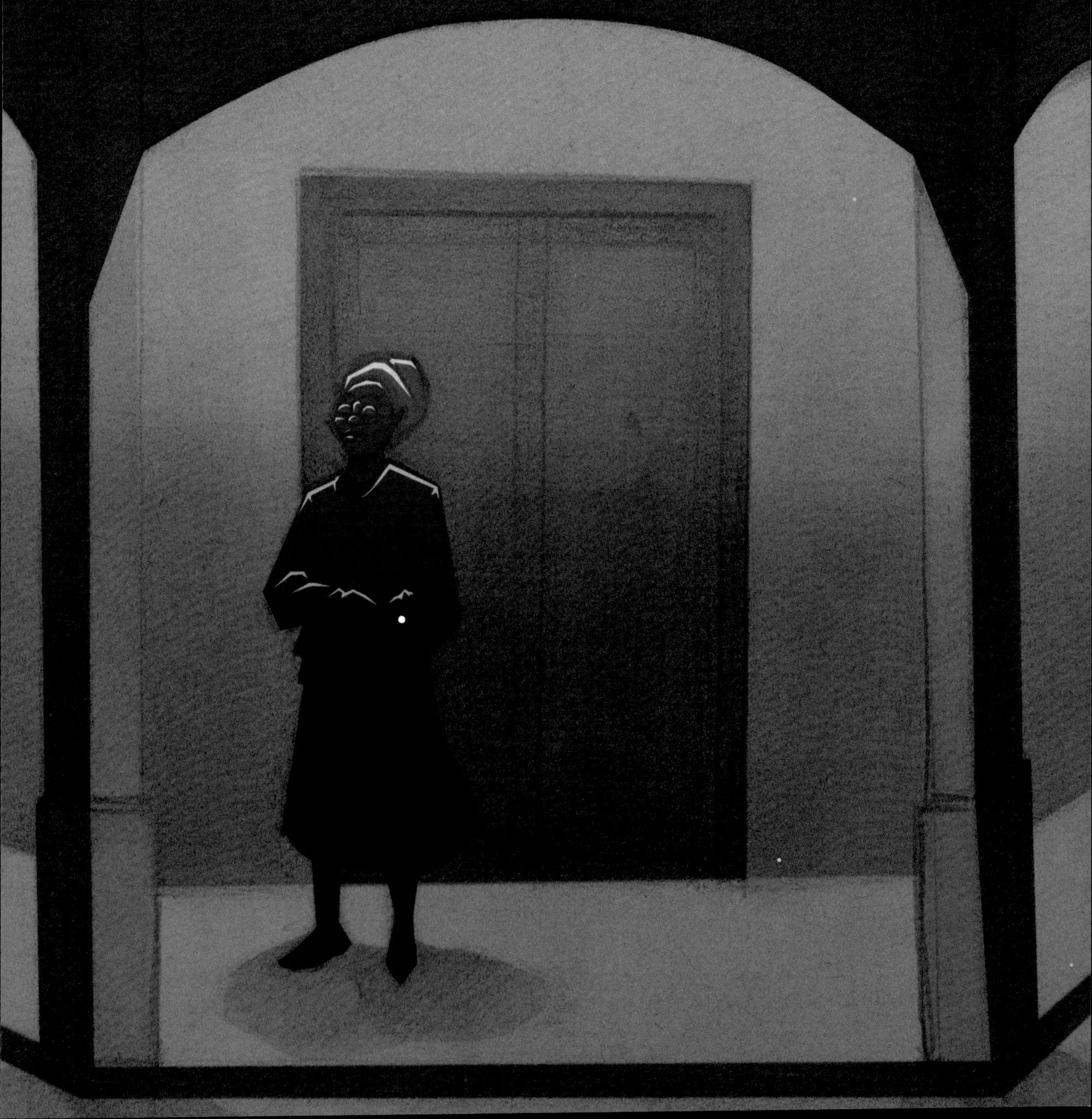

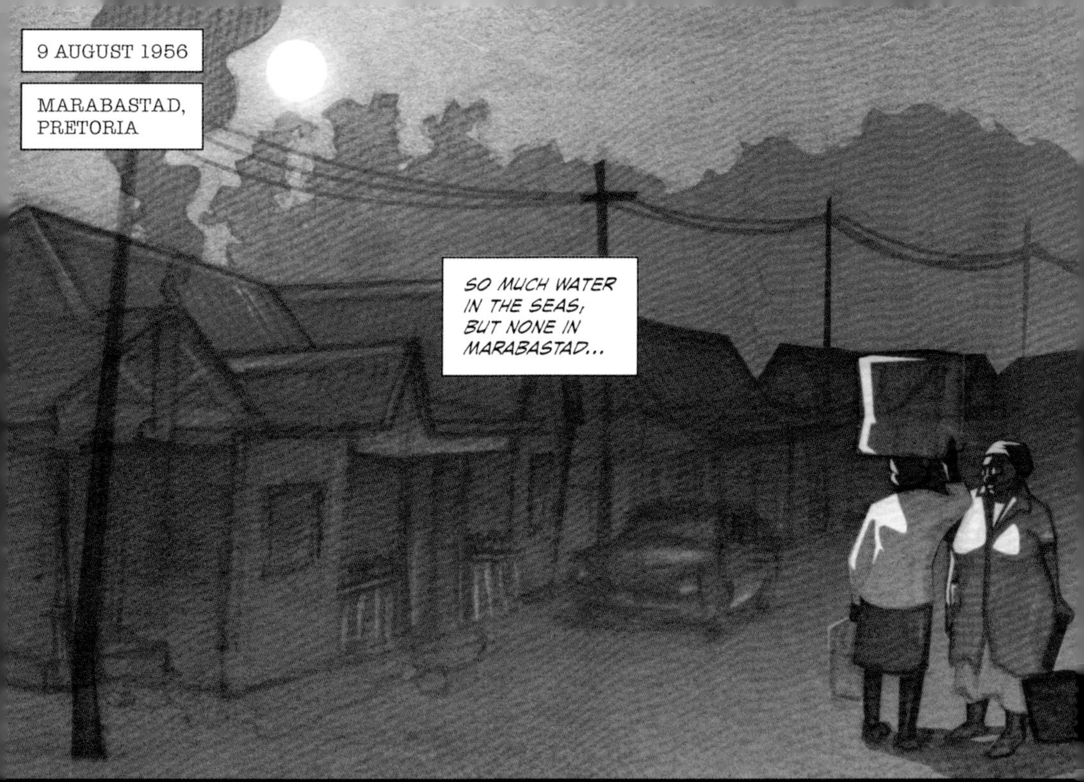
9 AUGUST 1956
MARABASTAD, PRETORIA
SO MUCH WATER IN THE SEAS, BUT NONE IN MARABASTAD...

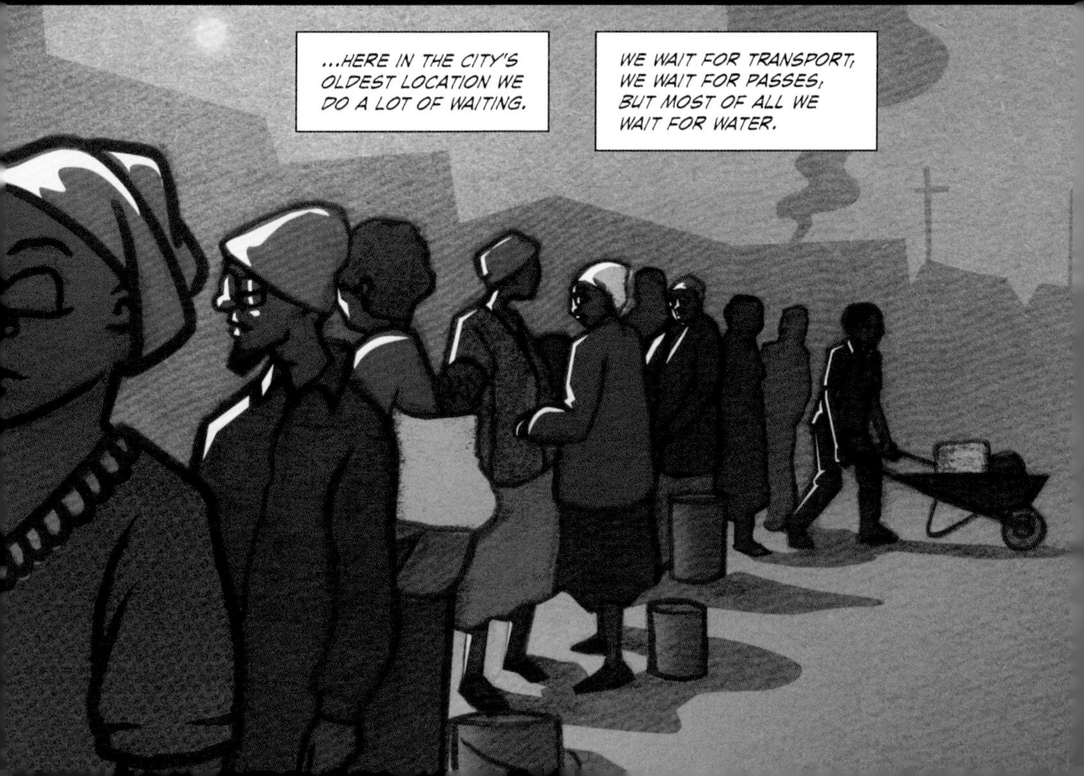
...HERE IN THE CITY'S OLDEST LOCATION WE DO A LOT OF WAITING.
WE WAIT FOR TRANSPORT, WE WAIT FOR PASSES, BUT MOST OF ALL WE WAIT FOR WATER.

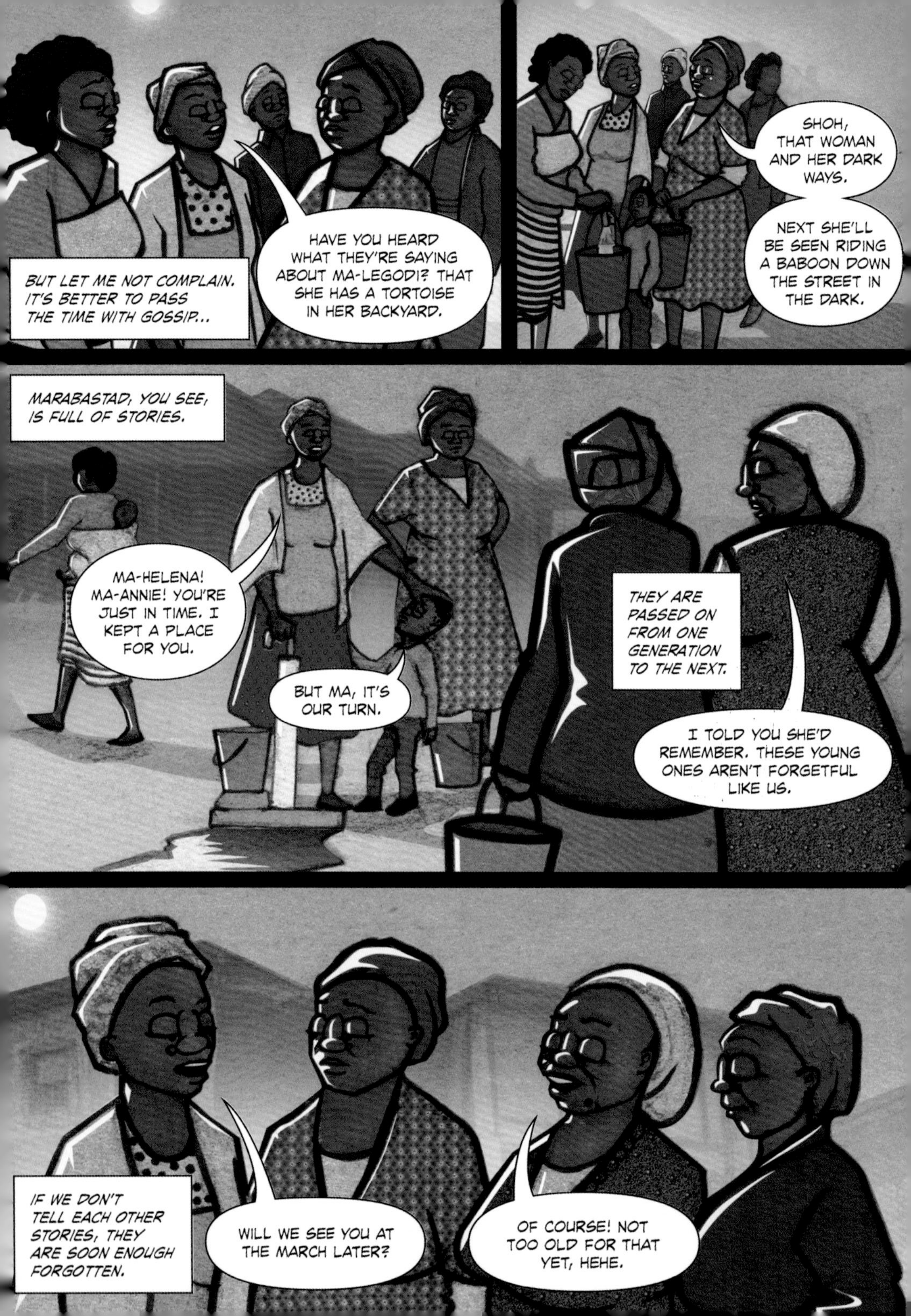
BUT LET ME NOT COMPLAIN. IT'S BETTER TO PASS THE TIME WITH GOSSIP...
HAVE YOU HEARD WHAT THEY'RE SAYING ABOUT MA-LEGODI? THAT SHE HAS A TORTOISE IN HER BACKYARD.
SHOH, THAT WOMAN AND HER DARK WAYS.
NEXT SHE'LL BE SEEN RIDING A BABOON DOWN THE STREET IN THE DARK.
MARABASTAD, YOU SEE, IS FULL OF STORIES.
MA-HELENA! MA-ANNIE! YOU'RE JUST IN TIME. I KEPT A PLACE FOR YOU.
BUT MA, IT'S OUR TURN.
THEY ARE PASSED ON FROM ONE GENERATION TO THE NEXT.
I TOLD YOU SHE'D REMEMBER. THESE YOUNG ONES AREN'T FORGETFUL LIKE US.
IF WE DON'T TELL EACH OTHER STORIES, THEY ARE SOON ENOUGH FORGOTTEN.
WILL WE SEE YOU AT THE MARCH LATER?
OF COURSE! NOT TOO OLD FOR THAT YET, HEHE.

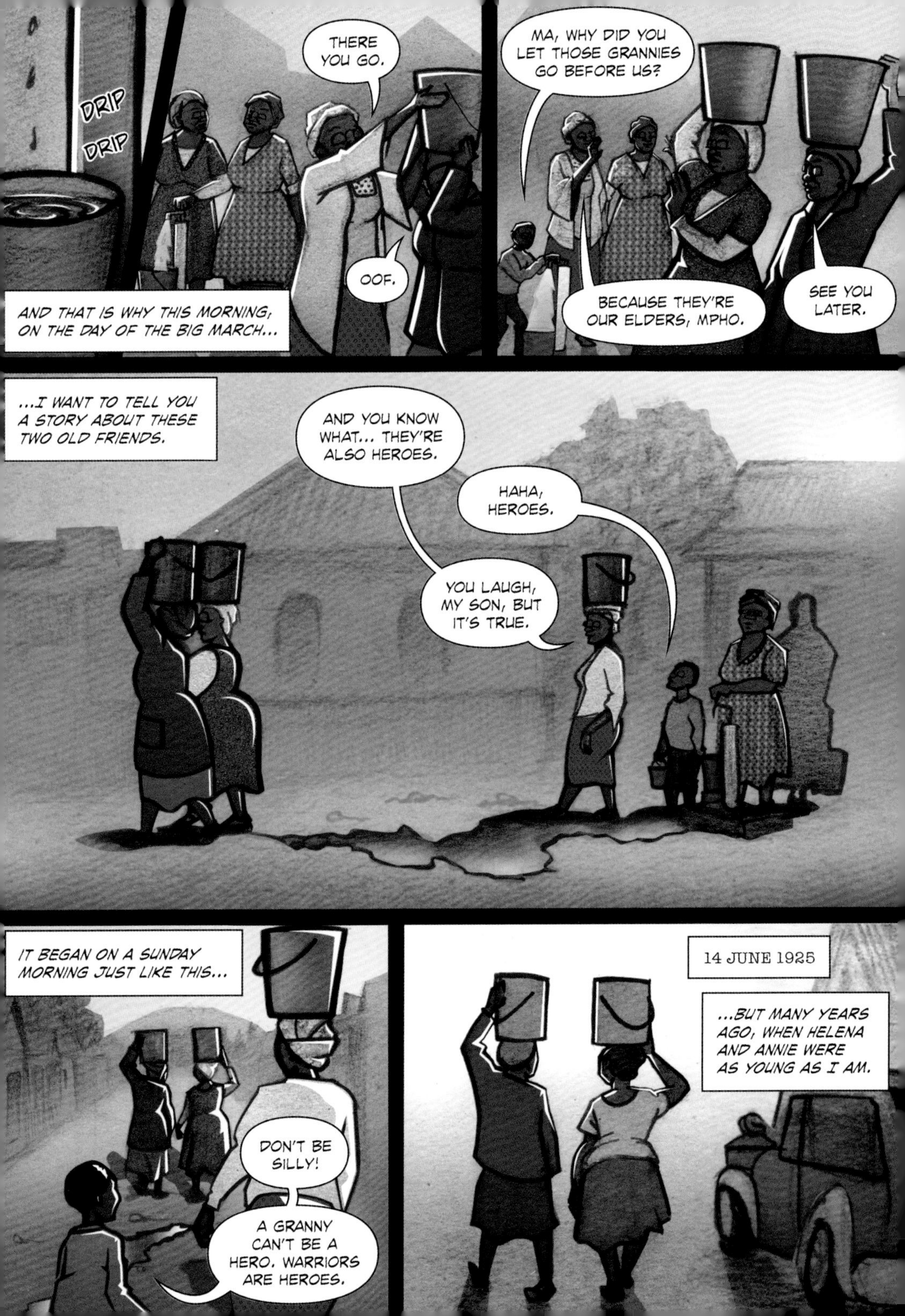
DRIP
DRIP
THERE YOU GO.
OOF.
AND THAT IS WHY THIS MORNING, ON THE DAY OF THE BIG MARCH...
MA, WHY DID YOU LET THOSE GRANNIES GO BEFORE US?
BECAUSE THEY'RE OUR ELDERS, MPHO.
SEE YOU LATER.
...I WANT TO TELL YOU A STORY ABOUT THESE TWO OLD FRIENDS.
AND YOU KNOW WHAT... THEY'RE ALSO HEROES.
HAHA, HEROES.
YOU LAUGH, MY SON, BUT IT'S TRUE.
IT BEGAN ON A SUNDAY MORNING JUST LIKE THIS...
DON'T BE SILLY!
A GRANNY CAN'T BE A HERO. WARRIORS ARE HEROES.
14 JUNE 1925
...BUT MANY YEARS AGO, WHEN HELENA AND ANNIE WERE AS YOUNG AS I AM.

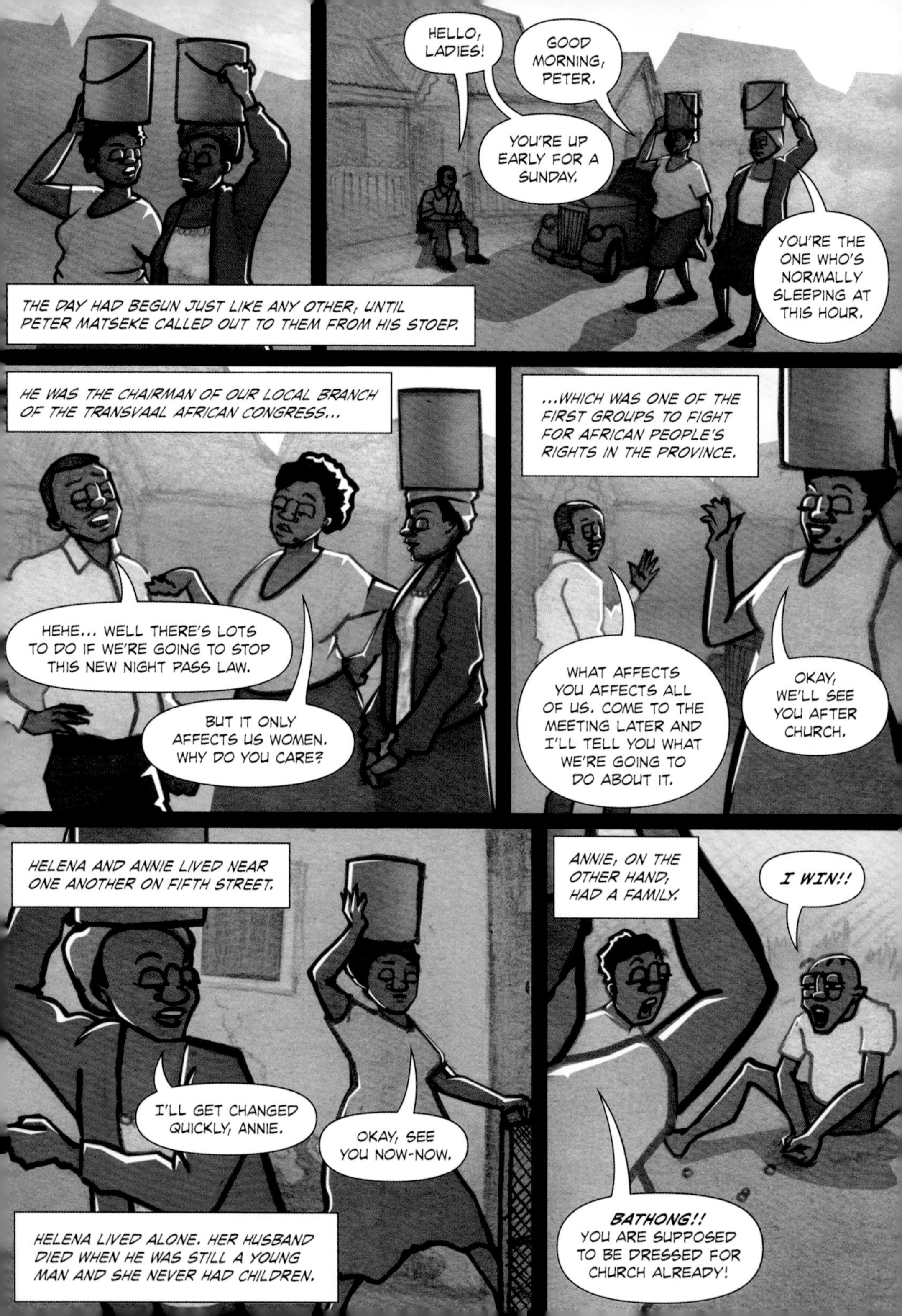
THE DAY HAD BEGUN JUST LIKE ANY OTHER, UNTIL PETER MATSEKE CALLED OUT TO THEM FROM HIS STOEP.
HELLO, LADIES!
GOOD MORNING, PETER.
YOU'RE UP EARLY FOR A SUNDAY.
YOU'RE THE ONE WHO'S NORMALLY SLEEPING AT THIS HOUR.
HE WAS THE CHAIRMAN OF OUR LOCAL BRANCH OF THE TRANSVAAL AFRICAN CONGRESS...
HEHE... WELL THERE'S LOTS TO DO IF WE'RE GOING TO STOP THIS NEW NIGHT PASS LAW.
BUT IT ONLY AFFECTS US WOMEN. WHY DO YOU CARE?
...WHICH WAS ONE OF THE FIRST GROUPS TO FIGHT FOR AFRICAN PEOPLE'S RIGHTS IN THE PROVINCE.
WHAT AFFECTS YOU AFFECTS ALL OF US. COME TO THE MEETING LATER AND I'LL TELL YOU WHAT WE'RE GOING TO DO ABOUT IT.
OKAY, WE'LL SEE YOU AFTER CHURCH.
HELENA AND ANNIE LIVED NEAR ONE ANOTHER ON FIFTH STREET.
I'LL GET CHANGED QUICKLY, ANNIE.
OKAY, SEE YOU NOW-NOW.
HELENA LIVED ALONE. HER HUSBAND DIED WHEN HE WAS STILL A YOUNG MAN AND SHE NEVER HAD CHILDREN.
ANNIE, ON THE OTHER HAND, HAD A FAMILY.
I WIN!!
BATHONG!! YOU ARE SUPPOSED TO BE DRESSED FOR CHURCH ALREADY!

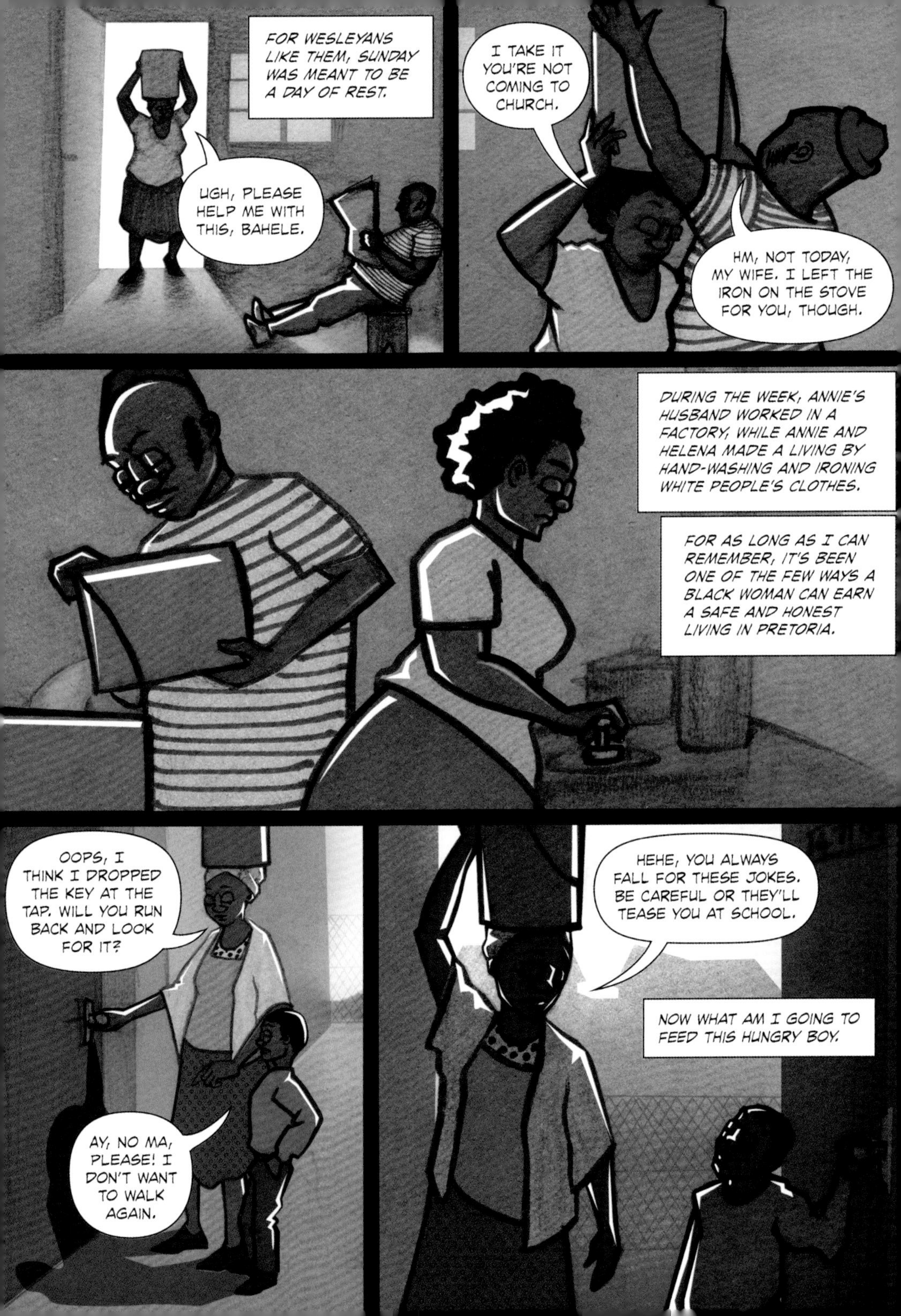
FOR WESLEYANS LIKE THEM, SUNDAY WAS MEANT TO BE A DAY OF REST.
UGH, PLEASE HELP ME WITH THIS, BAHELE.
I TAKE IT YOU'RE NOT COMING TO CHURCH.
HM, NOT TODAY, MY WIFE. I LEFT THE IRON ON THE STOVE FOR YOU, THOUGH.
DURING THE WEEK, ANNIE'S HUSBAND WORKED IN A FACTORY, WHILE ANNIE AND HELENA MADE A LIVING BY HAND-WASHING AND IRONING WHITE PEOPLE'S CLOTHES.
FOR AS LONG AS I CAN REMEMBER, IT'S BEEN ONE OF THE FEW WAYS A BLACK WOMAN CAN EARN A SAFE AND HONEST LIVING IN PRETORIA.
OOPS, I THINK I DROPPED THE KEY AT THE TAP. WILL YOU RUN BACK AND LOOK FOR IT?
AY, NO MA, PLEASE! I DON'T WANT TO WALK AGAIN.
HEHE, YOU ALWAYS FALL FOR THESE JOKES. BE CAREFUL OR THEY'LL TEASE YOU AT SCHOOL.
NOW WHAT AM I GOING TO FEED THIS HUNGRY BOY.

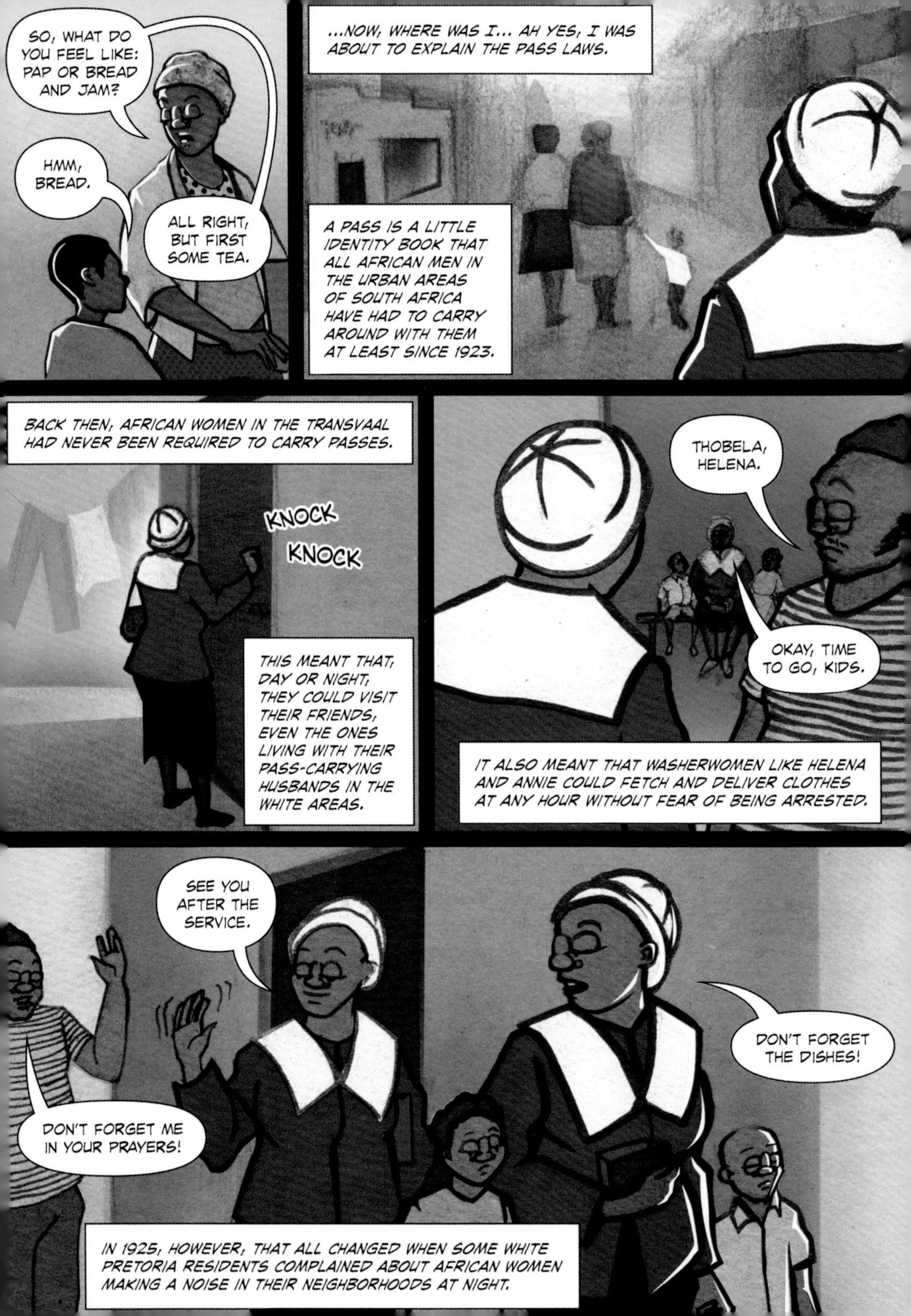
SO, WHAT DO YOU FEEL LIKE: PAP OR BREAD AND JAM?
HMM, BREAD.
ALL RIGHT, BUT FIRST SOME TEA.
...NOW, WHERE WAS I... AH YES, I WAS ABOUT TO EXPLAIN THE PASS LAWS.
A PASS IS A LITTLE IDENTITY BOOK THAT ALL AFRICAN MEN IN THE URBAN AREAS OF SOUTH AFRICA HAVE HAD TO CARRY AROUND WITH THEM AT LEAST SINCE 1923.
BACK THEN, AFRICAN WOMEN IN THE TRANSVAAL HAD NEVER BEEN REQUIRED TO CARRY PASSES.
KNOCK
KNOCK
THIS MEANT THAT, DAY OR NIGHT, THEY COULD VISIT THEIR FRIENDS, EVEN THE ONES LIVING WITH THEIR PASS-CARRYING HUSBANDS IN THE WHITE AREAS.
THOBELA, HELENA.
OKAY, TIME TO GO, KIDS.
IT ALSO MEANT THAT WASHERWOMEN LIKE HELENA AND ANNIE COULD FETCH AND DELIVER CLOTHES AT ANY HOUR WITHOUT FEAR OF BEING ARRESTED.
SEE YOU AFTER THE SERVICE.
DON'T FORGET ME IN YOUR PRAYERS!
DON'T FORGET THE DISHES!
IN 1925, HOWEVER, THAT ALL CHANGED WHEN SOME WHITE PRETORIA RESIDENTS COMPLAINED ABOUT AFRICAN WOMEN MAKING A NOISE IN THEIR NEIGHBORHOODS AT NIGHT.

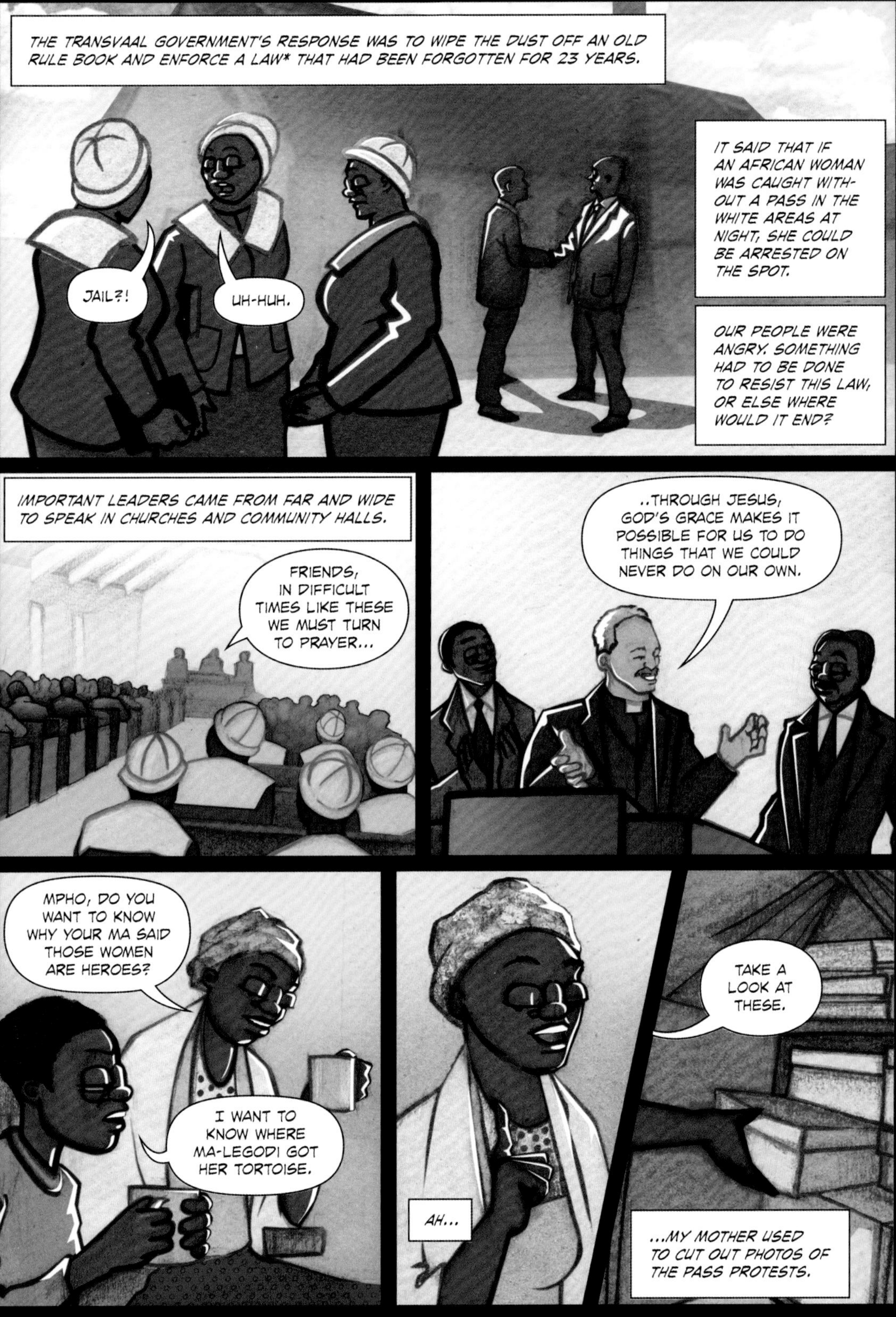
THE TRANSVAAL GOVERNMENT'S RESPONSE WAS TO WIPE THE DUST OFF AN OLD RULE BOOK AND ENFORCE A LAW* THAT HAD BEEN FORGOTTEN FOR 23 YEARS.
IT SAID THAT IF AN AFRICAN WOMAN WAS CAUGHT WITHOUT A PASS IN THE WHITE AREAS AT NIGHT, SHE COULD BE ARRESTED ON THE SPOT.
JAIL?!
UH-HUH.
OUR PEOPLE WERE ANGRY. SOMETHING HAD TO BE DONE TO RESIST THIS LAW, OR ELSE WHERE WOULD IT END?
IMPORTANT LEADERS CAME FROM FAR AND WIDE TO SPEAK IN CHURCHES AND COMMUNITY HALLS.
FRIENDS, IN DIFFICULT TIMES LIKE THESE WE MUST TURN TO PRAYER...
..THROUGH JESUS, GOD'S GRACE MAKES IT POSSIBLE FOR US TO DO THINGS THAT WE COULD NEVER DO ON OUR OWN.
MPHO, DO YOU WANT TO KNOW WHY YOUR MA SAID THOSE WOMEN ARE HEROES?
I WANT TO KNOW WHERE MA-LEGODI GOT HER TORTOISE.
AH...
TAKE A LOOK AT THESE.
...MY MOTHER USED TO CUT OUT PHOTOS OF THE PASS PROTESTS.

* Section 3, Transvaal Ordinance 43 of 1902.

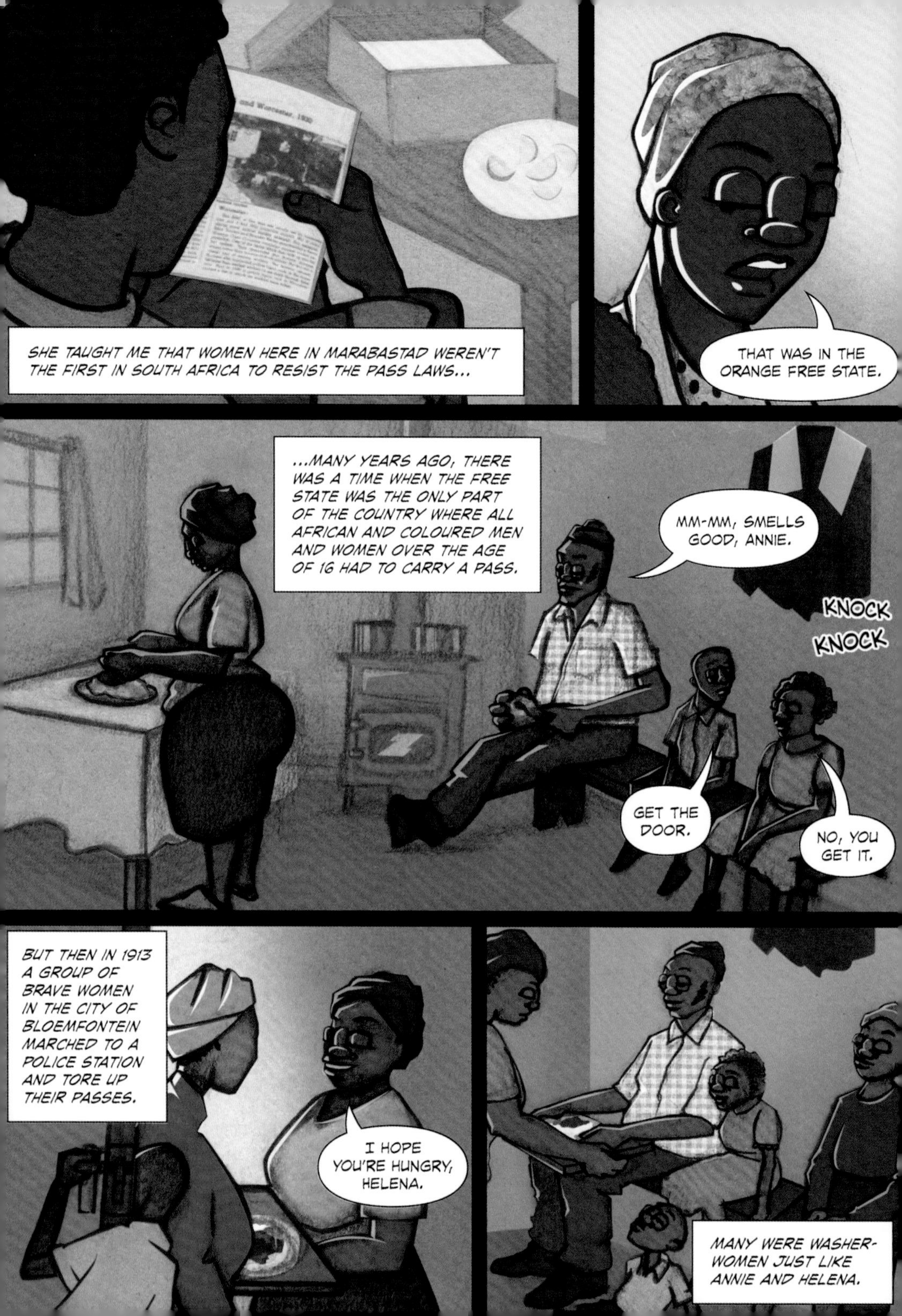
SHE TAUGHT ME THAT WOMEN HERE IN MARABASTAD WEREN'T THE FIRST IN SOUTH AFRICA TO RESIST THE PASS LAWS...
THAT WAS IN THE ORANGE FREE STATE.
...MANY YEARS AGO, THERE WAS A TIME WHEN THE FREE STATE WAS THE ONLY PART OF THE COUNTRY WHERE ALL AFRICAN AND COLOURED MEN AND WOMEN OVER THE AGE OF 16 HAD TO CARRY A PASS.
MM-MM, SMELLS GOOD, ANNIE.
KNOCK
KNOCK
GET THE DOOR.
NO, YOU GET IT.
BUT THEN IN 1913 A GROUP OF BRAVE WOMEN IN THE CITY OF BLOEMFONTEIN MARCHED TO A POLICE STATION AND TORE UP THEIR PASSES.
I HOPE YOU'RE HUNGRY, HELENA.
MANY WERE WASHER-WOMEN JUST LIKE ANNIE AND HELENA.

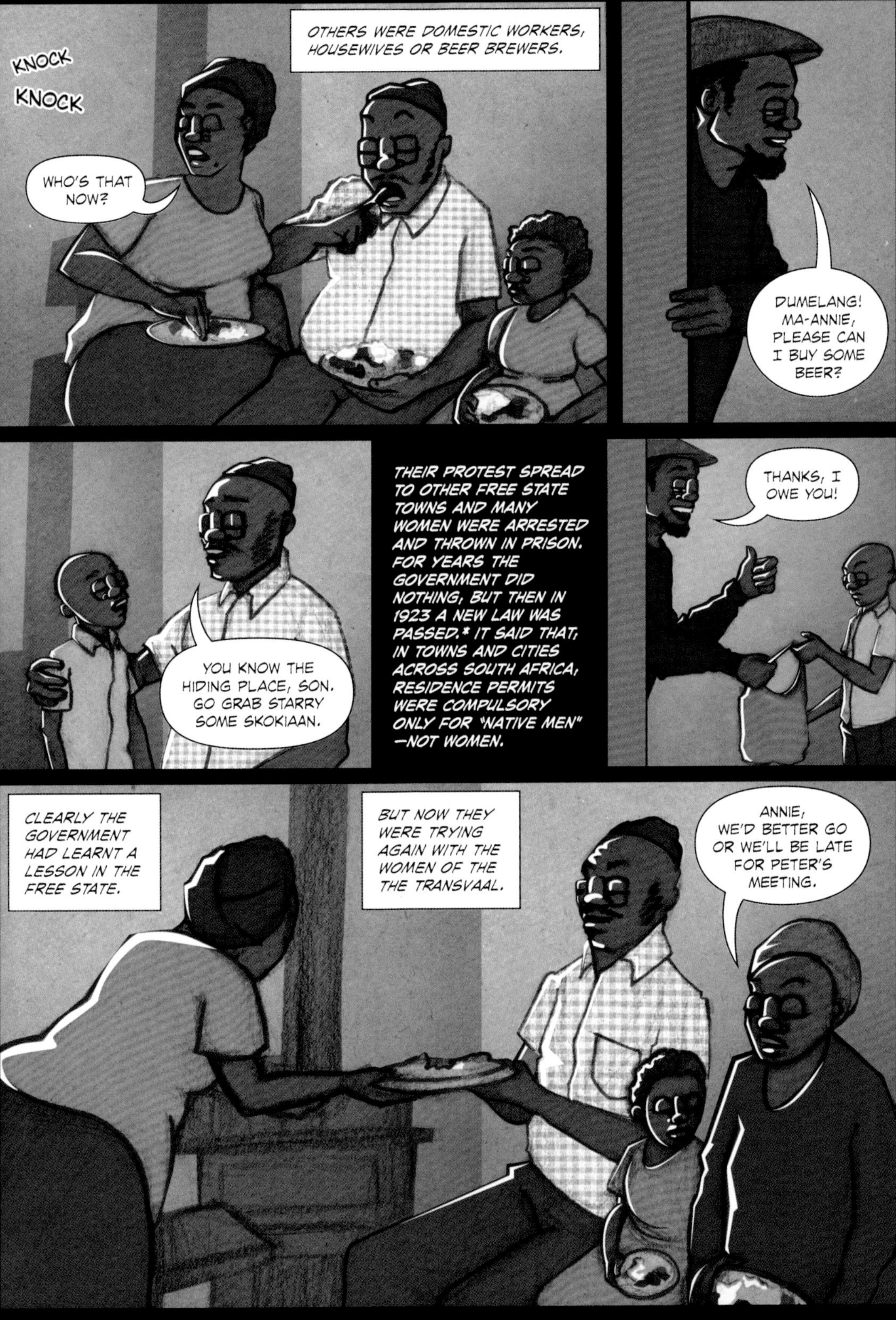
KNOCK
KNOCK
OTHERS WERE DOMESTIC WORKERS, HOUSEWIVES OR BEER BREWERS.
WHO'S THAT NOW?
DUMELANG! MA-ANNIE, PLEASE CAN I BUY SOME BEER?
YOU KNOW THE HIDING PLACE, SON. GO GRAB STARRY SOME SKOKIAAN.
THEIR PROTEST SPREAD TO OTHER FREE STATE TOWNS AND MANY WOMEN WERE ARRESTED AND THROWN IN PRISON. FOR YEARS THE GOVERNMENT DID NOTHING, BUT THEN IN 1923 A NEW LAW WAS PASSED.* IT SAID THAT, IN TOWNS AND CITIES ACROSS SOUTH AFRICA, RESIDENCE PERMITS WERE COMPULSORY ONLY FOR "NATIVE MEN" —NOT WOMEN.
THANKS, I OWE YOU!
CLEARLY THE GOVERNMENT HAD LEARNT A LESSON IN THE FREE STATE.
BUT NOW THEY WERE TRYING AGAIN WITH THE WOMEN OF THE THE TRANSVAAL.
ANNIE, WE'D BETTER GO OR WE'LL BE LATE FOR PETER'S MEETING.

* The Natives (Urban Areas) Act, Act No. 21 of 1923.

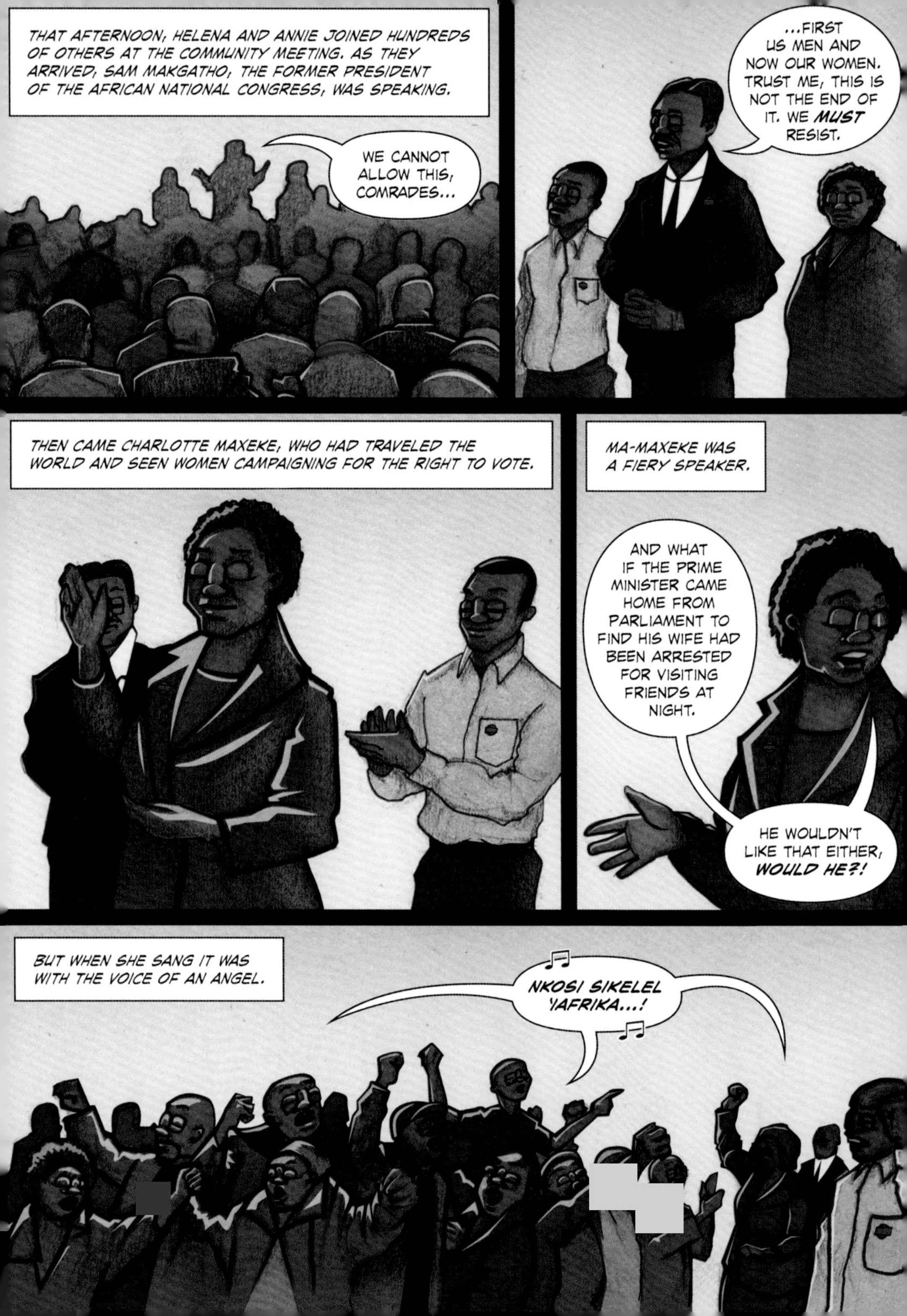
THAT AFTERNOON, HELENA AND ANNIE JOINED HUNDREDS OF OTHERS AT THE COMMUNITY MEETING. AS THEY ARRIVED, SAM MAKGATHO, THE FORMER PRESIDENT OF THE AFRICAN NATIONAL CONGRESS, WAS SPEAKING.
WE CANNOT ALLOW THIS, COMRADES...
...FIRST US MEN AND NOW OUR WOMEN. TRUST ME, THIS IS NOT THE END OF IT. WE *MUST* RESIST.
THEN CAME CHARLOTTE MAXEKE, WHO HAD TRAVELED THE WORLD AND SEEN WOMEN CAMPAIGNING FOR THE RIGHT TO VOTE.
MA-MAXEKE WAS A FIERY SPEAKER.
AND WHAT IF THE PRIME MINISTER CAME HOME FROM PARLIAMENT TO FIND HIS WIFE HAD BEEN ARRESTED FOR VISITING FRIENDS AT NIGHT.
HE WOULDN'T LIKE THAT EITHER, ***WOULD HE?!***
BUT WHEN SHE SANG IT WAS WITH THE VOICE OF AN ANGEL.
NKOSI SIKELEL 'IAFRIKA...!

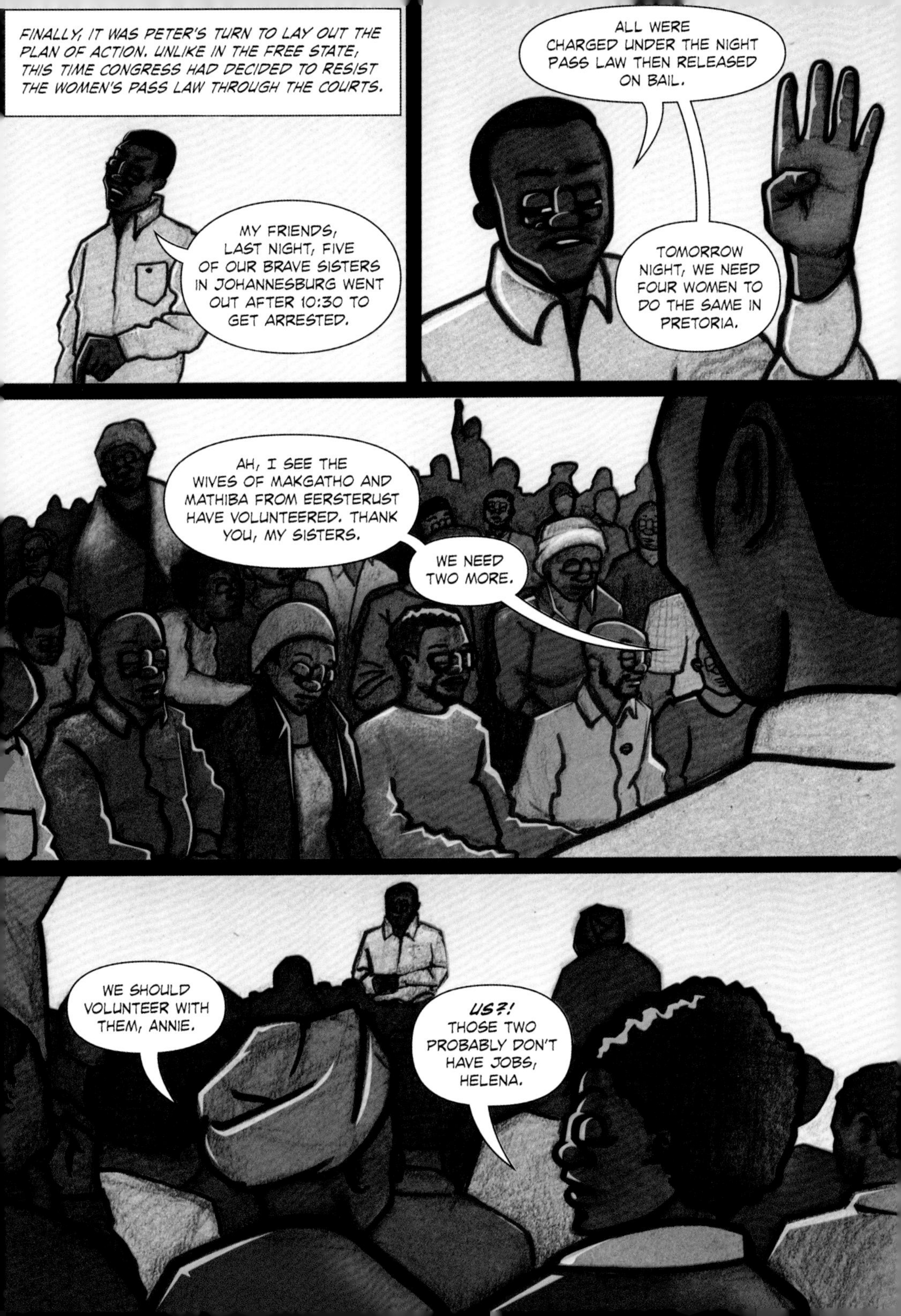
FINALLY, IT WAS PETER'S TURN TO LAY OUT THE PLAN OF ACTION. UNLIKE IN THE FREE STATE, THIS TIME CONGRESS HAD DECIDED TO RESIST THE WOMEN'S PASS LAW THROUGH THE COURTS.
MY FRIENDS, LAST NIGHT, FIVE OF OUR BRAVE SISTERS IN JOHANNESBURG WENT OUT AFTER 10:30 TO GET ARRESTED.
ALL WERE CHARGED UNDER THE NIGHT PASS LAW THEN RELEASED ON BAIL.
TOMORROW NIGHT, WE NEED FOUR WOMEN TO DO THE SAME IN PRETORIA.
AH, I SEE THE WIVES OF MAKGATHO AND MATHIBA FROM EERSTERUST HAVE VOLUNTEERED. THANK YOU, MY SISTERS.
WE NEED TWO MORE.
WE SHOULD VOLUNTEER WITH THEM, ANNIE.
US?! THOSE TWO PROBABLY DON'T HAVE JOBS, HELENA.

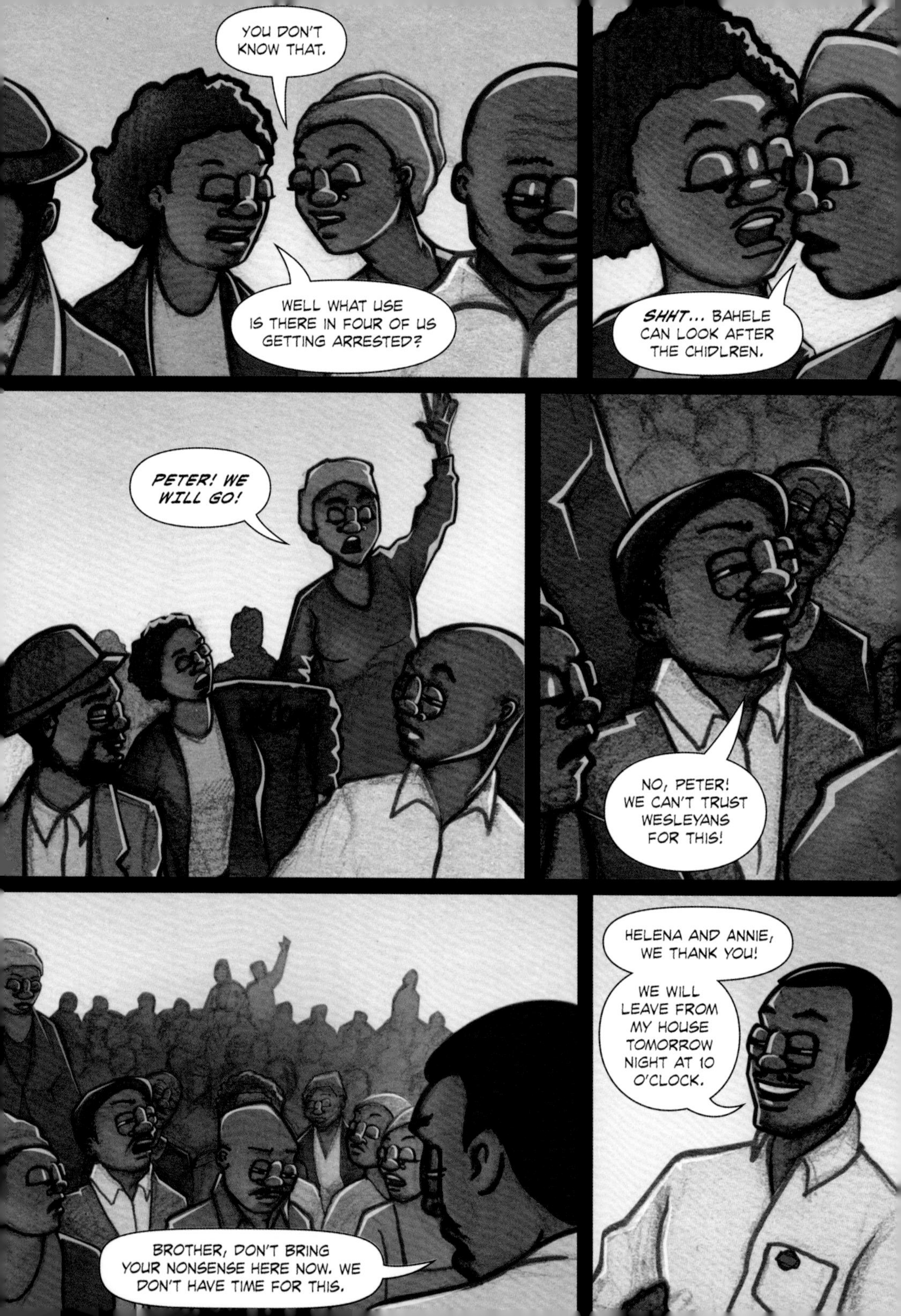
YOU DON'T KNOW THAT.
WELL WHAT USE IS THERE IN FOUR OF US GETTING ARRESTED?
SHHT... BAHELE CAN LOOK AFTER THE CHIDLREN.
PETER! WE WILL GO!
NO, PETER! WE CAN'T TRUST WESLEYANS FOR THIS!
BROTHER, DON'T BRING YOUR NONSENSE HERE NOW. WE DON'T HAVE TIME FOR THIS.
HELENA AND ANNIE, WE THANK YOU!
WE WILL LEAVE FROM MY HOUSE TOMORROW NIGHT AT 10 O'CLOCK.

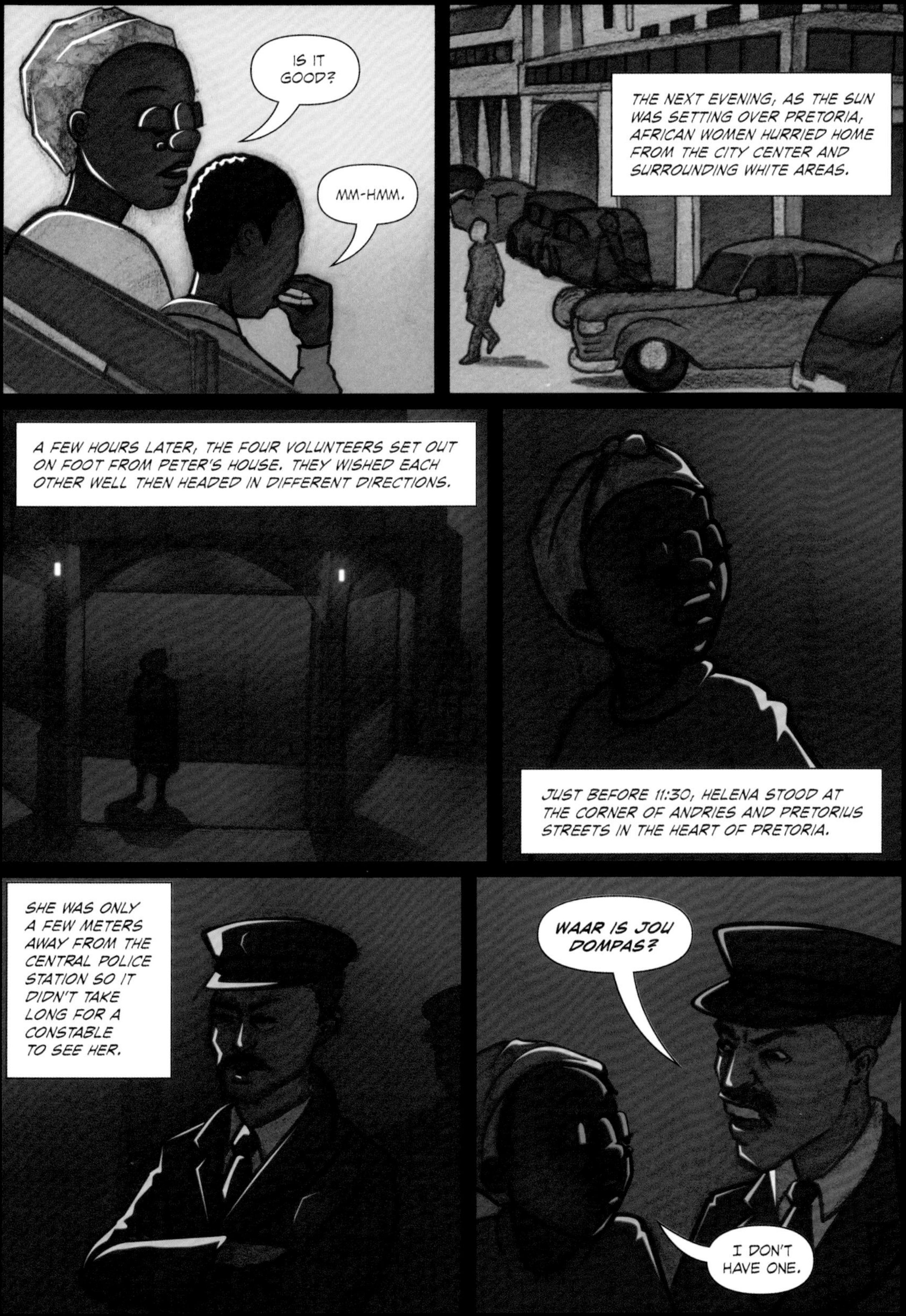
IS IT GOOD?
MM-HMM.
THE NEXT EVENING, AS THE SUN WAS SETTING OVER PRETORIA, AFRICAN WOMEN HURRIED HOME FROM THE CITY CENTER AND SURROUNDING WHITE AREAS.
A FEW HOURS LATER, THE FOUR VOLUNTEERS SET OUT ON FOOT FROM PETER'S HOUSE. THEY WISHED EACH OTHER WELL THEN HEADED IN DIFFERENT DIRECTIONS.
JUST BEFORE 11:30, HELENA STOOD AT THE CORNER OF ANDRIES AND PRETORIUS STREETS IN THE HEART OF PRETORIA.
SHE WAS ONLY A FEW METERS AWAY FROM THE CENTRAL POLICE STATION SO IT DIDN'T TAKE LONG FOR A CONSTABLE TO SEE HER.
WAAR IS JOU DOMPAS?
I DON'T HAVE ONE.

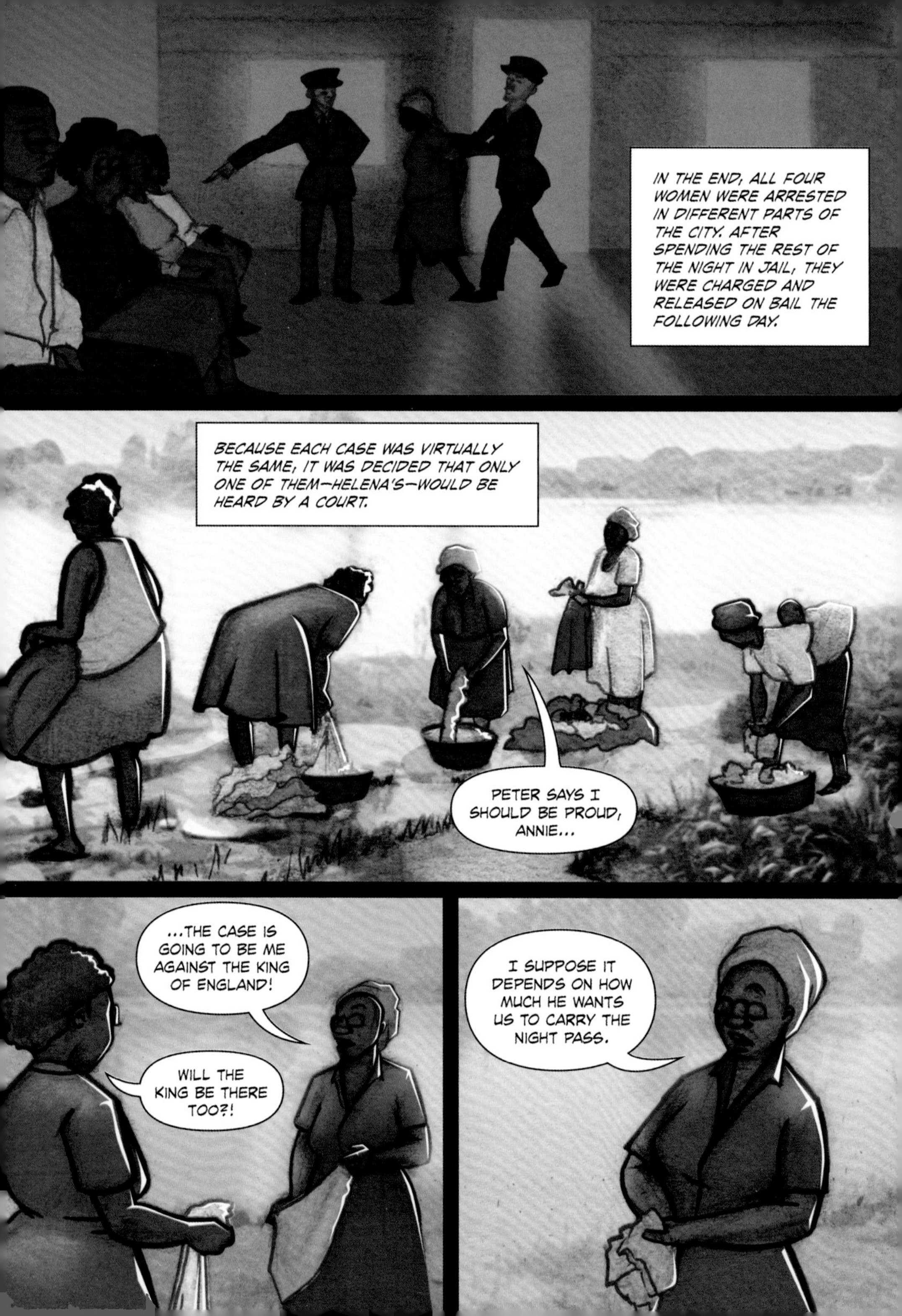
IN THE END, ALL FOUR WOMEN WERE ARRESTED IN DIFFERENT PARTS OF THE CITY. AFTER SPENDING THE REST OF THE NIGHT IN JAIL, THEY WERE CHARGED AND RELEASED ON BAIL THE FOLLOWING DAY.
BECAUSE EACH CASE WAS VIRTUALLY THE SAME, IT WAS DECIDED THAT ONLY ONE OF THEM—HELENA'S—WOULD BE HEARD BY A COURT.
PETER SAYS I SHOULD BE PROUD, ANNIE...
...THE CASE IS GOING TO BE ME AGAINST THE KING OF ENGLAND!
WILL THE KING BE THERE TOO?!
I SUPPOSE IT DEPENDS ON HOW MUCH HE WANTS US TO CARRY THE NIGHT PASS.

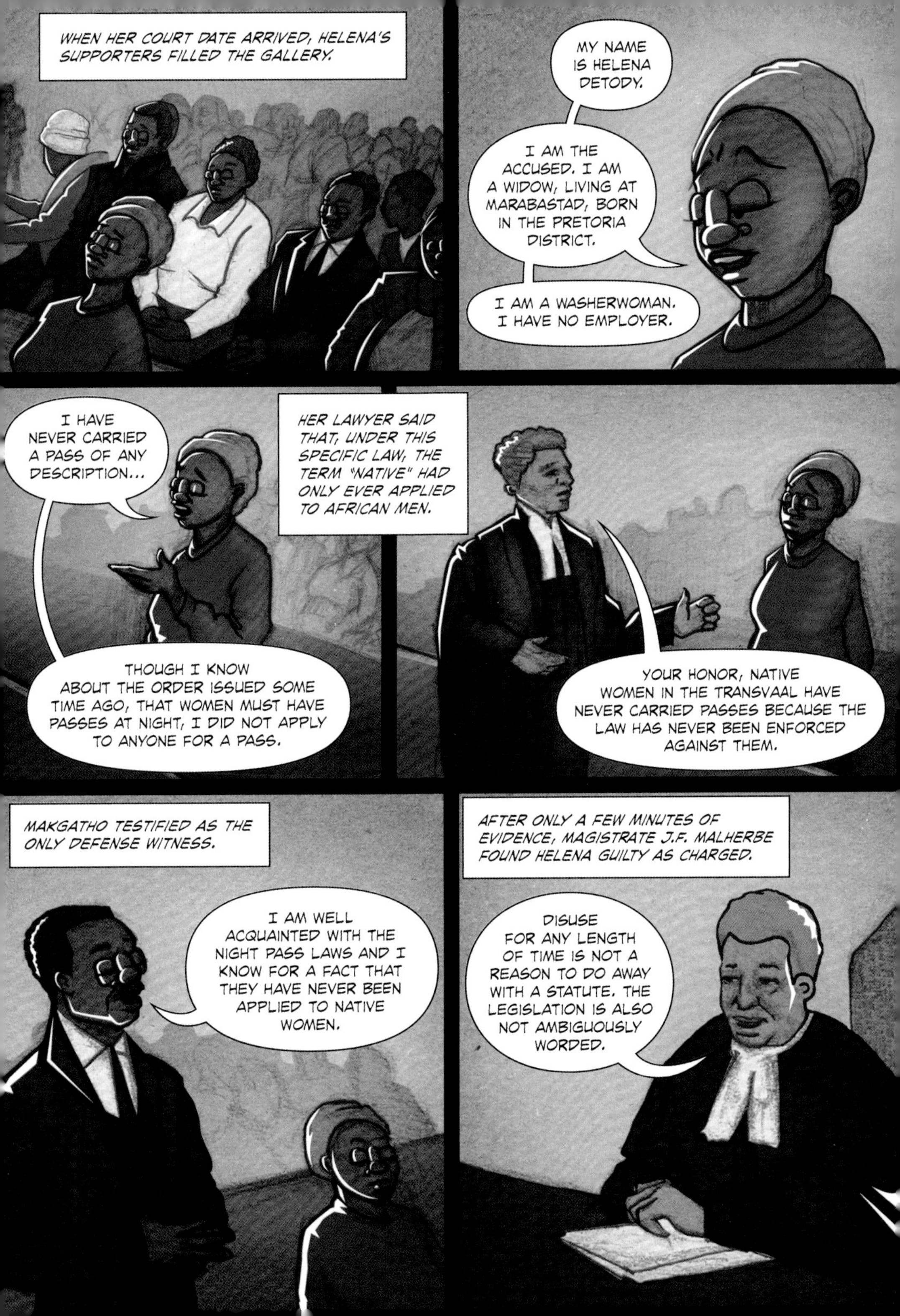
WHEN HER COURT DATE ARRIVED, HELENA'S SUPPORTERS FILLED THE GALLERY.
MY NAME IS HELENA DETODY.
I AM THE ACCUSED. I AM A WIDOW, LIVING AT MARABASTAD, BORN IN THE PRETORIA DISTRICT.
I AM A WASHERWOMAN. I HAVE NO EMPLOYER.
I HAVE NEVER CARRIED A PASS OF ANY DESCRIPTION...
THOUGH I KNOW ABOUT THE ORDER ISSUED SOME TIME AGO, THAT WOMEN MUST HAVE PASSES AT NIGHT, I DID NOT APPLY TO ANYONE FOR A PASS.
HER LAWYER SAID THAT, UNDER THIS SPECIFIC LAW, THE TERM "NATIVE" HAD ONLY EVER APPLIED TO AFRICAN MEN.
YOUR HONOR, NATIVE WOMEN IN THE TRANSVAAL HAVE NEVER CARRIED PASSES BECAUSE THE LAW HAS NEVER BEEN ENFORCED AGAINST THEM.
MAKGATHO TESTIFIED AS THE ONLY DEFENSE WITNESS.
I AM WELL ACQUAINTED WITH THE NIGHT PASS LAWS AND I KNOW FOR A FACT THAT THEY HAVE NEVER BEEN APPLIED TO NATIVE WOMEN.
AFTER ONLY A FEW MINUTES OF EVIDENCE, MAGISTRATE J.F. MALHERBE FOUND HELENA GUILTY AS CHARGED.
DISUSE FOR ANY LENGTH OF TIME IS NOT A REASON TO DO AWAY WITH A STATUTE. THE LEGISLATION IS ALSO NOT AMBIGUOUSLY WORDED.

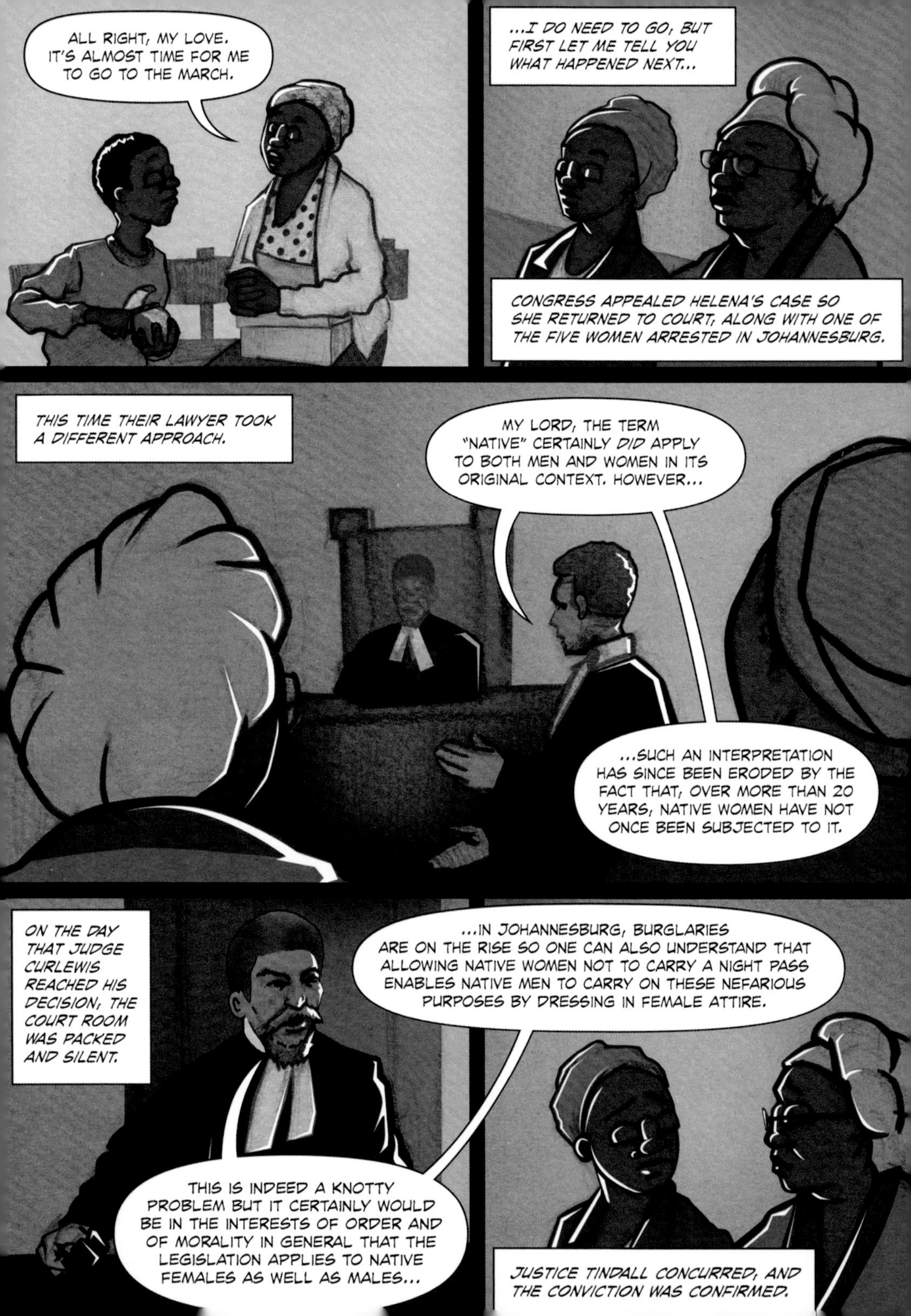
ALL RIGHT, MY LOVE. IT'S ALMOST TIME FOR ME TO GO TO THE MARCH.
...I DO NEED TO GO, BUT FIRST LET ME TELL YOU WHAT HAPPENED NEXT...
CONGRESS APPEALED HELENA'S CASE SO SHE RETURNED TO COURT, ALONG WITH ONE OF THE FIVE WOMEN ARRESTED IN JOHANNESBURG.
THIS TIME THEIR LAWYER TOOK A DIFFERENT APPROACH.
MY LORD, THE TERM "NATIVE" CERTAINLY DID APPLY TO BOTH MEN AND WOMEN IN ITS ORIGINAL CONTEXT. HOWEVER...
...SUCH AN INTERPRETATION HAS SINCE BEEN ERODED BY THE FACT THAT, OVER MORE THAN 20 YEARS, NATIVE WOMEN HAVE NOT ONCE BEEN SUBJECTED TO IT.
ON THE DAY THAT JUDGE CURLEWIS REACHED HIS DECISION, THE COURT ROOM WAS PACKED AND SILENT.
THIS IS INDEED A KNOTTY PROBLEM BUT IT CERTAINLY WOULD BE IN THE INTERESTS OF ORDER AND OF MORALITY IN GENERAL THAT THE LEGISLATION APPLIES TO NATIVE FEMALES AS WELL AS MALES...
...IN JOHANNESBURG, BURGLARIES ARE ON THE RISE SO ONE CAN ALSO UNDERSTAND THAT ALLOWING NATIVE WOMEN NOT TO CARRY A NIGHT PASS ENABLES NATIVE MEN TO CARRY ON THESE NEFARIOUS PURPOSES BY DRESSING IN FEMALE ATTIRE.
JUSTICE TINDALL CONCURRED, AND THE CONVICTION WAS CONFIRMED.

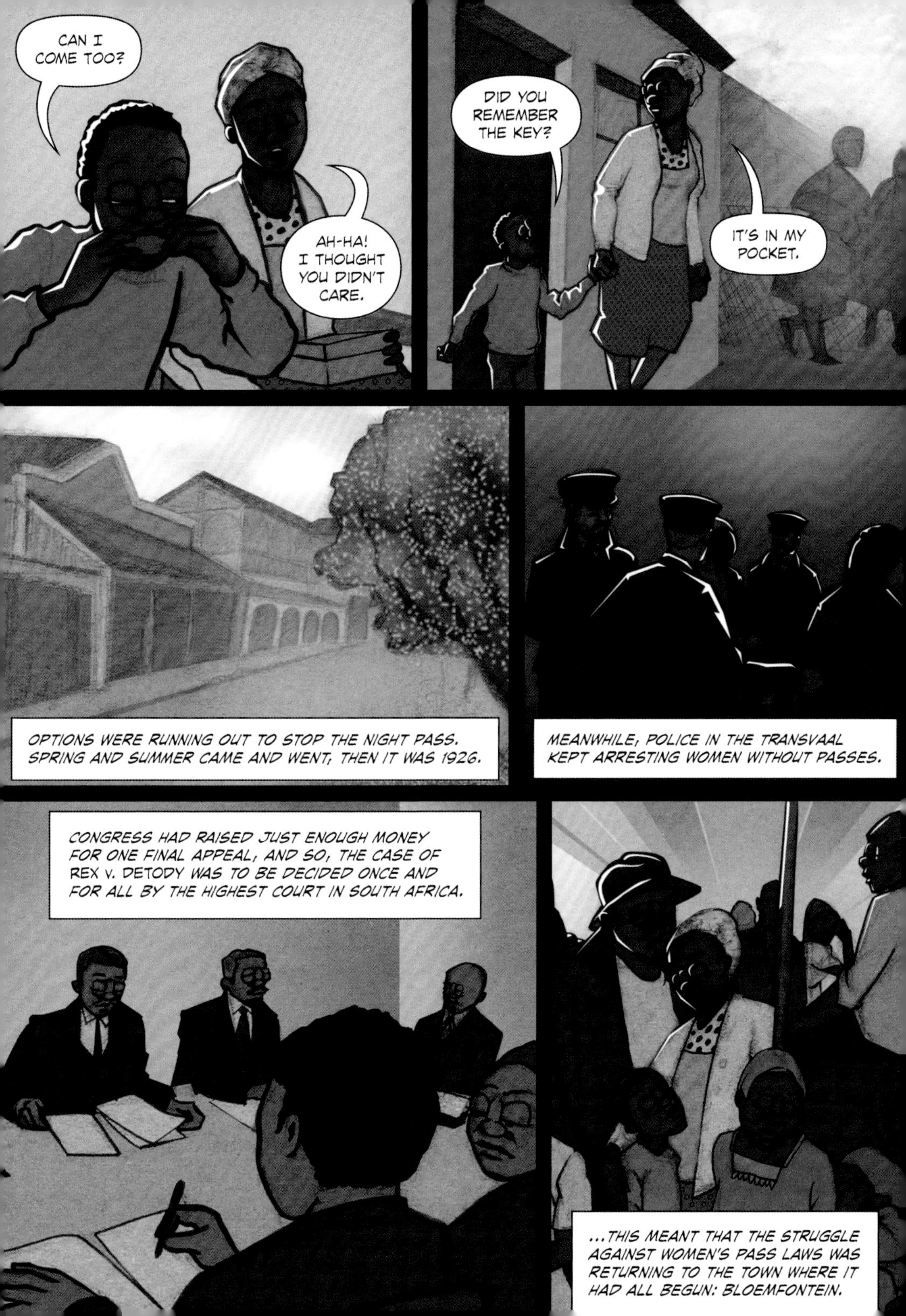
CAN I COME TOO?
AH-HA! I THOUGHT YOU DIDN'T CARE.
DID YOU REMEMBER THE KEY?
IT'S IN MY POCKET.
OPTIONS WERE RUNNING OUT TO STOP THE NIGHT PASS. SPRING AND SUMMER CAME AND WENT, THEN IT WAS 1926.
MEANWHILE, POLICE IN THE TRANSVAAL KEPT ARRESTING WOMEN WITHOUT PASSES.
CONGRESS HAD RAISED JUST ENOUGH MONEY FOR ONE FINAL APPEAL, AND SO, THE CASE OF REX v. DETODY WAS TO BE DECIDED ONCE AND FOR ALL BY THE HIGHEST COURT IN SOUTH AFRICA.
...THIS MEANT THAT THE STRUGGLE AGAINST WOMEN'S PASS LAWS WAS RETURNING TO THE TOWN WHERE IT HAD ALL BEGUN: BLOEMFONTEIN.

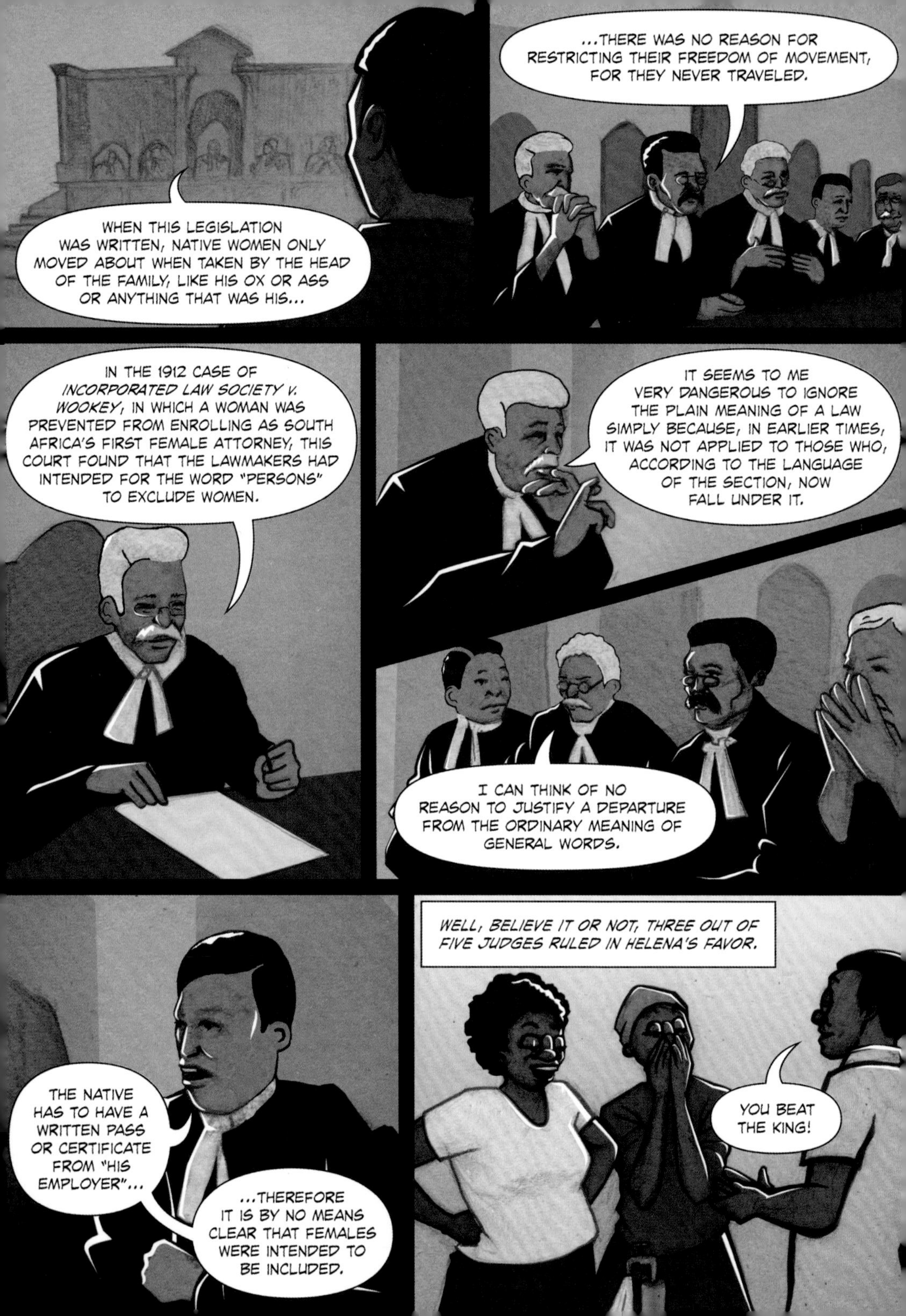
WHEN THIS LEGISLATION WAS WRITTEN, NATIVE WOMEN ONLY MOVED ABOUT WHEN TAKEN BY THE HEAD OF THE FAMILY, LIKE HIS OX OR ASS OR ANYTHING THAT WAS HIS...
...THERE WAS NO REASON FOR RESTRICTING THEIR FREEDOM OF MOVEMENT, FOR THEY NEVER TRAVELED.
IN THE 1912 CASE OF *INCORPORATED LAW SOCIETY V. WOOKEY*, IN WHICH A WOMAN WAS PREVENTED FROM ENROLLING AS SOUTH AFRICA'S FIRST FEMALE ATTORNEY, THIS COURT FOUND THAT THE LAWMAKERS HAD INTENDED FOR THE WORD "PERSONS" TO EXCLUDE WOMEN.
IT SEEMS TO ME VERY DANGEROUS TO IGNORE THE PLAIN MEANING OF A LAW SIMPLY BECAUSE, IN EARLIER TIMES, IT WAS NOT APPLIED TO THOSE WHO, ACCORDING TO THE LANGUAGE OF THE SECTION, NOW FALL UNDER IT.
I CAN THINK OF NO REASON TO JUSTIFY A DEPARTURE FROM THE ORDINARY MEANING OF GENERAL WORDS.
THE NATIVE HAS TO HAVE A WRITTEN PASS OR CERTIFICATE FROM "HIS EMPLOYER"...
...THEREFORE IT IS BY NO MEANS CLEAR THAT FEMALES WERE INTENDED TO BE INCLUDED.
WELL, BELIEVE IT OR NOT, THREE OUT OF FIVE JUDGES RULED IN HELENA'S FAVOR.
YOU BEAT THE KING!

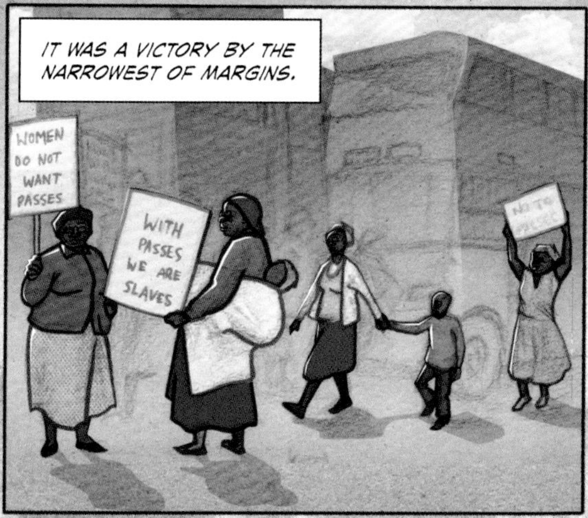
IT WAS A VICTORY BY THE NARROWEST OF MARGINS.
WOMEN DO NOT WANT PASSES
WITH PASSES WE ARE SLAVES

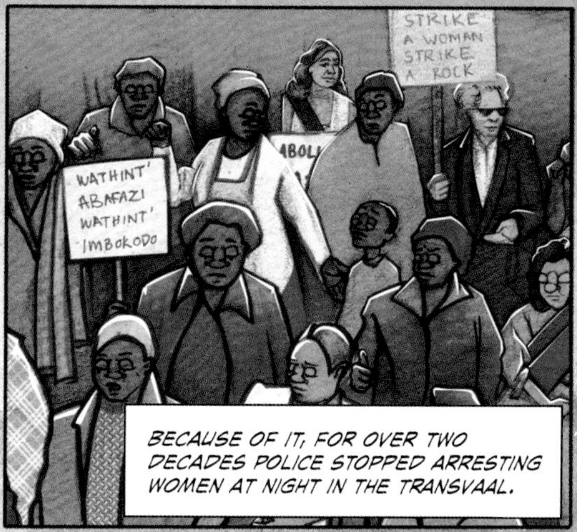
STRIKE A WOMAN STRIKE A ROCK
WATHINT' ABAFAZI WATHINT' IMBOKODO
BECAUSE OF IT, FOR OVER TWO DECADES POLICE STOPPED ARRESTING WOMEN AT NIGHT IN THE TRANSVAAL.

AND THAT, FRIENDS, IS WHY WE LET THOSE GRANNIES TAKE WATER BEFORE US...

Rex v. Detody is a near-forgotten landmark in the history of women's resistance to the pass laws in South Africa. Helena's victory in 1926, backed up by more than a decade of defiance by African and Coloured women in the Transvaal and Orange Free State, ultimately led the Union government to think again.

A quarter of a century later, under the apartheid regime, the proposal for women's passes resurfaced. This time, it was met with mass demonstrations across the country, culminating in the iconic women's march to the Union Buildings in Pretoria on 9 August 1956.

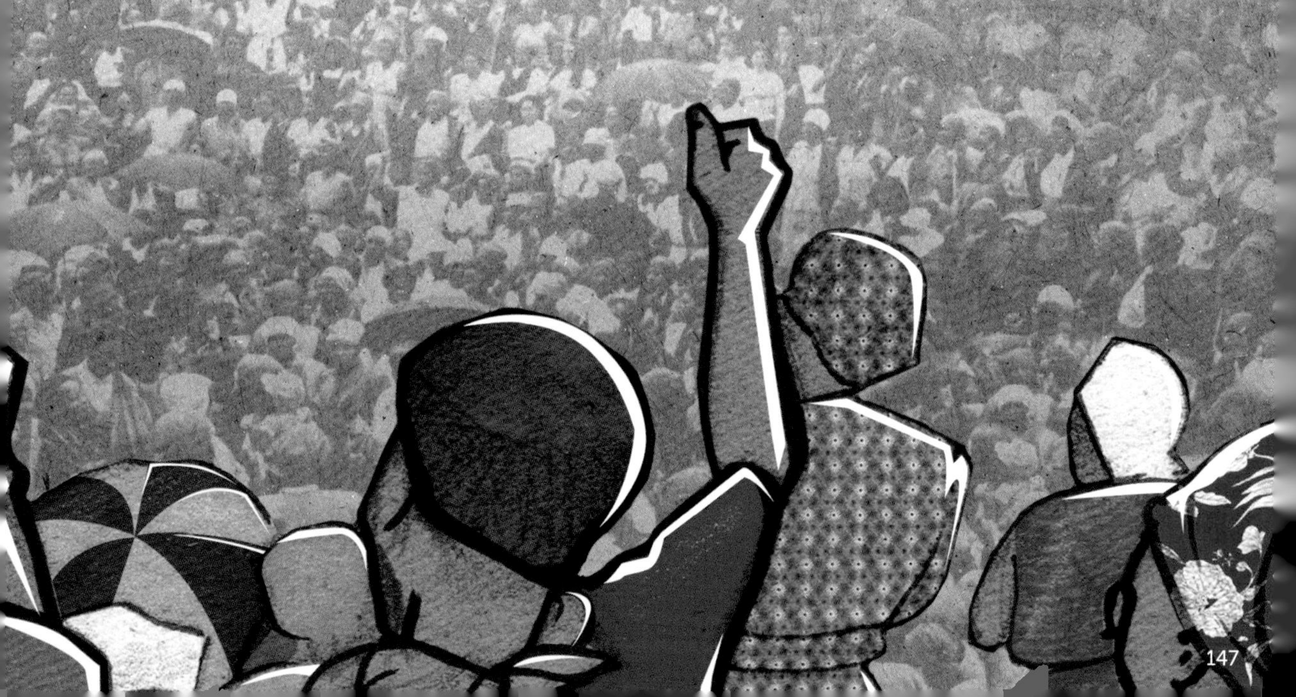

BEHIND THE STORY: SOURCES AND SKETCHES

CHAPTER 4: THE WIDOW OF MARABASTAD

Archives tend to be full of documents written by men. In pre-democratic South Africa, these men were almost always white. It should come as no surprise, then, that in researching the story of Helena Detody we faced a unique challenge. She was a widowed African woman who lived in Pretoria's impoverished Marabastad location during the early twentieth century. Her identity made her experience of oppression distinct from that of other groups, including African men and white women. She faced discrimination on multiple fronts, and today we see this reality reflected in the state archives, where millions of African women are virtually invisible as the individual subjects of historical research.

In the Appellate Division basement, the folder for *Rex v. Detody* is unusually thin compared with those for other case records. We cannot even be sure of the appellant's name: "Detody" is very likely an adaptation or misspelling by the Union courts of the Sotho-Tswana surname "Ditodi." Among the court papers is a brief transcript containing the 109 words that Helena spoke during her first court appearance. They offered us clues in the form of basic biographical information—"widow," "washerwoman," "living at Marabastad"—as well as the circumstances of her arrest.

In the National Archives, we were lucky to access a government file specifically related to the 1925 Transvaal night pass ordinance. It contains private correspondence between Department of Native Affairs officials and the Pretoria police; petitions and letters sent by leaders of the Transvaal African Congress; and most crucially, a single-page police spy report describing the gathering at which Helena and another woman, "Annie," volunteered to be arrested.

For the story's social environment, we found inspiration in Es'kia Mphahlele's memoir *Down Second Avenue*. The author was a young boy living in 1920s Marabastad during the time of the night pass ordinance. His recollections guided many of our assumptions about the day-to-day lives that Helena and Annie would have led.

TAILOR

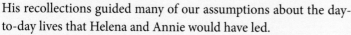

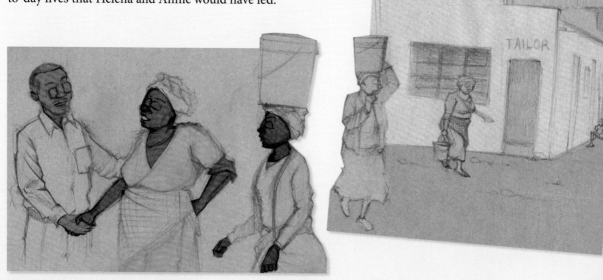

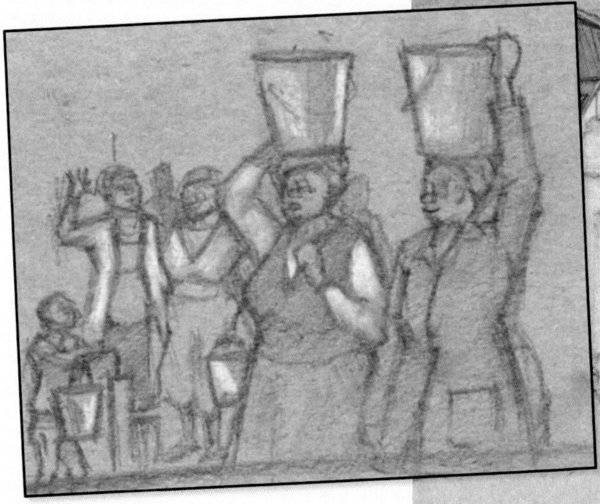

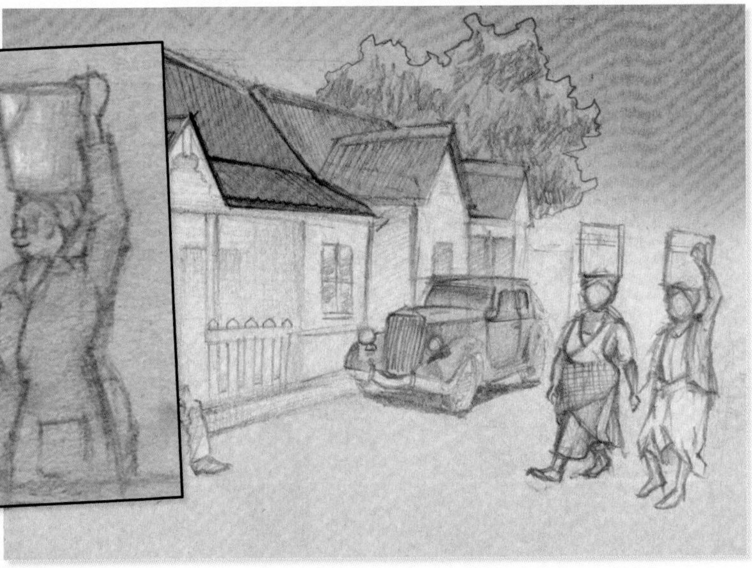

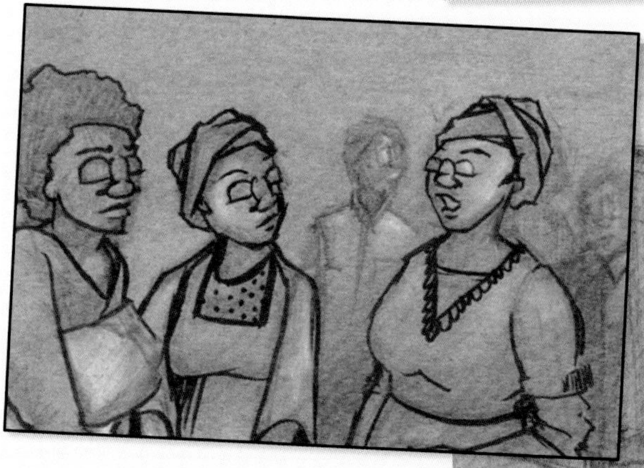

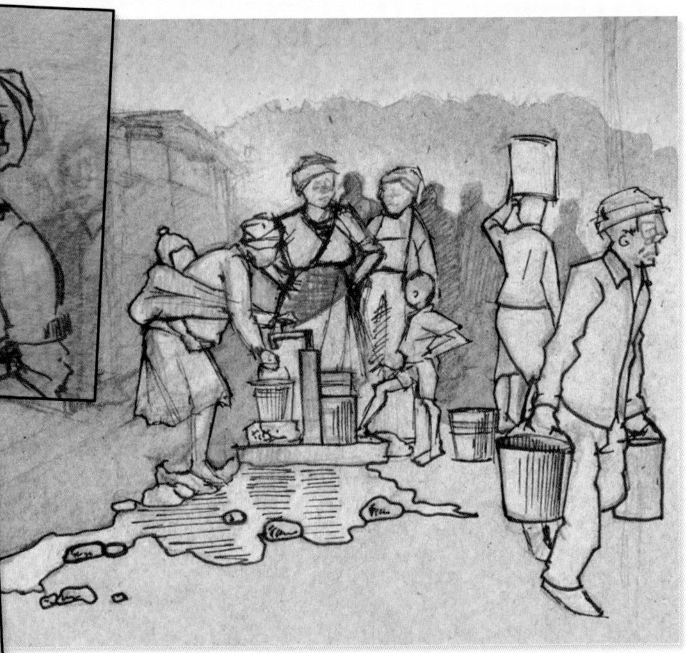

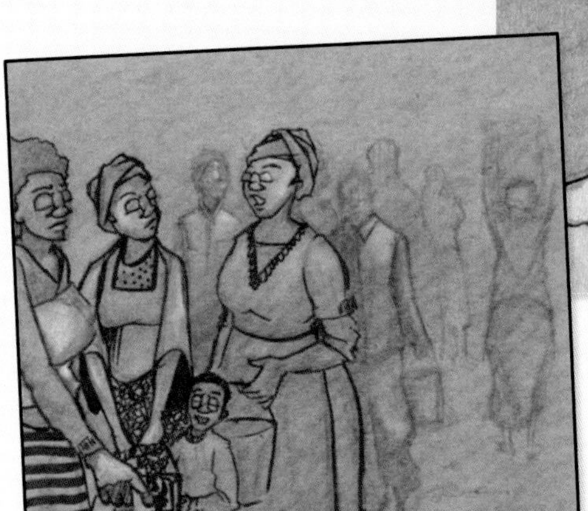

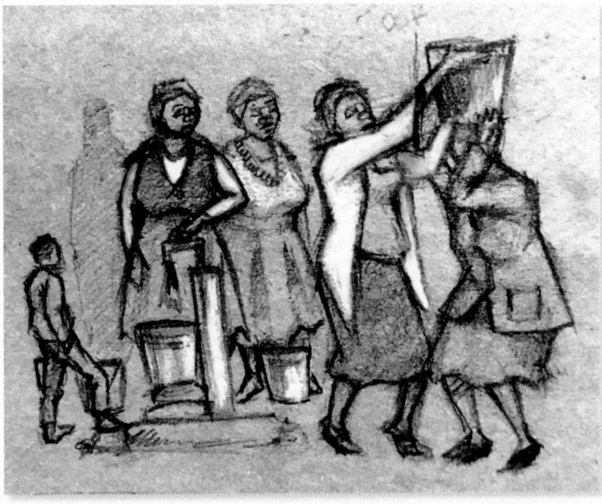

The opening street tap scene is inspired by Es'kia Mphahlele's memoir *Down Second Avenue.*

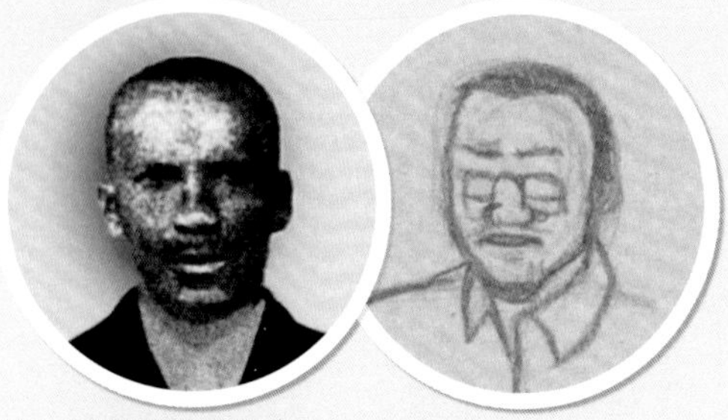

Peter Matseke (1878–1941) was the chairman of the Pretoria branch of the Transvaal African Congress during the 1920s. In the National Archives, his name appears regularly in government documents related to resistance efforts against the Transvaal women's night pass ordinance.

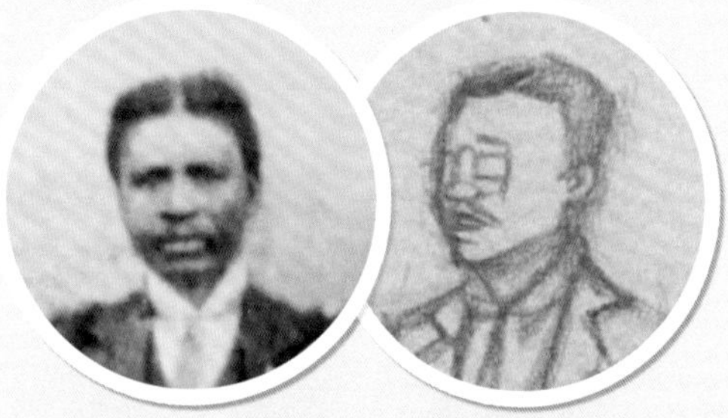

Sefako "Sam" Makgatho (1861–1951), a Methodist preacher and the second president of the African National Congress.

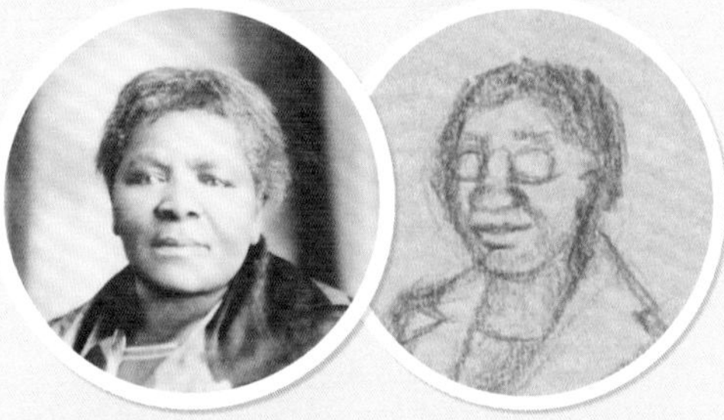

Charlotte Maxeke (1871–1939) was a social and political activist who played a leading role in women's anti-pass resistance in the early twentieth century.

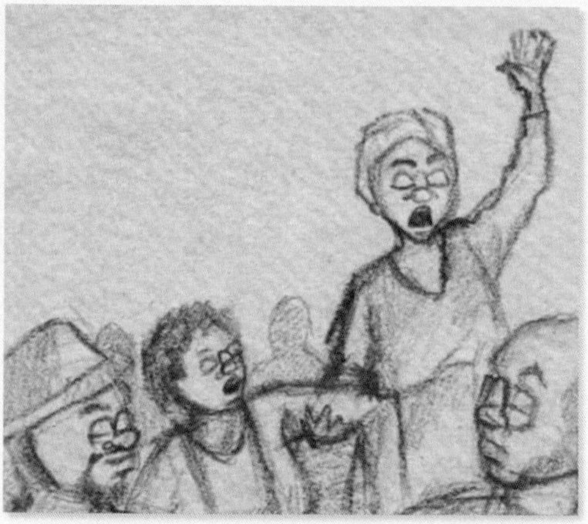

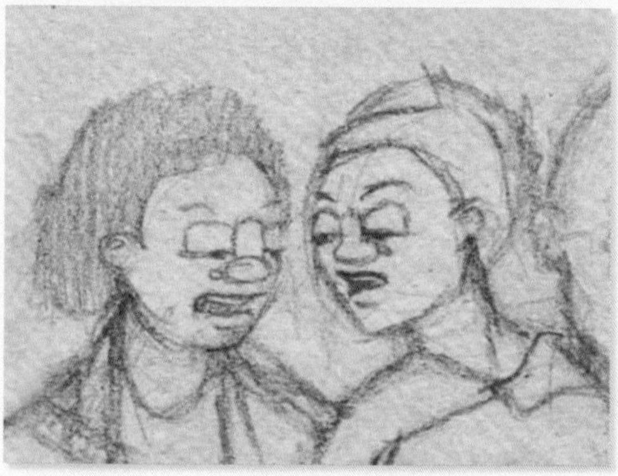

Right: The transcription of a police spy report written by "Native Detective Corporal" Hosiah Thagadi, describing the community meeting on 14 June 1925 at which "two women from Marabastad named Ellen (sic) and Annie came forward and were accepted."

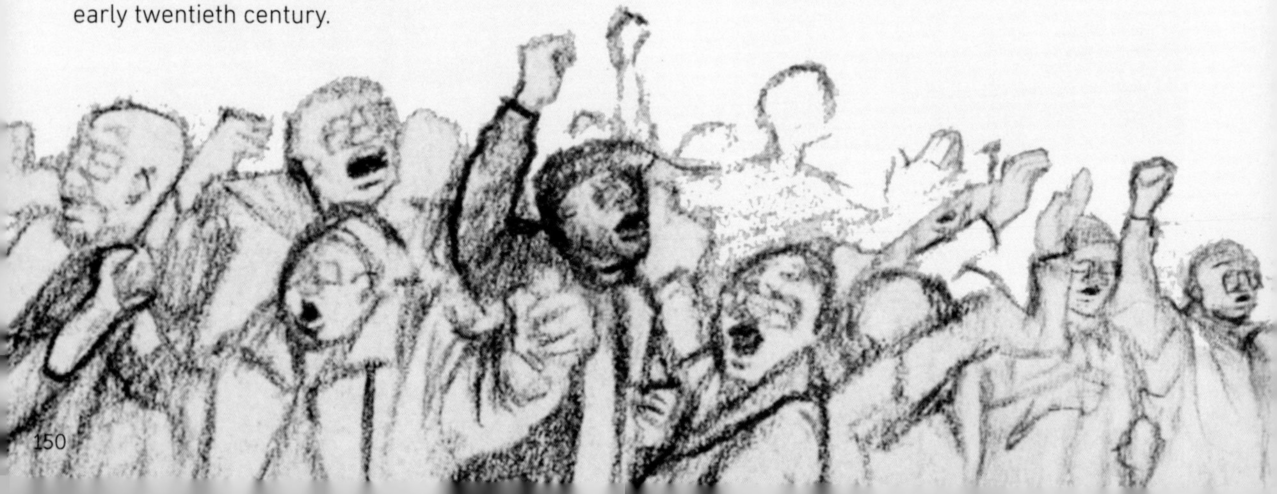

HOSEA THAGADI, states :-   I am a Nat. Det. Cpl of C.I. Department, Pretoria. In accordance with instructions received I attended a Meeting of natives held at the outspaan at 2 p.m. on the 14th instant. I was accompanied by Nat.Det. Klaas and Informant Asaf.

The principal speakers were Matseka, the District Organiser of the T.A.C., and Letanga of Johannesburg, who is a vice President of the T.A.C. for Transvaal.

Matseka first spoke and stated that they want money to fight the Government with respect to night passes affecting native women. That if they get sufficient money, they must be strong enough to have the Law removed. That by the women being compelled to carry passes, they become slaves. That if Mr. Tielman Roos and Gen. Hertzog returned from Parliament and found their wives arrested they would not like it. That they, the natives must defeat the Night Pass Law, even if they are compelled to be continually holding meetings.

That if the Government does not alter the Law, they will hold meetings to arrange that all native men and women discard their passes, so that they can be arrested and they will then see if the Government can keep them all in gaol.

That they are not afraid if they have to fight, as the European population is one million and the natives three millions, and if they get killed, it will be of no consequence. That five native women at Johannesburg had purposely been sent out at night to be arrested and had been arrested and their intention is to make a test before the court. That he wanted four native women at Pretoria to act in a similar way and that was the reason of calling the present meeting.

The native anthem "God help Africa" was then sung.

Letanga then addressed the meeting and expressed his agreement with the words of the previous speaker and stated that the purpose of the meeting was a serious one and that is to elect native women to walk in the street at night to be arrested. That at Johannesburg he took out five women at night and could see no Policeman in the street so he took them to the "Hungry Lions" meaning the Police, at the Charge Office at Jeppe, but arrest was refused and the women were afterwards arrested in the street and charged under the night Pass Ordinance and released on bail. That he now wants four native women from Pretoria to act similarly so that they can be arrested. That the natives must assist by providing money towards cost of bail for them.

A native women, whose name is unknown to me then spoke, and she stated that the women want to fight the Pass Law.

Matseka then stated that two women had offered their services, and they were the wives of Makgatho and Mathiba of Eerste Rust, and then two women from Marabastad named Ellen and Annie came forward and they were accepted. Another native got up and spoke against the use of the two latter women, and gave out that they were Wesleyans and could not be trusted, but the interupter was overruled.

The Matseka said that they, the said women, were to go to his home where they would be given instructions.

That he had T.A.C. badges for sale at 2/6 and those not in possession of one would not be allowed to enter the court to hear the case.

A collection was made and the total was announced to be £4. 0. 6.

Letanga stated that at Johannesburg at the hearing of the case against the native women, natives not possessing the badges were not allowed to enter the Court.

The meeting closed about 5.30 p.m.

There were about 200 natives, men and women, present and were quite orderly.

The meeting was advertised by pamphlet, one of which is attached.

(Sgd.) Hosiah Thagadi N.Det.Cpl.

Before me at Pretoria this 15th day of June, 1925.
(Sgd.) D.W. Lloyd. DET/H/Cst.

(5)

<u>HELENA Detody:-</u>

SWORN STATES:-

I am the accused. I am a widow, living at Marabastad. I was born in the Pretoria District. I am a washerwoman. I have no employer. I have never carried a pass of any description. I know about the order issued some time ago that women must have passes at night. I did not apply to anyone for a pass.

Above: Helena Detody's only surviving words: her short court testimony before Magistrate J.F. Malherbe found her guilty as charged in late July 1925.

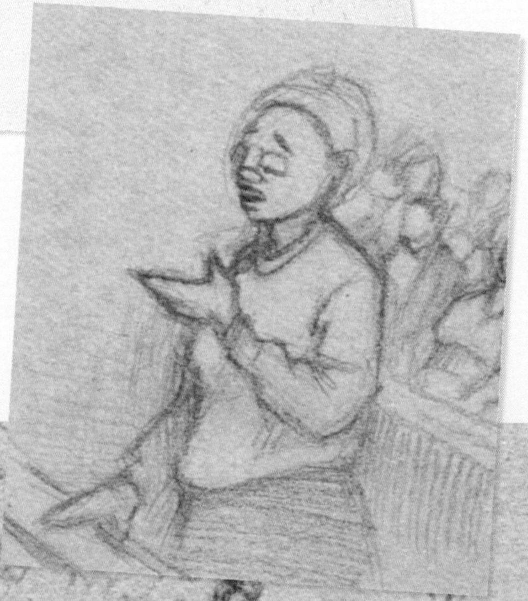

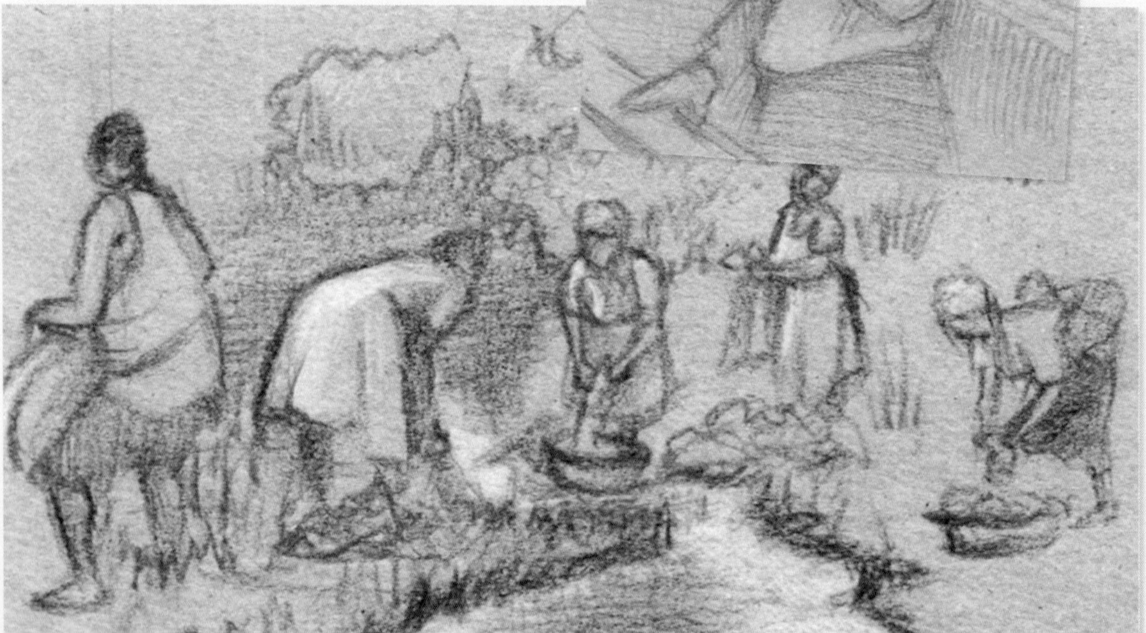

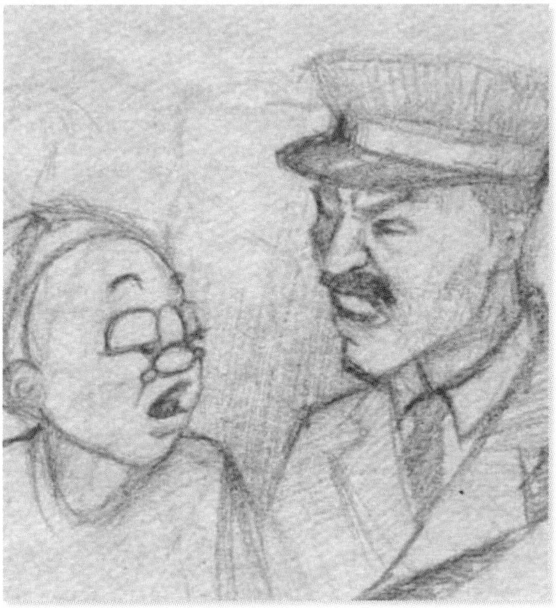

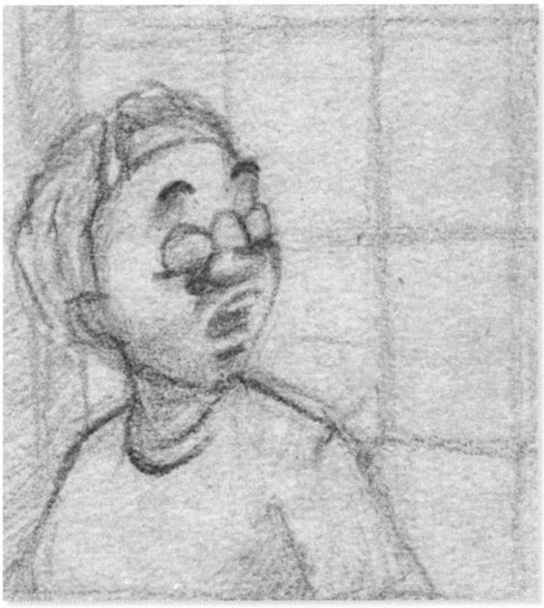

(6)

On the night of 15th June 1925, I and other women came into the streets of Pretoria without passes. We went to visit friends in Arcadia. We went out with the object of being arrested to test the validity of the order, requiring native women to have night passes.

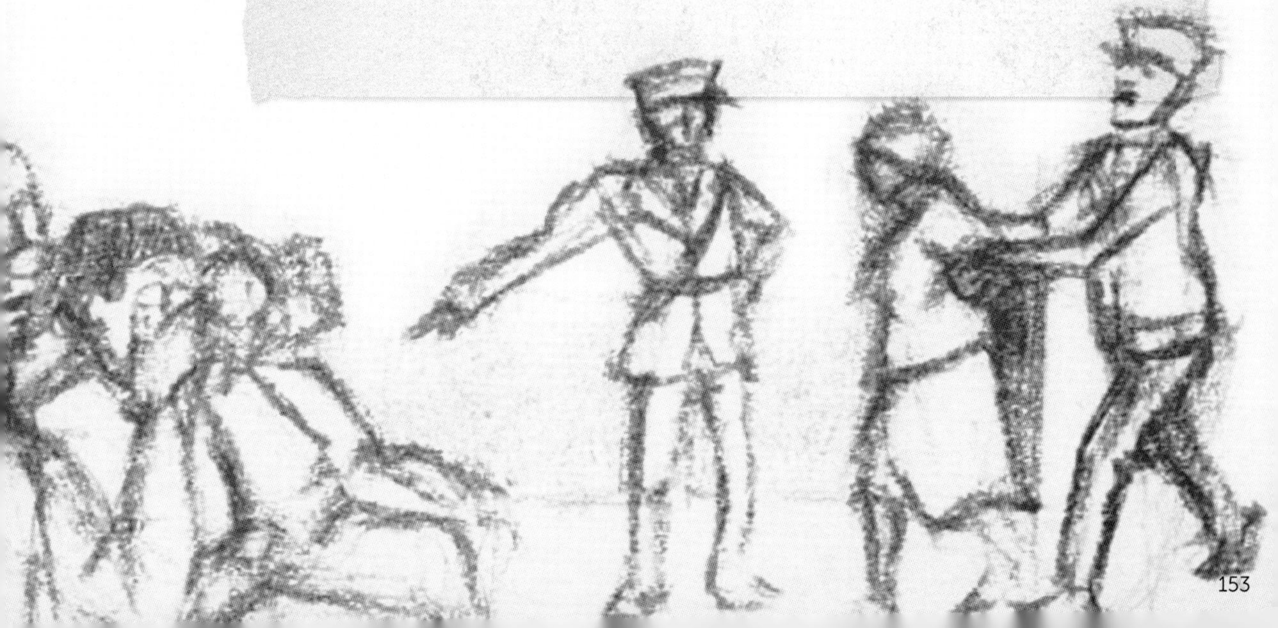

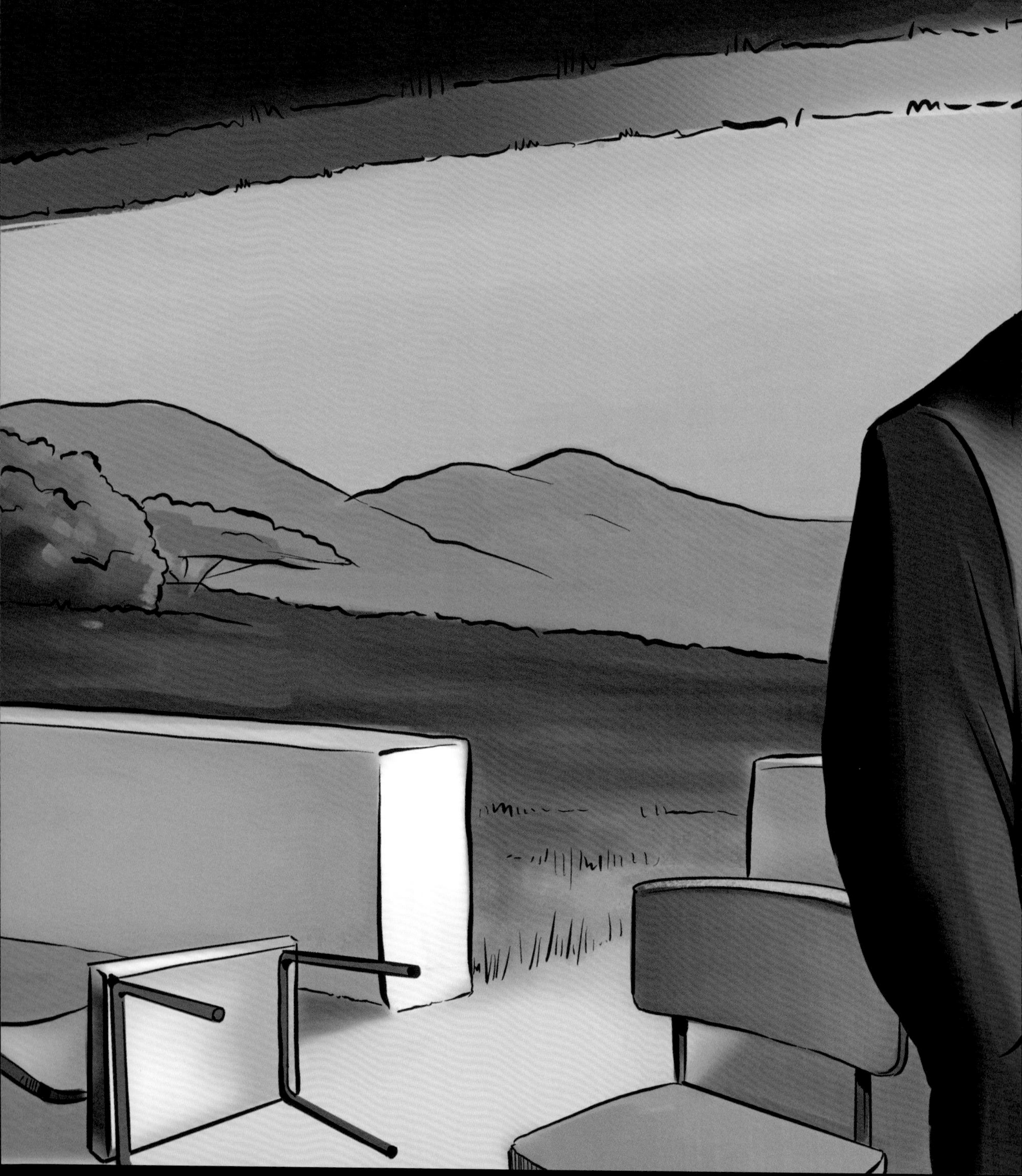

Chapter 5

A HOUSE DIVIDED

Illustrated by
Tumi Mamabolo

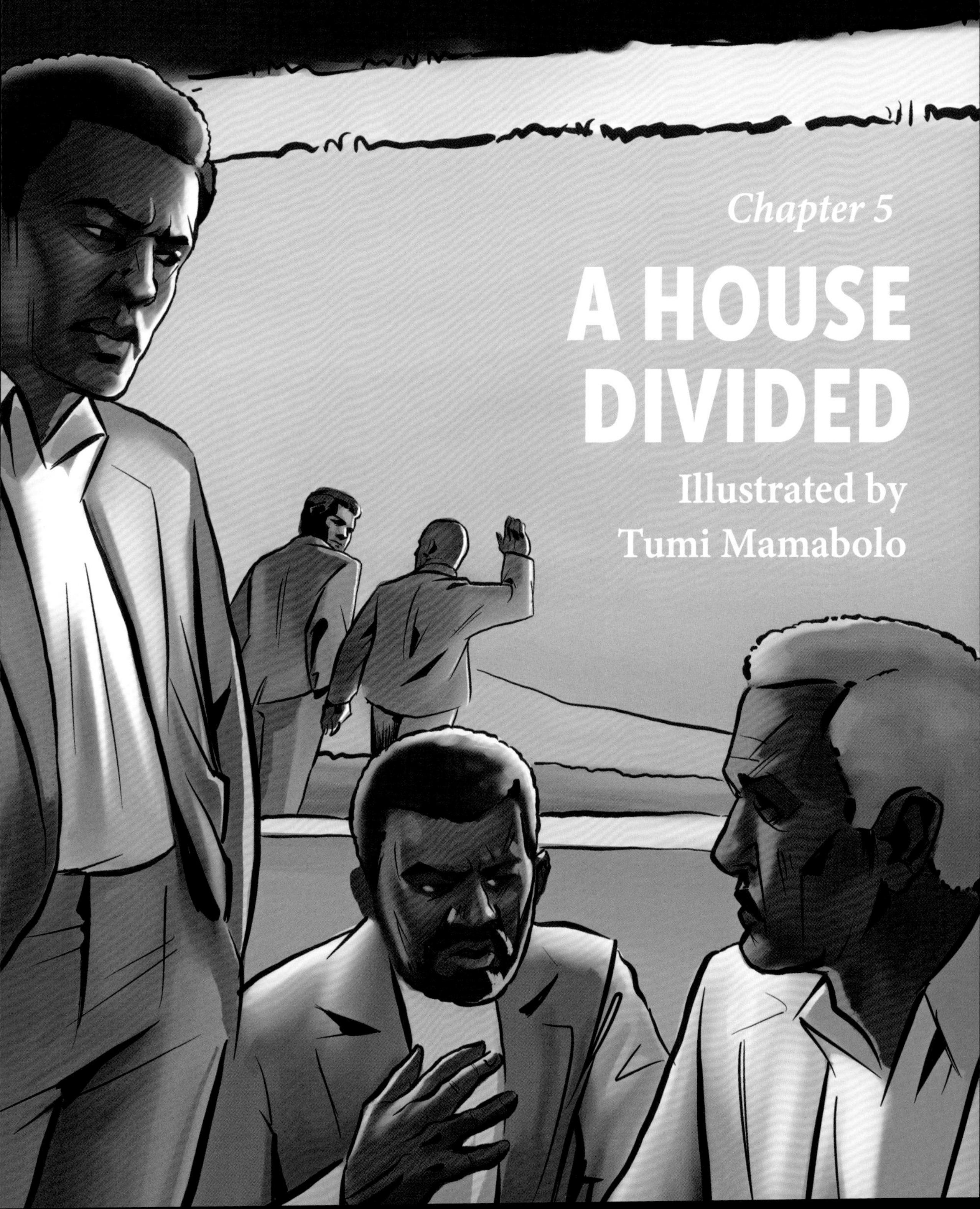

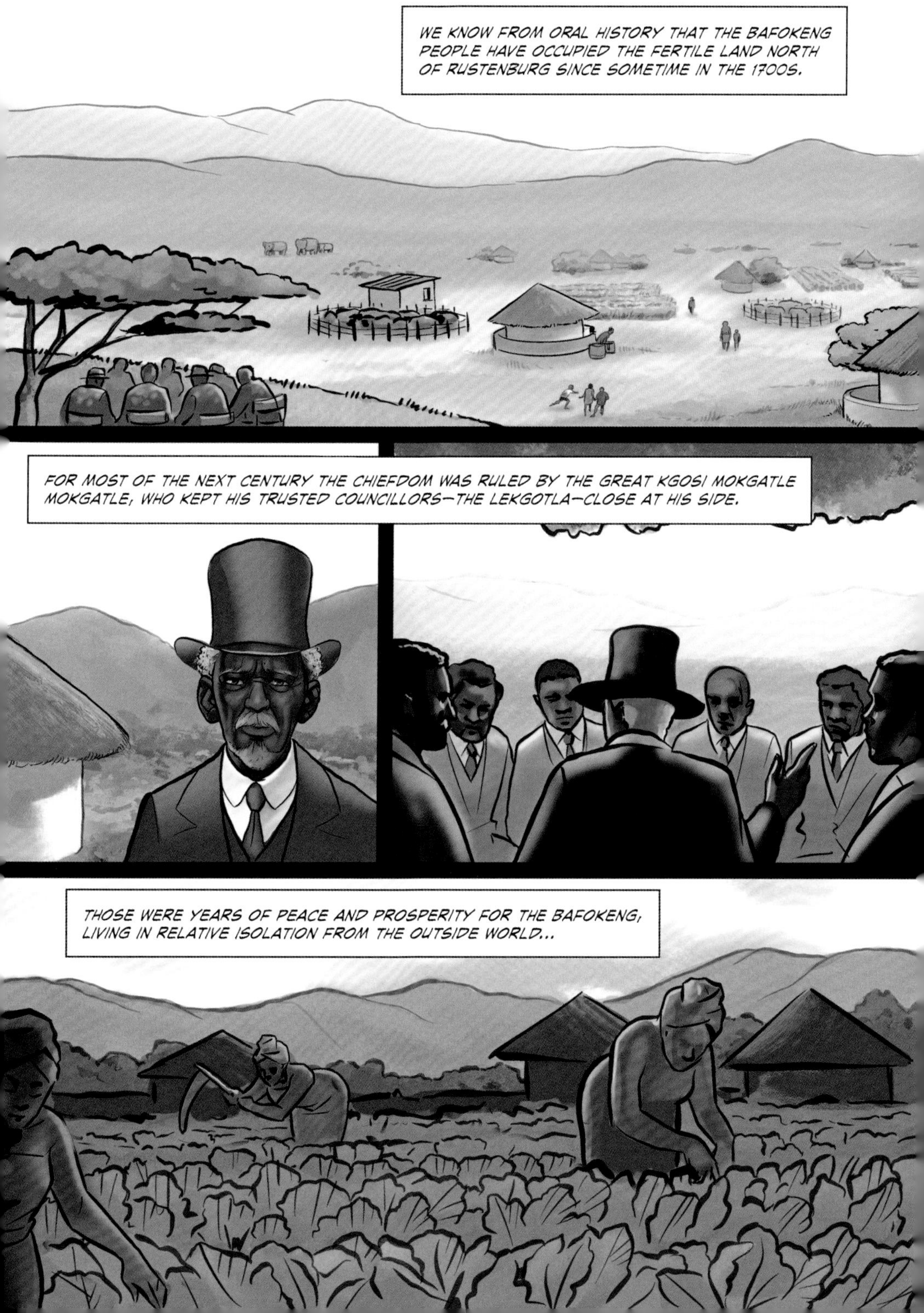
WE KNOW FROM ORAL HISTORY THAT THE BAFOKENG PEOPLE HAVE OCCUPIED THE FERTILE LAND NORTH OF RUSTENBURG SINCE SOMETIME IN THE 1700S.
FOR MOST OF THE NEXT CENTURY THE CHIEFDOM WAS RULED BY THE GREAT KGOSI MOKGATLE MOKGATLE, WHO KEPT HIS TRUSTED COUNCILLORS—THE LEKGOTLA—CLOSE AT HIS SIDE.
THOSE WERE YEARS OF PEACE AND PROSPERITY FOR THE BAFOKENG, LIVING IN RELATIVE ISOLATION FROM THE OUTSIDE WORLD...

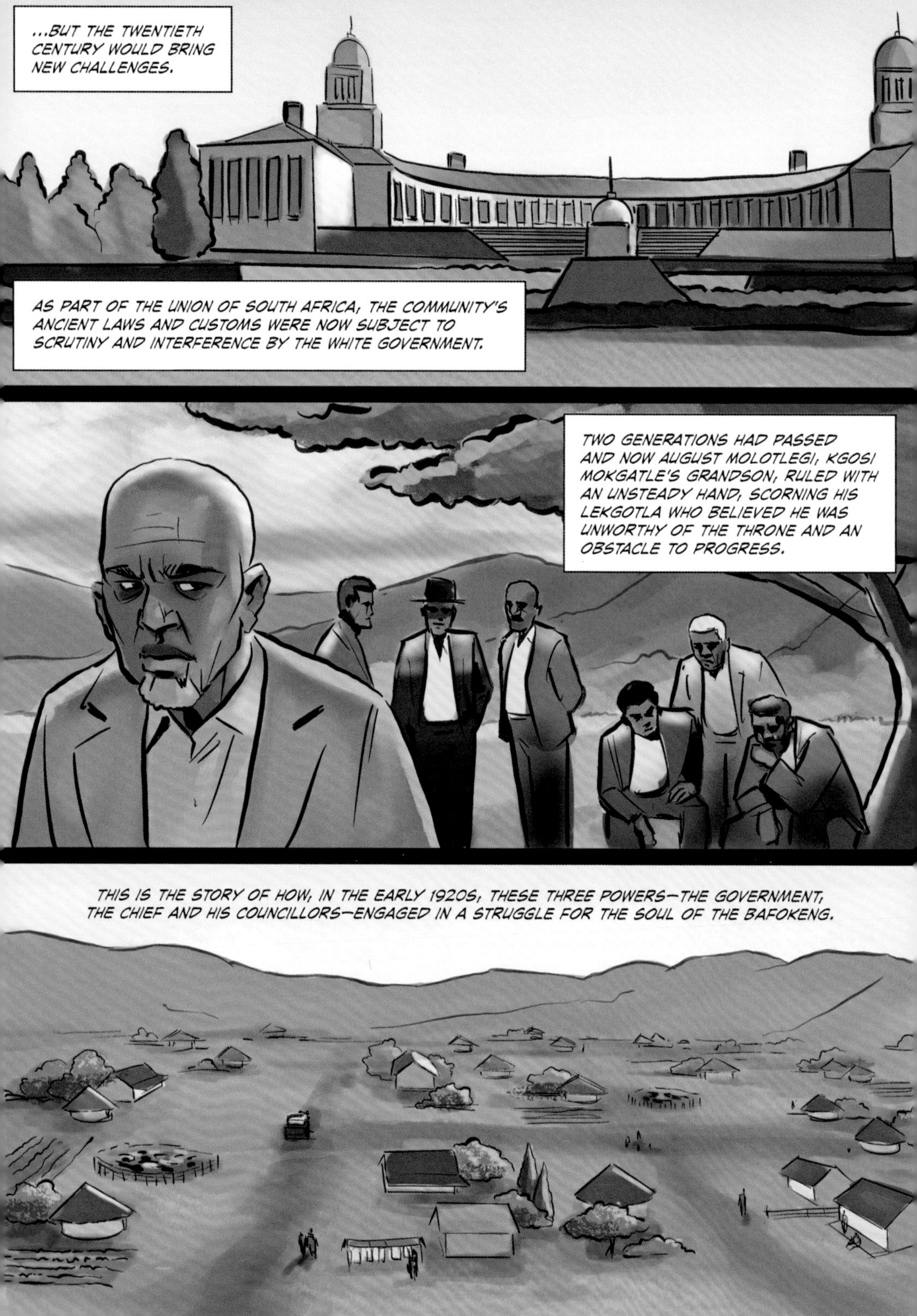
...BUT THE TWENTIETH CENTURY WOULD BRING NEW CHALLENGES.
AS PART OF THE UNION OF SOUTH AFRICA, THE COMMUNITY'S ANCIENT LAWS AND CUSTOMS WERE NOW SUBJECT TO SCRUTINY AND INTERFERENCE BY THE WHITE GOVERNMENT.
TWO GENERATIONS HAD PASSED AND NOW AUGUST MOLOTLEGI, KGOSI MOKGATLE'S GRANDSON, RULED WITH AN UNSTEADY HAND, SCORNING HIS LEKGOTLA WHO BELIEVED HE WAS UNWORTHY OF THE THRONE AND AN OBSTACLE TO PROGRESS.
THIS IS THE STORY OF HOW, IN THE EARLY 1920S, THESE THREE POWERS—THE GOVERNMENT, THE CHIEF AND HIS COUNCILLORS—ENGAGED IN A STRUGGLE FOR THE SOUL OF THE BAFOKENG.

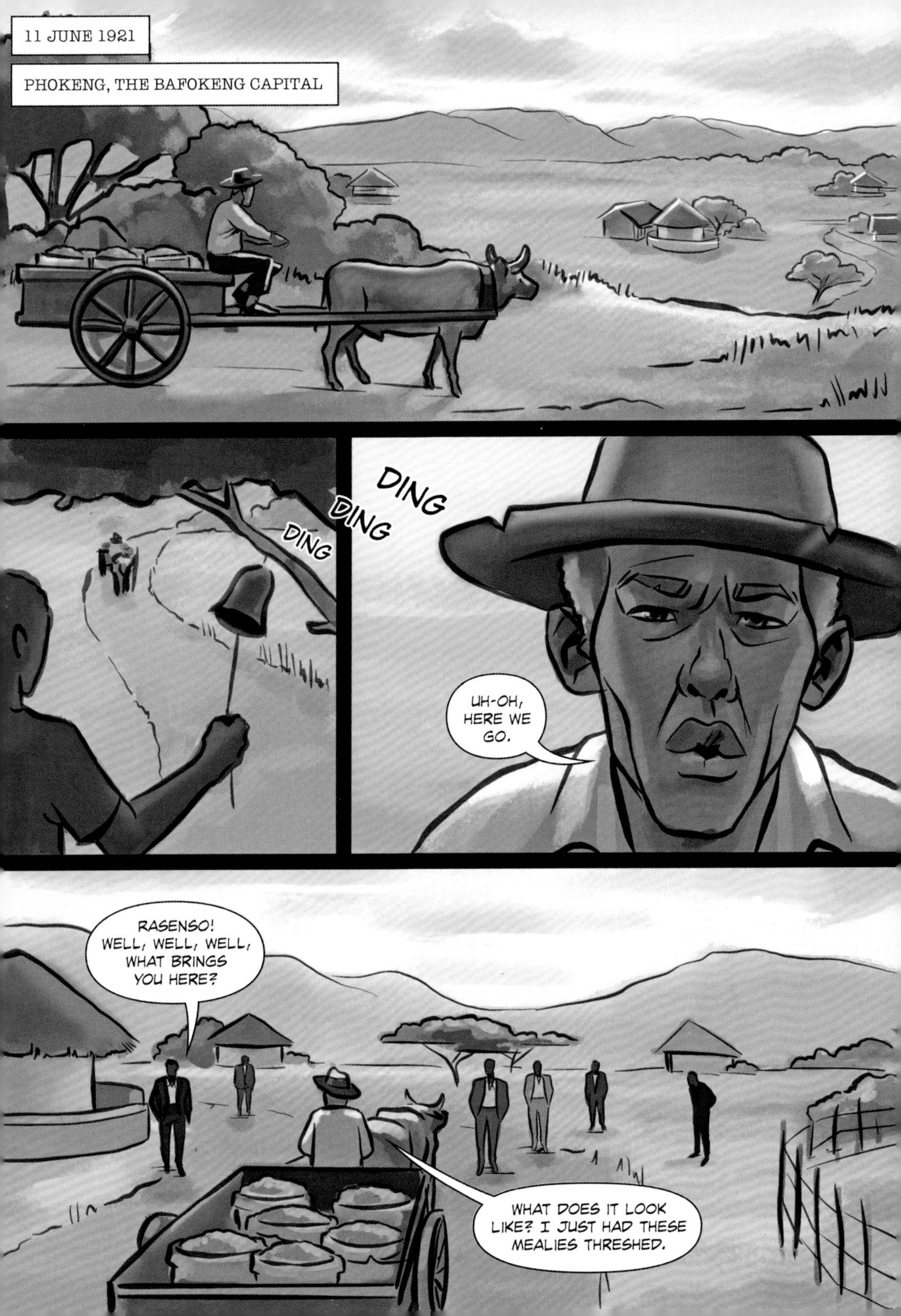
11 JUNE 1921
PHOKENG, THE BAFOKENG CAPITAL
DING
DING
DING
UH-OH, HERE WE GO.
RASENSO! WELL, WELL, WELL, WHAT BRINGS YOU HERE?
WHAT DOES IT LOOK LIKE? I JUST HAD THESE MEALIES THRESHED.

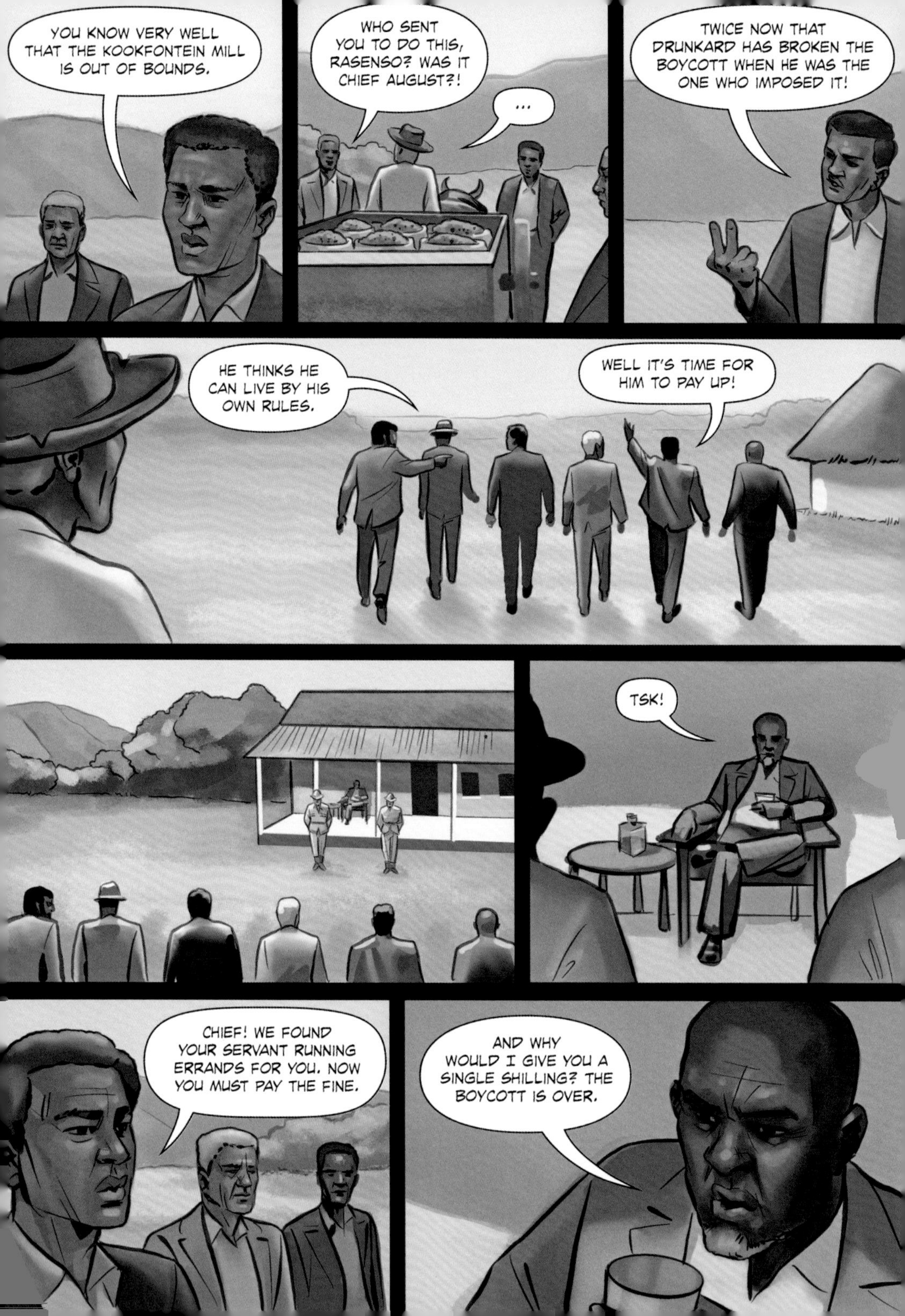
YOU KNOW VERY WELL THAT THE KOOKFONTEIN MILL IS OUT OF BOUNDS.
WHO SENT YOU TO DO THIS, RASENSO? WAS IT CHIEF AUGUST?!
...
TWICE NOW THAT DRUNKARD HAS BROKEN THE BOYCOTT WHEN HE WAS THE ONE WHO IMPOSED IT!
HE THINKS HE CAN LIVE BY HIS OWN RULES.
WELL IT'S TIME FOR HIM TO PAY UP!
TSK!
CHIEF! WE FOUND YOUR SERVANT RUNNING ERRANDS FOR YOU. NOW YOU MUST PAY THE FINE.
AND WHY WOULD I GIVE YOU A SINGLE SHILLING? THE BOYCOTT IS OVER.

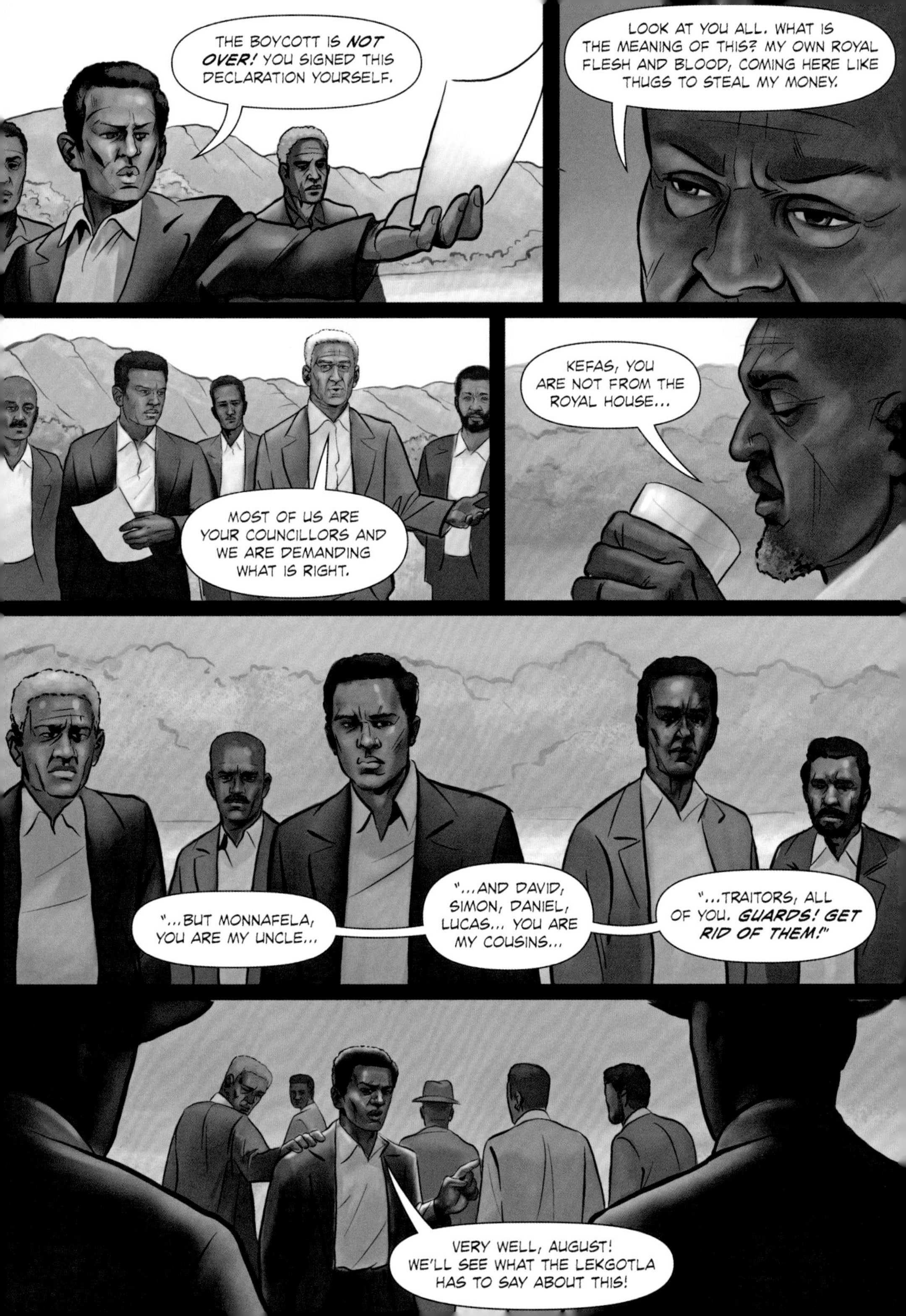
THE BOYCOTT IS *NOT OVER!* YOU SIGNED THIS DECLARATION YOURSELF.
LOOK AT YOU ALL. WHAT IS THE MEANING OF THIS? MY OWN ROYAL FLESH AND BLOOD, COMING HERE LIKE THUGS TO STEAL MY MONEY.
MOST OF US ARE YOUR COUNCILLORS AND WE ARE DEMANDING WHAT IS RIGHT.
KEFAS, YOU ARE NOT FROM THE ROYAL HOUSE...
"...BUT MONNAFELA, YOU ARE MY UNCLE...
"...AND DAVID, SIMON, DANIEL, LUCAS... YOU ARE MY COUSINS...
"...TRAITORS, ALL OF YOU. *GUARDS! GET RID OF THEM!*"
VERY WELL, AUGUST! WE'LL SEE WHAT THE LEKGOTLA HAS TO SAY ABOUT THIS!

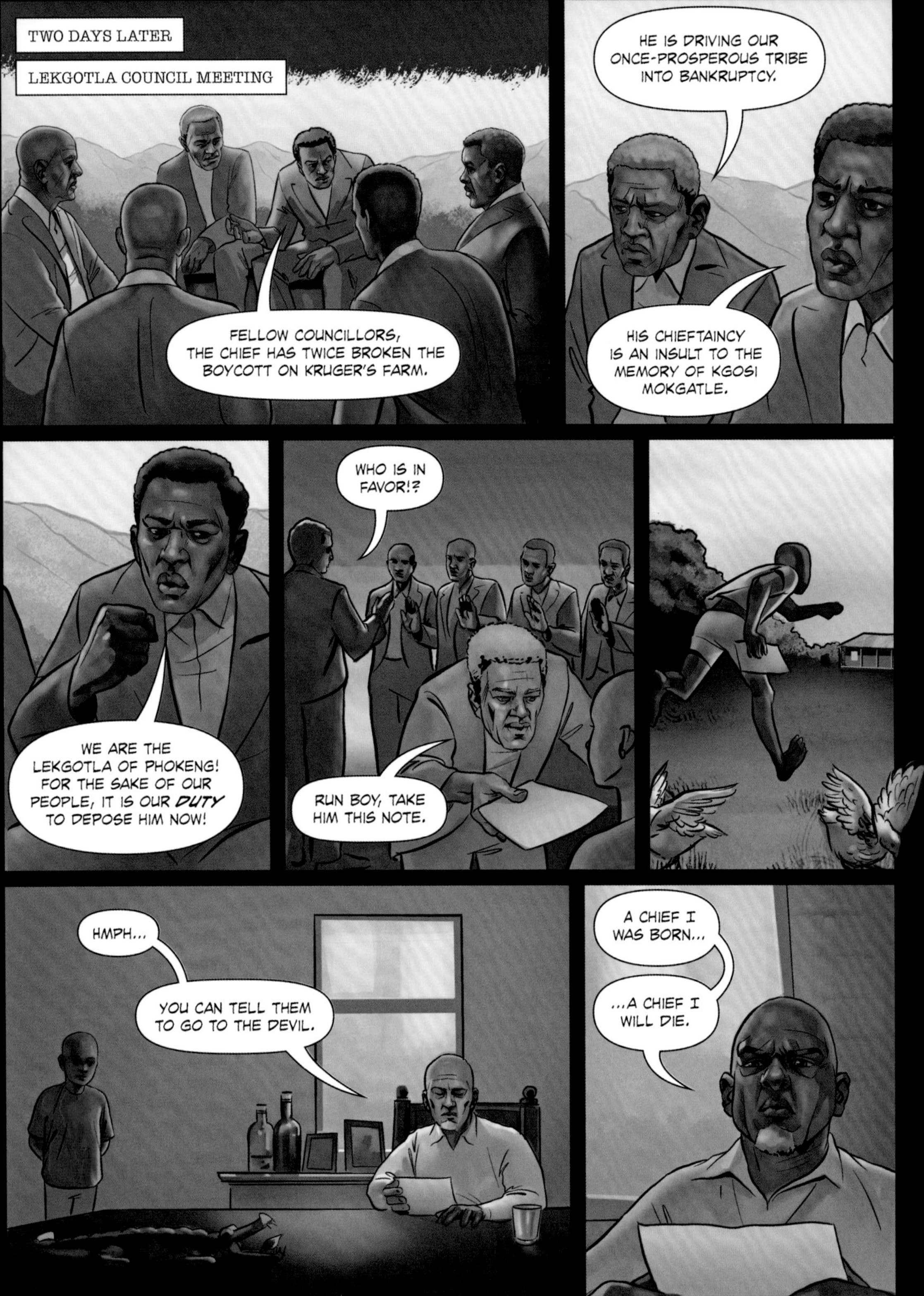
TWO DAYS LATER
LEKGOTLA COUNCIL MEETING
FELLOW COUNCILLORS, THE CHIEF HAS TWICE BROKEN THE BOYCOTT ON KRUGER'S FARM.
HE IS DRIVING OUR ONCE-PROSPEROUS TRIBE INTO BANKRUPTCY.
HIS CHIEFTAINCY IS AN INSULT TO THE MEMORY OF KGOSI MOKGATLE.
WE ARE THE LEKGOTLA OF PHOKENG! FOR THE SAKE OF OUR PEOPLE, IT IS OUR *DUTY* TO DEPOSE HIM NOW!
WHO IS IN FAVOR!?
RUN BOY, TAKE HIM THIS NOTE.
HMPH...
YOU CAN TELL THEM TO GO TO THE DEVIL.
A CHIEF I WAS BORN...
...A CHIEF I WILL DIE.

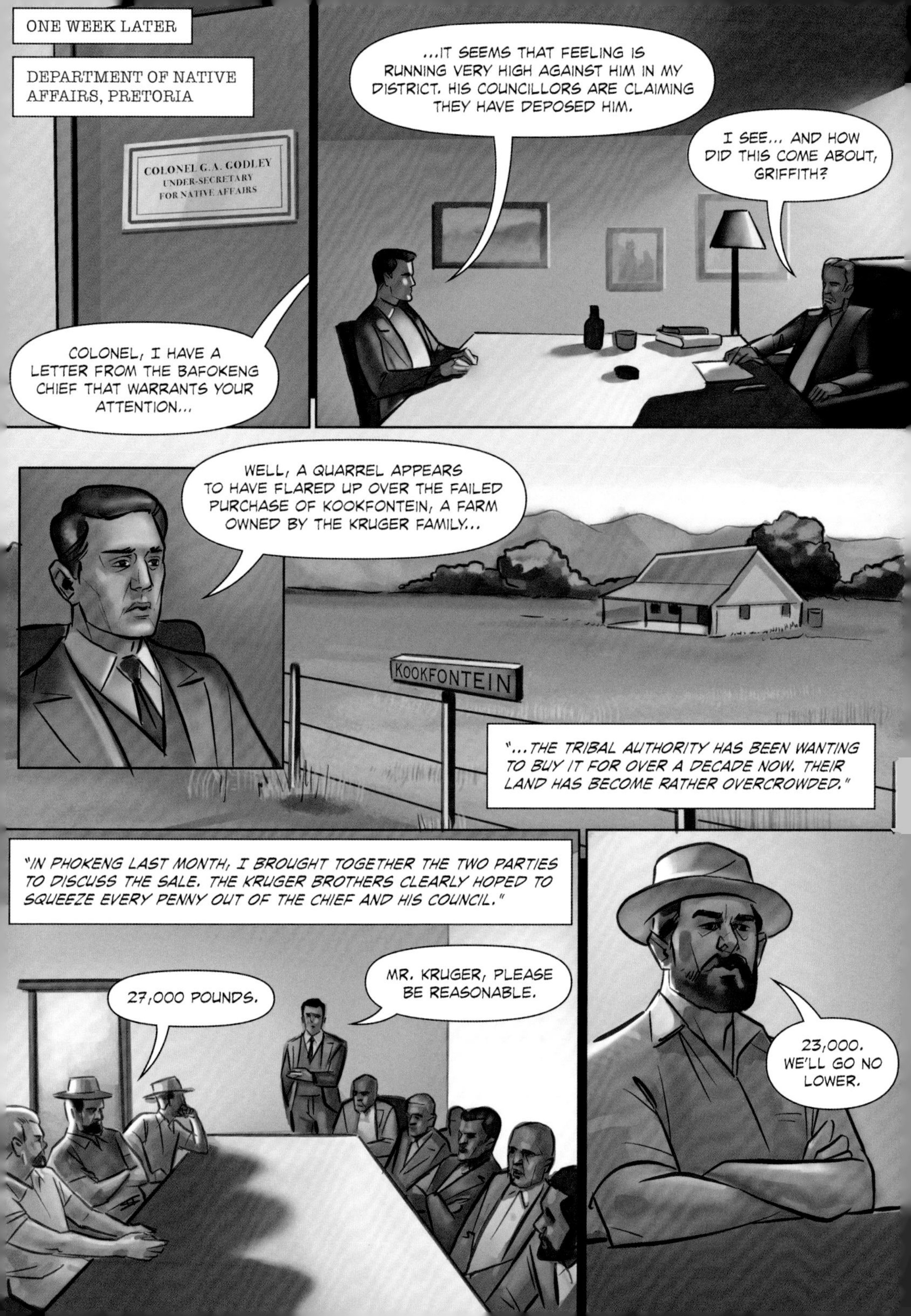
ONE WEEK LATER
DEPARTMENT OF NATIVE AFFAIRS, PRETORIA
COLONEL G.A. GODLEY UNDER-SECRETARY FOR NATIVE AFFAIRS
COLONEL, I HAVE A LETTER FROM THE BAFOKENG CHIEF THAT WARRANTS YOUR ATTENTION...
...IT SEEMS THAT FEELING IS RUNNING VERY HIGH AGAINST HIM IN MY DISTRICT. HIS COUNCILLORS ARE CLAIMING THEY HAVE DEPOSED HIM.
I SEE... AND HOW DID THIS COME ABOUT, GRIFFITH?
WELL, A QUARREL APPEARS TO HAVE FLARED UP OVER THE FAILED PURCHASE OF KOOKFONTEIN, A FARM OWNED BY THE KRUGER FAMILY...
KOOKFONTEIN
"...THE TRIBAL AUTHORITY HAS BEEN WANTING TO BUY IT FOR OVER A DECADE NOW. THEIR LAND HAS BECOME RATHER OVERCROWDED."
"IN PHOKENG LAST MONTH, I BROUGHT TOGETHER THE TWO PARTIES TO DISCUSS THE SALE. THE KRUGER BROTHERS CLEARLY HOPED TO SQUEEZE EVERY PENNY OUT OF THE CHIEF AND HIS COUNCIL."
27,000 POUNDS.
MR. KRUGER, PLEASE BE REASONABLE.
23,000. WE'LL GO NO LOWER.

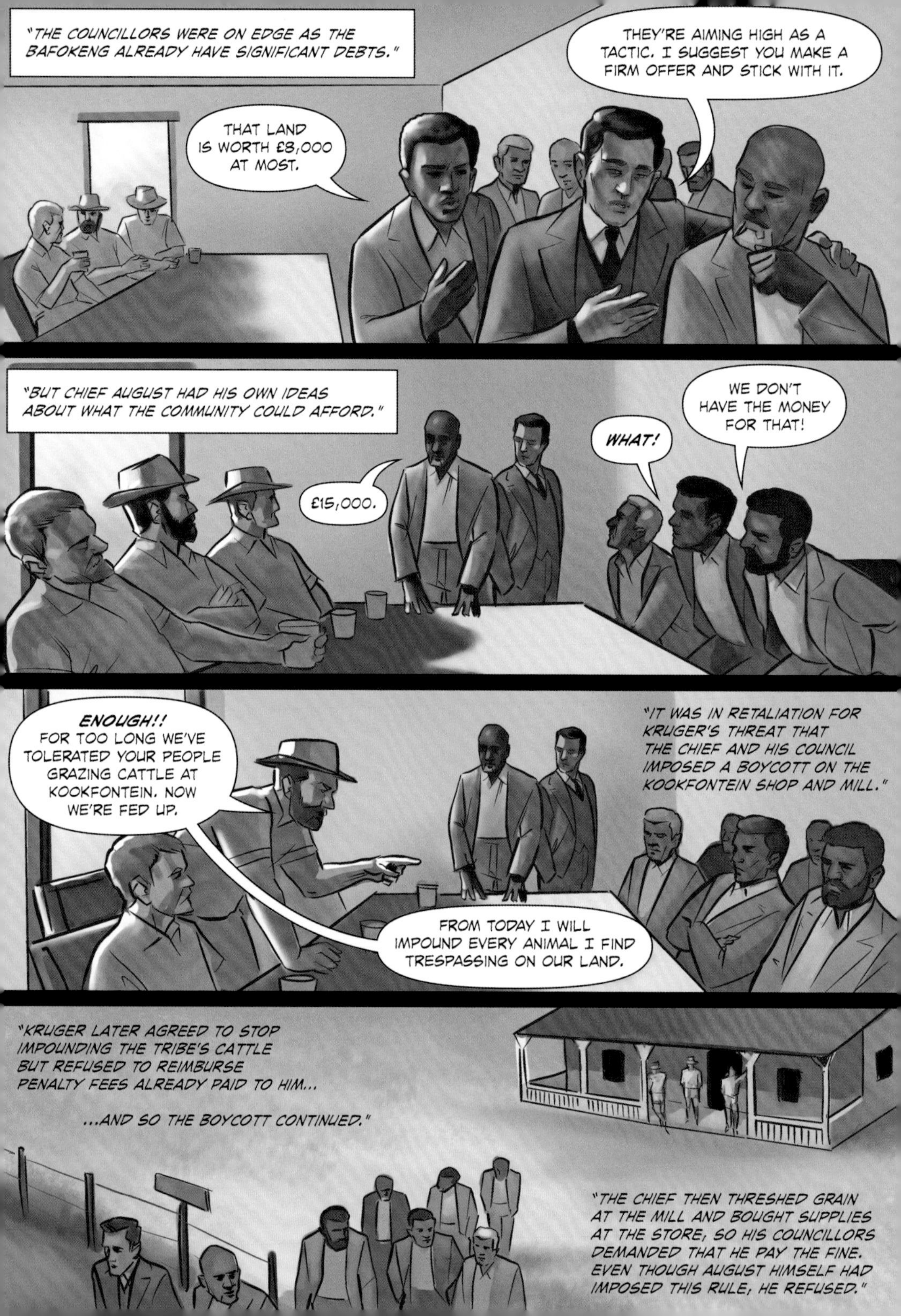
"THE COUNCILLORS WERE ON EDGE AS THE BAFOKENG ALREADY HAVE SIGNIFICANT DEBTS."
THAT LAND IS WORTH £8,000 AT MOST.
THEY'RE AIMING HIGH AS A TACTIC. I SUGGEST YOU MAKE A FIRM OFFER AND STICK WITH IT.
"BUT CHIEF AUGUST HAD HIS OWN IDEAS ABOUT WHAT THE COMMUNITY COULD AFFORD."
£15,000.
WHAT!
WE DON'T HAVE THE MONEY FOR THAT!
ENOUGH!! FOR TOO LONG WE'VE TOLERATED YOUR PEOPLE GRAZING CATTLE AT KOOKFONTEIN. NOW WE'RE FED UP.
FROM TODAY I WILL IMPOUND EVERY ANIMAL I FIND TRESPASSING ON OUR LAND.
"IT WAS IN RETALIATION FOR KRUGER'S THREAT THAT THE CHIEF AND HIS COUNCIL IMPOSED A BOYCOTT ON THE KOOKFONTEIN SHOP AND MILL."
"KRUGER LATER AGREED TO STOP IMPOUNDING THE TRIBE'S CATTLE BUT REFUSED TO REIMBURSE PENALTY FEES ALREADY PAID TO HIM...
...AND SO THE BOYCOTT CONTINUED."
"THE CHIEF THEN THRESHED GRAIN AT THE MILL AND BOUGHT SUPPLIES AT THE STORE, SO HIS COUNCILLORS DEMANDED THAT HE PAY THE FINE. EVEN THOUGH AUGUST HIMSELF HAD IMPOSED THIS RULE, HE REFUSED."

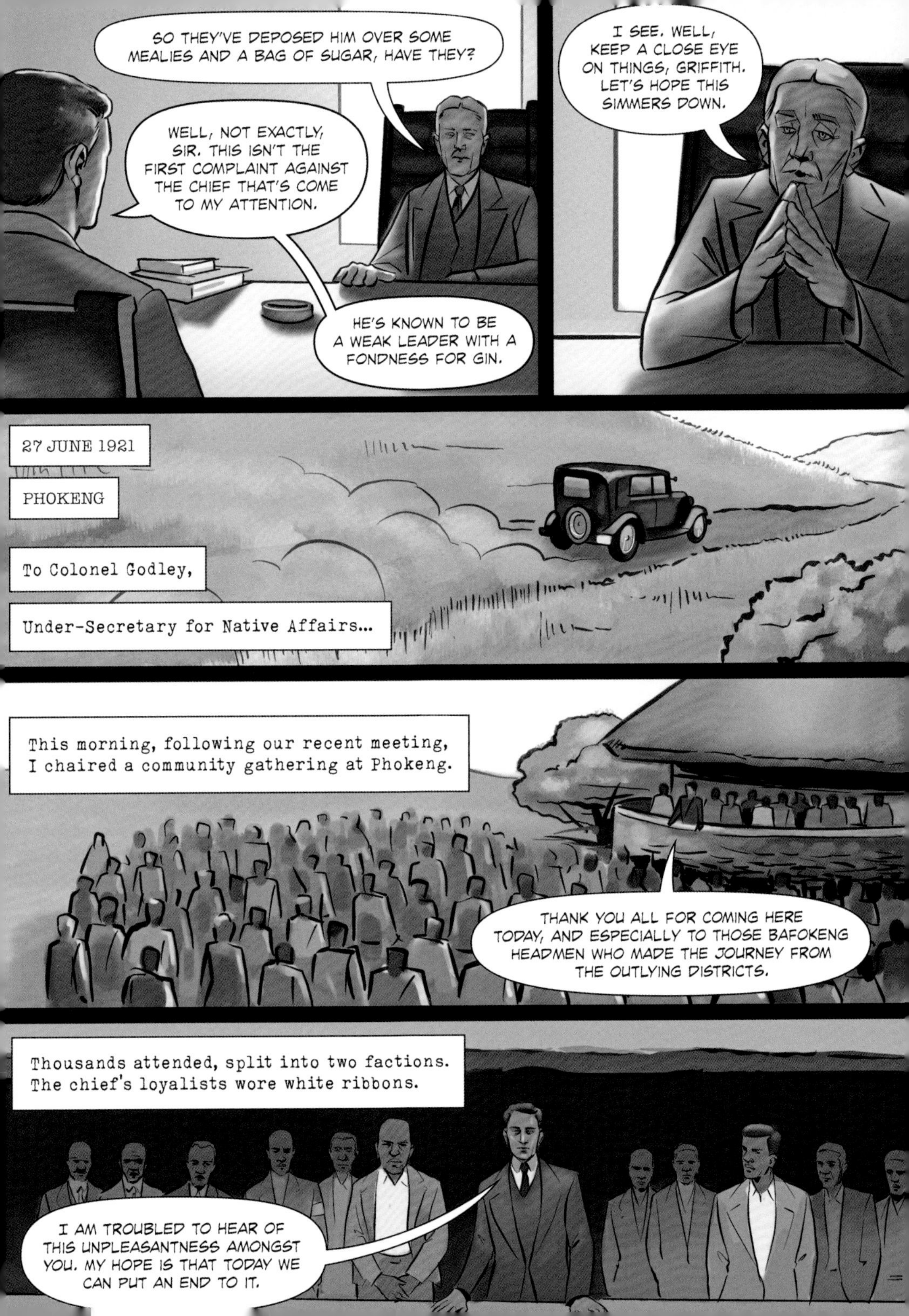
SO THEY'VE DEPOSED HIM OVER SOME MEALIES AND A BAG OF SUGAR, HAVE THEY?
WELL, NOT EXACTLY, SIR. THIS ISN'T THE FIRST COMPLAINT AGAINST THE CHIEF THAT'S COME TO MY ATTENTION.
HE'S KNOWN TO BE A WEAK LEADER WITH A FONDNESS FOR GIN.
I SEE. WELL, KEEP A CLOSE EYE ON THINGS, GRIFFITH. LET'S HOPE THIS SIMMERS DOWN.
27 JUNE 1921
PHOKENG
To Colonel Godley,
Under-Secretary for Native Affairs...
This morning, following our recent meeting, I chaired a community gathering at Phokeng.
THANK YOU ALL FOR COMING HERE TODAY, AND ESPECIALLY TO THOSE BAFOKENG HEADMEN WHO MADE THE JOURNEY FROM THE OUTLYING DISTRICTS.
Thousands attended, split into two factions. The chief's loyalists wore white ribbons.
I AM TROUBLED TO HEAR OF THIS UNPLEASANTNESS AMONGST YOU. MY HOPE IS THAT TODAY WE CAN PUT AN END TO IT.

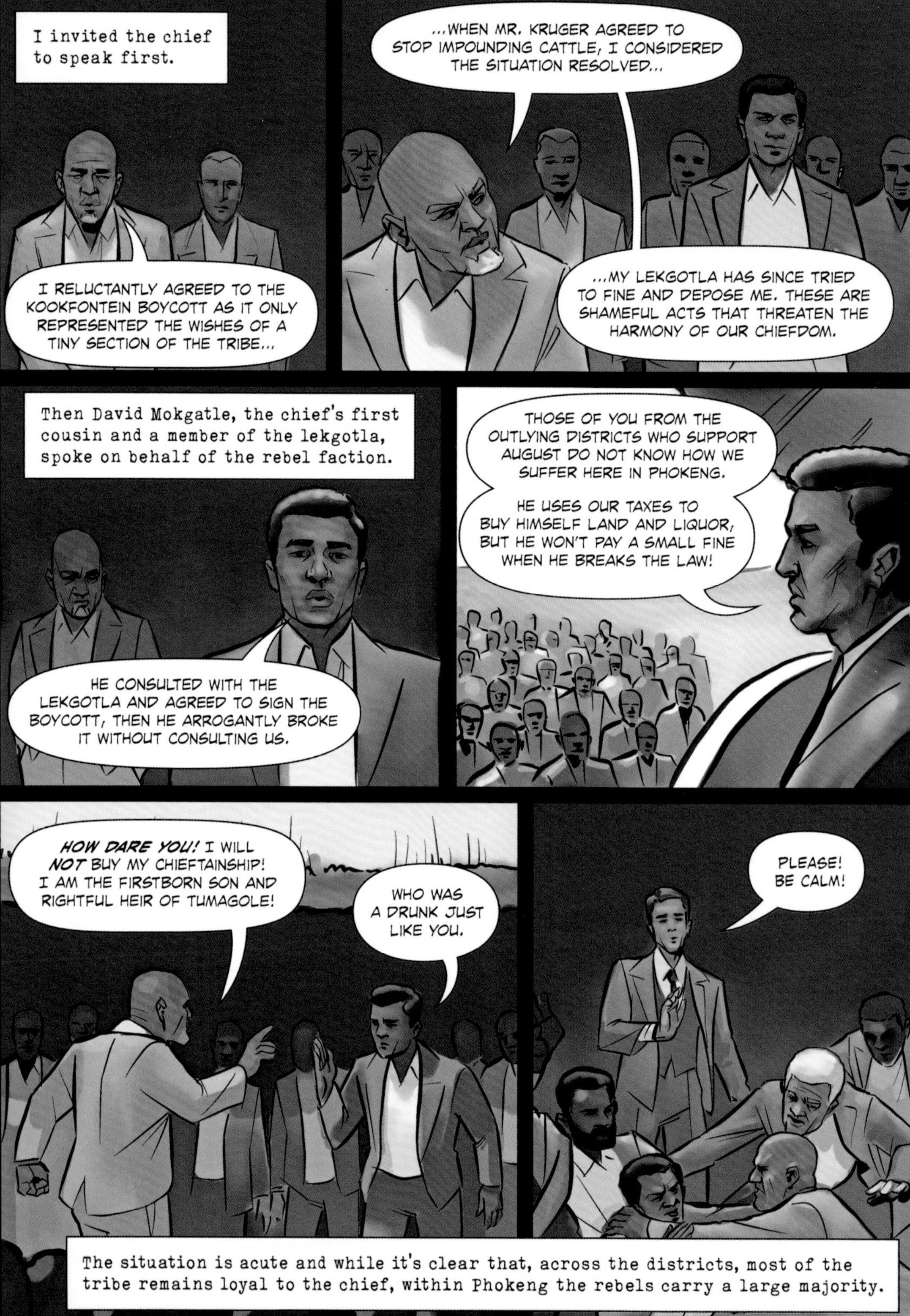

I invited the chief to speak first.
I RELUCTANTLY AGREED TO THE KOOKFONTEIN BOYCOTT AS IT ONLY REPRESENTED THE WISHES OF A TINY SECTION OF THE TRIBE...
...WHEN MR. KRUGER AGREED TO STOP IMPOUNDING CATTLE, I CONSIDERED THE SITUATION RESOLVED...
...MY LEKGOTLA HAS SINCE TRIED TO FINE AND DEPOSE ME. THESE ARE SHAMEFUL ACTS THAT THREATEN THE HARMONY OF OUR CHIEFDOM.
Then David Mokgatle, the chief's first cousin and a member of the lekgotla, spoke on behalf of the rebel faction.
HE CONSULTED WITH THE LEKGOTLA AND AGREED TO SIGN THE BOYCOTT, THEN HE ARROGANTLY BROKE IT WITHOUT CONSULTING US.
THOSE OF YOU FROM THE OUTLYING DISTRICTS WHO SUPPORT AUGUST DO NOT KNOW HOW WE SUFFER HERE IN PHOKENG.
HE USES OUR TAXES TO BUY HIMSELF LAND AND LIQUOR, BUT HE WON'T PAY A SMALL FINE WHEN HE BREAKS THE LAW!
HOW DARE YOU! I WILL *NOT* BUY MY CHIEFTAINSHIP! I AM THE FIRSTBORN SON AND RIGHTFUL HEIR OF TUMAGOLE!
WHO WAS A DRUNK JUST LIKE YOU.
PLEASE! BE CALM!
The situation is acute and while it's clear that, across the districts, most of the tribe remains loyal to the chief, within Phokeng the rebels carry a large majority.

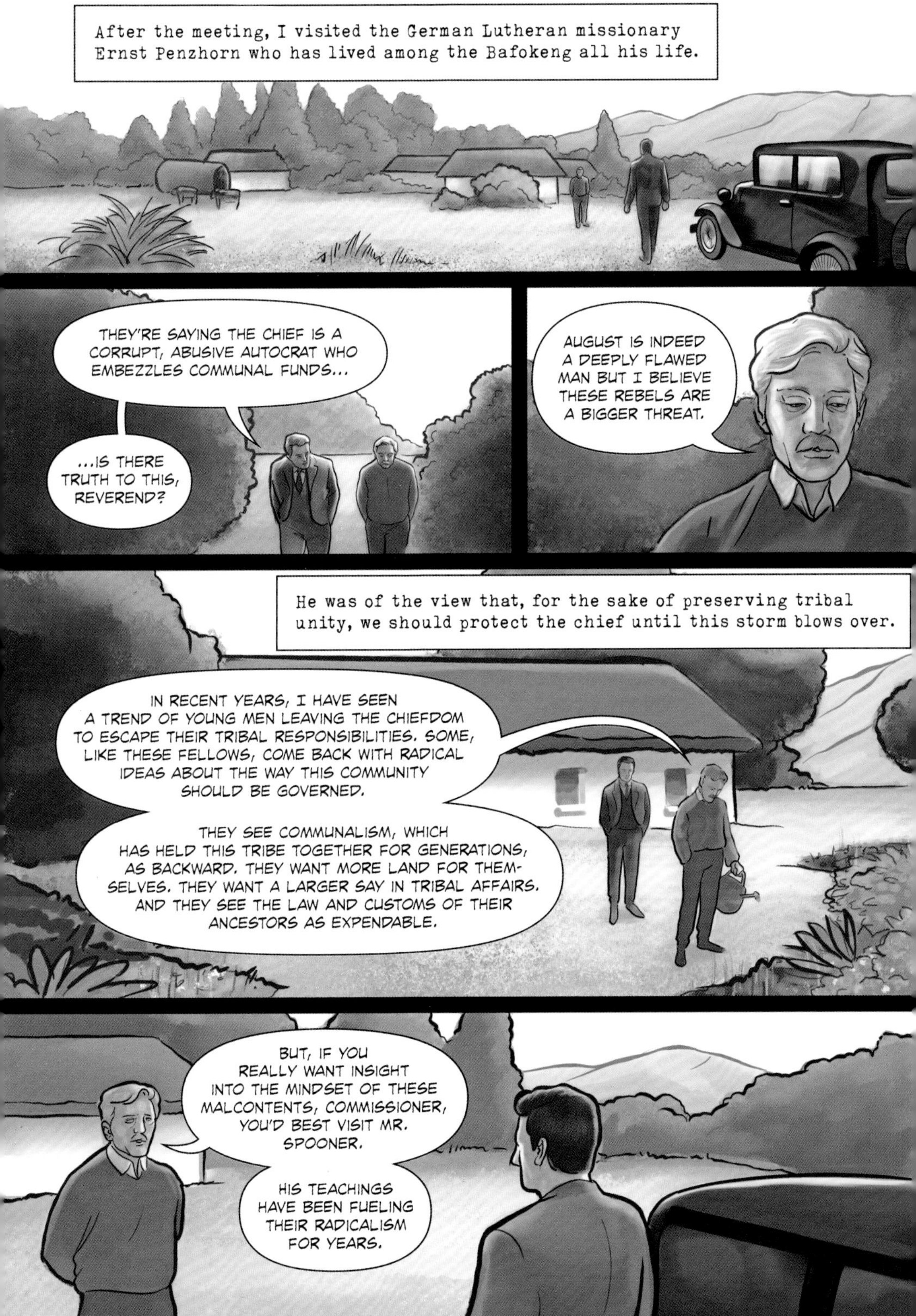
After the meeting, I visited the German Lutheran missionary Ernst Penzhorn who has lived among the Bafokeng all his life.
THEY'RE SAYING THE CHIEF IS A CORRUPT, ABUSIVE AUTOCRAT WHO EMBEZZLES COMMUNAL FUNDS...
...IS THERE TRUTH TO THIS, REVEREND?
AUGUST IS INDEED A DEEPLY FLAWED MAN BUT I BELIEVE THESE REBELS ARE A BIGGER THREAT.
He was of the view that, for the sake of preserving tribal unity, we should protect the chief until this storm blows over.
IN RECENT YEARS, I HAVE SEEN A TREND OF YOUNG MEN LEAVING THE CHIEFDOM TO ESCAPE THEIR TRIBAL RESPONSIBILITIES. SOME, LIKE THESE FELLOWS, COME BACK WITH RADICAL IDEAS ABOUT THE WAY THIS COMMUNITY SHOULD BE GOVERNED.
THEY SEE COMMUNALISM, WHICH HAS HELD THIS TRIBE TOGETHER FOR GENERATIONS, AS BACKWARD. THEY WANT MORE LAND FOR THEMSELVES. THEY WANT A LARGER SAY IN TRIBAL AFFAIRS. AND THEY SEE THE LAW AND CUSTOMS OF THEIR ANCESTORS AS EXPENDABLE.
BUT, IF YOU REALLY WANT INSIGHT INTO THE MINDSET OF THESE MALCONTENTS, COMMISSIONER, YOU'D BEST VISIT MR. SPOONER.
HIS TEACHINGS HAVE BEEN FUELING THEIR RADICALISM FOR YEARS.

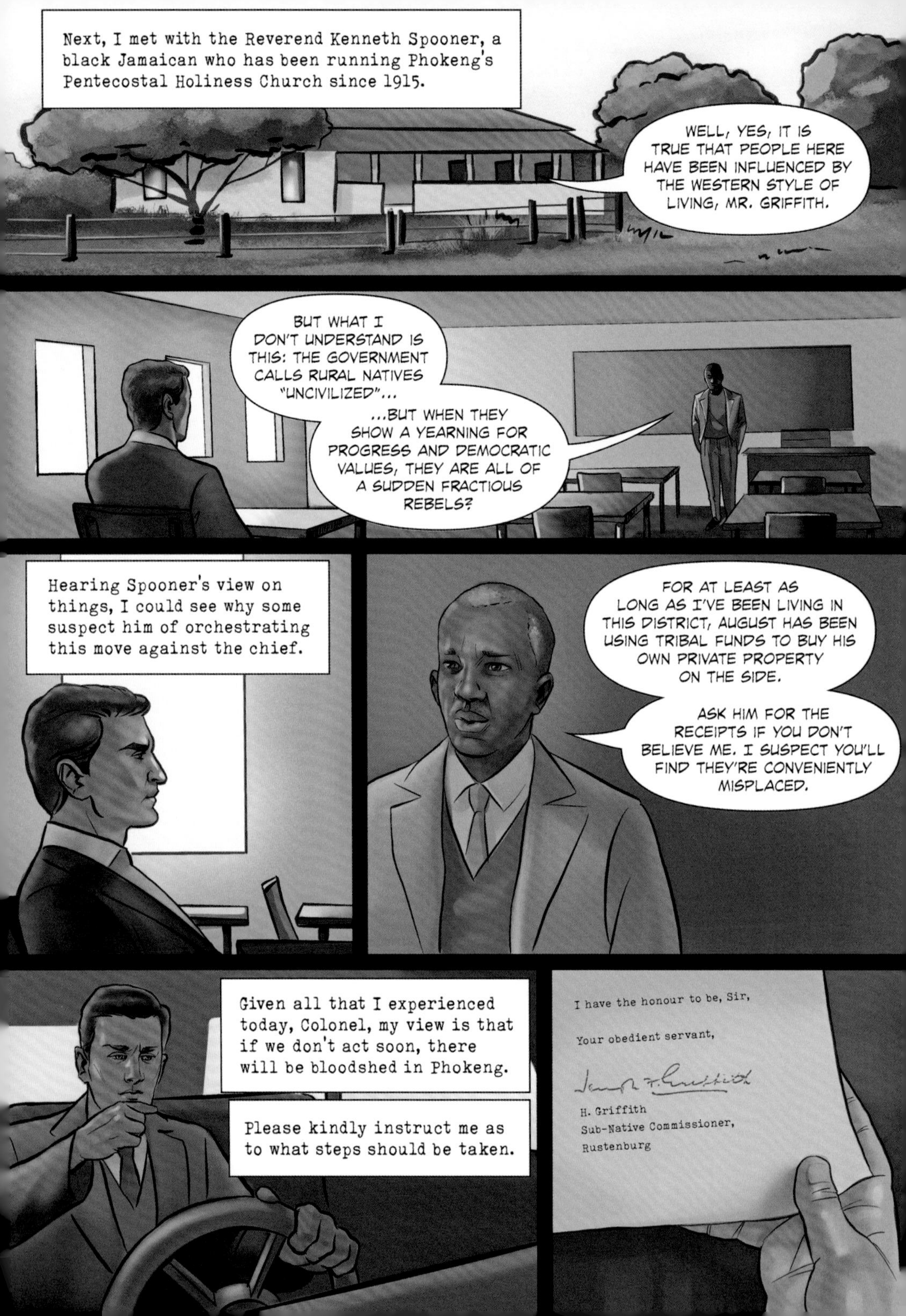

Next, I met with the Reverend Kenneth Spooner, a black Jamaican who has been running Phokeng's Pentecostal Holiness Church since 1915.
WELL, YES, IT IS TRUE THAT PEOPLE HERE HAVE BEEN INFLUENCED BY THE WESTERN STYLE OF LIVING, MR. GRIFFITH.
BUT WHAT I DON'T UNDERSTAND IS THIS: THE GOVERNMENT CALLS RURAL NATIVES "UNCIVILIZED"...
...BUT WHEN THEY SHOW A YEARNING FOR PROGRESS AND DEMOCRATIC VALUES, THEY ARE ALL OF A SUDDEN FRACTIOUS REBELS?
Hearing Spooner's view on things, I could see why some suspect him of orchestrating this move against the chief.
FOR AT LEAST AS LONG AS I'VE BEEN LIVING IN THIS DISTRICT, AUGUST HAS BEEN USING TRIBAL FUNDS TO BUY HIS OWN PRIVATE PROPERTY ON THE SIDE.
ASK HIM FOR THE RECEIPTS IF YOU DON'T BELIEVE ME. I SUSPECT YOU'LL FIND THEY'RE CONVENIENTLY MISPLACED.
Given all that I experienced today, Colonel, my view is that if we don't act soon, there will be bloodshed in Phokeng.
Please kindly instruct me as to what steps should be taken.
I have the honour to be, Sir,
Your obedient servant,
H. Griffith
Sub-Native Commissioner,
Rustenburg

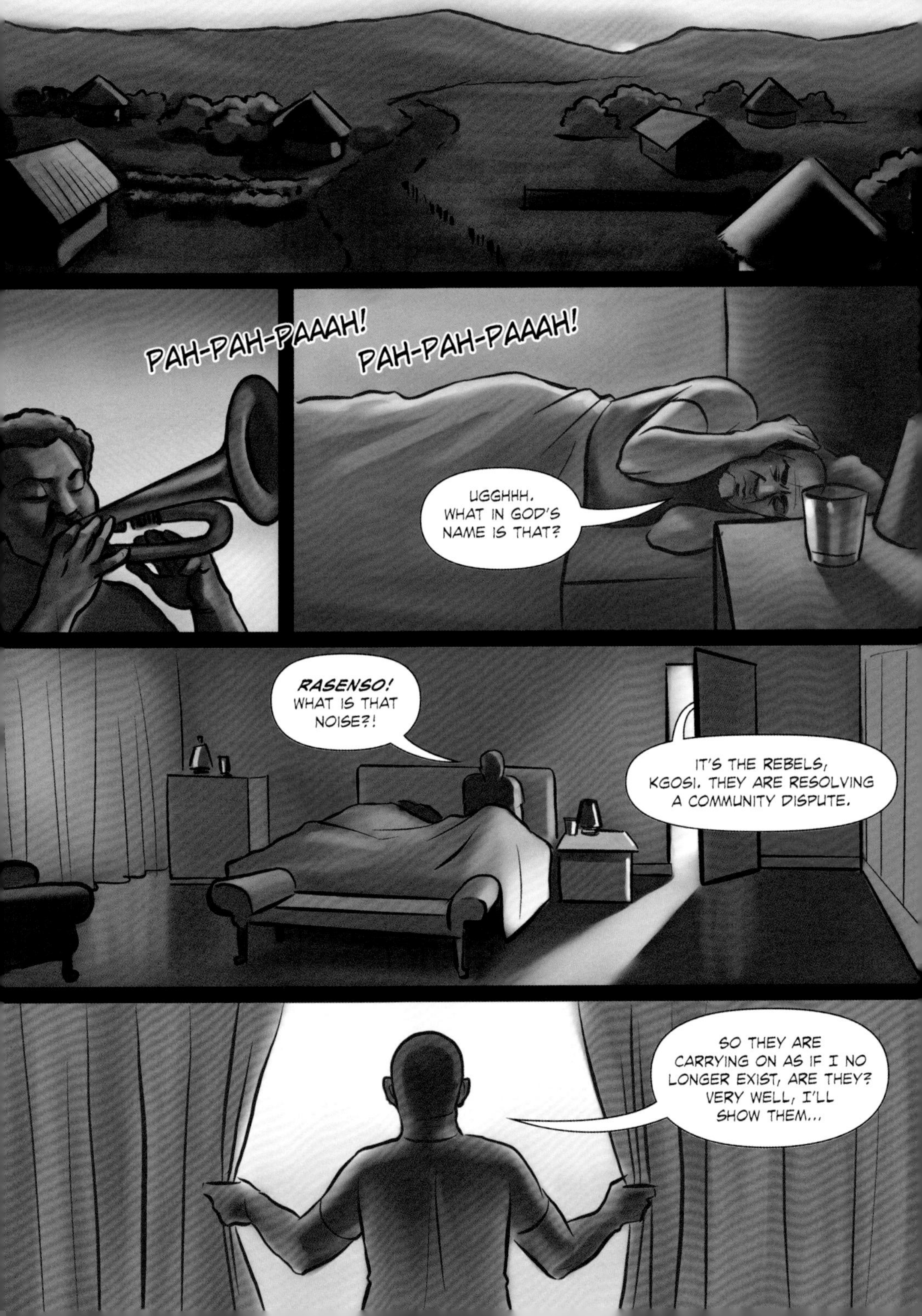
PAH-PAH-PAAAH!
PAH-PAH-PAAAH!
UGGHHH. WHAT IN GOD'S NAME IS THAT?
RASENSO! WHAT IS THAT NOISE?!
IT'S THE REBELS, KGOSI. THEY ARE RESOLVING A COMMUNITY DISPUTE.
SO THEY ARE CARRYING ON AS IF I NO LONGER EXIST, ARE THEY? VERY WELL, I'LL SHOW THEM...

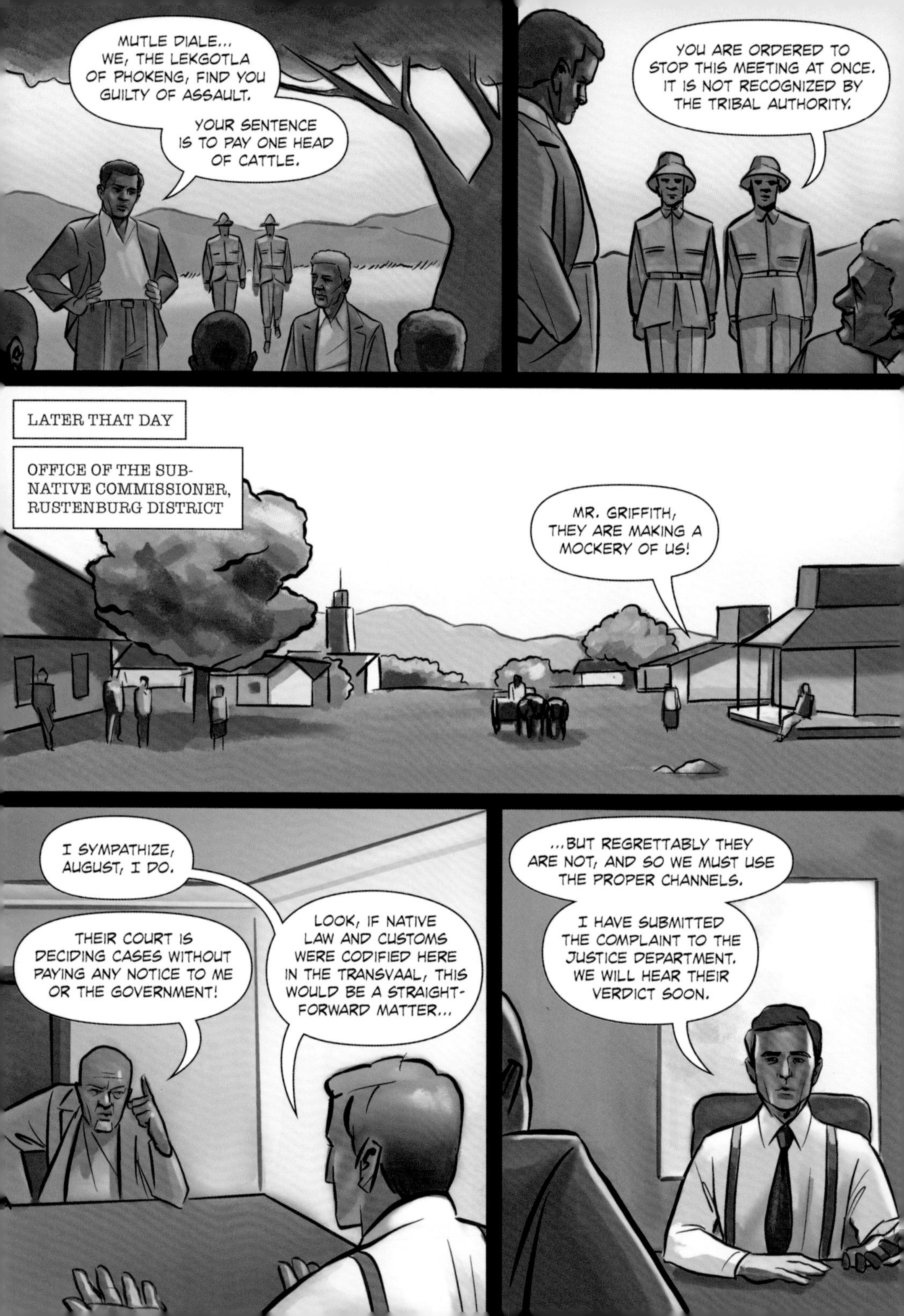
MUTLE DIALE... WE, THE LEKGOTLA OF PHOKENG, FIND YOU GUILTY OF ASSAULT.
YOUR SENTENCE IS TO PAY ONE HEAD OF CATTLE.
YOU ARE ORDERED TO STOP THIS MEETING AT ONCE. IT IS NOT RECOGNIZED BY THE TRIBAL AUTHORITY.
LATER THAT DAY
OFFICE OF THE SUB-NATIVE COMMISSIONER, RUSTENBURG DISTRICT
MR. GRIFFITH, THEY ARE MAKING A MOCKERY OF US!
I SYMPATHIZE, AUGUST, I DO.
THEIR COURT IS DECIDING CASES WITHOUT PAYING ANY NOTICE TO ME OR THE GOVERNMENT!
LOOK, IF NATIVE LAW AND CUSTOMS WERE CODIFIED HERE IN THE TRANSVAAL, THIS WOULD BE A STRAIGHT-FORWARD MATTER...
...BUT REGRETTABLY THEY ARE NOT, AND SO WE MUST USE THE PROPER CHANNELS.
I HAVE SUBMITTED THE COMPLAINT TO THE JUSTICE DEPARTMENT. WE WILL HEAR THEIR VERDICT SOON.

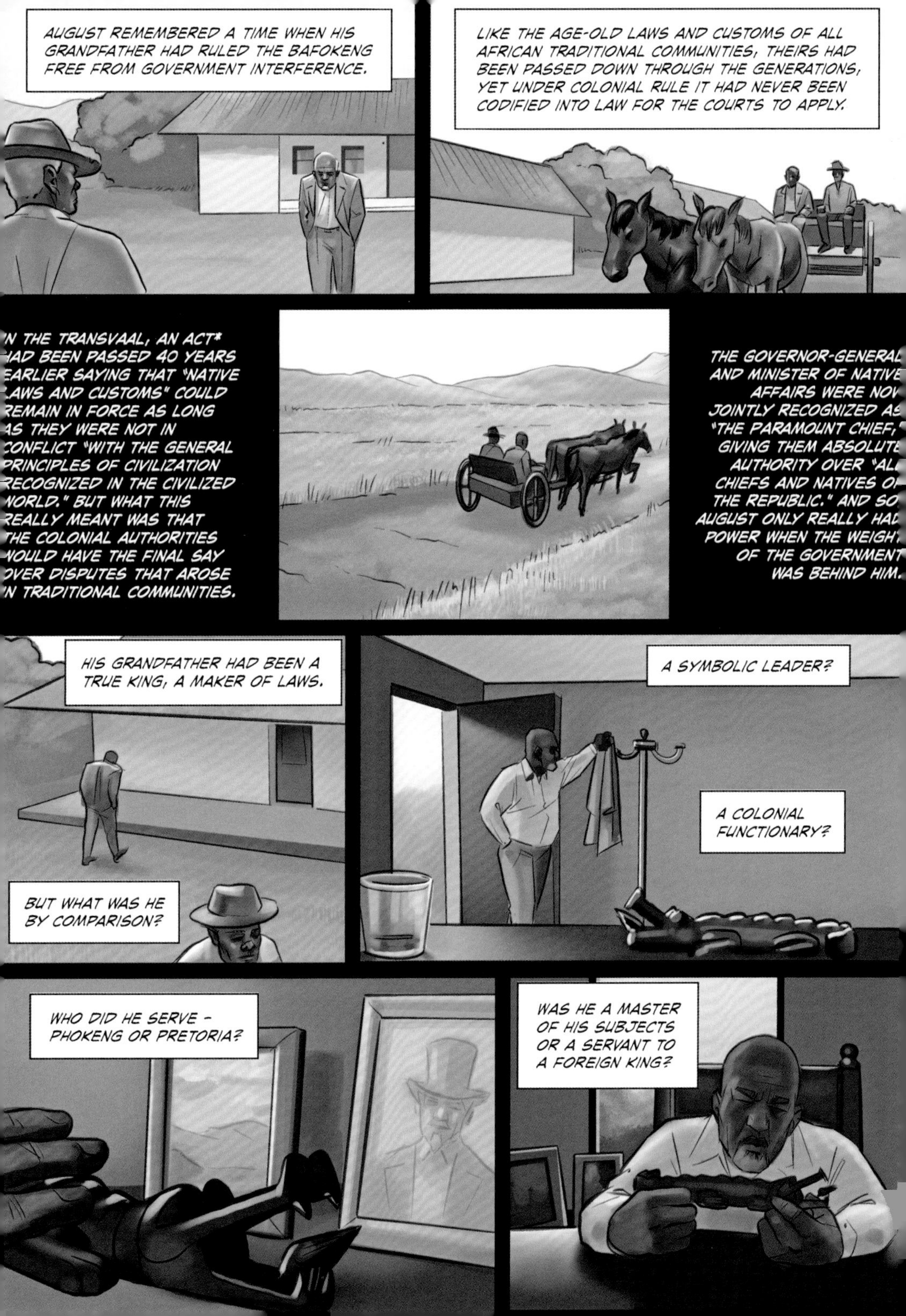
AUGUST REMEMBERED A TIME WHEN HIS GRANDFATHER HAD RULED THE BAFOKENG FREE FROM GOVERNMENT INTERFERENCE.
LIKE THE AGE-OLD LAWS AND CUSTOMS OF ALL AFRICAN TRADITIONAL COMMUNITIES, THEIRS HAD BEEN PASSED DOWN THROUGH THE GENERATIONS, YET UNDER COLONIAL RULE IT HAD NEVER BEEN CODIFIED INTO LAW FOR THE COURTS TO APPLY.
IN THE TRANSVAAL, AN ACT* HAD BEEN PASSED 40 YEARS EARLIER SAYING THAT "NATIVE LAWS AND CUSTOMS" COULD REMAIN IN FORCE AS LONG AS THEY WERE NOT IN CONFLICT "WITH THE GENERAL PRINCIPLES OF CIVILIZATION RECOGNIZED IN THE CIVILIZED WORLD." BUT WHAT THIS REALLY MEANT WAS THAT THE COLONIAL AUTHORITIES WOULD HAVE THE FINAL SAY OVER DISPUTES THAT AROSE IN TRADITIONAL COMMUNITIES.
THE GOVERNOR-GENERAL AND MINISTER OF NATIVE AFFAIRS WERE NOW JOINTLY RECOGNIZED AS "THE PARAMOUNT CHIEF," GIVING THEM ABSOLUTE AUTHORITY OVER "ALL CHIEFS AND NATIVES OF THE REPUBLIC." AND SO AUGUST ONLY REALLY HAD POWER WHEN THE WEIGHT OF THE GOVERNMENT WAS BEHIND HIM.
HIS GRANDFATHER HAD BEEN A TRUE KING, A MAKER OF LAWS.
BUT WHAT WAS HE BY COMPARISON?
A SYMBOLIC LEADER?
A COLONIAL FUNCTIONARY?
WHO DID HE SERVE - PHOKENG OR PRETORIA?
WAS HE A MASTER OF HIS SUBJECTS OR A SERVANT TO A FOREIGN KING?

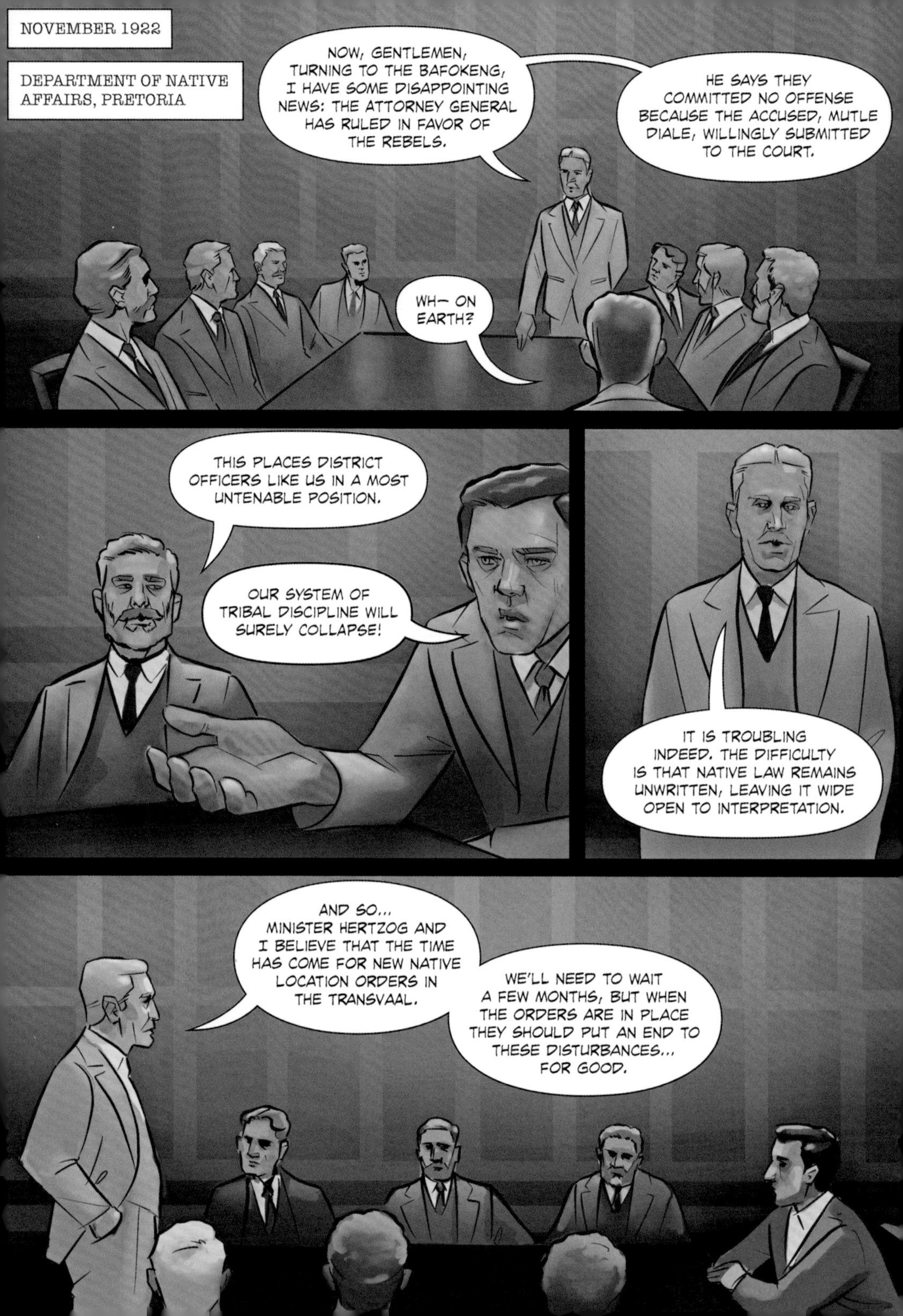
NOVEMBER 1922
DEPARTMENT OF NATIVE AFFAIRS, PRETORIA
NOW, GENTLEMEN, TURNING TO THE BAFOKENG, I HAVE SOME DISAPPOINTING NEWS: THE ATTORNEY GENERAL HAS RULED IN FAVOR OF THE REBELS.
HE SAYS THEY COMMITTED NO OFFENSE BECAUSE THE ACCUSED, MUTLE DIALE, WILLINGLY SUBMITTED TO THE COURT.
WH— ON EARTH?
THIS PLACES DISTRICT OFFICERS LIKE US IN A MOST UNTENABLE POSITION.
OUR SYSTEM OF TRIBAL DISCIPLINE WILL SURELY COLLAPSE!
IT IS TROUBLING INDEED. THE DIFFICULTY IS THAT NATIVE LAW REMAINS UNWRITTEN, LEAVING IT WIDE OPEN TO INTERPRETATION.
AND SO... MINISTER HERTZOG AND I BELIEVE THAT THE TIME HAS COME FOR NEW NATIVE LOCATION ORDERS IN THE TRANSVAAL.
WE'LL NEED TO WAIT A FEW MONTHS, BUT WHEN THE ORDERS ARE IN PLACE THEY SHOULD PUT AN END TO THESE DISTURBANCES... FOR GOOD.

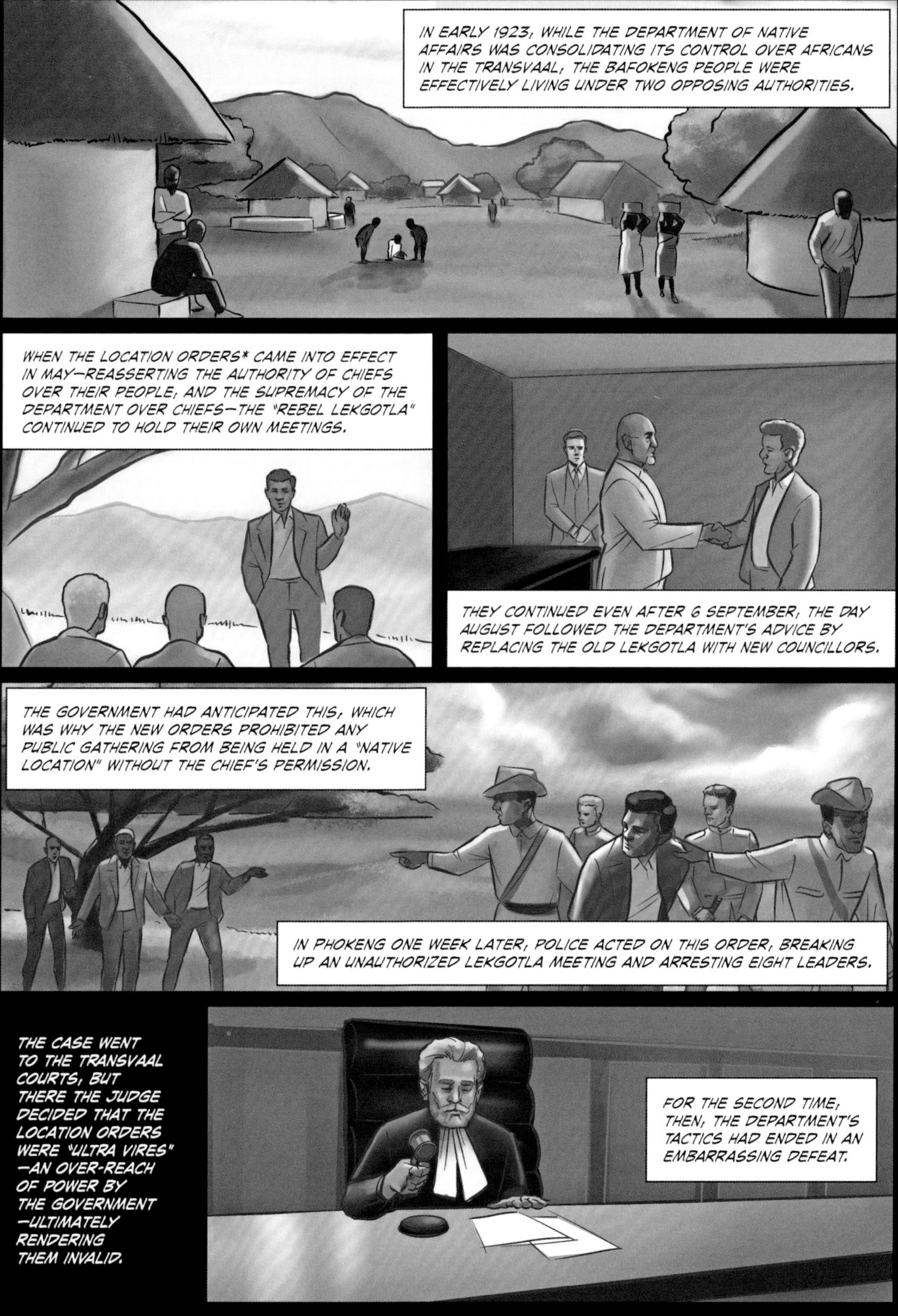
IN EARLY 1923, WHILE THE DEPARTMENT OF NATIVE AFFAIRS WAS CONSOLIDATING ITS CONTROL OVER AFRICANS IN THE TRANSVAAL, THE BAFOKENG PEOPLE WERE EFFECTIVELY LIVING UNDER TWO OPPOSING AUTHORITIES.
WHEN THE LOCATION ORDERS* CAME INTO EFFECT IN MAY—REASSERTING THE AUTHORITY OF CHIEFS OVER THEIR PEOPLE, AND THE SUPREMACY OF THE DEPARTMENT OVER CHIEFS—THE "REBEL LEKGOTLA" CONTINUED TO HOLD THEIR OWN MEETINGS.
THEY CONTINUED EVEN AFTER 6 SEPTEMBER, THE DAY AUGUST FOLLOWED THE DEPARTMENT'S ADVICE BY REPLACING THE OLD LEKGOTLA WITH NEW COUNCILLORS.
THE GOVERNMENT HAD ANTICIPATED THIS, WHICH WAS WHY THE NEW ORDERS PROHIBITED ANY PUBLIC GATHERING FROM BEING HELD IN A "NATIVE LOCATION" WITHOUT THE CHIEF'S PERMISSION.
IN PHOKENG ONE WEEK LATER, POLICE ACTED ON THIS ORDER, BREAKING UP AN UNAUTHORIZED LEKGOTLA MEETING AND ARRESTING EIGHT LEADERS.
THE CASE WENT TO THE TRANSVAAL COURTS, BUT THERE THE JUDGE DECIDED THAT THE LOCATION ORDERS WERE "ULTRA VIRES" —AN OVER-REACH OF POWER BY THE GOVERNMENT —ULTIMATELY RENDERING THEM INVALID.
FOR THE SECOND TIME, THEN, THE DEPARTMENT'S TACTICS HAD ENDED IN AN EMBARRASSING DEFEAT.

* Government Proclamation No. 760 (7 May 1923).

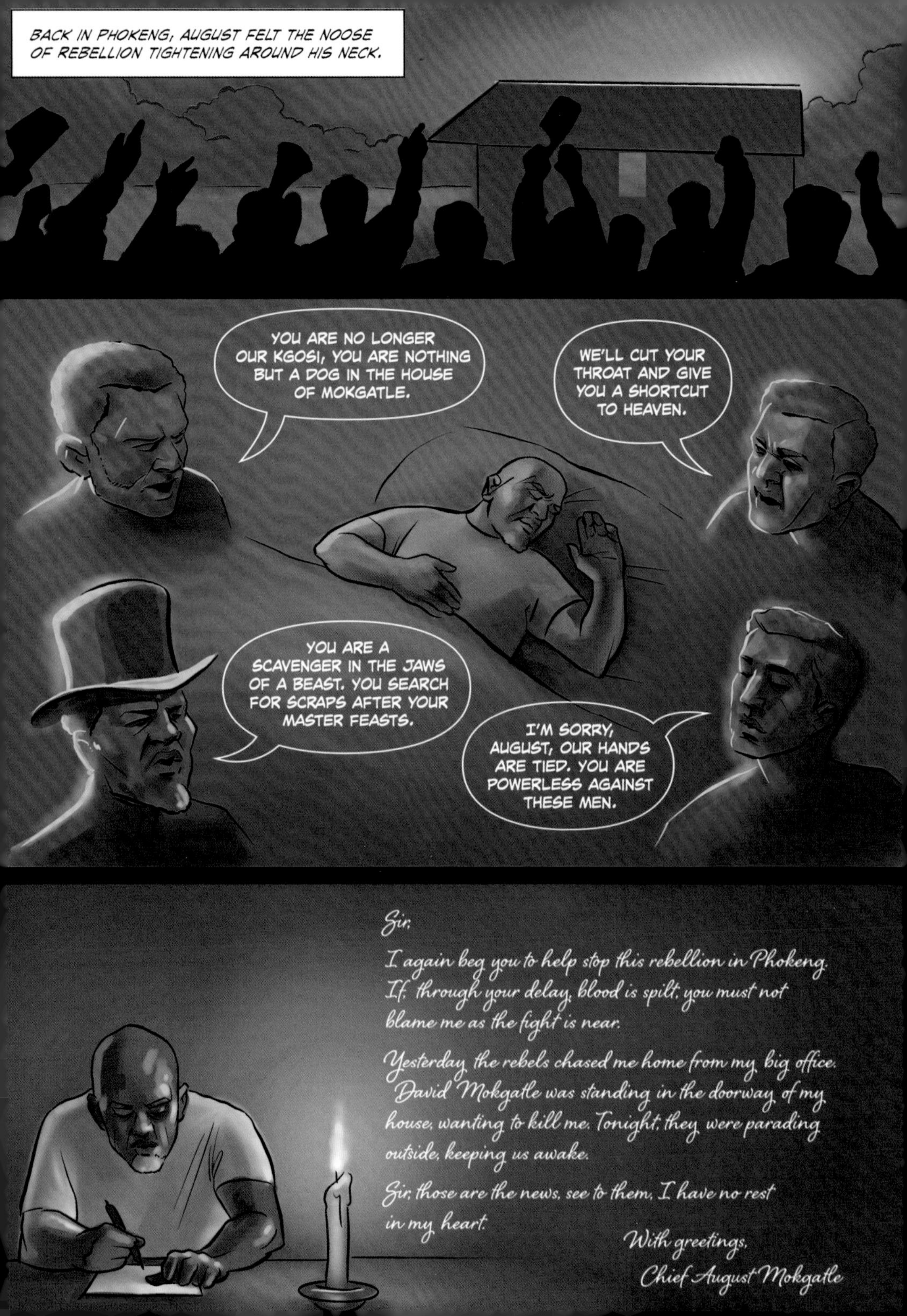
BACK IN PHOKENG, AUGUST FELT THE NOOSE OF REBELLION TIGHTENING AROUND HIS NECK.
YOU ARE NO LONGER OUR KGOSI, YOU ARE NOTHING BUT A DOG IN THE HOUSE OF MOKGATLE.
WE'LL CUT YOUR THROAT AND GIVE YOU A SHORTCUT TO HEAVEN.
YOU ARE A SCAVENGER IN THE JAWS OF A BEAST. YOU SEARCH FOR SCRAPS AFTER YOUR MASTER FEASTS.
I'M SORRY, AUGUST, OUR HANDS ARE TIED. YOU ARE POWERLESS AGAINST THESE MEN.
Sir,
I again beg you to help stop this rebellion in Phokeng. If, through your delay, blood is spilt, you must not blame me as the fight is near.
Yesterday the rebels chased me home from my big office. David Mokgatle was standing in the doorway of my house, wanting to kill me. Tonight, they were parading outside, keeping us awake.
Sir, those are the news, see to them. I have no rest in my heart.
With greetings,
Chief August Mokgatle

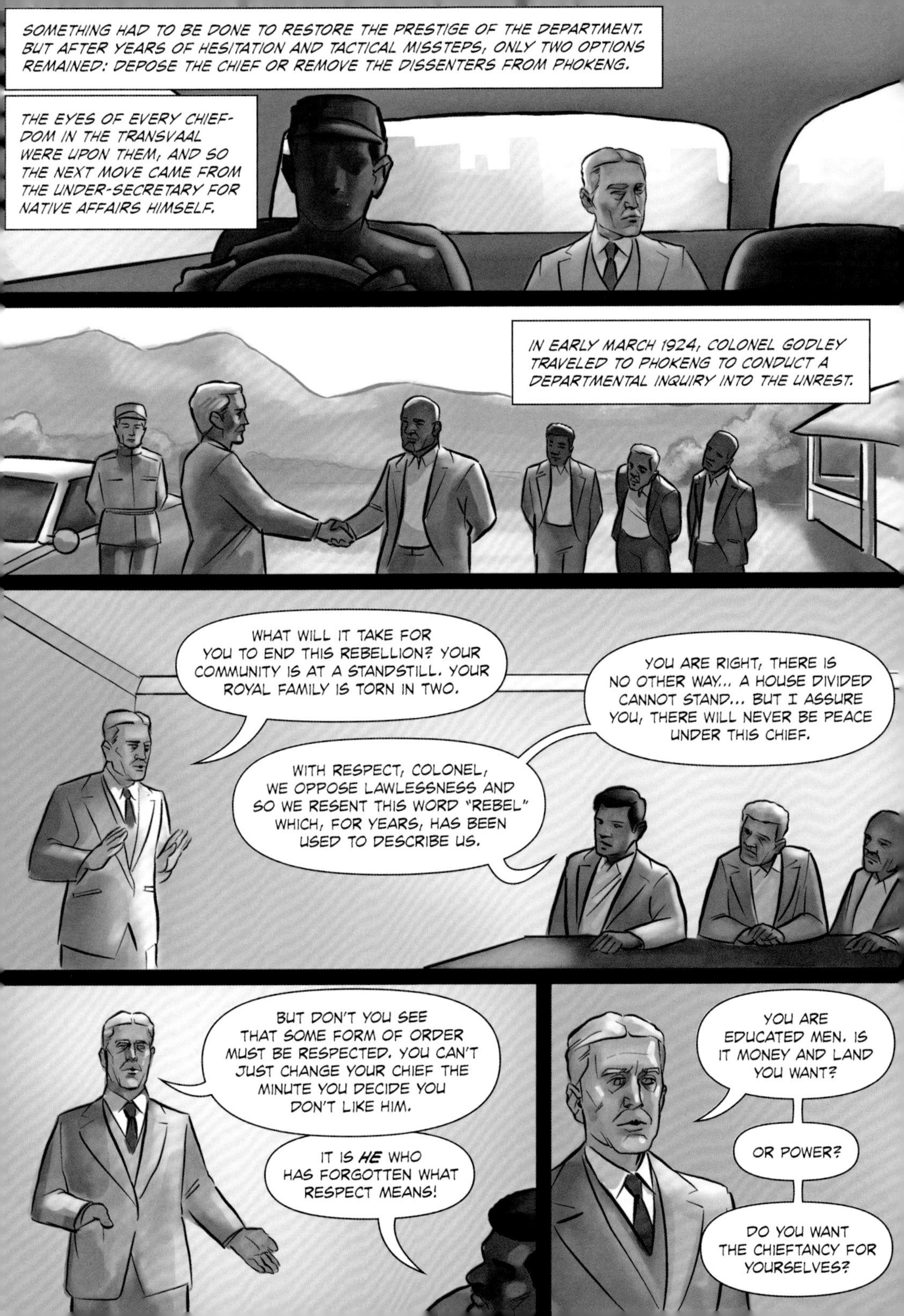
SOMETHING HAD TO BE DONE TO RESTORE THE PRESTIGE OF THE DEPARTMENT. BUT AFTER YEARS OF HESITATION AND TACTICAL MISSTEPS, ONLY TWO OPTIONS REMAINED: DEPOSE THE CHIEF OR REMOVE THE DISSENTERS FROM PHOKENG.
THE EYES OF EVERY CHIEF-DOM IN THE TRANSVAAL WERE UPON THEM, AND SO THE NEXT MOVE CAME FROM THE UNDER-SECRETARY FOR NATIVE AFFAIRS HIMSELF.
IN EARLY MARCH 1924, COLONEL GODLEY TRAVELED TO PHOKENG TO CONDUCT A DEPARTMENTAL INQUIRY INTO THE UNREST.
WHAT WILL IT TAKE FOR YOU TO END THIS REBELLION? YOUR COMMUNITY IS AT A STANDSTILL. YOUR ROYAL FAMILY IS TORN IN TWO.
WITH RESPECT, COLONEL, WE OPPOSE LAWLESSNESS AND SO WE RESENT THIS WORD "REBEL" WHICH, FOR YEARS, HAS BEEN USED TO DESCRIBE US.
YOU ARE RIGHT, THERE IS NO OTHER WAY... A HOUSE DIVIDED CANNOT STAND... BUT I ASSURE YOU, THERE WILL NEVER BE PEACE UNDER THIS CHIEF.
BUT DON'T YOU SEE THAT SOME FORM OF ORDER MUST BE RESPECTED. YOU CAN'T JUST CHANGE YOUR CHIEF THE MINUTE YOU DECIDE YOU DON'T LIKE HIM.
IT IS ***HE*** WHO HAS FORGOTTEN WHAT RESPECT MEANS!
YOU ARE EDUCATED MEN. IS IT MONEY AND LAND YOU WANT?
OR POWER?
DO YOU WANT THE CHIEFTANCY FOR YOURSELVES?

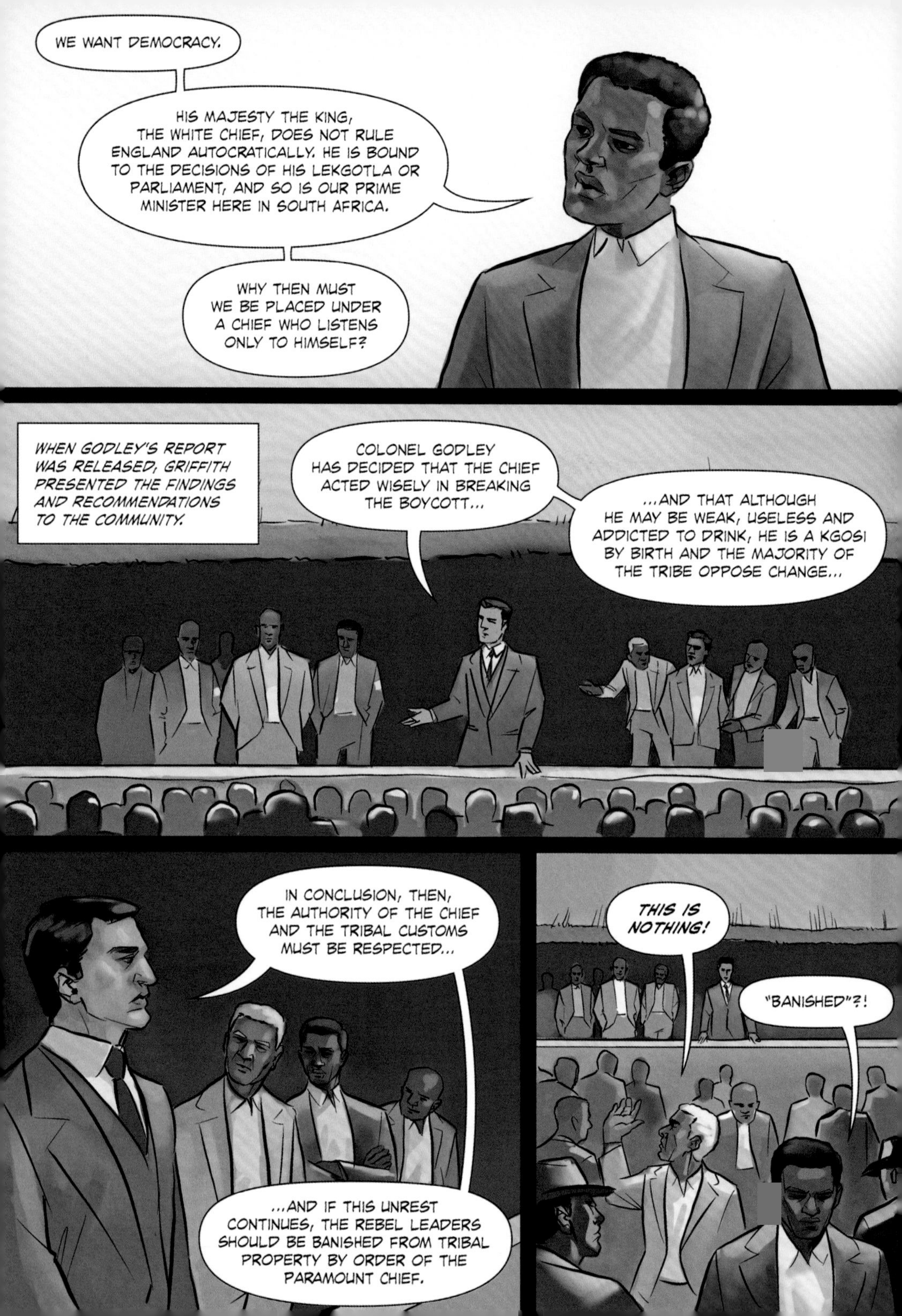
WE WANT DEMOCRACY.
HIS MAJESTY THE KING, THE WHITE CHIEF, DOES NOT RULE ENGLAND AUTOCRATICALLY. HE IS BOUND TO THE DECISIONS OF HIS LEKGOTLA OR PARLIAMENT, AND SO IS OUR PRIME MINISTER HERE IN SOUTH AFRICA.
WHY THEN MUST WE BE PLACED UNDER A CHIEF WHO LISTENS ONLY TO HIMSELF?
WHEN GODLEY'S REPORT WAS RELEASED, GRIFFITH PRESENTED THE FINDINGS AND RECOMMENDATIONS TO THE COMMUNITY.
COLONEL GODLEY HAS DECIDED THAT THE CHIEF ACTED WISELY IN BREAKING THE BOYCOTT...
...AND THAT ALTHOUGH HE MAY BE WEAK, USELESS AND ADDICTED TO DRINK, HE IS A KGOSI BY BIRTH AND THE MAJORITY OF THE TRIBE OPPOSE CHANGE...
IN CONCLUSION, THEN, THE AUTHORITY OF THE CHIEF AND THE TRIBAL CUSTOMS MUST BE RESPECTED...
...AND IF THIS UNREST CONTINUES, THE REBEL LEADERS SHOULD BE BANISHED FROM TRIBAL PROPERTY BY ORDER OF THE PARAMOUNT CHIEF.
THIS IS NOTHING!
"BANISHED"?!

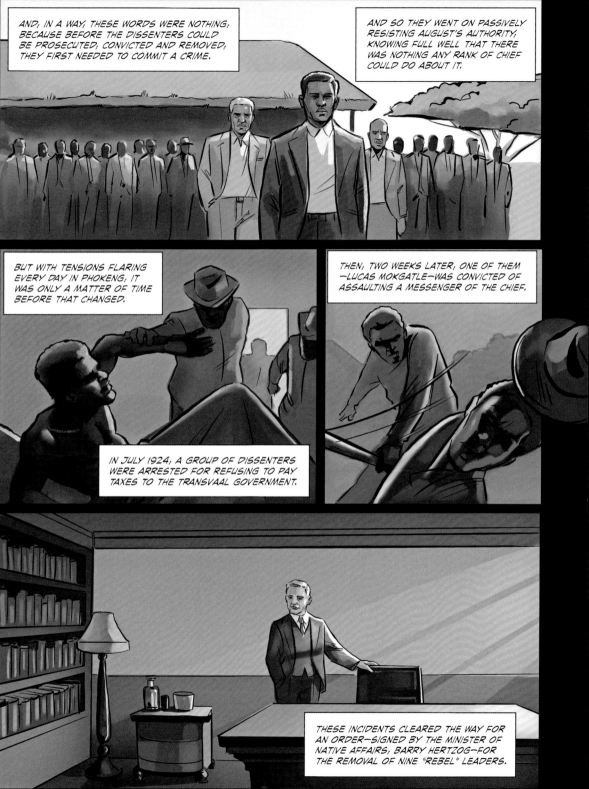

AND, IN A WAY, THESE WORDS WERE NOTHING, BECAUSE BEFORE THE DISSENTERS COULD BE PROSECUTED, CONVICTED AND REMOVED, THEY FIRST NEEDED TO COMMIT A CRIME.

AND SO THEY WENT ON PASSIVELY RESISTING AUGUST'S AUTHORITY, KNOWING FULL WELL THAT THERE WAS NOTHING ANY RANK OF CHIEF COULD DO ABOUT IT.

BUT WITH TENSIONS FLARING EVERY DAY IN PHOKENG, IT WAS ONLY A MATTER OF TIME BEFORE THAT CHANGED.

IN JULY 1924, A GROUP OF DISSENTERS WERE ARRESTED FOR REFUSING TO PAY TAXES TO THE TRANSVAAL GOVERNMENT.

THEN, TWO WEEKS LATER, ONE OF THEM —LUCAS MOKGATLE—WAS CONVICTED OF ASSAULTING A MESSENGER OF THE CHIEF.

THESE INCIDENTS CLEARED THE WAY FOR AN ORDER—SIGNED BY THE MINISTER OF NATIVE AFFAIRS, BARRY HERTZOG—FOR THE REMOVAL OF NINE "REBEL" LEADERS.

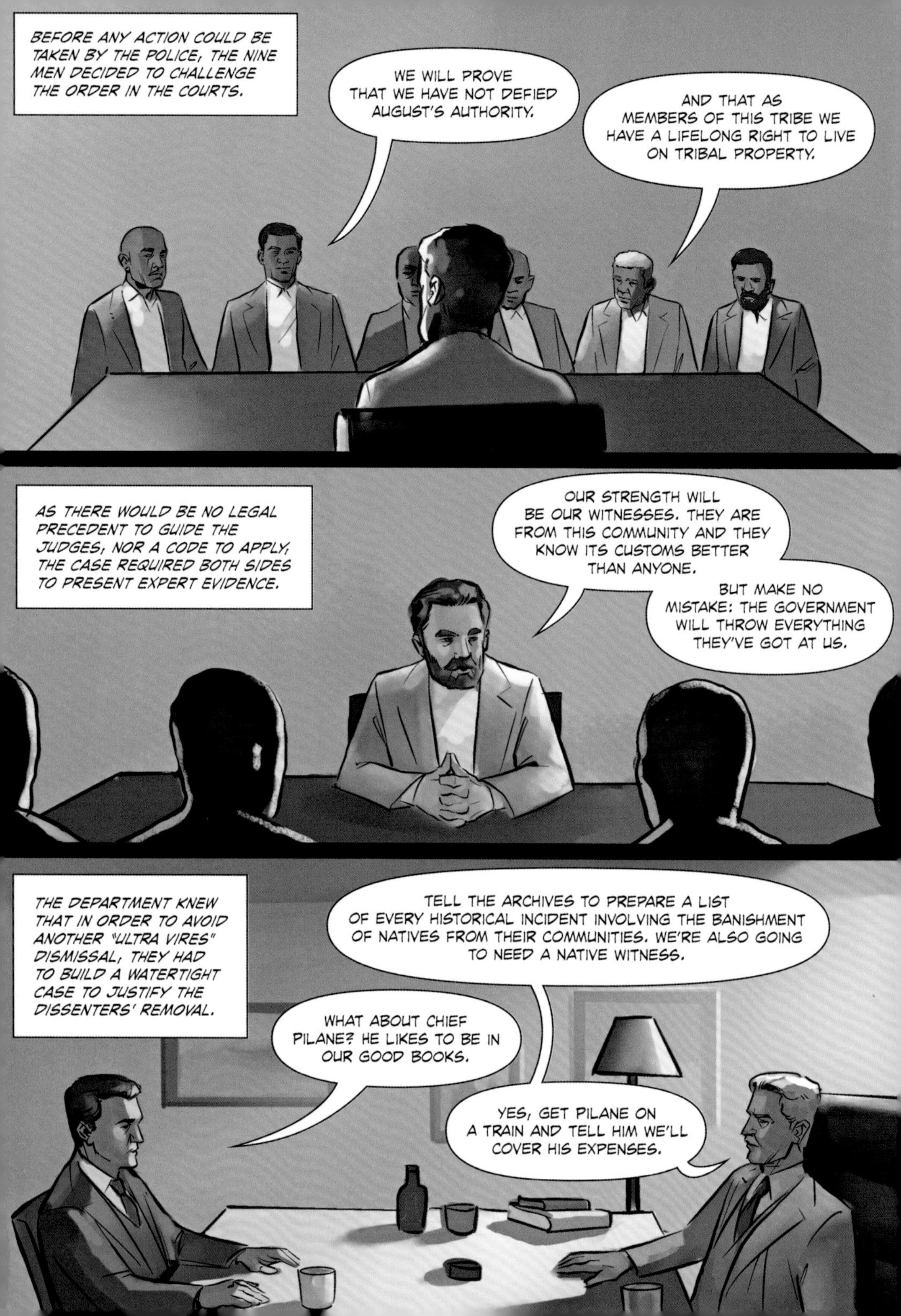
BEFORE ANY ACTION COULD BE TAKEN BY THE POLICE, THE NINE MEN DECIDED TO CHALLENGE THE ORDER IN THE COURTS.
WE WILL PROVE THAT WE HAVE NOT DEFIED AUGUST'S AUTHORITY.
AND THAT AS MEMBERS OF THIS TRIBE WE HAVE A LIFELONG RIGHT TO LIVE ON TRIBAL PROPERTY.
AS THERE WOULD BE NO LEGAL PRECEDENT TO GUIDE THE JUDGES, NOR A CODE TO APPLY, THE CASE REQUIRED BOTH SIDES TO PRESENT EXPERT EVIDENCE.
OUR STRENGTH WILL BE OUR WITNESSES. THEY ARE FROM THIS COMMUNITY AND THEY KNOW ITS CUSTOMS BETTER THAN ANYONE.
BUT MAKE NO MISTAKE: THE GOVERNMENT WILL THROW EVERYTHING THEY'VE GOT AT US.
THE DEPARTMENT KNEW THAT IN ORDER TO AVOID ANOTHER "ULTRA VIRES" DISMISSAL, THEY HAD TO BUILD A WATERTIGHT CASE TO JUSTIFY THE DISSENTERS' REMOVAL.
TELL THE ARCHIVES TO PREPARE A LIST OF EVERY HISTORICAL INCIDENT INVOLVING THE BANISHMENT OF NATIVES FROM THEIR COMMUNITIES. WE'RE ALSO GOING TO NEED A NATIVE WITNESS.
WHAT ABOUT CHIEF PILANE? HE LIKES TO BE IN OUR GOOD BOOKS.
YES, GET PILANE ON A TRAIN AND TELL HIM WE'LL COVER HIS EXPENSES.

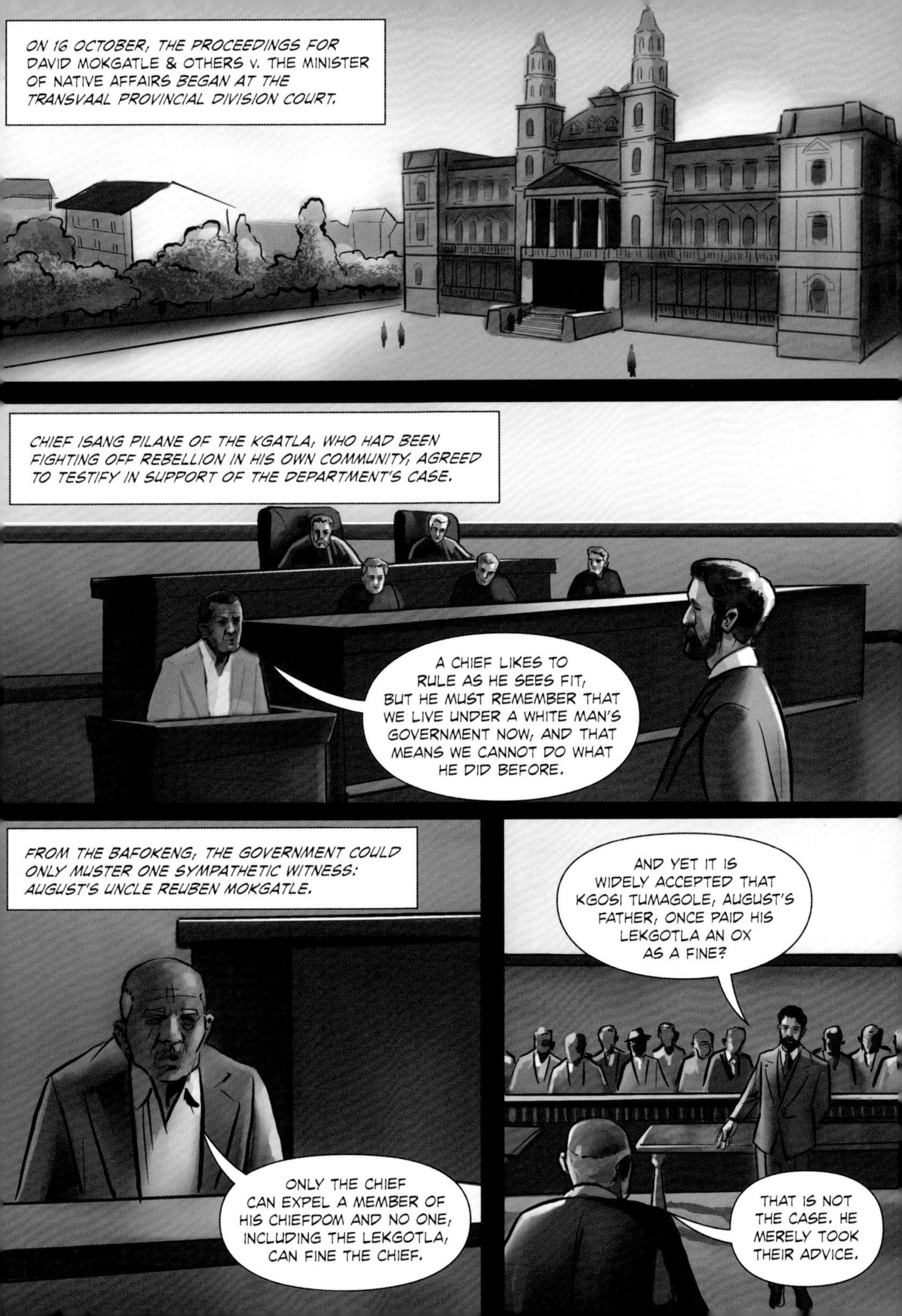
ON 16 OCTOBER, THE PROCEEDINGS FOR DAVID MOKGATLE & OTHERS V. THE MINISTER OF NATIVE AFFAIRS BEGAN AT THE TRANSVAAL PROVINCIAL DIVISION COURT.
CHIEF ISANG PILANE OF THE KGATLA, WHO HAD BEEN FIGHTING OFF REBELLION IN HIS OWN COMMUNITY, AGREED TO TESTIFY IN SUPPORT OF THE DEPARTMENT'S CASE.
A CHIEF LIKES TO RULE AS HE SEES FIT, BUT HE MUST REMEMBER THAT WE LIVE UNDER A WHITE MAN'S GOVERNMENT NOW, AND THAT MEANS WE CANNOT DO WHAT HE DID BEFORE.
FROM THE BAFOKENG, THE GOVERNMENT COULD ONLY MUSTER ONE SYMPATHETIC WITNESS: AUGUST'S UNCLE REUBEN MOKGATLE.
ONLY THE CHIEF CAN EXPEL A MEMBER OF HIS CHIEFDOM AND NO ONE, INCLUDING THE LEKGOTLA, CAN FINE THE CHIEF.
AND YET IT IS WIDELY ACCEPTED THAT KGOSI TUMAGOLE, AUGUST'S FATHER, ONCE PAID HIS LEKGOTLA AN OX AS A FINE?
THAT IS NOT THE CASE. HE MERELY TOOK THEIR ADVICE.

BY CONTRAST, EVERY WITNESS WHO TESTIFIED IN FAVOR OF THE BAFOKENG DISSENTERS WAS CLOSELY CONNECTED TO THE PHOKENG COMMUNITY.

MY HALF-BROTHER REUBEN WAS LYING. I SAT ON TUMAGOLE'S LEKGOTLA AND I AM TELLING YOU WE TRIED AND PUNISHED HIM THAT DAY.

ONE BY ONE, THEY REJECTED THE CHIEF'S RIGHT TO REMOVE ANYONE FROM THE CHIEFDOM...

BEFORE THE WHITE MAN GOVERNED THIS COUNTRY, NO ONE WAS EVER EJECTED FROM TRIBAL PROPERTY.

A MAN WHO IS CAST OUT MUST LIVE ON THE FLESH OF A DOG.

...WHEREAS THE DEPARTMENT OFFICIALS ARGUED PRECISELY THE OPPOSITE:

I HAVE ALMOST ALL MY LIFE STUDIED NATIVE CUSTOM, MY LORD.

AND OF COURSE THE CHIEF HAS THE POWER TO EXPEL UNRULY SUBJECTS IF IT'S WITH THE AIM OF PRESERVING TRIBAL UNITY.

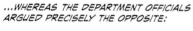

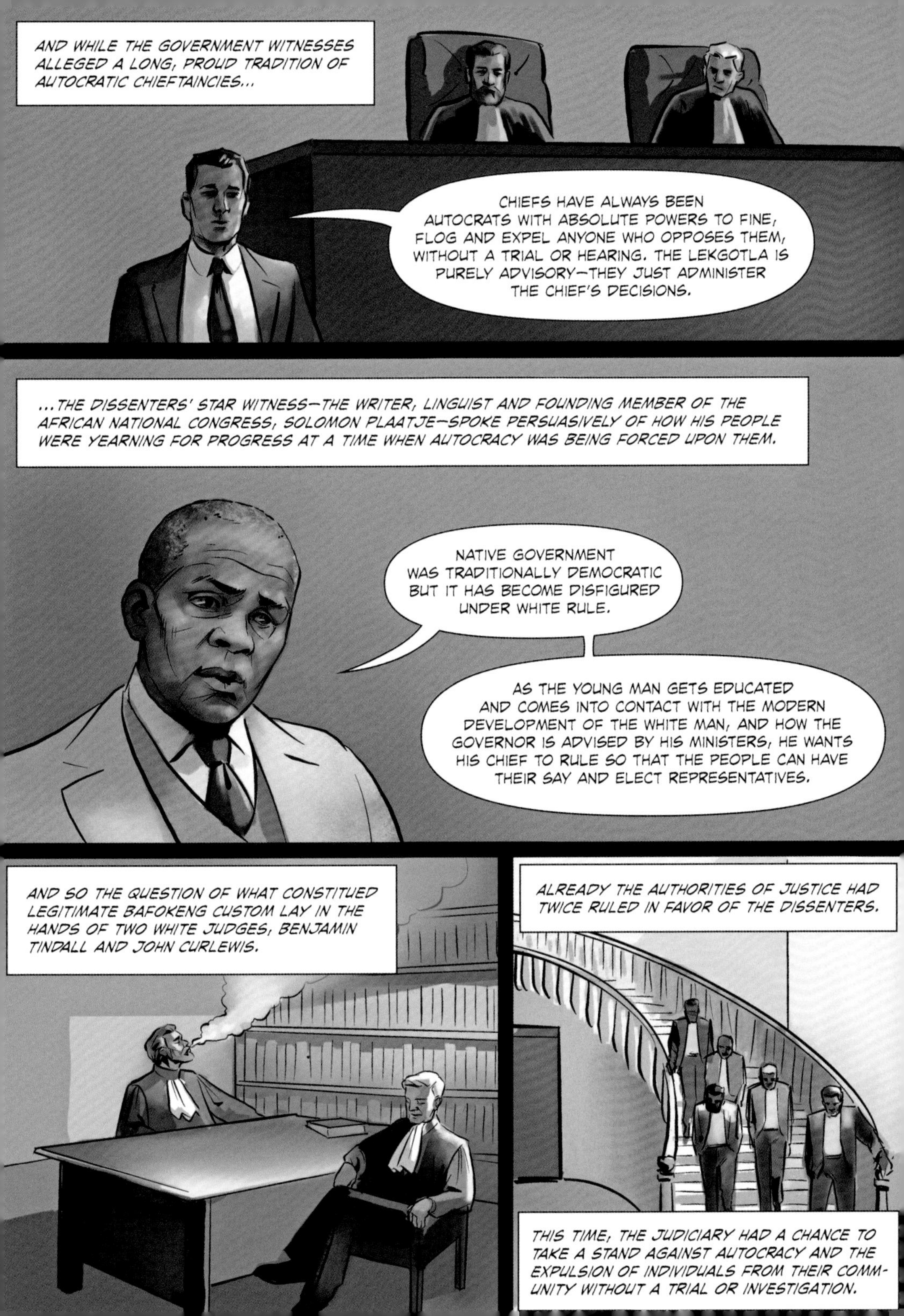
AND WHILE THE GOVERNMENT WITNESSES ALLEGED A LONG, PROUD TRADITION OF AUTOCRATIC CHIEFTAINCIES...
CHIEFS HAVE ALWAYS BEEN AUTOCRATS WITH ABSOLUTE POWERS TO FINE, FLOG AND EXPEL ANYONE WHO OPPOSES THEM, WITHOUT A TRIAL OR HEARING. THE LEKGOTLA IS PURELY ADVISORY—THEY JUST ADMINISTER THE CHIEF'S DECISIONS.
...THE DISSENTERS' STAR WITNESS—THE WRITER, LINGUIST AND FOUNDING MEMBER OF THE AFRICAN NATIONAL CONGRESS, SOLOMON PLAATJE—SPOKE PERSUASIVELY OF HOW HIS PEOPLE WERE YEARNING FOR PROGRESS AT A TIME WHEN AUTOCRACY WAS BEING FORCED UPON THEM.
NATIVE GOVERNMENT WAS TRADITIONALLY DEMOCRATIC BUT IT HAS BECOME DISFIGURED UNDER WHITE RULE.
AS THE YOUNG MAN GETS EDUCATED AND COMES INTO CONTACT WITH THE MODERN DEVELOPMENT OF THE WHITE MAN, AND HOW THE GOVERNOR IS ADVISED BY HIS MINISTERS, HE WANTS HIS CHIEF TO RULE SO THAT THE PEOPLE CAN HAVE THEIR SAY AND ELECT REPRESENTATIVES.
AND SO THE QUESTION OF WHAT CONSTITUED LEGITIMATE BAFOKENG CUSTOM LAY IN THE HANDS OF TWO WHITE JUDGES, BENJAMIN TINDALL AND JOHN CURLEWIS.
ALREADY THE AUTHORITIES OF JUSTICE HAD TWICE RULED IN FAVOR OF THE DISSENTERS.
THIS TIME, THE JUDICIARY HAD A CHANCE TO TAKE A STAND AGAINST AUTOCRACY AND THE EXPULSION OF INDIVIDUALS FROM THEIR COMM-UNITY WITHOUT A TRIAL OR INVESTIGATION.

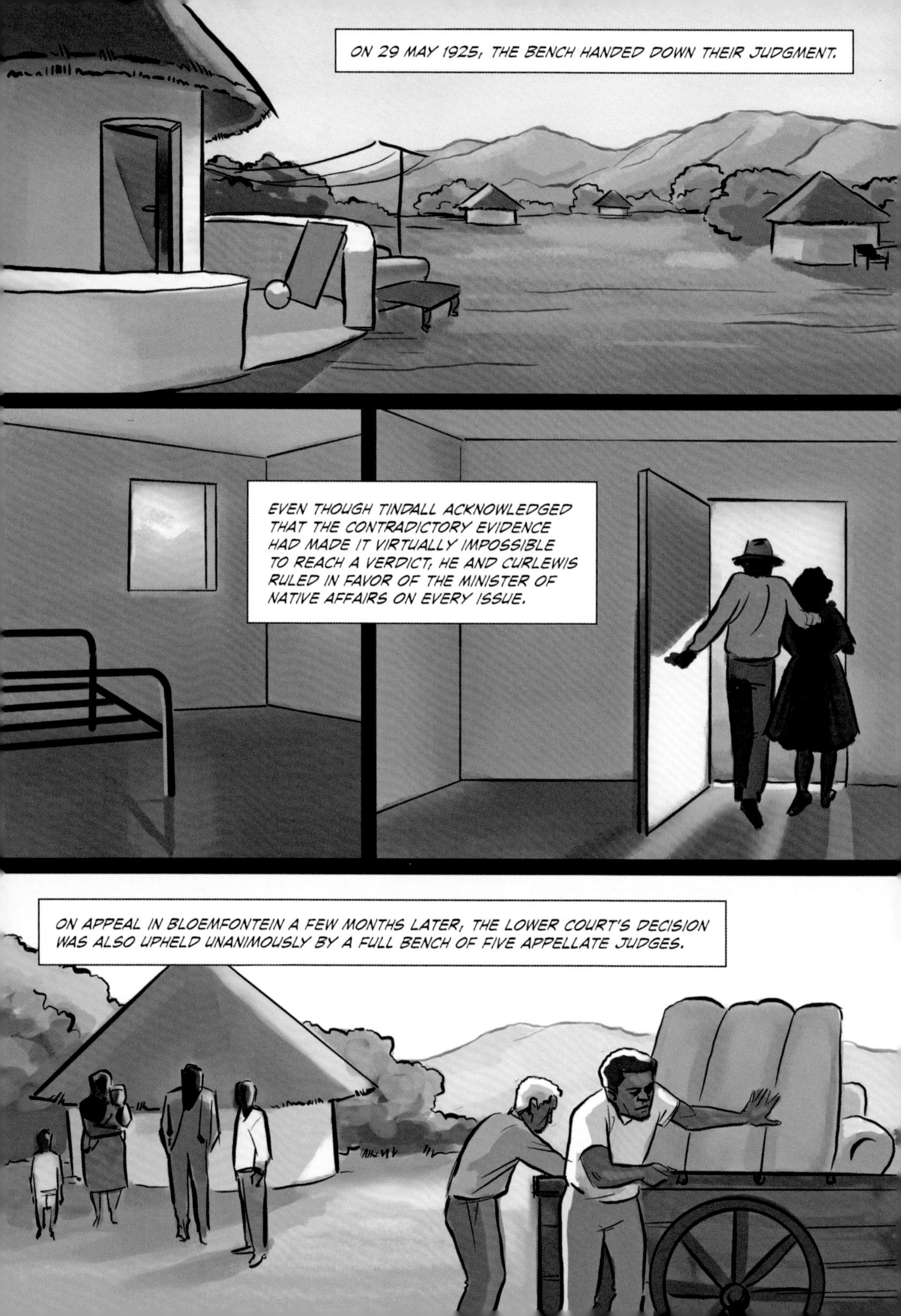
ON 29 MAY 1925, THE BENCH HANDED DOWN THEIR JUDGMENT.
EVEN THOUGH TINDALL ACKNOWLEDGED THAT THE CONTRADICTORY EVIDENCE HAD MADE IT VIRTUALLY IMPOSSIBLE TO REACH A VERDICT, HE AND CURLEWIS RULED IN FAVOR OF THE MINISTER OF NATIVE AFFAIRS ON EVERY ISSUE.
ON APPEAL IN BLOEMFONTEIN A FEW MONTHS LATER, THE LOWER COURT'S DECISION WAS ALSO UPHELD UNANIMOUSLY BY A FULL BENCH OF FIVE APPELLATE JUDGES.

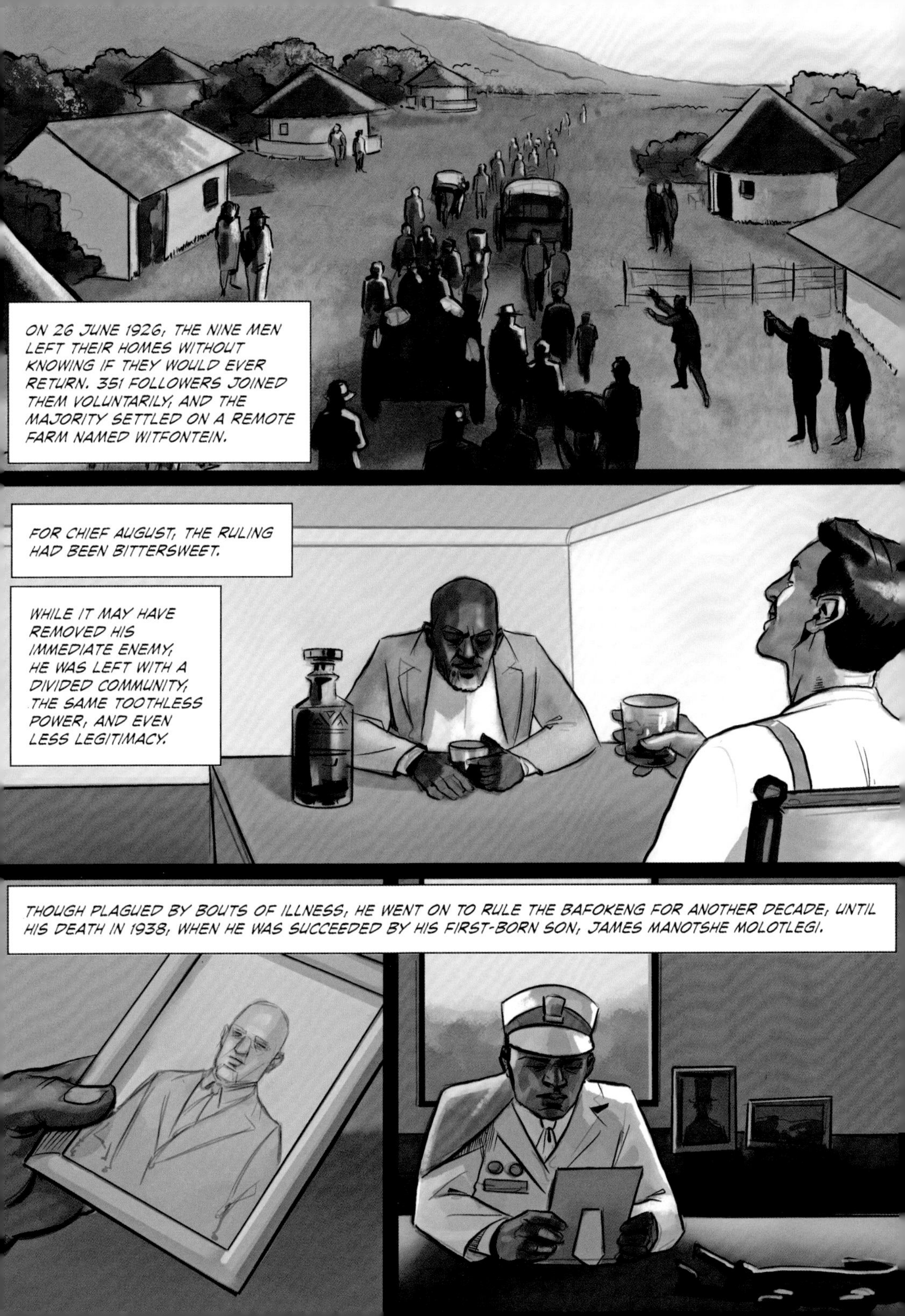
ON 26 JUNE 1926, THE NINE MEN LEFT THEIR HOMES WITHOUT KNOWING IF THEY WOULD EVER RETURN. 351 FOLLOWERS JOINED THEM VOLUNTARILY, AND THE MAJORITY SETTLED ON A REMOTE FARM NAMED WITFONTEIN.
FOR CHIEF AUGUST, THE RULING HAD BEEN BITTERSWEET.
WHILE IT MAY HAVE REMOVED HIS IMMEDIATE ENEMY, HE WAS LEFT WITH A DIVIDED COMMUNITY, THE SAME TOOTHLESS POWER, AND EVEN LESS LEGITIMACY.
THOUGH PLAGUED BY BOUTS OF ILLNESS, HE WENT ON TO RULE THE BAFOKENG FOR ANOTHER DECADE, UNTIL HIS DEATH IN 1938, WHEN HE WAS SUCCEEDED BY HIS FIRST-BORN SON, JAMES MANOTSHE MOLOTLEGI.

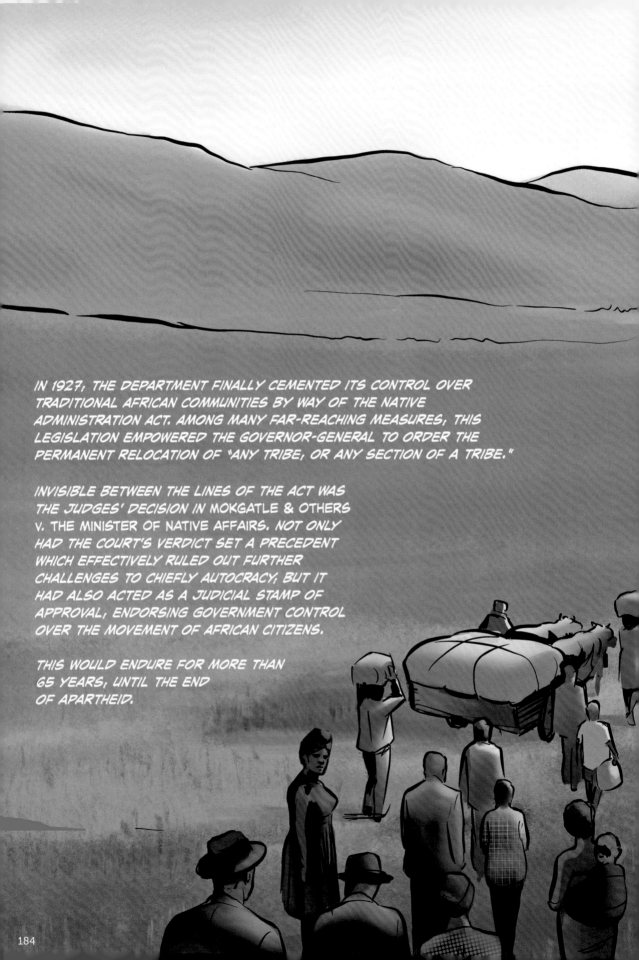

IN 1927, THE DEPARTMENT FINALLY CEMENTED ITS CONTROL OVER TRADITIONAL AFRICAN COMMUNITIES BY WAY OF THE NATIVE ADMINISTRATION ACT. AMONG MANY FAR-REACHING MEASURES, THIS LEGISLATION EMPOWERED THE GOVERNOR-GENERAL TO ORDER THE PERMANENT RELOCATION OF "ANY TRIBE, OR ANY SECTION OF A TRIBE."

INVISIBLE BETWEEN THE LINES OF THE ACT WAS THE JUDGES' DECISION IN MOKGATLE & OTHERS V. THE MINISTER OF NATIVE AFFAIRS. NOT ONLY HAD THE COURT'S VERDICT SET A PRECEDENT WHICH EFFECTIVELY RULED OUT FURTHER CHALLENGES TO CHIEFLY AUTOCRACY, BUT IT HAD ALSO ACTED AS A JUDICIAL STAMP OF APPROVAL, ENDORSING GOVERNMENT CONTROL OVER THE MOVEMENT OF AFRICAN CITIZENS.

THIS WOULD ENDURE FOR MORE THAN 65 YEARS, UNTIL THE END OF APARTHEID.

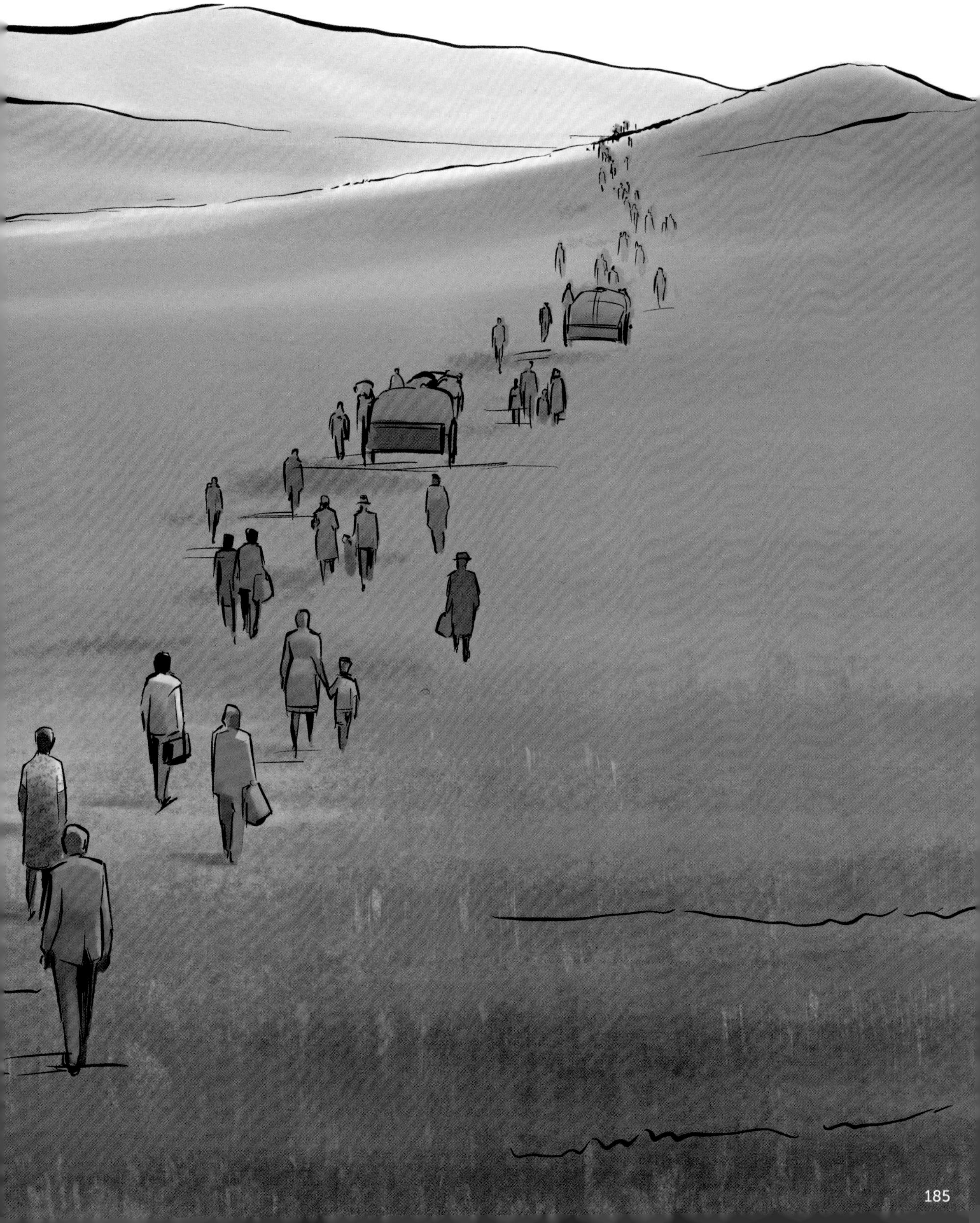

BEHIND THE STORY: SOURCES AND SKETCHES

CHAPTER 5: A HOUSE DIVIDED

The Royal Bafokeng Nation is largely unknown to the outside world. Only a handful of scholars have documented its centuries-old tales and traditions. These books, articles, and theses were an essential departure point for our "reconstruction" of the "Bafokeng Rebellion of 1921–1926." Where photographs were hard to come by, these texts provided the first layers of color and complexity to our understanding. They also led us to the one place where the visual narrative's finer details could be found.

Two cardboard folders, both housed in the National Archives, held the key to creating this chapter. They contain the records of the Secretary of Native Affairs and the Department of Justice from the period 1920–1927. Given their obvious inherent prejudices, these letters, dispatches, and reports needed to be approached with great caution. However, by staying attuned to biases, corroborating different accounts, and appraising each piece of evidence within its context, we were able to reach reasonable conclusions about events and the people caught up in them.

Importantly, the files' contents are not limited to correspondence between government officials (even though these papers are valuable in their own right for exposing the Union government's cynical tactics). Also included are original letters signed by kgosi August Mokgatle himself, as well as affidavits written by the dissenting councillors. These sources made it possible for us to quote or paraphrase the characters' original words throughout most of the story's dialogue.

Below: Phokeng in the 1880s, under the leadership of kgosi Mokgatle Mokgatle.

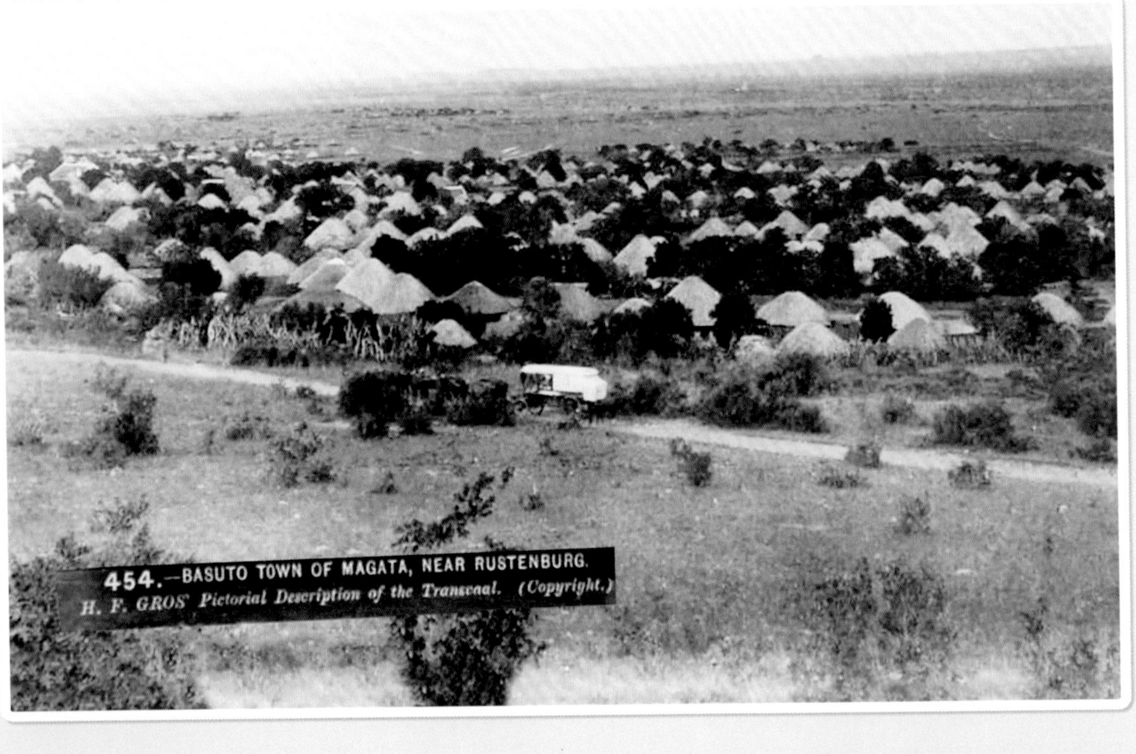
454.—BASUTO TOWN OF MAGATA, NEAR RUSTENBURG.
H. F. GROS' Pictorial Description of the Transvaal. (Copyright.)

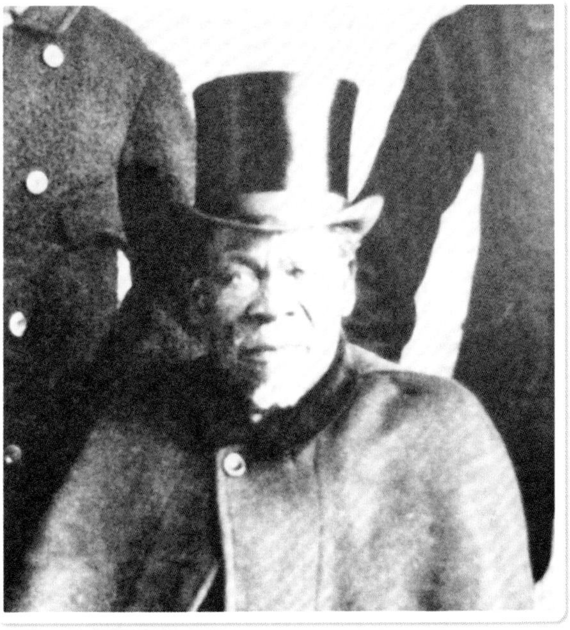

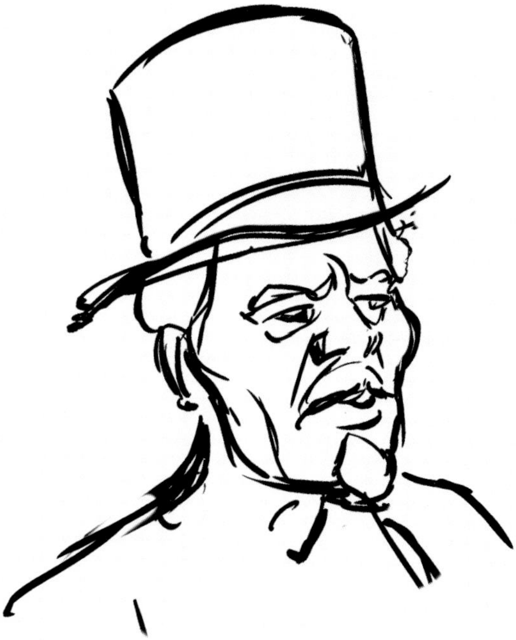

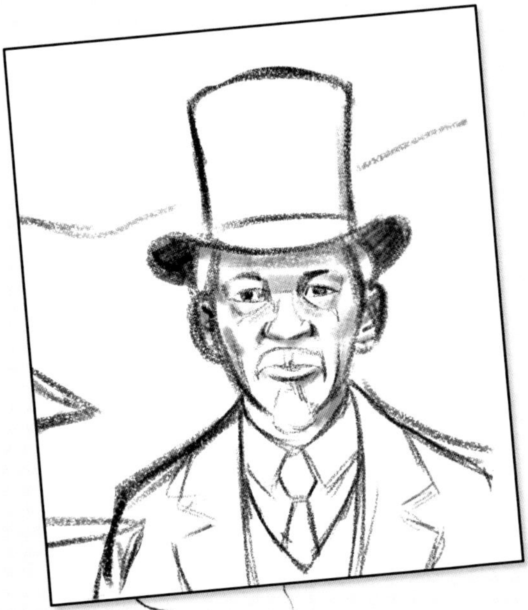

The great kgosi Mokgatle Mokgatle (chief of the Bafokeng from the 1830s until 1891), father of Tumagole Mokgatle (chief from 1891–1896) and grandfather of August Mokgatle (chief from 1896–1938).

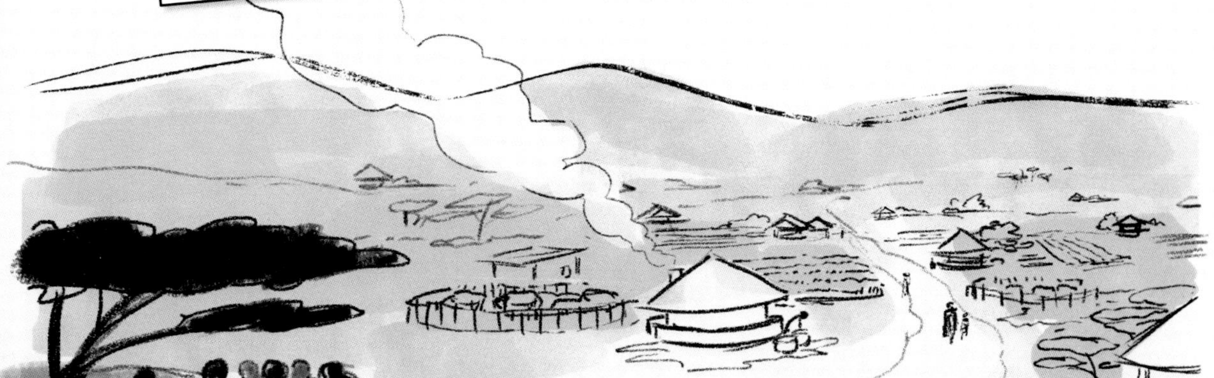

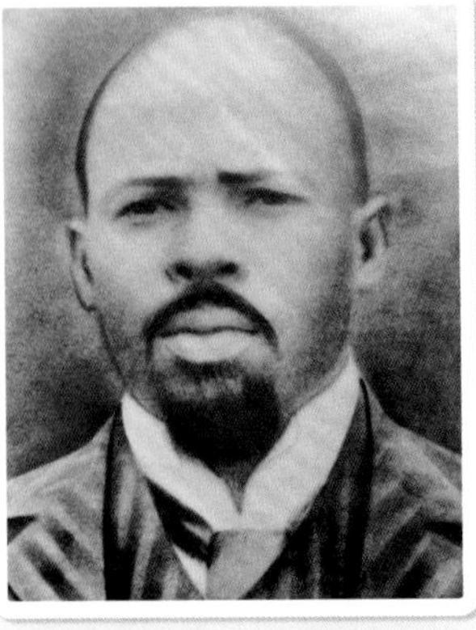

Above: Kgosi August Mokgatle in the early 1900s.

Right: A statement, signed by kgosi August Mokgatle in December 1923, which survives amongst the records of the Department of Native Affairs.

Below: Guards outside the headquarters of the Bafokeng's community administration in the 1920s.

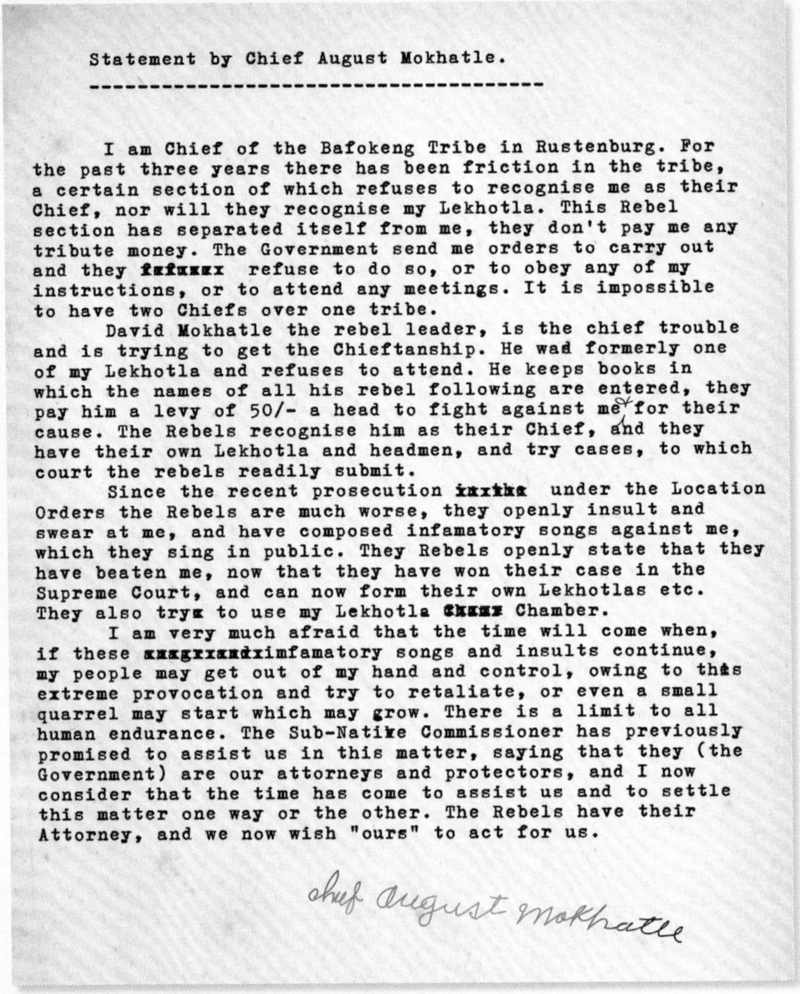

Statement by Chief August Mokhatle.

I am Chief of the Bafokeng Tribe in Rustenburg. For the past three years there has been friction in the tribe, a certain section of which refuses to recognise me as their Chief, nor will they recognise my Lekhotla. This Rebel section has separated itself from me, they don't pay me any tribute money. The Government send me orders to carry out and they fxfuxxx refuse to do so, or to obey any of my instructions, or to attend any meetings. It is impossible to have two Chiefs over one tribe.

David Mokhatle the rebel leader, is the chief trouble and is trying to get the Chieftanship. He wad formerly one of my Lekhotla and refuses to attend. He keeps books in which the names of all his rebel following are entered, they pay him a levy of 50/- a head to fight against me & for their cause. The Rebels recognise him as their Chief, and they have their own Lekhotla and headmen, and try cases, to which court the rebels readily submit.

Since the recent prosecution ixxthe under the Location Orders the Rebels are much worse, they openly insult and swear at me, and have composed infamatory songs against me, which they sing in public. They Rebels openly state that they have beaten me, now that they have won their case in the Supreme Court, and can now form their own Lekhotlas etc. They also tryx to use my Lekhotla Chxxx Chamber.

I am very much afraid that the time will come when, if these xxxgxxxndximfamatory songs and insults continue, my people may get out of my hand and control, owing to this extreme provocation and try to retaliate, or even a small quarrel may start which may grow. There is a limit to all human endurance. The Sub-Natixe Commissioner has previously promised to assist us in this matter, saying that they (the Government) are our attorneys and protectors, and I now consider that the time has come to assist us and to settle this matter one way or the other. The Rebels have their Attorney, and we now wish "ours" to act for us.

chief August Mokhatle

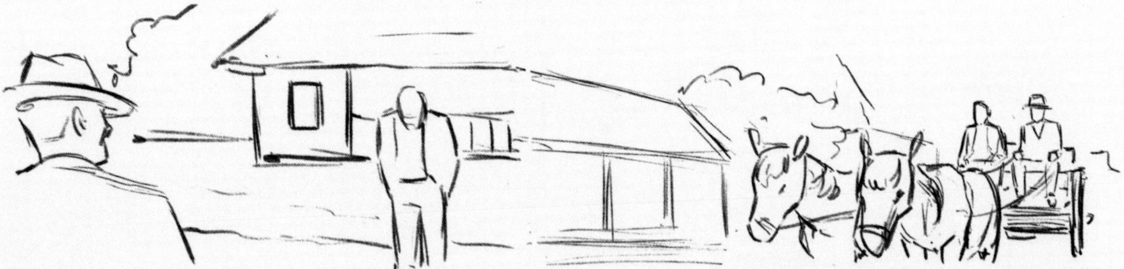

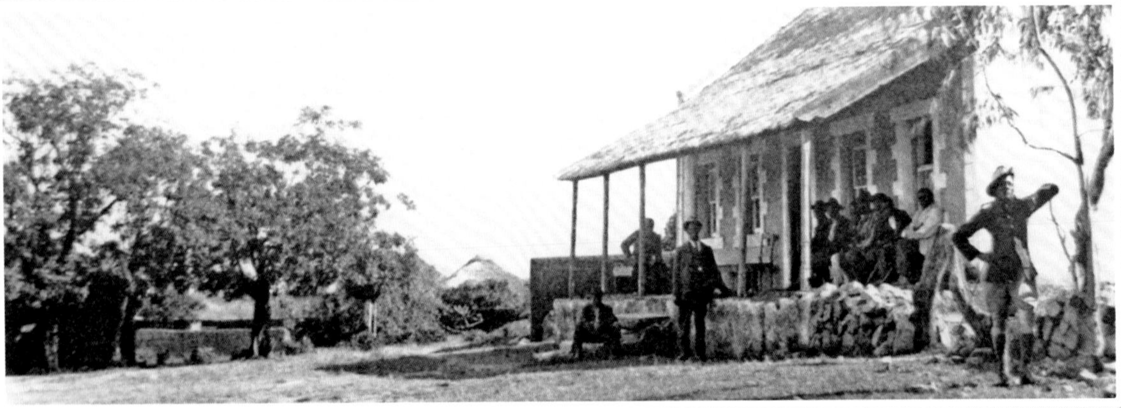

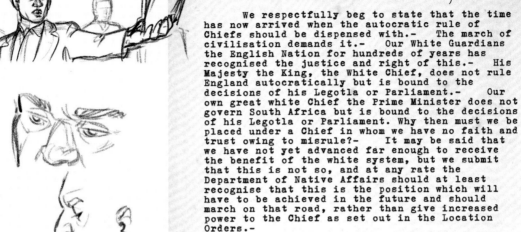

We respectfully beg to state that the time has now arrived when the autocratic rule of Chiefs should be dispensed with.- The march of civilisation demands it.- Our White Guardians the English Nation for hundreds of years has recognised the justice and right of this.- His Majesty the King, the White Chief, does not rule England autocratically but is bound to the decisions of his Legotla or Parliament.- Our own great white Chief the Prime Minister does not govern South Africa but is bound to the decisions of his Legotla or Parliament. Why then must we be placed under a Chief in whom we have no faith and trust owing to misrule?- It may be said that we have not yet advanced far enough to receive the benefit of the white system, but we submit that this is not so, and at any rate the Department of Native Affairs should at least recognise that this is the position which will have to be achieved in the future and should march on that road, rather than give increased power to the Chief as set out in the Location Orders.-

It is our united and urgent wish that peace should be restored as we recognise that a house divided cannot stand. We now in conclusion beg to ask you to convey to the Minister of Native Affairs our respectful greetings and a request which comes from our hearts that he take all necessary steps at once to have a Commission of Inquiry appointed with powers to take evidence on oath to enquire into to whole of the position of the Tribe, into its finances and into it's government. Let such a Commission then give it's report to the Minister and your Hon. will not find us backward in giving our wholehearted loyalty to the Government and the Laws of the Land.-

This document has been read to the assembled Legotla of Pokeng and has been approved, the undersigned have been appointed to sign the same on behalf of the whole of the Legotla and your Hon. has the assurance that this document has the support of everyone of us to whom the appellation "rebel" has been applied.-

Right: An opposing statement, signed by members of the Bafokeng lekgotla who deposed kgosi August Mokgatle.

S.N.C. 10/21/856/22.

UNION OF SOUTH AFRICA.

DEPARTMENT OF NATIVE AFFAIRS.

NATIVE AFFAIRS DEPARTMENT 19 OCT 1922 PRETORIA

.........................191.........

Complaint against Chief August Mokhatle.

The Secretary for Native Affairs,

Pretoria.

I beg to report that the trouble between the Chief August Mokhatle and a section of his tribe is still very acute, and I think a stage has now been reached when it is imperative for the Government to step in to force the disaffected section of the Tribe to obey the Chief's authority, showing him the respect due to a Chief, or alternatively to force them to vacate the tribal ground and live elsewhere in the Transvaal.

They are at present defying the Chief's authority. They have instituted a Court, presided over byt the rebel leaders David and Simon Mokhatle, at which all cases brought to it are settled. The proper Chief's Court being ignored by this section. They are most disrespectful and insulting in their attitude to the Chief. The Chief is continually asking that something be done to en this state of affairs as his patience is now exhausted .

You will remember that when you saw the two sections in Pretoria, you informed the rebel section that if they did not acknowledge the Chief's authority and show him the respect due to him, or words to that effect, they would have to be removed .

I think the time has now come, it is impossible for things to continue as they are at present, without there being serious trouble sooner or later.

Sub-Native Commissioner,
Rustenburg.

"The eyes of every chiefdom in the Transvaal were upon them..." fragments of correspondence written by Hugh Griffith (*left*), Sub-Native Commissioner for the Rustenburg District, and Colonel Godfrey Archibald Godley (*below*), Under-Secretary for Native Affairs, during the early 1920s.

Reverting to the matter more particularly under consideration, it is obvious that the present impossible state of affairs as regards the Bafokeng tribe cannot be allowed to continue and I am satisfied that the only effective solution of the difficulty lies in singling out the ring-leaders of the "rebel" section (David Mokhatle and his more prominent associates) and taking steps for their expulsion from the location under an order by the Governer-General, in his capacity as Paramount Chief of the Native population of the Transvaal, by virtue of the provisions of section thirteen of Law 4 of 1885 and of section one hundred and forty-seven of the South Africa Act.

Something must be done to restore The prestige of the Department which has undoubtedly suffered in the eyes of these people owing to the failure of the action taken under the Location regulations.

G.A.G.

Right: A meeting of Batswana chiefs and Union government officials in Rustenburg in December, 1924.

Right: Ernst Penzhorn, a second-generation Lutheran missionary of German ancestry whose political conservatism and paternalism made him a sympathizer of August Mokgatle.

Left: Reverend Kenneth Spooner, a Barbados-born Pentecostal missionary who supported the lekgotla's call for democratic change.

Right: Sol Plaatje, the writer, linguist, and founding member of the African National Congress, testified on behalf of the Bafokeng lekgotla in the case of *Mokgatle & Others v. The Minister of Native Affairs.*

Left: James Manotshe Mototlegi, August Mokgatle's first-born son, who was enthroned in 1938.

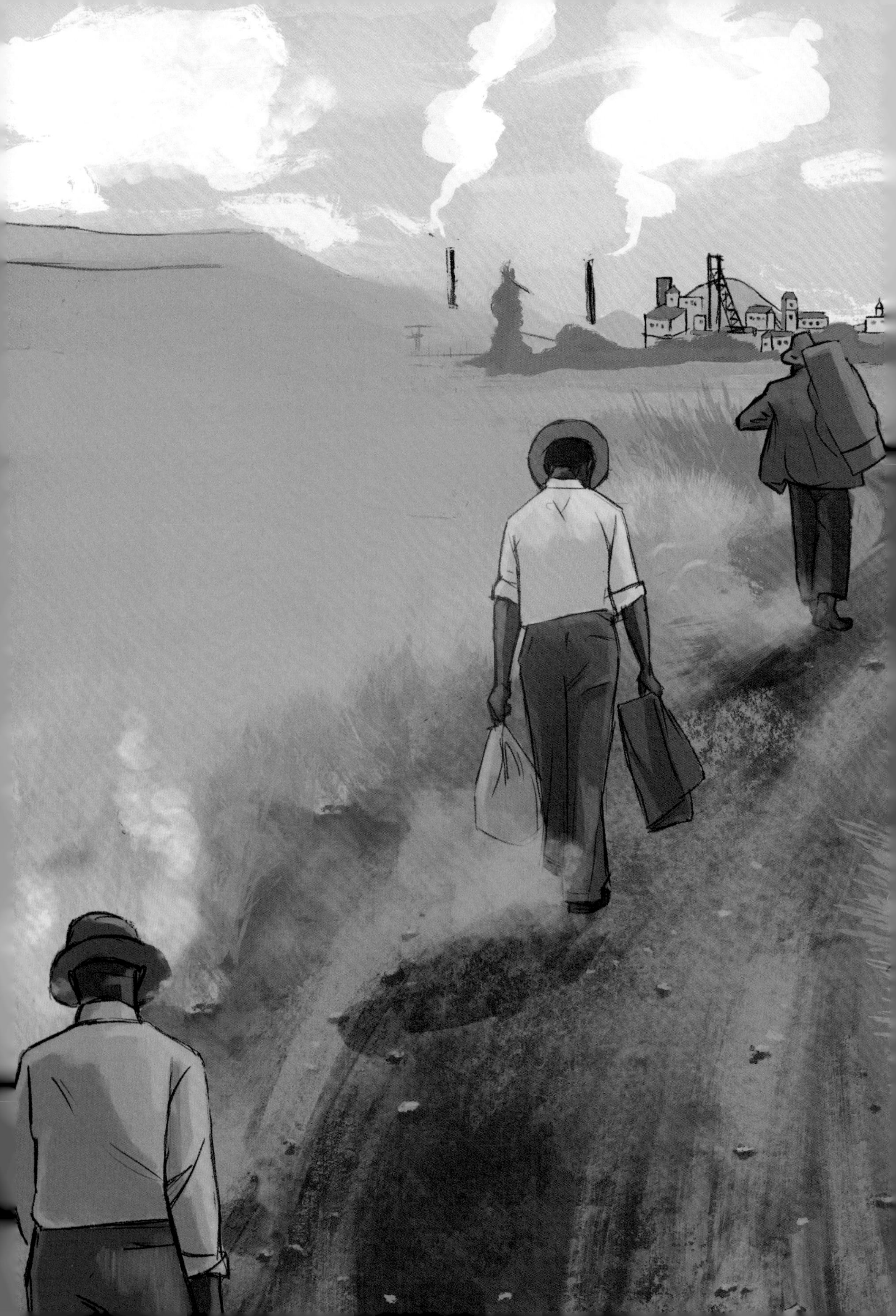

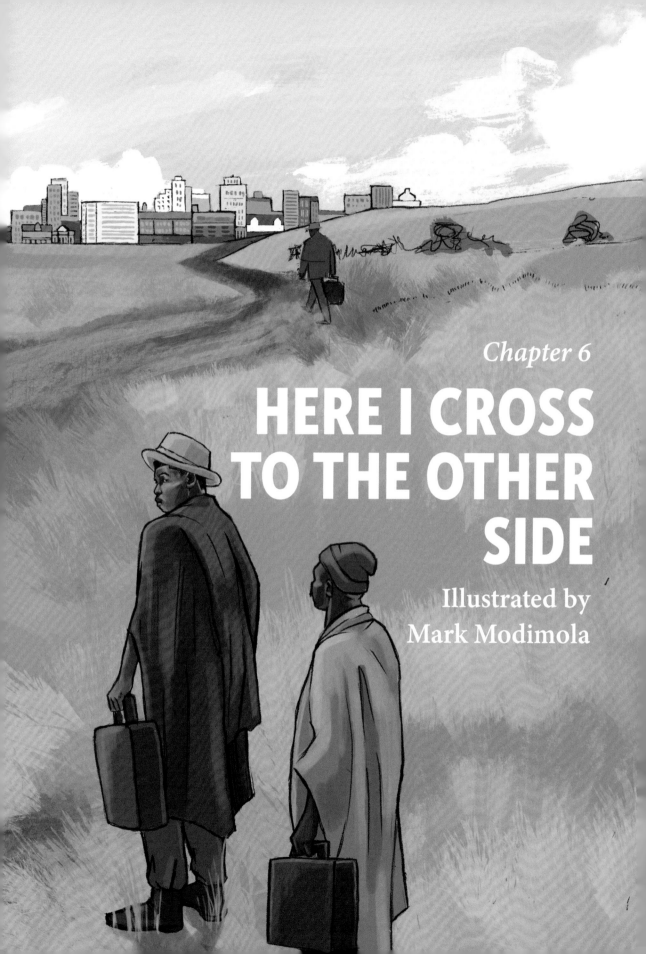

Chapter 6

HERE I CROSS TO THE OTHER SIDE

Illustrated by
Mark Modimola

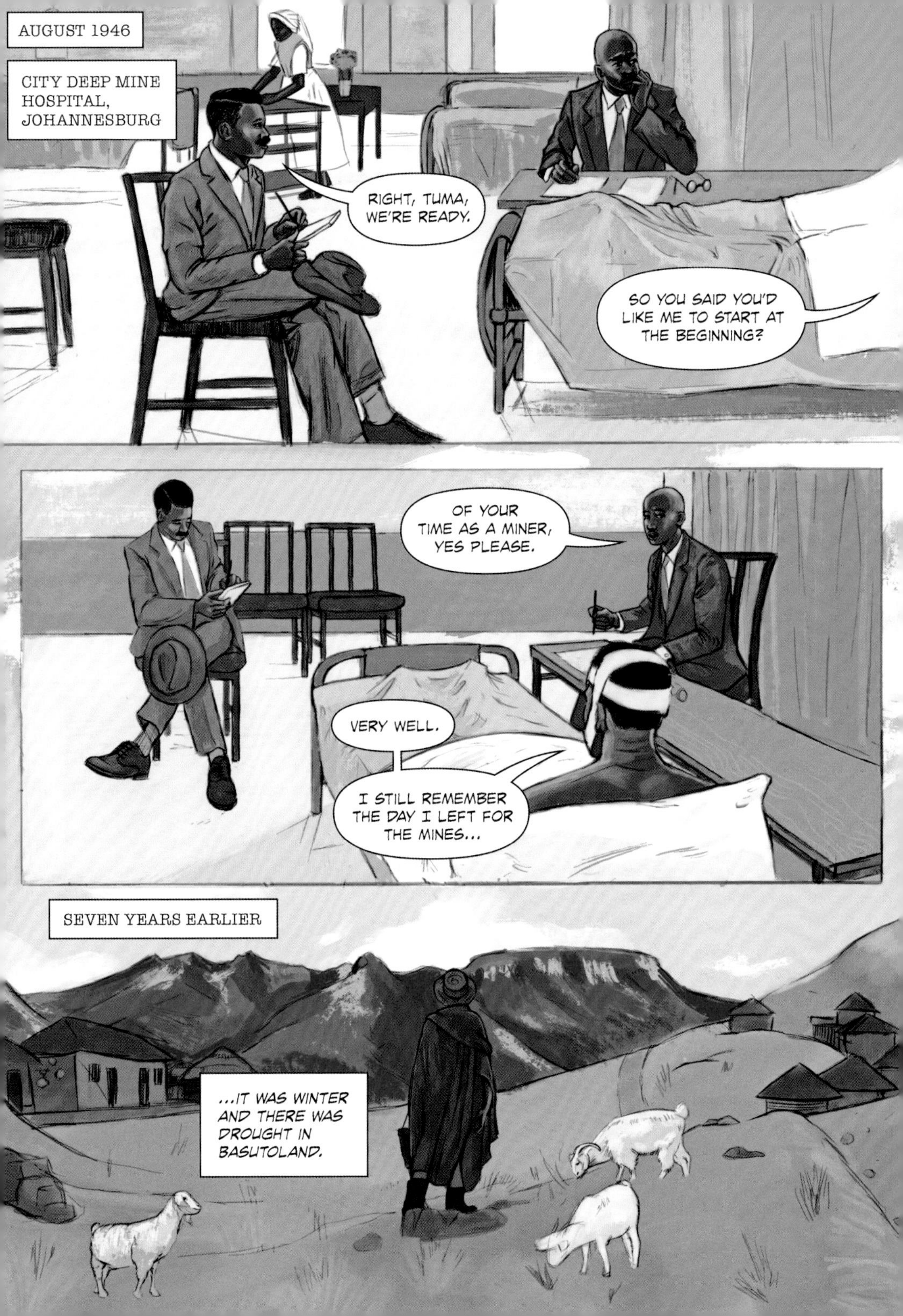
AUGUST 1946
CITY DEEP MINE HOSPITAL, JOHANNESBURG
RIGHT, TUMA, WE'RE READY.
SO YOU SAID YOU'D LIKE ME TO START AT THE BEGINNING?
OF YOUR TIME AS A MINER, YES PLEASE.
VERY WELL.
I STILL REMEMBER THE DAY I LEFT FOR THE MINES...
SEVEN YEARS EARLIER
...IT WAS WINTER AND THERE WAS DROUGHT IN BASUTOLAND.

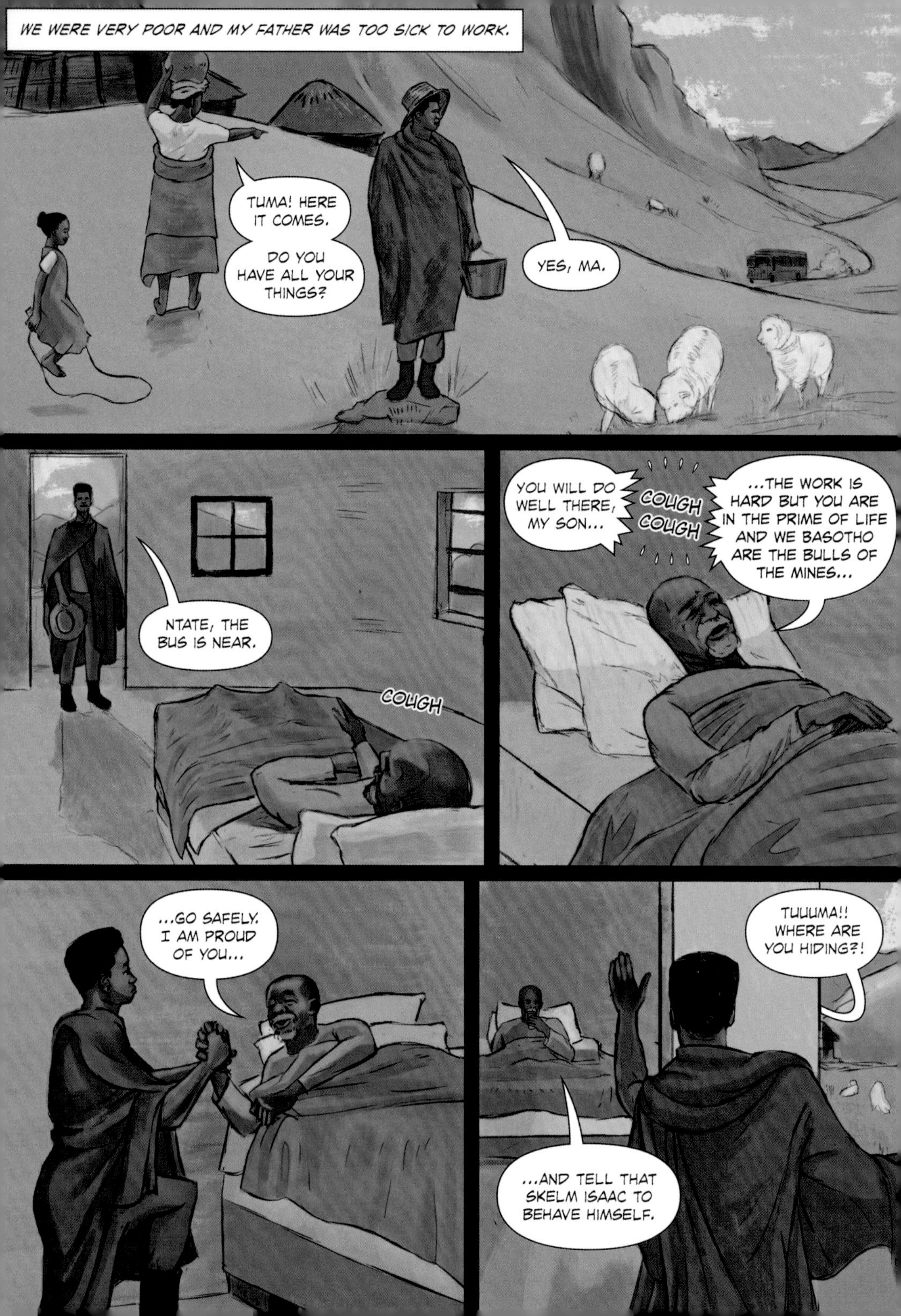

WE WERE VERY POOR AND MY FATHER WAS TOO SICK TO WORK.
TUMA! HERE IT COMES.
DO YOU HAVE ALL YOUR THINGS?
YES, MA.
NTATE, THE BUS IS NEAR.
COUGH
YOU WILL DO WELL THERE, MY SON...
COUGH COUGH
...THE WORK IS HARD BUT YOU ARE IN THE PRIME OF LIFE AND WE BASOTHO ARE THE BULLS OF THE MINES...
...GO SAFELY. I AM PROUD OF YOU...
TUUUMA!! WHERE ARE YOU HIDING?!
...AND TELL THAT SKELM ISAAC TO BEHAVE HIMSELF.

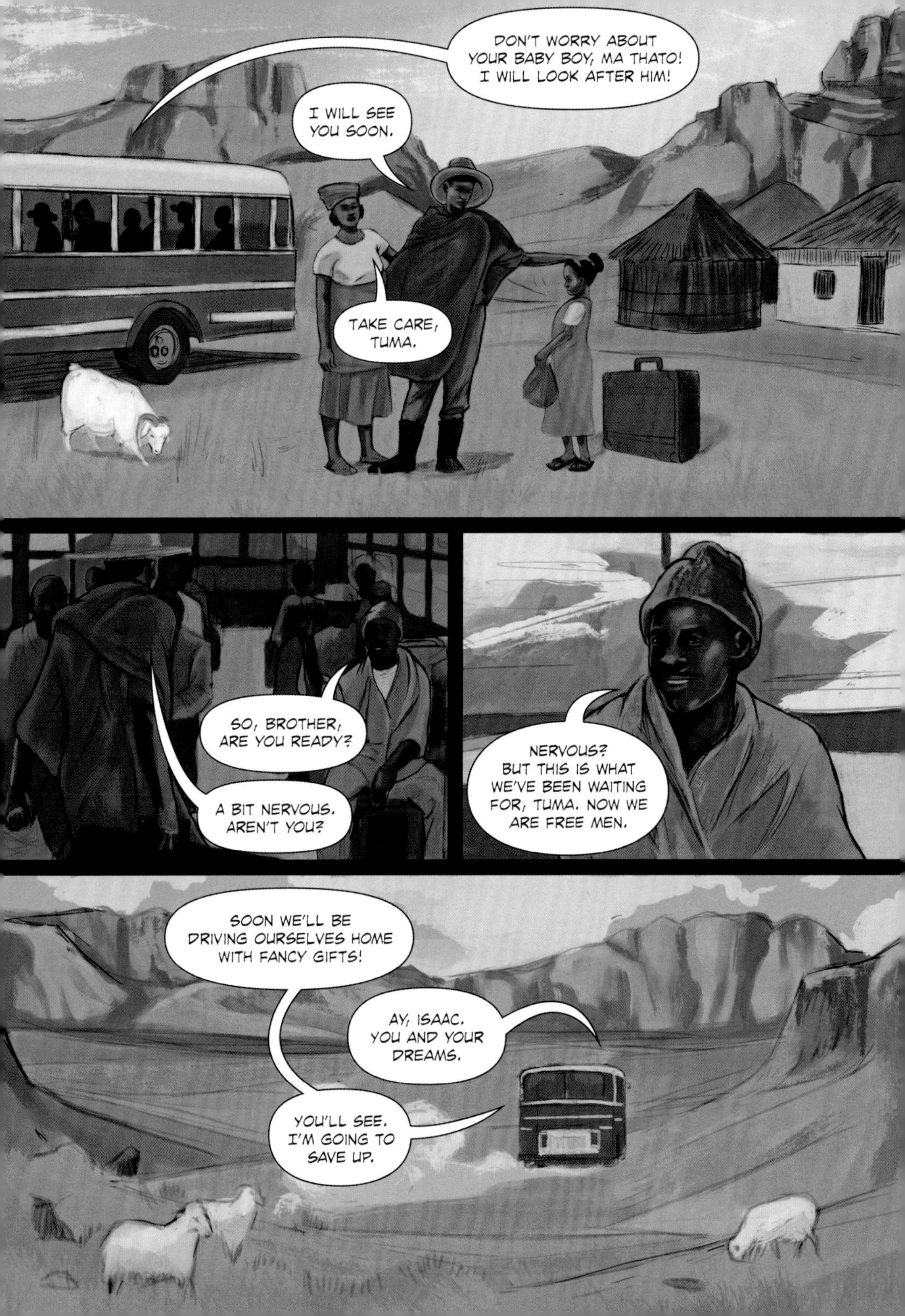
I WILL SEE YOU SOON.
DON'T WORRY ABOUT YOUR BABY BOY, MA THATO! I WILL LOOK AFTER HIM!
TAKE CARE, TUMA.
SO, BROTHER, ARE YOU READY?
A BIT NERVOUS. AREN'T YOU?
NERVOUS? BUT THIS IS WHAT WE'VE BEEN WAITING FOR, TUMA. NOW WE ARE FREE MEN.
SOON WE'LL BE DRIVING OURSELVES HOME WITH FANCY GIFTS!
AY, ISAAC. YOU AND YOUR DREAMS.
YOU'LL SEE. I'M GOING TO SAVE UP.

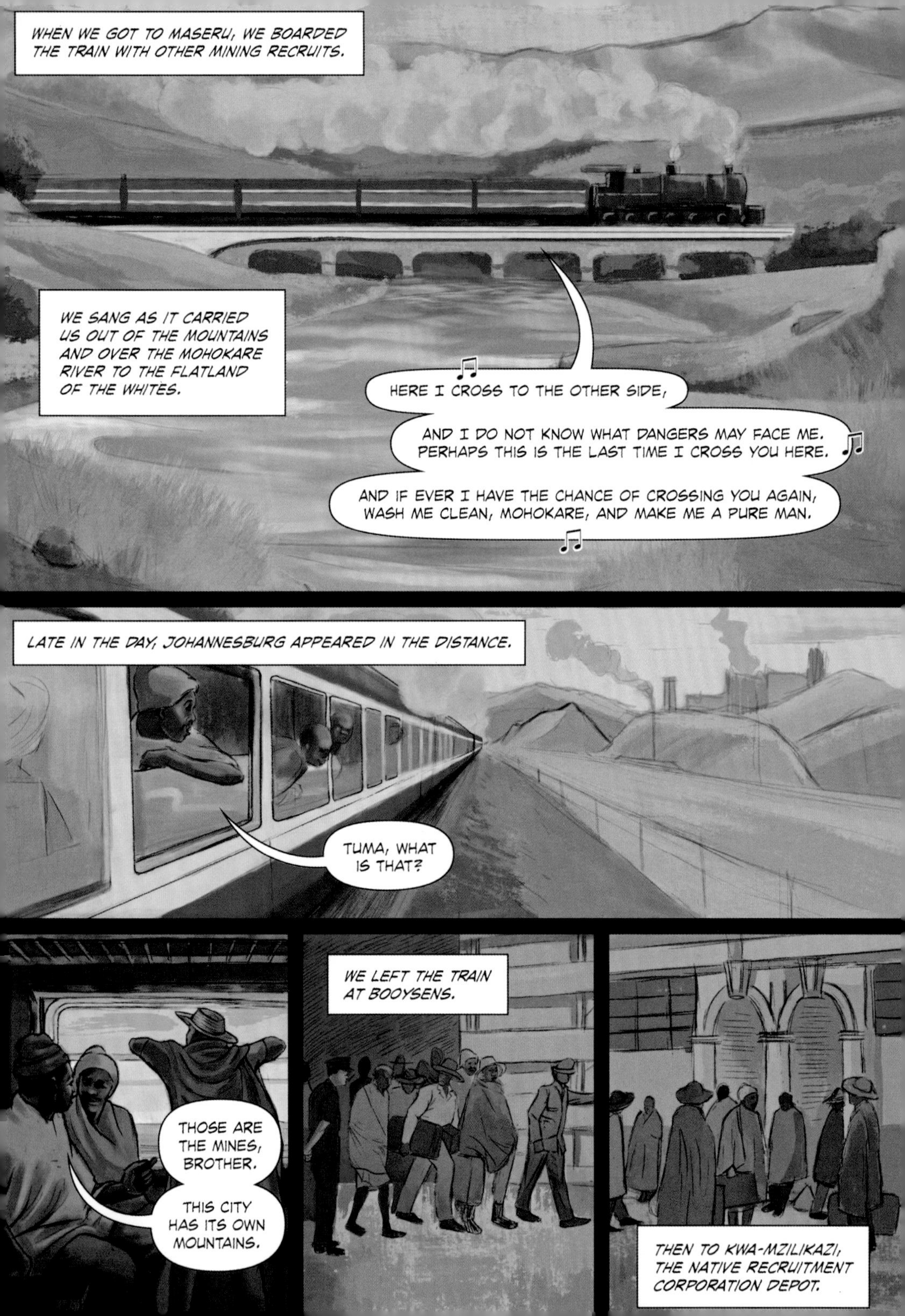
WHEN WE GOT TO MASERU, WE BOARDED THE TRAIN WITH OTHER MINING RECRUITS.
WE SANG AS IT CARRIED US OUT OF THE MOUNTAINS AND OVER THE MOHOKARE RIVER TO THE FLATLAND OF THE WHITES.
HERE I CROSS TO THE OTHER SIDE,
AND I DO NOT KNOW WHAT DANGERS MAY FACE ME. PERHAPS THIS IS THE LAST TIME I CROSS YOU HERE.
AND IF EVER I HAVE THE CHANCE OF CROSSING YOU AGAIN, WASH ME CLEAN, MOHOKARE, AND MAKE ME A PURE MAN.
LATE IN THE DAY, JOHANNESBURG APPEARED IN THE DISTANCE.
TUMA, WHAT IS THAT?
THOSE ARE THE MINES, BROTHER.
THIS CITY HAS ITS OWN MOUNTAINS.
WE LEFT THE TRAIN AT BOOYSENS.
THEN TO KWA-MZILIKAZI, THE NATIVE RECRUITMENT CORPORATION DEPOT.

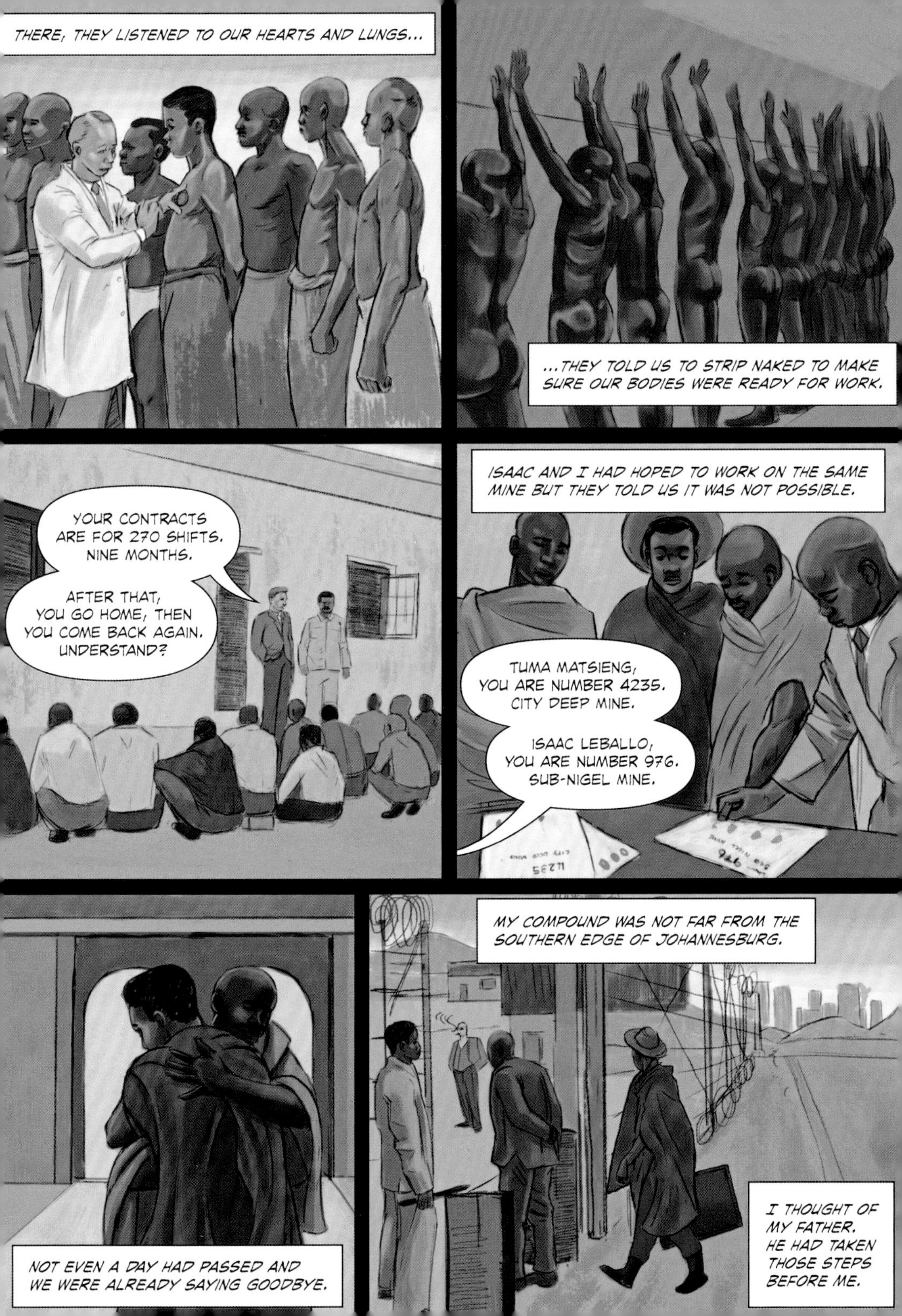

THERE, THEY LISTENED TO OUR HEARTS AND LUNGS...
...THEY TOLD US TO STRIP NAKED TO MAKE SURE OUR BODIES WERE READY FOR WORK.
YOUR CONTRACTS ARE FOR 270 SHIFTS. NINE MONTHS.
AFTER THAT, YOU GO HOME, THEN YOU COME BACK AGAIN. UNDERSTAND?
ISAAC AND I HAD HOPED TO WORK ON THE SAME MINE BUT THEY TOLD US IT WAS NOT POSSIBLE.
TUMA MATSIENG, YOU ARE NUMBER 4235. CITY DEEP MINE.
ISAAC LEBALLO, YOU ARE NUMBER 976. SUB-NIGEL MINE.
NOT EVEN A DAY HAD PASSED AND WE WERE ALREADY SAYING GOODBYE.
MY COMPOUND WAS NOT FAR FROM THE SOUTHERN EDGE OF JOHANNESBURG.
I THOUGHT OF MY FATHER. HE HAD TAKEN THOSE STEPS BEFORE ME.

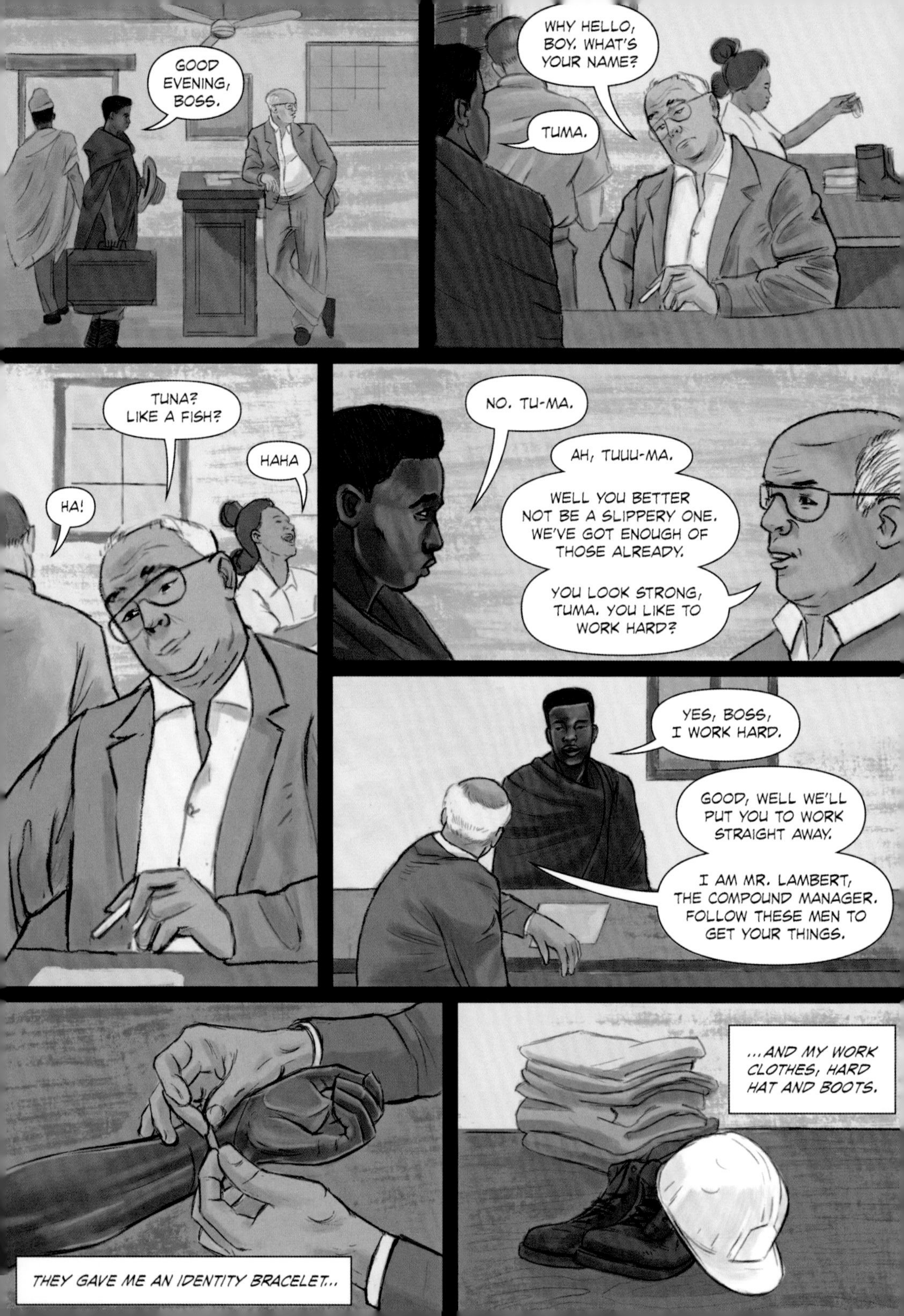
GOOD EVENING, BOSS.
WHY HELLO, BOY. WHAT'S YOUR NAME?
TUMA.
TUNA? LIKE A FISH?
HA!
HAHA
NO. TU-MA.
AH, TUUU-MA.
WELL YOU BETTER NOT BE A SLIPPERY ONE. WE'VE GOT ENOUGH OF THOSE ALREADY.
YOU LOOK STRONG, TUMA. YOU LIKE TO WORK HARD?
YES, BOSS, I WORK HARD.
GOOD, WELL WE'LL PUT YOU TO WORK STRAIGHT AWAY.
I AM MR. LAMBERT, THE COMPOUND MANAGER. FOLLOW THESE MEN TO GET YOUR THINGS.
THEY GAVE ME AN IDENTITY BRACELET...
...AND MY WORK CLOTHES, HARD HAT AND BOOTS.

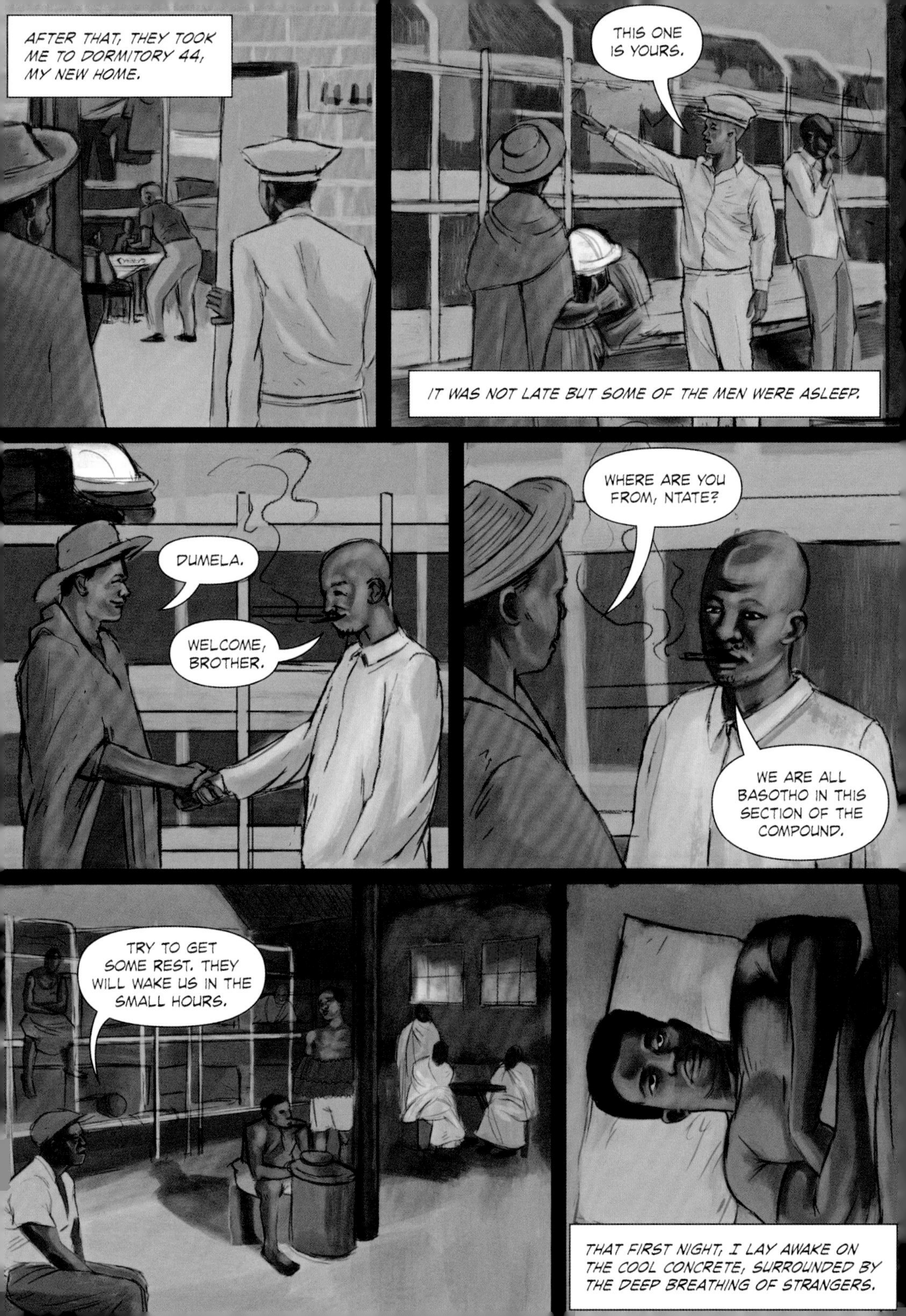
AFTER THAT, THEY TOOK ME TO DORMITORY 44, MY NEW HOME.
THIS ONE IS YOURS.
IT WAS NOT LATE BUT SOME OF THE MEN WERE ASLEEP.
DUMELA.
WELCOME, BROTHER.
WHERE ARE YOU FROM, NTATE?
WE ARE ALL BASOTHO IN THIS SECTION OF THE COMPOUND.
TRY TO GET SOME REST. THEY WILL WAKE US IN THE SMALL HOURS.
THAT FIRST NIGHT, I LAY AWAKE ON THE COOL CONCRETE, SURROUNDED BY THE DEEP BREATHING OF STRANGERS.

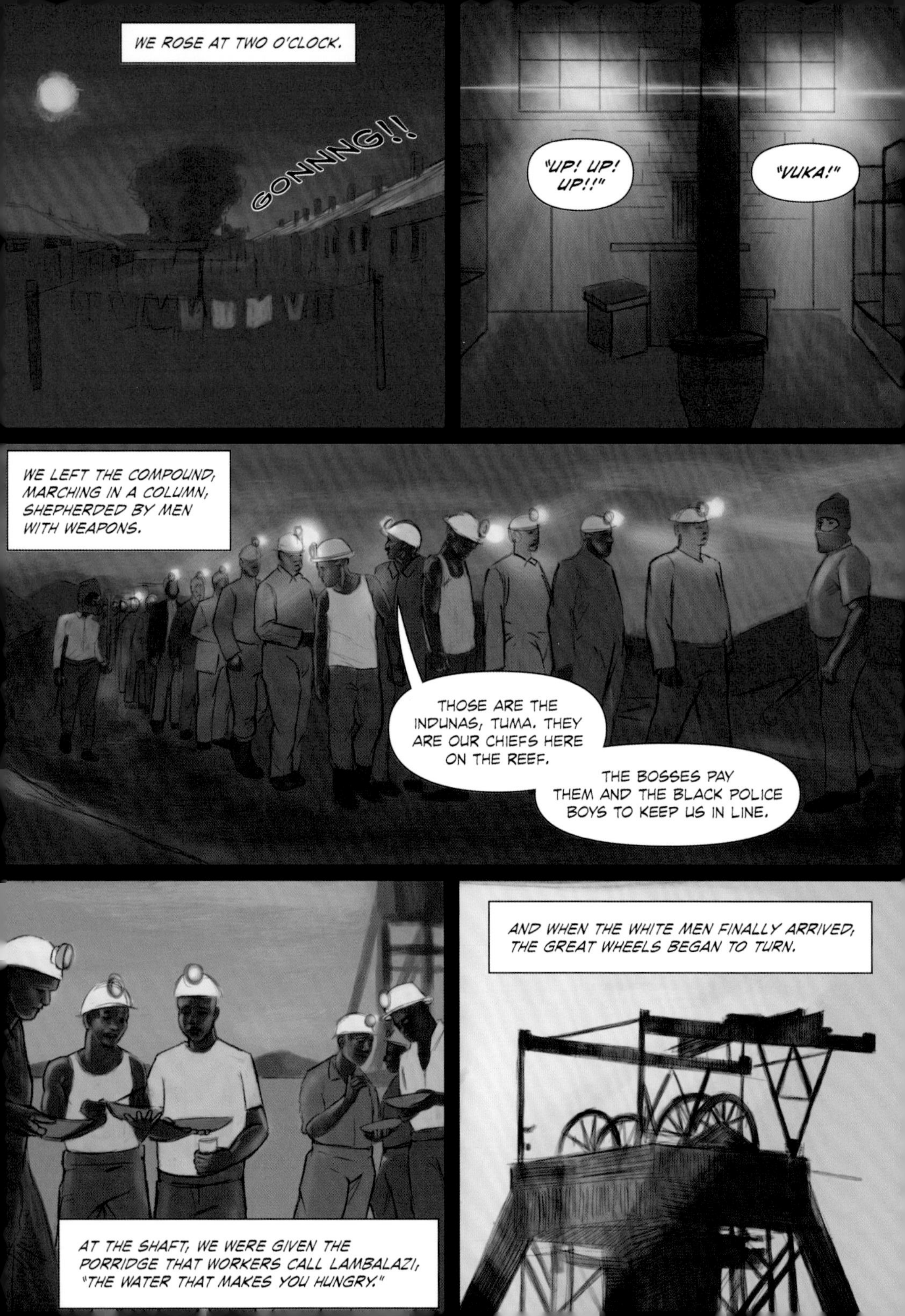
WE ROSE AT TWO O'CLOCK.
GONNNG!!
"UP! UP! UP!!"
"VUKA!"
WE LEFT THE COMPOUND, MARCHING IN A COLUMN, SHEPHERDED BY MEN WITH WEAPONS.
THOSE ARE THE INDUNAS, TUMA. THEY ARE OUR CHIEFS HERE ON THE REEF.
THE BOSSES PAY THEM AND THE BLACK POLICE BOYS TO KEEP US IN LINE.
AT THE SHAFT, WE WERE GIVEN THE PORRIDGE THAT WORKERS CALL LAMBALAZI, "THE WATER THAT MAKES YOU HUNGRY."
AND WHEN THE WHITE MEN FINALLY ARRIVED, THE GREAT WHEELS BEGAN TO TURN.

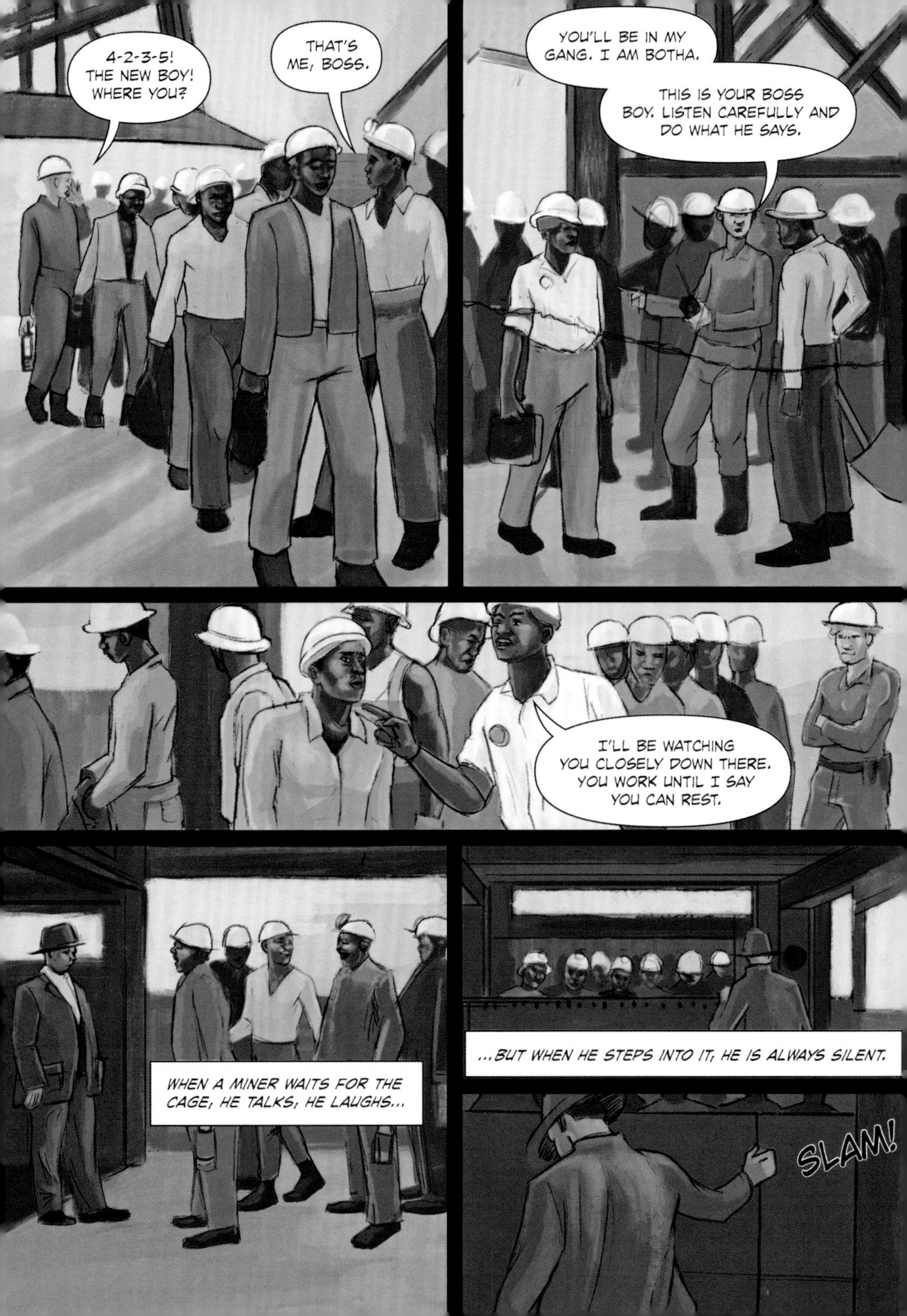
4-2-3-5! THE NEW BOY! WHERE YOU?
THAT'S ME, BOSS.
YOU'LL BE IN MY GANG. I AM BOTHA.
THIS IS YOUR BOSS BOY. LISTEN CAREFULLY AND DO WHAT HE SAYS.
I'LL BE WATCHING YOU CLOSELY DOWN THERE. YOU WORK UNTIL I SAY YOU CAN REST.
WHEN A MINER WAITS FOR THE CAGE, HE TALKS, HE LAUGHS...
...BUT WHEN HE STEPS INTO IT, HE IS ALWAYS SILENT.
SLAM!

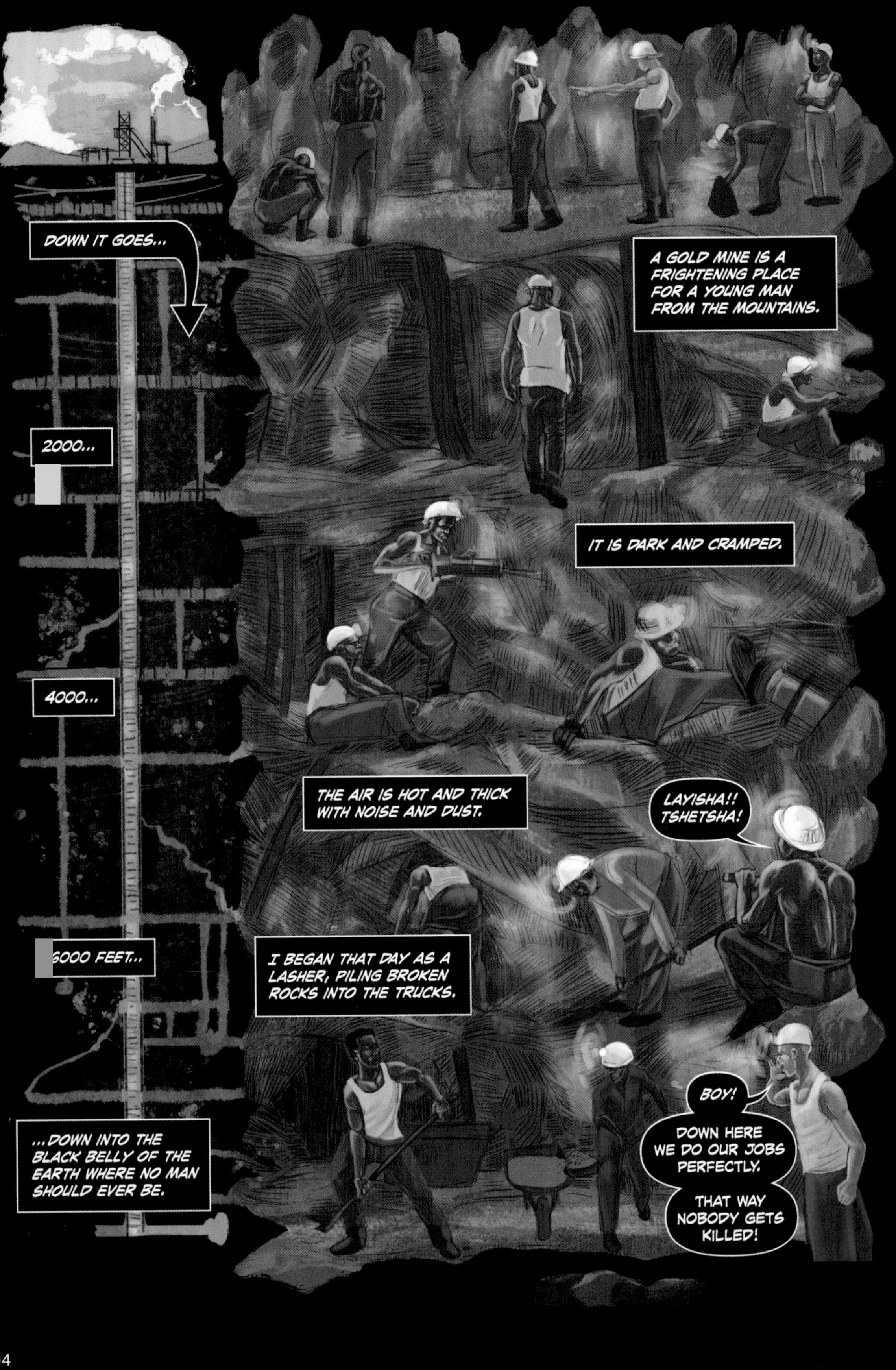
DOWN IT GOES...
A GOLD MINE IS A FRIGHTENING PLACE FOR A YOUNG MAN FROM THE MOUNTAINS.
2000...
IT IS DARK AND CRAMPED.
4000...
THE AIR IS HOT AND THICK WITH NOISE AND DUST.
LAYISHA!! TSHETSHA!
6000 FEET...
I BEGAN THAT DAY AS A LASHER, PILING BROKEN ROCKS INTO THE TRUCKS.
...DOWN INTO THE BLACK BELLY OF THE EARTH WHERE NO MAN SHOULD EVER BE.
BOY!
DOWN HERE WE DO OUR JOBS PERFECTLY.
THAT WAY NOBODY GETS KILLED!

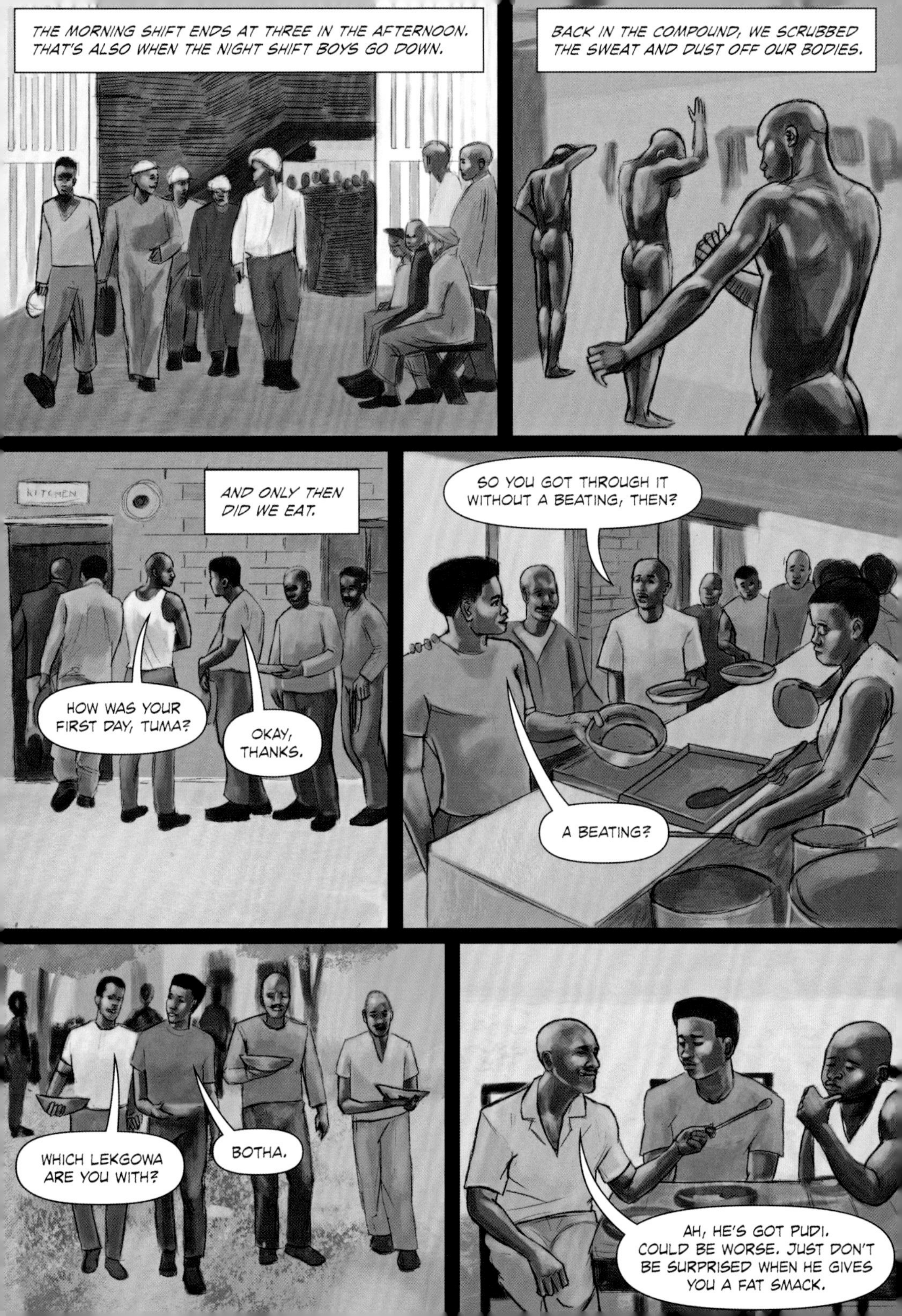
THE MORNING SHIFT ENDS AT THREE IN THE AFTERNOON. THAT'S ALSO WHEN THE NIGHT SHIFT BOYS GO DOWN.
BACK IN THE COMPOUND, WE SCRUBBED THE SWEAT AND DUST OFF OUR BODIES.
KITCHEN
AND ONLY THEN DID WE EAT.
HOW WAS YOUR FIRST DAY, TUMA?
OKAY, THANKS.
SO YOU GOT THROUGH IT WITHOUT A BEATING, THEN?
A BEATING?
WHICH LEKGOWA ARE YOU WITH?
BOTHA.
AH, HE'S GOT PUDI. COULD BE WORSE. JUST DON'T BE SURPRISED WHEN HE GIVES YOU A FAT SMACK.

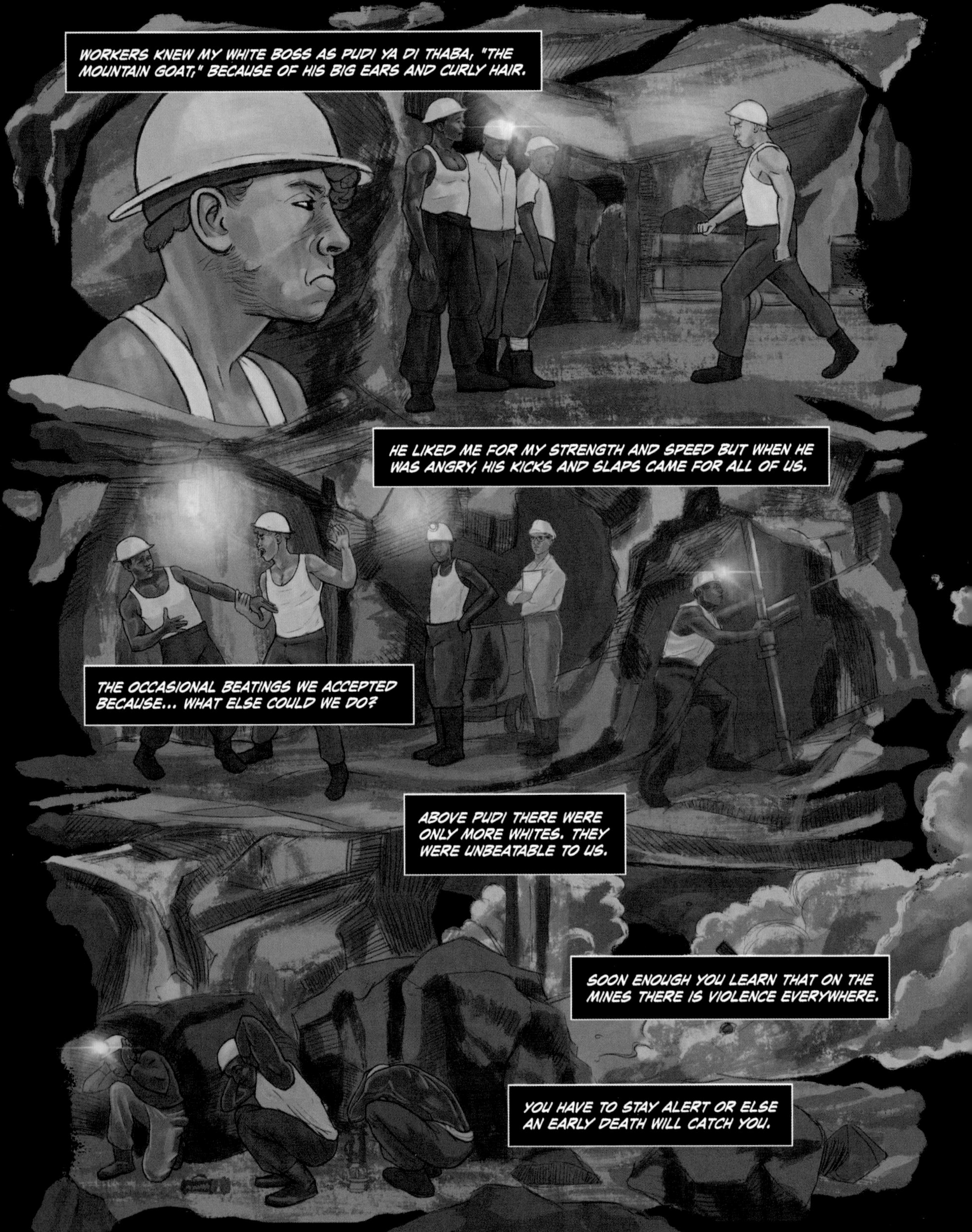
WORKERS KNEW MY WHITE BOSS AS PUDI YA DI THABA, "THE MOUNTAIN GOAT," BECAUSE OF HIS BIG EARS AND CURLY HAIR.
HE LIKED ME FOR MY STRENGTH AND SPEED BUT WHEN HE WAS ANGRY, HIS KICKS AND SLAPS CAME FOR ALL OF US.
THE OCCASIONAL BEATINGS WE ACCEPTED BECAUSE... WHAT ELSE COULD WE DO?
ABOVE PUDI THERE WERE ONLY MORE WHITES. THEY WERE UNBEATABLE TO US.
SOON ENOUGH YOU LEARN THAT ON THE MINES THERE IS VIOLENCE EVERYWHERE.
YOU HAVE TO STAY ALERT OR ELSE AN EARLY DEATH WILL CATCH YOU.

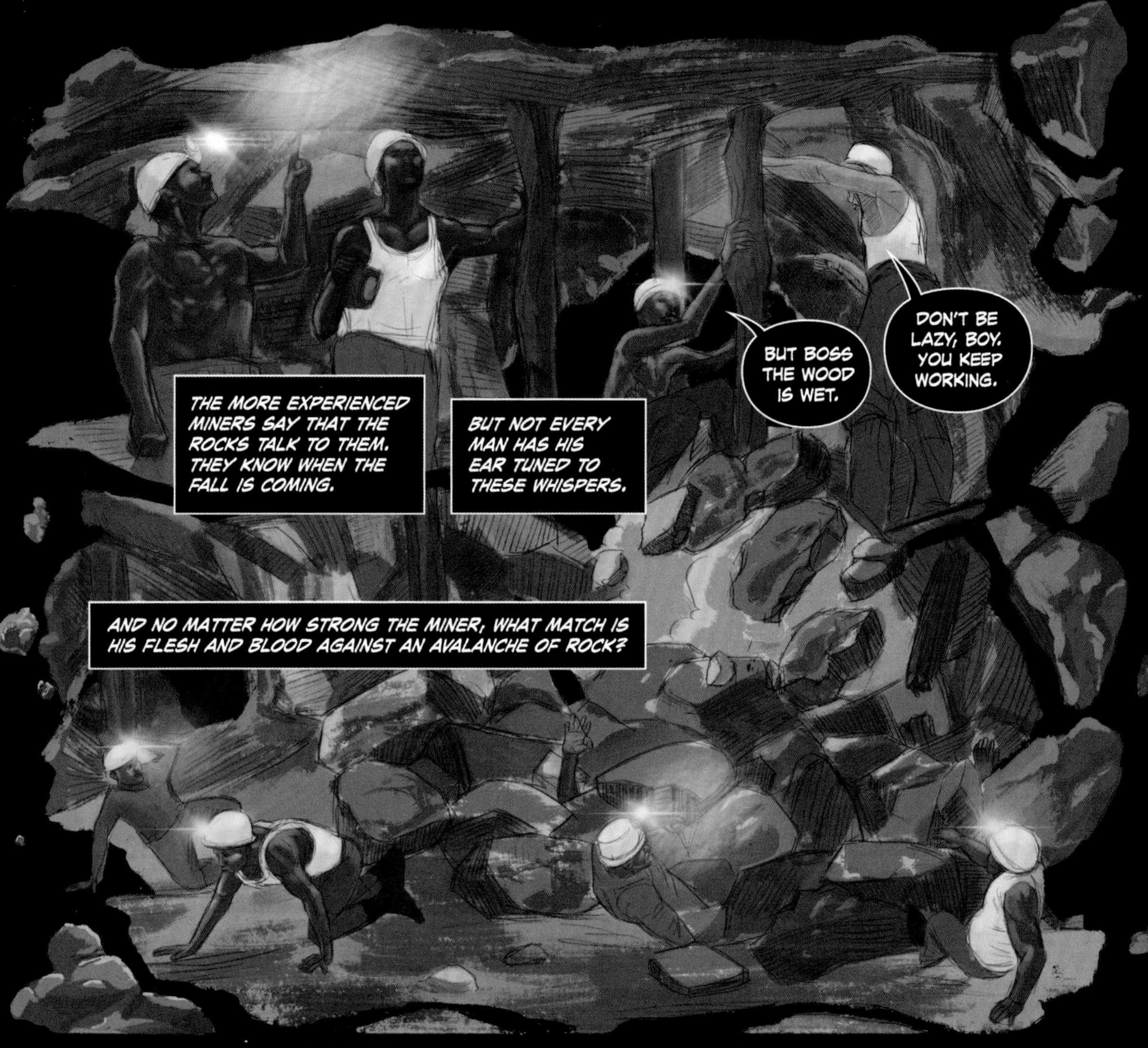
THE MORE EXPERIENCED MINERS SAY THAT THE ROCKS TALK TO THEM. THEY KNOW WHEN THE FALL IS COMING.
BUT NOT EVERY MAN HAS HIS EAR TUNED TO THESE WHISPERS.
BUT BOSS THE WOOD IS WET.
DON'T BE LAZY, BOY. YOU KEEP WORKING.
AND NO MATTER HOW STRONG THE MINER, WHAT MATCH IS HIS FLESH AND BLOOD AGAINST AN AVALANCHE OF ROCK?

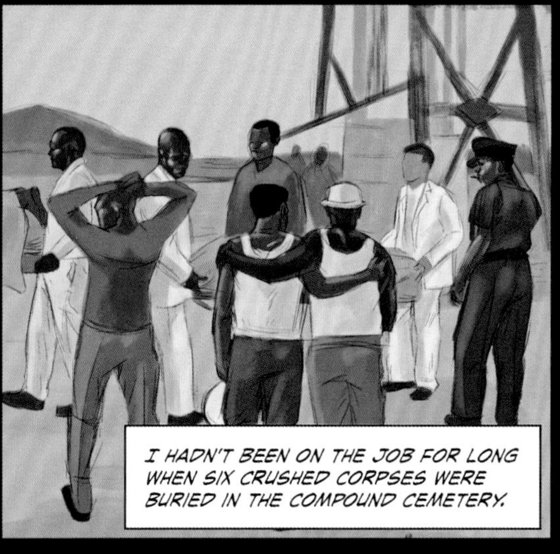
I HADN'T BEEN ON THE JOB FOR LONG WHEN SIX CRUSHED CORPSES WERE BURIED IN THE COMPOUND CEMETERY.

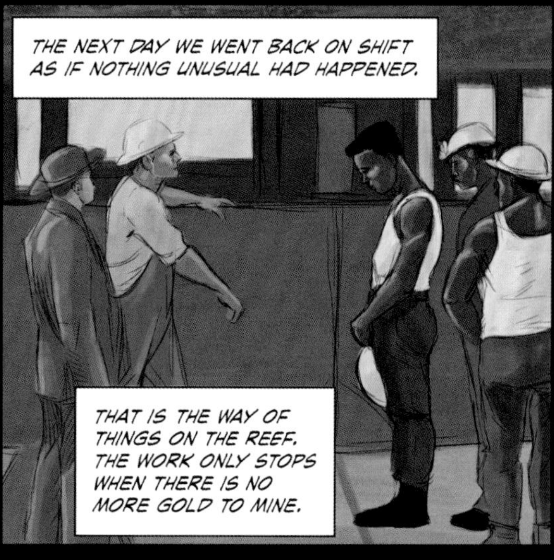
THE NEXT DAY WE WENT BACK ON SHIFT AS IF NOTHING UNUSUAL HAD HAPPENED.
THAT IS THE WAY OF THINGS ON THE REEF. THE WORK ONLY STOPS WHEN THERE IS NO MORE GOLD TO MINE.

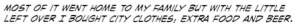

MOST OF IT WENT HOME TO MY FAMILY BUT WITH THE LITTLE LEFT OVER I BOUGHT CITY CLOTHES, EXTRA FOOD AND BEER.

EVERY 30 DAYS I WAS PAID THREE POUNDS AND EIGHT SHILLINGS.

ON WEEKENDS, I'D TAKE THE TRAIN TO SEE ISAAC AT SUB-NIGEL OR HE WOULD COME TO CITY DEEP.

WE'D GO TO THE SYRIAN BARS IN TOWN, THE SKOKIAAN QUEENS IN VREDEDORP AND THE NEWCLARE BEER HALLS.

TUMA! I'LL BE BACK!

DURING THOSE NIGHTS WE FORGOT ABOUT THE HARDSHIPS OF THE WEEK.

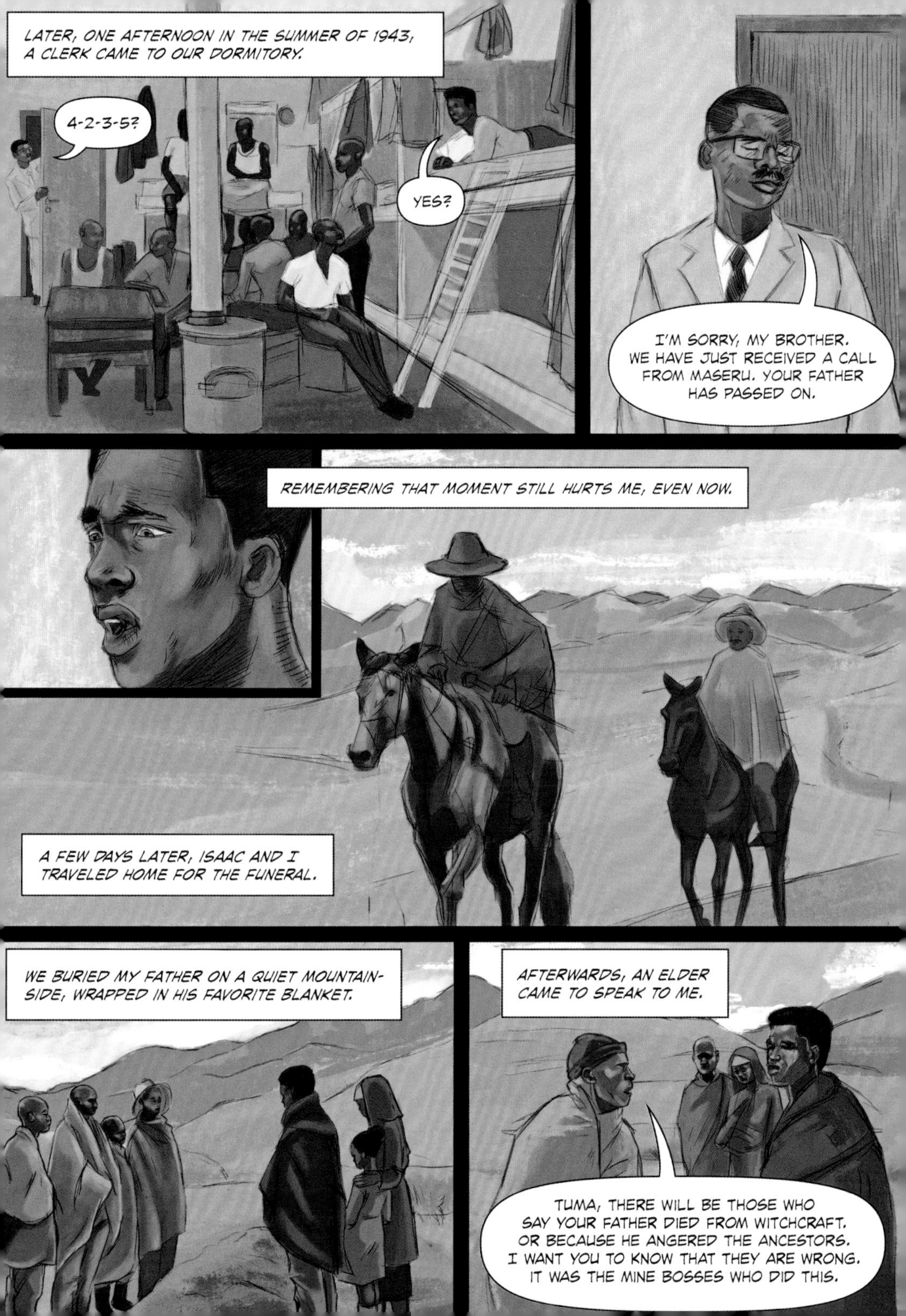
LATER, ONE AFTERNOON IN THE SUMMER OF 1943, A CLERK CAME TO OUR DORMITORY.
4-2-3-5?
YES?
I'M SORRY, MY BROTHER. WE HAVE JUST RECEIVED A CALL FROM MASERU. YOUR FATHER HAS PASSED ON.
REMEMBERING THAT MOMENT STILL HURTS ME, EVEN NOW.
A FEW DAYS LATER, ISAAC AND I TRAVELED HOME FOR THE FUNERAL.
WE BURIED MY FATHER ON A QUIET MOUNTAIN-SIDE, WRAPPED IN HIS FAVORITE BLANKET.
AFTERWARDS, AN ELDER CAME TO SPEAK TO ME.
TUMA, THERE WILL BE THOSE WHO SAY YOUR FATHER DIED FROM WITCHCRAFT. OR BECAUSE HE ANGERED THE ANCESTORS. I WANT YOU TO KNOW THAT THEY ARE WRONG. IT WAS THE MINE BOSSES WHO DID THIS.

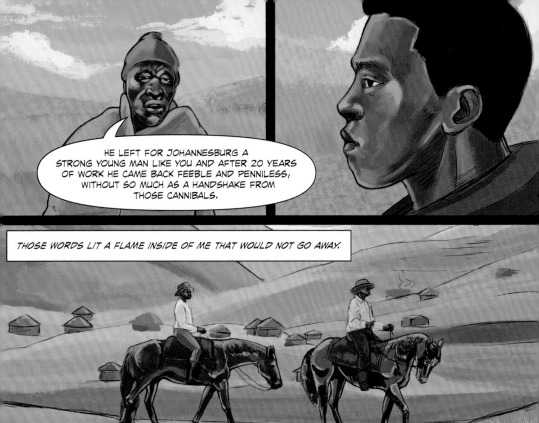

HE LEFT FOR JOHANNESBURG A STRONG YOUNG MAN LIKE YOU AND AFTER 20 YEARS OF WORK HE CAME BACK FEEBLE AND PENNILESS, WITHOUT SO MUCH AS A HANDSHAKE FROM THOSE CANNIBALS.

THOSE WORDS LIT A FLAME INSIDE OF ME THAT WOULD NOT GO AWAY.

THEY MADE ME SEE THE WORLD WITH DIFFERENT EYES.

WHY DO WE LET THE WHITES TREAT US LIKE THIS?

BECAUSE IF WE FIGHT BACK THEY WILL PROBABLY KILL US, BROTHER.

BUT THERE ARE SO MANY OF US ON THE MINES, AND SO FEW OF THEM.

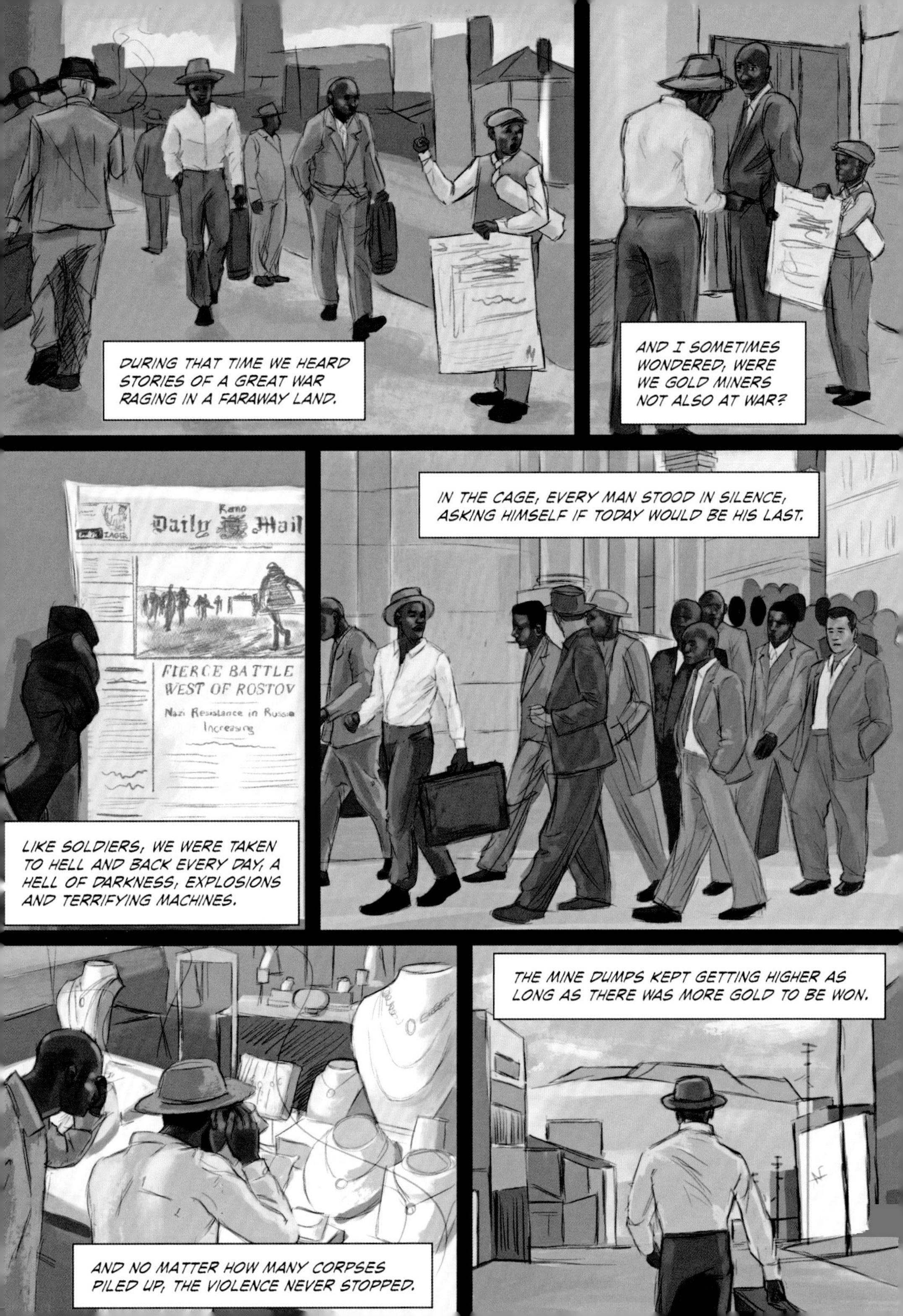
DURING THAT TIME WE HEARD STORIES OF A GREAT WAR RAGING IN A FARAWAY LAND.
AND I SOMETIMES WONDERED, WERE WE GOLD MINERS NOT ALSO AT WAR?
Rand Daily Mail
FIERCE BATTLE WEST OF ROSTOV
Nazi Resistance in Russia Increasing
LIKE SOLDIERS, WE WERE TAKEN TO HELL AND BACK EVERY DAY, A HELL OF DARKNESS, EXPLOSIONS AND TERRIFYING MACHINES.
IN THE CAGE, EVERY MAN STOOD IN SILENCE, ASKING HIMSELF IF TODAY WOULD BE HIS LAST.
AND NO MATTER HOW MANY CORPSES PILED UP, THE VIOLENCE NEVER STOPPED.
THE MINE DUMPS KEPT GETTING HIGHER AS LONG AS THERE WAS MORE GOLD TO BE WON.

IT WAS NOT JUST US, THOUGH.

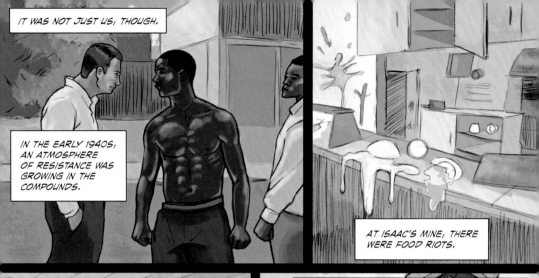

IN THE EARLY 1940S, AN ATMOSPHERE OF RESISTANCE WAS GROWING IN THE COMPOUNDS.

AT ISAAC'S MINE, THERE WERE FOOD RIOTS.

HERE AT CITY DEEP, LAMBERT TOLD US TO CLEAN OUR ROOMS, SO SOME WORKERS GAVE THE MANAGERS THEIR OWN MESS TO TIDY UP.

ELSEWHERE, WE HEARD OF STRIKES AND SIT-DOWNS WHERE THE POLICE WERE CALLED IN.

AND IT WAS ALSO AROUND THAT TIME THAT CLERKS AT CITY DEEP BEGAN TO SPEAK QUIETLY ABOUT A GROUP OF AFRICAN MEN WHO WANTED TO HELP US FROM THE OUTSIDE.

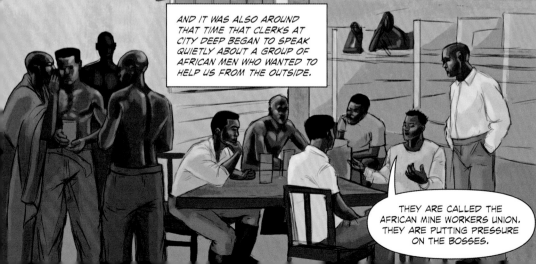

THEY ARE CALLED THE AFRICAN MINE WORKERS UNION. THEY ARE PUTTING PRESSURE ON THE BOSSES.

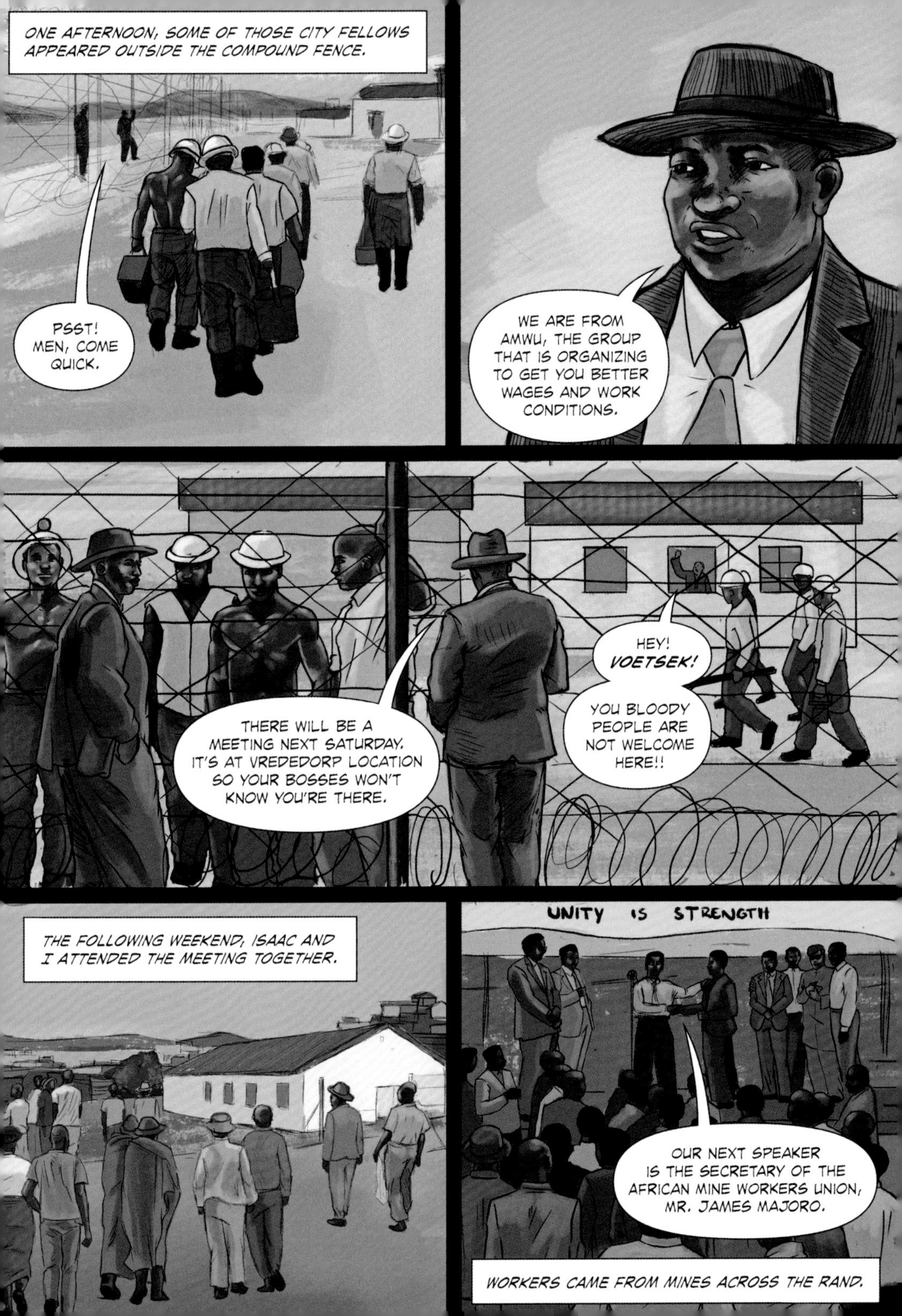
ONE AFTERNOON, SOME OF THOSE CITY FELLOWS APPEARED OUTSIDE THE COMPOUND FENCE.
PSST! MEN, COME QUICK.
WE ARE FROM AMWU, THE GROUP THAT IS ORGANIZING TO GET YOU BETTER WAGES AND WORK CONDITIONS.
THERE WILL BE A MEETING NEXT SATURDAY. IT'S AT VREDEDORP LOCATION SO YOUR BOSSES WON'T KNOW YOU'RE THERE.
HEY! VOETSEK!
YOU BLOODY PEOPLE ARE NOT WELCOME HERE!!
THE FOLLOWING WEEKEND, ISAAC AND I ATTENDED THE MEETING TOGETHER.
UNITY IS STRENGTH
OUR NEXT SPEAKER IS THE SECRETARY OF THE AFRICAN MINE WORKERS UNION, MR. JAMES MAJORO.
WORKERS CAME FROM MINES ACROSS THE RAND.

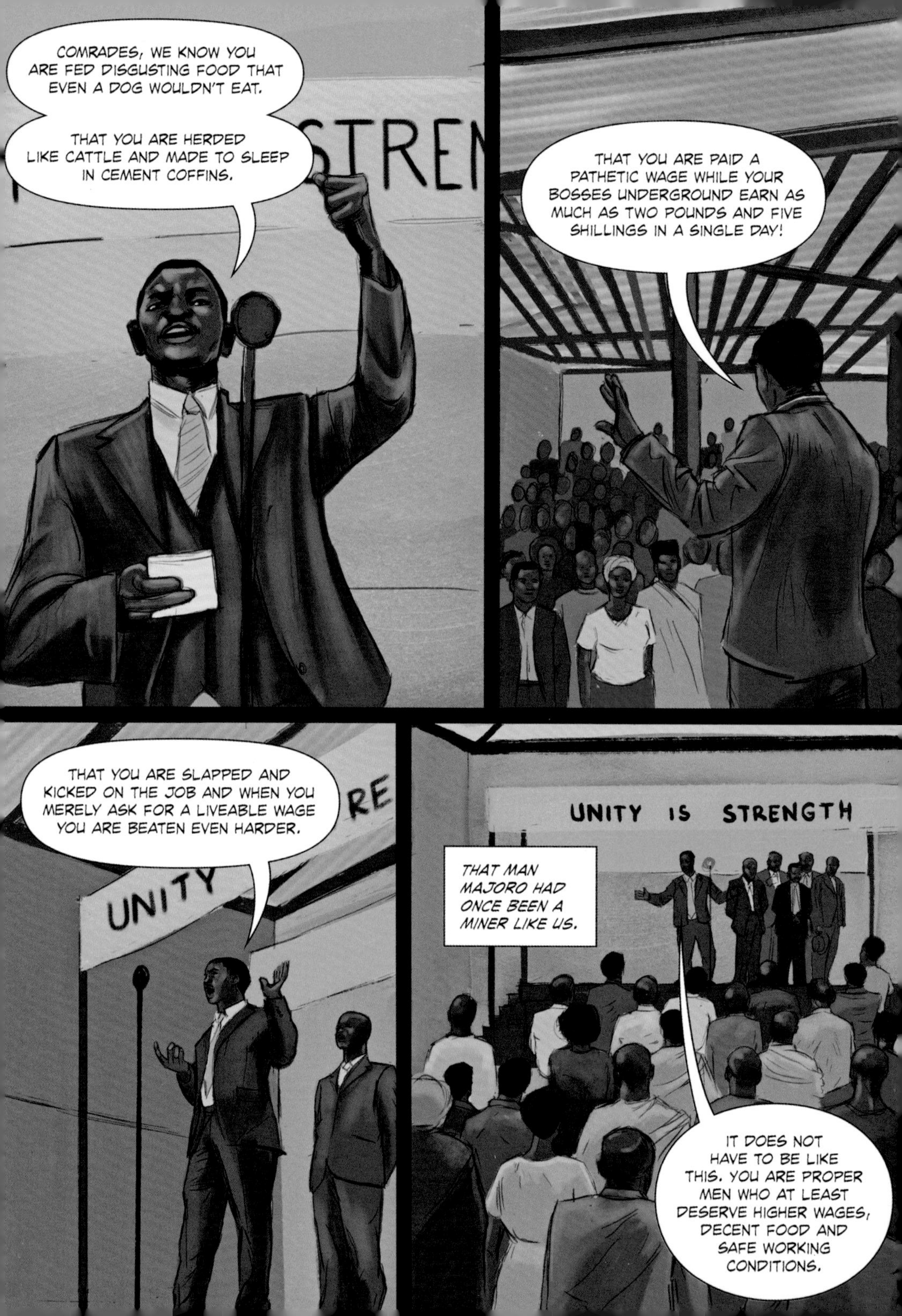
COMRADES, WE KNOW YOU ARE FED DISGUSTING FOOD THAT EVEN A DOG WOULDN'T EAT.
THAT YOU ARE HERDED LIKE CATTLE AND MADE TO SLEEP IN CEMENT COFFINS.
STREN
THAT YOU ARE PAID A PATHETIC WAGE WHILE YOUR BOSSES UNDERGROUND EARN AS MUCH AS TWO POUNDS AND FIVE SHILLINGS IN A SINGLE DAY!
THAT YOU ARE SLAPPED AND KICKED ON THE JOB AND WHEN YOU MERELY ASK FOR A LIVEABLE WAGE YOU ARE BEATEN EVEN HARDER.
RE
UNITY
UNITY IS STRENGTH
THAT MAN MAJORO HAD ONCE BEEN A MINER LIKE US.
IT DOES NOT HAVE TO BE LIKE THIS. YOU ARE PROPER MEN WHO AT LEAST DESERVE HIGHER WAGES, DECENT FOOD AND SAFE WORKING CONDITIONS.

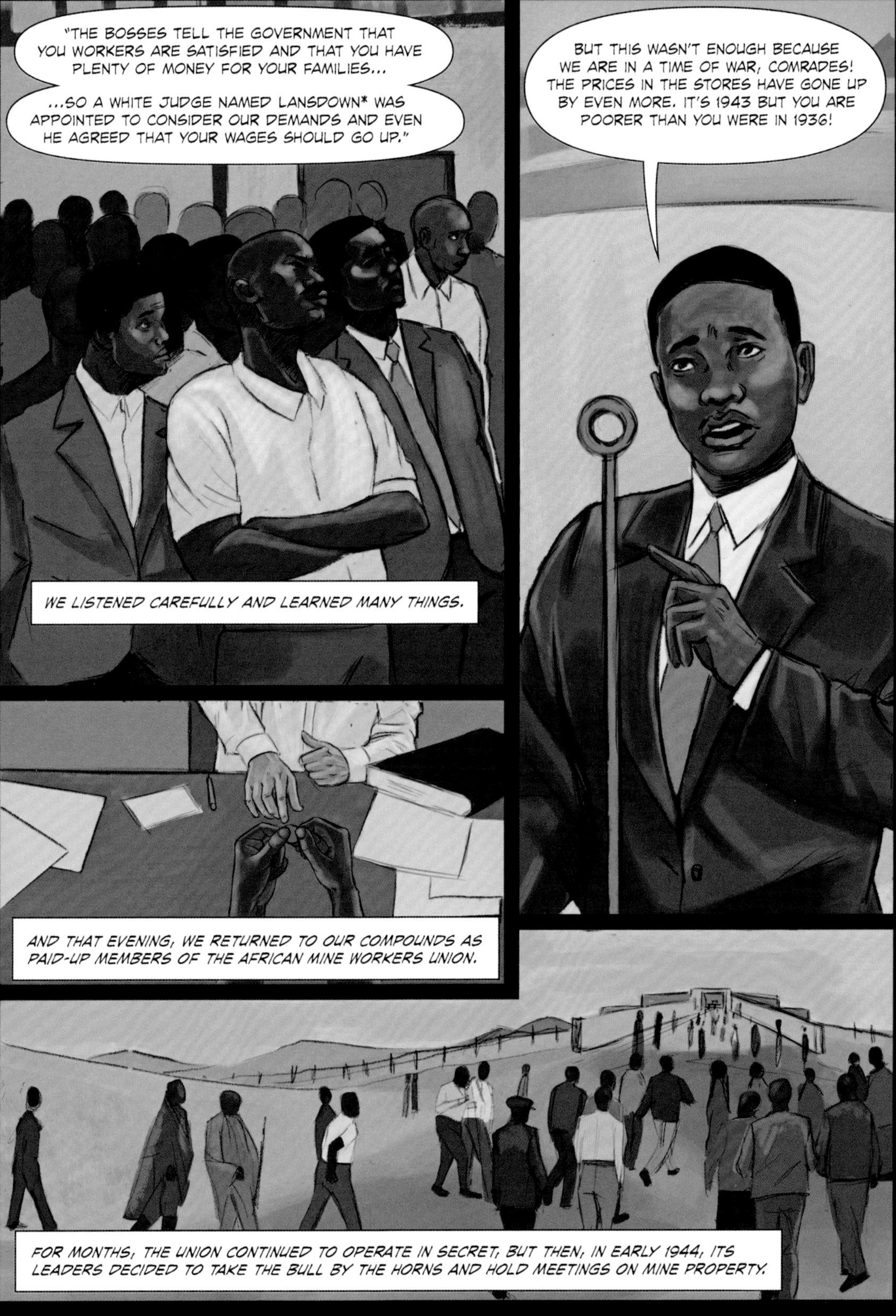
"THE BOSSES TELL THE GOVERNMENT THAT YOU WORKERS ARE SATISFIED AND THAT YOU HAVE PLENTY OF MONEY FOR YOUR FAMILIES...
...SO A WHITE JUDGE NAMED LANSDOWN* WAS APPOINTED TO CONSIDER OUR DEMANDS AND EVEN HE AGREED THAT YOUR WAGES SHOULD GO UP."
BUT THIS WASN'T ENOUGH BECAUSE WE ARE IN A TIME OF WAR, COMRADES! THE PRICES IN THE STORES HAVE GONE UP BY EVEN MORE. IT'S 1943 BUT YOU ARE POORER THAN YOU WERE IN 1936!
WE LISTENED CAREFULLY AND LEARNED MANY THINGS.
AND THAT EVENING, WE RETURNED TO OUR COMPOUNDS AS PAID-UP MEMBERS OF THE AFRICAN MINE WORKERS UNION.
FOR MONTHS, THE UNION CONTINUED TO OPERATE IN SECRET, BUT THEN, IN EARLY 1944, ITS LEADERS DECIDED TO TAKE THE BULL BY THE HORNS AND HOLD MEETINGS ON MINE PROPERTY.

* Witwatersrand Mine Natives' Wages Commission, 1943-1944.

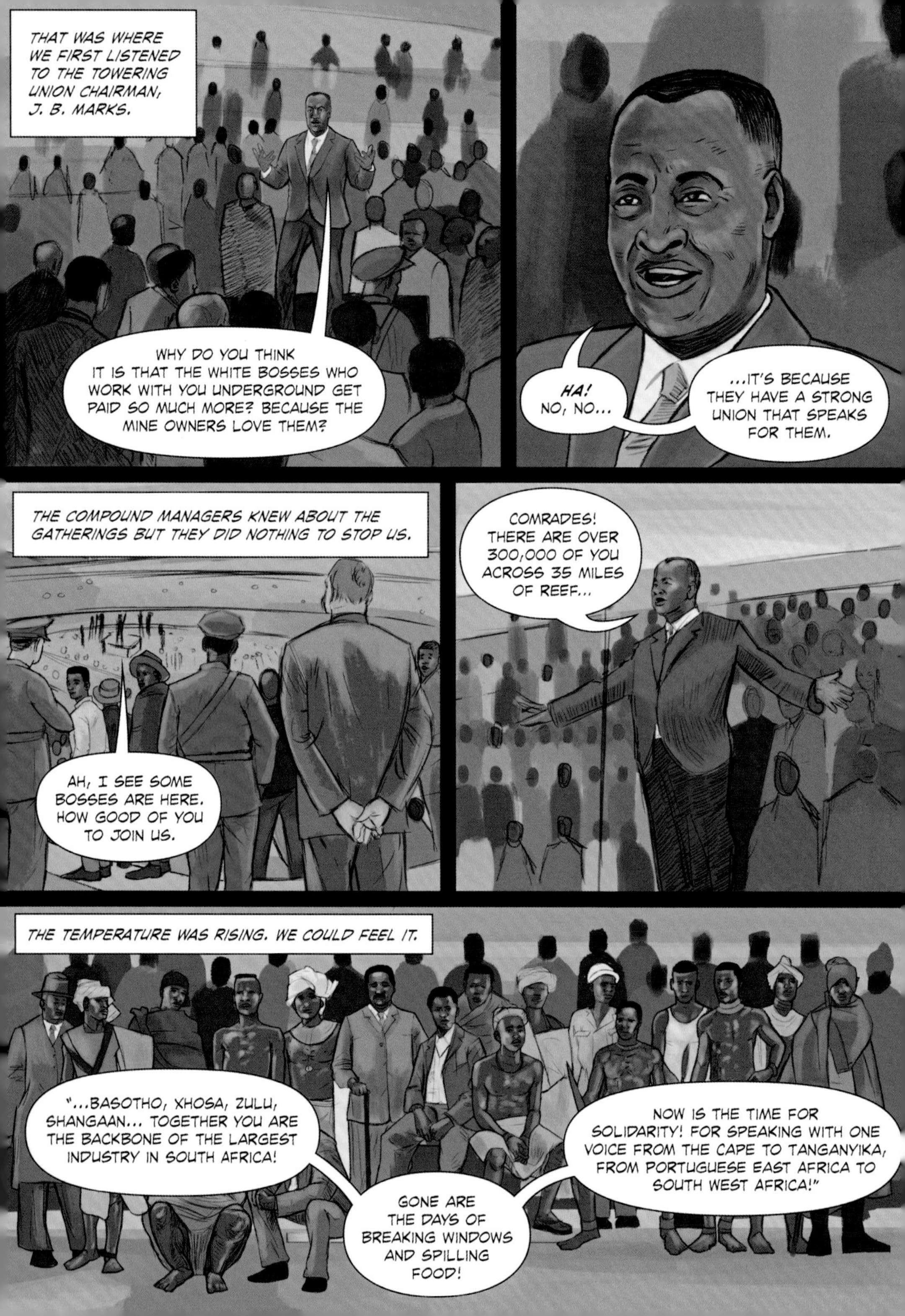
THAT WAS WHERE WE FIRST LISTENED TO THE TOWERING UNION CHAIRMAN, J. B. MARKS.
WHY DO YOU THINK IT IS THAT THE WHITE BOSSES WHO WORK WITH YOU UNDERGROUND GET PAID SO MUCH MORE? BECAUSE THE MINE OWNERS LOVE THEM?
HA! NO, NO...
...IT'S BECAUSE THEY HAVE A STRONG UNION THAT SPEAKS FOR THEM.
THE COMPOUND MANAGERS KNEW ABOUT THE GATHERINGS BUT THEY DID NOTHING TO STOP US.
AH, I SEE SOME BOSSES ARE HERE. HOW GOOD OF YOU TO JOIN US.
COMRADES! THERE ARE OVER 300,000 OF YOU ACROSS 35 MILES OF REEF...
THE TEMPERATURE WAS RISING. WE COULD FEEL IT.
"...BASOTHO, XHOSA, ZULU, SHANGAAN... TOGETHER YOU ARE THE BACKBONE OF THE LARGEST INDUSTRY IN SOUTH AFRICA!
GONE ARE THE DAYS OF BREAKING WINDOWS AND SPILLING FOOD!
NOW IS THE TIME FOR SOLIDARITY! FOR SPEAKING WITH ONE VOICE FROM THE CAPE TO TANGANYIKA, FROM PORTUGUESE EAST AFRICA TO SOUTH WEST AFRICA!"

BUT THE MEETINGS WENT ON UNCHALLENGED ALMOST EVERY DAY OF THE WEEK, FROM EAST TO WEST.

THEN, IN AUGUST, THE GOVERNMENT SUDDENLY MADE IT ILLEGAL* FOR ORGANIZATIONS TO HOLD GATHERINGS ON MINE PROPERTY.

THE GOLD YOU DIG IS *YOURS!* WHY SHOULD YOU LET PEOPLE WHO DO NOT WORK TAKE IT FROM YOU?

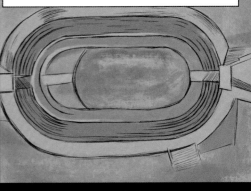

THE POLICE BEGAN TO DISRUPT UNION EVENTS.

UNDERGROUND AND IN THE COMPOUNDS, THE BOSSES PAID SPIES TO IDENTIFY ORGANIZERS.

DORM 32. TONIGHT, EIGHT O'CLOCK.

JUST LIKE THAT, THE MOVEMENT DISAPPEARED INTO THE SHADOWS AGAIN.

MOMENTUM WAS LOST DURING THOSE MONTHS, BUT BEHIND CLOSED DOORS THE UNION KEPT THE FLAME ALIGHT.

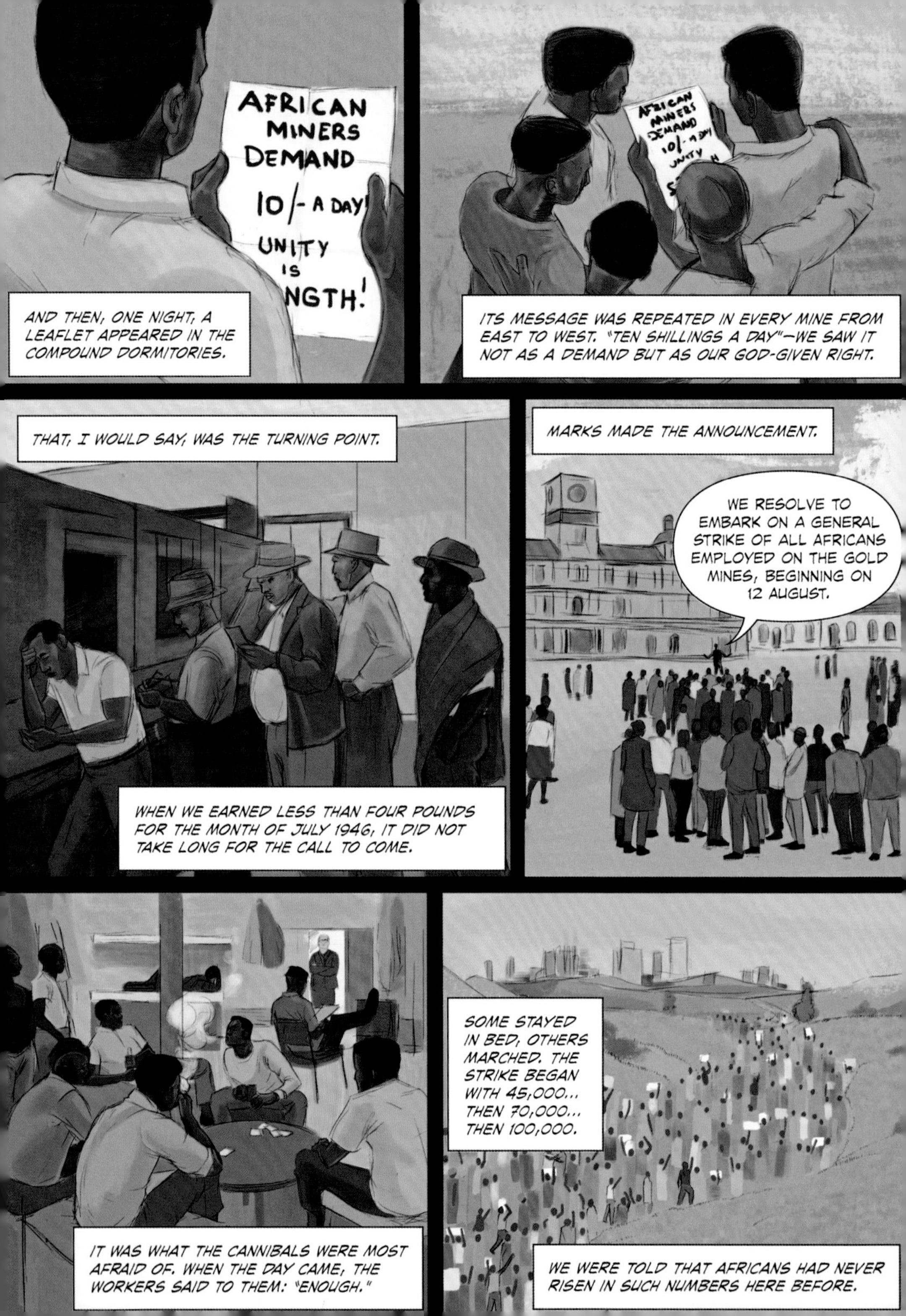
AFRICAN MINERS DEMAND 10/- A DAY! UNITY IS ...NGTH!
AND THEN, ONE NIGHT, A LEAFLET APPEARED IN THE COMPOUND DORMITORIES.
ITS MESSAGE WAS REPEATED IN EVERY MINE FROM EAST TO WEST. "TEN SHILLINGS A DAY"—WE SAW IT NOT AS A DEMAND BUT AS OUR GOD-GIVEN RIGHT.
THAT, I WOULD SAY, WAS THE TURNING POINT.
WHEN WE EARNED LESS THAN FOUR POUNDS FOR THE MONTH OF JULY 1946, IT DID NOT TAKE LONG FOR THE CALL TO COME.
MARKS MADE THE ANNOUNCEMENT.
WE RESOLVE TO EMBARK ON A GENERAL STRIKE OF ALL AFRICANS EMPLOYED ON THE GOLD MINES, BEGINNING ON 12 AUGUST.
IT WAS WHAT THE CANNIBALS WERE MOST AFRAID OF. WHEN THE DAY CAME, THE WORKERS SAID TO THEM: "ENOUGH."
SOME STAYED IN BED, OTHERS MARCHED. THE STRIKE BEGAN WITH 45,000... THEN 70,000... THEN 100,000.
WE WERE TOLD THAT AFRICANS HAD NEVER RISEN IN SUCH NUMBERS HERE BEFORE.

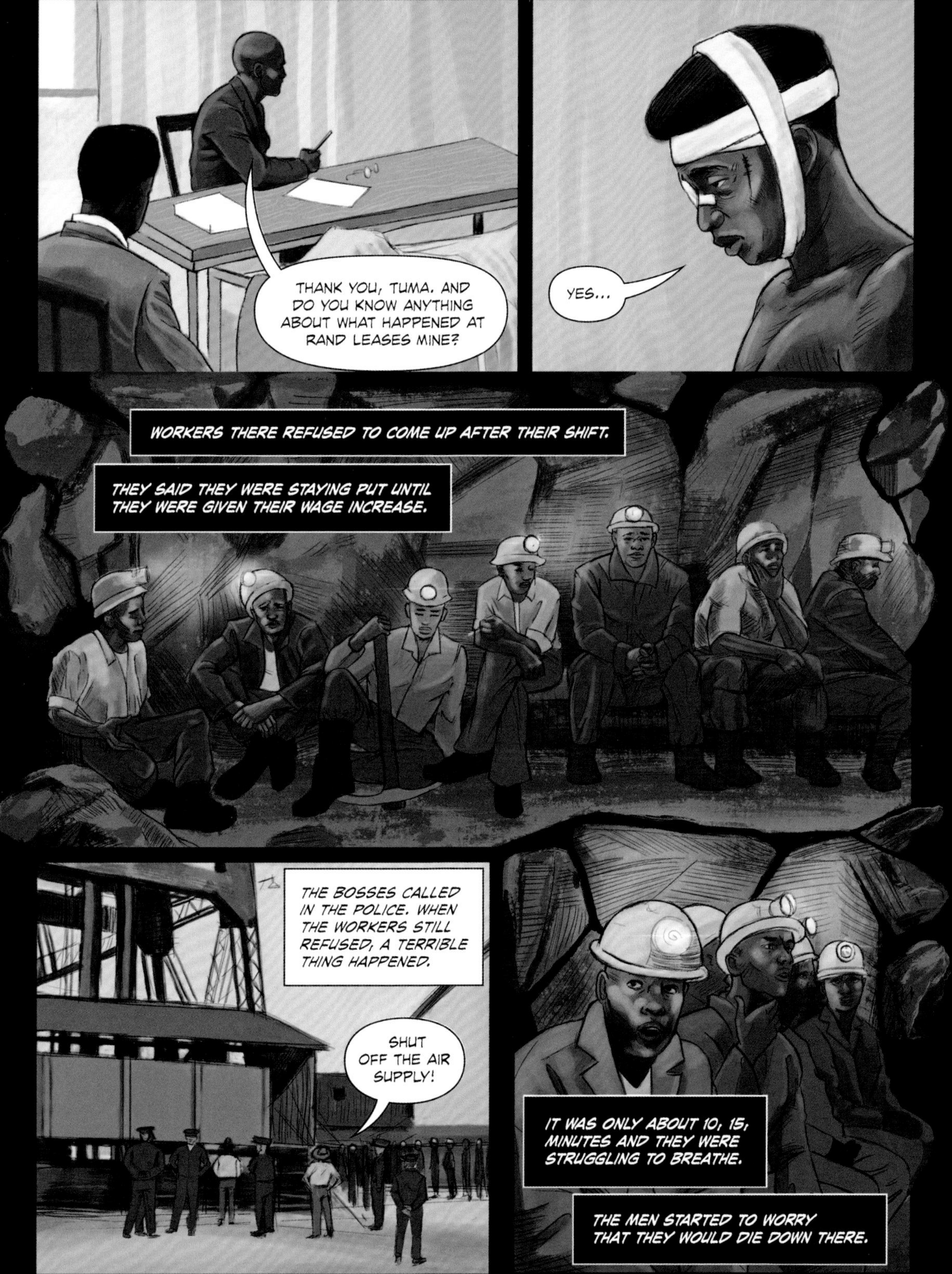
THANK YOU, TUMA. AND DO YOU KNOW ANYTHING ABOUT WHAT HAPPENED AT RAND LEASES MINE?
YES...
WORKERS THERE REFUSED TO COME UP AFTER THEIR SHIFT.
THEY SAID THEY WERE STAYING PUT UNTIL THEY WERE GIVEN THEIR WAGE INCREASE.
THE BOSSES CALLED IN THE POLICE. WHEN THE WORKERS STILL REFUSED, A TERRIBLE THING HAPPENED.
SHUT OFF THE AIR SUPPLY!
IT WAS ONLY ABOUT 10, 15, MINUTES AND THEY WERE STRUGGLING TO BREATHE.
THE MEN STARTED TO WORRY THAT THEY WOULD DIE DOWN THERE.

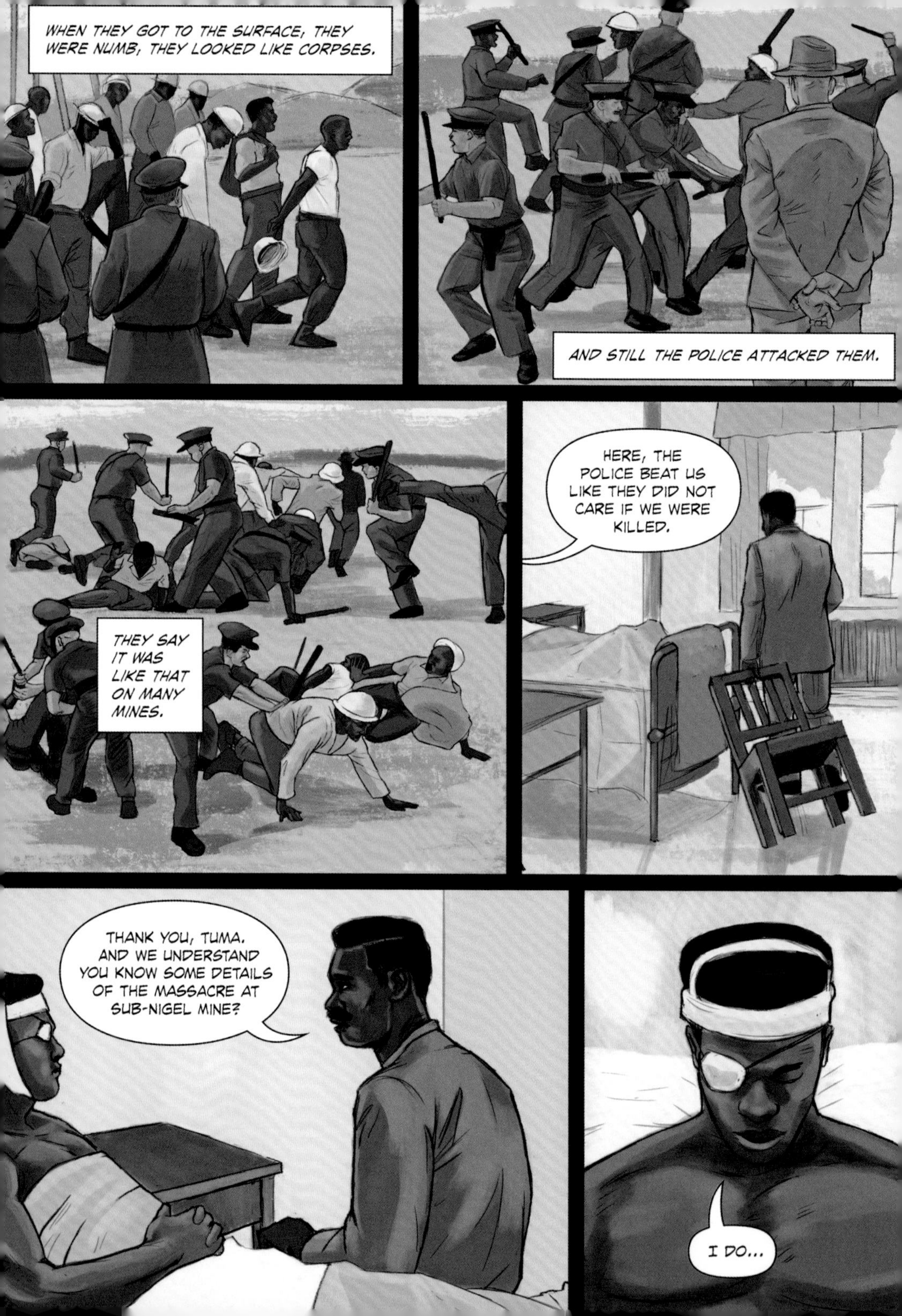
WHEN THEY GOT TO THE SURFACE, THEY WERE NUMB; THEY LOOKED LIKE CORPSES.
AND STILL THE POLICE ATTACKED THEM.
THEY SAY IT WAS LIKE THAT ON MANY MINES.
HERE, THE POLICE BEAT US LIKE THEY DID NOT CARE IF WE WERE KILLED.
THANK YOU, TUMA. AND WE UNDERSTAND YOU KNOW SOME DETAILS OF THE MASSACRE AT SUB-NIGEL MINE?
I DO...

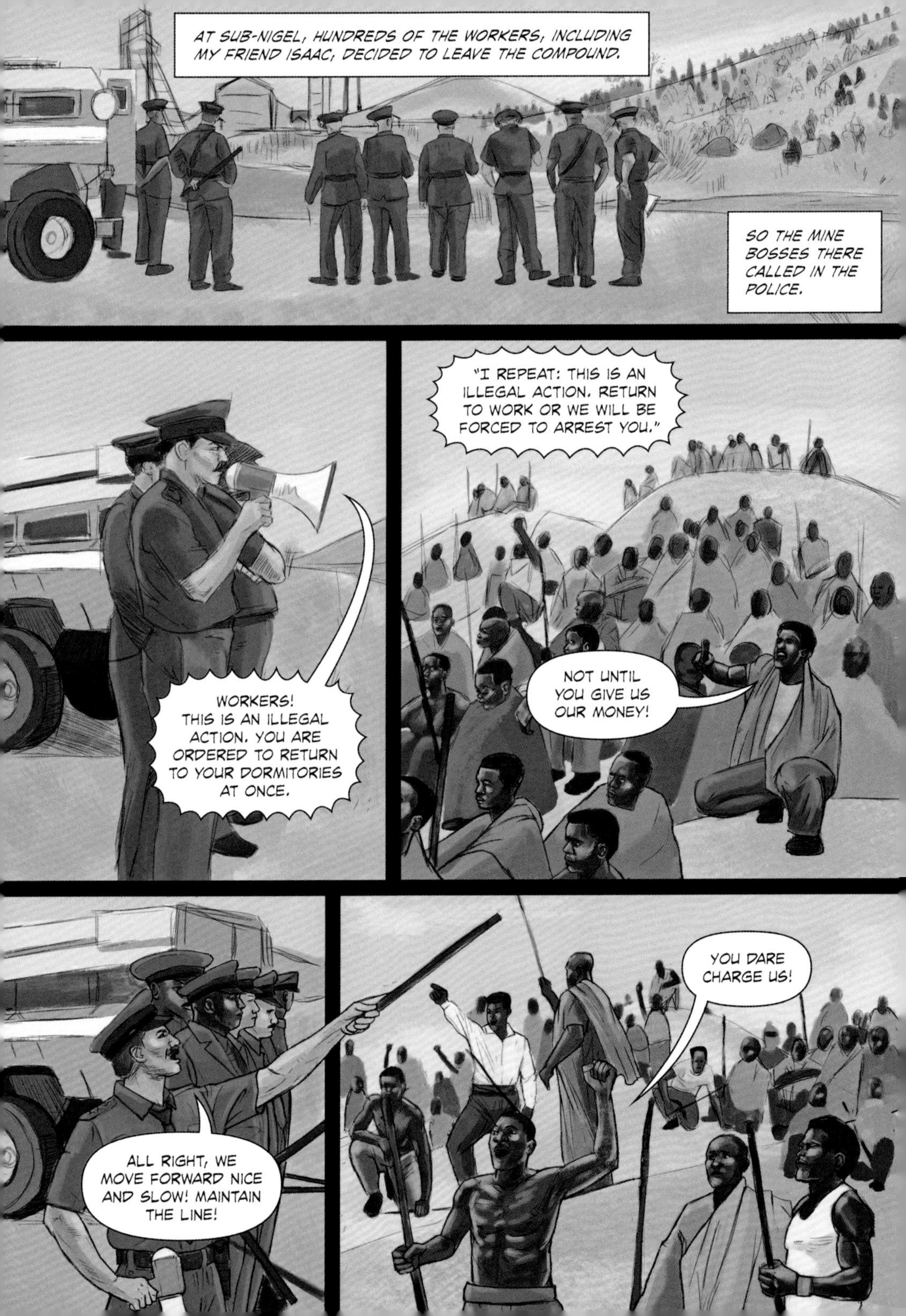
AT SUB-NIGEL, HUNDREDS OF THE WORKERS, INCLUDING MY FRIEND ISAAC, DECIDED TO LEAVE THE COMPOUND.
SO THE MINE BOSSES THERE CALLED IN THE POLICE.
WORKERS! THIS IS AN ILLEGAL ACTION. YOU ARE ORDERED TO RETURN TO YOUR DORMITORIES AT ONCE.
"I REPEAT: THIS IS AN ILLEGAL ACTION. RETURN TO WORK OR WE WILL BE FORCED TO ARREST YOU."
NOT UNTIL YOU GIVE US OUR MONEY!
ALL RIGHT, WE MOVE FORWARD NICE AND SLOW! MAINTAIN THE LINE!
YOU DARE CHARGE US!

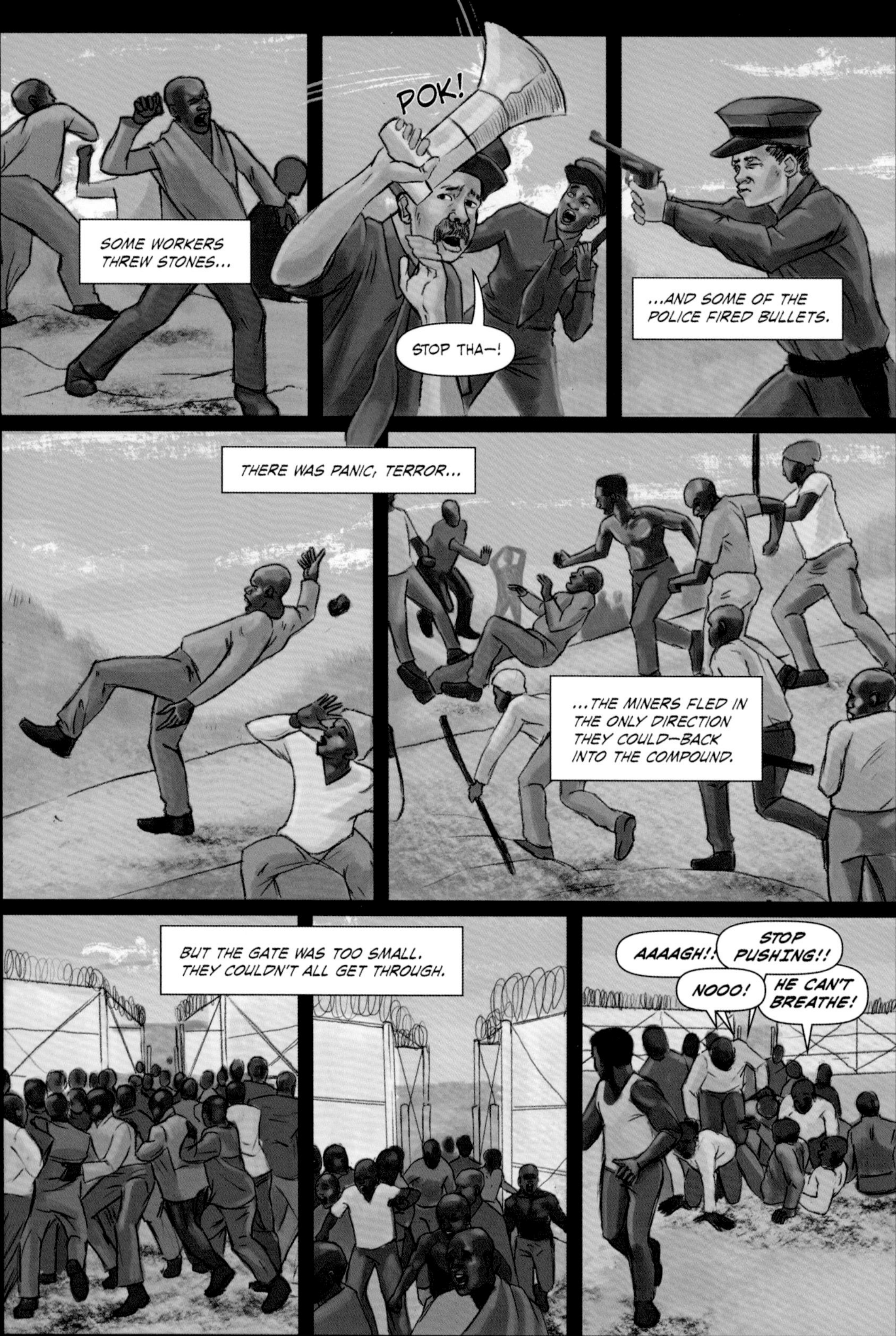
SOME WORKERS THREW STONES...
POK!
STOP THA—!
...AND SOME OF THE POLICE FIRED BULLETS.
THERE WAS PANIC, TERROR...
...THE MINERS FLED IN THE ONLY DIRECTION THEY COULD—BACK INTO THE COMPOUND.
BUT THE GATE WAS TOO SMALL. THEY COULDN'T ALL GET THROUGH.
AAAAGH!!
STOP PUSHING!!
NOOO!
HE CAN'T BREATHE!

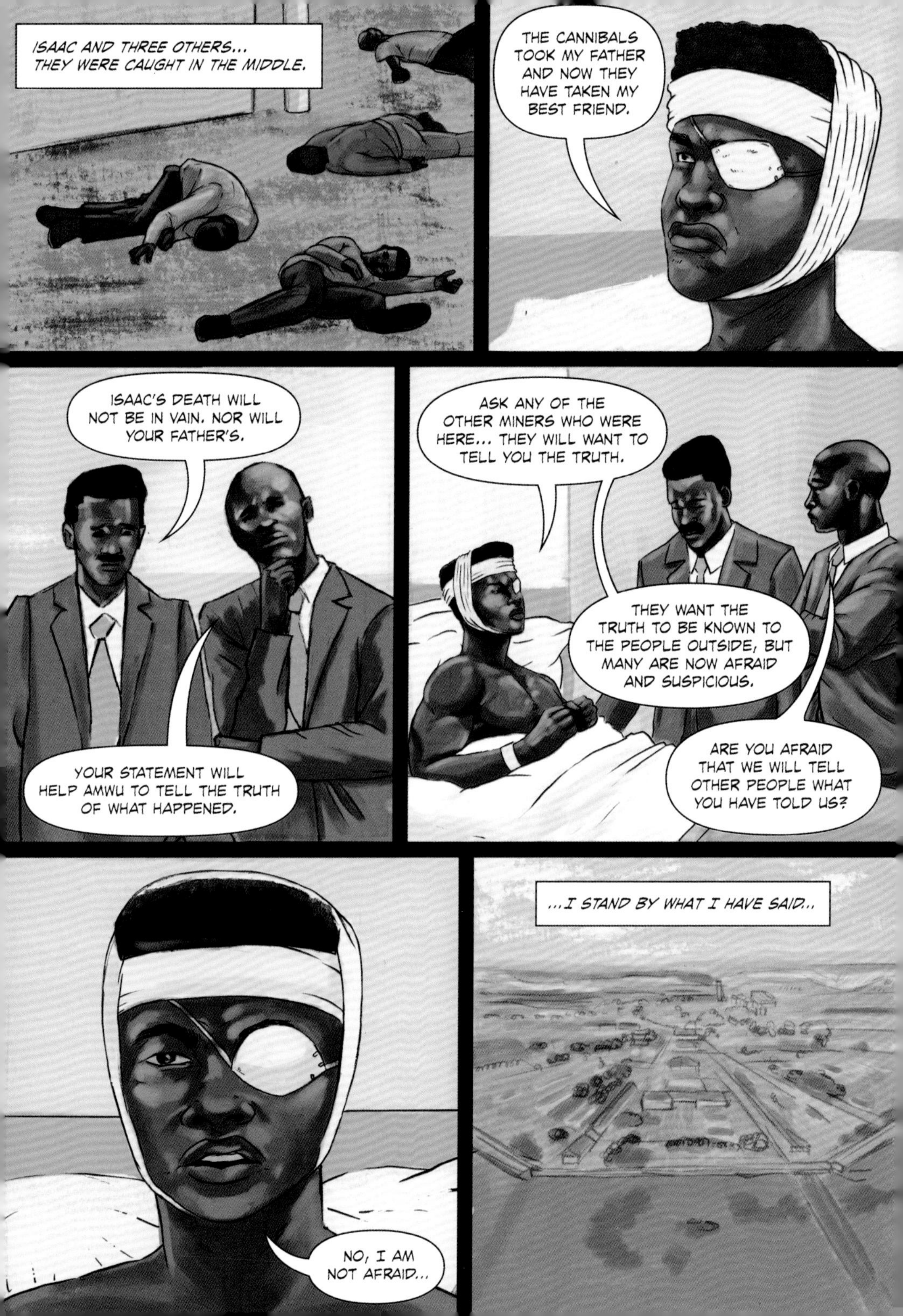

ISAAC AND THREE OTHERS... THEY WERE CAUGHT IN THE MIDDLE.
THE CANNIBALS TOOK MY FATHER AND NOW THEY HAVE TAKEN MY BEST FRIEND.
ISAAC'S DEATH WILL NOT BE IN VAIN. NOR WILL YOUR FATHER'S.
YOUR STATEMENT WILL HELP AMWU TO TELL THE TRUTH OF WHAT HAPPENED.
ASK ANY OF THE OTHER MINERS WHO WERE HERE... THEY WILL WANT TO TELL YOU THE TRUTH.
THEY WANT THE TRUTH TO BE KNOWN TO THE PEOPLE OUTSIDE, BUT MANY ARE NOW AFRAID AND SUSPICIOUS.
ARE YOU AFRAID THAT WE WILL TELL OTHER PEOPLE WHAT YOU HAVE TOLD US?
NO, I AM NOT AFRAID...
...I STAND BY WHAT I HAVE SAID...

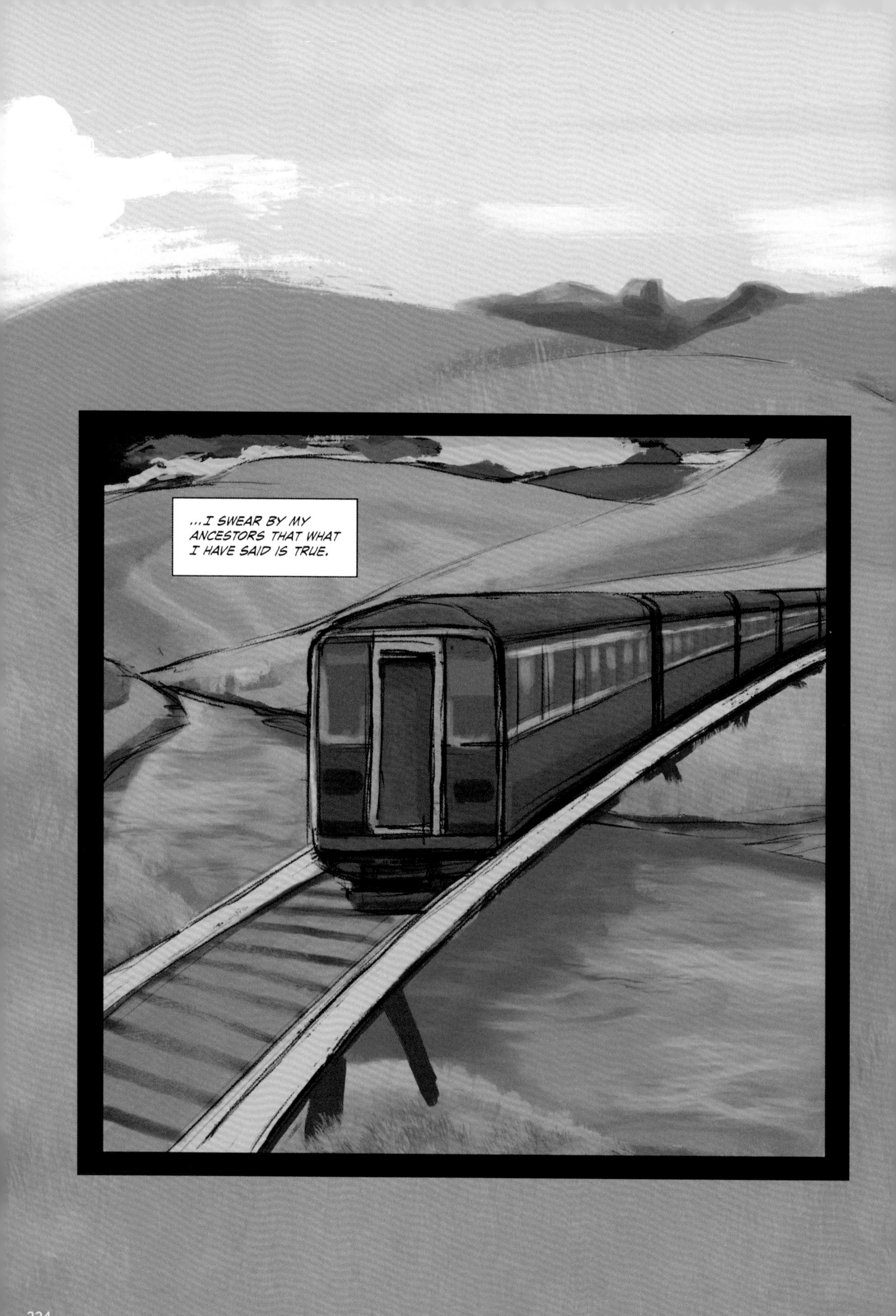
...I SWEAR BY MY ANCESTORS THAT WHAT I HAVE SAID IS TRUE.

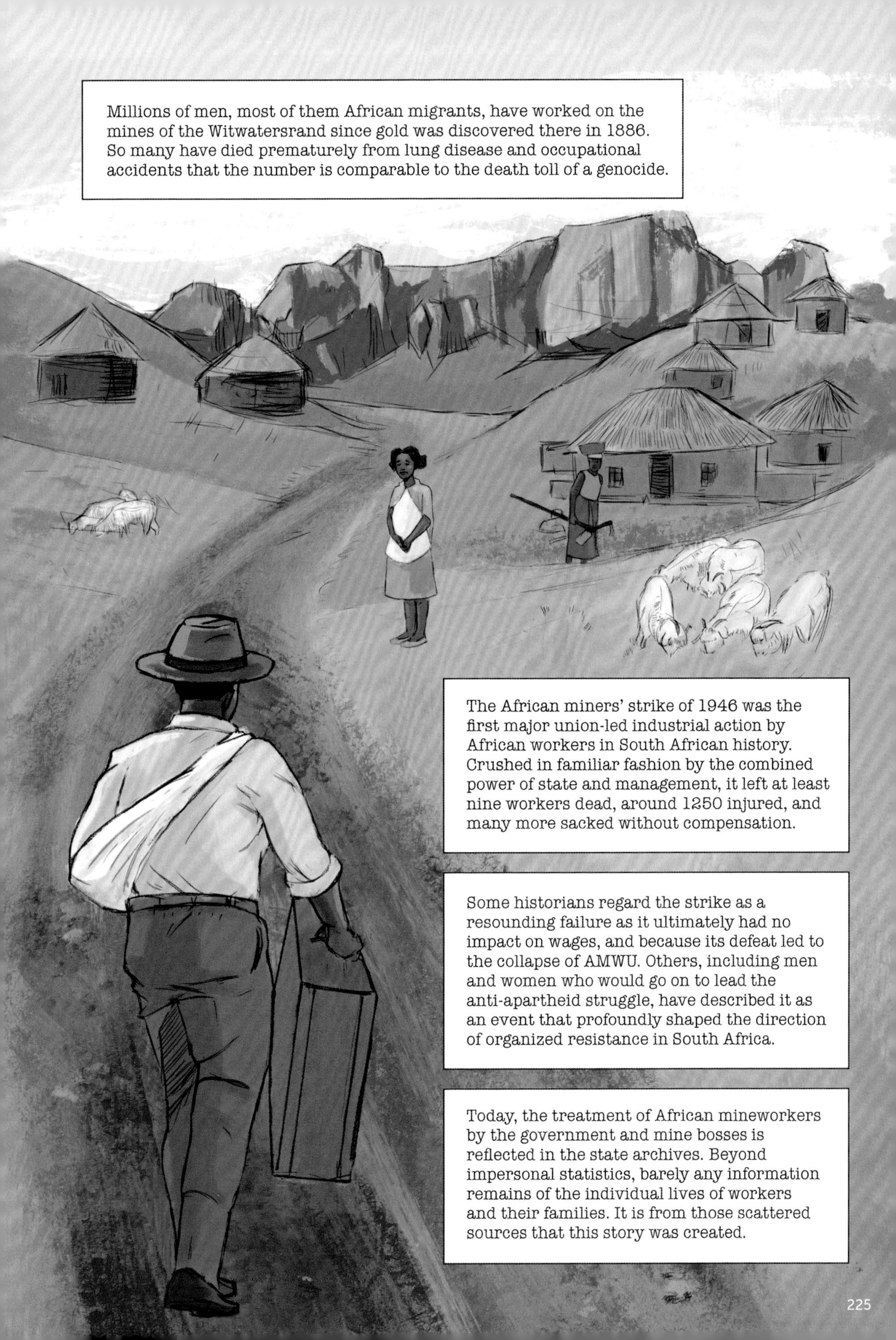
Millions of men, most of them African migrants, have worked on the mines of the Witwatersrand since gold was discovered there in 1886. So many have died prematurely from lung disease and occupational accidents that the number is comparable to the death toll of a genocide.
The African miners' strike of 1946 was the first major union-led industrial action by African workers in South African history. Crushed in familiar fashion by the combined power of state and management, it left at least nine workers dead, around 1250 injured, and many more sacked without compensation.
Some historians regard the strike as a resounding failure as it ultimately had no impact on wages, and because its defeat led to the collapse of AMWU. Others, including men and women who would go on to lead the anti-apartheid struggle, have described it as an event that profoundly shaped the direction of organized resistance in South Africa.
Today, the treatment of African mineworkers by the government and mine bosses is reflected in the state archives. Beyond impersonal statistics, barely any information remains of the individual lives of workers and their families. It is from those scattered sources that this story was created.

CHAPTER 6: HERE I CROSS TO THE OTHER SIDE

If there is one exception to the research approach we followed in this book, it is Chapter 6. Discerning readers would have noticed that this final narrative does not explicitly feature a legal case. There is an important reason for this. During the Union years, the Appellate Division heard very few cases that were directly related to the lived experiences of African mineworkers. When it did, the issues were generally several degrees removed from the miners themselves. *Basner v. Trigger*, to offer one example, was a defamation case involving the white senator and unionist, Hyman Basner, who accused the mines police of unlawfully spying on African mineworkers in the build-up to the 1946 strike.

There is a huge void of information about the individual lives of African mineworkers and their families in the nineteenth and twentieth centuries. Various commissions of inquiry were held during the Union years—including the 1943 Lansdown Commission cited by James Majoro in Chapter 6—but these mainly served to obscure or abstract the individuals involved: both the victims and violators. Realizing this, we decided to base this final narrative on fragments of source materials describing life on the mines in the 1940s. Every aspect of Tuma and Isaac's individual stories are based on these findings. Both are composite characters, representative of countless generations of young African men who, beginning in the 1880s, migrated from across rural Southern Africa to the Witwatersrand.

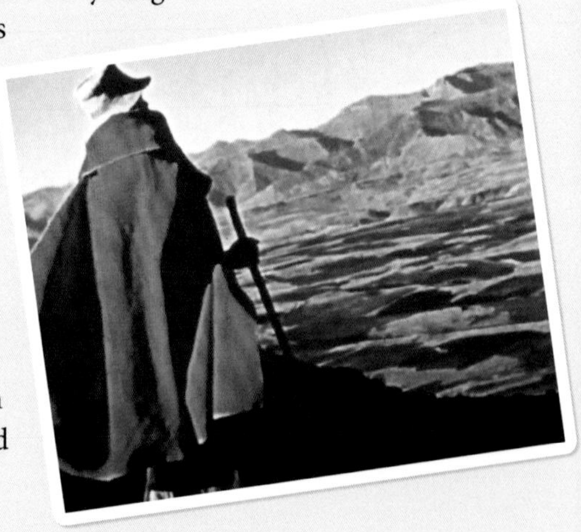

From a visual perspective, the photographic and motion-picture technology of the 1940s offered us unique advantages. During those years, a handful of eminent photographers, both local and international, gained access to some of the Witwatersrand's compounds and mines. The vivid scenes they captured in black-and-white were complemented by the mining companies' color propaganda recruitment films. For the latter, we are indebted to documentary filmmakers Catherine Meyburgh and Richard Pakleppa for their groundbreaking research, and generosity.

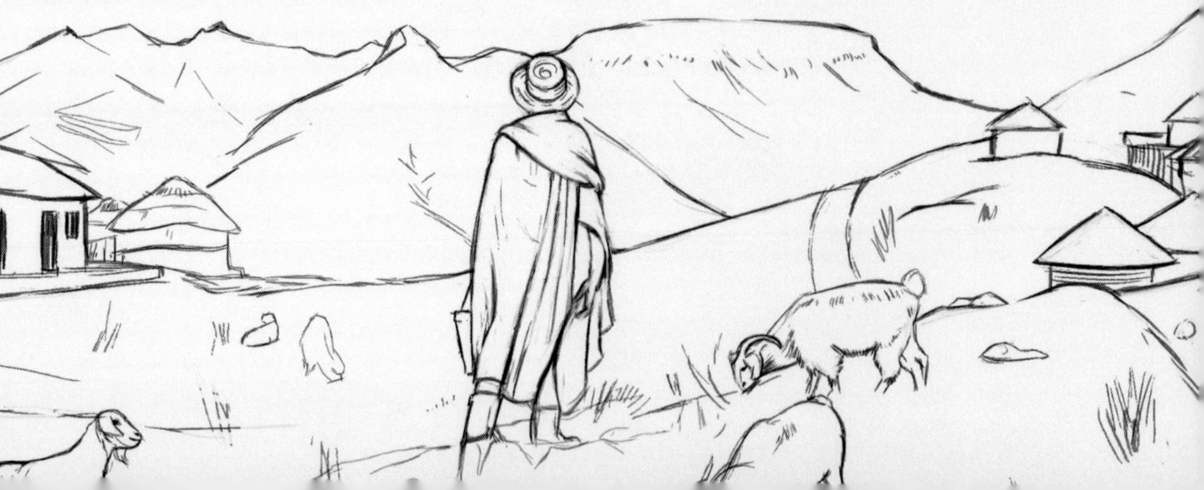

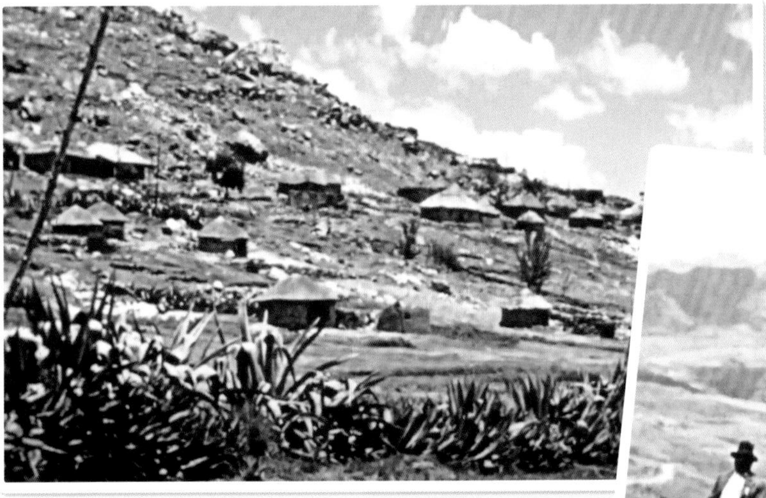

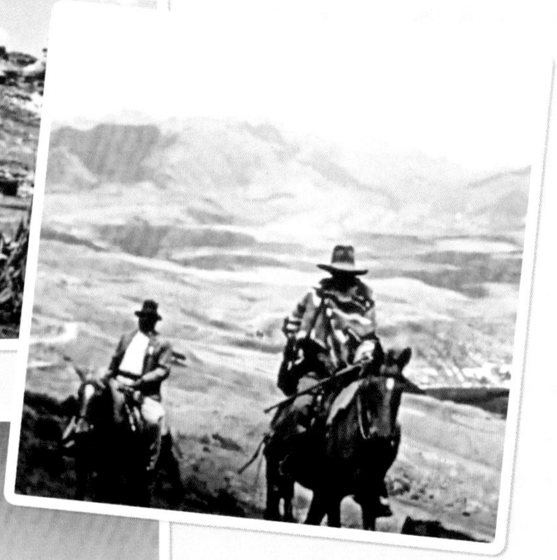

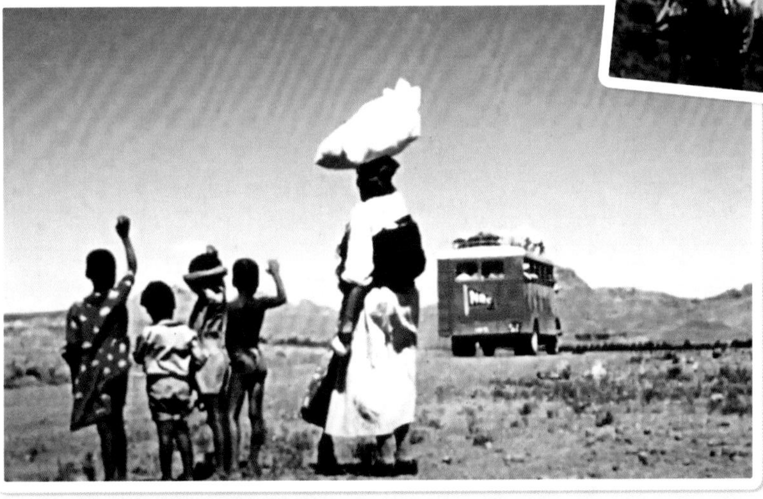

Scenes from rural Basutoland, c. 1940. Postal trucks (*left*) were used to collect migrant laborers from far-flung rural areas.

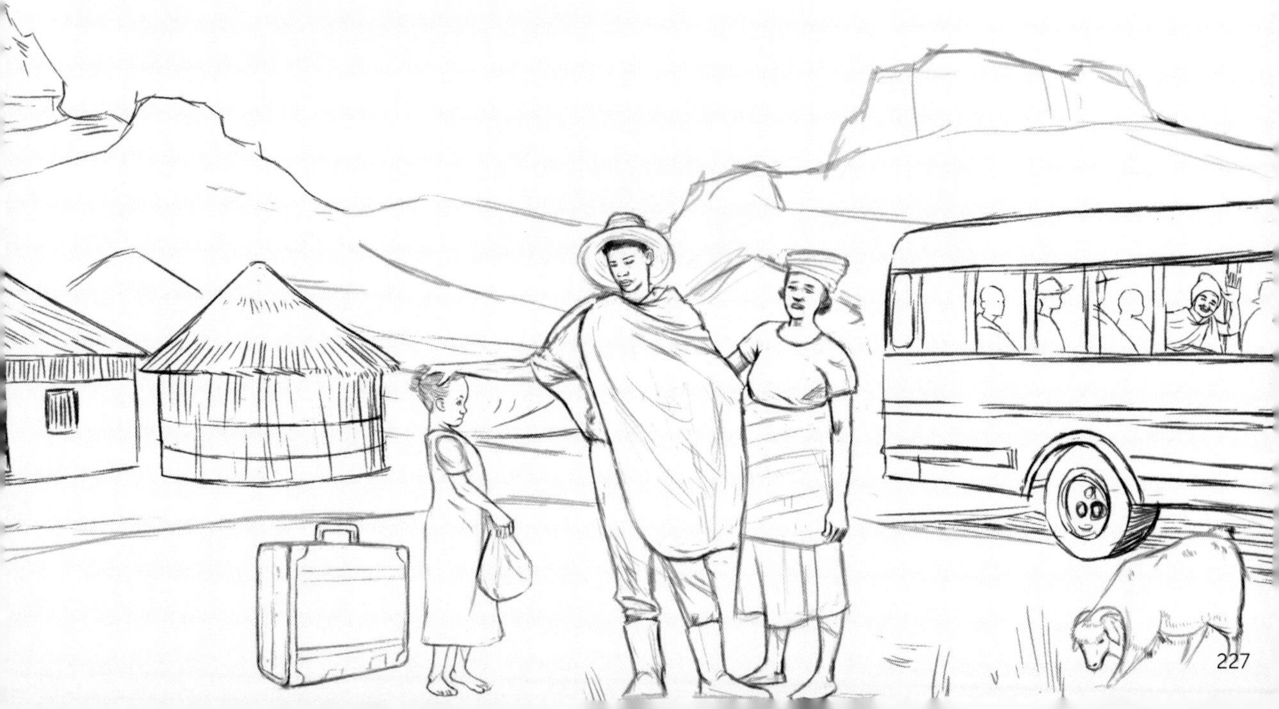

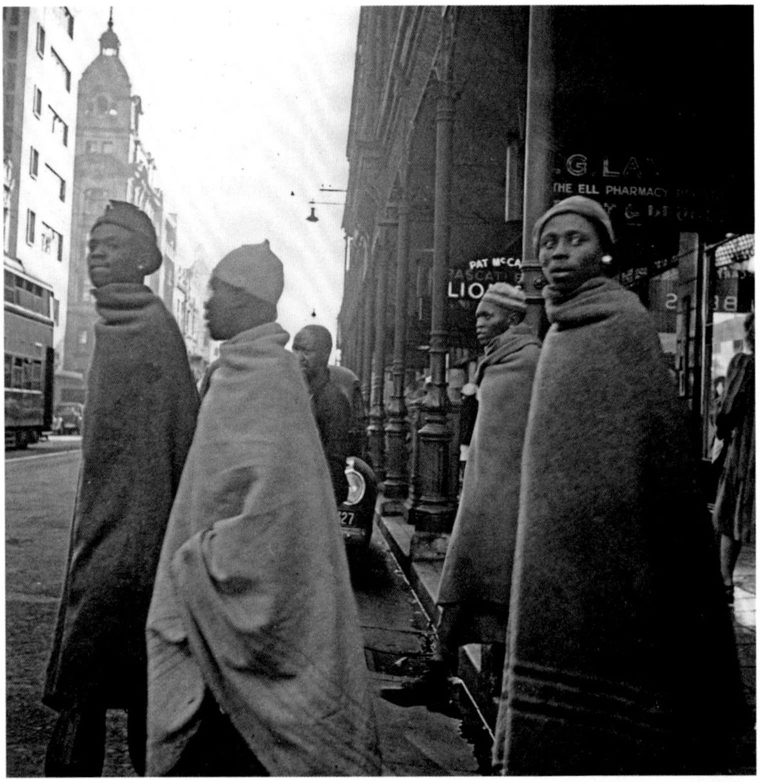
THE ELL PHARMACY

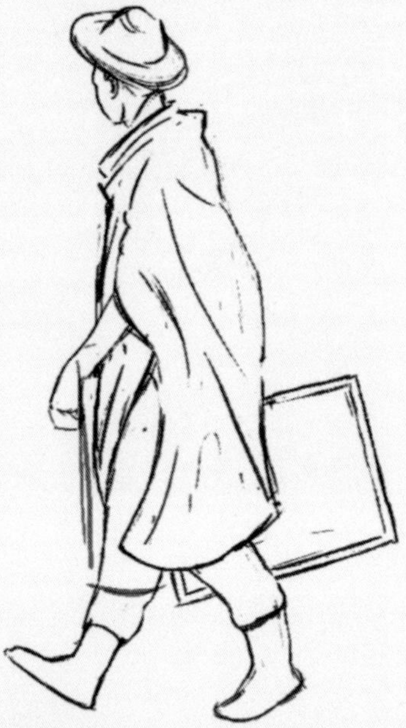

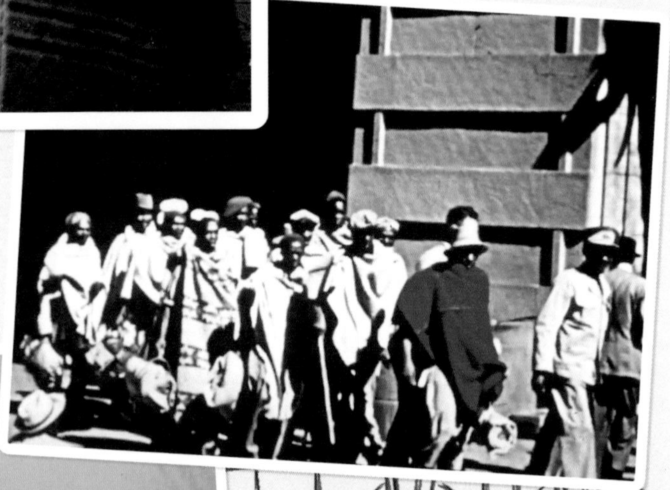

Above and right: Blanketed migrant workers arriving in Johannesburg from the rural areas. **Below:** A mine dump rising from the outskirts of 1940s Johannesburg.

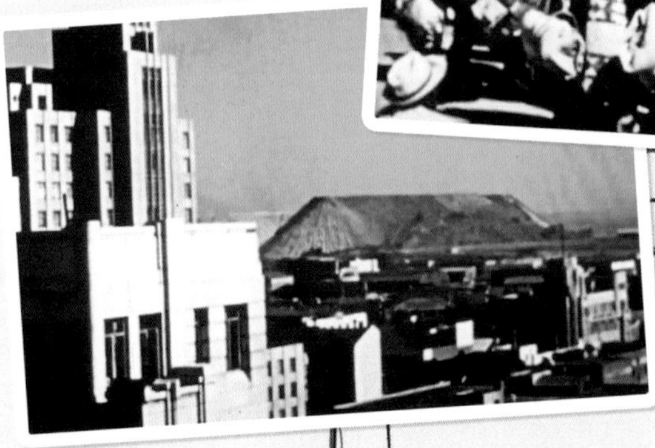

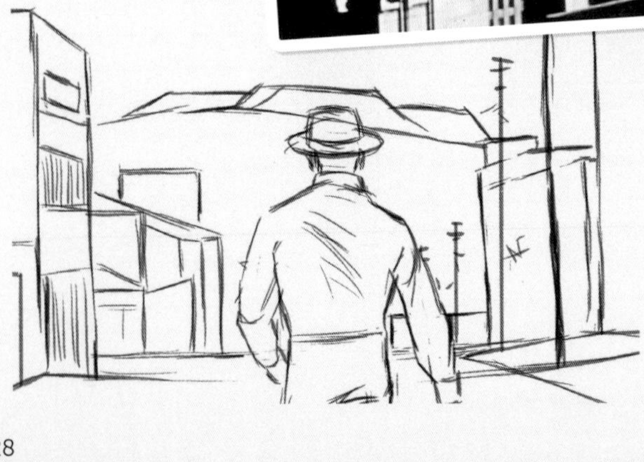

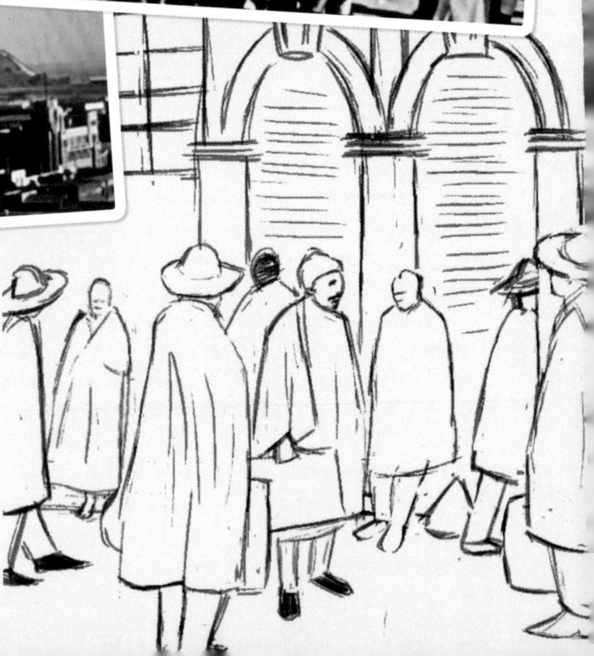

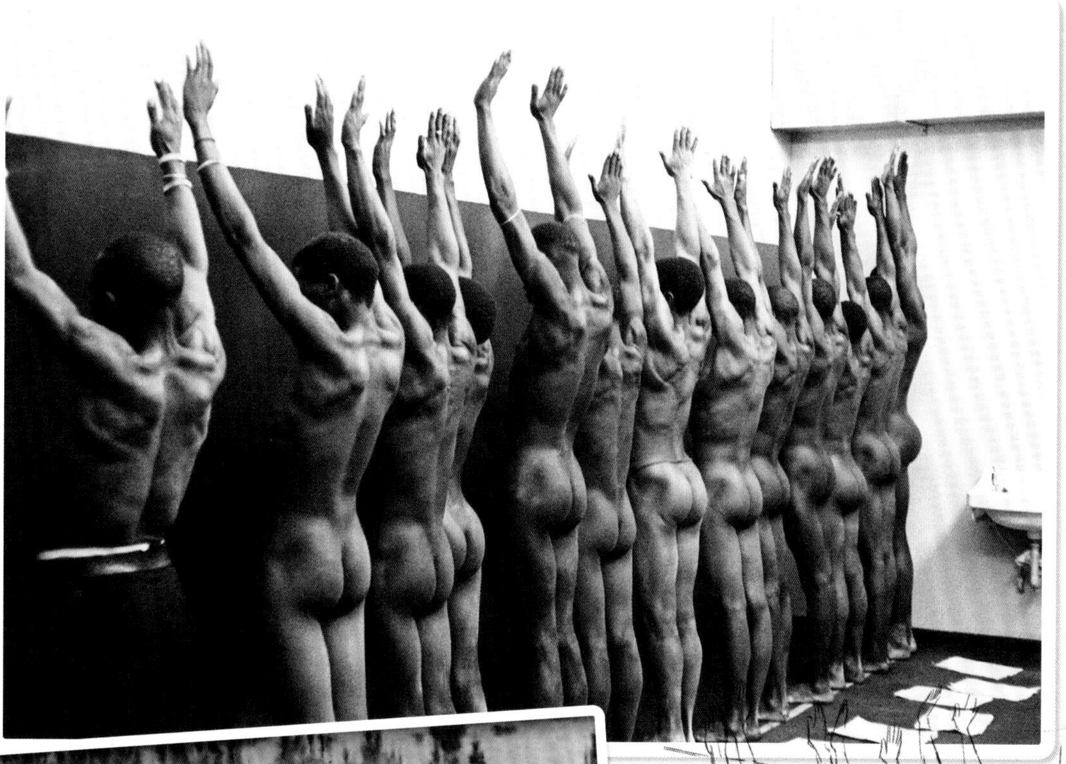

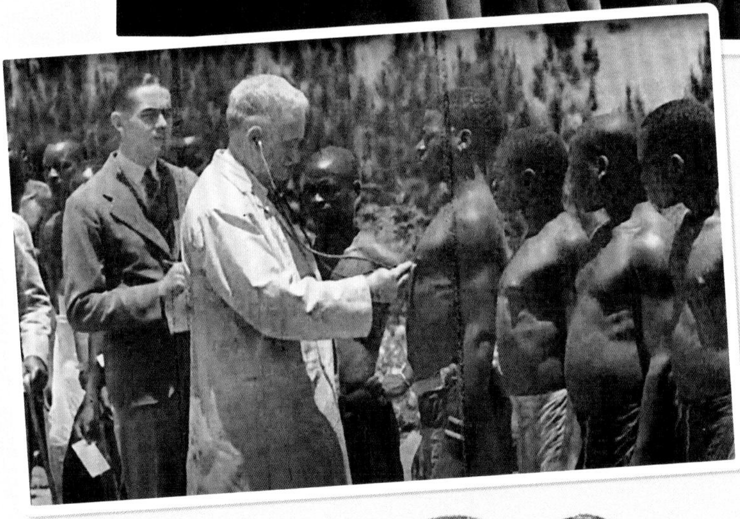

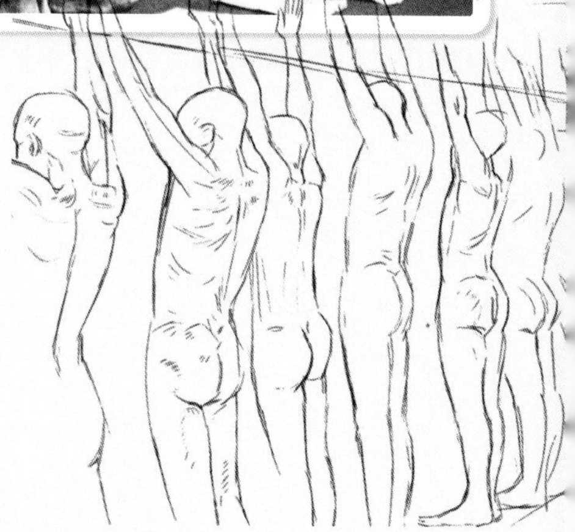

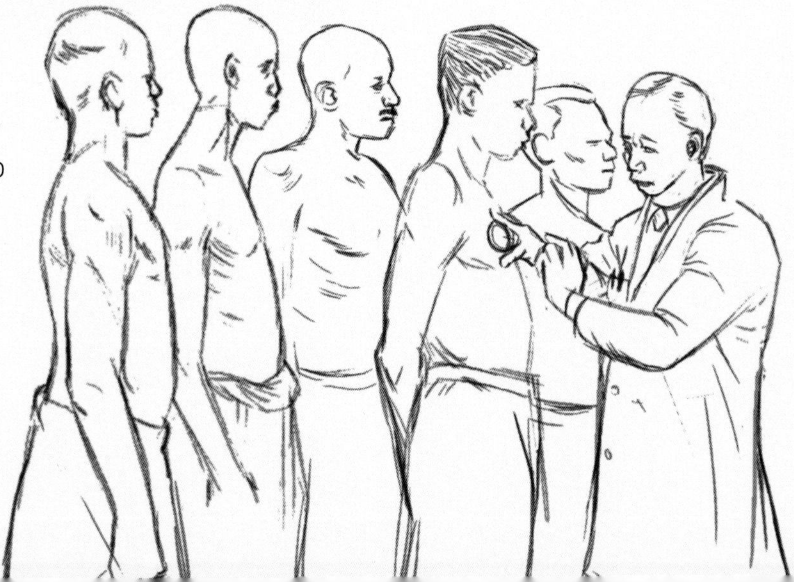

"They listened to our hearts and lungs... they told us to strip naked to make sure our bodies were ready for work..." migrants undergoing health checks prior to being contracted.

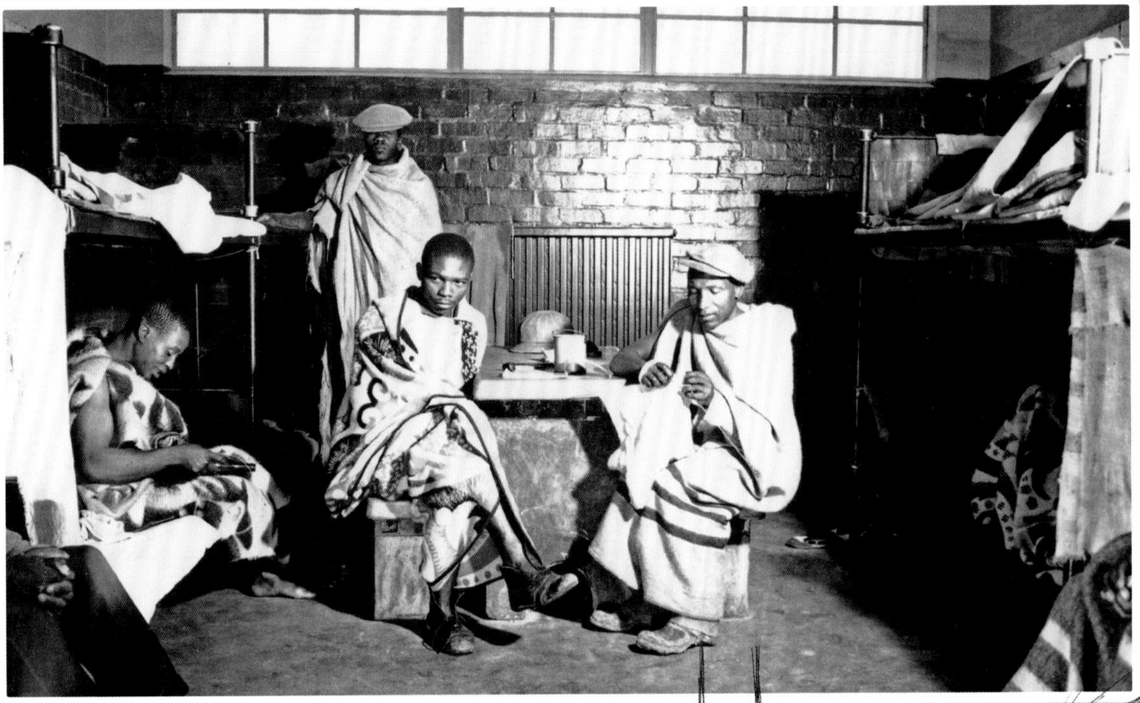

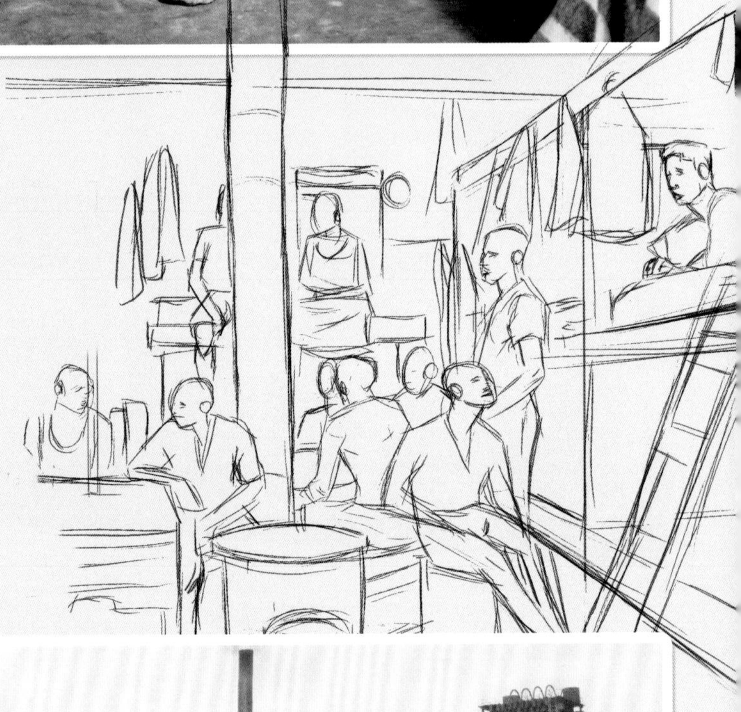

Above: Basotho miners at rest in a compound dormitory and others at work underground (*far right*) during the 1940s.

Below: Mid-twentieth-century mining infrastructure on the Witwatersrand.

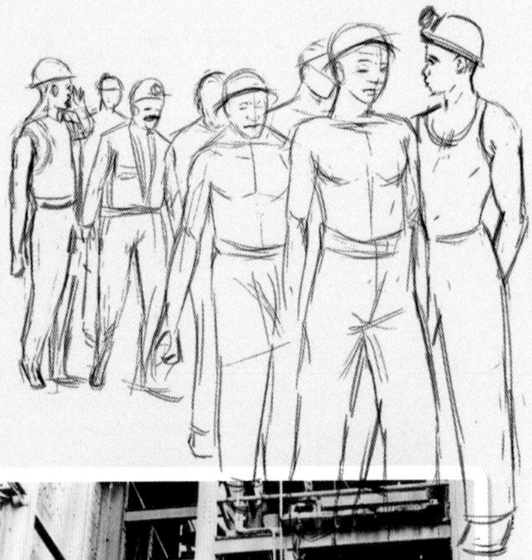

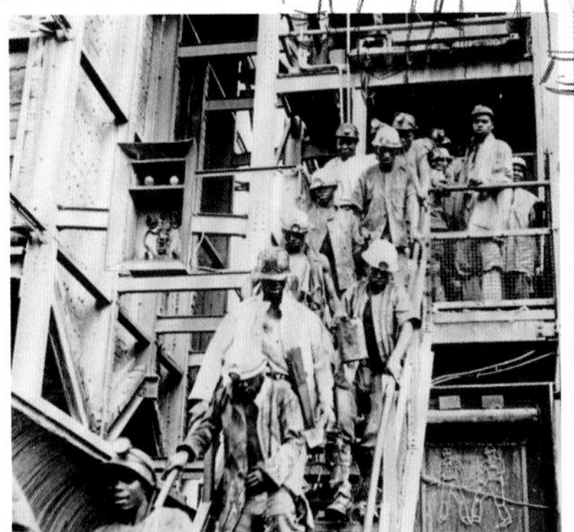

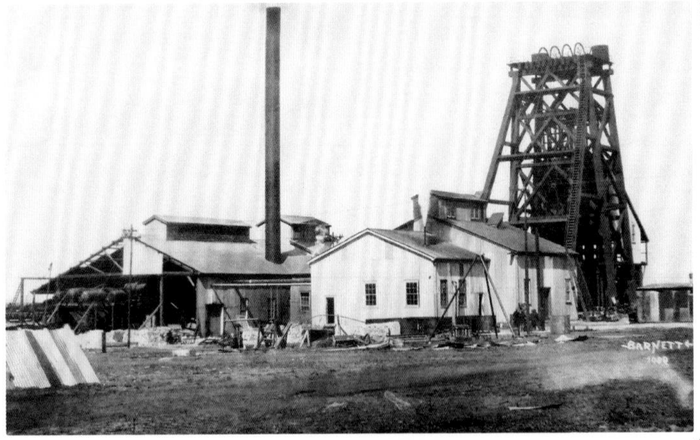

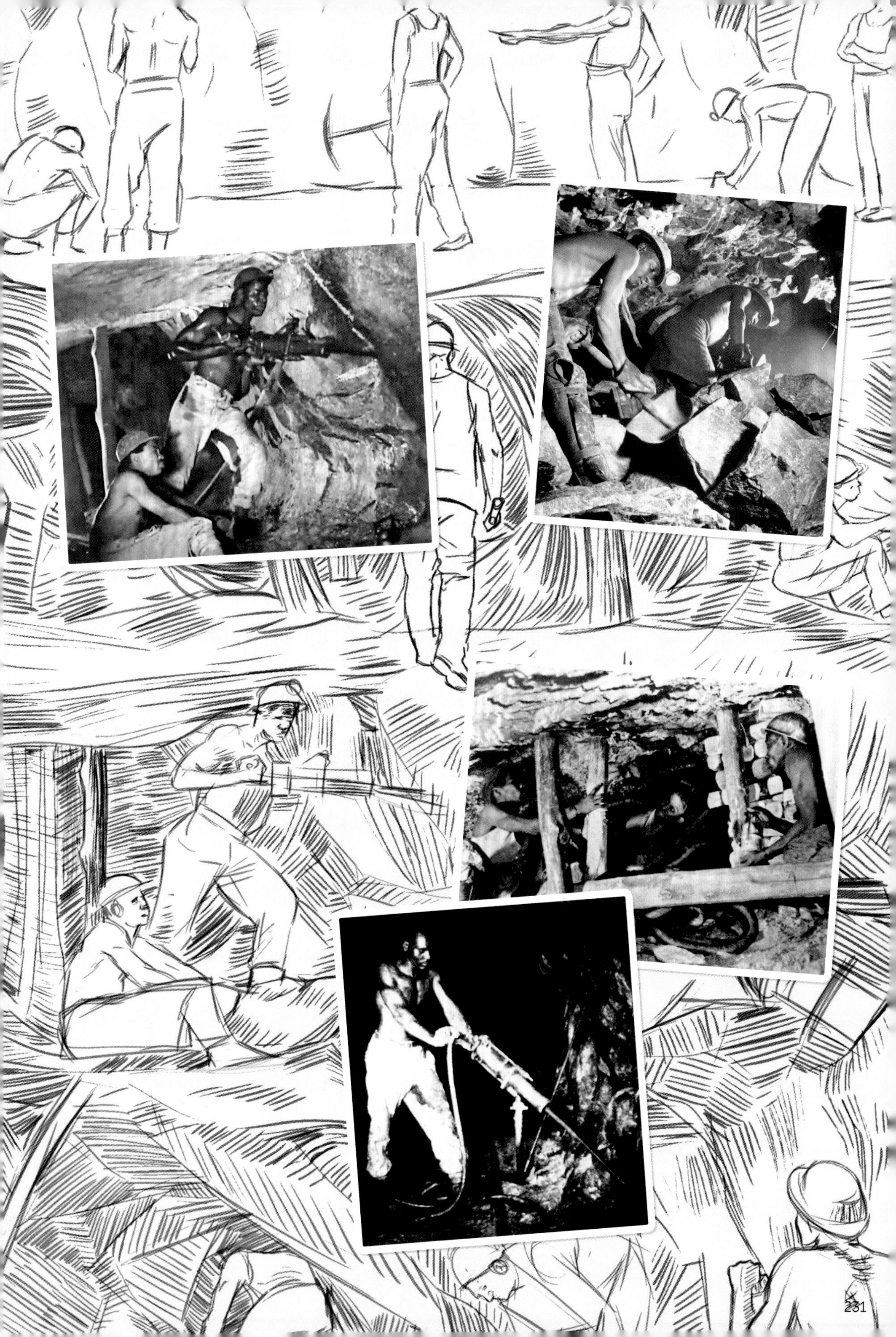

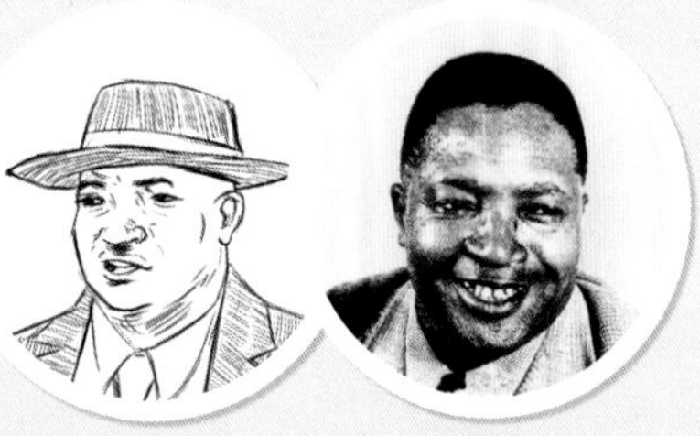

Communist leader and trade unionist **Moses Kotane** was a prominent recruiter around the Witwatersrand mine properties during the 1940s.

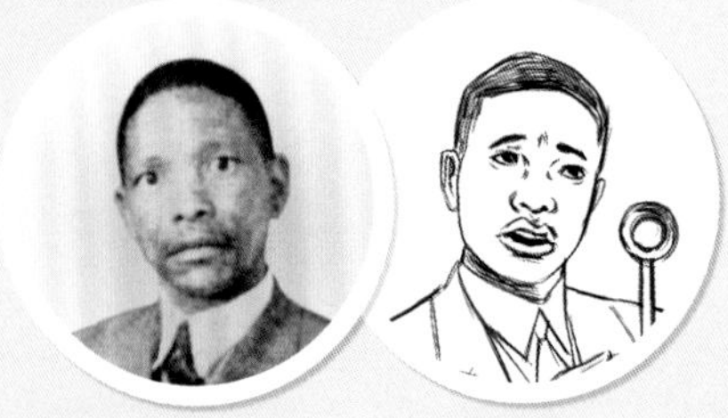

Formerly a miner, **James Majoro** was a founding member of the African Mine Workers' Union before becoming its secretary in the build-up to the 1946 strike.

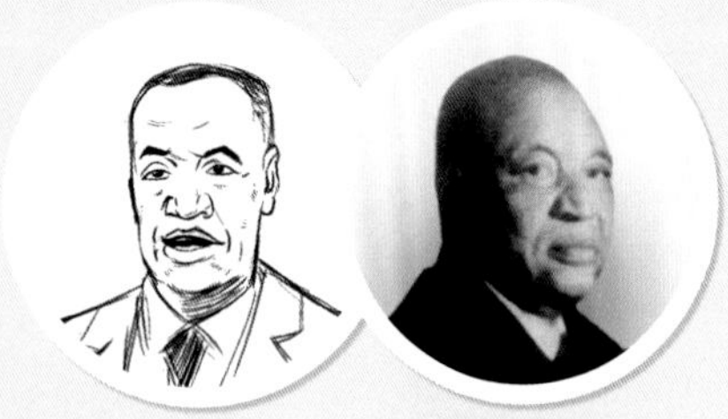

John Beaver ("J.B.") Marks was president of the African Mine Workers' Union during its rapid rise and fall between 1942 and 1946.

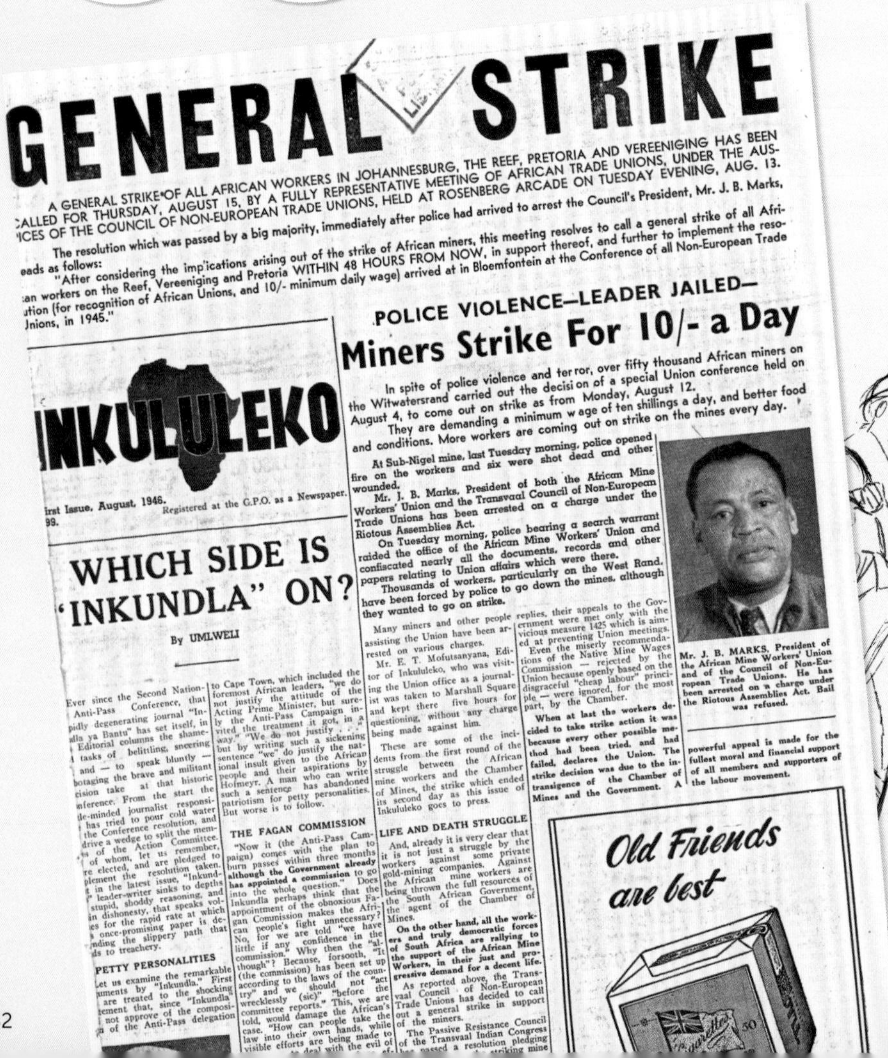

GENERAL STRIKE

A GENERAL STRIKE OF ALL AFRICAN WORKERS IN JOHANNESBURG, THE REEF, PRETORIA AND VEREENIGING HAS BEEN CALLED FOR THURSDAY, AUGUST 15, BY A FULLY REPRESENTATIVE MEETING OF AFRICAN TRADE UNIONS, UNDER THE AUS-ICES OF THE COUNCIL OF NON-EUROPEAN TRADE UNIONS, HELD AT ROSENBERG ARCADE ON TUESDAY EVENING, AUG. 13.

The resolution which was passed by a big majority, immediately after police had arrived to arrest the Council's President, Mr. J. B. Marks, eads as follows:

"After considering the implications arising out of the strike of African miners, this meeting resolves to call a general strike of all Afri-can workers on the Reef, Vereeniging and Pretoria WITHIN 48 HOURS FROM NOW, in support thereof, and further to implement the reso-ution (for recognition of African Unions, and 10/- minimum daily wage) arrived at in Bloemfontein at the Conference of all Non-European Trade Jnions, in 1945."

NKULULEKO

irst Issue, August, 1946. Registered at the G.P.O. as a Newspaper.
99.

WHICH SIDE IS 'INKUNDLA" ON?

By UMLWELI

Ever since the Second Nation- Anti-Pass Conference, that pidly degenerating journal "In-dla ya Bantu" has set itself, in Editorial columns the shame- tasks of belittling, sneering and — to speak bluntly — botaging the brave and militant cision take at that historic nference. From the start the le-minded journalist responsi- has tried to pour cold water the Conference resolution, and drive a wedge to split the mem-s of the Action Committee. of whom, let us remember, re elected, and are pledged to plement the resolution taken. t in the latest issue, "Inkund-" leader-writer sinks to depths stupid, shoddy reasoning, and in dishonesty, that speaks vol-es for the rapid rate at which once-promising paper is de-nding the slippery path that ds to treachery.

PETTY PERSONALITIES

Let us examine the remarkable uments by "Inkundla." First are treated to the shocking tement that, since "Inkundla" not approve of the composi-n of the Anti-Pass delegation to Cape Town, which included the foremost African leaders, "we do not justify the attitude of the Acting Prime Minister, but sure-ly the Anti-Pass Campaign in-vited the treatment it got, in a way." "We do not justify . . ." but by writing such a sickening sentence "we" do justify the nat-ional insult given to the African people and their aspirations by Hofmeyr. A man who can write such a sentence has abandoned patriotism for petty personalities. But worse is to follow.

THE FAGAN COMMISSION

"Now it (the Anti-Pass Cam-paign) comes with the plan to burn passes within three months **although the Government already has appointed a commission** to go into the whole question." Does Inkundla perhaps think that the appointment of the obnoxious Fa-gan Commission makes the Afri-can people's fight unnecessary? No, for we are told "we have little if any confidence in the commission." Why then the "al-though"? Because, forsooth, "It (the commission) has been set up according to the laws of the coun-try" and we should not "act wrecklessly (sic)" "before the committee reports." This, we are told, would damage the African's case. "How can people take the law into their own hands, while visible efforts are being made to deal with the evil of ...

POLICE VIOLENCE—LEADER JAILED—
Miners Strike For 10/- a Day

In spite of police violence and terror, over fifty thousand African miners on the Witwatersrand carried out the decision of a special Union conference held on August 4, to come out on strike as from Monday, August 12.

They are demanding a minimum wage of ten shillings a day, and better food and conditions. More workers are coming out on strike on the mines every day.

At Sub-Nigel mine, last Tuesday morning, police opened fire on the workers and six were shot dead and other wounded.

Mr. J. B. Marks, President of both the African Mine Workers' Union and the Transvaal Council of Non-European Trade Unions has been arrested on a charge under the Riotous Assemblies Act.

On Tuesday morning, police bearing a search warrant raided the office of the African Mine Workers' Union and confiscated nearly all the documents, records and other papers relating to Union affairs which were there.

Thousands of workers, particularly on the West Rand, have been forced by police to go down the mines, although they wanted to go on strike.

Many miners and other people assisting the Union have been ar-rested on various charges.

Mr. E. T. Mofutsanyana, Edi-tor of Inkululeko, who was visit-ing the Union office as a journal-ist was taken to Marshall Square and kept there five hours for questioning, without any charge being made against him.

These are some of the inci-dents from the first round of the struggle between the African mine workers and the Chamber of Mines, the strike which ended its second day as this issue of Inkululeko goes to press.

LIFE AND DEATH STRUGGLE

And, already it is very clear that it is not just a struggle by the workers against some private gold-mining companies. Against the African mine workers are being thrown the full resources of the South African Government, the agent of the Chamber of Mines.

On the other hand, all the work-ers and truly democratic forces of South Africa are rallying to the support of the African Mine Workers, in their just and pro-gressive demand for a decent life.

As reported above, the Trans-vaal Council of Non-European Trade Unions has decided to call out a general strike in support of the miners.

The Passive Resistance Council of the Transvaal Indian Congress has passed a resolution pledging ... striking mine ...

replies, their appeals to the Gov-ernment were met only with the vicious measure 1425 which is aim-ed at preventing Union meetings.

Even the miserly recommenda-tions of the Native Mine Wages Commission — rejected by the Union because openly based on the disgraceful "cheap labour" princi-ple — were ignored, for the most part, by the Chamber.

When at last the workers de-cided to take strike action it was because every other possible me-thod had been tried, and had failed, declares the Union. The strike decision was due to the in-transigence of the Chamber of Mines and the Government. A powerful appeal is made for the fullest moral and financial support of all members and supporters of the labour movement.

Mr. J. B. MARKS, President of the African Mine Workers' Union and of the Council of Non-European Trade Unions. He has been arrested on a charge under the Riotous Assemblies Act. Bail was refused.

Old Friends are best

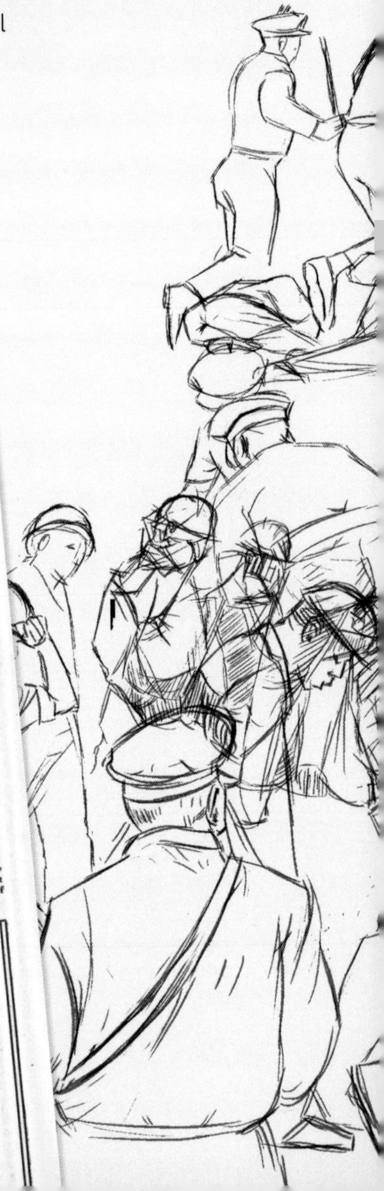

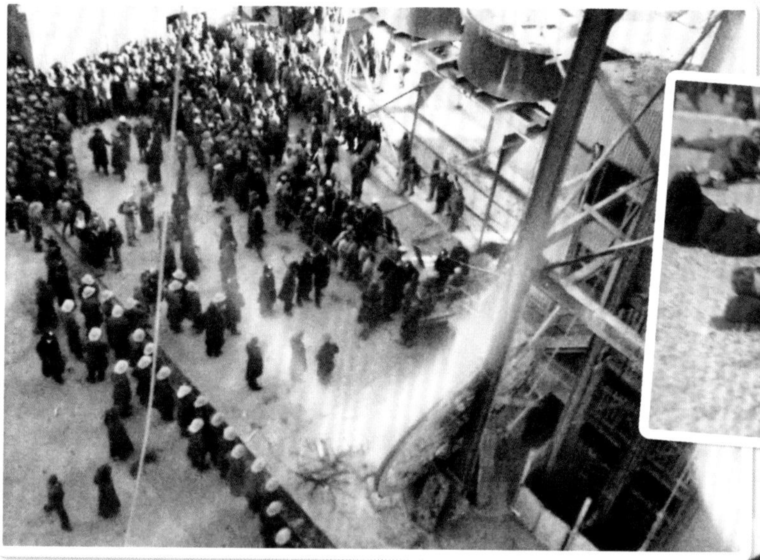

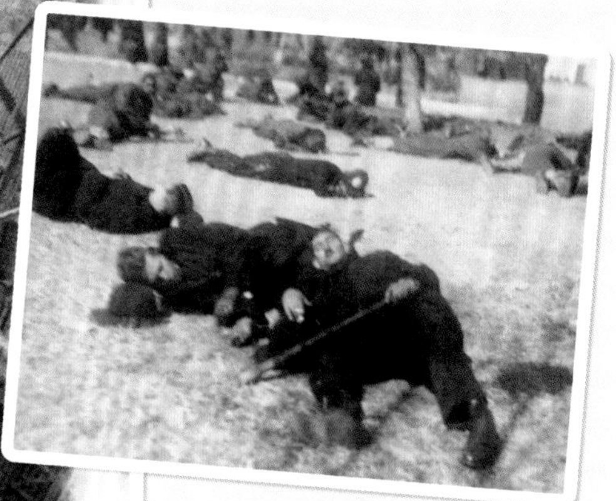

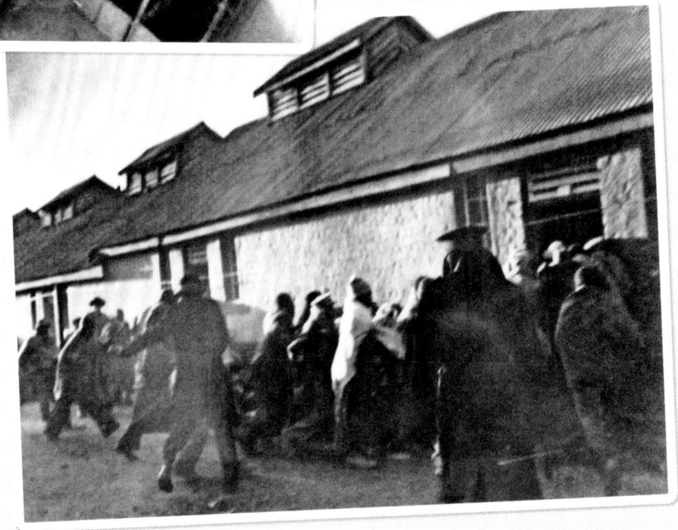

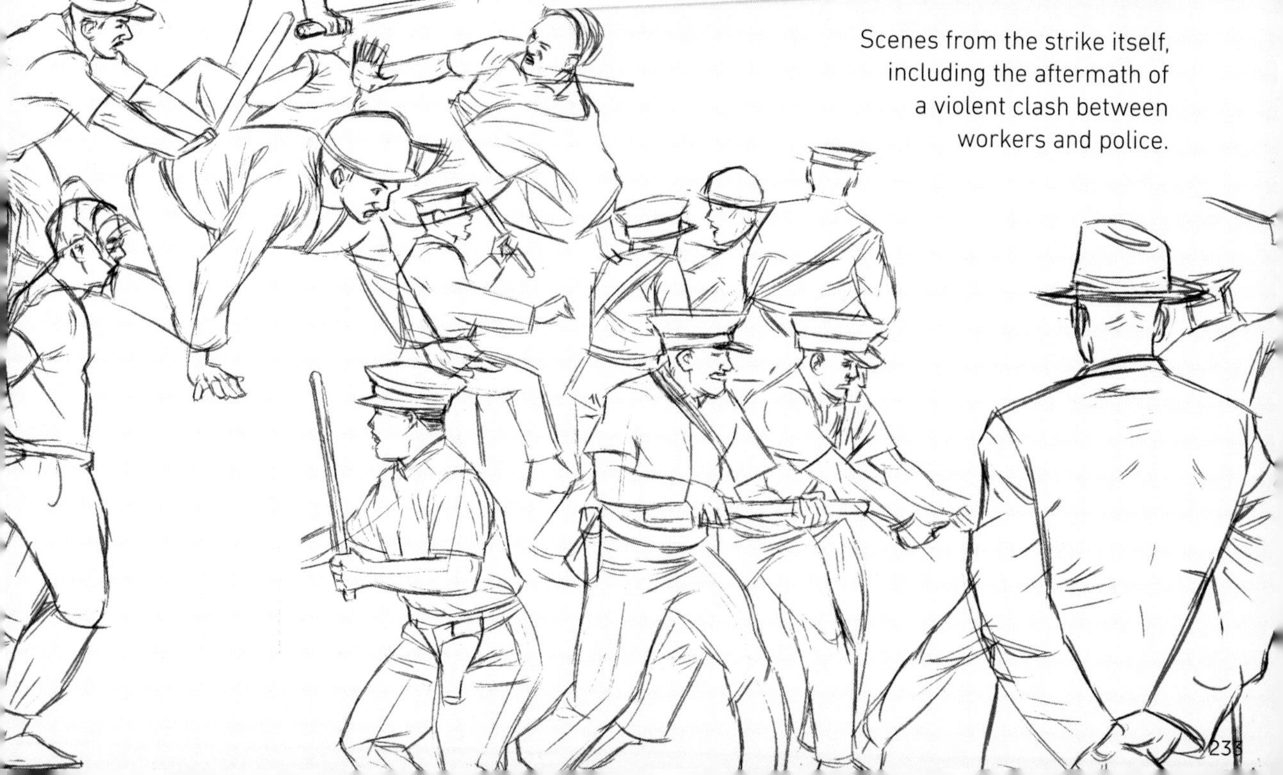

Scenes from the strike itself, including the aftermath of a violent clash between workers and police.

they ... brought them up gradually.

) And all that brought them in, brought them up gradually. And.. one day, these – my contacts – spoke with the .. other boss boys and.. all of a sudden they refused to come out from underground. You know what it means, when people refuse to come up. The management becomes mad ! People may die. So they just said, "We are sitting put, we are not going up, until we are paid, we are given an increase." Then, I
505 was called from the compound to go down. I just refused .... [inaudible] refused. Then they wanted to know why. I told them, "I don't want to be assaulted." "No, they won't assault you.The police are .. " "No, I might get hurt." You know, the police
513 were called, ...[inaudible] went down to beg the chaps to come up. They refused. After all attempts had failed, they did one of the most cruellest things I can never forget in my life – you know, I felt so depressed – They decided to close up the air. You know, I'm speaking from experience. You know, if you went underground and saw these people work, you'd never allow your child to go underground. You'd never do that. Oh, it was only about ten, fifteen minutes. You know [pause]the cage started rolling up .. you know, when these fellows came out of the cage they were just like, just ... just, you know, numb, like dead corpses. And .. the police on top of that were assaulting them ... ( ) And the mine officials looking on.

"debussing" from troop-carriers to join the attack.

Eight Natives Wounded, Four Trampled to Death at Sub-Nigel

STRIKERS yesterday clashed with the police at the Betty shaft of the Sub-Nigel Mine. The police opened fire, and eight natives were wounded. Four were trampled to death when the strikers fled in panic.

Trouble had been brewing since Monday morning, when about 2,000 natives at the shaft went on strike, and 14 policemen were sent there. They made seven arrests, but the strikers adopted a threatening attitude, and the police were forced to release their prisoners and withdraw.

Mine officials held a meeting on Monday afternoon. The natives refused to listen, and there were catcalls and shouting.

Subsequently Major J. J. du Toit, the District Commandant of Springs, went to the mine with 100 policemen. The natives were still in a dangerous mood, and he was forced to withdraw his men when it became dark.

Yesterday morning the strikers ...

some distance away, Major Du Toit sent in his unarmed policemen to surround the strikers and drive them back to their compound. The natives picked up stones from the embankment and hurled them at the police.

Eight policemen were injured, and the air became so thick with flying stones that the armed policemen were ordered forward. They fired 12 rounds, selecting individual targets. Eight natives were struck by bullets.

Panic immediately ensued among the strikers. They fled towards the compound gates, and it was at this stage that four were trampled to death. Eighty-three ...

Above: A fragment of an interview conducted in 1982, in which the former miner Philemon Mathole recalls an incident from Rand Leases Mine in 1946.

Right: An article published in the *Rand Daily Mail* on 14 August 1946, which describes the fatal confrontation between strikers and police at Sub-Nigel Mine.

Far right: A short interview with miner George Livi, record by AMWU members at City Deep Mine Hospital in the immediate aftermath of the '46 strike.

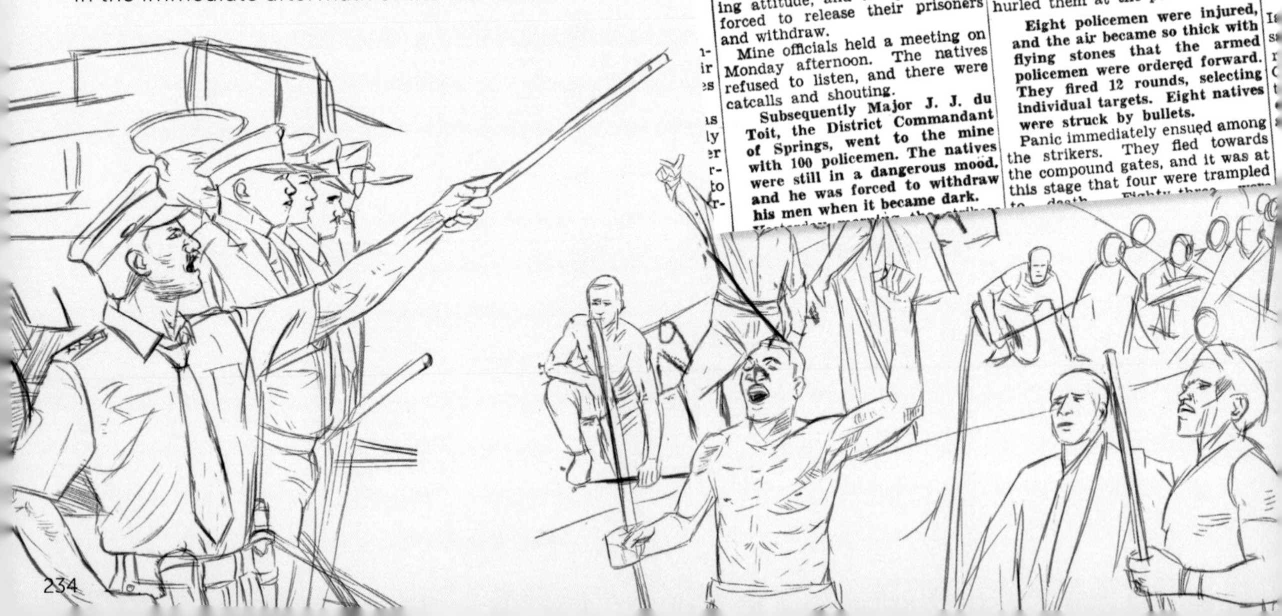

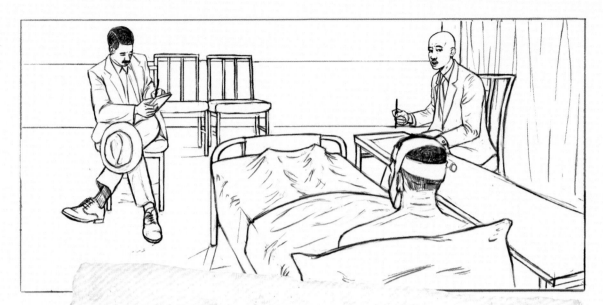

GEORGE LIVI. ROOM 69, City Deep. No 4047:   *Striker* —
"I was running away from the police who were ₩- rushing about
hitting everybody with batons. They caught me. They hit me on
the back and elbows. They were hitting people on the elbows and
knees and on their heads. There were others in the same room as
me who were injured and admitted to hospital. I did not see
anyone assaulting the police. It was the police who were
assaulting the miners. The Africans were soldiers. They had red
tabs on their shoulders. I think the white men also had red
tabs on their shoulders. The police were attacking anyone they
could catch. Many people were unconscious afterwards. They were
hitting the people as though they did not care whether they
killed them. They did not choose. Even some of the new recruits
were assaulted. They did not care whether they were supposed to
be working underground or not.
Yes, I supported the strike. I think we were right to strike.
The wages we get are very small wages - 2/5d. Per day - and we
have to do very hard work underground. I would support the
strike if there were another strike. Nothing has got better
since that time. The food is not as good as it was before the
strike. Many people were dismissed afterwards. Some of them
were from my room. Yes, I think they were given their wages. I
did not hear of any complaints about that. If you can go and
ask any of the miners who were here at that time they will want
to tell you the truth. They will tell you again what I have
told you. They will confirm what I am telling you. They all
want the truth to be known to the people outside. Some of the
people are afraid and some are now very suspicious. No, I am
not afraid. No, I do not mind if you tell other people what I
have told you. I will stand by what I have said. Yes, I swear
by my ancestors that what I have said is true.
This statement was made to me at City Deep Hospital and
interpreted by Sam Tuli and Stephen Modisane.

                                              7.11.46.

Glossary

ASIATIC
Historical term of racial classification, typically used to denote an Indian or Chinese person (obsolete and considered offensive).

BATHONG!
Expression of disbelief or surprise (Sesotho).

BOER
Historical term for a Dutch- or Afrikaans-speaking South African person of Dutch or Huguenot descent (Afrikaans).

BOSS BOY
African man in charge of a team of mineworkers or other laborers (obsolete and considered offensive).

BOY
Racist term for an African male, used irrespective of age, occupation or social position (obsolete and considered offensive).

COLOURED
Person, native to Southern Africa, of mixed heritage, including Khoi, San, African, Asian, white, and other descent. The term is embraced by members of this community though some view it as derogatory.

COMMANDO
Armed unit of soldiers, or strikers (as in the Rand Revolt), trained to carry out raids and engage in guerrilla warfare.

COMPOUND
Single-sex living quarters in which migrant laborers (usually African miners) live for the duration of their contracts.

COOLIE
Racist term for a person of Indian descent (obsolete and considered offensive).

DUMELA(NG)
Formal greeting (Sesotho-Setswana).

EUROPEAN
Historical term of racial classification used officially to denote a white person.

INDUNA
African foreman or supervisor on the mines (also used to denote a headman or councillor, especially in traditional Zulu society).

KGOSI
King or chief in traditional Batswana society (Setswana).

LAMBALAZI
"Water that makes you hungry," a term used by African miners to denote the thin porridge they were given for breakfast (Fanakalo, the lingua franca that was created on the mines as a language of instruction).

LAYISHA
"Lash," the mining activity of loading rock and ore into trolley cars for transportation to the surface (Fanakalo–see "Lambalazi").

LEKGOTLA
Council of elders in traditional Batswana society (Sesotho-Setswana).

LEKGOWA
White person (Sesotho).

LOCATION
Racially segregated urban residential area or township for Africans, Coloureds, Indians and other people of color.

MEALIE(S)
Maize cob or kernels (Afrikaans).

NATIVE
Historical term of racial classification used officially to denote Africans (obsolete and considered offensive).

NKOSI SIKELEL' IAFRIKA
"God, Bless Africa," the opening line of a hymn, composed by Enoch Sontonga, that was later adapted into the national anthem of democratic South Africa (isiXhosa).

NON-EUROPEAN
Historical term of racial classification used officially to denote Africans, Coloureds, Indians and other people of color, collectively (obsolete and considered offensive).

NTATE
Respectful term used to address an older man (Sesotho-Setswana).

PAP
Traditional South African porridge, made from coarsely ground maize.

PASS
Official certificate or letter required by law to be carried by specific groups (especially African men in urban areas) as a means of controlling movement and enforcing alcohol and curfew laws.

PERSON OF COLOR
In the South African context, this typically refers to a person of African, Coloured, Indian or Chinese descent.

PUDI YA DI THABA
Mountain goat (Sesotho-Setswana).

RAND
Unit of currency used in South Africa since 1961. "The Rand" is also the short form of geographical place name (*see* "Witwatersrand").

SAMMY
Racist term for an Indian man (obsolete and considered offensive).

SATYAGRAHI
Person who practices satyagraha, a form of non-violent resistance developed by Mohandas Gandhi during his time in South Africa (Sanskrit).

SCAB
Person who refuses to strike or join a union, or who takes the place of a striking worker (derogatory).

SKELM
Rascal or scoundrel, sometimes used affectionately (Afrikaans).

SKOKIAAN
Illegal home-brewed liquor made primarily of yeast, sugar, and water.

SKOKIAAN QUEEN
Woman who brews and sells illegal alcohol.

THOBELA
Greeting (Sepedi).

TRIBE
Historical term for chiefdom or community living within a traditional society. Today, "tribe" and "tribal" are considered problematic as they promote misleading historical and cultural stereotypes.

TSHETSHA
"Hurry" (Fanakalo–*see* "Lambalazi").

VOETSEK!
"Go away" or "Scram" (Afrikaans).

VUKA
"Wake up" (isiZulu as well as other Nguni languages).

WAAR IS JOU DOMPAS?
"Where is your pass?" (Afrikaans).

WATHINT' ABAFAZI WATHINT' IMBOKODO
"You strike a woman, you strike a grinding stone," a phrase sung by protestors at the 1956 women's march in Pretoria (isiXhosa and isiZulu).

WITWATERSRAND (also called "THE RAND")
35-mile escarpment which runs through the city of Johannesburg, and contains the richest gold deposits in the world (Afrikaans).

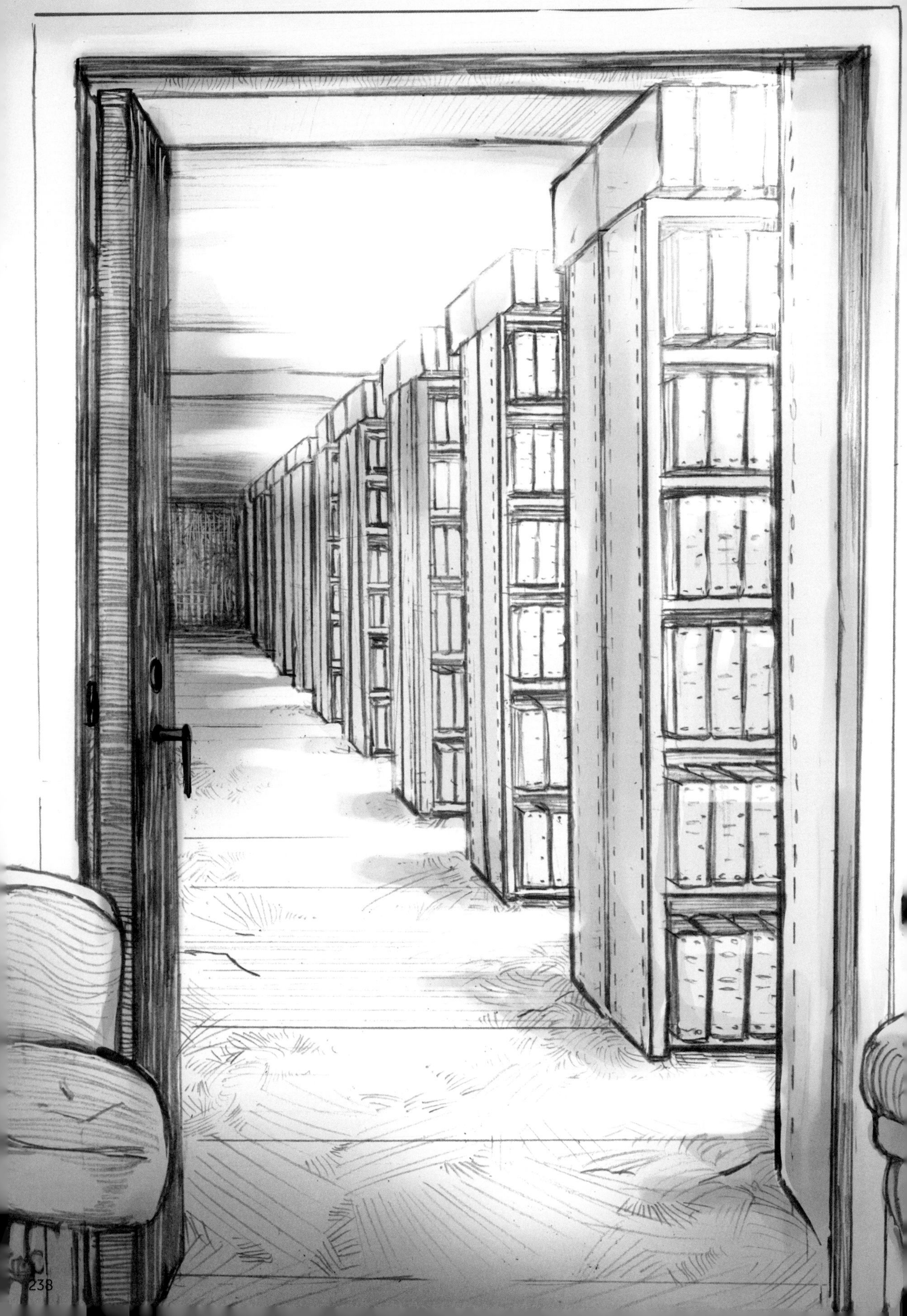

Bibliography

For convenience, the following abbreviations have been adopted in the court record citation:

AD: Appellate Division
CPD: Cape Provincial Division
TPD: Transvaal Provincial Division
UG: Union Government

The sources below are listed by chapter. As a preface to these titles, I wish specifically to acknowledge Hugh Corder's *Judges at Work: The Role and Attitudes of the South African Appellate Judiciary, 1910–50* (Cape Town: Juta, 1984) as it was an invaluable reference point for every chapter in *All Rise*.

CHAPTER 1: UNTIL THE SHIP SAILS

Court and archival records

- *Chotabhai v. UG (Minister of Justice) and Registrar of Asiatics*, 1910 TPD, 1911 AD.
- *Mahomed & Others v. UG (Minister of the Interior),* 1910 CPD, 1911 AD.
- National Archives (Pretoria), Registrar of Asiatics Files (IND): *Mahomed Ahmed Chotabhai*, 1906–1932.

Periodicals

- *The Cape Argus, Cape Times, Indian Opinion, The Krugersdorp Standard, The Natal Mercury, The Natal Witness, The Rand Daily Mail, The Star.*

Other sources

- Bhana, Surendra, *Setting Down Roots: Indian Migrants in South Africa, 1860–1911* (Johannesburg: Witwatersrand University Press, 1990).
- Chetty, K., *Indian Passenger and Ships List: 1860–1911*, Gandhi-Luthuli Documentation Centre, University of KwaZulu-Natal (https://scnc.ukzn.ac.za/doc/SHIP/shipndx.html).
- Cousins, Clarence, *Reflections of a Nineteenth Century Immigrant 1896–1950* (Tzaneen: Self-published, 1950), available in Clarence Wilfred Cousins Papers BC 1154, Manuscript Collection, University of Cape Town Libraries.
- Desai, Ashwin and Goolam Vahed, *Inside Indian Indenture: A South African Story, 1860–1914* (Cape Town: Human Sciences Research Council Press, 2010).
- Desai, Ashwin and Goolam Vahed, *The South African Gandhi: Stretcher-Bearer of Empire* (Stanford: Stanford University Press, 2016).
- Dhupelia-Mesthrie, Uma, "Betwixt the Oceans: The Chief Immigration Officer in Cape Town, Clarence Wilfred Cousins (1905–1915)," *Journal of Southern African Studies*, 42:3 (2016), 463–481.
- DiSalvo, Charles R., *M.K. Gandhi, Attorney at Law: The Man before the Mahatma* (Berkley, University of California Press, 2013).
- Gandhi, Mohandas K., *Hind Swaraj and Other Writings*, edited by Anthony J. Parel (Cambridge: Cambridge University Press, 1997).
- Gandhi, Mohandas K., *Satyagraha in South Africa,* trans. V.G. Desai (Stanford: Academic Reprints, 1954).
- Gandhi, Mohandas K., *The Collected Works of Mahatma Gandhi* (New Delhi: Government of India, 1969 edition).
- Guha, Ramachandra, *Gandhi Before India* (New Delhi: Penguin, 2013)
- Nundy, Edward, *The Transvaal Asiatic Ordinance, 1907: An Exposure* (Johannesburg: The Transvaal Leader, 1907).
- Swan, Maureen, *Gandhi: The South African Experience* (Johannesburg: Ravan Press, 1985).

CHAPTER 2: IN THE SHADOW OF A HIGH STONE WALL

Court and archival records

- *Rex v. W.J. Whittaker,* 1911 TPD.
- *Whittaker & Morant v. Roos & Bateman,* 1911 TPD, 1912 AD.
- National Archives (Pretoria), MM 331 / 11, *Tramway Strike Johannesburg: Report by Inspector of White Labour,* January 1911.

Periodicals

- *The Rand Daily Mail, The Star, Voice of Labour, The Nongqai.*

Other sources

- Beavon, Keith, *Johannesburg: The Making and Shaping of the City* (Pretoria: University of South African Press, 2004).
- Chubb, J.A., "The Jury System," *The South African Law Journal,* 73 (1956), 194–202.
- Gitsham, Ernest and James F. Trembath, *A First Account of Labour Organisation in South Africa* (Durban: E. P. and Commercial Printing Company, 1926).
- Hunter, Frances, *Mary "Pickhandle" Fitzgerald: Rediscovering a Lost Icon* (Durban: Just Done Productions, 2009).
- Hyslop, Jonathan, *The Notorious Syndicalist: J.T. Bain: A Scottish Rebel in Colonial South Africa* (Johannesburg: Jacana Media, 2004).
- Smith, Tony and Brian Patton, *Johannesburg Tramways: A History of the Tramways of the City of Johannesburg* (London: The Light Railway Transport League, 1976).
- South African Law Commission, *Simplification of Criminal Procedure: (Access to the Criminal Justice System),* Issue Paper 6, Project 73 (Pretoria: The South African Law Commission, 1997).
- Van Onselen, Charles, *New Babylon New Nineveh: Everyday Life on the Witwatersrand, 1886–1914* (Johannesburg: Jonathan Ball, 2001).

Illustrations

- Riis, Jacob, *Five Cents a Spot: Lodgers in a Crowded Bayard Street Tenement,* Preus Museum.
- *Board of Education, Toronto, August 14 1913, No. 94,* City of Toronto Archives, Series 372: 11, item 94.
- *1900s–1910s Woman Waiting on Customers Sitting around Counter in Restaurant Diner Silent Movie Still,* American Stock.

CHAPTER 3: COME GALLOWS GRIM

Court and archival records

- National Archives (Pretoria), Special Criminal Court Case No. 18/1922, *Rex v. S. A. Long,* September 1922.
- National Archives (Pretoria), Special Criminal Court Case No. 48/1922, *Rex v. S. A. Long,* October 1922.
- National Archives (Pretoria), JUS 713 1/200/22, *Constitution of a Special Criminal Court to Try Case of Rex v. S. A. Long,* September 1922.
- National Archives (Pretoria), URU 591, 2999, *Rex v. Samuel Alfred Long—Special Criminal Court: Indices, Exhibits and Appendices,* October–November, 1922.
- National Archives (Pretoria), GG 51 / 6525, *Sentences: Capital: Long, Lewis, Hull and Stassen,* "South Africa, Secret, Prince Arthur, Duke of Connaught to His Grace the Duke of Devonshire, K.G., G.C.M.G., G.C.V.O., &c., &c., &c., Colonial Office," London: 15 November 1922.

Periodicals

- *The Nongqai, The Rand Daily Mail, The Star.*

Other sources

- Bosman, Herman Charles, *Cold Stone Jug* (Cape Town: Human & Rousseau, 1969).

- Chanock, Martin, *The Making of South African Legal Culture 1902–1936: Fear, Favour and Prejudice* (Cambridge: Cambridge University Press, 2001).
- Godley, R.S., *Khaki and Blue: Reminiscences of Thirty-five Year's Service in South Africa* (London: Lovat, Dickson and Thompson, 1935).
- Gray, Stephen, *Life Sentence: A Biography of Herman Charles Bosman* (Cape Town: Human & Rousseau, 2005).
- Herd, Norman, *1922: The Revolt on the Rand* (Johannesburg: Blue Crane Books, 1966).
- Hirson, Baruch, "The General Strike of 1922," *Searchlight South Africa*, 3:3 (October, 1993), 63–94.
- Hoffmann, A.J., *On the Trail of Criminals*, Unpublished translation of the original Afrikaans *Op die Spoor van die Misdadiger* (Johannesburg: Afrikaanse Pers Boekhandel, 1948).
- Kahn, Ellison, "The Death Penalty in South Africa," *Tydskrif vir Hedendaagse Romeins-Hollandse Reg (Journal for Contemporary Roman-Dutch Law)*, 33:2 (1970), 108–141.
- Krikler, Jeremy, *The Rand Revolt: The 1922 Insurrection and Racial Killing in South Africa* (Johannesburg: Jonathan Ball, 2005).
- Reitz, Deneys, *No Outspan* (London: Faber & Faber, 1942).
- Roux, Edward, *S.P. Bunting: A Political Biography* (Cape Town: Mayibuye, 1993).
- Transvaal Strike Legal Defence Committee, *The Story of a Crime being the Vindication of the Transvaal Strike Legal Defense Committee in Connection with the Great Strike on the Witwatersrand in 1922* (Johannesburg: Transvaal Strike Legal Defence Committee, 1924).
- Turrell, Robert, *White Mercy: A Study of the Death Penalty in South Africa* (Westport, CT: Praeger, 2004).
- Van Niekerk, B.v.D., "Hanged by the Neck until You Are Dead," *The South African Law Journal*, 86 (1969), 457–475.

CHAPTER 4: THE WIDOW OF MARABASTAD

Court and archival records

- *Rex v. Detody*, TPD, 1925 TPD, 1926 AD.
- National Archives (Pretoria), *Secretary of Native Affairs Files* (S.N. A), 1920–1928.
- National Archives (Pretoria), *Department of Justice Files* (JUS), 1920–1928.

Periodicals

- *The Rand Daily Mail, The Star*.

Other sources

- Eales, K.A., "Gender Politics and the Administration of African Women in Johannesburg, 1903–1939" (M.A. dissertation, University of the Witwatersrand, 1991).
- Eales, K.A., "Patriarchs, Passes and Privilege: Johannesburg's African Middle Classes and the Question of Night Passes for Women," History Workshop paper (Johannesburg: University of Witwatersrand, 1987).
- Friedman, Michelle, "A History of Africans in Pretoria with Special Reference to Marabastad, 1902–23" (M.A. dissertation, University of South Africa, 1994).
- Mphahlele, Es'kia, *Down Second Avenue* (Johannesburg: Picador, 2004).
- Walker, Cherryl, *Women and Resistance in South Africa* (London: Onyx Press, 1982).
- Walshe, Peter, *The Rise of African Nationalism in South Africa: The African National Congress, 1912–1952* (London: C. Hurst and Co., 1970).
- Wells, Julia C., "The History of South African Women's Resistance to Pass Laws, 1900–1960" (Ph.D. dissertation, Columbia University Teachers College, 1982).
- Wells, Julia C., "The War of Degradation: Black Women's Struggle Against Orange Free State Pass Laws, 1913," *Banditry, Rebellion and Social Protest in Africa*, edited by Donald Crummey (London: James Currey, 1986), 253–270.
- Wells, Julia C., *We Have Done with Pleading: The Women's 1913 Anti-pass Campaign* (Johannesburg: Ravan Press, 1991).
- Wells, Julia C., *We Now Demand!: The History of Women's Resistance to Pass Laws in South Africa* (Johannesburg: University of the Witwatersrand, 1993).

- Wells, Julia C., "Why Women Rebel: A Comparative Study of South African Women's Resistance in Bloemfontein (1913) and Johannesburg (1958)," *Journal of Southern African Studies*, 10:1 (October, 1983), 55–70.

Illustrations

- *Pretoria South Africa–August: Women's March to the Union Buildings in August 1956,* Gallo Images, Johncom.

CHAPTER 5: A HOUSE DIVIDED

Court and archival records

- *Mokhatle & Others v. UG (Minister of Native Affairs),* 1925 TPD, 1926 AD.
- National Archives (Pretoria), *Secretary of Native Affairs Files* (S. N. A), 1906–1928.
- National Archives (Pretoria), *Department of Justice Files* (JUS), 1923–1924.

Other sources

- Bergh, J.S., "S.J.P. Kruger and Landownership in the Transvaal," *Historia* 59:2 (November, 2014), 69–78.
- Bozzoli, Belinda (with Mmantho Nkotsoe), *Women of Phokeng: Consciousness, Life Strategy, and Migrancy in South Africa, 1900–1983* (Johannesburg: Ravan Press, 1991).
- Mbenga, Bernard, "The Reverend Kenneth Mosley Spooner: African-American missionary to the BaFokeng of Rustenburg district, South Africa, 1915–1937," *New Contree,* 81 (December, 2018), 40–64.
- Mbenga, Bernard and Andrew Manson, *"People of the Dew": A History of the Bafokeng of Phokeng-Rustenburg Region, South Africa, from Early Times to 2000* (Johannesburg: Jacana Media, 2010).
- Mokgatle, Naboth, *The Autobiography of an Unknown South African* (Berkeley and Los Angeles: University of California Press, 1975).
- Simpson, Graeme, "Peasants and Politics in the Western Transvaal, 1920–1940" (M.A. dissertation, University of the Witwatersrand, 1986).
- Simpson, Graeme, "The Political and Legal Contradictions in the Preservation and Dissolution of the Precapitalist Mode of Production: The Fokeng Disturbances, 1921–1926" (B.A. Hons. dissertation, University of the Witwatersrand, 1981).

CHAPTER 6: HERE I CROSS TO THE OTHER SIDE

Court and archival records

- *Basner v. Trigger,* 1945 AD.
- SAIRR Oral History Archive, *Interview with David Bopape* (Johannesburg, 1982), Wits Historical Papers, AD1722/14.
- SAIRR Oral History Archive, *Interview with Philemon Mathole* (Johannesburg, 1982), Wits Historical Papers, AD1722/15.
- *Witwatersrand Mine Native Wages Commission Evidence,* Corey Library, Rhodes University, Grahamstown.

Periodicals

- *Inkululeko, The Guardian, The Rand Daily Mail, The Star.*

Films

- *The Golden Harvest of the Witwatersrand,* Chamber of Mines (1936).
- *Matsela,* Chamber of Mines (1946).
- *A Tour of Basutoland,* University of Johannesburg Special Collections (1947).
- *African Jim,* Donald Swanson (1949).
- *Phela Ndaba,* Antonia Caccia, Chris Curling, Simon Louvish, Nelson Nana Mahomo, Vus Make and Rakhetla Tsehlana (1970).
- *Dying for Gold,* Richard Pakleppa and Catherine Meyburgh (2018).

Other sources

- Abrahams, Peter, *Mine Boy* (London: Heinemann Educational Books, 1963).
- Bernstein, Rusty et al., *Memory Against Forgetting: Memoir of a Time in South African Politics 1938–1964.* Johannesburg: Wits University Press, 2017.
- Breckenridge, Keith, "The Allure of Violence: Men, Race and Masculinity on the South African Goldmines, 1900–1950," *Journal of Southern African Studies*, 24:4 (December, 1998), 669–693.
- Coplan, David B., *In the Time of Cannibals: The Word Music of South Africa's Basotho Migrants* (Chicago: University of Chicago Press, 1995).
- Drew, Allison (ed.), "The Impending Strike of African Miners: A Statement by the African Mineworkers' Union, 7 August 1946," *South Africa's Radical Tradition, A Documentary History,* Vol. 1 (Cape Town: Mayibuye Books, 1996).
- First, Ruth, "The Gold of Migrant Labour," *Review of African Political Economy, 25* (September–December, 1982), 5–21.
- James, Wilmot G., "Grounds for a Strike: South African Gold Mining in the 1940s," *African Economic History,* 16 (1987), 1–22.
- Leger, Jean and Monyaola Mothibeli, "'Talking Rocks': Pit Sense Amongst South African Miners," *Labour, Capital and Society*, 21:2 (November, 1988), 222–237.
- Maloka, Edward Tshidiso, "Basotho and the Mines: Towards a History of Labour Migrancy, c. 1890–1940" (Ph.D. dissertation, University of Cape Town, 1995).
- Mandela, Nelson, *A Long Walk to Freedom: The Autobiography of Nelson Mandela* (Boston: Little, Brown, 1994).
- Moodie, T. Dunbar (with Vivienne Ndatshe), *Going for Gold: Men, Mines and Migration* (Johannesburg: Witwatersrand University Press, 1994).
- Moodie, T. Dunbar, "Maximum Average Violence: Underground Assaults on the South African Gold Mines, 1913–1965," *Journal of Southern African Studies*, 31:3 (September, 2005), 547–567.
- Moodie, T. Dunbar, "The Moral Economy of the Black Miners' Strike of 1946," *Journal of Southern African Studies,* 13:1 (October, 1986), 1–35.
- O'Meara, Dan, "The 1946 African Mineworkers' Strike and the Political Economy of South Africa," *Journal of Commonwealth and Comparative Politics,* 13:2 (1975), 146–173.

Photo Credits

CHAPTER 1: UNTIL THE SHIP SAILS

p. 42:   Museum Africa

p. 43:   Peter Kallaway & Patrick Pearson

p. 44:   (*Top*) UWC-Robben Island Museum, Mayibuye Archives
          (*Bottom*) Keystone/Getty Images

p. 45:   (*Top*) National Archives (Pretoria)
          (*Bottom, left*) *Indian Opinion* (27 August 1910)
          (*Bottom, right*) *The Collected Works of Mahatma Gandhi*

p. 46:   *Indian Review*

p. 47:   *Indian Opinion* (22 October 1910)

p. 48:   Supreme Court of Appeal Archive (Bloemfontein)

p. 49:   Henry Polak – *Indian Opinion* (24 September 1910)
          Sonja Schlesin – *Souvenir of the Passive Resistance Movement in South
          Africa, Golden Number of Indian Opinion* (1914)
          Clarence Cousins – *Cousins Papers*, University of Cape Town
          Manuscripts Collection
          Johannes Wessels – National Library of South Africa

CHAPTER 2: IN THE SHADOW OF A HIGH STONE WALL

p. 75:   National Archives (Pretoria)

p. 76:   (*Top, left*) Museum Africa
          (*Bottom, right*) *Voice of Labour* (7 August 1909)

p. 77:   (*Middle, right*) *South African Pictorial, Stage and Cinema*
          (12 April 1919)
          (*Bottom, right*) *Transvaal Leader, Strike 1913*

p. 78:   (*Top*) *Transvaal Leader, Strike 1913*
          (*Bottom*) *Nongqai*, South African Police Service Museum

p. 79:   *Voice of Labour* (1 December 1911)

p. 80:   (*Top*) *Transvaal Leader, Strike 1913*

p. 81:   *Voice of Labour* (15 December 1911)

CHAPTER 3: COME GALLOWS GRIM

p. 116:   *The Star, Through the Red Revolt on the Rand (1922)*
          (*Overlay*) Museum Africa

p. 117:   (*Top*) *Herd, The Revolt on the Rand (1966)*
          (*Middle*) *Rand Daily Mail* (11 January 1923)

p. 118:   (*All*) *The Star, Through the Red Revolt on the Rand (1922)*

p. 119:   (*Top*) *Some Historic Walks and Drives of Johannesburg*, Johannesburg
          Historical Foundation
          (*Middle*) National Archives (Pretoria)

p. 120: (*Top*) Museum Africa
(*Bottom*) National Archives (Pretoria)
p. 121: (*Top*) National Archives (Pretoria)
(*Middle*) Museum Africa
P. 122: (*Top*) *The Star, Through the Red Revolt on the Rand (1922)*
(*Middle*) Museum Africa
(*Bottom*) National Archives (Pretoria)
p. 123: (*Top*) *Rand Daily Mail* (19 May 1922)
(*Bottom, left and right*) National Archives (Pretoria)
p. 124: National Archives (Pretoria)

CHAPTER 4: THE WIDOW OF MARABASTAD

p. 150: (*Top*) www.sahistory.co.za
(*Middle*) National Archives (Pretoria)
(*Bottom*) Historical Papers, Wits University
p. 151: National Archives (Pretoria)
p. 152: Supreme Court of Appeal Archive (Bloemfontein)
p. 153: Supreme Court of Appeal Archive (Bloemfontein)

CHAPTER 5: A HOUSE DIVIDED

p. 186: H.F. Gros, *Pictorial Description of the Transvaal* (1888)
p. 187: National Archives (Pretoria)
p. 188: (*Top, left*) Royal Bafokeng Nation Archive
(*Top, right*) National Archives (Pretoria)
(*Bottom*) National Archives (Pretoria)
p. 189: National Archives (Pretoria)
p. 190: (*Top, left*) National Archives (Pretoria)
(*Bottom*) National Archives (Pretoria)
p. 191: (*Top*) Historical Papers, Wits University
Ernst Penzhorn – *Pape, Hermannsburger Missionare in Südafrika* (1986)
Sol Plaatje – *Plaatje-Molema Papers,* Historical Papers, Wits University
James Manotshe Mototlegi – Royal Bafokeng Nation Archive

CHAPTER 6: HERE I CROSS TO THE OTHER SIDE

p. 226: *Matsela,* Chamber of Mines (1946)
p. 227: (*All*) *Matsela,* Chamber of Mines (1946)
p. 228: (*Top*) Leon Levson, History Workshop Collection, Historical Papers, Wits University
(*Middle and Bottom*) *Matsela,* Chamber of Mines (1946)
p. 229: (*Top*) © Ernest Cole Family Trust
(*Middle*) *Golden Harvest of the Witwatersrand,* Chamber of Mines (1936)

p. 230: (*Top*) Leon Levson, UWC-Robben Island Museum, Mayibuye Archives
(*Bottom, left*) History Workshop Collection, Historical Papers, Wits University
(*Bottom, right*) Museum Africa

p. 231: (*Top, left*) History Workshop Collection, Historical Papers, Wits University
(*Top, right*) Margaret Bourke-White, *Life Magazine/Getty Images*
(*Middle and Bottom*) History Workshop Collection, Historical Papers, Wits University

p. 232: Moses Kotane – History Workshop Collection, Historical Papers, Wits University
James Majoro – *Inkululeko* (August 1948)
J.B. Marks – History Workshop Collection, Historical Papers, Wits University
(*Bottom*) *Inkululeko* (August 1946)

p. 233: (*All*) Museum Africa

p. 234: (*Top*) SAIRR Oral History Archive, Historical Papers, Wits University
(*Bottom*) *Rand Daily Mail* (14 August 1946)

p. 235: Historical Papers, Wits University

Contributors

RICHARD CONYNGHAM is a Pietermaritzburg-born writer who lives in Mexico City. After graduating from the universities of Cape Town and Cambridge, he worked for South African civil-society organizations Equal Education, The Bookery, and Ndifuna Ukwazi, the London publisher Slightly Foxed, and the edtech organization MakeTomorrow. In 2016, Richard collaborated with the Trantraal Brothers to create *Safety, Justice and People's Power*, an illustrated companion to the O'Regan-Pikoli Commission of Inquiry into policing in Khayelitsha.

SAAID RAHBEENI lives in Maitland, Cape Town. A freelance illustrator with decades of experience, he previously worked for the Educational Support Services Trust, Jincom, Strika Entertainment, and MTE Studios. His drawings appear in a range of school textbooks published by Pearson, Pan Macmillan, and Oxford University Press, among others, and he has also contributed to the *Our Story* series by South African Heritage Publishers.

THE TRANTRAAL BROTHERS, André (*left*) and Nathan (*below*) are a sibling-illustrator duo who grew up in the Cape Town township of Mitchells Plain before moving to Bishop Lavis. They have published numerous cartoons and graphic works including *Coloureds* (2010) and *Crossroads* (2014–2020, written by Koni Benson). Independently, André has written and illustrated the children's book series, *Keegan and Samier*. Nathan has published three poetry collections in Kaaps—earning him numerous awards including the 2013 Ingrid Jonker Prize and the 2020 SALA Poetry Award—as well as a collection of his columns as published in the Afrikaans newspaper, *Rapport*.

LIZ CLARKE lives in Cape Town, where she works as an illustrator. She has contributed to the genre of graphic history internationally, and her work is featured in seven books published by Oxford University Press USA—including *Witness to the Age of Revolution* (written by Charles F. Walker), which won the Association of American Publishers PROSE Award for Nonfiction Graphic Novels, and *Abina and the Important Men* (written by Trevor R. Getz), which won the American Historical Association's James Harvey Robinson Prize.

DADA KHANYISA is an Umzimkhulu-born, Johannesburg-raised, Cape Town-based multi-disciplinary artist whose work explores the intersection of technology and contemporary social culture with respect to the Black experience. In 2016, they (Dada's preferred pronoun) were awarded the Simon Gerson Prize, and a year later, completed a commission for a 35-meter mural on Constitution Hill in Johannesburg. In 2018, the Stevenson Gallery in Cape Town presented Dada's first solo exhibition, *Bamb'iphone*, followed up two years later by the Johannesburg show, *Good Feelings*.

TUMI MAMABOLO hails from Polokwane in Limpopo province. He can't remember a time when he wasn't avidly drawing and painting, usually a comic or graphic novel from his own imagination. Since graduating with a degree in Information Design from the University of Pretoria in 2020, he has already won two Gold Loerie awards for his animation work. Still in his early twenties, Tumi is a rare talent and by far the youngest of the *All Rise* contributors.

MARK MODIMOLA was born in Pretoria of Sotho-Tsonga parentage. Originally a graphic designer, he studied at the University of Pretoria and later pursued a Fulbright Scholarship in the United States before returning to South Africa determined to illustrate full-time. Mark is a prolific and versatile creator, with a portfolio that explores African identity and spirituality, often through the cultural aesthetic of Afrofuturism.

Witpoort is proceeding normally. African Mineworkers

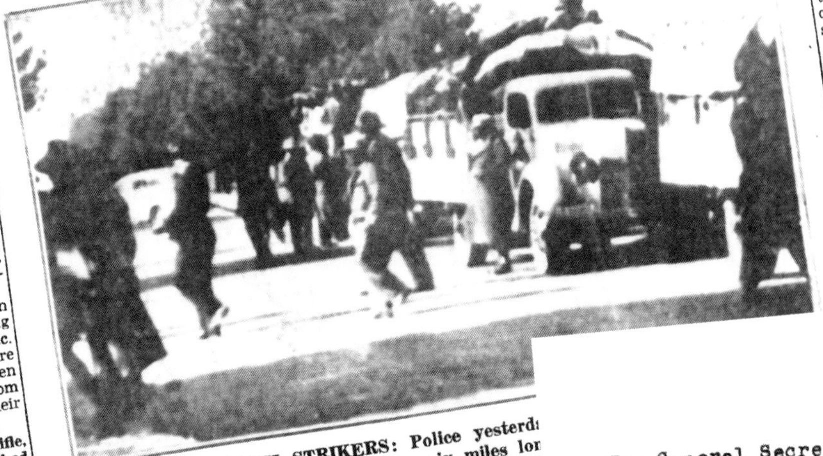

POLICE CLASH WITH STRIKERS: Police yesterd[ay] intercepted a column of native strikers six miles lon[g] 4,000 strong and armed with dangerous weapons, whi[ch] was marching from West Springs to Johannesburg. fight took place outside Brakpan where a number the strikers were injured. The photograph shows pol[ice] "debussing" from troop-carriers to join the attack

Eight Natives Wounde[d] Four Trampled to Death at Sub-Nigel

STRIKERS yesterdy clashed with the police at the shaft of the Sub-Nigel Mine. The police opene[d] and eight natives were wounded. Four were tramp[led to] death when the strikers fled in panic.

Trouble had been brewing since Monday morning, when about 2,000 natives at the shaft went on strike, and 14 policemen were sent there. They made seven arrests, but the strikers adopted a threatening attitude, and the police were forced to release their prisoners and withdraw.

Mine officials held a meeting on Monday afternoon. The natives refused to listen, and there were catcalls and shouting.

Subsequently Major J. J. du Toit, the District Commandant of Springs, went to the mine with 100 policemen. The natives were still in a dangerous mood, and he was forced to withdraw his men when it became dark.

Yesterday morning the strikers left their compound and gathered on a loose-stone embankment ... 200 yards away. A number ... were willing to ... on duty, but

some distance away, M... Toit sent in his unarme[d] men to surround the str[ikers and] drive them back to th[e com]pound. The natives [took] stones from the embank[ment and] hurled them at the poli[ce].

Eight policemen we[re ...] and the air became so [full of] flying stones that 1... policemen were order[ed ...] They fired 12 round[s ...] individual targets. Ei[ght ...] were struck by bulle[ts].

Panic immediately en[sued ...] the strikers. They f[led ...] the compound gates, a[nd it was at] this stage that four we[re trampled] to death. Eighty-t[...] slightly injured.

Shortly afterwards ... that all the natives, ... of their shift, wished ... ground. The cages ... time to lower them. ... The police seized three tr[uck]s ...pons, such as st... ...l balls, ...

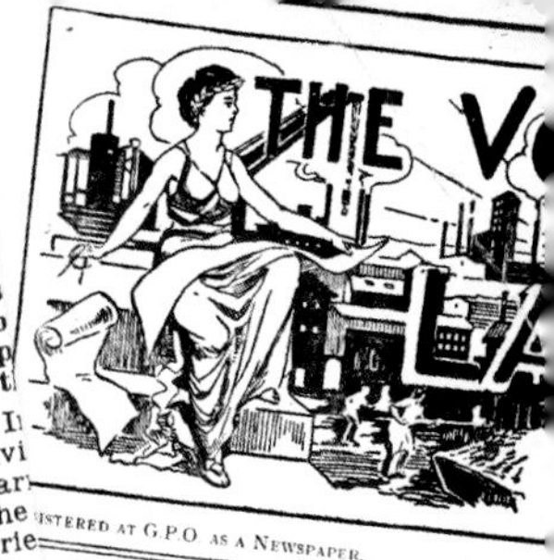

THE V[OICE OF]
LA[BOUR]

[REG]ISTERED AT G.P.O. AS A NEWSPAPER.

[Vol.] 5. No. 166. JOHANNESBURG,

June 2[...]

The General Secretary,
S.A.Trades and Labour Council,
Union Centre,
JOHANNESBURG.

Dear Sir,

I am attaching, as requeste[d ...] copies of our Constitution. I regret the [delay in this] matter, but I have no full-time staff ava[ilable and have] been extremely busy preparing our memoran[dum for the Wit]watersrand Gold Mines Native Wages' Commi[ssion].

In this connection I am al[so attaching a] copy of our memorandum, which I recommen[d to your] most careful consideration. My Union wil[l ...] much if your Council would see their way [...] representations. Your particular attenti[on ...] section on "Trade Unionism" (Pages 40 to [...] sure ... to suppor[t ...] vati...

Yours [...]

JAM[ES ...]
HON. [...]

From the Editor's Chair

"THE LAW IS AN HASS"

THE truth of this expression was never more realised than in the case of Mr. Chhotabhai's son. Sir John Wessels the man considers that, if the interpretation given to the Asiatic Law by the Government be true, it is "monstrous," it is "inhuman," and that it will create "a howl in the civilised world." Sir John Wessels the man considers that if the Minister of the Interior wishes not to molest the youth—Mr. Chhotabhai's son—he can easily manage it. So far, then, as man's judgment is concerned, it is against the threatened action of the Government.

But the Judge in man thinks differently. He can only consider the letter of the law. He, the Judge, is not concerned with the humanity or inhumanity of any Act. No matter how cruel an Act may be, if it is sanctioned by the legislature, the Judge is bound to enforce the intention of the legislature as expressed through its Acts. Sir John Wessels the Judge, therefore, has come to the conclusion, on reading the law, that however "monstrous" and "inhuman" the action of the Government is, it being in accordance with the Asiatic Act, he, the Judge, sanctions it. Under the present system he could not do otherwise. His oath binds him to enforce the laws of the land. He had, therefore, only two courses left open to him, either to give the interpretation of the law according to the letter of it or, it being repugnant to the dictates of humanity, to resign his office. The latter was too heroic a step. Judges, nowadays, do not adopt such a course. We have, therefore, the spectacle of the machinery of the law being prostituted to do a gross and monstrous injustice in the name of "law, order,

GENERAL ST[RIKE]

A GENERAL STRIKE OF ALL AFRICAN WORKERS IN JOHANNESBURG, THE REEF, PRETORIA ... CALLED FOR THURSDAY, AUGUST 15, BY A FULLY REPRESENTATIVE MEETING OF AFRICAN TR... [AUS]PICES OF THE COUNCIL OF NON-EUROPEAN TRADE UNIONS, HELD AT ROSENBERG ARCADE O[N] ...

The resolution which was passed by a big majority, immediately after police had arrived to arrest the C... reads as follows:

"After considering the implications arising out of the strike of African miners, this meeting resolves ...[afric]an workers on the Reef, Vereeniging and Pretoria WITHIN 48 HOURS FROM NOW, in support thereof, ...ution (for recognition of African Unions, and 10/- minimum daily wage) arrived at in Bloemfontein at the Co[nference of] Unions, in 1945."

INKULULEKO

[F]irst Issue, August, 1946.

Registered at the G.P.O. as a N...

POLICE VIOLENCE—LEA[DERS ...]

Miners Strike For[...]

In spite of police violence and terror, over ... the Witwatersrand carried out the decision of a ... August 4, to come out on strike as from Monday ... They are demanding a minimum wage of ten ... and conditions. More workers are coming out on str... At Sub-Nigel mine, last Tuesday morni[ng ...] fire on the worke[rs ...]

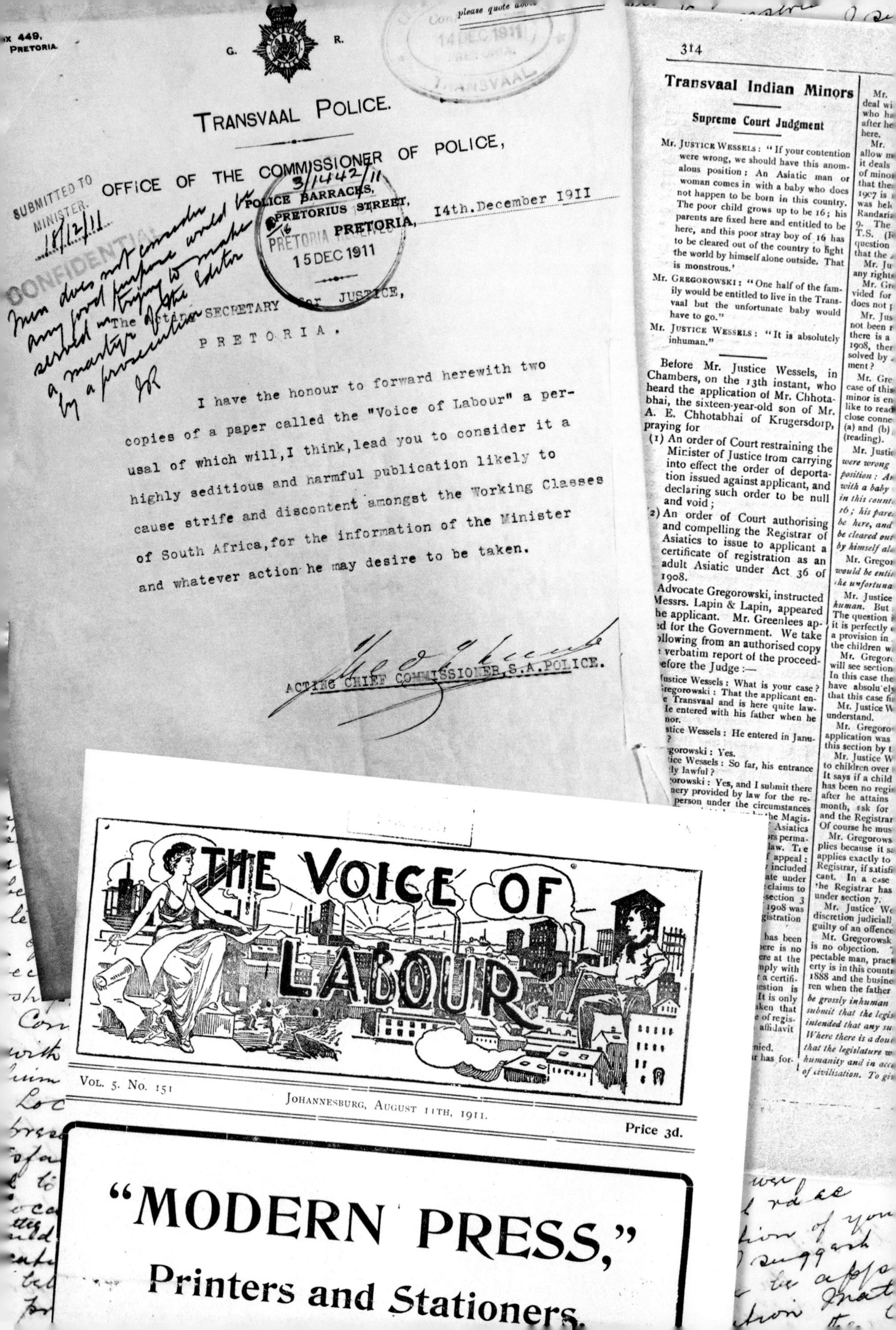

G. R.

TRANSVAAL POLICE.

OFFICE OF THE COMMISSIONER OF POLICE,
POLICE BARRACKS,
PRETORIUS STREET,
PRETORIA, 14th. December 1911

[handwritten, partly illegible:] CONFIDENTIAL
Men does not consider the
any food purpose would be
served in trying to make
a martyr of the Editor
by a prosecution

[stamp] 14 DEC 1911 PRETORIA TRANSVAAL

[stamp] PRETORIA RECEIVED 15 DEC 1911

SECRETARY for JUSTICE,

P R E T O R I A .

I have the honour to forward herewith two
copies of a paper called the "Voice of Labour" a per-
usal of which will, I think, lead you to consider it a
highly seditious and harmful publication likely to
cause strife and discontent amongst the Working Classes
of South Africa, for the information of the Minister
and whatever action he may desire to be taken.

[signature]

ACTING CHIEF COMMISSIONER. S.A. POLICE.

Transvaal Indian Minors

Supreme Court Judgment

Mr. JUSTICE WESSELS: "If your contention were wrong, we should have this anomalous position: An Asiatic man or woman comes in with a baby who does not happen to be born in this country. The poor child grows up to be 16; his parents are fixed here and entitled to be here, and this poor stray boy of 16 has to be cleared out of the country to fight the world by himself alone outside. That is monstrous.'

Mr. GREGOROWSKI: "One half of the family would be entitled to live in the Transvaal but the unfortunate baby would have to go."

Mr. JUSTICE WESSELS: "It is absolutely inhuman."

Before Mr. Justice Wessels, in Chambers, on the 13th instant, who heard the application of Mr. Chhotabhai, the sixteen-year-old son of Mr. A. E. Chhotabhai of Krugersdorp, praying for

(1) An order of Court restraining the Minister of Justice from carrying into effect the order of deportation issued against applicant, and declaring such order to be null and void;

(2) An order of Court authorising and compelling the Registrar of Asiatics to issue to applicant a certificate of registration as an adult Asiatic under Act 36 of 1908.

Advocate Gregorowski, instructed [by] Messrs. Lapin & Lapin, appeared [for] the applicant. Mr. Greenlees appeared for the Government. We take [the] following from an authorised copy [of a] verbatim report of the proceed[ings] before the Judge:—

[Mr.] Justice Wessels: What is your case?
[Mr.] Gregorowski: That the applicant en[tered the] Transvaal and is here quite law[fully,] [h]e entered with his father when he [was a mi]nor.

[Mr. Ju]stice Wessels: He entered in Janu[ary?]
[Mr. Gre]gorowski: Yes.
[Mr. Just]ice Wessels: So far, his entrance [was whol]ly lawful?
[Mr. Greg]orowski: Yes, and I submit there [is machi]nery provided by law for the re[gistration of a] person under the circumstances

[right column, fragmentary:]
deal wi...
who ha...
after he...
here.
Mr. ...
allow m...
it deals ...
of minor...
1907 is a ...
was hele...
Randaria...
9. The ...
T.S. (R...
question ...
that the A...
Mr. Ju...
any rights...
Mr. Gre...
vided for ...
does not ...
Mr. Jus...
not been r...
there is a ...
1908, ther...
solved by ...
ment?
Mr. Gre...
case of this...
minor is en...
like to read...
close conne...
(a) and (b)...
(reading).
Mr. Justice ...
were wrong ...
position: An...
with a baby ...
in this count...
16; his pare...
be here, and ...
be cleared out...
by himself ala...
Mr. Gregor...
would be entit...
the unfortuna...
Mr. Justice ...
human. But ...
The question ...
it is perfectly ...
a provision in ...
the children wi...
Mr. Gregor...
will see section ...
In this case the...
have absolu'ely...
that this case fi...
Mr. Justice W...
understand.
Mr. Gregoro...
application was ...
this section by t...
Mr. Justice W...
to children over ...
It says if a child...
has been no regi...
after he attains ...
month, ask for ...
and the Registra...
Of course he mus...
Mr. Gregorows...
plies because it sa...
applies exactly to ...
Registrar, if satisfi...
cant. In a case ...
the Registrar has ...
under section 7.
Mr. Justice We...
discretion judiciall...
guilty of an offence...
Mr. Gregorowsk...
is no objection. ...
pectable man, prac...
erty is in this count...
1888 and the busine...
ren when the father...
be grossly inhuman ...
submit that the legi...
intended that any su...
Where there is a doub...
that the legislature w...
humanity and in acc...
of civilisation. To gi...

THE VOICE OF LABOUR

VOL. 5. No. 151

JOHANNESBURG, AUGUST 11TH, 1911.

Price 3d.